THE GLORY OF THE LORD

Hans Urs von Balthasar

THE GLORY OF THE LORD:
A THEOLOGICAL AESTHETICS

By Hans Urs von Balthasar

VOLUMES OF THE COMPLETE WORK
Edited by Joseph Fessio, S.J., and John Riches

1. *SEEING THE FORM*
2. *STUDIES IN THEOLOGICAL STYLE: CLERICAL STYLES*
3. *STUDIES IN THEOLOGICAL STYLE: LAY STYLES*
4. *THE REALM OF METAPHYSICS IN ANTIQUITY*
5. *THE REALM OF METAPHYSICS IN THE MODERN AGE*
6. *THEOLOGY: THE OLD COVENANT*
7. *THEOLOGY: THE NEW COVENANT*

The publishers gratefully acknowledge the support of the Pro Helvetia Foundation in the preparation of the English translation.

THE GLORY OF THE LORD

A THEOLOGICAL AESTHETICS

BY

HANS URS VON BALTHASAR

VOLUME III: STUDIES IN THEOLOGICAL STYLE: LAY STYLES

Translated by Andrew Louth, John Saward, Martin Simon and Rowan Williams
Edited by John Riches

IGNATIUS PRESS • SAN FRANCISCO

First published in Great Britain by T. & T. Clark Limited, 1986
in association with Ignatius Press, San Francisco, U.S.A.

Originally published under the title
Herrlichkeit: Eine theologische Ästhetik, II: *Fächer der Stile*,
2: *Laikale Stile* by Johannes Verlag, Einsiedeln, 1962,
second edition 1969.

ISBN: 0–89870–038–8

Library of Congress Cataloging Number 82 – 23552

Typeset in Bembo by C. R. Barber & Partners (Highlands) Ltd,
Fort William, Scotland
Printed in Great Britain by Billing & Sons Ltd,
Worcester, England

CONTENTS

VOLUME III
STUDIES IN THEOLOGICAL STYLE:
LAY STYLES

DANTE

ST JOHN OF THE CROSS

PASCAL

HAMANN

SOLOVIEV

HOPKINS

PÉGUY

Que chaque type soit réalisé dans son exactitude et dans son plein. Que chaque type de pensée soit réalisé dans sa plus belle forme. Que chaque type de pensée soit récolté à son point, ἐν ἀχμῇ, dans sa plus haute et sa plus parfaite maturation. Et que celui qui a trouvé la faucille soit chargé de rapporter le blé.

PÉGUY

DANTE

I. UNTROD PATHS

Dante wrote his major works in the vernacular in about 1300 and, in so doing, was conscious of taking a momentous step in the history of mankind.[1] He was, of course, the inheritor of Latin scholasticism, but that tradition lay behind him. Apart from Thomas Aquinas (and even he was more of a philosopher than a theologian), and if we exclude Nicholas of Cusa's 'experiments' in theology, no theologian writing subsequently in Latin made a really significant contribution to the history of the human spirit. Even Suarez was of influence principally as a philosopher; the successive generations of commentators on St Thomas up to the Enlightenment are manifestly imitators of their master. Dante studied the Schoolmen, just as he studied Aristotle, Averroes and Siger, but when he meets scholasticism in the heights of Paradise, in the sun, in the lowest of the 'higher spheres', the impression left on him by the round dance of the 'twice twelve teachers of wisdom' (the two groups led by

[1] To facilitate accessibility, all citations from the works of Dante are from the complete *Inselverlag* edition (*Dantis Alagherii Opera omnia*, ed. H. Wengler, 2 vols., Leipzig, 1921). There is little point in providing even a brief survey of the immense literature devoted to Dante; but see: *Bulletino della Società Dantesca Italiana*, 1890–1921; the Dante bibliography of N. D. Evola: 1920–1930 (Florence, 1932), 1931–1934 (Milan, 1938), 1935–1939 (Aevum IV, 1941); and A. Vallone, *Gli studi danteschi dal 1940–1949* (Florence, 1950).

With regard to the *Comedy*, much research has gone into Hermann Gmelin's six-volume work, *Die Göttliche Komödie* (Klett, 1949–1957), but the emphasis is on the literary aspects. I know of no reliable work on Dante's theology in the strictest sense. Concordances: for the *Comedy*, E. Allen Fay (Cambridge, Mass., 1888); for the Latin works, Rand-Wilkins (Oxford, 1912); for the other Italian works, Sheldon-White (Oxford, 1905).

Abbreviations: Inf = *Inferno;* Pg = *Purgatorio;* Par = *Paradiso;* Canz = *Canzoniere;* VN = *Vita Nuova;* Conv = *Convivio;* M = *Monarchia;* VE = *De vulgari eloquentia.*

[The English translation of *The Divine Comedy* used throughout is the prose version of John D. Sinclair, rev. ed. (London, 1948); of the *Vita Nuova*, that of Barbara Reynolds (Harmondsworth, 1969); of the *Convivio*, the somewhat archaic version of W. W. Jackson (Oxford, 1909).]

Thomas and Bonaventure) is of the subtle interlocking mechanism of a clock with its chimes (*come orologio . . . che l'una parte l'altra tira ed urge, tin, tin, sonando*),[2] or of a holy mill (*santa mola*).[3] And so the Dominican sings the praises of Francis, and the Franciscan praises Dominic. Finally, Dante, entranced, sees a third round dance detach itself from the other two—'just as on the approach of evening new lights begin to appear in the sky so that the sight seems and seems not real' (*si che la vista pare e non par vera*).[4] This dance appears to him to be the 'very sparkling of the Holy Ghost' (*vero sfavillar del Santo Spirito*). His eyes, overcome, cannot bear the sight, and Beatrice, laughing, draws him on to another sphere. It is not inconceivable that Dante considered himself to be the originator of this new, third theology, taking his lead perhaps from Joachim of Fiore, whom he saw as the twelfth (and last) Doctor of the Church in the second group, just as Siger was the last of the first group. But even the fleeting sight of this third group dazzles Dante, and he tells us nothing of its actual character. For this we must turn to his work itself.

This work of his, inseparable both from its unique divine mission and from its historical existence, carved out like a statue or monument, Dante regarded as a venture into the new, the unknown. 'I want to demonstrate truths that no one else has dared to attempt (*intemptatas ab aliis ostendere veritates*). For what kind of contribution would it be if a man were merely to prove once again a theorem of Euclid, or to demonstrate for the second time the nature of happiness, which Aristotle has already done?'[5] And he says this at the beginning of the *Monarchy*! The opening sentence of his treatise on the mother tongue begins: 'Since we have found no one before us who has in any way tackled the subject of vernacular eloquence, and since we regard such eloquence as extremely necessary for all. . . .'[6] Since Dante lived in an age of discovery, images of putting to sea abound in his writing. Again and again, even in the heights of Paradise,[7]

[2] Par 10, 139, 142–143.

[3] Par 12, 3.

[4] Par 14, 72.

[5] M 1, 1.

[6] VE 1, 1.

[7] Par 33, 94. *Cf.* E. R. Curtius, *Das Schiff der Argonauten*. Kritische Essays zur europäischen Literatur, 1950, 398–428.

the legend of the Argonauts fascinates him: in Hell Jason arouses his admiration,[8] and even more so, Odysseus, who seems to him to be the bold explorer *par excellence*—thus anticipating what Columbus comes to mean for Bloy and Claudel. No one could conquer within Odysseus 'his passion to gain experience of the world' (*a divenir del mondo esperto*);[9] 'I put forth on the open deep with but one ship and with that little company, the few who never deserted me', travelling on past the columns erected by Hercules as a danger signal, in 'mad flight' (*folle volo*), in the sun's track (*diretro al sol*), to 'experience the unpeopled world' (*l'esperienza del mondo senza gente*).[10] Likewise, in Hell Dante follows a 'mad path' (*per la folle strada*)[11] and enters on 'the deep and savage way' (*lo camino alto e silvestro*).[12] He warns the great crowd, which attempts to follow him on his journey 'in his tiny craft'[13] (*in piccioletta barca*), to turn back in good time, for only 'ye other few' can 'hold my furrow before the water returns smooth again', for 'it is no passage for a little bark, this which the daring prow goes cleaving, not for a pilot that would spare himself'[14] Then follows the realistic, breathtaking descriptions of mountain climbing: in Hell, scrambling over rough boulders, the debris of demolished mountains,[15] and on to even dizzier heights, to the sheer face of the Mountain of Purgatory.[16] Dante experiences and describes what it is like to subsist on no more than the resources of the will, all bodily strength having drained away: 'I rose then, showing myself better furnished with breath than I felt, and said, "Go, for I am strong and fearless".'[17] Finally, come the images of flight: flying on the back of the fantastic monster Geryon, in whose presence Dante felt a greater dread (*maggior paura*) than did Phaethon and Icarus when they realized

[8] Inf 18, 85f.
[9] Inf 26, 98.
[10] Inf 26, 116–117, 125.
[11] Inf 8, 91.
[12] Inf 2, 142.
[13] Par 2, 1–12.
[14] Par 23, 67–69. The image constantly recurs: in the prelude to the *Purgatorio* (1, 1–3); in the second treatise of the *Convivio* (2, 1): 'With the mainsail of reason adjusted to the breeze of my desire I launch on the deep with hope of pleasant voyage.' *Cf.* Pg 24, 3.
[15] Inf 24, 1–60. On Dante's mountaineering imagery, see W. Heilermann von Heel, 'Der Bergsteiger Dante', *Dt. Dantejahrbuch* xiv (1932), 82–99.
[16] Pg 4, 22–51.
[17] Inf 24, 58–60.

their wings were melting:[18] both images of tragic hubris. Few indeed respond to the call of infinite space:

A questo invito vengon molto radi:
O gente umana, per volar su nata,
Perchè a poco vento così cadi?[19]

Dante is the first to undertake the flight to heaven,[20] although in Hell he follows in the footsteps of Virgil and Paul. Others may have been caught up to God in ecstasy, but no one else has undertaken a methodical exploration of Paradise or acquired *esperienza* of the hereafter. This last word—*esperienza*—recurs frequently, oscillating between its ancient meaning of 'mystical experience of God'[21], the even more ancient Irenaean sense of 'experience of grace through experience in the flesh of its opposite'[22] and a third, new sense—'experiential exploration of reality'—which looks towards modern times.[23] There is, of course, a long tradition, both in Antiquity and in the Christian era, of journeys to the hereafter, of transcendental adventure stories and reports of ecstatic experience.[24] However, Dante should be seen in stark contrast to this whole literary tradition because of his awareness, both theological and aesthetic, that he was setting down something that had never existed before and that in its own way is inimitable, a work that raises him high above his own age, plants him in the future (*s'infutura la tua vita*),[25] in eternity itself (*s'eterna*).[26] His sense of mission is without parallel in Christian history, inasmuch as it is not only lived out (as in the case of many saints) but is energetically impressed upon men and is ratified by the greatest poets of Antiquity as well as by the representatives of Christianity. How

[18] Inf 17, 79–82. See also U. Donati, *Il volo nella Div. Comm.* (Milan, 1942).
[19] Pg 12, 94–96.
[20] Par 2, 7.
[21] Par 1, 72.
[22] *Cf.* Inf 28, 48: Dante is led through Hell *per dar lui esperienza piena.* Pg 26, 74.
[23] Inf 26, 98, 116; Par 2, 95. Bibliography in Gmelin, *Komm.* I, 389f; Allen Fay, 240.
[24] A. Rüegg, *Die Jenseitsvorstellungen vor Dante*, 2 vols., 1945.
[25] Par 17, 98.
[26] Inf 15, 85.

could Dante's sense of being a new constellation have been so real to him, if he had not experienced the medieval synthesis he represents as something qualitatively new, open to the future?

Synthesis—that is just what Dante is: a synthesis of scholasticism and mysticism, of Antiquity and Christianity, of the sacral concept of Empire and the spiritual Franciscan ideal of the Church, and—even more stunningly—a synthesis of the courtly world of the *Minnesang* and the very different world of scholastic wisdom. In his own way we can class Dante with the great cathedral builders of the Middle Ages, with whom for the last time ethics and aesthetics peacefully coexisted and furthered and strengthened one another. And yet, whatever view one takes of the integration achieved by Dante, there is always an excess over and above the constitutive elements; despite its structure, his work is not a sum-total but an indivisible prime number, and it is this insoluble mystery that has bestowed upon him his power over history. This will be our concern in the following pages; and as our point of entry, let us try to discover, from the outside, what is new about Dante.

a. Conversion to the Vernacular

Dante saw and portrayed conversion to the vernacular as an innovation of the greatest historical significance. It is true, of course, that for more than a century there had been poetry in the vernacular—Gottfried's *Tristan* and Wolfram's Grail epic were already in the past. But Italy lagged behind, and, what is more important, for Dante it was not a question of composing verse romances (not even if their subject was an exalted symbol like the Grail). No, Dante was concerned with translating the knowledge of reality—hidden in the seven liberal arts, in philosophy, theology and history—from dead, fossilized Latin into the living, spoken language. The problem did not arise for the courtly poet of the *Canzoniere*, and scarcely for the prose writer of the *Vita Nuova*, but it arose suddenly and sharply for the author of the *Convivio*, who set himself the task of writing a philosophically orientated allegorical commentary on his *Canzoni*: but Latin in its grandeur is ill-suited for the role of servant of the vernacular, which is what the commentary must be vis-à-vis the text; Latin lacks the necessary obedience.[27] 'A Latin commentary would not be a servant but a lord, full of nobility, virtue and beauty. Full of nobility—for Latin is eternal and unchanging, while the vernacular, on the other hand, is unstable and subject to change. In the ancient comedies and tragedies, which can no longer change, we see the very same Latin we have today. This is not true, however, of the vernacular, which changes with the mood and mind of the age. Thus, in the cities of Italy, if we look back only fifty years, we see many words become extinct or newly coined or change their meaning. If a short passage of time produces such changes, how much greater will be the effect of a long time!'.[28] Dante, who in his work never lost sight either of his poetic reputation or of eternity, nevertheless threw caution to the winds and launched out on the inconstant, surging, unstable ocean that is the vernacular. He wrote a book specifically designed to justify this step. And whereas in the *Convivio* Latin seemed to be superior in nobility and beauty to the simple vernacular, in this new work he changed his point of view: the mother tongue is superior (*nobilior*), since it is 'natural, while the other is more artificial'; it is 'the original language of men and spread out throughout the world'; that language 'which children learn from those who look after them, when first they begin to form sounds', and which they accept 'without any rules, imitating their nurse'.[29] It is the language given to the first man by God himself, together with the original divine Word, to which Adam had responded (*per viam responsionis*).[30] At this time Dante believed that the primal language was preserved in Hebrew, because the Jews had not taken part in the building of the Tower of Babel, and that the incarnate Son had conversed with his heavenly Father in this God-given vernacular.[31] Later on he gave up this delightful theory. In Paradise Adam himself puts him right on the matter when he informs Dante that the primal language disappeared long before the building of the Tower and the confusion of languages, for, like everything else given over to man, it is subject to change.[32]

[27] Conv 1, 6–7.
[28] Conv 1, 5.
[29] VE 1, 1.
[30] VE 1, 4.
[31] VE 1, 6.
[32] Par 26, 124–129.

But Dante loved his mother tongue. It is that, not Latin, which is the contributory cause of his existence and which flows through his veins. 'This mother tongue of mine was the connecting link between my parents, and it was in this language that they spoke to one another. Just as the blacksmith's fire prepares the iron for him to make a knife, so my mother tongue took part in my begetting and is a contributory cause of my being'.[33] And because he loves it as part of himself, because its growth within him unites him more closely with the race itself, and every man 'loves best the soil upon which he dwells',[34] he wants to 'glorify' (*magnificare*) it and reveal its inner quality, its nobility.[35] It will be 'the new light, the new sun, which will rise where the old (scholastic Latin) sets'.[36] And indeed Dante now seeks for a vernacular that is *illustre, cardinale, aulicum et curiale*[38] amongst the countless Italian dialects (even the suburbs of Bologna had each their own langauge!)[37] but remains conscious of the fact that the imperial court was abroad; and when he sets out on the sea of dialects, it is with the secret ambition of creating for himself, out of the raw material of an unstable, historically conditioned language, a valid form of language that will unite two qualities: that of being alive and that of being valid. Professional theology will go on speaking Latin as before, but Dante does not want to be a professional; he wants to be the legislator of a living culture, as Virgil was for ancient Rome. To this end he makes use of all the learning of his age, but such learning is at the service of his action, not vice versa. His eyes are set on history; in opting for the common tongue, he is conscious of his specific responsibility to the people.[39]

b. Conversion to History

The Aeneid, for Dante, is history in the strictest sense, the history of a foundation. For Dante, conversion to history means from the very beginning rising above the *Minnesang* (which

[33] Conv I, 13. [34] Conv I, 12.
[35] Conv I, 10. [36] Conv I, 13.
[37] VE I, 16. On this whole subject, see B. Nardi, *Il linguaggio, Dante e la cultura medievale* (Bari, 1949).
[38] VE I, 9. [39] Conv I, 11.

could also on occasion include political songs), scholasticism and every other philosophical 'study of essences' that did not concern itself with the history of the Empire or of the Church. Dante, however, did not intend to write the history either of the past or of the present; no, from the lofty vantage point of one who has made an historic decision, he strives to leave his mark on present and future history. For this reason, in the *Divine Comedy* the history happening on earth is divided in two by a vertical stroke, which goes from Heaven to Hell and lays bare the absolute standards. But the stroke itself is a fact of history, an event of the year 1300 A.D.. Everywhere, from Hell to the highest Heaven, real history is present; individual historical personalities appear, beyond death, in their true light and importance; the lines of their historical destiny are traced right to the end, their form has left its mark on the earth. And like the individuals, so the families, cities, regions, countries, finally the whole Empire, the complete Church, come into view, are all weighed on the eternal balance and found to be too light, condemned and righted, rejected and endowed with new promises. Wolfram's *Grail* is a timeless story, but the poems of Dante refer very precisely to the history of the world. Man is not pure spirit; as an organic body, he loves the place and time of his birth.[40] The *kairos* of his appearing is determined partly but decisively by his horoscope. This is something the *Vita Nuova* already knows. Nothing is described more minutely in the *Divine Comedy* than the various astronomical constellations. If the most exalted spiritual faculty of man is *la discrezione*, the power of discernment, that true 'eye of the soul',[41] then the most terrible punishment of the damned is that they can recognize only past facts, possibly future events, but nothing in the present.[42] If the understanding of the present moment, of qualitative-cosmic time, is of fundamental importance, then so also is the utilization of time, as the *Divine Comedy* unceasingly reminds us: on the highway of time there can be no daydreaming or aesthetic dawdling.[43] Thus Dante has a special

[40] Conv 3, 3. [41] Conv 1, 11.

[42] Inf 10, 69f; 10, 103–108.

[43] Inf 9, 13f; Pg 12, 84; 17, 84; 18, 130f. (*Ratto, ratto, che il tempo non si perda!*); 23, 4f; 24, 91f. (*che il tempo è caro/In questo regno . . .*), etc. 'When we look into

interest in the ages of man's life and the canon of *virtù* relevant to them; what is suitable for the child is something quite different from what befits the youth, the grown man, the greybeard.[44] And yet time does not dissolve into merely empirical facts; in heaven, Dante's ancestor, Cacciaguida, sees the whole of historical time present in God in a single point,[45] without prejudice to the contingency and freedom of what occurs above, for here the times unite to form a *dolce armonia*.[46]

Yet while Dante takes seriously all the important personalities of his epoch, all the cities and regions in their individuality, his real concern bears finally upen the historical totality, which for him has two aspects: the *imperium* and the Church. His obstinate attachment to the Empire—expressed in the *Convivio*, the *Monarchy*, the *Divine Comedy*—goes against all the national aspirations of the late Middle Ages, especially in Italy. Such attachment could only be seen as mere romantic Utopianism or nostalgia, were it not linked with an image of the Church that has its living source in St Francis and the Spirituals and leads towards a much more rigorous distinction between the two realms than the Middle Ages had ever known. No, we can go even further and say that in the *Monarchy* Dante expresses a vision of a supranational unification of mankind, still thought out and expressed in medieval categories, of course, but more up-to-date than all the nationalisms of his age. With this vision in mind he first of all gives precise formulation to what Thomas Aquinas quite deliberately left in suspense: the doctrine of the double end of man, earthly and heavenly. Man is earth and Heaven, he is the 'horizon' between the two, he 'tastes the nature of both realms' (*sapit utram naturam*). And so, unique in all creation, the ultimate goal of man is twofold; 'man . . . is the only being who is ordered towards two ultimate goals. One of these constitutes his goal in so far as he is subject to change and decay and the other in so far as he is indestructible. Unerring Paradise has therefore set man to attain two goals: the first is

the cause of what annoys us, we find that in every case it comes from not knowing how best to use time (*dal non conoscere l'uso del tempo*).'

[44] The whole of the end of the *Convivio* (4, 23–30) is concerned with this question.

[45] Par 17, 16–18.

[46] Par 17, 37–43, 45.

happiness in this life, which consists in the exercise of his own powers and is symbolised by the earthly paradise; the second is the happiness of eternal life, which consists in the enjoyment of the divine countenance (which man cannot attain to of his own power unless aided by divine illumination) and is signified by the heavenly paradise'.[47]

The *Empire* is the perfect realization and representation of earthly order and human law: *imperii fundamentum jus humanum est*.[48] This in turn is rooted in the unity of the human race, a unity that is both real (the story of Paradise) and ideal (Plato's idea of man).[49] However, human law is founded upon what is most positive about man, his struggle for justice, and what is right and just in human terms is the renunciation of egotism, man's openness to the universal; in other words, love. This is magnificently expounded by the Emperor Justinian in the Sphere of Mercury:

Che, per voler del primo amor ch'io sento,
D'entro le leggi trassi il troppo e il vano.[50]

And this is affirmed once again by the great imperial eagle in Jupiter.[51] Just as in the order of things the individual is related beyond himself to the family, the family to the village, the village to the city, the city to a particular kingdom, so the different kingdoms must be integrated in a universal kingdom of man, for *totum humanum genus ordinatur ad unum*.[52] This unity is not the empty form of abstract power, but, as became clear, a true integration. But nonetheless it is *forma ordinis*, and, as the supreme form, it leaves its imprint upon all: imperial man begets beneath him a humanity marked by his nobility.[53] If the particular subordinate authorities are characteristically dominated by concupiscence, envy, ambition and party spirit, the Emperor, who possesses everything and has no rival, is essentially disinterested and stands free above all as the supreme embodiment of justice, for he rules men as men and so can be the embodiment of selfless love—*caritas*, Dante explicitly says.[54] His

[47] M 3, 16.
[48] M 3, 10.
[49] Conv 4, 13.
[50] Par 6, 11–12.
[51] Par 18, 116–117.
[52] M 1, 5.
[53] M 1, 13.
[54] M 1, 11.

power is universal in its scope, and at the same time it represents the whole before God, and so, viewed from this most exalted and unambiguous point, the whole of ethics assumes the form of free, selfless service.[55] For Dante, the principle of human love and of human law can only be made effective in the natural domain when particularism—which he sees devastating the Italian cities—is surpassed in favour of the universal. But, as at every stage in the realization of the Kingdom of God, Dante can think of the universal only in terms of personal love, so the unity of the earthly empire is secure only if the centre of unity is occupied by a person. Dante is perfectly well aware that, in saying this, he is proposing only the best possible *form*, which does not itself guarantee its authentic realization; he speaks constantly only of *posse*, of *debere*,[56] and thus of an opportunity that the form of the monarch's dignity gives him, an opportunity that he can let mankind in its totality share. This form does not exclude the kind of progressive particularization in the lower echelons of society that gives expression to the individual characteristics of the governed nations and states; on the contrary, it makes full provision for them.[57] Nevertheless, the ethical point of view, the justice embodied in the monarchical will, outweighs any purely political consideration. Only thus will humanity be able to achieve that oneness that enables it to stand as man before God, for man needs the *voluntas una, domina et regulatrix* if the desires that draw him towards the particular are to be dominated and mastered in a way that is worthy of him.[58]

This order is the rights of man, implanted at the time of creation, and so, for Dante, the tree of Paradise is at the same time the tree of the Empire,[59] and Christ alone is greater than it. It was stripped of its foliage by original sin, it received the power of rejuvenation from the Church of Christ, but it remains a mystery of creation,[60] which springs directly from God, and

[55] M I, 12. *Quamvis consul sive rex respectu viae sint domini aliorum, respectu autem termini aliorum ministri sunt, et maxime Monarcha, qui minister omnium procul dubio habendus est.*

[56] M I, 11, 12, 13.

[57] M I, 14 in connection with Aristotle and with Plato's theory of the state.

[58] M I, 15.

[59] Pg 32, 38–60.

[60] Pg 33, 56f.

needs no ecclesiastical intermediary. Ancient Rome existed, in all its power, before the Church;[61] God conferred upon it the office, and also the power, of embodying universal justice and, in consequence, the universal spirit, for *quicumque finem juris intendit, cum jure graditur.*[62] Yet only God can justify and order the interplay between the kingdom of the world and the kingdom of God. Dante sees the supreme legitimation of the imperial power (much higher than any the Church could ever confer on the emperor)[63] in the fact that Christ, who bore the guilt of all mankind, is condemned to death by the lawful representative of all mankind, is, that is to say, therefore lawfully condemned by the emperor. In Paradise Justinian will expound this doctrine once again, with this addition: that if the deicide of Golgotha was 'lawful', so also was the vengeance of God wrought by Trajan on Jerusalem.[64] This is a knot (*nodo*), that Dante cannot untie, and that, as the emperor points out, only finds its resolution *nella fiamma d'amor*, in the flame of God's love, in the mystery of his loving decree.[65] This is the vital point, because now the key to the problem of the relationship between the kingdom of the world and the kingdom of God, which in human terms remains for ever insoluble, is constituted not only by God as such (*ipse Deus, in quo respectus omnis universaliter unitur*),[66] but by the God of incomprehensible love, who has not only established all human justice but has used it, beyond itself, for his own purposes.

The task given to the emperor of uniting the world in justice and love, of stamping upon it the most sublime human form through the power of representative service, is a task given at creation and so is one that cannot be abandoned. The Donation of Constantine, which Dante regarded as historical, is null and void twice over—even though made by the emperor in good faith[67]—because it tried to concede a right that emperors cannot concede, and that the Church, by its very nature, cannot accept.[68] For 'the Church was in no sense properly fitted

[61] M 3, 13.
[62] M 2, 6.
[63] M 2, 12.
[64] Par 6, 91–93.
[65] Par 7, 58–60.
[66] M 3, 12.
[67] Par 20, 55–57.
[68] M 3, 10–13.

(*indisposita*) to receive temporal things, on account of the express prohibition recorded by Matthew: "Possess not gold nor silver, nor money in your girdles, nor purse for your journey, et cetera". And although the severity of this precept is tempered in certain respects in Luke, still I have been unable to discover that permission to possess gold and silver was granted to the Church subsequent to that prohibition.'[69]

The *Church*, for Dante as for Francis, is shaped solely by the form of Christ: 'The form of the Church is none other than the life of Christ, including both his deeds and his words. Now his life was the model and exemplar (*idea et exemplar*) for the Church militant, for its pastors in particular, but above all for the chief pastor whose office is to feed the lambs and the sheep. For this reason in John he himself gives his life to his disciples as the form of their lives: "I have given you an example, that you also should do as I have done to you"; and in the same Gospel we read what he said specifically to Peter after bestowing upon him the office of pastor: "Peter, follow me." But in the presence of Pilate Christ expressly renounced the kind of power we are discussing: "My kingdom," he said, "is not of this world; if my kingdom were of this world, my servants would fight, that I might not be handed over to the Jews; but my kingdom is not from the world." This must not be taken to mean that Christ, who is God, is not lord of this kingdom . . . but it means that, as the supreme exemplar of the Church, he has no responsibility for this kingdom.'[70]

This is why the great lover of every embodiment of form, of all radiant beauty, has no interest at all in the visible beauty of the Church on earth. For its beauty consists entirely in its humility and obscurity, and not at all in its structure. Dante, who in the heights of Paradise dedicates two songs to the nine angelic hierarchies of Dionysius the Areopagite, nowhere in his works echoes the idea of their earthly reflection in an 'ecclesiastical hierarchy', whose grades, offices, sacred duties might lay claim to a beauty of their own and might deserve, because of their representative function, to be put into the light. It is with bitter irony that he applies the title of *servus servorum* to

[69] M 3, 10. [70] M 3, 15.

his arch-enemy, Boniface VIII.[71] He will forgive neither him nor his successor Clement V, for their theocratic ways, and he certainly shows no mercy to Boniface's predecessor, Celestine V, for his 'great refusal' (*il gran rifiuto*) to render service to the Church, which, for the Pope, would have been the real 'great renunciation'.[72] The majority of the Popes are in Hell; he meets only two of them on the Mountain of Purgatory and only one in Heaven. Dante's criticisms of the worldliness of the medieval Church are unending; from the Empyrean Beatrice and Peter pour out their reproaches on the decadent Church, and, in a terrible image, the poet sees the transfigured Peter suddenly become incandescent with anger, fulminating against the 'atrocious' Boniface VIII, who has turned the apostle's tomb into a cesspit of blood and excrement. All heaven is coloured the same angry red, Beatrice grows pale and the spheres are darkened because 'the Bride of the Lord' has become a cheap whore, to be bought with gold.[73] Peter reproaches the popes for their ambition and their passion for pomp,[74] which divide the Church, and for their abuse of the power of the keys for the purposes of earthly warfare and of excommunication for political ends;[75] he reproaches them for their simony.[76] They commit adultery with the Bride of Christ;[77] they turn her into the whore of Babylon and permit the kings of the earth (especially the King of France, who will soon haul the popes off to Avignon) to commit fornication with her. Once purified by his confession before Beatrice, Dante is entrusted with the task of observing the full horror of Church history through the medium of symbolic images, viewing thus the gradual transformation of the pure Bride into the *Magna Meretrix*.[78] Moreover, in Paradise he is solemnly charged by Peter to make heaven's wrath known on earth, and 'not to hide what I hide not'.[79] And he spares the bishops and clergy no less than the

[71] Inf 15, 112.
[72] Inf 3, 60.
[73] Par 27, 19–45.
[74] Par 21, 127–135; Pg 16, 106–111.
[75] Pg 3, 133–135; Par 18, 127–129.
[76] Inf 19. The whole canto deals with the Simonists, who 'prostitute' the gifts of God: v 4; Par 18, 122–123; 27, 52–54.
[77] Inf 19, 57; 19, 100–114; Par 9, 142; M 3, 3: *matrem prostituunt*.
[78] Pg 32, 142–160.
[79] Par 27, 66.

popes; the clergy find themselves in Hell specially placed among the hypocrites,[80] the avaricious,[81] the homosexuals:[82] 'O divine Patience, that endurest so much.' [83] Later, the decadence of the religious orders is bemoaned, even, or rather, particularly, the great new mendicant orders,[84] and there is a denunciation of the wretched sermons that no longer expound the gospel, so that 'the poor sheep that know nothing return from pasture fed on wind'.[85] A constantly renewed lament rings out from the Kingdom above over the Church below. Alas, 'the good plant that was once a vine . . . is now become a thorn',[86] the holy city is laid waste;[87] Rome, bent on uniting the two powers, has sunk deep into the mire.[88] Even in the spiritual realm the successors of Peter do not exercise their functions in conformity to their mandate, for they imagine that divine authority has been granted to them, mere servants, in their own right. Boniface VIII, the 'prince of the new Pharisees', takes a terrible share of the guilt for the damnation of Guido da Montefeltro, whom he incited, allegedly by means of preventive absolution, to treachery.[89] If the Pope were omnipotent, 'he would be able to absolve me even if I were not penitent; which even God himself cannot do'.[90]

Dante is devoted, in a childlike way, to the Church of Christ, to her sacraments, to the divine Word that she dispenses. And just as he hopes for a saviour-emperor, so he longs for the purification of the Church.[91] His anger over her defects (not so much over the private sins of ecclesiastics, towards whom, as in the case of the Abbot of San Zeno or Hadrian V, he can adopt a respectful tone.[92] as over the deep-seated perversion and

[80] Inf 23, 58f (the whole passage is full of clerical terms).

[81] Inf 7, 46–48.

[82] Inf 15, 106: *In somma sappi che tutti fur cherci.*

[83] Par 21, 135.

[84] Par 11, 118–139 (against the Dominicans); Par 12, 106–124 (against the Franciscans); Par 21, 119 (against the ruination of the cloister); Par 22, 73–99 (St Benedict's speech about his rule, which has become a useless piece of paper).

[85] Par 29, 85–126.

[86] Par 24, 111.

[87] Pg 33, 1.

[88] Pg 16, 129.

[89] Inf 27, 100–102.

[90] M 3, 8.

[91] Par 27, 61–63.

[92] Pg 18, 113f; Pg 19, 91f.

exploitation of the august Bride of Christ) has nothing sectarian about it, nothing of the heterodoxy of a Joachim; it springs solely from the loving zeal of a Christian layman, who sees himself cheated of his rightful inheritance of the Spirit and of the riches of Christ, and who, on behalf of those who have been led astray, indeed on behalf of the Lord of the Church himself, laments the dereliction of the holy city.

c. Conversion to the Laity

For Dante, conversion to the laity means turning away from the scholastic study of essences to reflection on the reality and the conditions of the possibility of an authentic Christian existence; indeed—and this in contrast to the mendicant orders and the mysticism of the day—of an ethicopolitical existence in the world. From Dante to our own times this has been the route taken by every theology that has made its mark on history. For himself, such reflection has three components: it deals with his own personality, his own destiny, his own *eros*—three immensely portentous issues.

At the centre of Dante's work stands his personality—in extreme contrast to Thomas Aquinas, with whom personality completely and intentionally disappears—a personality to which nothing human, but also nothing divine, is alien, a personality that stretches out to the furthermost limits of the cosmos and pursues its own Christian fulfilment within the cosmic context of the fulfilment of the Kingdom of God. This leads directly to the central paradox that, as a created reality, this person will attain the heights of fame, but as a Christian reality, he will at the same time be thrust down into the profoundest humility and humiliation. Behind this paradox lies what Dante refers to as nobility (*nobiltà*, *onestade*) and vocation, from which it is clear that for him the concept of higher rank signifies equally greater grace and, in consequence, a greater vocation and responsibility. The fourth treatise of the *Convivio* strives to clarify the notion of nobility and, respectfully yet resolutely contradicting a saying of the venerated Emperor Frederick II, arrives at the conclusion that nobility does not depend on 'ancient wealth and gracious manners' (*antica ricchezza e be' costumi*), and so not on anything passed down within particular families.[93] Neither wealth nor any exterior power can confer nobility of soul, and it is difficult to see how a common herd could become noble simply through the progress of time.[94] Nobility is primarily an individual matter and denotes the perfection of an individual member of a particular class.[95] Following Aristotle, Dante argues that this perfection is found first of all in the attainment and possession of one's own proper virtue (*aretê*, *virtù propria*), and this includes the 'moral virtues', as the 'fruits most truly peculiar to man', which, again following Aristotle, are given as courage, self-control, liberality, love of splendour (*magnificenza*), greatness of soul (*magnanimità*), proper ambition, gentleness, sociability, veracity, good humour (*eutrapelia*), justice.[96] But all these virtues spring from an attitude, a fundamental predisposition (*abituale elezione*), as effects from their cause (*siccome effetto da sua cagione*). This attitude is the foundation of personal nobility, which is 'thus a more comprehensive notion than that of virtue'. The virtues are like stars, but nobility is the heaven in which they appear: 'The intellectual and the moral virtues shine in it; good dispositions given by nature shine in it, namely tenderness and religion, and the praiseworthy emotions, namely chasteness and compassion, and many others. There shine in it the excellencies of the body, namely beauty, courage and unspoilt health. And so many are the stars that extend over this heaven that it is no wonder that human nobility produces so many and various fruits, so manifold are its natural characteristics and potentialities, comprised and united in one simple substance; and in them, as in different branches, it bears different fruits. Indeed I venture to say that human nobility as regards its fruitfulness surpasses that of the angels, although the angelic be more divine in its unity.' But it is the task of divine grace and of the cosmic constellation to determine how the individual soul is receptive to the forces and faculties God has breathed into it, and it is the degree of this receptiveness that decides its intrinsic and habitual nobility of soul. 'For the divine seed does not fall onto

[93] Conv 4, 3.
[94] Conv 4, 10, 14.
[95] Conv 4, 16.
[96] Conv 4, 17.

the race or tribe but comes down upon the individual. And so it is not the race that makes the individual noble, but the individuals make noble the race.' According to the ancient doctrine of procreation to which Dante subscribes, the heavenly powers are the decisive agents in drawing out living reality from the potency of matter, God only completing the cosmogonic work by stooping in love before nature's miracle: 'Know that as soon as the articulation of the brain is perfected in the embryo The First Mover turns to it, rejoicing over such handiwork of nature, and breathes into it a new spirit full of power, which draws into its own substance that which it finds active there and becomes a single soul. . . .'[97] For this reason, the nobility of soul derived from nature and that derived from grace can only be thought of in strict union; the cosmological aspect, which has the Aristotelian virtues in view, and the theological, which is concerned with the gratuitous infusion of the Spirit's gifts into the soul, are well-nigh two aspects of the same process.[98] Thus Augustine and Aristotle are together invoked as witnesses to the truth that man must boldly lay hold of his own nobility by realising the good that he is (*s'ausi a ben fare*), trusting the *hormê* in his heart, the *hormê* that at first sight seems like a purely natural instinct but, when pursued, can be seen increasingly clearly to be an impulse received from divine grace.[99] It is now that it becomes clear also which souls possess personal nobility, and which not, as the apostle says: 'All the runners compete, but only one receives the prize.' Here Dante's own self-understanding becomes clear: the noble soul, following its own flight, discovers that it must reach out beyond itself; its apparently natural *magnanimità* requires it to submit to the ways of grace and to take upon itself the burdens of its Christian vocation. We shall see later how much Dante experienced his election as an incomprehensible and superabundant grace. But this grace is counterbalanced by the weight of the commission: 'The day was departing and the darkened air releasing the creatures on the earth from their labours, and I, alone, was preparing to endure the conflict both of the way [through Hell] and of the pity of it. . . . O my spirit,

[97] Pg 25, 68–74. [98] Conv 4, 21. [99] Conv 4, 22.

that noted what I saw, here shall be shown thy worth (*la tua nobilitate*)!'[100] Dante demands inner greatness of himself and relies on it to be a match for his countermovements. The *Convivio* says magnificently: 'The man who has true largeness of soul always makes himself great (*sempre il magnanimo si magnifica in suo cuore*), and the small-souled man makes himself less than he is. . . . And because with the same measure with which a man measures himself he measures the things that are his, which are as it were part of himself, so it is that the large-souled man's things always seem to him better than they are, and the things of others worse; and the small-souled man always thinks his things of little worth, since he overvalues the things of others.'[101] The vision of the unity of natural and Christian greatness of soul is, for Dante, the presupposition of his sense of vocation, and Virgil, Beatrice and the three chief apostles confirm this for him. It is also the reason why his hope is directed simultaneously toward both earthly and heavenly glory, so that right into old age he is still hoping for the poet's crown at the Florentine baptistery[102] as well as the crown of faith from Peter.[103] Such a sense of nobility is quite distinct from mere hereditary nobility (*O poca nostra nobilità di sangue!*);[104] rather, Dante is aware that he is profoundly indebted to his spiritually noble ancestor, despite all the unworthy intervening generations, and that through his ancestor, in the noble blood itself, Dante can become more than he is himself (*voi mi levate sì, ch'io son più ch'io*).[105] The ancestor gives tongue to this sense of nobility with a tenderness that knows the inseparability of love and blood (*O sanguis meus, o superinfusa gratia Dei!*[106] *O fronde mia . . . , io fui la tua radice*),[107] but which, on the other hand, bases all its interiority on Dante's charismatic vocation. Such a sense of nobility stands in a unique place between the Middle Ages and modern times at a moment of truth, a *kairos*, completely fulfilled in itself and seemingly unrepeatable. It is the same moment at which intellectual scholasticism stoops to drink at the deep fountains of the mother tongue and recognizes there its source, while the popular poetry

[100] Inf 2, 1–9.
[101] Conv 1, 11.
[102] Par 25, 7–9; Par 1, 28f; first eclogue, 42f.
[103] Par 25, 10–12.
[104] Par 16, 1.
[105] Par 16, 18.
[106] Par 15, 28–29.
[107] Par 15, 88–89.

of the *Minnesang* discovers its own redemptive truth in the sublime lovesong in honour of Beatrice. It is also the same moment when ancient culture and Christian theology flow smoothly together, when Virgil, at the end of his protégé's first journey, can place him unquestioningly in the hands of Beatrice. Now, of course, this conjunction, which constitutes the entire inner structure of the *Convivio*, the *Divine Comedy* and the *Monarchy*, is Dante's own conscious creation; it is in no sense something that was merely 'in the air' or that was produced, as it were, by simply taking a cross-section at random through the main stream of the evolution of the Middle Ages into the Renaissance. It is the creative work of an adventurous spirit, who, in bringing it to completion, has boldly seized hold both of himself and of his vocation and has drawn both Virgil and Beatrice into his own orbit. Antiquity has an unsurpassable value for him; he *loves* Virgil and Statius and Aristotle and all the other great figures of the past as the fathers of his soul; during his journey, in moments of terror, he clings to the maternal breast of his sacred friend, Virgil, and truly lets him be his conscience.[108] Christianity has ultimate value, because the love of Dante for Beatrice can be fulfilled nowhere but in Heaven. If pre-Christian Antiquity has its proper place in Hell, and if the mythological figures of the classical *Walpurgisnacht* are its true population (Charon, Minos, Cerberus, Pluto, the Megaera, the Minotaur, the Centaurs, Chiron, Geryon, Cacus, the giants (but none of the gods)); if the Christian saints and angels, who have taken the place of the ancient gods (planets and stars) reign in Paradise, then the mountain of Purgatory is properly the place for the two worlds to meet and intermingle: The audacity with which Dante systematically places Antiquity and Christianity in parallel, for example by offering to the penitents a model of virtue drawn in each case from mythology, and from the Bible,[109] is a further advance on the *Secunda Pars* of St Thomas's *Summa Theologiae*. For Dante the poet, like Aquinas, makes the ethics of Antiquity in its abstractness the broad basis of Christian morality; but he does more than that; he takes over all its

[108] Inf 19, 34–36; 23, 37f; 23, 51; Pg 8, 42. Virgil as conscience: Inf 30, 130–148.

[109] E.g., Pg 12, 25–63.

historical and mythological substance as well. If poetic inspiration is the province of Apollo and the Muses, then Apollo and the Muses must be summoned, even if it be to sing the praises of the Christian Heaven.[110] There is no flowery rhetoric or 'conventional wisdom' about this (as there was so often in the preceding centuries); it is not even a matter of broadening one's 'cultural range'; no, it is the work of the *eros* in Dante's soul, that in the last analysis knows itself indebted to both worlds, that loves both with a perceptive and appreciative love, that, it is true, clearly recognizes the relative hierarchical positions of Christianity and Antiquity—Beatrice sent Virgil to Dante, and Virgil takes him to Beatrice and then leaves him—but that never repudiates the rightful value of nature to the advantage of supernatural values. Moreover, for Dante 'nature' means cosmos, which as such is thoroughly permeated by the divine *eros*, as indeed we saw when we considered the question of the relationship between monarchy and Church; without *amor* (Dante even says *caritas*) there is no order in the kingdom and so none in Antiquity, philosophy or poetry.

Since the knot that ties together the different parts of Dante's work is to be found in his personality, his personal destiny also becomes a matter of some urgency. Dante wrestled with the problem of when and how far it was right for him to speak of himself. His name only appears once in the *Divine Comedy*: at the climax of his meeting with Beatrice, when, still veiled, she looks at him and calls him (. . . *suon del nome mio, che di necessità qui si registra*).[111] And yet the whole *Divine Comedy* is a poem written in the first person. Dante refers to Boethius, who, 'in a pressing situation, to save himself from the eternal shame of his captivity', found himself also compelled to use the first person; he refers to Augustine and his *Confessions*, where the saint speaks of himself 'because his assessment of himself was a lesson for others and so of great benefit'. He observes a total silence on the subject of Abelard's *historia calamitatum*; here existence cannot serve as a lesson, here the personal destiny is not sufficiently illuminated by Christian love. But Boethius is close to him; like Boethius unjustly condemned politically and deprived of his

[110] Par 1, 13f.

[111] Pg 30, 63.

liberty, Dante passed his life in humiliating exile, in 'poverty', a 'pilgrim, almost a beggar', 'a vessel without sail or helm'.[112] Like one of the giants in chains, Dante groans under the terrible injustice and does not tire of exposing it and, in the process, by his own example, of exposing all the ethical and political injustice of Italy and the world. But at the same time his own destiny must enable him to grasp the Christian account of the meaning of existence: 'O my brother, we are every one citizens of one true city; but thou wouldst say that thine lived in Italy a pilgrim.'[113] In Paradise Dante's ancestor speaks prophetically about the banishment and uprooting that are coming to him, the loss of what is dearest to him, the 'salty taste of the bread of strange lands', the 'hard way up and down another man's stairs', the wickedness and senselessness of his companions, the difficult task of reconciling the prudence and wisdom incumbent on one who has been politically humiliated with the fearlessness demanded by his mission.[114] This whole prediction nevertheless depends on a vision of what God has foreordained for Dante, which gives it the tone of a *dolce armonia*,[115] while 'that lady who was leading me to God' wondrously speaks the concluding word: 'Change thy thought; think that I am in his presence who lightens the burden of every wrong'.[116] Earth is *esilio di Babilon*, to be at home is to be with God.[117] One so attached to the earth as Dante was would never have discovered the meaning of Christian resignation if it had not been for the glaring injustice of his humiliation; it is this to which he must bear witness. This is the price he pays for being able to look down from the spheres on the *insensata cura dei mortali*, with their *deffetivi sillogismi*, and to rise above the concerns of the four faculties: 'One was going after law and another after the medicine, one was following the priesthood and another seeking to rule by force or craft, one was set on robbery and another on affairs of state, one was labouring in the toils of fleshly delights and another given to idleness; while I, set free from all these things, was high in heaven with Beatrice, received thus gloriously.[118] Whoso laments that we die

[112] Conv 1, 3.
[113] Pg 13, 94–96.
[114] Par 17, 46–142.
[115] Par 17, 44.
[116] Par 18, 4–6.
[117] Par 23, 133–135.
[118] Par 11, 1–12.

here to live above has not seen there the refreshment from the eternal showers of grace.'[119] From this height man's hectic life on earth appears as a universal immersion in *cupidigia*. 'O covetousness, who so plungest mortals in thy depths that none has power to lift his eyes above thy waves! The will blossoms well in men, but the continual rain turns the sound plums withered and sour.'[120] But what is more, this bitter privation makes a hope surpassing all human calculation grow within him, a hope that is the reason for his being given the privilege of visiting the royal mansions of God: 'So that, having seen the truth of this court, thou mayst with that strengthen in thyself and others the hope that begets true love below. . . . The Church militant has not a child more full of hope . . . therefore it is granted him to come from Egypt to Jerusalem that he may see it before his warfare is accomplished.'[121] Thus Dante arrives in Heaven like the Nordic barbarian in Rome who marvelled at the superhuman grandeur of the Lateran, like the pilgrim who looks about him *nel tempio de suo voto* and 'hopes to tell of it on his return'.[122] Pilgrim here below, pilgrim above, Dante is given, by his exile, the right distance from which to measure everything in its true value.

There is however a third and most important aspect of Dante's conversion to the laity to be considered. In addition to the preoccupation with individual personality and destiny, there appeared, for the first time in Christian theology, the theme of individual, personal and fateful love. Dionysius and Bonaventure had indeed found divine Eros in the cosmos, and in his *Confessions* Augustine had recognized and confessed personal Eros, but the first was not personal, and the second was not in the least degree theological. Likewise, the amorous adventures of the heroes of Artus made no claim to theological relevance. But this is the claim that Dante makes for Beatrice. The thoroughly earthly love of the *Vita Nuova* is carried as far as the heights of Heaven; indeed, it is extolled as the motive power for the whole journey through the hereafter. The love, which began on earth between two human beings, is not denied, is not

[119] Par 14, 25–27.

[120] Par 27, 121–126.

[121] Par 25, 40–45, 53–57.

[122] Par 31, 31–39, 43–45.

bypassed in the journey to God; it is not, as was always, naturally enough, hitherto the case, sacrificed on the altar of the classical *via negativa*; no, it is carried right up to the throne of God, however transformed and purified. This is utterly unprecedented in the history of Christian theology. As Charles Williams rightly saw, it transcends the whole neo-Platonic scheme of *via positiva*, *negativa*, *eminentiae*.[123] It is true that the figure of the beloved is enriched with symbolic content, but it would be ridiculous to maintain that she is only a symbol or allegory—of what? of faith? of theology? of the vision of God?. Only dusty academics could fall for something as abstruse as that. No, the figure of the beloved is a young Florentine girl of flesh and blood. Why should a Christian man not love a woman for all eternity and allow himself to be introduced by that woman to a full understanding of what 'eternity' means? And why should it be so extraordinary—ought one not rather to expect it—that such a love needs, for its total fulfilment, the whole of theology and Heaven, Purgatory and Hell?

One can surround the real figure of Beatrice, as also Dante's real life of love, with as many question marks as one wishes. Nevertheless, the principle is established for the first time, and never again so magnificently: for the sake of infinite love, it is not necessary for the Christian to renounce finite love. On the contrary, in a positive spirit, he can incorporate his finite love into that which is infinite—but at the cost of terrible sufferings, of course, as Dante shows us.

It is only in the light of this principle, which justifies the life and work of Dante, that one can resolve the enigma of the *Convivio* (with which Gilson was so concerned, though without resolving it):[124] why does Dante, in harsh and almost incomprehensible opposition to his masters Aristotle and Thomas, declare that the supreme philosophical discipline is not metaphysics but ethics? Dante establishes a parallel between the sciences and the ten heavenly spheres that surround the earth. For the seven planetary spheres there is no difficulty; they represent the seven liberal arts: the *trivium* of grammar, dialectic

[123] *The Figure of Beatrice*. A Study in Dante (1943, 7th impression, 1958).
[124] *Dante et la philosophie* (1939), pp. 100–113.

and rhetoric, and the *quadrivium* of arithmetic, music, geometry and astronomy. The tenth sphere, the Empyrean of God, is reserved for theology. But the eighth and ninth spheres, the heavens of fixed stars and crystal, must accommodate the highest philosophical disciplines: the science of the nature of the world (physics), of right conduct (ethics), and of the being of existents (metaphysics). However, an abstract science can simply lay no claim to a place in Dante's cosmos; by following an Aristotelian and Thomist path, Dante sees in physics the science of visible (material) essences, symbolized by the visible pole star in the sky, and, on the other hand, in metaphysics the science, known only by deduction; of invisible essences—the celestial intelligences, First Matter, divinity—symbolized by the invisible pole star. Thus, physics and metaphysics form, henceforth together, the sphere of the fixed stars, dominated by the heaven of transparent crystal, the *Primum mobile*, which moves all things, even metaphysics: this is ethics.[125]

For Dante, however, ethics or the science of right conduct, means, as we have already seen, the building of one's individual perfection (*virtù*) on the foundation of the soul's perfection, its nobility, a nobility that is the 'divine germ' in man, derived from both nature and grace. It is infused into man by celestial intelligences and, beyond them, directly by God; and, as *hormê*, it directs man towards his eternal good; in other words, it is Eros. In long expositions of the nature of philosophy (to which we shall return) Eros is defined as the union of the two moments of love (*philo-*) and wisdom (*sophia*), whose encounter is loving, erotic and, for that very reason, aesthetic.[126] This Eros, supreme principle of the world, *l'amor che muove il sole e l'altre stelle*,[127] cannot, for the poet Dante, refer to 'principles of being', but only to beings that actually exist.

The correct attitude towards all things can also be expressed by the supreme ethical concept of *giustizia* (with whose glorification Dante intended to conclude his *Convivio* and, though subordinated to it, by all the Aristotelian virtues, above all the cardinal virtues, which can also be represented by the

[125] Conv 2, 4; 2, 14–15.
[126] Conv 3, 14–15; *cf.* the next chapter.
[127] Par 33, 145.

courtly virtues, preeminently *cortesia*. In adult life Dante recommended *temperanza e fortezza*, or *magnanimità*, which, in 'Virgil, our greatest poet', Aeneas shows when he leaves Dido, or even when he 'hardened himself to enter alone with the Sybil into Hell and search for the soul of his father Anchises, in the face of so many perils'. But Dante adds immediately that, to be perfect, this period of life 'needs without question to be loving' (*d'essere amorosa*), which he also illustrates by the example of Aeneas.[128] Dante, the political man of cosmic-Christian justice, and Dante, the erotic man in quest of Beatrice, are one and the same, and above this ethical two-in-one-ness he knows of nothing except the inner mysteries of the Godhead. This primacy of ethics in Dante's thought should not be construed as the primacy of *praxis* over *theoria*, of action over contemplation, since he often stands up for the old hierarchy of values, but rather as the primacy of concrete personal existence over the essentialist world view of scholasticism. That is Dante's new way.

2. EROS AND AGAPE, OR WHO IS BEATRICE?

Dante must be interpreted from the summit of his work. The *Comedy* remains the key to the *Canzoniere* and the *Convivio*, which means that the Beatrice of the *Comedy* is the key to the earlier writings. The *Vita Nuova* is symbolic and melancholy, the *Convivio* is philosophizing and fragmentary, but the *Comedy* achieves a completeness of expression that raises the two previous works above themselves, liberates them and leads them to their true realization. At every stage of his life Dante strove for integration. The *Vita Nuova* is already qualitatively much more than what his poet friends, Guinizelli, Cavalcanti, Lapo Gianni, had achieved. And it is only in virtue of this 'more' that Dante, who meets these friends at various stages on his journey through Heaven, can greet them and put in their mouths the songs of his youth: Casella—'*Amor che nella mente mi ragiona*';[129] Bonagiunta—'*Donne ch'avete intelletto d'amore*'.[130] But in the case

[128] Conv 4, 26. [129] Pg 2, 112. [130] Pg 24, 51.

of the former, Cato warns the indolent, negligent spirits who hang on his words in rapture to 'haste to the mountain', and the latter is a poet of the old school, who concedes preeminence to the other. Dante climbs past both of them to a higher level. But if he is to study philosophy, he must first of all seek a superior point of view:

'We are not to call any man a real philosopher who is friendly with wisdom for the sake of pleasure, as are many who delight in composing odes and who zealously devote themselves to rhetoric and music. . . . We are not to call him a real philosopher who is a friend of wisdom for profit, as are lawyers, physicians, and almost all the clergy, who do not study in order to know, but in order to get money or office; and if anyone would give them that which it is their purpose to acquire, they would linger over their study no longer.' Beyond the delightful (*delectabile*) and the useful (*utile*) there is a love for wisdom for its own sake; wisdom alone is worthy of man (*honestum*). And just as love between men is genuine when each loves the other without reserve, so the true philosopher embraces wisdom in her totality, and wisdom in her totality opens herself to the whole man. 'And just as real friendship, abstracted from the individual soul and considered only in itself, has as its object the knowledge of right action, and for its form has the striving for right action, so philosophy considered in itself, apart from the individual soul, has as its object understanding, and as its form an almost divine love for the intellect (*quasi divino amore allo 'ntelletto*).'[131] So it is that the *Convivio*, which provides a philosophical exposition of the *Canzoni*, seeks a standpoint raised above the Eros of the run-of-the-mill poets and philosophers. And just as divine *hormê*, that gift of grace, is gradually distinguished from a purely natural drive or instinct by virtue of the superior goal for which it strives,[132] just as the developing embryo at first assumes the form of a plant, sponge and animal before there is revealed in it the spiritual form, which nonetheless was already in it as its motive power,[133] so the Eros of the poet rises up with a sudden start (the *Convivio* was left unfinished) to the height of its realization in the *Comedy*. The love referred to in the *Vita*

[131] Conv 3, 11. [132] Conv 4, 22. [133] Pg 25, 49–51.

Nuova, which in the *Convivio* sought, by means of philosophy, to gain interior space, only comes to itself when it is exteriorized and enlarged till it assumes universal proportions, whereby the universe itself receives its true form, the form of love. Whoever the consoling *Donna gentila*, on whom Dante depended after the death of Beatrice, may be, whatever the place in his earthly life occupied by Gemma, whom he married and who bore him sons and daughters but who (according to Boccaccio) did not follow him into exile, the *Comedy* proves that Dante wants to see his life and work, indeed his whole Christian existence, as resting on an unshakeable fidelity, which he preserves from the dreamlike days of his youth, and which persists, purified, right on to the summit of his holy faith. If Helen were Gretchen, Faust would be a counter to Dante; but Helen's garments are dissolved, in dionysiac fashion, into the All, and while Gretchen can intercede for Faust to Mary, she cannot be his muse. And in Hegel's unending degrees of mediation there is no eros and no fidelity, because what is mediated is only ever the Absolute Spirit mediating itself to itself. Only Claudel's *Le Soulier de Satin* again achieves Dante's dimension, in which personal love and the shaping of the universe are mutully conditioned, taking the same path through the hell of the hardest renunciations and the purgatories of expiated infidelity. As Augustine says, 'Etiam peccata'. And yet the woman Claudel loves is not dead, so everything remains that much more passionate. Philosophy, which came to Dante's aid, is not at Claudel's disposal, and so a tragic dualism between the two images of women becomes inevitable in his work (*cf.* among the *Grandes Odes*, *La Muse qui est la grâce*). This muse could and ought to carry out Beatrice's work, but instead the muse dashes herself on the erotic defiance of the poet. Beatrice's purificatory and redemptive power in the end remains unique; she alone leads from Eros to Agape, or rather she is that Eros that is transfigured into agape. 'For the lady who guides thee through this divine region has in her look the same virtue as had the hand of Ananias.'[134] And the poet replies by referring to the integrating power of heavenly love, whether *quanta scrittura* refers to the *Minnesang* or philosophy or

[134] Par 26, 10–12.

both: 'The good that satisfies this court is alpha and omega of all the scripture that love reads to me in tones loud or low.'[135] The disciple John, who in Heaven examines Dante's love, asks him to enumerate the elements of which his ultimate love is composed, out of which it achieves wholeness. 'Therefore I began again: "All those things whose bite can make the heart turn to God have wrought together in my charity; for the world's existence and my own, the death he bore that I might live, and that which every believer hopes for as I do, with the living assurance of which I spoke [of the good], have drawn me from the sea of perverse love and have brought me to the shore of that love that is just."'[136] Dante has been suspected of Averroism, in the respect that for him, to an increasing extent, all good activity originates from Heaven, while the human heart—as it were, the stuff into which the heavenly forms are embedded—is again and again compared to a passive 'wax' which can at most contribute a greater or lesser pliability to the form.[137] But this, however, is only one side of the dialectic of love, in which the ascent of the love results both wholly from the grace bestowed upon him by the beloved and from his own efforts, is as much an unmerited favour as his own deserts, as much an unfathomable absolution as his own repentance and conversion. That is why the full concept of love in Dante cannot be adequately described either as Eros (striving upwards) or as Agape (condescending); from the first, love is seen and described as lying beyond this opposition, and this 'beyond' becomes ever clearer in the successive stages of the work.

The *Canzoniere*, and more especially the *Vita Nuova*, are, as Dante says in the *Convivio*, like 'presentiments in a dream' (*quasi sognando già vedea*);[138] they are in the strictest sense an 'aesthetic anticipation' of the later, consciously accepted totality. Dimly and sadly aware of the value of the treasure that is still hidden from him, the young lover enshrines it in a prose whose subtlety verges on preciosity. The real vision of the girl, who at their first

[135] Par 26, 16–18.

[136] Par 26, 55–63.

[137] Conv 1, 8; 2, 10; M 2, 2; Inf 11, 49f; Pg 18, 38; 33, 79f; Par 1, 40–42; 8, 127; 13, 67–69; 13, 73–75. A. S. Cook, 'Dante's Figure of the Seal and the Wax', *Mod. Lang. Notes* (1900), 511f.

[138] Conv 2, 13.

meeting was nine years old, carries on in the form of a dream, in a *miravigliosa visione*, in which Amor, lordly and terrible and yet full of the promise of inner joy, appears and addresses the poet with the words, *Ego dominus tuus*: 'In his arms I seemed to see a naked figure, sleeping, wrapped lightly in a crimson cloth. Gazing intently I saw it was the gracious girl who had bestowed her greeting on me the day before. In one hand the standing figure held a fiery object, and he seemed to say, *Vide cor tuum*. After a little while I thought he wakened her who slept and prevailed on her to eat the glowing object in his hand. Reluctantly and hesitantly she did so. A few moments later his happiness turned to bitter grief, and, weeping, he gathered the figure in his arms and together they seemed to ascend into the heavens.'[139] The apparent favour he subsequently bestows on other women assists the poet in concealing his true love from the world. The first lady, who at Amor's bidding had served as a screen, leaves the city. Amor then reappears 'like a traveller, dressed in simple, humble clothing' and tells him of a second lady who will be his defence. But the homage he now gives her gets the poet talked about, so that Beatrice refuses to greet him in the street. He implores Amor for mercy. The latter appears to him while he sleeps and says, *Fili mi, tempus est, ut praetermittantur simulacra nostra*, but then bursts into tears. Dante, dismayed, then asks him, 'Lord of all nobility, why do you weep?' Amor replies with the prophetic words: *Ego tamquam centrum circuli, cui simuli modo se habent circumferentiae partes: tu autem non sic.*[140] Amor is at the centre and from there surveys all the paths that should lead the lover, still on the circumference, to the centre, and when he considers their height and their depth, he weeps. Death, everywhere present in the *Vita Nuova*, stalks these paths, death which from moment to moment comes ever nearer and finally snatches away Beatrice herself. Meanwhile, the poet remains ensnared by the bittersweet dialectic of erotic preexistence. Love is good, because it turns the faithful lover's mind away from all that is less worthy; it is not good because it brings more and more pain; and yet, on the other hand, it is good, because such pain is itself sweet and the beloved is unique.

[139] VN 3.

[140] VN 12.

The sight of the beloved, the pleasantries she exchanges with others about him, make him say, mysteriously: *io tenni li piedi in quella parte della vita, di là dalla quale non si può ire più per intendimento di ritornare.*[141] Anyone who thought of returning would not be able, or rather would not be permitted, to go out beyond that extremity. But what would it mean to return? What one day will it mean for Dante to return from Heaven? Everything presses him toward the final truth. The poet decides from then on to compose only 'what was praise of this most gracious being', and at once inspiration complies with that decision in the famous canzone, *Donne ch'avete intelletto d'amore*, in which the angels and the blessed souls in Paradise ask that Beatrice return home to God. But God in his mercy grants the lover still on earth a short reprieve; for all women who look upon her she is the archetype, but none can resist her eyes or her smile.[142] And yet these eyes make beautiful everything they survey.[143] Beatrice's father dies, the poet falls seriously ill, and, as if in delirium, there appears to him the unavoidability of his beloved's death, and other hallucinatory figures whisper to him: 'You too are already dead'. In a dream Beatrice lies dead before him, her face full of gentleness and humility; she seems to say: 'I now go to behold the fountainhead of peace.' Then he too calls passionately on death: 'Sweet death, come to me . . . see, I already wear your colour.' Soon after that Amor says to him: 'Bless now the day I took you in my power for this you must surely do.' The poet then sees, coming first, Giovanna, the 'mistress of his best friend', and behind her, Beatrice. The name of the first reminds him of the Forerunner, 'who preceded the true light. . . . And afterwards Amor seemed also to say these further words: "Anyone who thought carefully about this would call Beatrice Amor because of the great resemblance she bears to me."'[144] Now Beatrice dies, yet the fact is just registered. The poet is not capable of describing it, and, what is more, he would have to put himself in the limelight, which must be avoided at all cost, perhaps because, in dying, Beatrice

[141] VN 14.
[142] VN 19.
[143] VN 21.
[144] VN 24.

has let him know she returns his love? It is possible; we do not know. The number nine has constantly accompanied her to the point where she becomes the very embodiment of the number, 'that is, a miracle, of which the root is nothing other than the glorious Trinity itself. Perhaps a more subtle mind could find a still more subtle reason for it'.[145] If, as three times three, she has been God's radiance, has grace, then, as the next canzone says, hers is no ordinary return to God, but rather God's calling back to himself what is his own. Then follows the account of the anniversary of Beatrice's death when the poet first catches sight of the *gentil donna*, who, full of compassion, watches him from a window. For the sake of this compassion he becomes fond of her, seeks her presence, is bewildered by it and is brought to that state of division that the first canzone of the *Convivio* will describe and allegorically interpret. The *Vita Nuova*, however, does not embark on this allegorical path but returns 'with bitter regret' and 'a heart full of shame' to the most lovely Beatrice. The book closes with two sonnets of longing and pilgrimage. They sing of the 'new understanding, which Love, by weeping, gave him' and which draws him up above the highest heavens, where he sees the transfigured Beatrice. But the 'pilgrim spirit . . . speaks of what it sees in subtle words I do not comprehend within my heart forlorn': 'Yet of that lady sweet I know it speaks, for oft it brings my Beatrice to thought; and this, dear ladies, well I understand.' The last vision reveals to the poet things which make him decide to write no more of the beloved 'until I could do so more worthily'. 'If it shall please him by whom all things live that my life continue for a few years, I hope to compose concerning her what has never been written in rhyme of any woman. And then may it please him who is the Lord of courtesy that my soul may go up to see the glory of my lady, that is of the blessed Beatrice, who now in glory beholds the face of him *qui est per omnia secula benedictus*.'[146]

Fundamental Christian ideas run through the whole book. Above all, the idea of humility constantly recurs: Beatrice herself is crowned with *umilità*, and at the sight of her the poet's

[145] VN 30.
[146] VN 42–43.

heart becomes humble. The grace of the woman whom he adores is immediately characterized, here and in the *Canzoniere*, by *pietà*, compassionate love. To meet Beatrice means for Dante, to enter in upon the heart of Christianity: 'Whenever and wherever she appeared, in the hope of receiving her exquisite salutation I felt I had not an enemy in the world. Indeed, I glowed with a flame of charity that moved me to forgive all who had ever injured me.'[147] It is Christianity but, as it were, in an atmosphere of aesthetic reverie, whose distinctive charm is the deliberate failure to distinguish between dream and reality. The Platonic motifs, from which the *Convivio* branches off, and which regard the beloved as an idea, a heavenly power, an emanation from the Godhead, at the same time provide a philosophical justification for this half-real dream-like existence. It is possible to offer an interpretation of Dante principally in terms of this early stage, to present the Christian element in his work in mythical-Platonic terms and to see the associated doctrine of love, which emerges at precisely the same time as the *dolce stil nuovo*, as the hypostatisation of an enclosed, self-contained world of human emotion. This is how he was treated in the symbolism of Rossetti in England and of all those like Rossetti on the continent; the atmosphere of Tristan, of Petrarch's, Michelangelo's, and Shakespeare's sonnets is not far away. Indeed, the same wind was blowing in the circle of Dante's friends, where Eros ruled over the heart as an all-powerful *fatum*, a sweet calamity, and this problem was not really overcome by Guido Guinizelli, where the Platonic tendency breaks through, the contemplation of heavenly beauty in the nobility of form, in the eyes, mouth and words that reveal the *cor gentile*. Dante has this air in his lungs; he exhaled it once again, with inner sympathy and passion, in his song in Hell about Francesca da Rimini,[148] only to leave it behind him, once and for all, in Hell. He preserves something of it in Purgatory and Hell—apparently a great deal, because even the divine Eros in Paradise is clothed in the language of the *dolce stil nuovo* and could never have been expressed without that

[147] VN 11.
[148] Inf 5, 73–142.

language.[149] Yet what is preserved is a transfigured Eros, cleansed of all tragedy and the melancholy of decay.[150]

But one must not overlook the fact that, in the dream world of the *Canzoniere*, essential themes of the *Comedy* are announced. The hardness of Hell is anticipated in the terrible '*canzoni* of stone', which portray the stony, pitiless heart of the beloved; for example in *Amor tu vedi ben*, whose hammered rhythm Dante boasts of having invented, and in the truly formidable *Così nel mio parlar*, which cruelly depicts Eros as a vampire and kindles a war without mercy. Many of the punishments and forms of torture that the damned suffer in Hell are inflicted on the lover in the *Canzoniere*. The heart, turned to stone, glass and ice,[151] is first smashed, then healed again for its further undoing.[152]

L'imaginar dolente che m'acide
Davanti mi dipinge ogni martiro. . . .[153]

Seen here in advance, the torments of Hell are also a function of heavenly Eros, as can be read on the gate of Hell (*fecemi . . . il primo Amore*), and it is from there that they derive their meaning.

The *Convivio* is Dante's attempt to find a bridge that will take him to his beloved, now disappeared. The first intermediary was the *donna della finestra* at the end of the *Vita Nuova*. But the Platonic doctrine of love, there already sketched out, presents a second intermediary: philosophy, love of wisdom. And because Dante always works like an architect, he establishes an interior connection between the two: the songs to the *donna pietosa* are interpreted, in the 'allegorical sense', as expressing love for *sophia*. There is in all this a measure of existential obscurity and intentional mystification. The most important canzone, *Voi che intendendo il terzo ciel movete*, describes the conflict in Dante's

[149] Pg 18, 1–75; above all, Par 27, 88–99, where the *Minnesang* style is transferred to the heavenly realm.

[150] For this whole theme, see B. Nardi, *Filosofia del amore nei rimatori del duecento e in Dante. Dante e la cultura medievale* (Bari, 1949), pp. 1–92.

[151] Sestine, '*Al poco giorno*', Canzone, '*Io son venuto*', '*Ai fals ris*', Str. 3.

[152] Canzone, '*Amor dacchè convien*', Str. 4.

[153] Canzone, '*Ion non posso celar*', Str. 2.

heart between the old love, which lifted up his thoughts to the 'glorified lady' and filled him with a longing for death, and a new love, which struggles bitterly against the old. This new love fills his heart with anxiety until he understands that there is only one Eros, the Eros which assigns to him the new, noble love, the Eros to which he must respond.

Amor, signor verace,
Ecco l'ancella tua, fa che ti piace.

Words, literally, of manifest infidelity and near blasphemous in their presumptuous use of other, most sacred words; only allegorical interpretation could remove the double scandal. But this interpretation remains profoundly ambiguous, especially if one considers Dante's bitter confession in Purgatory, when he acknowledges the insanity of his life since the death of Beatrice. In the *Convivio* there is willful dissimulation: does the literal sense have historical reality, the allegorical being secondary and metaphorical? Or is the allegorical the only true sense,[154] the literal being only its poetic garb? Or, finally (and this might be the solution), is the allegory intended to justify the historical reality? Beatrice has been carried away to be inaccessible above the highest spheres; even love for her threatens to evaporate into unintelligibility. In order to live, this love needs mediation, and since these intermediaries are only functions of the ultimate love, the poet believes he is permitted to identify them with it. Another woman, who embodies all the noble qualities of *umilità, pietà, cortesia,* keeps alive the reality of the beloved, and philosophy, by means of its universality, provides a bridge to the one who is now so far away. Philosophy teaches us about the cosmic system, the circling spheres and the intelligences that govern them, upon which the poet climbs to the Empyrean. It teaches us to see the symbolism of all the cosmic forms and to perceive, through them, the ultimate Beloved, the *eschaton orekton.* Philosophy also teaches us to understand man's ethical and political behaviour, according to the Platonic/Aristotelian doctrine of *politeia,* as of a piece with his philosophical Eros, and to apply such understanding to the way we live. Beatrice, as the

[154] '*E da procedere all, esposizione allegorica e vera*' (Conv 2, 13).

goal of both intermediaries, is in Heaven—Dante knows this through a 'revelation of love'. There is no need to speak further of her, for all things, even the *Convivio*, go on their pilgrim way to find her.[155]

We can leave the question of Dante's love life on one side. It is certain that the *donna pietosa* is someone other than his wife, Gemma, and both the poems and the *Comedy* make us suspect that there were other women too who kept alive the image of Beatrice for him as much as they obscured it. It is the problem of 'Platonic love', inasmuch as the *via positiva* Dante follows had to demand the compatibility of both the contemplation of the beautiful and the renunciation of its possession—and here, of course, we meet the problem of Dante's marriage. Gemma can be only the woman passed by and humiliated by the poet-genius. But about all this the *Convivio* is silent.

On the other hand, it speaks abundantly about philosophy, especially of those sciences that together give it completeness: physics the science of the cosmos, metaphysics the science of the intelligences and ethics. This is the *donna pietosa* who takes pity on him and by whom he moves upward to the highest love. We must take seriously the description of the erotic-anagogic beauty of philosophy, the transfer to it of all the praises of the *Minnesang*. Her eyes and her glances, when they are 'turned to her lovers', are overpowering, they 'enflame the soul when it is inwardly free',[156] make 'a great fire from a spark', a longing for vision, even in the depths of sleep.[157] A glance is a revelation of the soul that lies hidden within, and the glances of philosophy flash before the thinker like incandescent revelations of the absolute, like eruptions into this present world of what is eternal and essentially hidden. 'The sight of this lady has been dispensed to us so bountifully not only through beholding her face which she shows to us, but through the longing to acquire the things that she keeps hidden from us.'[158] 'At the window of the eyes' appear the interior dispositions of the soul, and likewise, in her smiling mouth, 'the soul shows herself . . . like colour under glass (*siccome colore dopo vetro*)'.[159] 'I do not say without good

[155] Conv 2, 9.
[156] Conv 2, 16.
[157] Conv 3, 1.
[158] Conv 3, 14.
[159] Conv 3, 8.

cause "where she taketh heed of me", and not "where I take heed of her". But hereby I wish to intimate the great power (*virtù*) that her eyes exercised over me, for their rays pierced through me on all sides as if I had been transparent.'[160] This piercing can also seem to 'kill', precisely when, in dialectic, philosophy's dilemmas seem to be torn in two.[161] Here she can behave unfeelingly as the beloved rejecting her lover and thus not reveal herself.[162] This does not prevent love being 'the form of philosophy', and this love manifests itself in its dealings with wisdom, which 'brings in its train wondrous beauty'.[163] In brief: 'Philosophy has wisdom for her material object and love for her form',[164] and since wisdom is ultimately eternal, the love that loves the eternal can also only have the character of eternity. Just as 'the divine light radiates into the intelligences without any intermediary (*senza mezzo*) . . .': because it is eternal, so also must its objects be, and *vice versa*. This is why love of philosophy confers on man a resemblance to divine love.[165] This personal view, both of the divine wisdom that looks and smiles upon us and of love's answer, leads Dante to link this same love with faith and hope. Through philosophy's revelatory glance of love, which, like a flash of lightning, fleetingly reveals for us the obscurity of God's mysteries, 'we are helped to believe that every miracle may be accounted for in a more lofty understanding and consequently may exist. Whence our excellent faith has its origin, and from faith comes the hope that dares to long for things foreseen, and from hope springs the workings of charity. And by these three virtues men rise to the pursuit of philosophy in that celestial Athens where Stoics and Peripatetics and Epicureans through the skill of eternal truth willingly complement each other in harmony of spirit'.[166]

From philosophy comes both the clear-eyed glance, the convincing demonstration, and the 'enigmatic smile': the *persuasioni*, the persuasive force of the beautiful woman, who 'seduces' us into what is higher, who veils and unveils her charms, only veiling with the promise of unveiling. And what is

[160] Conv 3, 10.
[161] Conv 2, 16.
[162] Conv 4, 1.
[163] Conv 3, 13.
[164] Conv 3, 14.
[165] *Ibid.*
[166] *Ibid.*

unveiled is so overwhelming for us that Dante can regard the final communion of lover and beloved as simply the conclusion, of the yearning and striving, which have now assumed form and shape. For Dante 'eternal striving' is a contradiction, an impossibility, in fact a moral outrage.[167] Of course, Eros draws us upward ever higher, purifying, humbling and demanding renunciations, for the simple reason that the beloved is with God, and philosophy implants in us the love of what God himself loves. But this is only for the sake of the discovery and vision of that ultimate figure, which Dante reveals to us in the image of the Celestial Rose.

For Dante, looking truth or wisdom in the eyes—and that can mean seeing oneself in *reflexio completa*[168]—means not stopping before one has encountered the object of God's approval and love. But Beatrice is precisely the definitive object of God's approval and love, a part of eternal wisdom, and since one cannot really speak of a part where all things interpenetrate, she is that wisdom herself. In fact, now it becomes unimportant whether it is the *donna gentile* who symbolizes philosophy; all that matters is that the ineffable grace, which once and for the first time was encountered on earth in Beatrice, is the manifestation of that eternal grace, which loved us in advance, from eternity: 'Open your eyes and perceive that before you were made she loved you, guiding and ordering your whole life, and after you were made, in order to direct you aright, she came in your own likeness to you.'[169] Is this meant to refer to Beatrice? Or Wisdom incarnate, Christ? At this point does the blasphemy of offering the *Ecce ancilla* to the god, Eros, become intelligible and pardonable?

Dante cannot be suspected of having hypostasized eternal Sophia, which for him is nothing other than the means of eternalising Eros in God, of understanding Eros not merely as the love of the heart striving toward God or as God's love of the world pouring itself on creation, but as the fulfilled archetype of the erotic reciprocity between man and woman. On the one hand, God recognizes himself when he recognizes his love for

[167] Conv 3, 15. [168] Conv 4, 2.
[169] Conv 3, 15.

the world, for the things he intends to create, and his love is so great that it is not troubled by his foreknowledge that some creatures will perish, no more than would nature prevent a tree from blossoming, supposing that it had consciousness and knew that some flowers would fall off. On the other hand, 'although God in beholding himself sees all things as one (*insiemente tutto*), he nonetheless also sees all things as distinct from himself and from one another, *in quanto la distinzione delle cose è in Lui*'.[170] And so wisdom is God himself and yet is not God himself (just as Eve, taken from his rib, was Adam and yet not Adam). Thus

> God, who comprehends everything in a unifying manner (for his comprehension is his encircling) sees nothing so gentle as he sees when he looks where this philosophy abides. . . . For if we recall to memory what has been said earlier, philosophy is a loving converse with wisdom, which is found in God most of all, since in him dwell highest wisdom and highest love and highest act (*atto*), and it cannot exist elsewhere except in so far as it proceeds from himself. Divine philosophy is therefore part of the divine essence . . . and she exists in him in true and perfect fashion as if eternally wedded to him (*quasi per eterno matrimonio*). In the other intelligences she exists in lesser degree, almost like the beloved prostitute (*quasi come druda*) of whom no lover has complete enjoyment, but in whose aspect he finds satisfaction for his desires and enthusiasm (*vaghezza*).[171]

This is the key word in the *Convivio*: philosophy is 'prostitution' as long as it is still on the way to the highest love. However, it becomes a perfect participation in the eternal nuptials the moment Beatrice is discovered to be the one who is in God, the one whom God loves, and who is just as God loves her to be. For this reason, once she is found, she can never be lost.[172] But, on the other hand, 'philosophy not only lodges in the wise, but also . . . wherever the love for her finds lodging . . . whose true home is in the Holy of holies of the divine Mind.'[173]

The *Divine Comedy* realises the truth of the *Convivio*, which was left unfinished, probably because ultimate Christian truth and transparency cannot be attained through the distinction

[170] Conv 3, 12.
[171] *Ibid.*
[172] Par 33, 100–105.
[173] Conv 4, 30.

between literal sense and allegory. For if the literal sense was true, it was infidelity to Beatrice, and no allegory could disguise the fact that it was an illusory form of self-redemption and not the receiving of divine grace. But if the literal sense was not true but purely fictitious, then the plane of existence had not been fully attained, and the study of philosophy was really just Dante's way of consoling himself for the loss of Beatrice. Only a totally new starting point could clarify this blurred distinction. From now on, all mediations between Heaven and earth are seen in principle as the ways of grace, occasioned by Christian, not philosophical, powers. Beatrice then proves herself to be a reality (not a symbol), for, in her *pietà* for Dante and in graciously sending Virgil to him, she is stirred into action by the highest creaturely sanctity: Mary is the one who has taken pity and who sent St Lucy to Beatrice in order to spur her into helping her beloved. Thus stirred, Beatrice descends into Limbo and beseeches Virgil to hurry to the aid of her 'friend': 'I fear he may already be so far astray that I have risen too late to succour him. . . . Love moved me and makes me speak.'[174]

The *Comedy* begins with Dante being lost in the dark wood of sin. This would have been fatal to him, and no self-constructed philosophy could have helped him out of it had not grace thrown him both a life-belt and a fish-hook. Love alone led him to the terrible warnings of Hell and to purification in Purgatory, at the end of which he must encounter, withstand and declare himself for love. The key to the whole journey, as Virgil says to the poet, is to be found in Beatrice: 'When thou art before her sweet radiance whose fair eyes see all, thou shalt know from her of thy life's journey.'[175] If in the *Convivio* the eyes and the smile of philosophy flashed like lightning and led the poet upwards, the whole of the *Comedy* is filled with the eyes and the smile, indeed laugh (*riso*), of Beatrice. The thought of it was enough to lead Dante up to her; but the sight of her leads him to the vision of God. The whole journey is constantly called a grace, indeed an unimaginably exalted grace. That Dante, a living man, a citizen of this world, should proceed through the kingdom of the world to come 'is so strange a thing to hear that it is a great

[174] Inf 2, 64f.

[175] Inf 10, 130–132.

token that God loves thee'.[176] Thus speaks Sapia, and immediately after, Guido del Duca: 'Thou makest us marvel . . . at the grace given thee.'[177] Likewise, Hugo Capet: 'I will tell thee . . . because so great grace shines in thee even before thy death.'[178] Dante gives this reply to the lustful: 'I go up hence to be no longer blind. A lady is above who gains grace for me by which I bring my mortal part through your world.'[179] And to the angry, recalling the unique mission of Isaiah: 'I came here through the anguish of Hell; and since God has so received me into his grace that he wills that I see his court in a way quite strange to modern use. . . .'[180] *Per modo tutto fuor del moderno uso.* Cacciaguida, however, on seeing his 'son', cries out: 'O grace of God poured forth above measure! To whom as to thee was heaven's gate ever opened twice?'[181] Justinian addresses him thus: 'O born for good, to whom grace has given to see the thrones of the eternal triumph.'[182] His own constellation, Gemini, 'light pregnant with mighty power from which I acknowledge all my genius, whatever it be', speaks to Dante of the same 'grace' granted to him 'to enter into the high wheel that bears you round'.[183] Finally, his protectress herself:

E Beatrice cominciò: 'Ringrazia,
Ringrazia il Sol degli angeli, ch'a questo
Sensibil t'ha levato per sua grazia.'[184]

Bernard, who tells him to look up finally at Mary, addresses him as 'child of grace'.[185] It is a grace that imprints upon him the visible signs of election[186] and grants him nothing less than that special grace of certainty of salvation, which Thomas Aquinas

[176] Pg 13, 144.
[177] Pg 14, 13–14; likewise, 14, 80–81.
[178] Pg 20, 41–42.
[179] Pg 26, 58–60.
[180] Pg 16, 39–42.
[181] Par 15, 29–30.
[182] Par 5, 115–116; likewise, the apostle James, Par 25, 40f.
[183] Par 22, 112–120.
[184] Par 10, 52–54, 'And Beatrice began: "Give thanks, give thanks to the Sun of the angels, who to the visible one has raised thee by His grace".'
[185] Par 31, 112.
[186] Pg 21, 22–24.

confirms for him.[187] All this divine grace flows down, as Bernard's prayer in the final canto proclaims, from Mary, the womb of the incarnation of God: 'Thou, Lady, art so great and so prevailing that whoso would have grace and does not turn to thee, his desire would fly without wings . . . in thee is mercy, in thee pity, in thee great bounty, in thee is joined all goodness that is in any creature.'[188] It is the grace of God flowing down to him through Mary, the mediatrix of graces. But this grace is also mediated by the whole of the 'Jerusalem above', by the community of the saints, who were and are entirely real, historical human beings, and from whose midst arises a multitude of helpers, guides and intercessors, each of whom, in his own way, expresses the community of love in its totality. Beatrice, formed by God as the poet's eternal beloved, has, without doubt, the same degree of reality as the other saints. Here is no allegory or symbol; here we are simply dealing with the laws of the *communio sanctorum*. This fact constitutes the foundation of the *Divine Comedy*, which is, therefore, not just one of the transcendental adventure stories of the Middle Ages. There is nothing about the *Comedy* of that curiosity found in the visionary literature of this and later periods. It is existential theology.

From Dante's point of view the journey through the three realms is two things at the same time: first, the history of his redemption from perdition, his progressive realization of what it is to be a Christian; and second, his discovery of how his first and deepest love can become, in a Christian way, truly eternal. For Dante these two are one. The possibility of man's fulfilment existentially demands eternal life. But this is not given as a kind of vague hope, the object of which would always be beyond man's grasp, quite unrealizable in terms of his actual experience of mortality. No, what man, the creature of God, is given, or more specifically, what the Christian is given, is an anticipated incorporation, even in the experiential sense, into eternal life, for he is already a real partaker of divine life in that Christian grace received in the sacraments of the Church. Whoever truly

[187] Par 10, 82–87.
[188] Par 33, 13–15, 19–21.

wishes to be a Christian must keep his psychological experience open and allow it to be determined, to the very last, by the experience of eternal realities. And of course, as Dante knew only too well, that does not mean bypassing the theological virtues, but realizing their inner depth. Even in the heights of Paradise the poet submits to an examination by the chief apostles on the orthodoxy of these three virtues of his. Indeed, on his journey he must also seek to realize what, from the perspective of faith, the experience of life beyond death is as such. What he said of that is of unprecedented profundity and could spring only from a most pure and humble Christian contemplation. It is sufficient to recall how he bathed in the rivers Lethe and Eunoe, how he was able to forget all his past faults without detriment to his own spiritual integrity and yet to remember all that is good and of grace. The words of Cunizza in the sphere of Venus recall her manifold amorous adventures and affairs on earth: 'Yet here we do not repent; nay, we smile, not for our fault, which does not come back to mind, but for the power that ordained and foresaw. Here we contemplate the art that makes beautiful the great result and discern the good for which the world above wheels about the world below.'[189] These words are essentially forgetful only of the experience of sin and lust, and they transfigure all events in the light of God's grace, which, setting aside the former, depraved manner of life, is the true and definitive way by which the blest may appropriate and realize their own earthly life. But such immersion in the correct perspectives of existence would have been difficult for a poet like Dante had he not been able to contemplate at length the spirit, soul and total character of his beloved in glory. Just one look at her was enough for him to perceive in his heart the moral taste and discernment that regulate, in a Christian and definitive way, situations on earth; just one look was enough to communicate that courtesy of heart that sets the tone *nell'aula più segrata* of the heavenly Emperor and his court.[190] This has never been tried in poetry before or since. It would be ludicrous to say that Dante is indeed a great poet but 'still' bound by the

[189] Par 9, 103–108.
[190] Par 25, 40–42, 'in the inner chamber'.

dogma of the Middle Ages or of Catholicism in general: as a poet he can be interpreted only from the centre of this dogma; he identifies himself existentially with it, plunges his inspiration into its waters in order to receive that same inspiration anew from it. Thanks to the concrete, Christian reality of grace, his poetic preexistence in the *Vita Nuova* and his philosophical explorations in the *Convivio* are subsumed without remainder in this new inspiration. Even his political passion, his judgment on his own era and cities and provinces, can be interpreted only from this dogmatic centre.

In this Beatrice is his model. She is what is called, from Origen to the medieval commentaries on the Canticle, the *anima ecclesiastica*,[191] the soul whose experience and sensibility, thoughts and desires have been assumed into the universality of the *Sponsa Christi*, the bride of the Lamb, the heavenly Jerusalem, the company of all the living and of the saints. Dante is given complete Christian authority to identify his beloved, whom he knows to be with God, with this incarnation of the loving Church, and, in so far as she is this, to expect from her mediation of divine grace for his redemption, purification, illumination and union. In the earthly Paradise appears the triumphal procession of the Church, her chariot drawn by Christ in the form of a griffin, accompanied by the four living creatures from Ezekiel, the four and twenty elders, the theological and cardinal virtues and the hagiographers of the Bible. All sing: 'Blessed art thou among the daughters of Adam and blessed forever be thy beauty!'—a paraphrase of the Ave. When the chariot, the 'seven-starred constellation of the first heaven', stands still, three times the cry is heard, '*Veni sponsa de Libano*', without doubt intoned by the author of the Canticle. Hundreds of angels descend from the chariot, strewing flowers to the cry of *Benedictus qui venis* and *Manibus o date lilia plenis*. Then, 'girt with olive over a white veil, clothed under a green mantle with the colour of living flame', Beatrice comes down from the chariot like the sun rising. Dante recognizes this veiled figure immediately by the mysterious power that she radiates, and *d'antico amor sentì la gran potenzia . . . cognosco i segni*

[191] *Cf.* my '*Wer ist die Kirche?*' in *Sponsa Verbi* (1960), pp. 148–202.

dell'antica fiamma . . . il santo riso a sè traeali con l'antica rete.[192] These are words from the world of the *Minnesang*, recalling his youth when first the lovely one appeared to him. The poet does all he can to impress upon his reader the identity of the one who appears now with the completely real Florentine girl; there is no question here of allegory. And yet the mariological and, frankly, christological attributes, together with the cardinal virtues, are later[193] presented as Beatrice's handmaidens, who serve her before she descends to earth—as if she were the Church preexistent with God. The theological virtues form a circle around her: 'Beatrice, turn thy holy eyes. . . .'[194] When the festal procession has gone on to the tree of Paradise, she descends once again from the chariot,[195] and later (Dante sleeps between this and the disappearance of the procession) she is seated 'beneath the new foliage' of the tree of the kingdom, 'upon its root', in the company of the virtues. Now begins the transformation of the Church-chariot, the history of the Church in the form of symbols. Beatrice intervenes here only to drive away the lean fox, the image of heresy.[196] She plays no part in the transformation of the Church into the Great Harlot, but while the virtues sing their lament about the ruin of the holy city, she listens to them 'sighing and compassionate . . ., so altered that Mary changed little more at the cross'.[197]

All this can have only a theological interpretation; any other kind of interpretation, especially of a simply aesthetic-symbolic kind, would have to convict the poet here of extreme bad taste. And if Dante has done everything he can to make us believe in the identification of his *antica fiamma* with the heavenly Beatrice now merged with the Spirit of the Church, if, consequently, he directs his earthly Eros, in all seriousness, at this heavenly object, he is also willing to pay the existential price for it and to submit himself, in confession, to the sacramental judgment of his

[192] 'Felt old love's great power. . . . I know the mark of the ancient flame. . . . so did the holy smile draw them to itself with the old net.' The procession of the Church: Pg 29. The cries: Pg 30, 11, 17; the acknowledgment of love's great and ancient power: Pg 30, 39, 48. The old net: Pg 32. 6.

[193] Pg 31, 106f.

[194] Pg 31, 133.

[195] Pg 32, 36, 86f.

[196] Pg 32, 122.

[197] Pg 33, 4–6.

beloved, who now—across the purifying water—looks down upon him from the heart of the Church.

3. *PURGATORIO*, CONFESSION AND INSPIRATION

The whole of the *Divine Comedy* is unequivocally constructed around Dante's meeting with Beatrice in the *Purgatorio*. The journey through Hell is motivated by the compassion of Beatrice, who sees no other way of setting Dante free from his *follia*,[198] and the various levels of the Mountain of Purgatory are, for Dante, preliminary stages of, and preparation for, that meeting. Aesthetically, it is Paradise that is in the most difficult position. To pass muster as poetry, it must disclose the inner dimensions of Dante and Beatrice's first reunion, for that is where the sole centre of gravity in the drama is to be found and where the decisive catharsis occurs. This scene is fashioned with the utmost aesthetic and theological tact and seriousness, for in it Eros must strip itself bare even to the point of a complete and supremely humiliating nakedness of soul; it must consent to Christian *katorthôsis*, amendment and restoration, which means inseparably both confession and Purgatory. Dante has understood that confession must be precisely a purifying, cauterizing fire, and that Purgatory after death can be no less than the final existential confession: confrontation with love, as it is, really and in Heaven, the total destruction of all on earth that presumptuously called itself by that name. And this ideal-typical, eschatological confession cannot even be practised by man himself; instead it must come down upon him like a judgment, as true love reveals itself to man. That is how Jesus confessed the Samaritan woman at Jacob's well, when he seized upon her evasive, allusive replies and told her everything that she had done. This purification of Eros before its final transfiguration is possible only in the Church, and so the beloved must assume the objective and inexorable countenance of Ecclesia. Here the whole world of Tristan is transcended, as is that of Wolfram's *Parzival* with its symbolic twilight and its

[198] Pg 1, 59.

existentially insoluble ambiguity (*zwîvel*), its objective and fateful guilt. Here the soul is illuminated like a crystal and can and must, without reserve, face up to its baseness and cowardice (*viltà*).[199] There no longer can be any question of an aesthetic 'slurring of the notes', of invoking the ideas of destiny and tragedy. During judgment there can be no side-glance at other people who are also sinners, perhaps greater sinners, no side-glance at mitigating circumstances, no side-glance at the forgiveness that is soon to follow. Existence in its entirety must force itself into the judgment of confession like a river through a narrow gorge.

The central scene is already prepared for in the *Inferno*, and the whole ascent up the cliffs and ledges of Purgatory is a preparation for it. Hell begins with the gloomy anguish (*paura*) of the one who has gone astray in the *selva oscura* of guilt, who has lost the *verace via*. The beasts, the symbol of sins, press him hard. He could deal with them if there were only two of them, but not three. The sight of the she-wolf arouses such fear (*paura*) 'that I lost hope of the ascent'; she drives him back 'to where the sun is silent'. What good is it to the sinner that it is 'the beginning of the morning and the sun is mounting with those stars that were with it when Divine Love first set in motion those fair things' if the fear (*paura*) he had known all through the night 'in the lake of his heart' still continues?[200] He only returns to the light when love makes him set out on 'the journey to the end of night', when the man without hope enters the gate beneath which 'all abandon hope'.[201] The whole journey seems like a dream,[202] and from that dream-like quality the landscape of Hell derives the strange conjunction of great plasticity and ultimate elusiveness. Nonetheless again and again there is an awakening from the snares of sleep,[203] and his own reality is constantly brought before his eyes: the weight of his body makes Charon's boat cut deeper into the water than it was

[199] As self-accusation: Inf 2, 45, 122; Inf 9, 1.

[200] Inf 1–60.

[201] Inf 3, 9.

[202] Inf 1, 11; *cf.* Par 32, 139: 'But since the time flies that holds thee sleeping. . . .'

[203] Pg 15, 115f.

wont;[204] he alone casts a disconcerting shadow in Purgatory. For his salvation and to his horror, he will have to see damnation, but not without, by way of suggestion, experiencing it first hand. Before the city of Dis, where the demons guard the entrance, he must experience the impotence of Virgil,[205] and he thinks of having to return 'alone on his mad way'.[206] 'Judge, reader, if I did not lose heart at the sound of the accursed words; for I did not think I should ever return home.'[207] Shortly after, the travellers meet the Furies, who call upon Medusa to turn Dante to stone. Virgil commands him to hide his face: 'For should the Gorgon show herself and thou see her, there would be no returning above.'[208] Fear must unceasingly overwhelm him: during his mad flight on Geryon's back, when it shakes him like the shudder of an intermittent fever;[209] when the devil accompanies him to the pit of boiling tar;[210] again in the pit of the hypocrites, where fear ruffles his hair,[211] and then at the sight of the wrestling giant, Antaeus, when fear nearly kills him.[212] Before crossing the portals of Hell, Dante has given his consent to all that is to come; he entreats Virgil: 'In order that I may escape this evil and worse, lead me where thou hast said, that I may see St Peter's gate.'[213] It is the gate of confession in the middle of Purgatory. This is the mountain of penitence, expiation and confession in one. At the bottom Dante begins by washing himself in the dew of Heaven to cleanse himself of the soot of Hell and by donning his ascetic garb of rushes.[214] Then follow the terraces of the mountain, and each step upward is like a 'shedding of skin' (*spogliarvi lo scoglio*),[215] a stripping away of the darkness of the world,[216] the untying of a knot,[217] and thus the opening of his heart to the waters of peace,[218] a self-purification in order 'to return fair to him that made thee'.[219] It is an ascent, that would not be possible 'on foot', but only 'with

[204] Inf 8, 30.
[205] Inf 9, 1f.
[206] Inf 8, 91.
[207] Inf 8, 94–96.
[208] Inf 9, 56–57.
[209] Inf 17, 85f.
[210] Inf 21, 94, 127f.
[211] Inf 23, 19f.
[212] Inf 31, 109.
[213] Inf 1, 132–134.
[214] Pg 1, 121f.
[215] Pg 2, 122.
[216] Pg 11, 30.
[217] Pg 23, 15.
[218] Pg 15, 131.
[219] Pg 16, 31–32.

the swift wings and plumage of great desire',[220] only with the singleness of purpose of one who does not have the time to look to right or left, but stands 'like a firm tower that never shakes its top for blast of wind'.[221] The higher one goes, the easier the climb.[222] But for Dante climbing can be only by day,[223] in stark contrast to the way of purification shown in St John of the Cross, a way that can be walked only by night. The *via purgativa* is at the same time *illuminativa*; hence, Virgil's beautiful, ancient prayer to the sun.[224] The ascent is speeded by the intercession of the living, thanks to which penitent love can accomplish in a single flight what otherwise would occur so slowly.[225] Dante also discovers that one can be carried away by grace, as if in a dream or rapture, like Ganymede, which enables one to leap over the terraces.[226] As in Hell, Dante shares, more or less, in the pains of the penitent, depending on how strongly aware he is of having fallen into the kind of sin in question. He knows himself to be almost free of envy, but he has far more to fear from the punishment of pride;[227] he walks there in the company of a penitent who carries a heavy burden of stone on his back 'as oxen go in a yoke',[228] and finally he will have to pass through the naked fire of the lustful.[229]

What, however, gives Purgatory its proper form is the gate of confession, which at the beginning of the Inferno already beckoned as the gate of St Peter and the hoped-for destination of the penitent's journey. The silent doorkeeper is an angel with clothes the colour of ashes, a face and sword so brilliant that Dante is drawn again and again to look in his direction but cannot. He sits upon the diamond threshold, to which three steps lead: the first, smooth and shining, made of white marble that mirrors the sinner's face and opens up his conscience to him; the second of deepest purple, of rugged and burnt stone; and then the third—repentance—porphyry 'flaming red like blood that spurts from a vein', the absolution that flows from the wounds of Christ. '"Say from there, what would you?" he

[220] Pg 4, 28–30.
[221] Pg 5, 14–15.
[222] Pg 4, 90.
[223] Pg 7, 44, 49–51; Pg 27, 74–75.
[224] Pg 13, 16–21.
[225] Pg 6, 37–39.
[226] Pg 9, 1–69.
[227] Pg 13, 134–138.
[228] Pg 12, 1–2.
[229] Pg 27, 10f.

began. "Where is the escort? Look that the ascent be not to your hurt."' That is the almost brutal question; the angel of confession incarnates the objectivity of the sacrament. Dante must throw himself at his feet and humbly (*umilemente*) beg the doorkeeper to withdraw the bolt. Beating his breast, he begs for mercy (*misericordia*). With the point of his sword the angel traces seven *P*s on Dante's forehead signifying the seven deadly sins (*peccata*), each of which must be atoned for on a cornice of the mountain. Two keys, one of gold, the other of silver, are brought out, *quarum una pertinet ad judicium de idoneitate ejus qui absolvendus est, et alia ad ipsam absolutionem* (St Thomas).[230] These are the keys of Peter, which have been entrusted to the angel. The door creaks and opens; the way of penance begins.

Nevertheless, the liturgy at St Peter's gate lacks the main element in confession: acknowledgment of sin and absolution. These are reserved for the meeting with Beatrice. Before that happens Dante must climb the cornices, and as he leaves each one, an angel wipes away with its wing one of the *P*s, or sins, from his forehead. In contrast to Hell, sins here are classified from the point of view of love. Love can fail its purpose, and such failures are the most serious sins; reparation for these sins—pride, envy, anger—must be made at the bottom of the mountain. But love can also be lacking in proportion—through defect (sloth, *acedia*), or through excess (avarice, gluttony, lust). The last of these, as the most easily excusable of sins, stood at the entrance to Hell; likewise, according to the same evaluation, it stands by the exit to Purgatory. But whereas in Hell the poet was overcome by pity for tragic lovers, here in Purgatory, on the seventh terrace of purification, he must himself pass through the trial by fire, which seems to him like molten glass. The angel sings, 'with a voice far clearer than ours', 'Blessed are the pure in heart': 'Then: "There is no way farther, holy souls, unless first the fire's sting is felt; enter into it and be not deaf to the singing beyond."'[231] Dante grows numb and rings his hands. He seems to see bodies burning in the flames. Virgil encourages him, and seeing that he is still somewhat dazed and abstracted, 'he said a

[230] *S. Th.* 3, Suppl. 17, 3. 'Of which one relates to the perception of the fitness of the one who is to be absolved. And the other to the absolution itself.'

[231] Pg 27, 10–12.

little impatiently: "Look now, my son, between Beatrice and thee is this wall."' Now his longing soars upward. Virgil strides forward, with Statius following behind, and in the flames speaks unceasingly of Beatrice. He says: 'It seems as if I see her eyes'. On the other side they are received into the earthly Paradise, at which point Virgil takes his leave, for Dante no longer has any need of a guide. He has been purified; he has come of age in those natural virtues about which antiquity can instruct him: 'No longer expect word or sign from me. Free, upright and whole is thy will, and it were a fault not to act on its bidding; therefore over thyself I crown and mitre thee.'[232] From now on Dante can stroll freely round the glorious garden of Paradise, which the ancient poets celebrated under the names of the 'Golden Age' or 'Parnassus'; the tops of its trees rustle in the breeze of the spheres circling so near. The passage that serves as a sign of the hiatus between this natural perfection—indeed of its rejection—and the great confession scene that is still to come, is one of the strangest and yet one of the most expressive in the whole of the *Comedy*. The man now become autonomous has not yet been justified in the sight of God and of love. For, meanwhile, the procession of the Church has approached, and Beatrice, still veiled, has come down from her chariot. Dante, distressed by the disappearance of Virgil, bursts into tears, but Beatrice raises her voice for the first time and gives him this warning: 'Weep not yet, for thou must weep for another sword.'[233] The words that she now utters plunge him deeper and deeper into shame, to its bottommost limit—*tanta vergogna!*[234] 'So does the mother seem harsh to her child as she seemed to me, for the savour of stern pity tastes bitter.'[235] *Amaro*, *acerbo*—the words are repeated. Without tears Dante stands before the veiled figure, until, moved by the compassion of the angels' song, the ice cracks into sighs and tears. But the confession must pitilessly follow its course. What a gift—no, what a summons from grace—was here squandered! And the higher the demands of heaven, the greater the fall. Scarcely had his beloved died than he betrayed her and entered the service of others,

[232] Pg 27, 139–142.
[233] Pg 30, 56–57.
[234] Pg 30, 78.
[235] Pg 30, 79–81.

'following after false images of good that fulfil not promise'. No prayer for his enlightenment had been of avail; only one thing would work: he had to be shown the damned. Here is the place for self-knowledge, repentance, confession. 'God's high decrees would be broken if Lethe were passed and such a draught were tasted without some scot of penitence and shedding of tears.'[236] For this reason the confession discourse relentlessly proceeds on its way, and now, like the point of a sword, the word points straight at the guilty man. So serious a charge demands an admission. An agitated, scarcely audible Yes forms itself on his lips 'such that to hear it there was need of sight'. What obstacles have you met with, asks cruel Love, what ditches, what chains, have prevented your love from rising up to me? 'And what attractions and advantages showed in the aspect of other things for which thou must be at their service?' The sinner's acknowledgment that he has been led astray by the treachery of false pleasure profits him nothing but is accepted as a matter of course, in fact is shrugged off as being of no importance. 'And she: "Hadst thou kept silence or denied what thou confessest, thy fault would be not less plain, by such a judge is it known."' And so that the useless tears might be of some benefit to him, the bitter consolation of confession is given, that if ever again he is 'enticed by the Sirens' he will feel terror before them in his very members. After Beatrice's departure, everything, compared with her, could only be a movement downward. The grace of being permitted to meet the most beautiful of all women entails the renunciation of all other seductive beauty. This is the asceticism of the *Minnesang* and takes us a long way beyond the allegories of the *Convivio*. Beatrice speaks of 'a young girl or other vanity' (*pargoletta o altra vanità*) and admits that, while a 'young chick' (*nuovo augelletto*) may well be ensnared twice or three times, no full-fledged bird would be. This convinces Dante that he has committed an unpardonable offence. Then, finally, comes the final blow: 'Since by hearing thou art grieved, lift up thy beard and thou shalt have grief by looking.' Beatrice turns to look at Christ. When Dante sees her do that, he is stung by the nettle of remorse, he becomes like a sturdy oak tree

[236] Pg 30, 142–145.

uprooted by a storm. Everything he once loved he now hates, what he has just seen eats away at his heart, and he collapses, vanquished, to the ground. 'What I became then she alone knows who was the cause of it.'[237]

No other part of the *Comedy* has anything like the force of this scene; it is the heart of the whole work. Here Eros has grown out of its subjectivity and into the objective form of a sacrament. On the other hand, here too we see sacramental, ecclesial form unveiled and justified and convincingly shown to be love. This is ecclesiology of a most modern kind. Supremely personal love breaks forth from the centre of the Church, but it will not tolerate subjectivity unless it has been purified, ordered, overcome and gathered up in the subjectivity of God himself. That is why 'perverse love' (*amor torto*)[238] is trained by all kinds of methods to conform to the all-embracing norms of true love. Moreover, such 'methods' may be as much ancient and natural as Christian and supernatural. Penitents weighed down by their heavy burdens move round the mountain, the ground of which is paved with images of the virtues and authentic love. Voices cry out and spur them on, watchwords imprint themselves on the memory of the soul, the Beatitudes entice them ever higher. The fact that representatives of Antiquity make their appearance not only in Hell but also on the mountain of purification underlines the gravity and inescapability of the punishments and purifications. The Christian commandment might easily appear to be heteronomous were it not for its accord with the natural law of human existence, an accord that the constitutions of Caesar and Justinian and the poetry of Virgil and Statius express.

The confession scene is not just an episode in the *Comedy*; it is the dynamic goal of the whole journey. And yet it is just as much the point of departure for Paradise. The fire of Beatrice burns Dante's soul to the quick and recasts it in pure light, and the immediate result is an unprecedented intimacy and boldness of access. When Beatrice has finished confessing Dante and has seen him break down before her, three things happen. First, Matilda, the sovereign of the earthly Paradise, draws Dante

[237] Pg 31, 1–90.
[238] Par 26, 62.

through the river, and a very drastic affair it is, with his head ducked under 'so that I needs must drink the water'; it is the symbol of an eschatological absolution, whereby earthly sin definitively becomes a thing of the past, trivial and rightly forgotten. Second, straightway there follows the contemplation of Church history. Dante, who henceforth has a pure and shriven heart, can now become, indeed must become, the observer and father confessor of the sinful, historical Church that has degenerated into the Whore of Babylon.[239] Third, Dante's relationship with Beatrice is raised to the level of intimacy: 'I no longer call you servants but friends.' Having shattered Dante, Beatrice now calls him to her side 'so that, if I speak with thee, thou shalt be ready to listen to me.' And as he approaches: 'She said to me: "Brother, why dost thou not venture to question me, now thou comest with me?" As with those that are too reverent before their superiors with whom they seek to bring the voice distinctly to their lips, so it was with me, and with imperfect utterance I began: "My lady, you know my need and what will meet it." And she said to me: "From fear and shame I will have thee free thyself henceforth, that thou mayst no longer speak like one that dreams."'[240] And so, as his last action in Purgatory, Dante must drink from the second river of Paradise, Eunoe, which replaces the negative forgetting of guilt with the positive knowledge of all the good he has done on earth, the indispensable foundation of his existence not just as a poet but as a man. After the confession Beatrice does away with artificial respect and distance and admits Dante into Paradise and so into the essence of love. And the *cortesia* of that love is not a kind of formality but nature elevated. It is that tenderness of the heart, that, so to speak, at every beat, as an expression of innermost emotion, looks at the beloved in order to glean and receive from her the meaning and form of existence. At first Beatrice had perforce to represent for Dante the hard form of the Church, but now in Paradise she is inspiration at its freest, at once both the love of his heart and the polestar high above him. For Dante, poetic inspiration and Catholic veneration of the saints flow effortlessly and necessarily

[239] Pg 32, 145–160.

[240] Pg 33, 20–33.

together, and if anyone were to protest that St Beatrice was an obstacle to his vision of God, Dante would count him worthy of no more than a pitying glance. In the *Paradiso* all formality has disappeared from the relationship of the lovers. Beatrice is nothing but blessed and eternal laughter (*riso*), an abyss of gaity, from which Dante sees his own happiness pouring down towards him: 'Within her eyes burnt such a smile that I thought I touched with mine the depth of my grace and of my paradise.'[241]

Beatrice's gaity is not without a certain sovereign humour, as, for example, in the scene with the somewhat exaggeratedly emotional Cacciaguida, whom Dante, his great-great-grandson, conscious of his ancestor's celestial nobility, decides to address with the honorific 'Voi', 'At which Beatrice, who stood a little apart, seemed by her smile like her who coughed at the first fault written of Guinevere.'[242] Beatrice smiles indulgently and with a gentle irony, like Dame Malehaut in the old courtly romance, drawing attention to herself with a slight cough when Guinevere wants to kiss Lancelot. At the end, when Beatrice returns to her place in the Celestial Rose, high above Dante, yet unremotely near—for in the Rose there is no more space—this intimacy does not prevent the poet from addressing a heartfelt prayer to the saintly object of his love.

O donna in cui la mia speranza vige . . .
Tu m'hai di servo tratto a libertate . . .
La tua magnificenza in me custodi.[243]

Love's inspiration takes this constantly recurring form, namely, that whenever Dante has before him a thought, word or deed to conceive or carry out, he first searches with his eyes for the gaze of his beloved to assure himself that it is right. And this turning toward love, well nigh imperceptible yet each time almost ceremoniously reported, does not mean for Dante that he is a stranger and slave, but rather that he is truly autonomous and

[241] Par 15, 34–36.

[242] Par 16, 13–15.

[243] Par 31, 79, 85, 88. 'O lady in whom my hope has its strength. . . . It is thou who hast drawn me from bondage into liberty. . . . Preserve in me thy great bounty.'

free. 'I turned to Beatrice, and she heard before I spoke and smiled to me a sign that made the wings grow on my will.'[244] Or when Dante has a question for someone on his lips: "Therefore my Lady said to me: 'Pour forth the flame of thy desire, so that it may issue marked clearly with the internal stamp. . . .'[245] When Beatrice is silent, then the poet recognizes that it is time for him to be silent too, but only while there is no sign. 'But she on whom I wait to know how and when to speak and when to be silent keeps still, so that I do well, against my desire, to ask no question. She, therefore, who saw my silence in seeing Him who sees all said to me: "Satisfy thy eager desire."'[246] Beatrice looks at God, Dante looks at Beatrice and sees in her, as in a clear mirror, the sign from God. The beloved does not imprison the poet within herself; on the contrary, she opens up for him the perception of all reality. *He* would be tempted to confine himself to her; he feels himself to be bereft of word and thought whenever it is a case of describing the love that breaks forth from her sacred eyes. 'So much I can tell again of that moment, that, as I gazed at her, my heart was freed from every other desire so long as the eternal joy that shone direct on Beatrice satisfied me from the fair eyes with its second aspect. Overcoming me with the light of a smile, she said to me: "Turn and listen, for not only in my eyes is Paradise."'[247] This greater world to which Beatrice points him is the world of the testimony of faith, the world of politics and the empire, the world of the cosmic orders that ascend to God himself. She thus becomes his sole muse and far outpasses the muses to whom Dante appeals in the *Inferno* and *Purgatorio*, even though in Paradise Virgil is once again gratefully acknowledged as *la nostra maggior musa*,[248] and at the beginning of the *Paradiso* mention is made of the guidance of Apollo, the inspiring breath of Minerva, and the nine accompanying muses.[249] For Dante the ancient gods are only 'principles'; Beatrice, on the other hand, is pure, personal reality.

[244] Par 15, 70–72.
[245] Par 17, 7–9.
[246] Par 21, 46–51.
[247] Par 18, 13–21.
[248] Par 15, 26.
[249] Par 2, 7–9; Par 1, 13f.

4. *PARADISO*. ANCIENT COSMOS AND CHRISTIAN COSMOS

If Dante's Paradise is being considered from the perspective of a theological aesthetic, then one cannot avoid the question as to what kind of world view it rests on and presupposes: is it the mythological world view of Antiquity or the Christian world view of the Bible? The organization of Hell with its concentrically descending circles and pits, of the Mountain of Purgatory with its ascending cornices and the Earthly Paradise at its summit—all this one might accept as poetic licence, the poet's freedom to give what shape he likes to the invisible. But then we have the ten spheres of the *Paradiso* revolving round the earth, the furthest of them, also the most rapid in its orbit, embedded in the divine Spirit of creation and love. All ten represent so very clearly the heavenly cosmology of Antiquity and, to all appearances, are too bound up with its philosophy and theology for the question not to be asked in the most urgent manner, But it also applies retrospectively to the Platonic aesthetics of the *Vita Nuova* and, even more so, to the *Convivio*. In these two works we have Beatrice as the celestial 'intelligence' and angelic being whose heavenly radiance shines down on earth, and Philosophy as the *gentil donna* who leads the intelligences into the cosmos and who in that capacity alone can act as the intermediary between earthly and glorified reality. We must look at the theology implied by this image of the cosmos; then we must ask what Christian theology of both the Middle Ages and today can and should take from it.

Let us understand an initial point. During the Middle Ages the cosmic powers were believed to constitute, in their entirety, the way God's power and activity are present and transmitted in the universe and could be called the 'world soul'. Moreover, on earth they were thought to determine the existence and way of life of all living things, of plants and animals, even of man himself, except in so far as the 'apex of his spirit' was a direct emanation from the breath of God; these powers were also thought to determine the destiny of the individual and of all history. This view was universally accepted during the Middle Ages. Dante could have derived it from Boethius as well as from

Albert and Thomas and the Arabs; with even stronger astrological emphasis it also held sway in Byzantine theology. The cosmic powers, ruled by special intelligences (angels), are active, fundamental qualities of reality; each intelligence makes its mark on its constellation and thereby on an aspect of the cosmos and of the history of the world.[250] This qualitative aspect of Dante's cosmos (this also applies, incidentally, to Hell and Purgatory) prevents an exaggerated emphasis being given to the moment when the soul climbs higher, the systematic, mystical 'ascent' from sphere to sphere. Justinian in the lower sphere of Mercury does not fundamentally have less dignity than the emperors in the sphere of Jupiter, and so on. A definite group of souls belongs to each of the fundamental cosmic qualities that have been marked by an angelic intelligence. These souls set out toward their earthly destiny under the sign of Mars, Venus or Saturn and, having accomplished it, return to their star in order thereafter (here the Christian doctrine of the communion of saints comes in) to influence the destinies of those still on earth. But Dante makes a precise distinction between the abode of the blest, which is with God and so in the highest heaven, in the Empyrean, transcending any concept of space, and their 'stars', which are only, as it were, the places of their appearing and the centres of their activities. Thus, on his arrival in the sphere of Venus, he sees the lights of the Venus souls descending, like high winds,[251] from the Empyrean to greet him. *Tutti sem presti al tuo piacer*.[252] For this reason Dante also makes a clear distinction between, on the one hand, what man owes indirectly to God and directly to cosmic life and, on the other hand, what he receives directly from God. But since God's direct and indirect actions are one and the same, so also are its effects: man as nature and person. With this qualification Dante can show himself very well disposed toward Plato's *Timaeus*; Plato might well have had the right idea about the connection between soul and star, or at least one can fairly interpret it thus.[253] The Empyrean

[250] Par 2, 130–132.

[251] Par 8, 22f. Similarly, St Peter Damian in the Sphere of Saturn, Par 21, 64–66.

[252] Par 8, 32–33. 'We are all ready at thy pleasure, that thou mayest have joy of us.'

is the place of blessedness, the star is the place of mission. When the blest turn from the Empyrean to the constellation, it is their own free, loving cooperation with the providence that governs the world. That is how Dante understands the matter when St Peter Damian comes out to meet him:

> 'I see indeed, holy lamp,' I said, 'how free love serves in this court for fulfilment of the Eternal Providence'.[254]

But when the blessed souls go from the place of God's glory to the place of their mission, they bring their blessedness with them, which is the reason why the stars shine as they do. It is the shining forth of their eternal origin, like the beam of joy from radiant, living eyes.

> *Per la natura lieta onde deriva*
> *La virtù mista per lo corpo luce*
> *Come letizia per pupilla viva.*[255]

There can be no doubt about it: the most sublime and impressive passages in the *Paradiso* invariably portray the cosmos as being embedded in the glory and peace of divine love, shot through with angelic and spiritual powers that shine forth and are sent out by God as his living organs. And here Dante stresses alternately the chain of loving forces (Eros), that emanates from God or ascends from the world up to him; they receive their strength from above, they operate below:

> *Questi organi del mondo così vanno,*
> *Come tu vedi omai, die grado in grado,*
> *Che di su prendono, e di sotto fanno.*[256]

The *Paradiso* begins with the praise of 'the glory of him who moves all things' and concludes with the same universal movement, this time ascribed to Amor. The theology of Dante

[253] Conv 3, 5; 4, 21 = Par 4, 49f. Commentary and bibliographical references in Gmelin, *Kommentar zum Par.* 84–89.

[254] Par 21, 73–75.

[255] Par 2, 142–144. 'By the joyous nature whence it springs the mingled virtue shines through the body as joy through the living pupil.'

[256] Par 2, 121–123. 'These organs of the universe proceed thus, as thou seest now, grade by grade, each receiving from above and operating below.'

presents itself, perhaps more than any other, as a theology of glory. The light of the stars, the inaudible music produced by the harmony of their everlasting orbit,[257] enflames the heart with ardent desire for God: 'The newness of the sound and the great light kindled in me such keenness of desire to know their cause as I had never felt before.'[258] But this departure and return to God is in no sense a process of exteriorising and reassuming the Absolute; on the contrary, the order of the cosmos is itself an expression of divine love and is loved by individual beings for its likeness to God. Just as all beings tend toward God, so they tend *con istinto* towards this order, and both movements—the one toward the Absolute beyond all form, the other toward the eternal form—are one and the same.[259] Being at the same time attached to both of these, love for one's fellow creature can become a permanent and positive way to love of God, and conversely, everything outside of God is a ray of light from God, and so radiant goodness is loved in all, and without the All needing to be denied for the sake of the One.[260] The 'beginning and end' of the 'nature of the world' is not only, as Aristotle saw, the love of the cosmos for God; it is also the Divine Mind itself which is the 'light of love' by which the movement and activity of the world is enkindled.[261] In this respect it can be said of the angelic hierarchies that eternal love (Eros) has revealed itself in new loves[262] and that their orders, as mediators of the love of God, have a contemplative function as they gaze at God above and an active ministry below.[263] But while eternal art plays on, without obstacle, in Heaven and among the stars, it does run against opposition from inert matter, which can turn *l'intenzion dell'arte* from its course, and upright love can be deformed into a *torto e falso piacere*,[264] bitter fruit can sprout from sweet seed.[265] But perfect reception of the divine seed effected by 'the one almost divine', and the unsurpassable fruit 'of which the earth was made worthy (*degna*)' is the Son of God himself.[266] Here all things are held together in a great bond of simultaneity, as

[257] Par 1, 76–78.
[258] Par 1, 82–84.
[259] Par 1, 103–126.
[260] Par 26, 28–36.
[261] Par 27, 106–114.
[262] Par 29, 18.
[263] Par 28, 127–129.
[264] Par 1, 135. 'Distorted and false pleasure.'
[265] Par 8, 93.
[266] Par 13, 73–84.

scripture says: *creavit omnia simul* (Ecclus 18.1)—from pure form, pure matter and their union arise all things that come into existence and pass away.[267] That is why even the angelic world cannot exist before the creation of matter, for it is upon matter that the angels work and thereby find their perfection.[268] When Dante sings an authentically medieval song about the 'goddess' Fortuna and her turning wheel,[269] he has in mind the eternal movement, composed of elements of both chance and order, between the heavenly forms and matter, which as a 'third arrow' proceeds from God. Men, of course, often curse Fortune: 'But she is blest and does not hear it. Happy with the other primal creatures, she turns her wheel and rejoices in her bliss.'[270] In fact, why should the heavenly intelligences, whom the people call angels, not be called 'gods'[271] if elsewhere their created status is clearly affirmed? What we find in Dante is not the Greek gods, but the powers that represent whatever reality they have, which is why there can be real giants in Hell who 'chose to try their strength against supreme Jove'. Ephialtes stands in chains, because he 'made the great attempt when the giants put the gods in fear'.[272]

This cosmos, permeated with divine energies, is understood in a Christian way. Its entire aesthetic power of expression serves to support a Christian theological aesthetic. We may seriously ask whether such an undertaking is justified. There can be no doubt that the world view of Antiquity gives the poet marvellous advantages in terms of vividness, and the daring images, that he himself creates to make his journey in the hereafter credible, fit comfortably into the framework prepared for them. This in marked contrast to others like Milton and Klopstock. Ancient astronomy in conjunction with a geography enlarged to cosmic proportions gives the whole

[267] Par 29, 22–24.

[268] Par 29, 45.

[269] Inf 7, 91–96.

[270] *Ibid.*, 94–96.

[271] *Ibid.*, 87; Par 5, 123; Conv 2, 5: '*intelligenze, le quali la volgare gente chiama angeli. . . . E chiamale Plato Idee, che tanto è a dire quanto forme e nature universali. Li Gentili le chimavano Dei e Dee, avvegnachè non così filosoficamente intendessero quelle come Plato.*'

[272] Inf 31, 91–96.

work an imaginative power that approaches the hallucinatory. To recall just one image, though an important one: before the lovers risk the *passo forte* from the last of the planetary spheres to 'ultimate salvation' (*ultima salute*), Beatrice demands that the poet look back once again 'down' (*in giù*) on the way he has now traversed. 'With my sight I returned through every one of the seven spheres, and I saw this globe such that I smiled at its paltry semblance; and that judgment that holds it for least I approve as best. . . .'[273] Here the ascetical *de-spicere* is given its properly geographical sense. Once more there follows, at the moment of ascent from the fixed stars to the sphere of crystal, one final look back: 'and see how thou dost turn'. This time it is the revolution of the stars, which is portrayed with conscious art: 'So that I saw on the one hand, beyond Cadiz, the mad track of Ulysses, and on the other nearly to the shore where Europa made herself a sweet burden; and more of the space of this little threshing floor would have been disclosed to me but the sun was moving on beneath my feet and was a sign and more away.'[274] Here is a journey through space to induce vertigo, following the revolutions of the concentric spheres, astronomically exact, and yet soaring out of space, for the sphere of crystal, which is pure invisible transparency, adjoins what is beyond space; Dante is conscious, with the ancients, of the paradox he thereby expresses. This and other passages raise a question as to what extent Dante did or did not understand this cosmic symbolism fully and consciously as *symbolism*; in other words, to what extent does the spiritual sense predominate over the image that expresses it. This is very beautifully made clear at the time of the sudden great tremor that shakes the Mountain of Purgatory. Statius explains its significance to the poet: the physical laws of the terrestrial world no longer apply here; the mountain quakes every time a soul feels itself purified, whenever the purifying punishment ceases to weigh down upon it like a law imposed from outside but is accepted by the soul in complete freedom. Thus the soul reaches the end of its purification, and the whole of Purgatory greets this breakthrough into everlasting freedom with a cry of 'Gloria' that shakes its very foundations.[275]

[273] Par 22, 133–137. [274] Par 27, 82–87. [275] Pg 21, 40–75.

Another example, no less magnificent, is the wind of the spheres, which blows through the treetops of Paradise. The astronomical image, in its exactness, has a much deeper significance: this constant wind scatters the seeds of the trees of Paradise unceasingly—yes, even now—on the sinful world below.[276] The third and most important example is the detailed explanation, again given by Statius, of what for Dante is a paradoxical fact; namely, that Dante sees the souls in the hereafter in bodily form and that it is from their bodily appearance—their tears, their thinness, and so on—that he can read the state of their soul. The explanation given is that the soul, as the substantial form of the body, has an attractive power over matter even after death. When the solid matter slips from its grasp, it takes hold of the air that surrounds it and gives it form, and from this fashions for itself new, shadowy limbs in expectation of the future resurrection of the solid body.[277] But this means that the souls of the departed are not separated from the world but are inserted into the community of this single, real cosmos, and as cosmic beings help to determine, in their turn, the destiny of the world. Even a demythologized theology will find it difficult to waive aside this idea so boldly maintained by Dante against Platonism and against St Thomas.[278] What these examples show is that one can at least question whether, with the demythologization of the cosmos by modern natural science, the ideas behind the 'cosmo-theology' of Plato, Aristotle and Scholasticism have been superseded.

It may be that what in fact has been removed is precisely what hinders, rather than helps, the development of an authentically Christian theological aesthetic. Dante has gone to the limits in extracting from the imaginative resources of the ancient cosmos what can be of service to theological and Christian poetry. But in so doing he has inevitably had to take on, at the same time, things that are prejudicial to it. To omit these can only assist the emergence of other, new mysteries of the Christian revelation.

Such geographical distance from earth, earth sinful and in the grip of death, cannot remain without existential consequences,

[276] Pg 28, 88–120. [277] Pg 25, 88–105.

[278] *Cf.* K. Rahner, *Zur Theologie des Todes*; ET, *On the Theology of Death*, 2nd ed. (1965).

despite the steep ascents and intoxicating raptures of the *Paradiso*. In his Paradise Dante can work only with the materials of pure light and love and blessedness, contrasting light with even deeper light, surpassing love with even more ardent love, and because he allowed himself to acquiesce in a prefiguration of the resurrection body, he can offer unprecedented delights to the five bodily senses: symphonies of exquisite melodies, fragrances, sweetnesses, spectacles of an unparalleled kind for eye and ear, the intermingling and mutual enrichment of the sensory impressions, even the most unlikely syntheses and works involving all the arts. His fantasy here verges on the fabulous and has hardly been surpassed by any of the modern symbolists. Nothing remains abstract; as if under a spell, everything has form and is perceptible by the senses. Choreography on a grand sale is unrolled; the teachers of Wisdom dance around Dante, then a second and finally a third round dance flows forth. In the sphere of Jupiter the souls form first of all a living inscription, *Diligite Justitiam*. From its final *M* there develops the living image of the imperial eagle, which proclaims, through a choir speaking in unison, the triumph of justice. In the sphere of Mars the souls of the martyrs come together in the shape of a cross, and in the sphere of Saturn the souls of the contemplatives, all together, form Jacob's ladder 'to such a height that my sight could not follow it'.[279] Just like the strings of triumphal processions in late Renaissance drawings, two processions, one with Christ, the other with Mary, pass through the heaven of the fixed stars, and finally, the souls surge upward, like snowstorms, into the Empyrean, where the nine choirs of angels encircle the luminous heart of the Godhead in a kind of 'metaphysical carousel of light'.[280] In the lower part of the Empyrean the light from the bodies of the blest is so blinding that Dante's mortal eyes cannot discern in them any bodily form. But they reveal their inner mobility in that they revolve round one another like 'wheels in the structure of a clock', or glass balls.[281] All these displays affect the reader like a breathtaking drama—theatre, ballet, and fireworks rolled into

[279] Par 21, 30.
[280] Gmelin, *Komm. zur Par.*, 479.
[281] Par 24, 13f, 151, etc.

one—and yet behind it all there is a certain embarrassment, even emptiness. It is as if the poet were sparing no pains to satisfy a traditional *representation* of Heaven, which nonetheless is still more a representation than an idea with profoundly Christian content. However, what gives rise to this feeling of emptiness are precisely the elements of neo-Platonism and Antiquity, the remoteness from earth and that remoteness of the heart which, at least in part, follows from the geographical distance, and which then easily degenerates into a didactic reasoning. Dante works hard at putting dramatic life into every scene, but the threefold examination of his faith (by Peter), his hope (by James) and his love (by John) succeeds only in being boring. Other motifs are more in the nature of weaker repetitions. For example, there is the scene where Dante drinks from the river of fire;[282] whatever its justification, it inevitably calls to mind the occasion when the poet drank from the Lethe and Eunoe.

Nevertheless, within the framework of the world view he inherited, Dante explores every possibility of taking up what is neo-Platonic into what is Christian. We see this whenever he shows us Heaven bending down to Earth and contributing to its destiny. Only the Christian heart of Dante could overcome all his scholastic prejudices and portray Beatrice, in heavenly bliss, pouring out bitter tears for the sake of the world. This fact is mentioned three times, first of all by Virgil at the entrance to Hell when he explains that he has been sent by Beatrice: '*Gli occhi lucenti lagrimando volse*.'[283] It is again mentioned by Virgil when Dante, come of age, is released from Purgatory. Now he must wait for the woman with the beautiful eyes, 'which weeping made me come to thee.'[284] Finally, it is mentioned by Beatrice herself, who, during the confession scene, reproaches the guilty man for having forced her to lead him through Hell. 'For this I visited the threshold of the dead and to him who has brought him up here my prayers were offered with tears.'[285]

Amor, the weeping god of the *Vita Nuova* and the whole *Minnesang* tradition may have been of influence here, but, from a Christian point of view, such influence is only to the good. In

[282] Par 30, 73f.
[283] Inf 2, 116.
[284] Pg 27, 137.
[285] Pg 30, 139–141.

this way Dante breaks with the abstract scholastic theology of the *visio beata*, but he acts in line with a long tradition that is Patristic, even medieval, and especially modern, a tradition to which we will return when we come to Péguy.

Moreover, to this tradition belongs the blood-red anger of Peter and, with him, of the whole incandescent company of Heaven at the shame of the Church on earth. Dante is not afraid to let the final explosions of wrath go before him into the highest spheres of Heaven—first, the fulmination of the Prince of the Apostles in the heaven of the fixed stars,[286] then that of Beatrice in the Crystalline Sphere.[287] Indeed, even in the Empyrean, in the immediate presence of God's throne, it breaks out once more in a devastating attack on the Popes. And Beatrice's final words in the *Comedy* push Boniface VIII even further down into his fiery pit.[288]

However, once again the decisive question is inevitably about the reality of earthly/heavenly Eros. The earthly component was recast in the confession in Purgatory; in order to evolve into objective reality, Eros had to submit, through death, to a final humiliation. But, thus transformed, it is compatible with Heaven. *Il terzo cielo*, the Sphere of Venus, had already played a leading role in the *Canzoniere* and the *Convivio*;[289] in the *Paradiso* it becomes the abode of the purified and transfigured courtesans. By means of marvellous symbolism Dante explains how, according to Alfragan, the earth casts its shadow as far as the third heaven, thus establishing a mysterious bond of destiny between earth and Heaven. Cunizza da Romano, the sister of the notorious Ezzelino, reigns here, like a transfigured Magdalene, after her many intricate amorous adventures on earth. Dante has known her in addition as a respectable old lady in Florence. In her we see the joint effect of Lethe and Eunoe: she 'can gladly pardon herself',[290] for 'here we do not repent; nay, we smile, not for our fault, which does not come back to mind, but for the power (*valore*) that ordained and foresaw'.[291] Here also we find Folco of Marseilles, a fervent troubadour of love, then a monk and leader of the crusade against the Albigenses.

[286] Par 27, 10f.
[287] Par 29, 88f.
[288] Par 30, 128–148.
[289] Conv 2, Canzone v. 1f. and commentary.
[290] Par 9, 34.
[291] Par 9, 103–105.

Finally, we come upon Rahab, the prostitute of Jericho, outside of whose house there is no salvation, and who has been, from of old, the great *figura Ecclesiae*: 'she was taken up before any other soul at Christ's triumph.'[292] While there are no prominent virgin figures to enliven Dante's Paradise, these women occupy a place of honour, and the same is true, in the sphere of the moon, of those women who through compelling fate—family or politics—have been prevented from fulfilling their vow of virginity. Dante goes into great detail about the theological problems raised by such a fate, especially by the commutation of a vow. It is clear that this question exercised him at the personal level a great deal: can a human being who has given himself for eternity to the love of God and pledged his troth be dispensed from that vow? Dante's solution is severe and unequivocal: whoever has given himself away cannot take himself back. At most, what has been vowed (the 'matter' of the vow) might be commuted by the Church with her power of the keys, but the vow itself can never be.[293] 'Whatever, therefore, is of such worth that it weighs down every balance cannot be made good by other outlay.'[294] This is directed against any too casual exercise of the keys. If the Eros that unites man and woman is as eternal and definitive as the love between Dante and Beatrice, how on earth could the marriage bond between humanity and God be untied or replaced by something else?

Eros *concludes* the covenant. For Dante, it only opens up into the infinity of God because at the same time it completes the relationship. It is form and gives form. Ultimately nothing remains unaccounted for, indeterminate; everything that is nebulous is clarified and given a recognizable form. Thus there remains in all the blest in Heaven a longing for the risen body, *disio dei corpi morti*,[295] for the immortalization of flesh and blood and thus also of the solidarity of the generations. Yes, there is a longing 'not perhaps for themselves alone, but for their

[292] Par 9, 119–120. *Cf.* the section on the Rahab motif in my 'Casta Meretrix', in *Sponsa Verbi* (1961), pp. 222–239.

[293] Par 5, 34f.

[294] Par 5, 61–63. Here Dante takes up a position opposed to that of St Thomas. *Cf.* Gmelin, *Komm.* 3, 102–103.

[295] Par 14, 63.

mothers, for their fathers, and for the others who were dear before they became eternal flames'.[296] In a profound speech Solomon explains that the present shadowy or luminous body of the souls in Heaven receives its radiance from spiritual beatitude. One day, though, it will be the other way: the transfigured resurrection body will react upon the glorified soul's beatitude and power of vision, thus raising it to new heights.[297]

The luminous bodies in Paradise are so radiant that they blind Dante, and this blinding reaches its maximum intensity in the vision that greets Dante on his entry into the Empyrean, the seat of the Godhead and of all the blessed angels and souls. Beatrice shows Dante the highest heaven in its definitive form, but the light so overwhelms him that at first he can see nothing at all. But then, endowed with a new power of vision, he becomes aware, albeit indistinctly, of something quite overpowering: 'And I saw light in the form of a river pouring its splendour between two banks painted with marvellous spring. From that torrent came forth living sparks, and they settled on the flowers on either side, like rubies set in gold; then, as if intoxicated with the odours, they plunged again into the wondrous flood, and as one entered, another came forth.'[298] Beatrice praises the high desire this blurred vision evokes in the poet. Nevertheless, he must first drink of this water and bathe his eyes in it; then he will see what the river of fire with its swarms of sparks and the flowers on its banks really are. As soon as his eyes are moistened he is given all the power of sight that he requires, and the unendingly flowing river then becomes a lake (*di sua lunghezza divenuta tonda*).[299] Like men who appear first behind masks that distort their faces but then cast them off, so now all is disclosed: the sparks that fly hither and thither are in reality angels emerging from God's sea of light; and the riverbanks decked with flowers, upon which the sparks settle only later to plunge back intoxicated into the river, in reality are the vast outer circle of the white, Celestial Rose, which, reflected in the sphere of crystal, is formed by the assembled company of all human souls

[296] *Ibid.*, 64–66.
[297] *Ibid.*, 37–60.
[298] Par 30, 61–69.
[299] Par 30, 90.

in bliss. And so this Rose, the final image of Paradise, is perpetually visited by the angels, who swarm down upon it like bees; they bring it divine life and thence return that life anew to God. This is the supreme image of Dante's inspiration. It is dominated by notions of rank and the strictest order, which Dante painstakingly describes; and yet no spatial distance separates the various ranks. Beatrice, having returned to her heavenly place in the third circle of the highest rank, is, *sì lontana*, nonetheless not remote from Dante, who looks up at her. She seems to smile at him before turning completely towards the *eterna fontana*. The *Doctor marianus*, Bernard, directs the gaze of the poet towards the highest created beauty, the *pacifica orifiamma*,[300] the Mother of the Lord. Everything has now assumed form: 'In all the breadth of this kingdom nothing of chance can find a place . . . for all thou seest is ordained by eternal law, so that here the ring exactly fits the finger.'[301] In the *Convivio* Dante has already attacked every kind of unresolved, aimless infinity in human desire. Precisely because his love for Beatrice is *final*, he is the foe of all that moves in the direction of Faust or Don Juan. His understanding of the will in terms of form is based on Aristotle's: the law of the form of being, with its living entelechy, is not aimless and uncertain; it is clear and definite and demands obedience.[302] Man's *desiderium naturale* may tend toward God and the vision of God, but because it is nature, it has a goal to attain, at which to come to rest, beyond which it cannot reasonably strive. Time and again the words *termine*, *terminato*, *finito*, *misurato* are repeated. If a certain kind of knowledge is impossible for our nature, then we may not 'naturally desire to have this knowledge'.[303] For 'this world exists without certain limits. . . . The jurisdiction of universal nature is therefore limited within certain bounds, and consequently the particular nature likewise'.[304] In Dante we see

[300] Par 31, 127.

[301] Par 32, 52–57.

[302] Conv 1, 7 discusses the 'obedience of nature'. Conv 4, 9 deals with obedience to imperial authority. Such obedience is strictly limited according to the powers invested in the Emperor.

[303] Conv 3, 15.

[304] Conv 4, 9.

the modesty of Antiquity in its estimate of man and the limitations of his existence transferred, without qualification, to a Christian ethos. He describes the soul of the child, 'setting forth on the new and ever untrod path of life', endowed at the same time with the thought of a final and supreme goal. The soul thinks first that it can find this goal in all the paltry little good things of life; what is nearest seems to it to be the pinnacle of all that is worth striving for, while he who is truly the most high, God, seems far away. This false evaluation leads to the vice most severely censured by Dante, the 'thirst for more and more', avarice and *auri sacra fames*.[305] The same applies to spiritual things; even striving for knowlege is essentially finite, just as all man's natural tendencies have a definite goal (*certo fine*). He even invokes St Paul, who said: 'I bid every one among you not to think of himself more highly than he ought to think, but to think with sober judgment' (Rom 12.3). Yes, insatiable desire is Hell, as Virgil, from his own experience, teaches his protégé: '"Foolish is he who hopes that our reason can trace the infinite ways. . . . Rest content, race of men, with the facts; for if were you able to see all, there would have been no need for Mary to give birth, and you have seen the fruitless desire of men such that their desire would have been set at rest which is given them for an eternal grief—I speak of Aristotle and of Plato and of many others." And here he bent down his brow and said no more and remained disquieted.'[306] In Paradise Thomas Aquinas gives a similar warning, though without the sense of the tragic that surrounds the man excluded from the vision of God.[307] And as the poet is admitted to the threshold of the vision of God, he experiences the bliss of the End.

Ed io ch'al fine di tutti i disii
Appropinquava, sì com'io dovea
L'ardor del desiderio in me finii.[308]

To see all this aright, we must not lose sight of the fact that, throughout his journey, but especially in Paradise, Dante is

[305] Conv 4, 12.
[306] Pg 3, 34–45.
[307] Par 13, 112f.
[308] Par 33, 46–48. 'And who was drawing near to the end of all desires, ended perforce the ardour of my craving.'

continually overcome and overwhelmed by what he experiences. He constantly asserts that what he has seen is far more splendid that he could possibly describe. Not only is the dazzling brightness of the blest more intense than he can bear, but the beauty of Beatrice, growing more and more from sphere to sphere, reaches such proportions that finally, in a long and solemn passage, he lays down his poetic office before her, for he is certain not only that he cannot say how beautiful she is, but also that she is far more beautiful than he understands, and only her creator may enjoy that beauty to the full: 'I own myself beaten at this pass more than ever comic or tragic poet was baffled by a point in his theme. . . . From the first day I saw her face in this life until this sight the pursuit in my song has not been cut off; but now must my pursuit cease from following longer after her beauty in my verse, as with every artist at his limit.'[309] There is thus a limit to being overwhelmed, and even this renunciation has still a poetic form! For the poet does not turn away from Beatrice, but rather stands his ground in the face of the immeasurable. This theme is magnificently realized when, at the very end of his whole journey, Dante prepares to look up into the luminous abyss of the Godhead itself. Only by steadfastness in the face of the immeasurable can he survive. To turn away for self-preservation would be fatal: 'I think, from the keenness I endured of the living flame, that I should have been lost if my eyes had been turned from it.'[310] Dante's moderation is born of withstanding the immoderation of the object; it comes of submitting, in an act of blessed renunciation, to the overwhelming force. It is to this mystery that the central doctrine of the *Paradiso* points, the doctrine, namely, of human subordination to the divine will, which is not only recommended to men on earth but actually constitutes the form of eternal blessedness. Every desire is taken up into the divine form; obedience coincides with a blessed fulfilment that is beyond desire. 'Brother, the power of charity quiets our will and makes us will only what we have and thirst for nothing else. Did we desire to be more exalted, our desire would be in discord with his will who appoints us here, which thou wilt see cannot

[309] Par 30, 19–36. [310] Par 33, 76–78.

hold in these circles if to be in charity is here *necesse* and if thou consider well its nature. Nay, it is the very quality of this blessed state that we keep ourselves within the divine will, so that our wills are themselves made one. . . . And in his will is our peace. It is that sea to which all things move, both what it creates and what nature makes.'[311] The human mind finds rest in this will like the beasts in their lairs.[312] For this will—as Dante is instructed when he raises a question about predestination—is identical with eternal wisdom. The mind can understand this, and for this reason God's will applies to it *a priori* as the norm of the good; to ask for anything beyond this norm is folly. 'Whatever accords with it is in that measure just'.[313] In Heaven the lovers precisely love the incomprehensibility, the impenetrability (even for them) of the divine plan of salvation. 'And this very lack is sweet to us, because in this good, our good is perfected, that which God wills we will too.'[314] Because of its creative depth and diversity (*creando . . : diversamente*), God's will is different for each individual creature, and this differentness is part of the beauty and delight of the world.[315] Moreover, the cooperation of creatures with God's will is necessary and indeed expected by God. In their eternal happiness the souls of the blest can contemplate the proportion of grace and merit and thereby come to see the supreme justice that lies at the heart of love. Indeed, precisely because that proportion itself rests entirely upon love, it is a part of eternal happiness. It is Justinian who expresses this profound truth and then adds: 'Thus the living justice sweetens our affections so that they can never be warped to any evil.'[316] But finally, the humble subordination of the human to the divine will is also a Christian mystery, the mystery of love, and so something very different from the ancient idea of submission to fate. Just as man, out of love, says Yes to God, so from eternity has God, in love, said Yes to the creature. And it is in this exchange of love between such dissimilar partners that we find the mystery of God's hearing of our prayers: God lets himself be conquered by man in accordance with the original decree of his loving will: '*Regnum coelorum* suffereth violence

[311] Par 3, 70–87.
[312] Par 4, 127.
[313] Par 19, 88.
[314] Par 20, 136–138.
[315] Par 32, 65–66.
[316] Par 6, 121–123.

from fervent love and lively hope, which conquer the divine will, not as man masters man, but conquer it because it would be conquered, and, being conquered, conquers with its own goodness.'[317] This doctrine (Thomist, albeit orchestrated with the distinctive sounds of Dante's Eros) takes up the old Augustinian formula, that God, by rewarding, crowns his own grace. Dante has built into this Christian schema the entire cosmos of Antiquity: the Platonic doctrine of Eros, which already in the *Symposium* bases human Eros on a primordial, descending grace; and the Aristotelian doctrine of form and matter, according to which the complete fulfilment of form depends on the maximum receptivity of matter. This pliancy of matter Dante understands as grace: the grace of the astronomical hour, the grace of a noble vocation and mission, upon which any merit on man's part depends.[318] All man must do is boldly reach up to the high level of his vocation.[319]

And so we are left with this final image: the Celestial Rose. It is people who form the calyx of the flower, and in its lower part are the fragrant souls of children, who are there by pure grace. Its bees are the angels, who bring God's descending love to the company of the blest. We are left with the final reciprocity of Eros and Agape, which for Dante are but two names for the same thing: Amor, God's most truly proper name. This reciprocity is nuptial, and the existential experience of this ultimate reality is called—if we are to judge the matter on the poet's level and by his criteria—Dante and Beatrice. This criterion is explicitly subordinated to the criterion of the glorified Church: Mary, not Beatrice, is the final image; Bernard, not Dante, speaks the last word of prayer. But what Bernard cannot say and cannot be, the archangel can make visible—the divine Eros itself, which, by the mediation of the angel glowing with love, rushed down upon the Virgin. Already in Mary's triumph in the sphere of the fixed stars we see Gabriel configured to her: 'There descended through the sky a torch that, circling, took the likeness of a crown that encircled her and wheeled about her. . . . "I am angelic love who encircles

[317] Par 20, 94–99.
[318] Conv 4, 20.
[319] Conv 4, 21.

the supreme joy which breathes from the womb that was the inn of our desire."'[320] In the Empyrean the figures that further down appeared to the poet as no more than lights now appear with their proper characteristics revealed. The poet asks Bernard about the figure of the angel: '"Who is that angel that gazes with such rapture on the eyes of our Queen, so enamoured that he seems on fire?" . . . And he answered me: "All confidence and gallant bearing that can be found in angel or in any soul are in him; and we would have it so".'[321] Dante would like to have been this angel. It can therefore be said that ultimately his Paradise has a Marian form. Christ stands higher, dwelling in the heart of the Trinity. Only 'in the mirror and enigma' of supreme rapture can man have an inkling of him as the humanly incomprehensible 'quadrature of the circle'—the dazzlingly glorious identity of God and man. His triumphal procession through the eighth heaven makes only a faint impression,[322] and if his outline is to be seen in the great living image in Mars, the cross formed of souls, it is still only an image, to which Dante is not prepared to concede the full presence.[323] The cross of Christ, in all its reality, is met nowhere in the *Divine Comedy*.

5. *INFERNO:* BETWEEN THE TIMES

This last affirmation opens the way to a proper appreciation of the *Inferno*, which until now has not been taken into account in our interpretation, and which now finally calls that entire interpretation into question, perhaps explodes it. The central scene of the *Comedy*, we said, was the conquest of the inner, psychological world of Dante's personality by the demands of a heavenly Eros. This corresponded to the objective Church, to humanity redeemed and reunited by God, and finally to the Eros of God, which imprints itself and burns through her with the fire of love. Such transcendence of the narrow and sinful 'I', such liberation for 'thou' and for love, was worth all the

[320] Par 23, 94–96, 103–105.
[321] Par 32, 103–105, 109–111.
[322] Par 23, 19f.
[323] Par 14, 103f.

sufferings and humiliations. These humiliations could also produce the humble act of postponing the poet's own blessedness for the sake of consenting to the incomprehensible, loving decrees of divine predestination. But what if that mystery involves eternal damnation? And what if the Eros that shapes and governs all worlds also rules over a kingdom from which love is totally and eternally excluded? And if Dante's theological aesthetic is based precisely upon the resemblance of *amor* and *bellezza*, then is a poem about Hell at all conceivable? In the first place it must be said that it is aesthetically possible only if and insofar as it is theologically possible (that is to say, as it can be justified by Eros). It must therefore be as much aesthetically questionable as it is theologically problematic.

In an impressive book on *Die Rechtsmetaphysik der göttlichen Komödie* (1942) (*The Metaphysics of Law in the Divine Comedy*) Hugo Friedrich has shown that Dante is dependent upon the same objective cosmology of order and law as Thomas Aquinas, Boethius and Augustine, and before them in Antiquity the great defenders of the *theios kosmos*. The *Convivio* was to have concluded with the glorification of *giustizia*; the *Monarchia* defines it as much ethically and politically as metaphysically—in this last respect it is the earthly expression of the *lex aeterna*, '*similitudo divinae voluntatis*; therefore nothing out of accord with the divine will can be right, and everything consonant with the divine will is right'.[324] Guilt or sin is contrary to right, and because it is the disruption of that ordered right or right order (*rectitudo*) implanted by the Creator in the nature of things, it contains within itself its own punishment. Indeed, the order perverted by the creature still affirms itself in its very perversion: when No is said to God, the louder Yes resounds; in the pain of chastisement, the unity of goodness and pleasure is acknowledged. The affirmation of the cosmos in its totality, with both its light and shadows, was the supreme and admirable achievement of the ancient theodicy; it was also without doubt the main reason why Dante entrusted himself unhesitatingly to the guidance of Virgil in his journey through the realm of darkness.

[324] M 2, 2.

However, one cannot avoid the question—and we have already asked it in the case of Augustine—as to whether this ancient theodicy, which regards the world as a universe of law, could be quite so easily adopted by a Christian theology burdened not only with the problem of suffering in general, but also with the specific problem of eternal Hell. Friedrich, while seeing that, as a matter of fact, this adoption took place in the work of Augustine and his medieval successors, does not ask himself whether it was necessary or right for it to take place. He has not considered the other traditions of Christian theology, that of the Greek fathers and of the medieval mystics who did not think along the same lines as Augustine. Likewise, he regards the Augustinian-Thomist cosmos as no more than an edifice of 'eternal law' and hence does not do justice to the fact that the Christian gospel is above all one of redemptive love. Augustine certainly tried to incorporate even eternal Hell in his aesthetic justification of creation: the world is a 'marvellous poem' (*pulcherrimum carmen*) adorned with the antitheses of good and evil, light and darkness. Moreover, he was able to cite a scriptural text to this effect, albeit one that shows clear signs of Hellenizing influence: 'Good is the opposite of evil, and life the opposite of death; so the sinner is the opposite of the godly. Look upon all the works of the Most High; they likewise are in pairs, one the opposite of the other' (Sir 33.14f). Augustine, the former Manichaean, could let this text pass without comment and takes it to include even the New Testament opposition of the two eternal kingdoms of light and darkness, love and hate, thus also proving that ultimate unity and harmony come from God.[325] Aristotelian influence through St Thomas, as well as neo-Platonic influence through Boethius, heightens the cosmic and philosophical aspects of this vision without essentially altering it. On the other hand, it lessens the biblical and dramatic aspects, such as we see, for example, in the Eastern Church's image of the Redeemer descending into Hell and conquering the powers of darkness. Here, then, we have a quite unprecedented objective sense of the order and goodness of being in its totality, a totality before which every particular

[325] *Civ. Dei* 11, 18.

point of view must give way—whether in knowledge, in faith or in face-to-face vision. This objectivism forms, as it were, the pedal note of all the images of the world that have had decisive influences on Dante. Their strength lies in 'their regard for the whole, in their renunciation of subjective individualism. What counts is not man but order, or rather, with respect to man, only what validates order, by means of a participation as much positive as negative'.[326]

However, perhaps it is that Augustine and Thomas had just not reckoned with the possibility of a man, with his living body, descending into Hell, and there meeting, face to face, the individual souls of the damned, his former friends and enemies, the great and admired men of Antiquity and Christendom, popes and emperors. In the realm of abstract thought the aesthetic justification of Hell could be carried out without special difficulty, but not so easily when Scholastic theology was transformed by a layman into existential theology. Thus Dante's journey into Hell turns out to be a crucial test for that entire Christian theodicy derived from Antiquity. Can it stand up to this test? More to the point, can it stand up to the test when it is considered as what it claims to be, as Christian theology? This searing test of Christian existence, or more precisely, this searing test of Scholastic theology through Christian existence, is taken so seriously by Dante that he does not hesitate to transform its paradoxes into lived reality. To do that, he has to make real two very different things at the same time: true and living encounters with his fellow human beings, now damned, and their final and absolute deprivation of all relationship with him—both the establishment and the breakdown of communication. Communication is restored in the all-inclusive framework of divine order. Surprisingly, this Hell is older than mankind, as old as the world, and a work of art of the triune God (this is indicated by the three names of God inscribed on the gate of Hell: *divina potestate*, *somma sapientia*, *primo amore*, although *giustizia* is set above all three).[327] This Hell is *di giustizia orribil arte*,[328] a construction of the Almighty,[329] an artistic

[326] Friedrich, 121.

[327] Inf 3, 4–6.

[328] Inf 14, 6; *cf.* Inf 11, 100.

[329] Inf 10, 37; 12, 23; 15, 12; 31, 85.

creation of supreme Wisdom as good as Heaven and earth.[330] It is significant that, when Cato sees the two travellers emerging out of Hell, he cries in his astonishment: 'Does order thus no longer rule in the abyss? *Son le leggi d'abisso così rotte*?'[331] Communication is established by the form of punishment (*contrappasso*) appropriate to the offence, its every detail full of significance. This form of punishment so lays hold of the sinner from within that the punishment becomes the complete expression of his guilt. In fact, content and form are so intertwined that the sinner himself presses toward the place of his punishment and eagerly embraces its particular form: 'Divine justice so spurs them that fear turns to desire'.[332] This is why there is a confessional at the entrance to eternal Hell: for the acknowledgment of one's own guilt (*tutta si confessa*) before the judge of Hell, Minos, and the apportioning of suitable punishment; confession in the full sense, but without any love or absolution, a sacrament without grace.[333]

But if Hell is the artistic creation of love, it is nevertheless only of a rigidified, petrified love, of which there remains only the 'form', only punitive justice. This work can, therefore, only be traversed and inspected in an attitude of complete objectivity, devoid of any emotion of the heart, only with a rigidified and petrified heart. That is to say, communication in the form of pure justice and truth—and without this form there would be no dialogue between Dante and the damned—is at the same time the breakdown of personal communication, which cannot occur except through the self-giving of the heart, except, at least partly, through love. It is of course true that in the *Inferno* there are many memorable encounters that resoundingly display greatness of soul, indeed, greatness of heart, tenderness and respectful veneration. But it must in fairness be pointed out that all these scenes take place within the unrelenting grip of Hell. They thus rest on the presupposition that Dante can offer nothing to these lost souls, nothing Christian, nothing personal, nothing except that strangest of gifts: a little bit of posthumous fame when he returns to earth as the poet of Hell. This is truly an

[330] Inf 19, 10.
[331] Pg 1, 46.
[332] Inf 3, 124–126.
[333] Inf 5, 7–8.

idea from Antiquity, but equally a truly Augustinian idea, drawn from the *Civitas Dei*. On the other hand, nothing Christian can be given them; not even a little hope, a little love, can be procured for them.

For this reason the journey through Hell, despite all the conversations there, is a matter of getting information, of observing and remembering. Virgil presses on like an impatient museum guide. Delay is pointless, because nothing can be gained from it. '*Guarda e passa.*'[334] '*Vassi per veder le vostre pene*',[335] '*a veder lo strazio*'.[336] '*Ma Virgilio mi disse: Che pur guate? . . . Ed altro è da veder che tu non vedi.*'[337] This becomes especially obtrusive in the lower reaches of Hell, where the damned, like animals, lie in ditches into which the travellers look down from above, 'just as we look at wild animals in their enclosures, for example into bear pits, which the cities of Dante's time had already constructed'.[338] For Dante, his progress through Hell would therefore mean initiation into pure objectivity and thus his weaning away from an excessively human compassion not yet in conformity with the supreme order of the world. Friedrich has shown that for Augustine compassion, although admittedly not condemned as it was by the Stoics, is nonetheless subordinated and rigorously brought into line by reason; compassion is only admissible when the movements of the passions correspond to law and to justice. As mere sensible emotion, as philanthropic fellow feeling, compassion in itself is neither good nor evil; to attain ethical value, it must first allow itself to be guided by the *cor rectum* to the objective *rectitudo* of divine order. But when it is a case of God having damned, compassion for the souls of the damned would plainly be a secret revolt against the wisdom of God. When the poet weeps over the terrible deformity of the diviners, whose heads have been turned round on their shoulders so that their tears drop down their backs, Virgil reprimands him: 'Art thou too as witless as the rest? *Qui vive la pietà quand'è ben morta.* Piety here

[334] Inf 3, 51; *cf.* Inf 30, 60, *Guardate ed attendete.*
[335] Inf 12, 21.
[336] Inf 13, 140.
[337] Inf 29, 4, 12.
[338] Gmelin, *Komm. zur Hölle*, 280; Inf 18, 1–18.

consists in no longer having pity. Who is more guilty than he who has pity on the damned?'[339] Dante wept because he saw 'our beautiful image so distorted', the image of divine resemblance here mutilated by God himself as the just and exterior punishment for the interior sin. Here it is a question of understanding, even of admiring, the fitness, the beauty of all this. At the very entrance to Hell Dante knows that the hard 'battle' he will have to fight is against his own pity (*la guerra della pietate*).[340] After the story of Francesca da Rimini he swoons out of pity.[341] Likewise before Ciacco,[342] with the avaricious[343] and especially with the suicides,[344] his pity makes itself felt. And then, when in the lower reaches of Hell he catches sight of the horrific mutilations, the demonic metamorphosis of man into snake, the stinking infirmaries of the sick, when he listens to the severed head of Bertran de Born speaking to him, with acres of souls in torment stretching beyond what the eye can see, he still wishes only to weep: 'The many people and the strange wounds had made my eyes so drunken that they were fain to stay and weep.'[345] Virgil, for his part, in fore-Hell, his own dwelling place, had been overcome with compassion for those who yearn eternally without hope.[346] But now he reproves the poet, for Dante's tears have no point, 'and only a little time is given us'. It is as if in the nethermost regions Dante has at last learnt impassibility, for he listens to Ugolino's story without any expression of emotion, indeed as if turned to stone within (*dentro impietrai*).[347] It is left to Ugolino himself to appeal to his compassion. 'Thou art cruel indeed if thou grieve not now . . . if thou weep not now, at what dost thou ever weep?'[348] But the poet can also express other feelings and passions: disgust, contempt, anger, and even with these at first purely earthly reactions, it is a case of adapting them to the all-inclusive, divine order. When God is angry, then man can and must be angry alongside him. In one strange scene the poet promises Alberigo, the traitor and murderer of his own kin, that he will break away

[339] Inf 20, 27–30.
[340] Inf 2, 4–5.
[341] Inf 5, 140–142; 6, 2.
[342] Inf 6, 58f.
[343] Inf 7, 36.
[344] Inf 13, 36f, 84.
[345] Inf 29, 1–3; *ibid.*, 36, 43–44.
[346] Inf 4, 13f, 21.
[347] Inf 33, 49.
[348] Inf 33, 40, 42.

the frozen tears from his eyes so as to stir him into telling the poet his name. But he does not do it, for this reason: *E cortesia fu lui esser villano* ('it was courtesy to be a churl to him').[349] This scene may refer to a verse from the Psalms: 'With the pure thou dost show thyself pure; and with the crooked thou dost show thyself perverse (*et cum perverso perverteris*)' (17.27; 2 Kings 22.27, Vulg). It may well be only through inadvertence that Dante strikes with his foot against the head of one of those frozen beneath the lake of ice, one who is shown to be Dante's brother:

Guarda come passi!
Va sì che tu non calchi con le piante
Le teste dei fratei miseri lassi.[350]

Or it could be that this chance is also 'fate or will'?[351] On the other hand, there is also the incident where Dante comes to blows with the frozen man and angrily tears out a few tufts of his hair in order to find out his name.[352] It can even happen that Virgil praises this display of indignation, whereupon Dante expresses the desire to see the sinner, Filippo Argenti, thoroughly punished, a wish that Virgil in his turn grants.[353] The standard by which all these emotions are measured remains the will of God ruling over the damned. It is into the mystery of that will that the poet is initiated, and it is there that every human emotion finds its measure and limit. This is *apatheia*, which surpasses the *apatheia* of the Buddhist, for whom compassion is the supreme norm of morality, precisely because no being can be totally and definitively lost on the wheel of Samsara.

What, then, we must ask, is the net result of this existential testing of theology? Does it prove it to be biblical, evangelical, Christian, or not? It may be that the dialectic of the establishment and breakdown of communication is not a real possibility from the Christian point of view, because it is neither prescribed nor conceivable. But should this turn out to be the case, the blame would not lie with Dante, but with the system, which he tried to put to the test. Then the *Inferno* would at the

[349] Inf 33, 150.
[350] Inf 32, 19–21.
[351] Inf 32, 76.
[352] Inf 32, 103f.
[353] Inf 8, 43–60.

same time be both the system's *reductio ad absurdum* (through the test) and its spiritual full stop, even though in later centuries it would continue to be tested. All artistic depictions of Hell—from Orcagna to Breughel, from Bosch to Michelangelo's *Last Judgment* and Rubens' forays into of Hell, to Milton also, and right up to Rimbaud's *Saison en Enfer* and Sartre's *Huis-clos*—all these depend, though less consciously and systematically, on a dialectic, the essential content of which Dante exposed, and this he carried out with extreme and relentless clarity, even though it was not he who invented the dialectic.[354] It only remains to ask whether he was able to carry this out in complete consistency with his theological and aesthetic presuppositions, or only in contradiction to them, thus exposing a fatal flaw in his Christian poem about the cosmos. But once again we must say that it is not the poet who is responsible for this flaw, but the system handed to him. As a layman he simply took up the system imparted to him and to the best of his ability defended and glorified it.

Nothing can happen in Dante's Hell, because love is absent. And according to his own doctrine, as well as that of Antiquity, of Augustine and of Thomas, love is the interior motive force of all living things. No matter how much feeling and imaginative power is imparted to the dramatization of the scenes, they take place entirely within the mighty grip of damnation and second death; thus, from the existential point of view, they demonstrate total meaninglessness. The symbol of this is that the damned can have no knowledge of the present; all they can know is past and future, so long as the future remains at all. For this reason what passes for their spiritual life is but a function of earthly events and will be completed extinguished on the last day when those events come to an end.[355] As we shall presently see, within the grip of Hell there are enormous differences of value, but they must all be seen in relation to the eternal standard: what has been excluded for eternity from the vision of God must together constitute a single realm of shadows and sorrow. This

[354] See, for example, the *Disputationes* of Simon of Tournai (ed. J. Warichez, 1932), where the question of Christian communication with the damned is constantly and fervently discussed.

[355] Inf 10, 100f.

affirmation becomes fundamental for subsequent ages. For Luther and thorough-going Protestantism, as well as for Jansenism, the sinful world in its entirety is removed from the light of divine Eros and has fallen into a state of general damnation—with the exception of those for whom Christ died on the Cross. Here then Dante's infernal confines are generalised; they have become the confines of the world itself. Within them, of course, there may well be all the degrees of value, of true and false, good and evil, beautiful and ugly and so on. But none of these has the absolute sense they had in ancient philosophy, because none is animated by the Eros of divine truth: in damnation philosophy is an impossibility. Within its confines there is only deadness, only 'material', only 'facts'; even philosophical thought itself becomes 'fact', a filing cabinet for facts. Philosophy sinks to the level of the other profane sciences. But then, as a consequence, theology becomes disincarnate, for it lacks its proper connection with the transcendence of human reason. And so, as was argued in the first volume, every theological aesthetic becomes impossible.

It follows inescapably from this that in Hell the love of God is completely veiled by justice, and the divine beauty can only consist in the right proportioning of punishment to guilt. Thus the divine *vendetta*,[356] a word that constantly recurs in Dante, signifies the divine recompense; to experience this produces, even in man, a profound satisfaction.[357] And so we find ourselves transported to a religious world entirely dominated by law, in conformity, on the one hand, to Antiquity and, on the other, to the Old Testament and its *lex talionis* (this is the *contrappasso*); and wherever Hell is enlarged to become a kind of model for the whole of worldly existence, Christian juridical thought necessarily has its back against the wall.

Dante has two lines of resistance against the logic of his *Inferno*, which seemed to him to be demanded by theology. The disparity of these two ways shows us the extent to which his poem on Hell stands at a turning point between eras. The first way is the aesthetic attempt to go as far as possible toward

[356] The instances are listed by Gmelin, *Komm. zur Hölle*, 139–140; *cf.* also 428.

[357] Pg 20, 94–96; *cf.* Pg 33, 34–36.

relaxing the remorseless grip of Hell, and this aesthetic attempt is consequently also theological. But first of all, the poet proceeds aesthetically, giving as a backdrop to his journey through Hell the most magnificent landscape. His imaginative power as a poet is inflamed and at the same time held in check by his great models from Antiquity—Virgil, Ovid, Statius—but beyond all these it is fed by his own inexhaustible spring. He constructs stage sets, one after the other, of titanic and hallucinatory power: rocks by night, heaps of boulders, bridges, walls, rivers of fire and of blood, cities aflame, glowing pits, flights through the air on the backs of monsters, lakes of ice, the circle of giants like the battlements of a fortified city, finally the icy blast of wind from the bat wings of Lucifer. On these stage sets he presents a profusion of diverse figures, each sketched with its own unique characteristics. The travellers meet these figures and hold the briefest of conversations with them on matters of the greatest importance. In so doing they learn more and more new and strange things about Hell, but also about the past, present and future of the world above. This torrent of events, as it sweeps along, completely captivates all the senses, all feeling and thinking, and so allows no respite in which to call to mind the vice-like grip in which everything is held. But the course of events is not just enlivened at an aesthetic and external level; the emphasis on differences in value generates a spiritual and philosophical excitement. These differences are so marked that Dante gives the impression that Hell has hardly any unity, that fundamentally it is an analogical, perhaps even equivocal, construction. The poet has every reason to give these equivocations full scope and takes full advantage of them.

Virgil is the guide through Hell, not least because in the sixth book of the Aeneid he himself created a journey through Hell for his hero. Indeed, he was familiar with Dante's Hell at first hand, for he was already one of the dead, in its lowest depths, before the birth of Christ.[358] For this reason, and because for Dante the whole ancient, pre-Christian world is excluded from the vision of God, Dante's Hell has just as many features derived

[358] Inf 9, 22f. On this, see F. von Falkenhausen, 'Erichthos Beschwörung', *Dt. DanteJahrbuch* xxi (1939), 144–147.

from the Hades (Sheol) of Antiquity (and thus of the Old Testament) as those of Christian inspiration. It is inhabited and literally articulated by figures from ancient mythology, who here appear as people just as real as the poets and philosophers in the Limbo and Elysium of the fourth canto. The dwelling place of the great luminaries of Antiquity seems like an island of light in the sombre ocean of Hell. Its predominant manners are those of courtesy of the heart; the noblest human values are not only known but practised, and Dante is welcomed by the great poets into their circle and is honoured as their equal.[359] Here, as elsewhere in Hell, there reigns the authentic nostalgia of Antiquity for the beautiful life above, close to the sun, *la vita serena*,[360] *la dolce terra latina*,[361] and fame, in the sense of earthly immortality, as for Dante himself, is considered to be one of the supreme values.[362] Of course, this ancient image of Hell is given certain characteristics that foreshadow the Christian idea, but not such as would deprive it of its own characteristics. It is located, admittedly, inside the first gate of Hell, which has remained open since Christ's descent into Hell, but it is outside the second gate, which the devil and the shrews keep so tightly shut. Outside the second gate there is first of all—theologically strange but how characteristic of Dante!—the numberless host of futile existences who are too insubstantial for either eternal reward or eternal punishment. Neither the mercy nor the justice of God can do anything with them (*misericordia e giustizia li sdegna*). All that the poet can do is let them run round in circles for eternity behind a banner—a slogan, an ideology. And they are so numerous 'that I should never have believed death had undone so many'.[363] We also meet outside the second gate those who have succumbed to earthly, mythical Eros. As befits the this-worldly sublimity of that love, these souls are driven

[359] Inf 4, 97–105.
[360] Inf 15, 49.
[361] Inf 27, 26.
[362] Inf 16, 31, 85. For Dante it is a sure sign of the destruction of the hierarchy of values that in nethermost Hell the thought of posthumous fame no longer has any appeal, that the sinners desire only to be forgotten. Inf 18, 46; 18, 118f; 19, 64f; 23, 112; 24, 133f; 27, 61f; 32, 92f.
[363] Inf 3, 50, 56–57.

onward by the hurricanes of Hell like starlings and cranes—Paris, Tristan, Dido's troop, *le donne antiche e i cavalieri*.[364] Within Hell itself the distances are no less great: between the great heroes, like Odysseus and Jason; the presumptuous, like Farinata; those who were nearly saints and missed Heaven for the sake of a single sin, like Guido da Montefeltro and other Florentine nobles led astray by the Pope; tragic figures, like Piero delle Vigne and even Ugolino; those whom Dante respects for their intrinsic merit or their art, like Bertran de Born[365] and the aforesaid Montefeltro[366]—between all of these and those crafty scoundrels who inhabit the lower circles of Hell the distance is small. There would seem to be no limit to the number of distinctions the poet makes in his value judgments. Compared with the subtlety of his power of moral discernment, the overall confines of damnation seem almost external and artificially contrived. When considered in the light of these intra-infernal differences, the true reason why one nobleman is to be met with in Hell and another in Purgatory can no longer be made plain. By contrast, the decisive factor is the seriousness with which the poet in general takes the perspective of eternity. This is applied to earthly destinies and historical developments and leads to the great series of examples distributed among the three kingdoms of the hereafter without, however, any compelling reasons being given for the ultimate destiny that has befallen each.

Something that goes even further in this direction is the strange communication that exists between the kingdoms, and which is not simply set up by the wandering poets. It is astonishing enough that the angels can dive into Hell,[367] but what is even more surprising is that Beatrice herself can go down to Virgil from highest Heaven[368] and 'leave her footprints in Hell',[369] or that an inhabitant of Hell, Virgil, can leave Hell and go as far as the earthly Paradise and the vision of the glorified Church—by way of an extended interpretation of the prophecy in the fourth eclogue.[370] Greetings are exchanged

[364] Inf 5, 67, 71–72, 85.
[365] VE 2, 2; Conv 4, 11.
[366] Conv 4, 28.
[367] Inf 9, 64f.
[368] Inf 2, 50f.
[369] Par 31, 81.
[370] Pg 29, 57.

between the kingdoms; for example, on his return Virgil brings back the greetings of Cato, who has been transferred from Limbo to ante-Purgatory, for his wife Marcia who remains behind.[371] And precisely in the personal circle of Virgil there is undoubtedly human communication established on the basis of the noblest values of mind and heart. The conversation between Virgil and Statius[372] (who was a secret Christian and as such has passed through Purgatory) takes place in the light of love. The word 'love' recurs several times and in different forms in that conversation; it is a real bond of love that leads to Statius' finding faith through Virgil's eclogue.[373] Thereupon Virgil gives him information about fore-Hell where dwell the great poets of former ages whom Statius loves so much, and where they often speak of Parnassus,[374] which is in truth the earthly Paradise[375]—what heartfelt thought for one another across the borders of the kingdoms! There are also some, like Cato whom we have mentioned, who dwelt first in the kingdom of darkness and have now been transferred to the kingdom of hope or the kingdom of fulfillment. Adam did penance down below for more than five thousand years;[376] now he sits on a throne in the heaven of the fixed stars.[377] Cato, though a suicide, is allowed to join the souls led out from Hell by Christ at his descent; this is because of his Roman virtue and because he is the representative of man's freedom of conscience. So likewise we meet two pagans in Heaven. First there is the Emperor Trajan, who was redeemed by the prayer of Pope Gregory I. In fact, the Pope was moved to prayer by the *gran valore del romano principato* and his *viva speme*,[378] so that now in Heaven Trajan experiences the opposition of the two kingdoms (*per l'esperienza di questa dolce vita e dell'opposta*).[379] The other pagan is the mysterious Trojan, Ripheus,[380] who came from Hell into Heaven simply as an example of the election of divine grace,[381] but he too is not without a certain merit, for he sought moral justice *per tutto suo*

[371] Pg 1, 82f.
[372] Pg 22, 10, 15, 16, 19, 24.
[373] Pg 22, 73.
[374] Pg 22, 104.
[375] Pg 28, 141.
[376] Pg 33, 61.
[377] Par 26, 82f.
[378] Pg 10, 73–76; Par 20, 106–117.
[379] Par 20, 47–48.
[380] Par 20, 67.
[381] Par 20, 68–72.

amor.[382] For Dante there is such a thing as baptism of desire in the sense of an anticipated sharing in the theological virtues before the coming of Christ.[383] This participation is not sharply distinguished from natural morality, which is why any transition from Hell to the kingdoms above is motivated by these two factors taken together. All this relaxes the grip of Hell, indeed finally submits its existence to the providence of God. What are we to think if Beatrice in Heaven before God's throne proclaims the praises of Virgil?[384] What if, at the entry to Paradise, Virgil after such a long and intimate association with Dante discharges him as a pupil come of age but without really taking leave of him? Perhaps such a leave-taking (for eternity) could not be made existentially credible within the framework of this theological aesthetic. We may not be able to demonstrate convincingly that Dante bequeaths his Virgil any sort of chance, because like all the noble souls of Antiquity 'he secretly regarded him as worthy of redemption',[385] but the opposite cannot be proved either. For the human heart may well be able to transcend its limitations and enter into heavenly love (despite all the suffering that involves), but to transcend those limitations in order to achieve an understanding of Hell remains unattainable at the existential level. Dante has come up against this limitation, and he is very clearly aware of it.

So, if Dante is not able to follow the first way right to the end, there remains only the second. And while the first (which took place within the continuing objective confines of Hell) betrays its roots in the historical past, the second looks historically forward. At the command of a weeping Beatrice, Dante is guided through Hell, because no other way leads to his conversion. He must see where his life is leading him. And if this obligation humbles him, it is accompanied by a privilege—the privilege, by virtue of a unique election, of descending into that kingdom reserved for God most high, and of coming to know it and of telling about it. Aeneas, whom Dante regards as an absolutely historical figure, was able to undertake this journey into Hell in virtue of his status as founder of Rome: 'In the

[382] Par 20, 121.

[383] Par 20, 127–129.

[384] Inf 2, 73–74.

[385] Gmelin, *Komm. zur Hölle*, 82.

heaven of the Empyrean he was chosen to be father of glorious Rome and of her Empire.'[386] And Rome was chosen as the seat of both the Empire and the Papacy. 'By this journey for which thou honourest him he heard things which fitted him for his victory and prepared for him the Papal mantle.'[387] According to the medieval *Visio Pauli*, a second founder descended into Hell,[388] in order to see the torments of the damned; he too was reproved by an angel for his misplaced compassion: was he trying to be more merciful than God? Dante was clearly familiar with this text.[389] According to him, Paul, the *vas d'elezione*, had descended into Hell 'that he might bring thence confirmation of the faith'.[390] Dante, who feels himself to be unworthy—'I am not Aeneas; I am not Paul'—is afraid that he will be thought presumptuous. The response to this, which does not diminish Dante's mission but only renders it, as it were, psychologically bearable, refers to Beatrice's command; the election is at the same a humiliation, 'may' is also 'must' and what grace does for Dante is to unite these two meanings: 'Necessity brings him here, not pleasure.'[391] Because he is a sinner, Hell is bound to terrify and deter him; because he has been specially chosen, he is bound to proclaim that terror on his return. He plunges deep into the mysterious, objective judgments of God, there to be purged; then, later on, with the accent now on the objectivity of theology and the Church, he conveys to sinners the message of divine justice. What he reports is not conjecture but first-hand experience, and just to recall it makes him shudder and tremble. When Dante remembers the dark wood of sin in which he lost his way, the mere thought of it renews his fear.[392] He breaks into sweat when he thinks of the earthquake in Hell.[393] His blood runs cold when he thinks back on the hideous throng of snakes and naked men in the seventh ditch.[394] And when he reflects on what he saw in the eighth ditch, 'it pains him even today', and he tightens the reins on his

[386] Inf 2, 19–21. [387] Inf 2, 25–27.
[388] Bibliography in Gmelin 1, c. 51; Rüegg I, 255–291.
[389] Rüegg 391. [390] Inf 2, 28–29.
[391] Inf 12, 87. [392] Inf 1, 6.
[393] Inf 3, 131–132; *cf.* also Inf 14, 78; 16, 12; 22, 31.
[394] Inf 24, 82–84; *cf.* 25, 4.

mind, lest it run away with him and deprive him of his mission.[395] When on one occasion he eavesdrops, out of curiosity, on the quarrel of two of the damned, Virgil angrily reprimands him, and Dante looks upon him 'with such shame that still it haunts my memory'.[396] Very understandably, he has never forgotten the men frozen up to their heads beneath the lake of ice, with only their faces, blue with cold, projecting out: 'shuddering comes over me, and always will, at frozen pools.'[397] Correspondingly, when he remembers the Mountain of Purgatory, he says: 'May I see it again!'[398] St Bernard, with 'Beatrice and so many of the blest', prays the Mother of God to keep his affections pure, as befits one who has seen Paradise.[399] The existential turmoil expressed in these passages is more than just a poetic device to give a semblance of reality to his journey; it has the same degree of reality as that passage in the *Paradiso* where Dante in Heaven is confirmed in his mission of proclaiming on earth what he has seen above. When confronted with aesthetic visions of such theological rigour, the reader has no hesitation in accepting the theological seriousness of the aesthetics, and vice versa. It is not as if Dante had followed his personal inclinations, making Hell an outlet for his hate and Heaven the embodiment of his love and desire. Dante's mission is to throw eternal light on temporal affairs, to place human destiny on the scales of eternity, to raise up to full and clear definition what is blurred and incomplete and therefore, from the earthly point of view, unintelligible; such definition befits man's true meaning, and, through God's justice and grace, is his due. Already in the *Canzoniere* and *Vita Nuova* we find that no aspect of love can become an object of faith except through 'the intelligence of the third sphere'. This is even more true of the *Comedy*, where the reality of faith, which, for the Christian, alone gives meaning to existence, is not only believed in by the poet, but is seen in the light of faith to such an extent that in the perfected figure of truth he can present an aesthetic vision that anticipates the heavenly vision. If it is true that this vision is the

[395] Inf 26, 19–25.
[396] Inf 30, 133–135.
[397] Inf 32, 71–72.
[398] Pg 2, 16; *cf.* 2, 114.
[399] Par 33, 34–39.

poet's divinely ordained mission, then it is only logical that it should at the same time become the most terrible kind of moral exhortation to the whole of Christendom and be regarded as such by the poet.

The experience of the hereafter is made relevant to the man who experiences it; he in turn, in obedience to his mission, makes it relevant to the experience of those to whom he addresses himself, his fellow Christians. The reality of what he has seen is still, of course, completely objective (it is not in any sense a mere function of the subject's power of imagination or, for that matter, hallucination), but its objectivity consists now entirely in its kerygmatic function, which is also true, as we shall see, of the visions in the Johannine Apocalypse, whatever differences there might be in the theological quality of the two visions. Both testify to what they have seen, and both have seen not only Purgatory and Heaven but also the lake of fire and the monsters from the abyss. But the total realism of the vision prevents neither seer from seeing 'images', or rather effigies, of evil. For Dante's encounters in Hell can be nothing else, if one considers the existential dialectic into which such encounters draw the traveller who witnesses them. Effigies have no *motus*, no vital interior conative life in the Aristotelian and Thomistic sense, no entelechy, no hope, no *amor*; they are without rapport. That is why the rapport Dante establishes with them is intrinsically impossible. Bernanos sees the full implications of this when his country priest describes Hell for the Comtesse: 'Alas, if God's own hand were to lead us to one of these unhappy things, even if once it had been the dearest of our friends, in what language could we address it? Truly if one of us, if a living man, the vilest, most contemptible of the living, were cast into those burning depths, I should still be ready to share his suffering, I would claim him from his executioner. To share his suffering! . . . The sorrow, the unutterable loss of those charred stones which once were men, is that they have nothing more to be shared.'[400]

And it is only because they are effigies that they can be looked at. In no sense, then, as Bernanos, being a true Christian, knew

[400] *Journal d'un curé de campagne* (1936), p. 181.

well, can they be compared to our suffering, fellow human beings. This is why Hugo Friedrich's analysis of the *Inferno* misses the essential point when it presents us with the alternative: either sentimental, humanitarian compassion or (in company with Dante) rising above such compassion to the point of view of divine and cosmic justice. This alternative is Hegelian, at best Spinozist; it is not Christian. It overlooks the third possibility: the Cross, the substitutionary death of Christ. Or perhaps Friedrich has subsumed this third possibility and Christology under the heading of an *amor fati* and has drawn for us the image of a Christ who, in his surrender to the Father's cosmic will, was always prepared to abandon the redemption of mankind.[401]

The *Divine Comedy* is so very much a transverse section through the cosmos that the historical event of Christ's redemption of mankind (which can be shown only in longitudinal section) makes hardly any appearance at all. Hell is as eternal as the creation of the world and will be as eternal as the heavenly Paradise. There is no question, absolutely no question, of Hell in its innermost structure having been transformed by Good Friday and Holy Saturday—the two days during which Dante carries out his journey through Hell—while Easter morning finds him precisely in the Earthly Paradise. The Eastern Church's image of redemption is alien to Dante. Christ has opened the outer door of Hell and led out a few souls from fore-Hell, but the inner door remains as tightly shut as ever.[402] And the wretched memorial of his progress through the interior of Hell is a geographical image: a landslide, which Virgil observes with amazement, since the last time he came that way the road was still clear.[403] Dante does not distinguish theologically between the pre-Christian Hades (Sheol) and the Hell of the New Testament, nor does he grasp the connection between this Hell and the distinctive kerygma of the New Testament. This journey through Hell, therefore, follows in the footsteps of Virgil rather than of Christ, which for the Christian would be the only possible way of entering this 'place'.

[401] Friedrich cites Hugh of St Victor as a shocking example of such a christology (pp. 164–165). Unfortunately, there are other examples.

[402] Inf 8, 126.

[403] Inf 12, 34–45.

The mythological image of the world was able to fit the redemptive events tidily and neatly into the geographical and astronomical structure of the cosmos—in very much the same way that Thomas Aquinas does in his great eschatology in the *Commentary on the Sentences*. The inadequacies of that image of the world now stand out as theological. The lack of christological (and thus also of trinitarian) influence on the *Inferno* (the inscription above the gate is far from being sufficient) has its effect on the *Purgatorio*, which places much greater emphasis on the moral restoration (*katorthôsis*) of man than on the imitation of Christ and the inexorable confrontation with his Cross. Above all, it affects the *Paradiso*, where the reality of Christ as universal mediator is almost entirely absent. Glory here is indeed the glory of a Heaven aflame with the Eros of God, but the distinctively Christian quality of this—God's descent into death and Hell, his humiliation to the point of complete kenosis, God taking our place and bearing the sin of the whole world—this kind of glory does not come into view. For this reason the *Comedy*'s image of God is not really trinitarian but an extraordinarily intensified, Christian version of the Eros of Antiquity. And it is quite clear that the relationship of Dante and Beatrice, of Gabriel and Mary, of earthly and heavenly love, of Eros and Agape within an Eros that is regarded as embracing all, is the last word of the poet.

6. THE ETERNAL FEMININE

The classical and Patristic notion of the beauty of the cosmic order does, of course, hold sway in Dante's work, but the question, prominent in Bonaventure, of how that beauty is to be expressed is stressed to the point where it becomes the dominant concern. It is the question of whether the ineffable ground of being can express itself in the form of created being: the two, ground and form, meet in the human beauty of Beatrice. Even in Dante's early work her earthly figure is an expression of Heaven—so precious indeed is she that Heaven is always on the point of recalling and reclaiming this image of itself, and in the *Comedy* there is nothing greater than her on earth: 'Never did nature or art set before thee beauty so great as the fair members in which I was enclosed. . . .'[404] But it is the eyes of Beatrice in which this beauty is concentrated, like lightning, those eyes, which even from behind the thick veil that conceals her before the confession, enflame the poet,[405] and which in Paradise transport him upward from sphere to sphere. Beatrice looks up to God, and her eyes mirror Heaven. Dante looks into that mirror and finds himself gradually carried up above.[406] The Eternal Feminine that draws us up is more than just a symbol, far more than an allegory; it is reality and extends, without break, up through all the gradations of reality, from the tangible, earthly body of the beloved, past her glorified figure, as far as St Lucy, who represents the *Ecclesia sanctorum*, as far as Mary, the archetype and foundation of the receptive and virginally fruitful Church. This principle has nothing to do with any passing, mythological image of the world; it can be justified by Catholic theology so long as one does not aestheticise it but rather recognizes that in it is mediated the full seriousness of the biblical message, the seriousness of the Cross and the remission of sins, the seriousness of conversion and confession.

It cannot be said that Dante has, as it were, 'sexualised' Christian Eros, even though it is by erotic similes that he constantly tries to illuminate the most profound relationships of human existence. For example, he distributes the transcendental qualities of truth and goodness between man and woman, and makes beauty the fruit of their union. Then again he ties a bond of friendship between nobility of soul (*nobilitade*; husband) and philosophy (wife), a bond that unites so inseparably in Eros that Eros becomes one with philosophy and at the same time, as love for philosophy, constitutes true nobility.[407] In the *Canzoniere* there is still a certain dualism between the two supreme values, virtue and beauty, and the question is asked how the heart, without infidelity, can serve two mistresses:

[404] Pg 31, 49–51.

[405] Pg 30, 66.

[406] Par 2, 22f; 5, 86f; 8, 15f; 10, 37; 14, 79f; 18, 52f; 21, 1f; 22, 100f; 27, 97f; 30, 13f.

[407] Conv 4, 30.

Parlan bellezza e virtù all'intelletto,
E fan quistion: come un cuor puote stare
Infra duo donne con amor perfetto.[408]

The answer is that beauty can be loved for the sake of joy, and virtue for the sake of noble deeds, but this is not satisfactory. The more profound answer, already in outline in the *Canzoniere* and developed in the *Convivio* and the *Comedy*, sees in beauty the expressive form of the good and the true. For one who has still not had access to the deeper mysteries there is the reflected splendour of beauty, in all its colours, concealing within it, of course, a sacred mystery, just as a sacrament contains a hidden grace.[409] This relationship determines philosophical Eros: 'Morality is the beauty of philosophy, for just as the beauty of the body follows from the proper disposition of the members, so the beauty of Wisdom, which is the body of philosophy, as has been said, follows from the disposition of the moral virtues that enable her to give pleasure perceptibly to the senses (*che fanno quella piacere sensibilmente*).'[410] The body of truth and goodness is beautiful, but for Dante the three are inseparably connected, because Eros has also been characterized as form (soul) and Sophia as the matter (body) of philosophy (or truth). There can be no ethics without Eros and thus without beauty, but even more so, there can be no beauty without ethics, for the latter, according to Dante, constitutes the highest of the intellectual spheres that lie closest to God. Thus, for Dante, the ethical and the aesthetic remain a tightly intertwined unity. This is important with regard to the objection that for Dante erotic beauty has displaced ethics and that everything is absorbed in an ecstatic and ultimately irresponsible kind of contemplation. On the contrary, the *Divine Comedy* is also a proclamation of penitence, a rigorous initiation into just ethical and political behaviour, into a supreme sense of responsibility on the part of every individual with regard to this present world. Thus Dante's relationship with Beatrice is in no sense intended as an

[408] Sonetto, '*Due donne in cima*'.
[409] Final strophe of the canzone for the second book of the *Convivio*. *Cf.* Pg 33, 73–78.
[410] Conv 3, 15.

aesthetic libertinism; the Francesca episode shows how seriously he takes the ethics of the state of marriage. But it is true that Eros for Beatrice goes beyond the states of this life and indeed unites the two of them, though only when they are seen in the vanishing point of Paradise. Dante praises those men, who after a life in the state of matrimony, or indeed even during that life, turn toward the religious state. 'No one ought to excuse himself by reason of the marriage tie that still binds him in extreme age; for not only does he who assumes a habit and rule of life like that of St Augustine, or St Francis, or St Dominic, join the ranks of the professed, but a man may also become truly and properly professed while married, for God does not require us to be professed save in heart.'[411] Here, then, we have Dante, the married layman with the image of his eternal beloved on his heart. And here too we may apply the words of the canzone that the one for whom the meaning of the figure is not disclosed must carry that figure respectfully. And so in the kingdom of beauty there is an image of truth when Beatrice, in the place of Christ, leaves her mark on the kingdom of the lost:

O donna in cui la mia speranza vige,
E che soffristi per la mia salute
In inferno lasciar le tue vestige. . . .[413]

[411] Conv 4, 28.

[412] Par 31, 79–81. 'O lady in whom my hope has its strength and who didst bear for my salvation to leave thy footprints in Hell. . . .'

ST JOHN OF THE CROSS

THE PERFECT ADVENTURE

Between Dante and St John of the Cross come Luther and the Reformation. But also in between come Columbus and the new experience of a spherical earth, and Copernicus and the opening up of space, which was to render the old theological image of the cosmos obsolete. The Carmelite reform is a conscious response to the first of these revolutions and reflects the second in passing; the third will not be confronted until Pascal. The Reformers banished aesthetics from theology; John of the Cross, the uncompromising ascetic, and Pascal, the man influenced by Jansenism, respond to that banishment with a new aesthetic theology that stands in sharp confrontation with the German Reformation.

The effect of both the new sense of the earth's spherical nature and of the new science of the cosmos was to destroy the myth of the 'perspicuity' of the *analogia entis* as presupposed and developed in Dante's cosmos—the analogy between earth and Heaven, the former age and the new age, the world of the body and the world of the spirit, nature and grace, knowledge and faith, man and God. And the destruction of the *analogia entis* prepares the way for the Lutheran dialectic between the kingdoms and for the principle of *sola fide*. The latter was not only a declaration of war against the philosophizing of the Middle Ages but also an act of defiance against the approaching new era. The two authors we are now to consider resist *sola fide* but daringly combine its Christian radicalism with a new form of perspicuity, a profound aesthetic experience. Christian tradition makes its contribution to this new aesthetic. John of the Cross reforms an old contemplative order with its roots in Palestine; he responds, fundamentally, with the theology of the Christian East. If we are to see St John in his right setting, we must never forget that as a young theological student in Salamanca he sketched out a programmatic treatise on the nature of Christian mysticism. In this—evidently to find firm ground from which to combat Illuminism and everything for which it had been condemned by the Church[1]—he draws upon Patristic tradition, 'especially on Dionysius and Gregory the Great'.[2] It is precisely in these two theologians that he finds his justification for representing the mystical way as absolutely *the* way to God: it is the Christian way that contains within itself the truth of Platonism, even the whole Far Eastern quest for God, including Buddha and Lao-tse. And, although mysticism is a way taken by only a very few, it is nonetheless the model for every way of faith, precisely because it is the way of the one and only faith. The challenge and the scandal of the Carmelite response to Luther lie in the fact that it incorporates the whole of monastic tradition from the Greeks up to and including the Middle Ages into the new Christian radicalism; indeed, with its modern orientation toward personal, experiential and psychological categories, the Carmelite response makes the new radicalism more radical than ever.[3]

In contrast, Pascal responds to the Reformation from the perspective of Luther's own Augustinian, Western tradition, which he combines (this had never been done before) with the outlook of modern science to form something unique and remarkable. However, both John of the Cross and Pascal stress, albeit in different ways, the aspect of the experience of faith over the Reformers' assurance of faith. This experience of faith is a verification, at once both subjective and objective, of the Christian mystery in the believing person and, for both authors, stands in outright opposition to the light of reason. The *illuminatio* of Plato and Augustine is no longer a mediating link between philosophy and theology; the distinction has clearly become a division, and only from above, from the point of view

[1] On the Index of 1559, beside John of Avila, Francis of Osuna and Luis of Granada, we also find the Spanish translations of Tauler, Dionysius the Carthusian and Heinrich Herpff.

[2] Crisogono de Jesus OCD, *Vida de San Juan de la Cruz*, cited from the text in *Biblioteca de Autores Cristianos* (BAC), *Vida y Obras de S. Juan de la Cruz*, 2nd ed. (Madrid, 1950), 85.

[3] This tradition is described in a book, in the tradition of Abbot Butler's *Western Mysticism*, by A Benedictine of Stanbrook, *Mediaeval Mystical Tradition and St John of the Cross* (Burns & Oates, 1954).

of faith, can the two orders be understood as a unity. Natural theology may be possible 'in itself', but it no longer has any existential force. 'The truth is that one must ever adhere to Christ's teaching, and that everything else is nothing.'[4] The shadowy notion of God that natural reason can gain from its own resources does not interest John. He desires God as he is in himself, and this God can be known only through God. Pascal, likewise, does not deny the 'God of the Philosophers', but concerns himself only with the God of Abraham and of Christ.

[4] A ii, 22, 8. The works will be cited as follows: A = *The Ascent of Mount Carmel*; N = *The Dark Night*; C = *The Spiritual Canticle*; L = *Living Flame of Love*; Ep = Letters; P = Poetry.

Except for C, all works will be cited according to the text and paragraph numbering of P. Silverio de S. Teresa, 3rd ed. (Burgos, 1943). This same numbering is used in the BAC edition mentioned in n. 2.

The *Canticle* exists in two redactions: the shorter (A) and the longer (B). Since the critical work of Dom Chevallier (*Le Cantique Spirituel de St Jean de la Croix*, Notes historiques, Texte critique, vers. française, 1930), Redaction B, though still reproduced in Spanish editions, has been considered by an increasing number of scholars to consist of later interpolations into the Redaction A, the genuine redaction. Our quotations will be from Chevallier's text, and the commentary on each of the thirty-nine five-lined strophes is cited as in Chevallier, according to strophe and line number.

[The English translation used throughout is that of Kieran Kavanaugh OCD and Otilio Rodriguez OCD, *The Collected Works of St John of the Cross* (Washington, 1963).]

The most important studies: For biography, P. Crisogono (seen n. 2), P. Fr Bruno, *St Jean de la Croix* (1929); E. Allison Peers, *Handbook to the Life and Times of St Teresa and St John of the Cross* (1954); *ibid, Studies of the Spanish Mystics* (1927–1930). For personality and works, Jean Baruzi, *St Jean de la Croix et le problème de l'expérience mystique* (1924; 2nd ed., 1931), a standard work written from a neo-Kantian perspective, which Georges Morel SJ (*Le sens de l'existence selon St Jean de la Croix*, 3 vols, 1960–1961) has attempted to refute from the perspective of a quite definite neo-Hegelianism. For general interpretation, Irene Behn, *Spanische Mystik* (1957).

Standard authorities today on the aesthetic aspect of St John's work: Damaso Alonso, *La poesia de San Juan de la Cruz* (Madrid, 1942), as well as two sensitive French studies, Max Milner, *Poésie et vie mystique chez St Jean de la Croix* (Seuil, 1951); Michel Florisoone, *Esthétique et mystique d'après St Thérèse d'Avila et St Jean de la Croix* (Seuil, 1956). Further literature on the aesthetics: P. Crisogono (BAC, 2nd ed., 515, n. 12); many articles in the journal *Études Carmélitaines*. A good, though not comprehensive, concordance has been produced by Fr. Luis de San José, *Concordancias de los Obras y Escritos de . . . S. Juan de la Cruz* (Burgos, 1948).

God alone suffices. Man is created, called, endowed with grace, for the sake of the vision of God, for participation in the inner, triune life of eternal love. Man, who is relative, is what he is for the sake of the Absolute, and inasmuch as the Absolute outweighs the relative, so in human desire God must outweigh all created things. God for his part is pure, radiant love, a love that is open to the creature and desires its participation in the absolute and ontological unity of the Godhead. Such participation is possible when divine love becomes the loving action of the creature itself. 'So great a union between God and the soul is caused that all the things of both God and the soul become one in participant transformation (*unas en transformación participante*), and the soul appears (*parece*) to be God more than a soul. Indeed, it is God by participation (*y aun es Dios por participación*). Yet in truth its being (even though transformed) is naturally as distinct from God's as it was before.'[5] This, this alone, is 'man in truth'. Compared with this idea of God as man's origin and destiny, all other representations of human nature are lifeless abstractions.[6] Man is the 'image and likeness of God', but compared with the truth, he remains an image and a likeness.

What does it matter if only a few recognize and respond here on earth to this natural vocation, which everyone else will attain one day after terrible purification and retraining in the fire of Purgatory? Since when has the 'little flock', the 'strait gate', the 'narrow way' been any kind of objection or counterargument in a Christian context?[7] There are only a few, but 'not because God wishes that there be only a few of these spirits so elevated; he would rather that all would be perfect, but he finds few vessels that will endure so lofty and sublime a work'.[8] And yet this work is also a commitment to the unrelenting imitation of Christ, the *vida apostolica*, by which the world is crucified to me, and I to the world, and here John is faithful to tradition, which sees such imitation as transcending the opposition between contemplation and action.[9] Elsewhere John acknowledges that

[5] A ii, 5, 7.
[6] Morel, vol. ii, ch. 5: *L'homme en vérité: Dieu par participation* (229—261).
[7] N (Introduction, Silverio, 322); N i, 8, 1; N i, 11, 4; L i, 24; L ii, 12; L ii, 27.
[8] L ii, 27. [9] Ep 7.

God selects specific individuals to share in this ultimate 'truth about man', those namely who in turn are destined to be imitated themselves, men who must be, like Moses, Elijah, Paul, 'sources of the spirit in the church',[10] spiritual 'founding fathers', whose 'virtue and spirit are to be diffused among their children'.[11]

The challenge of St John of the Cross is that he flings the old slogan, 'God alone suffices', in the face of a world increasingly convinced of its own importance, and he does this with an exclusiveness that effectively makes the realization of 'man in truth' the preserve of a few. It is certainly the case that throughout all his works there is an unrelenting reductionism that knocks down everything in its way. All truths, every good and worthy object, anything that is not 'God in himself' is relativized and set in motion, and must be abandoned and transcended for the love of God. That the good things of creation should be in this category is not especially surprising from a Christian point of view, but it is surprising that in this he includes no less emphatically, even more emphatically, all that is supernaturally valuable and good, everything that is in any sense God's 'operation' in the world or in man yet which, as such, can be distinguished from God himself: virtues, charisms, illuminations, consolations, visions, and so on. Indeed, in this respect the reformer of Carmel seems to want to be more radical than Luther, because he too, without any suggestion of scepticism, interprets everything with objective form in the historical relevation utterly and completely in terms of the making present of God's interiority. Such a devastating and sweeping programme was unheard of in the Church since the days of Evagrius Ponticus. And we may reasonably ask whether such an attempt to pierce through the historical form to the Absolute does not already bring us close to the spirit of the Enlightenment; certainly the comparison with Hegel becomes unavoidable. And yet, for all that, John of the Cross has been raised up to be a Doctor of the Church, not least because of his remorseless power of discrimination.

John goes along, and points us toward, the essential way to

[10] A ii, 24, 3.

[11] L ii, 12.

God, and so he too, like Dante, brings the 'hereafter' into existence in this world, or rather, since in Christ the hereafter has entered the here and now, he shows us the depths of eternity within life itself. He too, like Dante, must enter the night of Hell, for only in the absolute distinction between the sinful creature and the absolute God in his total purity can the divine in its truth be perceived. But it is a demythologized night; there is no Virgil for a guide, no conversations with the damned; I myself am Hell. 'Sometimes this experience is so vivid that it seems to the soul that it sees Hell and perdition open before it. These are the ones who go down into Hell alive.'[12] Placed before the naked reality of the Absolute, which presents itself to her in the mode of privation and dispossession, the soul endures an 'infinite death' in her languishing and suffering, 'a living image of that infinite privation'.[13] This experience clarifies for John the meaning of the Old Testament, and he quotes in long passages from Job, Jeremiah and Jonah, whose lot it was to experience the wrath of God, total abandonment by God. '"Your wrath weighs upon me, and all your waves you have let loose" . . . for in truth the soul experiences the sorrows of Hell, all of which reflect the feeling of God's absence, of being chastised and rejected by him. . . . The soul experiences all this and even more, for now it seems that this affliction will last for ever.'[14] The soul 'feels terrible annihilation as an event in its very substance',[15] her hope in God vanishes, and with it any prospect of an end to the night,[16] she 'resembles one who is imprisoned in a dark dungeon, bound hands and feet, and able neither to move, nor see, nor feel any favour from heaven or earth'.[17] 'She must feel a withdrawal, deprivation, emptiness, and poverty regarding these blessings. And a person must be brought to think that he is far removed from them, and become so convinced that no one can persuade him otherwise or make him believe anything but that his blessings have come to an end.'[18] Prayer becomes impossible for the soul; it cannot be that God hears.[19] We must

[12] N ii, 6, 6.
[13] L iii, 22.
[14] N ii, 6, 2–3; *cf.* ii, 7, 4.
[15] N ii, 6, 6.
[16] N ii, 7, 2–3.
[17] N ii, 7, 3.
[18] N ii, 9, 9; *cf.* 10, 8.
[19] N ii, 8, 1.

have great compassion for a soul such as this,[20] pursued in such a manner by the fire of God,[21] for what happens to her remains beyond her understanding until the end: the darknesses cannot comprehend the light.[22]

Abandonment is experienced subjectively as the fire of Hell, but from God's perspective it is the fire of Purgatory.[23] For St Thomas Aquinas the two fires were but one.[24] And John says that the agonies of the soul abandoned by God are 'almost like the agonies of Purgatory'.[25] The trials, which the soul on the way to total union with God has to undergo here on earth, correspond to the fire that the rest will face in Purgatory.[26] Souls in both cases suffer great doubts about whether they will ever be released from these afflictions[27] (an idea that Pascal will defend). Thus we are invited to 'form an idea of the sufferings of Purgatory'[28] from this experience of night. We should not see all this as mere simile; no, as regards the suffering, there is an identity between the two states, even if objectively the 'dark fire' that purifies here below is a 'dark, loving spiritual fire'.[29]

This love penetrates and purifies the soul. Its effect is like that of fire on wood. First, the fire blackens and dries the wood, causes it to sweat and this envelops it with smoke, but then, when it has been purified in this way, the wood is burnt through from within and transformed into fire.[30] So too, when the living flame of love in which the soul burns has reached its goal, heaven is anticipated. It is, first of all, an 'earthly paradise' resulting from the purgation of the senses and of the spirit in which the soul attains baptismal innocence and complete subjection to God.[31] But later it becomes an anticipation of eternal blessedness itself, from the final perfection of which the soul is separated by only a thin veil, while at the same time she is already bathed in its glory.[32] St John's work reaches its peak in the description of these explosions of glory (*gloria*) from the fire

[20] N ii, 7, 3.
[21] N ii, 6, 5.
[22] L i, 22.
[23] *Cf.* L i, 25.
[24] Suppl. q. 74 a 8.
[25] L i, 21.
[26] L ii, 25.
[27] N ii, 7, 7.
[28] N ii, 10, 5.
[29] N ii, 12, 1.
[30] N ii, 10, 1–4; ii, 12, 5; C 38, 5; L i, 19–21.
[31] A iii, 26, 5; C 31, 5; C 37, 2–5.
[32] L i, 29f.

of unifying love. This flaring up of divine sunlight, this 'flashing of sparks and flames',[33] this eruption of the habit of love in the act of love[34] promotes 'love full of divine sweetness and power' in the soul; 'it is as if [the soul] were being given eternal life to taste, since it raises her up to the activity of God in God'.[35] It is a direct touch (*toque*) of the soul by God, and she would be bound to die, were it not for the fact that the hand that wounds her very being at the same time preserves her life.[36] 'And thus this soul will be a soul of heaven, truly heavenly and more divine than human.'[37] Her life consists in being transported to glory, and 'God is constantly on the point of finally giving her eternal life'.[38]

Here is a Dante deprived of all images and concentrated in a single interior experience. Instead of ditches, cornices and spheres there is nothing except God: the purifying God of the night, who transfigures the soul, raising her higher and higher. And this is the message: it really exists, this way out of the sombre prison of human nature, this flight that the first stanza of the poem of the *Dark Night* describes:

En una noche oscura
Con ansias en amores inflamada'
¡Oh dichosa ventura!
Salí sin ser notada,
Estando ya mi casa sosegada.
A oscuras, y segura
Por la secreta escala, disfrazada,
¡Oh dichosa ventura!
A oscuras y en celada
Estando ya mi casa sosegada.[39]

Yes, this is the night, this is love's venture in darkness and disguise, by a secret stair, leaving everything behind and passing over to attain another, divine and unlimited world. John's

[33] L Prologue.
[34] L i, 3.
[35] L i, 4–5.
[36] L i, 8; i, 27.
[37] N ii, 13, 11.
[38] L iii, 10–11.
[39] 'One dark night, / Fired with love's urgent longings / —Ah, blessed adventure— / I went out unseen, / My house being now all stilled; / In darkness, and secure, / By the secret ladder, disguised, / —Ah, blessed adventure— / In darkness and concealment, / My house being now all stilled.'

whole work is a summons to this unique and necessary adventure. In place of Dante's images there are images of world discovery with all the pathos of the age of the Conquistadores. The Bridegroom is asked to look at the companions of the Bride, who go 'with her through strange islands' (*de la que va por insulas extrañas*),[40] which are interpreted as 'modes and ways that are foreign to all the senses and to common natural knowledge'. Elsewhere the Bridegroom is compared to 'lonely wooded valleys' and 'wonderfully strange islands'. This is explained as follows: 'The wonderfully strange islands are surrounded by water and situated across the sea, far withdrawn and cut off from communication with other men. Many things very different from what we have here are born and nurtured in these islands; they are of many strange kinds and powers never before seen by men, and they cause surprise and wonder in anyone who sees them. Thus, because of the wonderful new things and the wonderful strange knowledge (far removed from common knowledge) that the soul sees in God, she refers to him as "wonderfully strange islands". A man is called *strange* for either of two reasons: he is withdrawn from people, or, compared with other men, he is singular and superior in his deeds and works. The soul calls God "strange" for these two reasons. . . . It is no wonder then that God is strange to men who have not seen him, since he is also strange to the holy angels and to the blessed. For the angels and the blessed are incapable of seeing him fully, nor will they ever be capable of doing so.'[41] Thus the image of the strangely seductive island is lost in the image of the all-engulfing ocean: 'to assert that the way and the road to God by which the soul travels toward him is in the sea and her footsteps in many waters and the way thereby is unknowable is to say that the way to God is as hidden and secret to the sensory part of the soul as are the footsteps of one walking on water imperceptible to the bodily senses';[42] the joy that she finds in God 'is like the sea, which does not diminish for all the water that is drawn of it or for the rivers that run into it'.[43] And the image of the sea in

[40] C 32, 5.
[41] C 13, 3.
[42] N ii, 17, 8.
[43] C 29, 5.

turn blends with that of darkness (*esta agua tenebrosa*),[44] and of the unending wilderness (*un immenso desierto*).[45] The existentially interpreted images of the Old Testament are also taken up here: the exodus from Egypt, the drowning of the foe in the sea of contemplation so that the soul may be brought 'into the freedom and holy rest of the children of God, into the wilderness',[46] and likewise the rocky mountain of Carmel, upon which 'our holy father Elijah' found his God.[47]

Whatever its diversity, the only function of the imagery is to point to the *conquista* that leads the soul, which feels its way through the darkness, *per caminos nuevos nunca sabidos*[48] to a *sabiduria oscura*.[49] The notion of secrecy is central to the thought of St John of the Cross, although his doctrine betrays no trace of any kind of 'secret knowledge', is infinitely far removed from all Cabbalism, from Böhme and Swedenborg, for it makes no claim to anything particular or definite by way of experience and encounter; all it offers is the imageless, limitless expanse of the incomprehensible God. What is secret here is precisely what is proclaimed and taken for granted in all public places and (especially) in every part of the Church. And yet no one knows the secret, no one can make it his own. Of its very nature it can be recognized only as a mystery, and an eternal mystery it remains and becomes so more and more for one who encounters it once and eternally. John retains the traditional term 'mystical theology', used from Denys onward; indeed, there are several explicit references to the Areopagite. For John 'mystical theology' is not primarily a subjective, secret learning, but rather, knowledge about the objective mystery of God.[50] The *skotous aktis*, the 'ray of darkness',[51] is dark precisely because the soul is not adapted to the extreme light, but the adaptation, so far as it is possible, consists in being caught up in the essential mystery. But the soul's adaptation and initiation can be only secondary reasons for this learning being secret,[52] and the

[44] N ii, 16, 13.
[45] N ii, 17, 6.
[46] L iii, 38.
[47] A ii, 8, 4; ii, 24, 3; C 13, 5; L ii, 17.
[48] N ii, 16, 8.
[49] N ii, 16, 10.
[50] A ii, 8, 6; N ii, 12, 5.
[51] N ii, 5, 3; C 13, 5; L iii, 49.
[52] *La ciencia sabrosa . . . es la teologia mística que es ciencia secreta de Dios, que llaman los espirituales contemplación.* C 18, 2; *cf.* C 38, 4.

distinction from ordinary knowledge consists not in the knowledge as such, but in the love that it alone mediates and in which it selectively operates.[53] What God communicates directly to the soul of himself 'always remains secret and ineffable . . . the soul is like a man who beholds an object never before seen in itself or in its likeness: he understands, he finds satisfaction in it, and yet he cannot give it a name. . . . The language of God has that trait'.[54] His wealth is all the greater, because it is 'concealed in his infinite unity and simplicity'.[55] It is an 'absolute secret between the spirit and God',[56] a haven and hiding place in the face of God: 'You dwell permanently hidden within them. . . . As a result "you hide them in the secret of your face", which is the Word, "from the disturbance of men"' (*cf.* Ps 30.21).[57] The soul then understands the meaning of the text from the Apocalypse: 'To him who conquers . . . I will give . . . a precious stone, with a new name written on the stone that no one can read except him who receives it' (2.17).[58]

This secret alone is the absolute 'refuge' (*refugio*)[59] beyond all worldly danger and the soul's own acts and habits, the 'concealment' (*escondrijo*),[60] where she remains in great security (*seguridad*), surrounded by the 'wall' (*muro*) and 'enclosure of peace' (*vallado de paz*),[61] and thus in 'great solitude away from all things' (*gran soledad de todas las cosas*).[62] It is the solitude into which God led his people to speak to them and to marry them (Hos 2.16),[63] the silence in which the words of infinite wisdom are heard.[64] What is hidden is also secure: 'If the soul possesses these things in secret [*a solas*], she also understands them in secret; her desire is that her secret may be very hidden, very deep, as far as possible from any external communication. In this she is like the merchant with the pearl, or even better, like the

[53] N ii, 17, 2.

[54] N ii, 17, 3; *cf.* L iv, 6, the discovery of the 'incomparable newness of God', of his absolute vivacity (he is 'more mobile than all mobile things' [according to Wisd 7.24], more active than all active things), and the contemplation of all creatures within this eternal newness.

[55] L iii, 17.

[56] N ii, 23, 3.

[57] L ii, 17.

[58] L ii, 21.

[59] N ii, 23, 4.

[60] N ii, 23, 1.

[61] C 30, 4.

[62] C 24, decl; C. 34, 2–3.

[63] L iii, 34; C 34, 5.

[64] L iii, 67.

man who found a treasure hidden in a field, covered it up and then went off in joy to buy that field.'[65] This is not secrecy for its own sake; no, it is of the nature of love that she 'reveals her mysteries only to her friends'.[66] So the soul presses for permission to go deeper and deeper into the 'thicket' (*espesura*)[67] of God, 'which is so deep and immense that no matter how much the soul knows she can always enter it further'. This fact must always be taken into account and considered whenever one is dealing with the revelation of God in Christ and the interpretation that in the course of the Church's history the revelation has been given; God's triune wisdom is 'so well concealed that however numerous are the mysteries and marvels that holy doctors have discovered and saintly souls have contemplated in this earthly life, far more is yet to be said and understood. There is much to fathom in Christ, for he is like an abundant mine with uncounted recesses of treasures, so that however deep men go they never reach the end or bottom, but rather in every recess find new veins with new riches everywhere'.[68]

Medieval ways to God were, for the most part, 'ascents', ladders that were meant to lead the soul closer to God by means of an ingenious series of spiritual acts and habits (active renunciations and contemplative dispositions). St John of the Cross lived within this tradition and even availed himself of entire sections of these schemes of ascent in his works (such as the *decem gradus amoris sec. S. Bernardum* of pseudo-Thomas Aquinas).[69] Nonetheless, his criticism of all acts and habits places him far beyond these ways of ascent. His approach is no matter of cleverly dovetailing the *via negativa* and the *via positiva* into the *via eminentiae*. No, John is much closer to the original rhythms of Denys, although he is much more consistent and relentless in his logic: everything is gained when everything is abandoned, the ship lands when it is wrecked, you leap on to firm ground when all the rungs of your ladder break. It is like St John of the Cross's own leap when he escaped by night from the Toledo convent after nine terrible months in the custody of the

[65] C 32, decl.
[66] C 18, 1.
[67] C 35, 5.
[68] C 36, 3.
[69] N ii, 19–20; Opusc. 54, ed. Vivès, vol. 28, 351–367.

Calced Carmelites. He improvised a rope by knotting together his sheets, but it did not reach far enough, and so he had to jump down onto the ramparts, narrowly missing the chasm of rocks by the banks of the Tajo, where he would have been dashed to pieces. It is true that the 'night' is a way through, a purifying emergence into an exceedingly great light,[70] and yet it is the permanent means of making the decisive spiritual jump, and it remains absolutely identical with contemplation. If the commentaries pay more attention to the first aspect, the poems concentrate more on the second, and the poems, as we shall see, are decisive. This is true of the powerful poem, composed in the Toledo prison, with its refrain about the night:

Que bien sé yo la fonte que mana y corre
Aunque es de noche—[71]

the spring known well only through faith (although it is night), whose origin is unknown, because it has none, and yet from it, it derives its whole being (although it is night), and there is nothing so beautiful, Heaven and earth drink refreshment there (although it is night); it is a bottomless abyss and no ford to cross it can be found (although it is night), its clarity is never darkened, and from it proceeds all light (although it is night):—'Rich are the streams and full—this know I well; / They water nations, heav'ns and depths of Hell, / Although 'tis night.'[72]

With this we should take the other poem from the time of John's imprisonment, perhaps the most daring he wrote, a transposition of the psalm 'By the waters of Babylon'. Babylon here is the world (including the earthly Church in her external aspect), Sion is God, the soul's true homeland, for which she longs. 'The strangers (outsiders, *extraños*) among whom I was captive rejoiced; they asked me to sing what I sang in Sion: "Sing us a song from Sion, let's hear how it sounds." I said: "How can I sing in a strange land where I weep for Sion, sing of the happiness that I had there?" I would be forgetting her if I

[70] This notion of a 'way through' is most clearly emphasized in L ii, 28–31.

[71] 'For I know well the spring that flows and runs, / Although it is night.'

[72] P viii (Silv. 809). [These lines quoted in the text are taken from the English version of E. Allison Peers, *St John of the Cross: The Complete Works*, vol. ii (London, 1934), p. 454.]

rejoiced in a strange land. May the tongue I speak with cling to my palate . . . if I celebrate one feastday or feast at all without you.' In place of the original Jewish conclusion ('O daughter of Babylon, you devastator, . . . happy shall he be who takes your little ones and dashes them against the rock!'), there is a profound allegory:

¡Oh hija de Babilonia,
Misera y desventurada!
Bienaventurada era
Aquel en quien confiaba,
Que te ha de dar el castigo
Que de tu mano llevaba.
Y juntará sus pequeños,
Y a mí, porque en ti lloraba,
A la piedra que era Cristo,
Por el cual yo te dejaba.[73]

Accursed Babylon must be dashed, with her children, on the rock of Christ; that is all that can be sung when deprived of Sion. But the singer's revenge, the punishment he wants to inflict on his tormentress, is the revenge of eternal love, and the singer himself wants to suffer that with her—indeed, he is already in the midst of suffering, for he too has been dashed.

This is an adventure in the atmosphere of extreme secrecy—escaping to Sion from captivity in Babylon, by night, disguised, on a secret stair, not approaching by degrees, but dancing to the rhythm of *nada-todo*.

To reach satisfaction in all
Desire its possession in nothing.
To come to the knowledge of all,
Desire the knowledge of nothing.
To arrive at being all,
Desire to be nothing.
To come to the pleasure you have not,
You must go by a way in which you know not.

[73] 'O Daughter of Babylon, / Miserable and wretched! / Blessed is he / In whom I have trusted, / For he will punish you / As you have me; / And he will gather your little ones / And me, who wept because of you / At the rock who is Christ / For whom I abandoned you.' P xiv (Silv. 817–818).

To come to the possession you have not,
You must go by a way in which you possess not.
To come to be what you are not,
You must go by a way in which you are not.[74]

This has a dramatic force beyond that of any human drama. The soul goes into the night of the All. First she enters the night, then she is swallowed up in it. Thus she learns that the All that she walks toward is not a Something. God is not only the 'wholly other'; he transcends the most extreme opposition as the *non-Aliud*. The soul has herself to realise something that transcends the distinction between subject and object, and yet which, of her very nature, she can realise only by means of that distinction. But if she is to do this, the soul is required to come out from all the confines of life, and such emergence is possible only through a love stronger than Hell, a life stronger than death. This love does not attain the beloved by its own powers, but jumps and is caught by the open arms of the love of God, who transforms the soul from being a lover into a beloved. But this happens only when love of itself goes to the outer limit, like the love of Mary Magdalene who sought the beloved alive among the dead. Beatrice lives, and Dante, by practising penance and renunciation, can live and approach her. But Christ has died and withdrawn himself from the Bride, and she must seek him in real death by dying with him. What Mary Magdalene does at Simon the Pharisee's banquet is bold and shows the enthusiasm of her love, but what she does by the tomb flies in the face of reason, 'yet it is of the nature of love to regard everything as possible'. That is why the Bride in the Canticle likewise goes out into the streets to ask about her lover when he disappears. She is like 'the lioness or she-bear that goes in search of her cubs when they are taken away and cannot be found. So the soul in her loss goes out in search of her God. Since she is immersed in darkness, she feels his absence and that she is dying with love of him. She is like Rachel in her longing to bear children when she says to Jacob, "Give me children, otherwise I will die"' (Gen 30.1).[75] The nights she spends going hither and thither serve not only to purify her but, above all, also to give her that breadth of vision

[74] A i, 13, 11.

[75] N ii, 13, 6–8.

required of her if she is to see that 'he is nothing of all that I know and am, and only if all becomes nothing for me can he become my All'. 'Whoever refuses to go out at night in search of the Beloved . . . but rather seeks him in his own . . . comfort . . . will not succeed in finding him.'[76]

2. THE PARADOX OF MYSTICAL POETRY

The love that survives every death but which also has to undergo every death in order to survive: this is the solution of the agonizing paradox of how supreme poetic beauty can blossom forth from such negation. For there is no doubt about it: the reformer of Carmel responds to the negation of the Protestant reformers with beauty; to the destructive dialectical Word with the constructive poetic Word. The poems are the decisive statement in St John of the Cross's work. Compared with the poems, the commentaries are of a lower level; by his own admission they are quite inadequate and incapable of doing justice to the content of the inspired words in all their simplicity.[77] The commentaries refer the reader to the more compact, more pregnant *figuras, comparaciones y semejanzas*. These disclose their meaning, says the poet, only if read 'in the simplicity of the spirit of love'; otherwise they 'seem to be absurdities rather than reasonable utterances', as is true of the poetic parts of the Bible. 'Since these stanzas, then, were composed in a love flowing from abundant mystical understanding, I cannot explain them adequately. . . . Though we give some explanation of these stanzas, there is no reason to be bound to this explanation. For mystical wisdom, which is the subject of these stanzas, is understood through love and need not be understood distinctly in order to cause love and affection in the soul, for it is given according to the mode of faith, through which we love God without understanding him.'[78] And lest we be tempted to think that this poetry is the mere product of a

[76] N ii, 24, 4.
[77] C Prol. 1.
[78] C Prol. 2.

heart tormented by overflowing love, John brings it all back to the revelation of God, to the Word in scripture: he 'submits himself in advance . . . unconditionally to the judgment of our holy Mother the Church'. 'I do not intend to affirm anything of myself nor trust in any of my own experiences nor in those of other spiritual persons whom I have known or heard of. Although I plan to make use of these experiences, I want to explain and confirm at least the more difficult matters through passages from sacred Scripture.'[79] And this can be seen not only in the prose commentary, which seeks to safeguard, as it were, the boldness of the verse by means of scriptural quotations, but also in the poetry itself. The poems consist of a paraphrase, in the case of the Spiritual Canticle, of the Song of Songs (although precisely how much of it is paraphrase, it is impossible to say), an adaptation of one of the psalms and the transposition of themes from the gospels, especially St John's prologue (as in the case of the great romance on the Trinity and the Incarnation). But scriptural influence is particularly evident in the most characteristic creations of St John of the Cross's genius: the poems of the *Dark Night*, the poems of the *Living Flame*, the verses about the ecstatic hunt for divine game.

Here the literary problem presents itself, although as yet we are only on the threshold of St John's work. St John's poems are praised by many as the crown of Spanish lyric poetry: consequently, they have a certain affinity with other poetry of the period. Ramon Lull, in his most interior work (*The Book of the Lover and the Beloved*), consciously imitated the forms of the Sufi mystic poets. Similarly, St John explicitly refers to the great lyric poet Garcilaso, who died young (+ 1536. It is true that John speaks of Garcilaso's friend, Boscan, who died in 1542, but the poetry of both writers appeared together, and both are founders of the Italian style in Spain). We find in Garcilaso's work the pastoral motifs familiar to us from St John: springs and thickets, nymphs, sirens and nightingales, shepherds and shepherdesses; indeed we even find themes that we tend to think of as being peculiar to the mystic. In Garcilaso we find the stanza:

[79] C Prol. 4.

Finally on the fifth night my cruel fate departed,
to lead me to where the thick texture of life
was to be broken up
and my little house was to leave me
in the silence of the dark night.

Alonso,[80] however, has shown that there was an intermediate link, the work of a certain Sebastián of Córdoba, *Las Obras de Boscán y Garcilaso trasladadas en materias cristianas y religiosas* (Ubeda, 1757), in which, for example, the lament of two shepherds is transformed into the allegorical lament of the divine shepherd Christ, which, like St John's magnificent pastoral poem, even speaks of 'a shepherd, lifted up upon that tree, his face and forehead wounded and crowned with thorns'. But it was not only in these naive, complicated allegories that the synthesis of classical/worldly and biblical/spiritual poetry was already established and taken for granted. It was also an accepted part of the late-humanist, early Baroque *milieu* Juan de Yepes encountered in the Jesuit College at Medina del Campo and, above all, in the 'Castilian Athens', the University of Salamanca. The great Fray Luis de León, who in the most difficult periods of the Inquisition and the Index sought to translate the Bible (especially the poetic books) into Castilian, at the same time translated the Eclogues and Georgics of Virgil, Pindar, Horace and Tibullus, and wrote the sublime, neo-Platonic Ode to Salina (who had published a work on music) on the subject of the harmony of God in the world.[81] Other elements that contribute to this synthesis in St John's work are the old folk songs with their *coplas* (stanzas with refrains) and romances (epic poems on themes of national history). The latter too had undergone spiritual transposition (*glosas a lo divino*) and echo throughout nearly all of John's poetry. Like Theresa of Avila, John was a great lover of song. 'He used to sing as he walked', testifies a brother who often accompanied him on the stony path from Beas to the hermitage of Calvario. Folk poetry spoke directly to the heart and had none of the affectation of the

[80] For the following see the summary in Max Milner 1, 61f.

[81] *Obras completas castellanas de Fray Luis de León*, ed. Gardia, BAC, 2nd ed. (1951), 1436–1438. Translated (and abridged) in Irene Behn, *Spanische Mystik*, 262–263.

theological travesties of Garcilaso. John's refrains—'I know not what', 'Dying because I do not die'—have their origin in simple love songs, now transposed into the highest sphere.

It is precisely against this background of a synthesis of biblical/theological, classical/humanist and popular/national elements that the Song of Songs emerges in all its original, pastoral freshness. This was the imperishable jewel for which the Christian tradition had forged an inestimably precious monstrance of spiritual commentaries in mystic filigree. And the Song of Songs, in its turn, does not stand alone, but is a treasury of images and symbols, whose effectiveness depends on their place within the total meaning of divine revelation. Thus they require no 'strange speech' (*allegoria*) to make them religiously comprehensible and tolerable. No, their authenticity derives from the *conubium* between God and mankind. The word of the old covenant has, ultimately, a rigidity and narrowness from which it is set free when the new and everlasting covenant, the totality of revelation dawns, in which the Logos of scripture is expounded in the freedom of the Holy Spirit. This whole free treatment of the biblical *Canticum* in the Spanish mystic's *Cantico* (for which he claims divine inspiration) is a reflection of what is certainly an unprecedented and audacious achievement: the 'appropriation' of the entire sphere of the Logos by the Holy Spirit of the Church. All manner of creatures come into this new poem, although they are inconspicuous in the commentary and do not even receive any particular emphasis: 'the nymphs of Judaea' (St. 31), the 'singing sirens' (St. 30), the 'sweet nightingale' (St. 38). Likewise, completely unemphasized (as so often with great poets), the whole worldly/spiritual atmosphere of folk song comes into the work.

It would be absurd to deny these influences, as would be the attempt to exclude specific literary names in favour of a merely indefinite atmospheric influence in order to prove that St John's inspiration was not profane but purely spiritual, purely mystical.[82] To resist such attempts is not to deny the fact now to

[82] Thus argues P. Emerito de Jesus Maria, 'Las raices de la poesia sanjuanista y Damaso Alonso' (in the journal *El Monte Carmelo*, Sept. 1950). *Cf.* Milner 1, 125–134.

be considered; namely, that all these influences do not, do not in any way, place in doubt the creative power of St John's genius. He soars like an eagle up to the lofty solitude of his experience of God, and thence alone is born the language that will be the vehicle for his equally solitary artistic works. Eckhart describes the divine birth of the eternal Son in the soul. It is the same Word of God, encountering and dwelling in the soul together with his Spirit, which constitutes the only sphere from which, in the final analysis, Eckhart's word and John's poetry originate. But how are the spheres within this larger sphere of influence to be distinguished? There is, first of all, the direct perception of 'substantial locutions'[83] from substance to substance, the evocations of man's most primitive symbols—night, light, water, ringing sounds—flowing almost directly from the same profoundly interior source. Then there is the recalling of the hallowed words and images of the Bible, which are theologically interwoven and caught up to the heights of interior inspiration. Finally, there is the whole range of expressive material formed by natural images and the beloved and long-cherished symbols familiar from literature. Who can confirm this and neatly separate the various levels? Who can divide the spheres of supernatural and natural inspiration? Why shouldn't the direct in-spiration of the Holy Spirit at the same time awaken all of the powers of artistic enthusiasm and creative inventiveness where such powers exist? And who would want to maintain that such elevation of man's creative ability to the service, both passive and active, of the divine Word is impossible or inadmissible from a Christian point of view or incompatible with supreme holiness? On the contrary, this poetry claims to be a direct expression and incontrovertible testimony to such engraced holiness, a reflection of its splendour. The expression as such, of course, is not 'necessary', because the holiness could occur without poetry, but the two originate from the same sphere of loving freedom in the soul's relationship with God; both are the overwhelming splendour of grace, an 'inundation with glory' (*toda la sustancia del alma bañada en gloria;*[84] *aquella llama, acada vez que llamea, baña al alma en*

[83] A ii, 31; C 13, 5.

[84] C 37, 1–2.

gloria).[85] Baruzi tried to insert a clearly defined series of stages between the symbolism, in the strict sense, of the poems of the *Dark Night* and the allegorical imagery of the *Canticle* and the *Living Flame*; only the former spring from the highest and most interior sphere. But the transition (which in several places is noticeable) is much smoother; it is precisely the *Canticle* that contains stanzas or at least lines of supreme symbolic inventiveness, such as the incomparable eleventh:

O cristalina fuente
Si en esos tus semblantes plateados
formases de repente
Los ojos deseados
que tengo en mis entrañas dibujados.[86]

It is entirely logical that the prose commentary should interpret the flowing spring as faith (we must, of course, recall what this word means for St John) and the 'silvered-over face', the 'external appearance', as the individual 'propositions of the faith', which here on earth are 'silver' and only in the life to come will reveal the gold that lies beneath. Equally logically, the 'eyes I have desired' are interpreted as 'divine rays' and 'divine truths', which here below enlighten us through the articles of faith, though still obscurely. The fact that these eyes are 'hinted at', 'sketched', within the heart of man means certainly that in the infused virtues the heart possesses these truths, albeit obscurely and imperfectly. Besides this, says the commentary, there is another sketch, the sketch of love. The lover carries the image of the beloved in his heart, and 'transforming love produces such likeness in the lovers that one can say that each is the other and both are one'. All this is beautiful and true, but how hopelessly it limps behind the vision! How wonderful is that unresolved, ardent 'yes': if only it could happen, if only on that smoothly flowing, simmering surface (and yet it is the surface of the spring itself, which is crystalline and transparent to the depths and for that very reason

[85] L i, 3.

[86] 'O spring like crystal! / If only, on your silvered-over face, / You would suddenly form / The eyes I have desired, / Which I bear sketched deep within my heart!'

is unfathomable) you would suddenly (*exaiphnês*) let the real vision, the unfathomable depths of the eye, burst open—*videntem videre!*—those depths, whose shadow, outline, intimation lies in the eye and spring of my own soul; if only you would stand in front of me and yet be in me, if only before my eyes and yet in my eyes you would open up your own eye. The commentary does well here to point, by restricting and defining, to the Credo in all its objectivity. For it is only when the objective dimension of the revelation of the triune God in the incarnate Son is opened up that this mutual regard of God and the soul in the Holy Spirit can be understood in all its true breadth and depth and can be preserved from all misleading identification.

This is but one example among very many of the qualitative superiority of the poetic statement over the prose restatement, although the poet is always aware that even the most accomplished poetic statement, together with its inspiration, is only ever an echo, an ardent pointer toward the original divine *spiratio*. The centre of the mystic act is beyond the centre of the poetic act. The centre of the latter is on the periphery of the former, even though the poem is conceived in the more secret womb of mystical experience; the poem is the echo of the experience, testifying and referring and pressing back to it. In no way does the mystic's poetry go beyond the word of revelation itself; his activity is confined to the sphere of imitation, the sphere of the Holy Spirit who infuses his existential interpretation into the soul and so sets it down deep inside the womb of Christ's Bride, the Church.

This means, then, that poetry at this high level must not be considered in separation from holiness. But holiness in this qualitatively distinctive sense has no other origin except the imitation of Christ, the total stripping away of everything, the following of the evangelical counsels, the affirmation of everything that the man of this world experiences as a renunciation of the aesthetic, dissatisfaction with all this-worldly, creaturely delights, and with all enjoyment of them, whether intentional or unintentional, sinful or lawful. It is precisely to the renunciation of the 'aesthetic' that this poetry must bear witness, if it is to be an authentic witness, in the Holy

Spirit, to the bridal love of Christ and the Church, of God and the world on the Cross. We are now a long way from Bonaventure and the whole neo-Platonic ascent by stages from type to archetype. We are closer to Francis, but closer still to the remorseless sword of the Gospel word, which for the love of the One demands the hatred of everything else. And the sword must pierce to the division of the joints and marrow of the soul, to the division of the soul from itself, before the promise of the hundredfold can be fulfilled on earth. To bear witness to this, poetry must therefore begin inside the division, as the scream of the vivisected soul in the middle of the night, in order to end in the song of praise of the soul, even more fully alive at a deeper level, wounded in the fire of glory. It is the fiery arrow of the seraph (John explicitly quotes this) that pierces the souls of Francis and Theresa—beyond pain and pleasure, wound and health, life and death: *¡Oh cauterio suave! ¡Oh regalada llaga!*[87] 'The very same cautery that touches the wound also heals it, but it heals only by penetrating deeper within it.'[88]

It is only in this context that we see the full paradox of this 'mystical aesthetics'. John's whole work strives to isolate the individual components of this paradox with extreme clarity so that no doubt is left as to the point, the height, at which these diverse factors are reconciled and indissolubly merged. We must now consider these factors one by one.

1. Throughout all of St John's works there runs a massive *negation*, or more precisely, reduction. No created thing is God, and because every created thing has form, all forms must be surmounted and abandoned if the vision of God is to be possible. It is self-evident that the senses do not comprehend God.[89] But, for John, it is no less self-evident that the intellect (*entendimento*) can only think something by means of the senses (*solo lo que alcanza por los sentidos*),[90] and so it needs the 'figures and forms of objects, which are present either in themselves or in their likenesses'. And so 'nothing which could possibly be imagined or comprehended in this life can be a proximate means (*medio*

[87] 'O sweet cautery, O delightful wound!' L ii.

[88] L i, 25; L ii, 7–10, 13.

[89] A iii, 24, 1–3.

[90] A ii, 3, 1–2.

proximo)[91] of union with God. In our natural way of knowing, the intellect can only grasp an object through the forms and phantasms of things perceived by the bodily senses. Since these objects cannot serve as a means, the intellect cannot profit from its natural knowing. As for the supernatural way of knowing, the intellect, according to the possibilities of its ordinary power and while in the prison of the body, is neither capable nor prepared for the reception of the clear knowledge of God. Such knowledge does not belong to this state, since death is a necessary condition for possessing it.'[92] Thus faith takes the place of the intellect and acts, like a guide for the blind,[93] to lead us to things 'we have never seen or known, either in themselves or in their likenesses; in fact nothing like them exists'.[94] We know them, literally, only by 'hearsay', for 'as St Paul says, "faith comes from what is heard, and what is heard comes from the preaching of Christ"'.[95] This has all the appearance of a Nominalist/Lutheran/Kantian starting point, which now leads directly to the sweeping critique of all means and ways to God that are not those of 'pure faith'.[96] This is a 'mystagogical', not a philosophical, critique, which therefore begins by drawing a line between relative and absolute being, an opposition to be instilled into the soul like the ABC. If God is being, the creature is nothing;[97] if God is beauty, the creature is ugliness;[98] if God is pleasure, the creature is aversion; if God is goodness, the creature is evil; if God is wisdom, the creature is folly;[99] if God is freedom, the creature is slavery.[100] God has one kind of taste, the creature has another, and the palate of the soul cannot experience two tastes at a time.[101] '"The animal man does not perceive the things of God; they are foolishness to him and he cannot understand them" (1 Cor 2.14). By the animal man he means here the man who still lives with natural appetites and

[91] It would not be surprising if the Scholastic *proximo*, which one finds frequently but is also on occasion absent, turned out to be a prudent addition made by the editor.

[92] A ii, 8, 4.

[93] A ii, 4, 3.

[94] A ii, 3, 3.

[95] *Ibid.*; on *fides ex auditu* see A ii, 27, 4.

[96] A ii, 24, 8; *la pura fe*

[97] A i, 1, 3–4.

[98] A i, 1, 4; Ep 10.

[99] A i, 1, 4.

[100] A i, 1, 5.

[101] A i, 5, 3–4.

gratifications.'[102] The fragrance of God is lost in a soul not wholly concentrated on him, just as the fragrance of a salve is lost when it is exposed to the open air.[103] 'Creature' here always has the meaning of that which is radically other than God, which for that very reason must transcend itself, if it is to attain that participation in the Godhead that God bestows upon it. From its tasting of the finite it must draw no 'conclusions' about how the Absolute may taste; what it must do is taste it at first hand.[104] It must, by whatever means possible—by its own utmost exertions, though knowing all the time that ultimately what it seeks must be experienced passively—give God noetically and existentially the predominance in its own self that he always has ontically.[105] This can be only a work of love, for in terms of being, the creature remains eternally the 'other than God'. But in transfiguring, nuptial love, the mutual otherness of God and man makes possible exchange and reciprocal indwelling.[106] Thus the idea of flight, of rapture, plays a decisive role, although ecstasy must be thoroughly purified and transformed from its present imperfection as a bodily or physiological state of rapture into a substantial, habitual state of being borne off.[107] This results when the soul—*me hice perdidiza y fuí ganada*—makes itself lose its very self and its way and so makes itself found by God. This *hice* is a reflection of the harsh anti-Reformation element in St John's life and work, although he is very much aware that the effort involved in what the soul does depends entirely on God's prevenient grace, the grace that flows from the crucified Son of God. Despite the negativity of what it undertakes, the achievement of human Eros in causing itself to be overwhelmed by the divine Eros is something very positive, though it is from the outset always a response to God's creative and elective word of grace.[108] Man, with all his intellectual capabilities, who 'cannot know, of himself, what God is like, must necessarily approach him like a vanquished man'.[109]

[102] L iii, 65.

[103] A i, 10, 1.

[104] N ii, 9, 1–2.

[105] C 38, 4.

[106] C 11, 5.

[107] C 12, 2a, where John refers to Theresa's descriptions of rapture.

[108] A ii, 31, 1–2.

[109] L iii, 58.

The work of demolition, of world critique, is thus, through the transcendent power that sustains it, something quite positive, the work of a love that has been chosen by God and that, for its part, responds by making a choice of its own (and thus excludes everything else from its love). The others, who seek their gratification and glorification in this world together with God, have their reward here below.[110] To many, of course, 'observing how we annihilate the faculties in their operations, it will perhaps seem that we are tearing down rather than building up the way of spiritual exercise'. In reality, though, it means for the 'beginner' that his faculties are to be 'drawn away from their natural props and capacities and raised above themselves'.[111] And if it seems to be 'the destruction of the natural activity and use of the faculties so that man becomes like the beasts, then we must not forget that this work is undertaken at God's initiative and for his sake, and that 'God does not destroy, but perfects nature'.[112] The image of the peel and the core is constantly repeated; the divine fruit of the core must be extracted from the creaturely peel.[113]

The attack, then, is against attachment to creaturely values, the attempt to quench man's essential 'thirst' at the murky waters of human transience. The whole abstract ontology of the God-world opposition, the law, formulated time and again, of their mutual exclusiveness,[114] subserves the purpose of educating the particular, fallen man with his disordered appetites.[115] The fault of this attachment does not depend on quantity: *one* grain of sand is sufficient to obstruct the vision of the eye, one thread to prevent a bird from flying.[116] Yahweh trained his people in the exclusiveness of love: St John cites many a passage that reveals the pointlessness of trying to find pleasure in something

[110] A iii, 28, 5–6.

[111] A iii, 2, 1–3.

[112] A iii, 2, 7.

[113] A ii, 14, 4; A iii, 13, 6. [114] A i, 4, 2; A i, 6, 1; A ii, 17, 5; A iii, 6, 1; A iii, 7, 2; A iii, 12, 2; A iii, 15, 1; A iii, 19, 4; N ii, 5, 4; N ii, 6, 1; N ii, 7, 5; N ii, 9, 3; C 8, 2. The law is very often expressed in comparative form, e.g. A i, 5, 6; N ii, 8, 2; N ii, 16, 3; N ii, 16, 11, etc.

[115] A i, 6, 6; A i, 15, 1; A ii, 5, 3–4; A iii, 16, 2.

[116] A i, 9, 3; A i, 11, 4; L iii, 72.

other than God.[117] In so doing he succeeds in satisfying the aspirations of the great Asian mystics to free men from their 'thirst', a thirst that is tragically intensified by the experience of human transience. Thus, at first sight, John's demands that the soul be detached from all 'forms' and 'images' can seem like the unquestioning adoption of the Platonizing mysticism of the Desert Fathers, especially that of Evagrius Ponticus. The notions of *nous katharos*, the *gnôsis aneidês*, *haplê*, *aülos*, recur freely, and many of St John's dicta, if translated into Greek, could be incorporated directly into the *Gnostic Centuries* of Evagrius.[118] And since John, like Evagrius, writes for contemplatives, the struggle is above all against the higher, spiritually disguised forms of the capital vices (Evagrius, *De octo vitiosis cogitationibus*=John, *Dark Night*, I, 2–7). And in connection with these concealed attachments and desires for possession, the conflict is also about the renunciation and abandonment of all supernaturally imparted 'forms', be they visions of the phantasy, or definite, clearly delineated insights of the intellect, or consolations and gratifications of the will, or reminiscences for the memory to store up and hark back to.[119] In so far as peel and core are here taken together, there is always danger of confusing the peel with the core. But even in the most exalted visions, consolations and insights, the peel remains creaturely and for that very reason, unless discerned by some higher criterion, can harbour a good or an evil or at least an ambiguous spirit. St John's intention is to train the soul away from all these treasures to complete poverty and destitution, to prevent love

[117] A i, 6, 6.

[118] The soul must be *pura (kathara) y sencilla (haplous, monoeidês), non limitada (apeiros) naitenida a alguna intellegencia particular, ni modificada con algun limite de forma (typos), especie (eidos) e imagen (eikôn)* (A, ii, 16, 7). Thus the soul attains likeness to God, who endows her *con su sencillez y pureza . . . que la deja limpia y pura y vacia de todas formas y figuras* (C 17, 3). *Cf.* C 31, 4; 35, 4 (*agua pura al entendimiento limpia y desnuda de accidentes y fantasias*); 38,4; L ii, 8 (*toque solo de la divinidad en el alma sin forma ni figura alguna intellectual ni imaginaria*); L ii, 20 (*el Verbo . . . ajena de todo modo (schesis) y manera (tropos) y libre de todo tomo, de forma y figura y accidentes*); L iii, 52; L iv, 14, etc, as well as many of the *Maxims* and *Counsels*.

[119] The whole of Books ii and iii of the *Ascent* are devoted to a critique of this kind.

from resting content with and clinging to the enjoyment of the form in which the divine manifests itself, so as to hurl it in complete nakedness into the naked reality of God. For the beginner, representative images may be helpful, indeed indispensable, for meditation;[120] even the proficient, whom God is already beginning to wean away from images, may have to return to them from time to time, to receive further help.[121] But the means toward the transcendence of love that are useful at the beginning later on become harmful when God himself causes essence to outweigh sign, the core to outweigh the peel.

Thus John lays down the following inexorable, broad rule of practical conduct with regard to 'forms and figures', all the supernatural ones as well as the natural: they must all, without exception, be rejected, be they from God or the devil or the soul's own powers, so that the soul may hold exclusively to the formlessness of the theological virtues. If the forms come from God, then they produce their effect *in actu primo* even before the soul has given her assent.[122] From the high vantage point of divine absoluteness John does not tire in his attempts to throw light on the relative nature of those gifts of God that have a definite, perceptible form. For example, he points to the relativity of the charisms, which can be bestowed even on the unworthy; of prophecy, the content of which is so often thought out hypothetically and can depend for its fulfilment on unknown factors; of spiritual apprehensions, which can be in part the product of man's secret desires; of spiritual admonitions, which would have to be passed on to the Church, and their apparently quite definite wording which would have to be understood in an extensive, heavenly sense. The trouble here is that the better a man thinks he has understood his mission the more incapable he is of understanding these gifts in their higher senses. To penetrate this supernatural universe seems to ordinary Christians a supreme honour, but John teaches the God-seeking soul to emigrate from it. All privileges with definite form that may come her way must be treated as if they

[120] A ii, 12, 5.

[121] There are later interpolations that try to argue thus; *cf.* the interpolation at the end of N i, 10 (Theatine edition, 47).

[122] A ii, 16, 10–11; A ii, 24, 8; A iii, 13, 3 (A ii, 11, 6).

were nothing; when confronted with them, the soul must remain uncommitted and indifferent, so that always and everywhere she can distinguish the Giver from the gift and seek and see only him in it.

On this point John is not in perfect accord with St Theresa, who was preoccupied with the configurations of visions and experiences for much longer and more deliberately than he was. Her ardent Eros was enkindled and purified precisely by the abundance of these particular graces, and in this connection she labelled John, whom she loved and treasured so much, as a spiritualist: 'God deliver us from people who are so spiritual that they want to turn everything into perfect contemplation, come what may.' She compares St John's method with the *Spiritual Exercises* of St Ignatius (apparently with regard to their fundamental agreement). 'It would be a bad business for us if we could not seek God until we were dead to the world. Neither the Magdalene, nor the woman of Samaria, nor the Canaanite woman was dead to the world when she found him.'[123] This high-spirited statement suggests a possible starting point for an anti-critique of St John's critique of all worldly forms. Whether it is justified or not, we shall see only at the end when we have gained an overall view of the way in which different aspects of John's system balance each other out.

2. The critique of forms and states in its full context is connected with the positive element of transcendence; it is for this that John makes his critique, and it is this that John, in one of his great architectonic simplifications,[124] identifies with the theological virtues. For him these are fundamentally a single reality (only differentiated by the three powers of the soul), the reality of participation in God. Faith is the transfer of all criteria for truth from the I that understands to the eternal Thou. Hope is the renunciation of all memories of humanly consoling subjects and themes. Love is the surrender of the whole of our being to the God we love. This triune attitude of a faith that

[123] *Obras de S. Teresa*, ed. Silverio, *Bibl. mist. carm.* (1915–1924), vi, 67; ET, E. A. Peers, *The Complete Works of St Teresa of Jesus*, vol. iii (London, 1946), p. 267.

[124] H. Delacroix calls him one of the '*grands simplificateurs du monde*' (*Études d'hist. et de psych. du mysticísme*, 1908, p iii, cited in G. Morel, 1, 180).

loves and hopes and of a love that believes and hopes is, however, now defined by John at both the *experience* of God (beyond all actual psychological experience) and as the state of *contemplation*. In making this assertion John refers especially to Denys and to Denys's identification of *thêôria* and *theologia mystikê*, which is fulfilled beyond all *gnôsis* in *pistis*. *Pistis* here has the (biblical) double emphasis of a total, trusting surrender of all personal security, and of a final certainty (*pistôsis*) beyond all finite reason in the divine. Together, this *pistis—thêôria* is *night* and *cloud* (*gnophos*), again with the double emphasis of genuine darkness for the finite subject and supereminent brightness in the infinite Godhead. All this follows the rhythm of God's ever-greaterness already established by Denys and taken up by Bonaventure: 'Faith, manifestly, is a dark night for man, but in this very way it gives him light. The more darkness it brings upon him, the more light it sheds. For the night by blinding illumines him.'[125] The reason for this lies ultimately in the nature of God: 'The loftier and clearer the things of God are in themselves, the more unknown and obscure they are to us.'[126] To this John applies the image so dear to him of the sun's ray and its shining upon the speck of dust that stands in its way. 'The more it is purified of these specks of dust, the more obscure and impalpable it seems to the material eye.'[127] It is in terms of this image that John explains the Areopagite's angelic hierarchies: they transmit the light of God to one another rather like totally pure panes of glass placed in a line, through which a single ray streams uninterruptedly.[128] Loving faith makes the world transparent to God, makes it disappear in its objectivity and configurated character. But because its light no longer strikes against anything, and because God himself is not an object, God can be experienced by the soul only as dark night. In loving and hoping faith the soul looks out into openness, indeed she becomes that openness, the open mouth that God alone can fill.[129] Faith is an 'infused virtue', that is, a 'divine, flowing

[125] A ii, 3, 4. [126] A ii, 8, 6.

[127] A ii, 14, 9; *cf.* A ii, 5, 6; A ii, 16, 10; N ii, 8, 3–4; L iii, 34.

[128] N ii, 12, 3–4.

[129] Ep 11 (published also as a fragment appended to the *Ascent*; ed. P. Gerardo, A iii, 46).

spring',[130] so much something from God that the substance of faith will be preserved even in the vision of eternal life.[131] Faith is the 'secret stair' that leads from this closed world into the divine openness[132]—darkness and certainty at the same time.[133]. All finite and individualistic 'wanting-to-see-for-myself' and 'wanting-to-make-sure-for-myself' would only disturb this infinite, dark and open light. For John, *intellectus fidei* does not consist in such finite assurances; to want to understand too much deprives faith of its meritorious character,[134] robs the adventurous quest for God in the Absolute of its 'force',[135] which grows only in the night; it weakens courage,[136] boldness,[137] which bestows upon faith all its nobility. It is precisely from worldly emptiness that security and stability in the absolute sense grow. The successors of Denys called this *hidrysis* and *bebaiotês*; John, for his part, called it *seguridad* (being secure),[138] *sosiego* (relaxed repose).[139] But in so far as faith is one with contemplation, John extolled it as 'loving obscure knowledge' (*noticia oscura amorosa*).[140] This is the interiorization of the ecclesial *fides ex auditu*, as in the young Augustine; it becomes an attentive forgetting of all exterior impressions, so that 'in silence only the ear of the spirit is open to listen to God'.[141] It no longer utters words with definite form, but 'substantial' words, which God communicates to the substance of the soul, and these far transcend any possibility of illusion.[142]

[130] C 11 expl. and 1.

[131] C 11, 2.

[132] A ii, 1, 1.

[133] A ii, 3, 1.

[134] A ii, 27, 5; A iii, 31, 8. Thus God works miracles for the strengthening of faith only 'out of necessity' (A iii, 31, 9). 'When the soul detaches her will from sensory testimonies and signs, she is exalted in a purer faith' (A iii, 32, 4).

[135] C 22, 1–2; N ii, 11 (the whole chapter).

[136] N ii, 11, 3.

[137] N ii, 20, 2; C 4, expl.; C 20, expl. and 1–3.

[138] Numerous passages: *Concordancias* 997–978. The soul is protected against possible deception by the devil, but also protected against herself (*amparada se si misma*, N ii, 16, 13).

[139] Numerous passages: *ibid.*, 1030–1032.

[140] A ii, 24, 4.

[141] A iii, 3, 5.

[142] C 13, 5.

For this reason the fulness of open faith/contemplation is again and again characterized, in contrast to the particular form, as *general*. 'The more spiritual [the soul] is, the more she discontinues trying to make particular acts with her faculties, for she becomes engrossed in one general, pure act.'[143] This gives a *noticia general y confusa*,[144] a *luz espiritual tan sencilla, pura y general, no afectada ni particularizada a ningun particular inteligibile, natural ni divino.*[145] And to 'such great poverty of spirit' the words of St Paul can be applied: *Nihil habentes et omnia possidentes.*[146] Particular knowledge can be inserted into this universal knowledge or experience[147] without danger, as in a *cognitio matutina* placed in the background. At the end of his final work[148] John gives a magnificent illustration of this possibility. The reality that truly attains to this universality is the 'love' that has set the soul free from all particular knowledge; as it soars upward to God this love is given the privilege of experiencing the downward sweep of the Three-in-One, the light of the Trinity.[149]

Nevertheless, this dark universality remains, for one who is only an aspirant, the experience of pure night: privation, annihilation, crucifixion; the experience of that process which John, with St Paul, describes as the stripping and dispossession of the old man and the putting on of the new man conformed to Christ (Eph 4.24)[150]; elsewhere he uses the bold phrase, 'the inner resurrection of the spirit'.[151] At first the night is subjectively death, although objectively it is already resurrection; but as the way of the soul's dying, it has its twilight, midnight and dawn that ushers in eternal life,[152] when the veil that separates her from the vision of God is stretched to the breaking point.[153] And yet

[143] A ii, 12, 6.
[144] A ii, 14, 6.
[145] N ii, 8, 5; *cf.* L iii, 49.
[146] N ii, 8, 5; *cf.* ii, 12, 4.
[147] N ii, 9, 5.
[148] L iv.
[149] N ii, 25, 4; C 38, 1f.
[150] N ii, 3, 3; N ii, 13, 11; L ii, 33; *cf.* on John 1.13 (*ex Deo nati*); A ii 5, 5.
[151] Ep 5.
[152] A i, 2, 1–5.
[153] A ii, 9, 3; A ii, 3, 4–5; A ii, 4, 6.

the midnight is already objectively the brightest of light, just as the *shekina* of the wilderness was a dazzling darkness above the temple.[154] All the time John stresses that God's light shines unchangingly and constantly, that it is only the unpurified state of those who approach that makes them experience it as darkness and purgatorial torment. This idea must not be interpreted in a weaker, neo-Platonic sense, as if the *bonum diffusivum sui* was shining in eternal serenity high above all the suffering destinies of man. One must rather consider that in this affirmation John has entirely in view the living, elective God of the Bible, who 'descends into Hell and leads back out again'; even the Cross, upon which the Son is abandoned by the Father, as seen by the Father, is purest light, the light that is glorified even *in extremis*.

Thus the following two statements can be reconciled: that God himself is prepared to open the way of perfection (contemplation) to all; but in fact, only the elect, as we saw, who for their part must be springs of life within the Church, attain it.[152] If the qualifications given to the light ('hell fire', 'purgatorial fire', 'heavenly flame') arise from the state of the soul, nevertheless at every stage the divine light is the active principle that produces true illumination by means of the night. And it matters little at what moment the soul begins to understand 'what sort of work is being accomplished within her'.[155] Equally unimportant is how many psychological factors (perceptible 'stages') are to be discerned in this entry into the night of God; this is primarily because leaving the night (the 'dawn') constitutes no kind of counterpart to entering it (the 'twilight of evening'). Perhaps in this respect John is asking a little too much when he gives the course of his own life a universal application (thus inducing his imitators to construct simplistic schemata). Nevertheless there are other factors that correct the picture and restore the balance. The 'active night' (to

[154] L ii, 27; L iii, 46; *cf.* L iii, 11 (*Dios no se mueve*); A ii, 5, 4; N ii, 9, 11; N ii, 10, 6; N ii, 13, 10: 'The darknesses and evils the soul experiences when this light strikes are not darknesses and evils of the light but of the soul itself. And it is this light that illumines it so it may see these evils. From the beginning the divine light illumines the soul.'

[155] N ii, 10, 6.

which the *Ascent of Mount Carmel* introduces us) and the 'passive night' (as described in the *Dark Night*) are not successive phenomena), but impinge extensively on one another; indeed, they are only two aspects of a single process. Moreover, the 'night of the senses' and the 'night of the spirit' (which may on occasion be separated by many years[156]), though distinguished with the same systematic lucidity, are nonetheless so thoroughly intertwined that 'the purgation of the sensory part is never adequately accomplished without the spiritual . . . and is not in earnest until the night of the spirit has at least begun'.[157] In the same way it is not possible to distinguish between the *via purgativa* and *illuminativa*. The illuminating light is in the first instance predominantly purificatory.[159] The loss of taste for the things of the senses and the finite is as such already the beginning of a tasting of God as he is in himself.

The relevance of this to the project of a theological aesthetics is as follows. Bathed in an obscure light, this present world is darkened as if at twilight and grows pale in an incurable state of disillusionment. But when the time comes, it will be in that same obscure light that the world rises anew, to go forward to the vision of God, to meet the God of the new Heaven and the new earth. However, this 'generality', the negation of the particular, of that which has specific form, is not in any sense an abstract universal, however much, to begin with, it exercises its power of reduction and abstraction on the particular. We must take special note here of the fact that St John of the Cross is not proposing a philosophical mysticism; he wants only to open up the experience of the living God of the Bible, the God of love, a dimension in which the theological virtues emerge into consciousness, in so far as they are infused, Trinitarian life, the realm of the Holy Spirit. At most one can ask whether the *beata nox* that he describes implies more a *theologia crucis* than a *theologia gloriae*. It is not easy to answer this. Following the tripartite division given at the beginning of the *Ascent*, a process is unfolded that passes through the glory of the Cross to the dawn of eternal life and eternal vision. And John stresses the gulf

[156] N ii, 1, 1.
[157] N ii, 3, 1.
[159] N ii, 7, 4.

between the highest earthly experience of God and eternal, heavenly vision with great vigour,[160] simply because a certain systematic logic (not just love's absolute longing for ultimate embrace) tends to suppress the lines of distinction. At the highest stages of spiritual progress, essentially it expresses something like the beginnings of eternal life,[161] when the face of God becomes transparent,[162] a shadow made of pure light (*resplandores*), for which the poet, stammeringly, finds the name *obumbraciones*.[163] 'Finally, [the soul] enjoys God's glory in the shadow of his glory, which gives knowledge of the measure and property of God's glory.'[164]

The 'night' is like a great curve. It begins with the asceticism of radical and active renunciation of the world and continues with the passive deprivation of all delight in things and even in God himself. Then it curves round the midnight of pure sightless faith until it reaches the dawn of a new substantial delight in the ways of God, the beginning of transparent vision. If this, then, is the 'curve' of the night, we must now ask what common features such different phases and experiences have. The answer of the poems is clear: it is love—without love John cannot for a moment even conceive what he calls faith. It is a love that has chosen her one and only beloved and therefore in a single flight soars audaciously above all created things, but also sinks humbled beneath them.

Cuanto mas alto llegaba
De este lance tan subido
Tanto mas bajo y rendido
Y abatido mi hallaba.[165]

It is love whose intrepidity withstands everything, even God himself, who takes her seriously and transfers her from All to Nothing so that she might find there the one whom alone she loves. Finally, it is a love as much robbed as ravished, whose

[160] C, 1 expl.; C 6, 2; C 13–14 expl. (end). John expresses himself in very cautious terms even about something that was almost universally taken for granted by Scholastic theology; namely, the direct vision of God of Moses and Paul.

[161] L iii, 10.

[162] L iv, 7.

[163] L iii, 12f.

[164] L iii, 15.

[165] P 6, stanza 3.

only longing is to do the will of the beloved, whether that means Hell or Heaven—'she has no more worldly hopes, no more spiritual longings'.[166] This love, which seeks in the void and is found 'in the hunt', is union; it is also the vehicle of contemplation and of what one must call vision in nonvision. Here John identifies himself with the teaching of the schools of Bernard and Bonaventure. As love, the will surpasses the intellect and leaves it behind.[167] One must remember that in ancient psychology the will/love occupies to a large extent the place of the biblical 'heart' and thus denotes what we mean today by 'person' and the 'centre of a person'. That is why, according to John, this transcendent will of love is quieted by God by means of what John calls 'substantial touches', by means of an immediate (*amesôs*) contact that surpasses all the particular acts of knowledge, feeling and desire, a contact between substance and substance, between person and person. God alone can enter into such substantial communion with his creatures, not only in the natural ontological sphere of the universal *analogia entis* (which to some degree can also be realized by mystics outside the Christian tradition), but also—and John quite explicitly distinguishes the two—in the supernatural sphere, in the reality (which emerges in the personal experience of love) of the loving grace of the triune God, who reveals himself to man, a reality that, in the theological virtues, is infused into the soul. That this touch of substance by substance does not in any way tend toward the pantheistic *unión esencial o sustancial*[169] John says with as much clarity as one could wish. John in no sense remains at an abstract level in his conception of substance, everything is set in the sphere of spiritual and personal actualizations. But these do not emanate just accidentally from the soul's obscure and undisturbed substance; no, they inflame and wound the soul at its very centre. The *toques*, the touches of substance by substance, that make present

[166] C 29, 5.

[167] N ii, 12, 7; C 17, 2 (in Redaction B of the *Spiritual Canticle*, stanza 26, 2); C 18, 2; L iii, 50; Ep 11.

[168] A ii, 5, 2–3 (in Redaction B of the *Spiritual Canticle*, stanza 11, 1, which is not found in Redaction A).

[169] A ii, 5, 3.

the heart of Thou in the heart of I are an experience, time and again described, that surpasses all delight and is almost mortal in its effect.[170] It is to be compared with the kiss at the beginning of the Canticle,[171] with fiery arrows,[172] with a wound, a 'death', which is at the same time 'a very deep knowledge of the Godhead,[173] sometimes descending as if from the serene heights of heaven,[174] or, like a wind sent from God, stirring up all God's gifts in the soul.[175] The very substance of the soul is wounded: *hiere en la sustancia del alma este . . . amor.*[176] Love brings the soul that ultimate, substantial openness that is beyond pain and pleasure,[177] and it tunes her to the key of divine love and wisdom. At first the wound seems like a severe and mortal attack on the soul's creatureliness, but when it has become her second nature, it becomes almost a game. 'The wounds imparted to the soul are the games of divine Wisdom.'[178]

Now it becomes clear why St John's mysticism achieves its complete form only in a Trinitarian context. His entire system struggles energetically against two opposed and false solutions: the pantheistic solution, which would be an unimaginable horror to him, and that other inadequate solution, which would limit loving union with the God of revelation to merely accidental acts. From work to work John's ship, sighting its destination ever more clearly, sails between and past these two rocks. He sets off from an idea that is still philosophical; namely, that God is the centre of the creature's sphere, into which God draws him in the deepest secrecy of night (at the end of the *Dark Night*).[179] Then he encounters the blissful amazement of the Bride in the Canticle, when the wind of the Holy Spirit blows into her all the perfumes and treasures of the Beloved, so that here already the mystery of the Holy Spirit shared by Bride and Bridegroom is glimpsed as the mystery of the infusing of the Spirit common to Father and Son, and creaturely love, through

[170] *Concordancias*: *Toques* (1061–1064), especially A ii, 32, 2–3; N ii, 12, 6; N ii, 23, 11 (*toques sustanciales de divina union*), 12 (end).

[171] N ii, 23, 12.

[172] C 1, 4.

[173] C 7 expl.

[174] C 16, 3–5.

[175] C 26, 3.

[176] N ii, 13, 3.

[177] L ii, 13.

[178] L i, 8.

[179] N ii, 20, 6 and chapters 15–25 *passim*.

grace, becomes a participation in the divine *spiratio*[180] itself; then finally he arrives at the sovereign exposition of this doctrine in the *Living Flame*.[181] From now on, at the level of the triune life, in which the creature through grace may participate actively and passively, we have passed beyond separating distance and the identification that threatens personal existence. Now the breathtaking miracles, the substantial touches of I and Thou, the awakening of Thou within I and of I within Thou, which only a miracle of grace can prevent from being mortal—now all this becomes the content of the life of love. The end of the *Living Flame* describes the disconcerting experience of Christ awakening in the heart and centre of the soul: 'Thou wakest, O Word, O Spouse, in the centre and depth of my soul, in its pure and most intimate substance.'[182] Christ awakes as Thou, as the 'only master' of my substance, in a *movimiento de tanta grandeza y señiorío y gloria y di tan íntima suavidad*, in a movement *de tan gran Emperador*,[183] so that with this awakening of the absolute in the heart, with this absolute awakening of the heart, everything, the entire creation, must awaken also. It is of crucial significance that the word *identity* is discarded as being abstract and much too weak. The one who awakens in the innermost part of the soul's substance is the Master, the sublime prince and emperor, and it is only as master that he is beloved. His awakening, therefore, raises up the soul in this ineffable way to her beloved and divine overlord only because at the same time it plunges her into the abyss, into the absolute distance of nothingness. Only now can we understand why disillusionment with the world, absolute distance, in which the descent of night teaches and immerses the soul, can already be the hidden glory of love. The distance of person in God in the womb of substantial unity is the presupposition of all love, both eternal and created. And so not only in the purifying night but also in the night of bliss we can say: 'He obtains more joy and recreation in creatures through the dispossession of them. . . . In detachment from things he acquires a clearer knowledge of them so that he has a better understanding of both natural and supernatural truths

[180] C 38, 1.
[181] L ii, 16; L iii, 17.
[182] L iv, 3.
[183] L iv, 4.

concerning them. ... He then whose joy is unpossessive of things rejoices in them all as though he possessed them all. ... He possesses them, as St Paul states, with great liberty (2 Cor 6.10).'[184]

We are a long way here from seeing man's relation to God as either one of opposition or immersion. Within the formless itself we can see once more something like a form emerging out of the Trinitarian distance of the persons. But this form is one with the formless glory of substantial union in love. The Son is 'the splendour of the eternal light, the unspotted mirror and image of the goodness' of the Father.[185] And so as 'touch', he makes the touching 'hand' of the Father perceptible. But the 'cautery applied with force' is again neither the hand nor the touch, but the third person, the Holy Spirit.[186] Thus God as set against man now takes on Trinitarian 'form' in so far as this relation is transcended by a pure indwelling in the fire and the wound. Similarly, when the soul is thrust into an (objective) encounter with God, she discovers the fundamental attributes of divinity, which she experiences as 'lamps of fire' (*lamparas de fuego*), burning torches. They make their appearance as much in their actual, clear and distinct form as in their reciprocal circumincession and mutual intensification, as much in their sovereign state of being *per se* as in their loving disposition of being *pro me*. 'Since (God) is the virtue of supreme humility, he loves you with supreme humility and esteem and makes you his equal, gladly revealing himself to you in these ways of knowledge, in this his countenance filled with graces. ... (He says to you:) "I am yours and for you and delighted to be what I am so as to be yours and give myself to you."'[187]

John searches for images to illuminate the unity of confrontation and indwelling, which seems to him here to be particularly 'indescribable'.[188] The 'splendours' of the lamps are the 'loving knowledge' that the divine attributes communicate to the soul by their radiance and by which the soul too is resplendent, transformed in such 'loving knowledge'. The

[184] A iii, 20, 2–3.
[185] L iii, 17; L ii, 16.
[186] L ii, 16.
[187] L iii, 6.
[188] L iii, 8.

illumination of the splendours is, for this reason, 'not like that produced by material lamps, which through their flames shed light round about them, but like the illumination that is within the very flames, for the soul is within these splendours. . . . More than that, it is itself transformed in them. It is like the air within the flames, enkindled and transformed in the flame, for the flame is nothing but enkindled air. The movements and splendours of the flame are not from the air alone, nor from the fire of which the flame is composed, but from both the air and the fire. And the fire causes the air, which it has enkindled, to produce these same movements and splendours. We can consequently understand how the soul with its faculties is illumined within the splendours of God.'[189] For St John it is never a case of the creature being engulfed by God; it is rather the incorporation of the creature in the whole of his being, with all his powers (and thus with his merit), into the depths of grace. 'The movements of these divine flames . . . are not alone produced by the soul that is transformed in the flames of the Holy Spirit, nor does the Holy Spirit produce them alone, but they are the work of both the soul and him, since he moves it in the manner that fire moves the enkindled air. Thus these movements of both God and the soul are not only splendours, but also glorification (*glorificaciones*). This activity of the flames and these flares are the happy festivals and games which . . . the Holy Spirit inspires in the soul.'[190] In this 'game' the only purpose of what may seem like identity is to render possible the reciprocity of giving, so that for the soul its supreme bliss is to be able to give back God (whom she has received and whom she bears within her) to God. 'Having him for her own, she can give him and communicate him to whomever she wishes. Thus she gives him to her Beloved, who is the very God who gave himself to her.'[191]

3. If we can now see clearly to what extent St John's faith is the experience of love, we should also understand, as a consequence, the justification of what at first sight seems surprising—the identification of his faith with *contemplation*. For

[189] L iii, 9–10.
[190] L iii, 10.
[191] L iii, 78.

faith is depicted as nonvision and noncomprehension, whereas contemplation means vision. Where the two are identified, then the act of 'mystical theology', with all its nonvision, dispossession, privation and night, must nevertheless involve vision: vision in the mode of nonvision, vision of someone present in the mode of absence or as through a veil or a quest, which is so absolute, tends so much towards the Absolute itself, that it cannot do other than ultimately find, 'hunt down', the Absolute; then again, the vision is love, which is set so much on the ultimate that it discovers the ultimate being itself as the mystery of love. One cannot say that it is the power of searching love that creates or forces out its object into the emptiness of the Absolute (like Rilke's idea that 'we . . . plan the gods' and grant the prayer of him who at the end hears ours).[192] For though love may throw herself into an encounter with the unknown, she knows that she has been taken hold of and carried further; rather than emptying herself, she is emptied; it is less a matter of her acting than of God's acting upon her. For this reason the basis of the soul's contemplation is the experience of being contemplated, as we saw in the stanza quoted earlier where the eyes of God are only 'sketched' in the soul, and she waits impatiently for the divine eye to make its appearance in the fluidity of faith. And yet what the soul desires is at the same time what she cannot endure, and so she has to implore her Beloved:

Apártalos, amado,
Que voy de vuelo.[193]

'Withdraw your eyes, Beloved, I am taking flight'; 'what she longs for so ardently . . . she cannot receive at the desired moment, save almost at the cost of her life'.[194] She implores her Beloved not to look at her while she takes flight; that is, while she hastens towards God with her love, and while she keeps her (unseeing) eyes of love fixed on him. This prayer of hers combines two thoughts: the soul knows by anticipation the unbearable beauty of God's eyes, and also acknowledges her incapacity for vision on account of her lack of strength.

[192] Sonette an Orpheus ii, 24.
[193] C 12, lines 1–2.
[194] Cant. 12. 1.

Nevertheless, she knows that at the heart of the mystery of the night lies the generous, creative eye of God himself:

Cuando tú me mirabas,
Tu gracia en mí tus ojos imprimían,
Por en eso me adamabas
Y en eso merecían
Los míos adorar lo que en ti vían.[195]

'When you looked at me', your contemplation rested upon me, 'your eyes imprinted your grace in me', for the *esse* of grace, *sequitur agere*, is produced by the divine gaze, divine love, and 'thus my eyes deserved to adore what they beheld in you'; the contemplative gaze is thus only made possible by the preliminary gaze of grace. Elsewhere this looking at God is called the 'unique eye' and is identified with faith.[196] Nonetheless, this unseeing faith is suspended between the gaze of the love of God, who by grace makes the soul beautiful (*que la hermosea*), and the gaze of the engraced soul at God, whom she adores as nothing less than the source of beauty.

The word and concept 'beauty' inevitably come in at this point. The 'general' (*general*) nature of the night of faith is in no sense a nothingness; it reflects the radiance of the invisible stars of love. It is itself the fluidity of love that passes all finite understanding, the fluidity that is in itself already the glory of God, so that it is only a question of time, of patient, expectant vision, before this obscure glory is transformed into a manifest, self-glorifying splendour. If the night is the *flight* of love, then it is the opposite of immobility. In the twilight gloom of this world we may still plot love's mobility by reference to the disappearing features of the earth's landscape. In the midnight of faith, however, love no longer has any such markers and can appear as pure *soledad* and *pura y oscura contemplación.*[197] Nevertheless, the greater the privations, the more the flight presses on toward the beloved, as the first part of the Canticle

[195] Cant. 23, stanza. ('When you looked at me / Your eyes imprinted your grace in me; / For this you loved me ardently; / And thus my eyes deserved/ To adore what they beheld in you.')

[196] Cant. 22, 5.

[197] N ii, 3, 3.

shows. The same night transfigures the experience of God from reprobation in Hell, through the severe torments of Purgatory, to the liberation of love's desire. This fact shows that the night is a drama, the most intense kind of activity in the darkness. This fulness of the night, which is at once both pure faith and contemplation, is in itself a vision, *inchoatio visionis*. It is the nonvision that comes between initial vision—when we hear the gospel preached and recognize that this is the truth and that God died on the Cross for us—and terminal vision, to which unseeing faith directly flies, and it is the anticipation of such terminal vision that enables us to withstand the darkest dereliction by God. Only thus is the beauty of this night comprehensible; only thus do we discover the transcendent spring from which the tremendous power of this lyricism flows. The spring is 'beyond all beauty (*sobre toda hermosura*) of what is, was or will be'. And for the sake of this 'beyond', which remains an 'I-don't-know-what', the poet knows that he will never be able to lose himself in the beauty of the world. No worldly magic can ensnare one whose 'noble heart' (*corazón generoso*) finds the Only One in pure faith outside of all law and necessity. Yes, as if by luck or chance (*por ventura*), he finds the Only One, the formless One, *solo . . . sin forma y figura*, 'without prop or stay'.[198]

It is the fact that St John of the Cross is given an anticipation of eternal vision (while remaining crucified to this world) that explains the paradox that, for him, the world, definitively abandoned and lost in God, is regained. In the *Spiritual Canticle*, which contains more Augustinian motifs than the other works, this idea emerges clearly for the first time. It is not a question of raising oneself to God by means of the ancient and mediaeval anagogical contemplation of créatures; no, it is the rediscovery of the creature in God, in the vision of God alone, in a sort of anticipation of the *cognitio matutina*. The only anagogical method in John is love; he even explicitly gives it that name. According to P. Eliseus of the Martyrs, 'he used to say that one could resist the vices in a manner at once more simple, more fruitful and more perfect' than direct attack. 'The soul combats

[198] P 16 (Silv. 819–821).

and destroys in this way all the temptations of the enemy . . . by using only anagogical acts inspired by love without any other alien practices.' Thus one must 'instantly resist by means of an act or movement of anagogical love, as one raises the heart to union with God. . . . Then the soul is no longer where the enemy wanted to strike and wound it; it has slipped away.'[199] But this anagogical love finds Trinitarian love, and in it God's decision to create the world. One of the Romances recounts this, and the Canticle draws certain conclusions from it:

Mil gracias derramando
Pasó por estos sotos con presura
Y yéndolos mirando
Con sola su figura
Vistidos los dejó de hermosura.[200]

'Pouring out a thousand graces', 'passing by' as if 'in haste', God has created the natures and elements. God gives his real attention to what comes second which he regards as first. God surveys (*mirar*) what he has created, and 'with his countenance (*figura*) alone [he] clothed them in beauty'. 'St Paul says, "The Son of God is the splendour of his glory and the form [or countenance: *figura*] of his substance"'. It should be known that only with this figure [countenance], his Son, did God look at all things; that is, he communicated to them their natural being and many natural graces and gifts and made them complete and perfect.' But not only that: 'with this countenance of his Son alone, he clothed them in beauty by imparting to them supernatural being. This he did when he became man and raised human nature, and with it all creatures, to the beauty of God, since in human nature he was united with them all. Accordingly the Son of God proclaimed: "I, when I am lifted up from the earth, will draw all men to myself."' . . . 'In addition to all this, from the viewpoint of contemplative experience, it should be known that in the living contemplation and knowledge of creatures, the soul sees such fulness of graces, powers and beauty with which God has

[199] Cited in Francois de St Marie, *Initiation à St Jean de la Croix* (1945).

[200] C 5, stanza. ('Pouring out a thousand graces, / He passed these graces in haste; / And having looked at them, / With his image alone, / Clothed them in beauty.')

endowed them that seemingly all are arrayed in wonderful beauty and natural virtue. This beauty and virtue is derived from above and imparted by that infinite supernatural beauty of the countenance (*figura*) of God; his look clothes the world and all the heavens with beauty and gladness, just as he also, upon opening his hand, fills every living thing with blessing, as David says (Ps 144.16).'[201]

Is the Son the face of the Father turned towards the world? Or is he the Father's facial expression, whom the Father contemplates? Is it in the Son, because of his love for the Son, for the sake of his love for the Son, that the Father loves all the creatures he has made in the Son? Is it because of the grace and beauty of the Son that he sees creatures as beautiful and full of grace? The two senses of *figura* come into play together: the sense that dominates the text of the Bible (expression, figure), and the other sense, which John brings to the fore (countenance, vision). But whichever aspect we emphasize, for this lover of contemplation the world gains its beauty from above: from divine love, which for its part, through the reflection of the persons, one in the other, is the archetype of all beauty. The contemplative sees not only the beauty of God and in it the beauty of the world; he also sees in the moment of vision, as it were, the *analogia entis*: 'Although the soul in this state is indeed aware that all things are distinct from God in so far as they have created being, and sees them in him with their power, their root and their tension, nonetheless, she knows precisely that God, by his being all these things with infinite eminence (*eminencia*), is such that she knows these things better in God's being than in themselves.'[202]

This statement does not come from the *Spiritual Canticle*, but from the last stanza of the *Living Flame*; with regard to what it says about the experience of God and the world, this is the supreme gift among everything we have received from St John. As if all the flights of the soul, all the love and knowledge up till now had been nothing, he describes this final experience as the awakening of God in him.

[201] C 5, 3.
[202] L iv, 5.

¡Cuan manso y amoroso
Recuerdas en mi seno¡

But if the absolute being opens his eyes in the heart of the creature, how then should the creatures, who depend on him for life, keep their eyes shut? The world awakens in the soul at the same time as God. When the divine Word awakens within her, 'it seems to the soul that all the balsams and fragrant spices and flowers of the world are commingled, stirred and shaken so as to yield their sweet odour, and that all the kingdoms and dominions of the world and all the powers and virtues of heaven are moved; and not only this, but it also seems that all the virtues and substances and perfections and graces of every created thing glow and make the same movement all at once. Since, as St John says, "all things in him are life", and "in him we live and move and have our being", as Paul declares, it follows that when, within the soul, this greatest of monarchs moves (whose principality—which consists of the three spheres, celestial, terrestrial and infernal, and the things contained in them—as Isaiah says, he bears upon his shoulders, upholding them all, as St Paul says, with the word of his power), all things seem to move in unison. This happens in the same manner as when at the movement of the earth all material things in it move as though they were nothing.'[203]

The description goes further. The soul sees not only how all creatures move in unison with God, but also how they too reveal themselves in unison with him when he reveals his glory, when he reveals his heart. God is the source of their being and duration, their power and perfection; it is also from God and together with God that all the value of creatures is revealed. 'Here lies the remarkable delight of this awakening: the soul knows creatures through God, and not God through creatures. This amounts to knowing the effects through their cause, and not the cause through its effects. The latter is knowledge *a posteriori*, and the former is essential knowledge.' And further: as God opens his eyes in the soul, it seems to her that God does indeed move 'in an incomparable newness', a newness that creatures also now share: 'The being and harmony of every

[203] L iv, 4.

creature . . . with its movements in God, is revealed to her with such newness, it seems to the soul that it is God who moves and that the cause assumes the name of the effect it produces.' Does not the book of Wisdom say: 'Wisdom is more mobile than any motion'? And rightly so, for 'it is the principle and root of all movement. "While remaining in herself", the wise man goes on to say, "she renews all things" (Wisd 7.24, 27). Thus what he wishes to say in this passage is that Wisdom is more active than all active things.'[204]

In all this vision the soul contemplates the face of God as if through a transparency, for not all the veils have been withdrawn. She sees how, by his power, he himself moves all creatures. His effects appear to the soul together with God and inseparable from him; he himself seems to be in motion in them, and they in him, perpetually.[205] This is a contemplation of the *analogia entis* in the terms fixed by Denys but with that Augustinian sense of a transparent *cognitio matutina* bestowed on earthly faith. From here until the end of the stanza everything is increasingly dominated by the *kabôd* of the Old Testament; the visionary, like Job, is afraid of being 'crushed by the weight of glory', unless he too be transformed into that same glory—*porque la gloria oprime al que la mira, cuando no le glorifica*;[206] the overwhelming glory is incomprehensibly 'gentle and full of love' and sustains all living creatures in their meekness; this glory is at the same time the gentle blowing of the Holy Spirit, whom the soul breathes in and out, that little breeze in which Elijah discovered God on the mountain—how else could a Carmelite conclude his work?

Thus the paradox is clarified and we can see how this most radical renunciation of the world, this systematic weaning away of the soul from all created form and figure, even in the deepest recesses of the heart and its attachments, even in the heights of the most exalted visions and locutions—how all of this can be compatible with a spirituality that can truly be called aesthetic. For this spirituality, *hermosura* signifies the supreme affirmation about God. 'Beauty' for John is an obsession; it is not only the

[204] L iv, 5–6.
[205] L iv, 7.
[206] L iv, 11.

end, it is also the means.[207] He may have rediscovered the beauty of the world through the beauty of God, but he could never have done this had he not known about beauty from the beginning; otherwise he would not even have been able to renounce it. Aesthetic sensitivity is part of his nature and accompanies him on the whole of his spiritual journey no less than it does his spiritual sister, the great Theresa. We know the love that both of them had for nature. For Theresa open country, running water, flowers are a 'book' in which she reads God. She wants convents to be, where possible, by the side of rivers. On one occasion she writes: 'The position of a convent is so important that it would be madness to worry about the cost. For a river and view I would be very glad elsewhere to give far more than this convent cost.' And again: 'I have a hermitage from which one can see the river, and a cell in which even from my bed I can observe what for me is such an agreeable sight.'[208] John fills his spiritual songs with all the detailed images of the open country, which are not just the requisites of bucolic verse but stem from direct and affectionate observation. Above all, he had, by nature, a love for the night, as is witnessed by the very large number of accounts that have been handed down. 'In the peace of the night he spent [according to the testimony of P. Alonso] many hours in solitary prayer. When he had finished, he fetched his companion, sat down on the green meadow and, with his eyes on the river flowing by, conversed with him about the beauty of the heavens, of the moon, of the stars. At other times he spoke about the gentle harmony of the moving spheres of Heaven and raised himself up to the Heaven of the blest, whose beauty and glory he praised in lofty words.' Others describe him 'praying all night long beneath the trees with arms outstretched'. Wherever he stayed, and right to the end of his life, he always sought out the open country to pray and instructed his *confrères* above all to pray outside in nature, in gardens, in fields, on cliffs and in forests; he knew the plants, the animals, he observed them and described their characteristics in

[207] *P. Crisogono de Jesus Sacramentado*, cited in Michel Florisoone, *Esthétique et Mystique d'après Ste Thérèse d'Avila et St Jean de la Croix* (1956), 161. We base what follows on this excellent little book.

[208] Florisoone, 17, 19.

his works. In the pastoral *Spiritual Canticle* his observation of nature is revealed in mystical form: 'My Beloved is the mountains [says the Bride] and lonely wooded valleys, strange islands and resounding rivers, the whispering of love-stirring breezes, the tranquil night at the time of the rising dawn, silent music, sound solitude, the supper that refreshes and deepens love' (St. 13–14). The imperceptible transition from simple natural imagery to mystical paradoxes (*la música callada, la soledad sonora*) shows that we are not dealing here with conventional anagogic contemplation of the world, but that John contemplates his God really, directly, in nature, and that he sees the natural images as only a function and elucidation of the divine attributes. *Mi amado las montañas*: the mountains *are* my Beloved, and of course precisely not in the pantheistic sense, but in that other sense given clear verbal expression in the fourth stanza of the *Living Flame*. In itself, nature is only a *dibujo*, a sketch or outline;[209] the completed picture is seen only in God, for only in him do the individual notes sound together in that symphony that only the substances of things, not their exterior accidents, can join together to perform. It is significant that the verse from the book of Wisdom is quoted: *Spiritus Domini replevit orbem terrarum, et hoc quod continet omnia, scientiam habet vocis* (Wisd 1.7). Only in the Spirit of God does 'the testimony to God that, in themselves, all things give' ring forth in the music that harmonizes the individual voices.[210] This is why the rigorous ascetical demand is made of the beginner not to submit to any illusions and not to desire to ascend immediately from the symphony of the accidents to the symphony of the substances: 'No one who has not yet mortified his pleasure in sensory things should dare to look for notable benefit from the vigour and activity of his senses regarding these goods in the belief that they are a help to the spirit. For the forces of the soul will increase more without these sensible things.'[211] The first movement of the soul must be to raise up all sensory things immediately to God. This will yield 'a truly extraordinary increase of joy and bliss'. For when the soul herself is purified, 'she experiences a

[209] C 11, 5.
[210] C 14, 3–4.
[211] A iii, 26, 7.

totally spiritual delight in turning directly (*luego*) toward God the joy she has in everything she sees'.[212] For as long as she is incapable of doing that, she must renounce all gratification, for one is not meant to 'celebrate oneself more than God'.[213]

St John of the Cross not only had the soul and perception of an artist, but, as is proved by the hastily sketched little drawing of the posture of the crucified Lord, whom he saw in a vision, he also possessed the technique of a master. In early youth, between six and eight years of age, he learnt different crafts, one after the other. He was apprenticed first to a carpenter, then to a tailor, a woodcarver and a painter. As a novice he spent his periods of recreation carving wooden crucifixes, and he continued this custom until the last years of his life. In his writings he used numerous images drawn from the different arts and crafts to illustrate the art of spiritual direction.[214] He loved music, sang a great deal and himself played at least one instrument. It is very clear that when he forsook the values of art, he was making a very hard decision, for him perhaps the hardest decision of all, and was performing a work of love, that can be justified neither by contempt for the world nor ascetical discipline, but which was solely in response to the call of Christ and out of love for him.

His attitude to ecclesiastical art, to its legitimacy and utility and to its dangers, can be understood only on the basis of this fundamental decision of his. It is a radical decision and yet profoundly different from the iconoclasm of Protestantism. He fought on two fronts: against the Reformation's depreciation of all religious images, of all church ornament, he defends the spiritual utility of these icons and refers to the mind and practice of the Church; against the development of a more passionate style of art in the Renaissance and early Baroque he advocates a rather medieval view of religious art. It is not, he argues, the enhancement of and submission to aesthetic values that in a work of art guarantees the communication of religious experience; no, that can be achieved only by a certain indeterminate transparency and, above all, simplicity. For the

[212] A iii, 26, 5.
[213] A iii, 38, 2.
[214] L iii, 42–43.

work is not meant to tie the soul down to itself but should point away from itself to God. This dialectic is authentic despite the doubts that can be raised about the authenticity of certain passages in the *Ascent*. Its powerful critique of devotional objects is played down at the end of each chapter by words whose unctuousness and feebleness seem to reveal that they are a later addition.[215] But even if these additions are authentic or contain a core of authenticity, they nonetheless do no more than temper the force of what is said in the third book of the *Ascent*, which critically examines artistic and other devotional aids. The whole book, pressing toward its conclusion like a rapidly flowing stream, proclaims unequivocally: Don't stand still! Climb higher! Seek God alone! Images? Certainly, the Church authorizes them and makes use of them, 'and yet there are many who pay more attention to the painting and decorating of the image than to what is represented'. Miraculous statues? Perhaps, but how outrageous to dress and undress them like dolls, so that for many they have become 'idols'. 'They are as attached to these images as were Michas and Laban to their idols'. The genuinely devout man 'has little need for many statues and uses those that conform more to the divine traits than to human ones'. 'Indeed, since some statues are truer likenesses than others and excite more devotion, it is fit to be attached more to some than to others.' But if the senses cling to this higher art, 'then what should be a help to the soul becomes a hindrance'.[216] What 'stupidity' to place one's trust more in this statue than another! God 'looks only upon the faith and purity of the prayerful heart.

[215] Examples of this are, in particular, the conclusion of A iii, 15, 2, where it is said that 'images will always help a person towards union with God' (which is precisely what John does not say); the conclusion of A iii, 42, 5–6, where it is said of holy places, such as Monte Gargano, the site of the miracle of snow at Sta Maria Maggiore, etc, that 'there is much greater chance of being heard by God in those places consecrated to his cult, since the Church has so marked and dedicated them'; and especially the conclusion of A iii, 44, 5, where the later interpolation is quite obvious: 'I do not condemn—but rather approve—the custom of setting aside certain days for devotions, such as novenas (alternative reading: 'fasts') and other similar practices. . . . ' These texts appear to be, at the very least, retouched. Of course, we have no originals and know that the text has been frequently mangled and interpolated.

[216] A iii, 35, 1–6.

If God sometimes bestows more favours through one statue than through another, he does not do so because of its greater ability to produce this effect . . . but because the devotion of individuals is awakened more by means of one statue than the other.' According to John's explicit statement, this also applies to 'images of extraordinary grace'. The image in itself 'is no more than a painting'. God 'works miracles only because of the faith and devotion shown toward the saint represented'. Moreoever, 'experience teaches that if God grants some favours and works miracles, he does so usually through statues that are not very well carved or carefully painted or that are poor representations (*imagines non muy bien talladas ni curiosamente pintadas o figuradas*), so that the faithful will not attribute any of these wonders to the statue or painting'. Images of special grace may now and then seem to move, to change their expression, give signs or communicate words: all of this may be good and genuine, but it may just as well come from the devil.[217] Rich decoration of oratories and churches is indeed fitting, but not if the beauty of churches is loved in place of the beauty of God. People who treat the objects of worship without respect ought, of course, to be 'reproved very sharply', but so should those who 'carve so inexpertly that the finished statue subtracts from devotion rather than adds to it. Some artists, so unskilled and unpolished in the art of carving, should be forbidden to practise their art'. 'Still, what pertinence has this to the possessiveness, attachment and appetite you have in these exterior decorations?' Ought one not to think of the wrath of Yahweh, the wrath with which he looked down upon so many of the religious festivals of the people? They were celebrated in his honour, 'yet men sought only their own ends in them'.[218] Christ told the Samaritan woman that genuine prayer does not depend on the temple and the holy mountain. He himself used to pray in the still of the night, in lonely and barren places, 'which raise souls to God such as the mountains that are raised above the earth and usually barren of the objects that would provide recreation for the senses'.[219] God places little value 'on your oratories and other

[217] A iii, 36.
[218] A iii, 37–38.
[219] A iii, 39; A iii, 44, 4.

places consecrated for prayer'; what he desires is 'the living temple', the interior recollection of the heart, spiritual poverty.[220] Likewise, no one should tie himself down inwardly to a place in which he once received a grace from God. God is free of all that, and man too is meant to be free.[221]

The final criticisms of the *Ascent*, at which point it breaks off uncompleted (unless the conclusion has been lost), are directed against preaching. It shows best where John wants to place his affirmative and negative emphases. Without doubt the preacher is a 'means' that God employs to bring his Word home to men. But 'the force and efficacy of preaching depend entirely on the interior spirit'. No matter how well chosen his words or how sublime his thoughts, the preacher usually only obtains an effect 'proportionate to his own interior spirit. God's word is indeed efficacious of itself . . . yet fire also has power to burn but will not burn if the material is not disposed. And so a twofold disposition is required if a sermon is to achieve its effect: that of the preacher, and that of his hearer. And usually the effect is commensurate with the interior preparedness of the preacher.'[222] 'The holier the life of the preacher, in so far as we on earth can judge, the more abundant the fruit, no matter how lowly his style, poor his rhetoric, and plain the doctrine.' The eloquence of a preacher sounds in the ears *como una música concertada o sonido de campanas*, but 'it does not possess the power to raise a dead man from his sepulchre'.[223] Thus nowhere (in sharp contrast to the Byzantine theology of icons) is there any emphasis on a quasi-sacramental 'presence' in images, holy places and customs, ceremonies and parts of the liturgy. To prevent any magical abuse of the creaturely means of grace, John refers everything back to the great open freedom of the Spirit—of the Holy Spirit, the intermediary between Heaven and earth. And if one were to try to point out the primordial sacramental reality and efficacy of the incarnate Image of God, the Son, then John's answer would be: 'Our Lord was indeed a living image during his sojourn in this world; nevertheless, those who were faithless received no spiritual gain, even though

[220] A iii, 40.
[221] A iii, 42.
[222] A iii, 45, 2.
[223] A iii, 45, 1–4.

they frequently went about with him and beheld his wondrous works. This is why he did not perform many mighty works in his own country.'[224]

The one motif is constantly repeated: the true abode of beauty is contemplation, contemplation raised up above all limited, worldly forms, contemplation that is identical with faith, with the night, with love. Not in the subjective sense of an act of contemplation, but in the sense of the all-embracing reality of the God who communicates himself and the reality of his grace, of God's triune life infused into man (in the theological virtues). It is against the dark night's golden back drop of love, hope and faith that the finite forms are illuminated in their true and everlasting beauty. It is only when the lover longs for the unique beloved's eyes to open that his own eyes are opened to all of beauty's reflected splendour, which the beloved, through the gaze of his eyes, has brought to birth in the world. The communicating link between the world's beauty and the beauty of God is love of God, by which the soul is conformed to God and thus transformed in grace. Now the word *beauty* flows unceasingly from John's pen. It is as if he were intoxicated by it: '*Y vámonos a ver en tu hermosura*—and let us go forth to behold ourselves in your beauty. This means, that we should be like one another in beauty and that this occurs in your beauty, so that when one looks at the other, you alone appear in your beauty, and each sees the other in your beauty, which happens when you transform me into your beauty; hence I shall see you in your beauty, and you shall see me in your beauty, and I shall see myself in you in your beauty, and you shall see yourself in me in your beauty; and I will resemble you in your beauty, and you resemble me in your beauty, and my beauty shall be your beauty, and your beauty my beauty; wherefore I shall be you in your beauty, and you shall be me in your beauty, because your very beauty shall be my beauty.'[225]

[224] A iii, 36, 3.
[225] C 35, 2.

3. VALUE AND LIMITS

Considering the dizzying heights to which St John soars, we cannot avoid the question as to the validity of such criteria in the Church of Jesus Christ. Nowhere is one so aware of the dubiousness of norms which reduce all to the same level as in the thought of this man, who is nonetheless a Doctor of the Church. Where the unique one, Jesus Christ, is the absolute norm, consideration of what is average or democratic has no place. What it truly is to be a Christian one learns from him, and secondly, one learns it from the few, the very few who in faith and love have chosen him as the exclusive law of their existence and have remained faithful to that choice to the end. If one man in a hundred thousand were a norm in this sense, because in this one man Christ's grace and the demands of his Gospel could be seen with all humanly possible purity, this would not be an objection to the value of the norm.

Faith, hope and love for Christ (which, in turn, through Christ and in the Spirit, is love for the Father) become the one and only law of existence and John, as one of the *grands simplificateurs du monde*,[226] believed it was his duty to concern himself with this kind of fundamental ideal of Christian life. The question still remains, however, whether such an ideal could be put into practice in the way John believes necessary. He defines 'pure faith' in two ways. First, there is the negative sense, the elimination of every *figura*, every finite form, that faith, as faith in God and for God alone, transcends in its formal object. Then there is the positive sense, when he identifies the 'night of faith' with the night of contemplation, which as such represents an existential relationship with God, a state in which one is affected by God—in other words, an experience of God, albeit formless, whether negative (in the night or privation) or positive (in the dawn of eternal vision). In both definitions John is dependent on the great spiritual tradition—Evagrius, Macarius, Denys, Gregory, Bonaventure and (especially where the night is concerned) Walter Hilton.[227] For the first, negative

[226] See note 124.

[227] It matters little whether John was familiar with Hilton's doctrine directly or indirectly or whether there is just circumstantial affinity.

aspect we may really have to go back as far as Evagrius to find a similar radicalism—unless one follows Asín Palacios and looks for a connection with Sufism.[228] But for the second, positive aspect, it must be said that John goes beyond the great tradition the notion represents and turns toward the modern age; his emphasis is on his own experience, on the way to God he himself has pursued. It is this experience, superimposed on tradition, that leads John to make the enormous demands he does. The fact is, in Denys especially and his medieval commentators or modifiers, the philosophical foundation is so dominant that the reproach is constantly made against them that they taught a superficially Christianized neo-Platonism, that they laid down the steps to be followed in the soul's ascent to God according to an altogether abstract schema of the dialectical relationship between God and the world, between divine transcendence and immanence. Especially in Aquinas, Denys takes his place as a philosophical authority alongside Aristotle and Augustine; and in Nicholas of Cusa and the Platonists of Florence later on, he performs a similar service. In comparison with all of this, the philosophical background in St John of the Cross disappears or rather is fully absorbed in the personally 'experienced' night of faith and contemplation. The 'I' whose experience is recounted nowhere explicitly steps into view, but no less than for St Theresa it is the necesary presupposition and invisible point of reference for all his statements.

The two simplifications, the negative and the positive, will now be considered in detail.

1. The faith that loves and hopes is that infinite, divine power that allows and requires all finite figures, objective as well as subjective, to be surmounted. For the earthly man the surmounting is crucifying; for the heavenly man it means the freedom of love. Here the question arises as to the religious value of all the figures of revelation—above all, of the form of God incarnate; then of the Church as a visible institution of salvation, as the communion of saints; and of Scripture in its objective, multiform facticity. Does not this mysticism fly past the incarnate Christ as it plunges, without mediation, into the

[228] *Huellas del Islam* (Madrid, 1941).

furnace of triune love? Still more, is not the Church as a concrete community of love left behind? Is not God's configured Word irresistibly reduced to a single, superhuman, ineffable Word?

There can be no doubt whatsoever that the incarnate Son of God, or more specifically, the crucified Son of God, determines the whole mystical way of this man who carries the cross even in his name. For him everything depends on the call of Christ in the Gospel, which is, of course, immediately heard and understood in the most radical manner. 'Christ, our Lord, instructing us about this way of renunciation, stated, according to St Luke: "Whoever of you does not renounce all that he has cannot be my disciple." This statement is quite clear, for the doctrine the Son of Man came to teach is contempt of all things (*fué il menosprecio de todas las cosas*) that we may receive the gift of God's Spirit. So long as the soul fails to rid herself of these possessions, she is incapable of receiving God's Spirit to work its pure transformation.[229] This essential definition of Christianity, reduced in this form, is found everywhere.[230] It is a call to the Cross, as the programmatic Chapter 7 of the second book of the *Ascent* shows in words of steel. 'A man makes progress only through imitation of Christ. . . . No one goes to the Father except through him.' He is door, way, truth, life. In what sense? 'First, it is clear that during his life he died spiritually to the world of the senses, and that at his death he died naturally. He proclaimed during his life that he had no place whereon to lay his head. And at his death he had less. Second, at the moment of his death he was certainly annihilated (*aniquilado*) in his soul, without any consolation or relief.[231] He was therefore compelled to cry out, "My God, my God, why hast thout forsaken me?" This was the most extreme abandonment that he suffered in his life. And in this way (*y asi*) he accomplished the most marvellous work (*obra*) of his whole life, surpassing all the works and deeds and miracles that he had ever performed on earth or in Heaven, that is, he brought about the reconciliation

[229] A i, 5, 2.

[230] A ii, 6, 4 (Lk 14.33 again); A ii, 7, 4 (Mk 8. 34–35); A ii, 7, 6 (Mt 10. 39; John 12. 25).

[231] The words *segun la parte inferior* and *sensitivamente* may be the prudent interpolations of an editor.

of the human race with God through grace. The Lord achieved this, as I say, at the very moment in which he was most annihilated in all things': in his reputation before the men who mocked him, in his human nature by dying and with regard to the Father, who left him without consolation or help, 'forsook him so as to pay the full price of sin.' For this reason the verse from the psalm applies to him: *Ad nihilum redactus sum et nescivi.* 'Union with God does not consist in recreations, experiences or spiritual feelings, but in the one and only living, sensory and spiritual, exterior and interior, death of the Cross.'[232]

According to the *Ascent*, Book I, Chapter 13, the foundation of all spiritual life is 'the habitual desire to imitate Christ in all things' by 'mortification and renunciation of self for the love of Christ, who in his life on earth had no other gratification, nor desired any other, than the fulfilment of his Father's will, which he called his meat and food.' And this mortification begins with the active choice and preference of 'the more difficult' instead of 'the easier,' and 'the less pleasant' instead of the gratifying, of 'the unconsoling' instead of the consoling, of 'the lowest and most despised' instead of the higher and more precious—in short, of 'total poverty in all the things of this world.'[233] For so long as we live, the depths of the mystery of Christ cannot be plumbed.[234] Imitation takes place in humility, which knows very well, and never forgets, that I myself was 'the cause of the Passion and death of Christ',[235] that if 'the knife is raised above our head',[236] we should not feel ourselves to be innocent victims. It is sufficient that we succeed in 'losing ourselves completely for Christ's sake',[237] and that we 'choose for love of Christ all that is most distasteful, whether in God or in the world.'[238]

One of the most magnificent chapters in the *Ascent* (II, 22) shows from what perspective John makes this last statement. It is God the Father's address to the man who hankers after new and personal revelations and answers from God. The discourse proceeds as follows: 'I have already told you everything in my Word, who is my Son. I have nothing more to reveal, no

[232] A ii, 7, 8–11.
[233] A i, 13, 2–5; *cf.* C 3, 3 and 5.
[234] C 36, 3.
[235] Ep 10.
[236] Ep 9.
[237] C 20, 3.
[238] A ii, 7, 5.

further answer to give you, there is nothing to add to him. Fasten your eyes on him alone, because in him I have spoken and revealed everything. *Ipsum audite*.'[239] 'If you desire me to answer with words of comfort, behold my Son, obedient and subject to me racked in pain, and you will see how much he answers. If you desire me to declare some secret truths or events to you, fix your eyes on him, and you will discern hidden "in him the most secret mysteries and wisdom, the wonders of God. . . ." These treasures of wisdom and knowledge will be far more sublime, delightful and advantageous than what you want to know. The Apostle, therefore, gloried, affirming that he had made it plain that "he knew no other than Jesus Christ and him crucified." And if you should still seek other divine or corporal visions or revelations, behold him, become human, and you will encounter more than you imagined, because the Apostle also says, "In him the whole fulness of deity dwells bodily".'[240]

All this proves unequivocally that St John's mysticism is meant to be understood christocentrically, and only through Christ is it theocentric. It is not philosophical but theological, grounded in the imitation of Christ, and all the words of the Bible, of both Old and New Testaments, are arranged concentrically around the annihilation of the Word of God on the Cross. John is a great lover of the Bible, and he knows the Bible. He quotes it in a wonderfully personal way, with vigour and penetration, but his choice of quotations, especially from the Old Testament, is wholly determined by his existential experience of love's death on the Cross and by the imitation of Christ, in grace, that goes as far as the Cross (or its inspired prefigurations in the Old Covenant). Abraham's, Moses' and Elijah's encounters with God in the darkness of faith, the dereliction by God experienced by Job, Jeremiah, Ezekiel, Jonah and others, are placed at the centre.[241] The Bible is concerned with neither 'spiritual sense' nor 'allegory', but with the Cross of Christ; everything else proceeds from it or leads to it. 'In place of Israel St John of the Cross substitutes every "chosen" soul

[239] A ii, 22, 5.
[240] A ii, 22, 6.
[241] Jean Vilnet, 'Bible et Mystique chez St Jean de la Croix', *Études Carmélitaines* (1949).

whom God wants as his Bride. It is the same event, identical with the divine guidance.'[242] We will have to return to the pressing question of whether this selective arrangement of texts around the night of the Cross does not perhaps have a constrictive effect, so that the night of the Cross itself, in its existential reflection in the mystic, is taken as the object and standard.[243]

The authentic image of God in the world is the image of crucified love—nothing else. All the profusion of imagery in the *Spiritual Canticle* can only be explained and justified as the deployment of the 'hidden treasures' of this one image. John carved crucifixes, but more than that, he drew a little oval sketch in Indian ink, about five centimetres in diameter, to explain to one of his brethren the vision he had of the crucified in the chapel gallery. The sketch shows the hanging body with such staggering foreshortening that the technique alone 'presupposes long practice'.[244] The image only becomes comprehensible if we picture the body to ourselves hanging not vertically (as it usually does in representations of the cross) but downward by its hands and feet, with the crossbeams lying horizontally, downward into the darkness of God's night, the night of the world and the night of Hell.

> It is in full downward flight that Christ appears to John; a stupendous vertical movement hurls him down, like a rock, the head first and straining the chest behind it, the neck vertical, the nape of the neck bent over, the arms distended and dislocated, the shoulder blades arched. The face is hidden, only the nape of the neck, the hair falling down in front of his face, the cranium, the upper part of the back, the hip, are visible. The lighting is violent, cast from above. A certain brutality produces this effect, while the lines of the drawing are supple and soft. The work has two main features: the first appears to be imposed upon the artist, the other is his own contribution. What is imposed is the soaring vision, the apparition hurtling madly downward in the light, the divine body with specks of shadow, made of nerves rather than

[242] Vilnet, 111.

[243] '*Ainsi la Bible . . . ne se présentera dans la composition des traités que sous l'aspect exact et limité où elle est intervenue dans la propre expérience intérieure de leur auteur*' (Vilnet, 160).

[244] Florisoone, 95.

> bones. What is imposed is to be seen in the arms composed of wounded, painfully swollen tissue, the suppleness of the narrow chest, which appears to be in flight from the unyielding wood, to be trying to detach itself and throw itself onto the ground. Under the force of gravity the left wrist has been torn, and the nail has been reinserted into the swollen soft hand. The heart bleeds in a long blackish stream on to the rigid chest . . . John's own personal contribution is the sovereign allure of this vibrant sketch, full of intensity and at the same time almost relaxed, so delicately and with such quickness of touch has the artist worked. Artistic effectiveness is completely subordinated to the significance of the event. The impression almost of cruelty is revealed in an uncompromising anatomical representation (we must not forget that the young Juan de Yepes, at the age of twenty, was an orderly at the hospital . . . of Medina del Campo)'.[245]

Florisoone reflects on the opportunities John might have had, at the time the sketch was drawn (1572–1577 in Avila), of seeing imitations of Italian originals in vertical perspective: Michelangelo's *Last Judgment*, which was imitated by Spanish artists, the early works of Tintoretto (El Greco only appears later). Elements of pictures, or of their copies, that John had seen may well have entered into his vision and its depiction, for 'God speaks the language of time and place'; 'yet in power of dramatic expression and in technical skill St John of the Cross surpassed the innovations of Michelangelo, Correggio, Tintoretto and El Greco, remarkable enough though they are'.[246]

The sketch of the crucifixion is illuminating in many respects. First, it shows that John was no iconoclast, that his characteristic doctrine of transcending configured imagery must be understood not in the letter but in the spirit. Seen like that, it points forcefully toward the central image, which, in its exaltation, draws all other images to itself, to judge and adjust them. For St John of the Cross it is the only 'possible' image, while in St Theresa there are many sensible visions of the body of the risen Lord. According to John, who here relies on an

[245] *Ibid.* 98–99.
[246] *Ibid.* 104.

ancient Patristic view, Christ almost never appears personally.[247] And yet there is a third idea indicated by the image of the Cross with its almost devastating force: the solitude of the one who walks toward Christ by imitating him, and the impossibility of placing the work of imitation on the same level as the work of Christ. This may explain the remarkable lacuna in St John's thought, the yawning gap where the Church should be.

An almost inexplicable modesty or reserve prevents John from presenting the 'work' of contemplation in its social aspect, as Theresa does so ingenuously and as little Thérèse does even more ingenuously. For the Little Flower, the self-oblatory Carmelite is the 'heart of the Church', 'mother of souls', the drive wheel of the entire motive power of the Church. It is an integral part of the bridal-nuptial love of the soul for God that she places at the disposal of God, her one and only beloved, everything that she is and thereby everything she might be able to accomplish. She never even raises the question of whether what she is doing is significant or fitting for God, let alone *how* he employs and distributes what she places at his disposal. Of St John's apostolic prayer and oblation there is hardly anything to see. It does not even seep through in the 'Prayer of a Soul Taken with Love'.[248] This culminates in the jubilation of absolute possession of God in love, in which—in the *cognitio matutina* already mentioned to which an *amor matutinus* here corresponds—all the world belongs to the loving soul. 'With what procrastinations do you wait, my soul, since from this very moment you can love God in my heart? Mine are the heavens and mine is the earth. Mine are the nations, the just are mine and mine the sinners. The angels are mine, and the Mother of God, and all things are mine; and God himself is mine and for me, because Christ is mine and all for me. What do you ask, then, and seek, my soul?'

Even in the passage from the *Living Flame* we have already considered, where one would undoubtedly expect the argument to turn toward the apostolate, it is absent. 'Having God for its own, it can give him and communicate him to

[247] N ii, 23, 7.
[248] Silverio, 745.

whomever it wishes. Thus it gives him to its beloved, who is the very God who gave himself to it. By this donation it repays God for all it owes him, since it willingly gives as much as it receives from him.'[249] The omission may, of course, just reflect a profound intention on the author's part. But even then is it not rather strange, disturbing? Where, in the whole of John's work, is the neighbour? Where is the communion of saints? Where is the Johannine criterion for love of God: love of the brother? This is taken for granted and receives no special emphasis, just as the Church in all her visibility is taken for granted; it is not forgotten but presupposed and so does not need to be specially mentioned, because every Christian knows about it from the Catechism. But he has not sufficiently reflected on the other matter—the seriousness of the Cross, the exclusiveness of God's demanding love. And yet—why is the *image* of God and of Jesus Christ, the human Thou in its misery and hidden glory, not taken up into transcendence, into the wind of the Holy Spirit? Does John take sufficiently into account the *reality* of the images, the reality of the God who *descends*, who comes down into flesh and pain and death? For it is that same God who decrees that the images are valid, definitively valid, for John. Are we not rather too close to the ancient neo-Platonic aversion (radicalized by Evagrius) to forms and figures, the *typoi* and *morphai* and *eidê*, from which the soul must be freed in order to attain as a *nous katharos* the *gnôsis aeidês* and *aülos*, which can also be called *apatheia*, *praotês* and *agapê*.

2. The second identification leads to a similar crisis. Here it is the identification of faith and contemplation. In this, as we have seen, the notion of contemplation is associated with that of experience in a measure that far outstrips that of the Patristic and medieval periods—experience, of course, in a very special, critically purified sense: experience of the Absolute in the nonexperience of all finite content and activity and thus, in truth, the transcendence of natural psychological criteria of experience, of a positive as well as a negative kind. In active purification, first of all, positive experiences—pleasurable sensory, spiritual and religious feelings and impressions to

[249] L iii, 78.

which the soul, consciously or unconsciously, again and again becomes attached—are renounced. This is a correct analysis, as is the statement that, to begin with, the negative ways of penance are to be preferred. However, John deliberately puts the emphasis on the absence of pleasure, not out of a desire for yet more suffering, but for 'complete poverty in all worldly things'; not to increase the negative aspect, but so that everything, positive as well as negative, may become transparent in the unique, obscure light of God.[250] But then, on the plane of the Absolute, 'experience in the Absolute' and 'experience with the Absolute' return, transferred from the plane of accidents to the plane of substance. The substance of the creature is affected, feels the privation to its roots, experiences in the night the touches (*toques*) of God in the core of its being, is conscious of the divine, triune life and love awakening within itself. And this 'experience with God' has a history, an evolution of the simplest kind, and refers to the simplest facts of religious philosophy as expounded in the West by neo-Platonism: the way of purgation, illumination and union. In the Christian mysticism of St John it becomes a way that, more and more predominantly, God himself takes in company with the soul. It is a way in which all 'techniques' are surpassed by God's gracious action, while the soul's only active task is to remove obstacles, and the spiritual director's, to clear the way for God.

It is the way up Mount Carmel, the way of the exclusive, contemplative vocation. Thus the question posed at the beginning is posed again: is it one particular way alongside other Christian ways, or is it absolutely *the* way, which contains the experience of God that is normative for all? The question is as old as Christian spirituality. The answer is more difficult and nuanced than the one usually given, whether it be affirmative or negative. It will depend on whether the special experience upon which John's mystical doctrine is based is understood as typical and normative or just illustrative; it can at least scarcely be denied that for John it is both of these at the same time. He describes *his* way to God, his unique experience with God, but he also describes it, partly out of humility, partly with exultant

[250] A i, 13.

assurance, as *the* way *par excellence*. This, according to his schema, was the way of biblical man, the way of Augustine, of Francis of Assisi and of his sister Theresa. It can be argued (with Baruzi) that the four treatises do not consist of a series of self-contained stages, but rather that each in its own way contains the whole on different levels that are not logically commensurable (so that, for example, the *Spiritual Canticle* cannot be placed simply between the *Dark Night* and the *Living Flame*). Nevertheless, the internal coherence of the entire corpus is so great that, despite all the open-ended freedom it imparts, it appears as *the* way to God.

It is possible, of course—especially for the noncontemplatives in the Church—to pass through the great purgative night in piecemeal fashion over the course of years. However, the way in which John speaks of this possibility shows that it is precisely only a remote participation in the real thing.[251] At this stage we must question the identification of the theological virtues with experiential contemplation (however fundamentally and generally this is to be understood). The possible varieties of perfect faith and contemplation cannot be canonically determined by one single experience, and within this variety the various forms of active Christian life must be allowed to make their contribution. It is equally mistaken (John does not do it directly, but defenders of his system may be tempted to) to argue that the theological virtues are founded upon the hypostatic union of the God-Man and thus also upon the consciousness of God by Christ in his human nature, which can be considered, rightly, as the archetype of all contemplation of the Father (in the immediacy of the Night). Inasmuch as this archetype provides the ultimate Christian rationale for the way of the 'ascent of the Mount Carmel' (which is 'redemptive contemplation' directed at the Father), we must reverse what we said earlier, since the 'redemptive action' includes the *renunciation* of divine experience by the Son in *forma Dei*; it leaves it behind and, for the sake of the sinner's redemption, is content with the *schêma anthrôpou* (Phil 2.7), the condition of the 'ordinary' man, who in his believing, hoping and loving does

[251] N ii, I, I–2.

not possess the experiential element of the contemplation enjoyed by the chosen.

Christ, the archetype, in this way is beyond the ways of contemplation and action, and love can be perfect in both ways. If this is so, then the contemplative way of those few who are chosen for it enters the realm of the charismatic. Although such unique experience points the way to the Church, it is now seen as one charism in the economy of grace in the mystical Body, as little Thérèse, above all, perceives. This charism, like others, even more than others, has representative and thus normative value for the whole Body. To this extent, then, John's doctrine becomes normative for the whole Church, but analogically, not as literally as he himself wanted this norm to be understood. The charismatic aspect of John's experience (and thus its individuality) is clarified by its relation to the only ultimate and normative archetype—Christ. Thus we can distinguish several degrees of its possible relevance: (1) In so far as it gives religious actuality to the philosophical *analogia entis* on the highest plane of revelation, it is in the broadest sense normative for every religious man who seeks to realize existentially the relation of absolute being to relative being. There can and must be analogies here with the great forms of human religion. (2) In so far as it makes real, by way of example, the infused and transcendent character of the Christian theological virtues, John's doctrine is normative for every Christian, even the active. The exclusively contemplative way has the special mission of making visible, with a purity that can be observed ('contemplated'), the form of Christian life. (3) In so far as it bears witness to an especially exalted and pure realization of the contemplative way, this doctrine in a stricter sense can be a guiding star for the contemplative ways in the Church, provided always God is given the freedom to lead other souls on other paths and according to different rhythms; guiding stars such as, for example, the founders of the religious orders, those founts of charismatic life, must not be presented by their successors as imitable in the literal sense, and even less should they present themselves as such. In any case little Thérèse set Carmel free from such a dangerous obsession.

If this analogical value of St John's doctrine is valid in the

Church, then the aesthetic character of his work is even more prominent. For what he gives the Church in the deadly earnestness of his personal struggle and his consciousness of being taken seriously by God constitutes for it a simile, a parable, a poem. And John was absolutely right to present the didactic part of his work as an unsuccessful, defective commentary on his poems, which constitute his message in the proper sense in a way that prose cannot rival. If we trust and agree with the correctness of John's judgment of himself, then we must see that it is as a poet rather than as a prose writer that he is a Doctor of the Church. He thus refers in an original and profound manner to the character of the Word of God itself, which is not simple prose nor can adequately be translated into prose. No, it is in its simplicity, like the meaning contained in an inexhaustible symbol, that the fulness of the Godhead dwells bodily.

PASCAL

Pascal's lonely genius, which finally does not want to identify itself with any particular school of thought—*je suis seul*[1]—nevertheless links us with the many ways that find their meeting in him. He is a humanist in Erasmus's sense: as an enemy of Scholasticism and monkery (for him it is the Jesuits, for Erasmus it was the older orders), he marks out the same bold path between the primitive, evangelical and patristic tradition and modern knowledge; as Erasmus was one of the founders of modern philology, so is Pascal one of the founders of modern, exact, natural science; and as with Erasmus the same religious pathos binds together the two sides of his nature, so with Pascal the same religious sense of structure bridges the tension between an ascetic Augustinianism, which embodies for him the primitive ecclesiastical tradition, and exact, scientific research—that is what marks Pascal off in a decisive and exemplary way, from all that stems from Descartes' approach to philosophy which, in itself dualistic, has led to the modern schizophrenia between exact science and imageless inwardness. Pascal, clearly aware of the poles that have to be united, but just as clearly aware of the rising power of the demonic, is possessed of an insurmountable will to draw all together into a single structure and has his place, by virtue of his achievement, among the supreme figures of theological aesthetics. He belongs to the ranks of those acerbic, ardent spirits of the French baroque,

[1] *Lettres Provinciales* 17, 867. The works are cited by page number after the new one-volume edition of the *Oeuvres Complètes*, edited by Jacques Chevalier with a commentary (Bibliothèque de la Pléiade, 1954). The *Pensées* (=P) are cited after the same edition, but by the number in Chevalier's enumeration, to which the number in the Brunschwicg Edition (=B) is added [and also the number in the Lafuma Edition (=L), from the translation of which (by A. J. Krailsheimer, Penguin, 1966) the English version is taken—Translator].

We have rejected the *Discours sur les passions de l'amour* as inauthentic; the best refutation of the thesis of authenticity is in E. Wasmuth, *Pascal, die Kunst zu überzeugen* (1950), 139–160. Also the fragment on the theatre (Pensées 208, B 11 L 764); *cf.* Louis Lafuma, 'Mme de Sablé et les dangers de la Comédie', *Ecrits sur Pascal* (1959), 117–124.

who, as laymen, ventured to force the sheerly impossible into the unity of a single visible form: combining the early Christian and Stoic pathos of death, of renunciation, of the spirit's world-conquering power with the spirit's own imperial claim to form in the ideal of the 'honnête homme'—the shaped and rounded personality manifest in ethical and aesthetic attitude—in the art of living, in the structure of drama, of palaces, of the state, even of the Church, whose deepest forming energies and claims about form, often inadequately represented among the clergy, would be perceived and tended by these great masters of form. It was not for nothing that these, the war of the Huguenots in their blood still, had the elemental impulse not to become the counterreformation party, but to carry forward in themselves the strongest impulses of the opposition party in the Church's political struggle in a creative way, in whatever variations this harsh, often almost iconoclastic earnestness found expression in them: in the mysticism of sacrifice of the 'French school' of Bérulle and Condren (whose views Pascal on occasion adopted unreservedly[2]), in the harsh, Christian Stoicism of Corneille and finally in that dark and gloomy Augustinianism of Port Royal, which glimmers from the pictures of Philippe of Champaigne and into whose all-too-powerful wake Pascal was drawn, although in the end—objectively and temporally—he distanced himself from it: *Je suis seul . . . , je ne suis point de Port-Royal.*[3] It is the France of the time before the Peace of Nijmegen, fired with the consciousness of a spiritual mission for Christendom and culture in its totality, fired with a will to carve out a Christian form for which no sacrifice is too great, a France that will give the world a living proof that Christianity is the sacrifice and self-oblation of life, and only at this price can it claim to be the representation of the divine in the world. It is in this claim that Pascal transcends that constricted form of the Augustinian tradition that is associated with the name of Jansen. Or, to put it another way, it is much more important to show clearly how far in Jansenism, despite its narrowing, the greatness and breadth of

[2] The famous letter to Gilberte Périer and her husband on the death of his father, Etienne Pascal, written in the style of the ancient *consolatio*, renders exactly and in detail the doctrine of sacrifice of the French School; 490–501.

[3] *Lettres Provinciales* 17, 867. [I am alone . . . I do not belong to Port Royal.]

Augustinianism was sought, sighted and actually realized, than to nail Pascal to a condemned theological position and to derive from this the right to ignore him. Pascal comes to Port Royal from something of his own that is greater, and he finally passes beyond Port Royal to something of his own that is greater yet. Through the greatness he transcended both that party in the Church which had already been censured in his lifetime and which after his death was fiercely persecuted and finally, with the destruction of Port Royal in 1709, stamped out, and also that other party which he himself had so frontally attacked and exposed with a verve perhaps never seen in the Church since the days of Tertullian: the Society of Jesus, whose lax moral theory was as frequently and as fundamentally condemned by the Church as was Jansenism, and which received from Pascal a wound from which it had not completely recovered when it was suppressed a century later. The terrible, inexorable polemicist, who with his war of letters created the first masterpiece of modern French prose, raised himself, despite all the conflict, above both parties; according to him, everything hangs on enduring the tensions between the contraries: 'Both Jesuits and Jansenists are therefore wrong to conceal them; but the Jansenists more so, because the Jesuits have been better at professing both [opposites].'[4]

1. THE BASIC THEMES

1. Like all great creators of form Pascal strives to get back to the *source*. A letter, six years earlier than the Memorial, reveals this basic experience: God and the divine is the ever new. Worldly learning can be learnt once and for all and held in the memory.

> To hear [in Holy Scripture] that secret language, a language foreign to those who are foreign to Heaven, it is necessary that the same grace, which can alone give the first understanding, continue it and make it always present by imprinting it unceasingly in the hearts of the faithful to keep it alive forever, just as among the blessed, God continually renews their

[4] P 790 B 865 L 786.

> blessedness, which is an effect and a result of grace, and just as, too, the Church holds that the Father begets the Son continually and maintains the eternity of his essence by an effusion of his substance that is both without break and without end. Thus the continuation of the righteousness of the faithful is nothing else than the continuation of the infusion of grace and not a single grace that subsists forever; and it is this that teaches us perfectly the perpetual dependence on the mercy of God in which we find ourselves, since, were he to interrupt its flow by however little, we would necessarily run aground. In this predicament it is easy to see that one must continually make new efforts to acquire this continual newness of spirit, since one can conserve the former grace only by the acquisition of new grace, and that otherwise one would lose what one thought one was retaining, just as those who want to trap the light catch only darkness. . . . Without uninterrupted renewal one is not capable of receiving the new wine that is not poured into old vessels.[5]

In man's relation with God there is only an ever-new love which it is the essence of being a Christian to strive after and preserve alive. 'The children of God must not put limits to their purity or their perfection. . . : "Be ye therefore perfect, even as your Father who is in heaven is perfect." It is therefore an error, very prejudicial and very ordinary among Christians and even among those who make profession of piety, to persuade oneself that there is a certain degree of perfection that, once achieved, makes one safe and beyond which one need not pass; since any degree becomes bad if one remains there, and one can prevent oneself falling only by climbing still higher.'[6] Now one can understand the acceptance of Condren's theory of sacrifice, according to which Christ presents before the Father 'an everlasting and continuous sacrifice', which is certainly offered on earth, but which is eternally consumed in the heavenly fire of the resurrection and the glory.[7] One can further understand the evangelical zeal to get back beyond all established and settled forms and 'uses' to primitive Christianity, which is evidenced in his burning essay, 'Comparison of the Christians of the First Ages with Those of Today.' At that time Christians had to

[5] Letter 4 (5 November 1648), 488.
[6] Letter 3 (1 April 1648), 485–486.
[7] Letter 5 (17 October 1651), 493–494.

realise the leap out of the world into the kingdom of God existentially in order to preserve sacramental baptism, whereas after the introduction of infant baptism any taking seriously of the demand that baptism makes is put off until later, is regarded as secondary and is often forgotten altogether.[8] One can understand above all the bitter struggle against Jesuit casuistry, which was basicaly concerned with a moral minimum, whereas for Pascal to be a Christian was to be concerned with the maximum. 'I will allow him no rest either in himself or in another, so that with no place to settle or rest . . .',[9] so a fragment begins. The casuists, who sought to allow in the practice of the confessional as much as was feasible, even what appeared to the undistorted consciences of the faithful as already a serious failure, and in their excesses went so far as to dispense from the love of God, to describe loving contrition as 'an obstacle rather' and then to set forth the attrition due to fear as sufficient even if there is no spark of love in it, to describe the commandment to love as a 'painful duty', a 'heavy and wearisome burden' that Christ has performed in our stead in the New Testament and which is replaced by the receiving of the sacraments[10]—such casuists seem to Pascal like the false teachers of the last days. It is 'a total reversal of the law of God, it attacks the very heart of piety, takes away the spirit that gives life and says that the love of God is not necessary to salvation. It goes so far as to pretend that the benefit that Jesus Christ brought into the world was to dispense from the love of God! Such is the height of impiety. The price of the blood of Jesus Christ was to obtain for us a dispensation from loving him. . . . Here is accomplished the mystery of iniquity.'[11]

The opposition comes to the surface in the Augustinian ethic, which measures everything by the either-or *caritas* and *cupiditas* as the final ethical criterion; in consequence a natural ethic that

[8] *Opuscules* V, 555–559.

[9] P 332 B 419 L 464 (trans. slightly modified).

[10] *Lettres Provinciales* 10, 776–778.

[11] *Ibid.*, 778. In the same eschatological tone, the justification, written by Pascal, for the protests of the Paris clergy against casuistry; above all the 'Cinquième écrit des curés de Paris' (928–938) and the 'Projet de Mandement', found among his remains (938–945).

takes no account of the orientation of an act towards the ultimate source of the divine love is from the outset determined by *cupiditas*, sinful self-love, as Pascal discloses. 'While the casuists replace the precepts of Scripture, which oblige us to relate all our actions to God, with a brutal permission to relate them all to ourselves . . . they fan the flame of concupiscence and put out the love of God.'[12] What Pascal finally holds against the Jesuits is the way they have of 'accommodating the precepts and rules of Jesus Christ to the interests, the pleasures and the passions of men',[13] which is meant to accredit the Church and especially the Society of Jesus among men—*autrement ils nous quitteraient*[14]—just what Dostoyevsky attributed to his 'Grand Inquisitor'. 'What is the relation, Father, between this teaching and that of the gospel?'[15] Pascal demands either a fundamental reform of the Jesuits or their suppression,[16] for it seems to him that they have departed completely from the attitude of their founder.[17]

The return to the source that Pascal seeks is not only a return to the patristic sources, but a return to the life of Jesus and through the undistorted facts of that life to the mystery of the suffering love of God. The first is served by the 'Outline of the life of Jesus Christ' that presses through all the veils of theological speculation to the basic phenomena and thereby knows that 'such a holy life . . . can be written only by the same spirit as brought about the birth [of Jesus]';[18] this spirit is then also necessary if the historical form is to be caught sight of. So Pascal accompanies any of the enumerated 'facts' with an interpretative contemplation: the cry of dereliction from the Cross, for example, that can be understood only soteriologically; or at the time of Christ's resurrection, the resurrection of the bodies of the saints which 'are raised in eternal glory' as witnesses and harbingers of the general

[12] 'Factum pour les curés de Paris', 908.
[13] *Ibid.*, 911.
[14] *Lettres Provinciales* 6, 720.
[15] *Ibid.*, 10, 772.
[16] 'Cinquième écrit des curés de Paris', 935.
[17] *Lettres Provinciales* 13, 817.
[18] *Abrégé de la vie de Jésus-Christ*, 626.

resurrection of the dead; or the marks of the wounds in the body of the Risen Lord, which remain displayed forever before the Father.[19] This way into the centre of the fact, which is at the same time the mystery of all history, is completed in the 'mystère de Jésus', of which more will be said here.

Such a return to the source leads finally to the ever-recurring closeness, indeed identity, between death and the end of the world. Pascal, who in his life was always sick and who died young, lived a life oriented toward the end of the world, and this feeling for life is expressed in his 'Prayer for a Right Use of Sickness': 'Grant that I may consider this sickness as a form of death, separated from the world, deprived of the objects to which I am attached, alone in your presence, so that I may implore of your mercy the conversion of my heart.' 'I praise you, my God, and will praise you all the days of my life, because you have been pleased to give me, for my own benefit, a foretaste of that dreadful day . . . on which you will consume Heaven and earth and all creatures that are in them . . . by removing all things from me by the weakness to which you have reduced me.'[20] Similarly in the treatise on 'The Conversion of the Sinner', which is probably correctly attributed to Pascal, and which depicts the way into love as an insight into not only the transience of things but into their 'having already passed away' and a breaking up of the earthly world.[21] Above all, the letters to Mlle de Roannez emphasize the thought, which he introduces right at the beginning: 'Because everything that happens to the Church happens to each individual Christian', what the Lord prophesied about the end of the world must be applied to the conversion of man to Christ: with the old man the old world as a whole perishes, with the temple the 'reprobate' is cast down in dust and ashes, no stone remaining on another.[22] And as the last judgment is the 'shaking of the universe', so there is in every conversion the 'universal shaking of the person'; only the merits of Christ, who on the Cross took upon himself for our sakes the eternal punishment, prevent this day of judgment

[19] *Ibid.*, 649, 650, 653.
[20] *Ibid.*, 606–607.
[21] *Sur la conversion du pécheur*, 549.
[22] First letter to Mlle de Roannez, 505–506.

on earth from being the beginning of eternal dissolution.[23] All these themes taken together already lead into a second, penetrating vision into the first causes, something peculiar to Pascal that he occasionally expresses in Platonic language, but which, as will be shown, has a structure that is quite other.

2. Pascal, in contrast to Descartes the thinker, is essentially a 'Seer'. The famous fragments on the 'thinking reed', on thought (*pensée*) as man's dignity and distinguishing characteristic,[24] in no sense contradict this, for the question is what Pascal means by thought. The first of Brunschwicg's fragments, that on the distinction between the mathematical and the intuitive mind (*l'esprit de géométrie et l'esprit de finesse*), makes this quite clear:

> With the intuitive mind, the principles are in ordinary usage and there for all *to see*. There is no need to turn our heads, or strain ourselves: it is only a question of good sight, but it must be good . . . one needs very clear *sight* to see all the principles as well as an accurate mind to avoid drawing false conclusions from known principles. All mathematicians would therefore be intuitive if they had good sight . . . and intuitive minds would be mathematical if they could adapt their sight to the unfamiliar principles of mathematics. . . . The reason why mathematicians are not intuitive is that they cannot see what is in front of them: for, being accustomed to the clear cut, obvious principles of mathematics and to draw no conclusions until they have clearly seen and handled their principles, they become lost in matters requiring intuition. . . . The thing must be seen all at once, at a glance. . . .[25]

Those who are devotees of the mathematical mind cannot see things in a single glance, '*voir d'une vue*'.[26]

These two ways of thinking, the one starting from clearly perceived principles, the other seeing things as a whole, are at first simply juxtaposed without any evaluation. Yet for Pascal the power of insight soon asserts its preeminence, as it is this that has the power to perceive causes behind things. 'All these people saw the effects but did not see the causes. In comparison with

[23] Ninth letter, 518.
[24] P 264 B 347 L 200; P 263 B 365 L 756.
[25] P 21 B 1 L 512.
[26] P 23 B 3 L 751.

those who have discovered the causes, they are like those who have only eyes compared to those who have minds. For the effects can, as it were, be felt by the senses, but the causes can be perceived only by the mind. And, although these effects can be seen by the mind, this mind can be compared to that which sees the causes as the bodily senses may be compared to the mind.'[27] There are three levels, therefore, the middle one of which is, seen from below, between the (relatively) perceiving mind and, seen from above, the relatively unperceiving senses. And with this one has already attained an insight into the heart of the *Pensées*, the fragment that draws the whole work together, the fragment on the three orders—Bodies-Mind-Charity—and the values that are realised in each order: 'All the splendour of wordly greatness lacks lustre for those engaged in pursuits of the mind. The greatness of intellectual people is not visible to kings, rich men, captains. . . . Great geniuses have their own power . . . they are recognised not with the eyes but with the mind, and that is enough. Saints have their power, their splendour . . . and do not need either carnal or intellectual greatness. . . . They are recognised by God and the angels. . . . With what great pomp and marvellously magnificent array Jesus came in the eyes of the heart, which perceive wisdom!'[28] Visible to the senses, to the mind, to the heart enlightened by love, but in each case visible on a new level! But if the things of the mind are hidden and remain dark to sense, and if the things of the love of God are hidden and remain dark to the mind, then the glory that the enlightened heart beholds is no other than that of love—the glories of the mysteries and humiliations of the divine love, and therewith the glories of the hidden one and the hiddennesses of the glory. But how can one see 'the presence of a God who hides himself'? All Pascal's interpretative skill is given to the question, the whole secret of his person is a response to it, the unveiling of which can take place only gradually. For the moment we have to be satisfied with the assertion that man, as he now is, is granted only a veiled vision, but still a real vision: 'He may not see nothing at all, nor may he see enough to think that he

[27] P 452 B 234 L 577.
[28] P 829 B 793 L 308.

possesses God, but he must see enough to know that he has lost him. For, to know that one has lost something, one must see and not see. . . .'[29]

This form of vision is for Pascal so essential that having been dissolved at one level it appears again at another; at every level there is a seeing in not-seeing, a true seeing that pressupposes a not-seeing, a seeing as a unity of things that are equally seen to be irreconciliable, a seeing 'of two situations' that are mutually exclusive and yet which 'one must know equally, if one is to see the truth',[30] or, more exactly, a seeing of two opposites 'that cannot exist alone because of their deficiencies, nor be united because they are contradictory, and which therefore destroy and annihilate one another in order to give place to the truth of the gospel—for it is that which reconciles opposites by an art wholly divine'.[31] Only in theology is the otherwise undemonstrable demonstrable, and therefore it is 'the centre of all truths . . . , because it embraces so visibly [*visiblement*] all truths that exist in [mutually exclusive] opinions. So I do not see how anyone can refuse to follow it.'[32] But this highest form of seeing, which contemplates the highest manifestation of divine art, does not simply transcend matters that are purely unintelligible, as, for example, concepts that destroy one another in a purely dialectic way; rather, it rests on deeper orders, at bottom on the science of bodies, geometry, which was always a form of seeing in not-seeing. Pascal's strange battle for the 'mathematical [or geometric] mind' against the abstractly logical mind is concerned precisely with this. The school logic against which he fought was a galimatias of mere abstractions, a deduction for principles not really perceived, which could not therefore see in its deduction the operation that it performed and so could mediate no fruitful knowledge. 'One must therefore ask how the thought exists in the mind of the thinker. . . . I would therefore ask of reasonable men if the proposition: "Matter is naturally and insuperably incapable of thought"; and that other, "I think, therefore I am", are really the same in the

[29] P 602 B 556 L 449.
[30] *Entretien avec M. de Saci*, 571.
[31] *Ibid.*, 572.
[32] *Ibid.*, 573.

mind of Descartes and that of Augustine, who said the same thing twelve hundred years before.' It is of course possible that Descartes too, without having 'taken it over' from Augustine, had really coined these sentences, 'for I know what a difference there is between simply writing something down without long and extended reflection and perceiving [*apercevoir*] in a saying a wonderful chain of consequences'. 'For one will say something spontaneously, without understanding its excellence, while another will grasp a marvellous chain of consequences, which leads us to say rashly that it is not in both cases the same saying. . . . The same thoughts sometimes develop quite differently in the mind of another than they did in the mind of the one who first thought them: infertile in their natural soil, they blossom when transplanted. But more often it comes about that a good mind produces himself from his own thoughts all the fruit of which they are capable, and that later others, having heard them esteemed, borrow them and deck themselves out with them, but without understanding their real excellence.'[33] For his apology Pascal frequently gathered material from secondary sources—from Montaigne, from the *Pugio fidei* of the Spaniard, Raymond Martin, et cetera, but he was quite clear that this constituted no objection to his own original vision and insight. 'Let no one say that I have said nothing new; the arrangment of the material is new. In playing tennis both players use the same ball, but one plays it better.'[34] Pascal's dexterity is of such an order that he not only plays with the greatest precision of each of the three levels of geometry, of mind and of the genius of love, but he also trained himself in the precision appropriate to mathematics and natural science as such, so as to attain that quite other precision appropriate to the realm of being and to the Christian realm. So he says that those who can 'see clearly [*verront clairement*]' the problems of spatial extension can therefore consider [*regarder*] their situation in the whole realm of being, and through this achieve self-knowledge and learn to value themselves at their own worth.[35]

3. There is yet another theme that must be considered before

[33] *De l'art de persuader*, 599–600.

[34] P 65 B 22 L 696.

[35] *De l'esprit géométrique*, 591.

any more detailed analysis is done, even though this theme appears to belong to Pascal's intellectual formation: his introduction to the world view of *Augustine*. Pascal's theology will always be associated with Jansenism, and historically that is right. As a lay theologian, first in Rouen through two disciples of Saint Cyran and later in Port Royal through Nicole and Arnauld, he received his initiation into a theology and spirituality from the dark side of which he cannot be abstracted. Of this his 'Writings on Grace' give proof enough, for despite their attempt to see the Augustinian-Jansenist doctrine of grace as a middle way between Calvinism on the one side and a Molinist Pelagianism on the other, they cannot shake themselves free of the constricting effect of Jansenism, which took over and developed only a completely one-sided Augustine. The way the first of the writings on grace begins with the 'dogma'—'*IL EST CONSTANT, qu'il y a plusieurs des hommes damnés et plusieurs sauvés*',[36] makes it amply clear how much the very manner in which the question is posed remains stuck in the context of the Middle Ages and the Reformation.

But there is quite another question, and one too rarely asked: how far did Pascal, with his remarkable gift for grasping the nature of great spiritual figures, achieve his intuition into the fundamental structure of Augustine's doctrine despite the constrictive teaching of Port Royal, and how far does this intuition, once it has been achieved, correspond to his own innermost aspirations? How far then does Pascal himself represent the original, creative tradition of Augustine? How much Pascal had read of the original text is uncertain but relatively unimportant, because already the many citations from Augustine in his writings show how much he was able, from fragments, to make out the spirit of the whole.[37] Jeanne

[36] *Op. cit.*, 948 (Pascal's underlining). [It is unshakably true that some men are damned and some are saved.]

[37] The following are cited in the Pensées alone: sermo 141 (*quod curiositate cognoverunt, superbia amiserunt* [what they knew through curiosity, they lost through pride]: P 5 B 543 L 190); ep. 48 (49) (on the use of force in religion: P 9 and B 185–186 L 172, 591); *de Civ. Dei* 21.10 (on the impossibility of grasping the connection between the soul and the body: P 84 B 72 L 199); ep. 120 (on the reasonableness of acquiescence in faith: P 462 B 276 L 983); *de Gen. contra*

Russier's intensive research into the sources of Pascal's theory of faith,[38] like so much work in the field, examines only the literature of Port Royal, where the parallels are so many that Pascal's originality seems to appear only in a few nuances. That may be so if one looks at the problems one by one under a microscope, but if one stands back and takes an overall view, the picture changes in important respects.

Here we can only mention in passing the decisive features of the spiritual relationship of the two world pictures. *Le cœur* (in contrast to *esprit, raison*) can be understood only in the light of the Augustinian *cor*, and not at all as pointing to a theology of feeling;[39] *cœur* is *sensorium* for the whole (the principles), the religious, for God[40]—whence the heart, guided by God (*inclina cor meum*),[41] made upright and ordered toward God (*cor rectum*),[42] whence the demand to return into the heart (*redire ad cor*), whence the definition of faith as *Dieu sensible au cœur*.[43] But only God can turn the heart to himself, only God can give to it *caritas*, the love of God. If the heart does not love God, then it loves itself and relates all its values to self-love, *cupiditas*. Theology therefore must essentially be *confessio*: conversation with God as the gracious Thou, who before all else gives with love the true knowledge of the Thou. Theology is necessarily

Manich. (on the six ages and their respective beginnings: P 549a B 655 L 283); *de Doctr. Christ.* (on the meaning of Scripture that can only be ascertained from Scripture itself: P 550 B 900 L 251); *de Civ. Dei* 11.22 (on the light of the Scriptures that is sufficient to enlighten the elect and blind the reprobate: P 582 B 578 L 236); *de Civ. Dei* 22.9 (on the essential role of miracle: P 625 B 812 L 169); *Enarr. in Ps 137* (for the doctrine on Jerusalem and Babylon and the meaning of the river of Babylon: P 696–697 B 458–459 L 545, 918). To that add a quotation from Augustine that has not been verified in P 659 B 513 L 930 for the Jansenist doctrine of grace, and many quotations in the letters and the writings on grace.

[38] *La foi selon Pascal*, 2 vols. (1949).

[39] *Ibid.*, 153f.

[40] P 478–479 B 281–282 L 155, 110.

[41] The verse of the psalm continually cited by Augustine (Ps 118 (119).36); *cf.* P 470 B 252 L 821; P 835 B 284 L 380; P 840 B 287 n. 2 L 382. [Incline my heart.]

[42] *Cf.* P 600 B 737 L 793; *cf. Vie de Pascal* by Gilberte Périer, 14. [An upright heart.]

[43] P 481 B 278 L 424. [God perceived by the heart.]

dialogic and existential.[44] The anti-Pelagian incapacity to attain to grace and love of oneself controls the structure of all that follows; it demands the radical reduction of ethics—personal ethics just as much as social and political ethics—to the two principles of *caritas* and *cupiditas*. Personal history and the history of the world is divided into the two cities: the city of God and the earthly city (*civitas Dei*, *civitas terrena*). The origin of this (anti-Manichaean) dualism must be explained in terms of the original fall of the human heart from God and of its incapacity to remove from below the difference in levels between the heavenly kingdom and the earthly kingdom. But because the earthly kingdom is only to be built up out of the elements of God's good creation (which elements carry from their creation his image and likeness), the *civitas terrena* must also be an image and likeness of the kingdom of Heaven, but outside it—that is, outside *caritas*. The relationship of the kingdom of God to the kingdom of the world can be determined only dialectically from the two elements: estrangement (fall) and image/likeness. Therefore the genuine dramatics of existence, its historicality, lie much less in the historical, horizontal sequence of the ages than in the vertical distention of the 'conditions' (*katastaseis*, as Origen and his school would say) of the heart between pristine state, the state of sin and redemption and the final state.

Thus one of the master keys for any understanding of Pascal, is the Augustinian *civitas dei* (not its Jansenist oversimplification, but an idea purely Augustinian in its structure), taken with the doctrine of the two states in the *Enarrationes*, which are cited so centrally in the *Pensées*.[45] Not even the position of Israel between

[44] P 602 B 556 L 449: 'The God of Abraham, the God of Isaac, the God of Jacob, the God of the Christians is a God of love and consolation; he is a God who fills the soul and heart of those whom he possesses; he is a God who makes them inwardly aware of their wretchedness and his infinite mercy, who unites himself with them in the depths of their soul, who fills them with humility, joy, confidence and love, who makes them incapable of having any other end but him.' P 102 B 536 L 99: 'Man carries on an inner dialogue with himself which it is important to keep under proper control. *Corrumpunt mores bonos colloquia prava*. [Evil communications corrupt good manners—1 Cor 15.33]. We must keep silence as far as we can and only talk to ourselves about God, whom we know to be true, and thus convince ourselves that he is.'

[45] *Cf.* n. 38. T. Spörri, *Der verborgene Pascal* (1955), has (147) referred to the significance of the *Civitas Dei*.

pagans and Christians can change anything essential in the dualism of figure and reality. Israel is prominent only in so far as it is a divinely appointed figure of Christ, and in that the dialectic is only intensified, reflecting the reality more exactly, but just for that reason more clearly revealing the lack (of grace and love). And because Israel is the divinely determined figure and foreshadowing of Christ, the New Covenant is already hidden among the pictures of the Old Covenant: the *civitas Dei* has existed on earth since the time of Abel, and Pascal proves in an exactly similar way the *perpétuité* of the true religion of love,[46] and so the Jewish dialectic between the image and the truth of love becomes for him an essential piece of the apology. The strange thing is that there can be a *figure de liberté* without true freedom,[47] a state of affairs on the whole achieved by the earthly state. The analyses of secular ethics, which in the social realm appear to border on Machiavellianism—where the power of justice cannot be enforced, then at least the justice of power should hold sway!—do not go ideologically beyond Augustine. But in the dialectic of the *katastaseis* there is found something that with Augustine, as with Pascal, can be called the 'method of immanence': the analysis of human existence in its concrete historicality as the place, or at any rate the starting point, of a theology of revelation. Man's not being in himself (as *divertissement* and *cor inquietum*), the way the mind has fallen under the powers of deception, of the senses, of imagination, of custom, and of all earthly vanities—all this is good Augustinianism. But it is also the relativisation of philosophy by the higher criterion of truth found in the illumination of grace; no thought and no ascetic-mystical practice can offer a way of redemption. Augustine, like Pascal, emphasises the vicious circle between gnosis, pride (*superbia*) and the darkening of the mind. Truth is—again a phrase from the Psalms—*adhaerere Deo* (cleaving to God), which is the beauty, ever ancient and ever new.[48] The schema, truth-image, reveals itself finally, accord-

[46] P 771–777 B 613–614, 616–617, 646, 851–852 L 280–282, 390, 573, 859, 903.

[47] P 569 B 683 L 268.

[48] '*Elle implore de sa miséricorde les moyens d'arriver à lui, de s'attacher à lui, d'y adhérer éternellement. Toute occupée de cette beauté si ancienne et si nouvelle pour elle.*

ing to Augustine, as the formula for the relationship between God and the creature, between absolute being and never-absolute becoming, which latter is continually held to be, as compared with God, merely unreality and untruth—an oriental and Platonic comparison. The young Augustine had passed through what Pascal calls Pyrrhonism, something which deeply influences both systems. If Augustine the philosopher saves himself from universal doubt by means of his theory of intuition and illumination, there remains Augustine the existential theologian of, say, the *Enarrationes in Psalmos*, tuned to that pitch which echoes purely in one of Pascal's fragments: 'Everything here below is partly true, partly false. Essential truth is not at home here for it is wholly pure and wholly true. Such mixture dishonours it and reduces it to nothing. Nothing is purely true, and so nothing is true in the sense of pure truth.'[49] Both Augustine and Pascal see the abyss that the analogy of being opens up between the qualities of eternal and of creaturely truth. And for Pascal, whose image of God is intended consciously to bear purely biblical traits and not those of the 'God of the philosophers', the Augustinian doctrine of illumination is forbidden at the levels of nature and philosophy as a bridging operation. For him, who derives his philosophical descent not from Plato and Plotinus but from Epictetus and Montaigne, the bridge over the gulf of the analogy of truth can only be built by the supernatural grace of the free, electing and reprobating God. While Descartes continues and establishes anew the line of the Augustinianism of Illumination and the Ideas, Pascal (in this closer to the Reformers) finds his point of departure in the Augustine of free grace and *caritas*, and

. . .': *Sur la conversion du pécheur*, 552. [She begs of his mercy the means by which to reach him, to be joined to him, to cleave there eternally. Completely absorbed in this beauty, so ancient and so new for her. . . .]

[49] P 228 B 385 L 905. *Cf.* too the passage crossed out by Pascal in P 438 B 434 L 131: 'Who will unravel such a tangle? This is certainly beyond dogmatism and scepticism, beyond all human philosophy. Man transcends man. Let us then concede to the sceptics what they have so often proclaimed, that truth lies beyond our scope and is an unattainable quarry, that it is no earthly denizen, but at home in Heaven, lying in the lap of God, to be known only in so far as it pleases him to reveal it. Let us learn our true nature from the uncreated and incarnate truth.'

therefore continues in the Augustinianism of the Hiddenness of God and the Night of the Heart, in which only the light of the Cross of Christ still shines.[50] But while here the divergence between Augustine and Pascal begins to open up, the consequences of which for theological aesthetics will be shown to be of great importance, the two are still close to one another in the realm of aesthetics in the narrower sense, for the beautiful is something that is found for the young Augustine wholly in the pattern and play of numbers, and indeed in a doctrine of an ordered system of numbers rising from matter to the soul; something that is, of course, found again as the foundation of any doctrine of the beautiful in the Pascal of geometry and scientific experiments, certainly without any conscious dependence on Augustine, but strikingly parallel to him and to the whole Pythagorean tradition. And for both the completed pattern of a Christian aesthetic must oscillate between the poles of the beauty of number and the beauty of grace as this is illuminated by the God who elects and rejects in a way beyond our understanding.

2. THE FIGURE IN THE INFINITE

In noticing the themes—a return to the sources, a graduated vision, an Augustinianism of figure (as creaturely and sinful form)—we have simply gathered the elements and have not attempted to put them together to form a structured world. If we are to perceive Pascal's unique achievement, we must consider again his position in intellectual history. He finds himself caught between modern science, rapidly and powerfully developing, and the thinking of the Reformers and the Jansenists, which is entirely governed by faith. What is missing from both poles is the unifying centrepiece of the philosophy of being. Pascal, schooled in his father's hostility to Scholasticism, falls irretrievably into the harsh dualism so

[50] E. Przywara, *Augustinus, Die Gestalt als Gefüge* (1934), Introduction, 42–53. [Reprinted (the introduction only) as *Augustinisch: Ur-haltung des Geistes* (1970), 45–49.]

characteristic of the future: the dualism between exact science and supernatural piety. In the interests of purity of method, both seem to demand the renunciation of philosophy. What might in spite of that bring them together is something handed down from the time of the troubadours and from Dante and taken up again by the humanists: the ancient ideal of the *cor gentile*, nobleness of the heart, of *cortesia*, of the *honnête homme*.[51] It is the period when the last great wave of Platonism has ebbed away and a new Stoic humanism holds sway, a humanism promoted by Justus Lipsius and du Vair, popularised though not approved of by Montaigne, and taken up by the great dramatists of France as well as by the theatre of the Jesuits.[52] 'Reticence, proportion, poise, *savoir faire* and *savoir vivre*, all that in unity and in accordance with law, restrained passion without emphasis, ordered according to the heroic, but the heroic only thinkable when it is revealed in the beautiful . . .: that is the aesthetic discipline that lies as the roots of the age. Ethics and aesthetics seek for once to be in complete agreement, even if they can never entirely succeed.'[53] This 'Stoic' anthropology, which for Pascal occupies the central position where earlier philosophy had held sway, he develops within the range of expression that is characterised by the opposite yet united poles of Epictetus and Montaigne. In conversation with M. de Saci he ingeniously characterises these extremes as dogmatism and scepticism, and also as anthropological optimism and pessimism, and they are for him as it were the nursery of Christian existence. It is a picture of man, contemplated with Christian eyes and filled from afar with Christian substance, which in its way contains within itself much latent philosophy; which through its ethical-aesthetic form, through its splendour and its worth, is the place from which Pascal forces into an astonishing unity a world that, under the force of dualism, is disintegrating into the here and the hereafter. It is a form made

[51] M. Magendie, *La Politesse mondaine et les théories de l'honnêteté en France au 17e siècle de 1600 à 1660* (Paris, 1925).

[52] Still fundamental: Léontine Zanta, *La renaissance du Stoïcisme au 16e siècle* (1914).

[53] Carl J. Burckhardt, 'Der Honnête Homme', in *Gestalten und Mächte* (1941), 80.

visible in man of a latent, lived philosophy, which allows Pascal in the structure of the *Pensées* to dispense with the metaphysical proofs of the existence of God in a quite offhand manner, so that almost playfully it is left open whether they are valid in themselves or not; it is enough that they lack the existential power of attraction[54] that Pascal requires of them. His aim is not to lead his reader from an abstract finitude to the absolute, but from an exact understanding of man's situation and condition to the living God: *anthropologia ancilla theologiae christianae.*

All this helps to explain whence, despite the disappearance of philosophy, a concept of sufficient metaphysical power could develop that could embrace the disintegrating parts of human existence and bind them into unity. The form that must be seen and which Pascal seeks to make visible is at its core man himself, who from his transitory position at the centre can look down and espy the scientific form, but who can also, looking up in faith, transcend himself and attain to the form—of the God-man—that makes him comprehensible to himself for the first time in his impossible middle position and therefore raises him up so that he can catch sight of himself. Therefore all orders have, in their basic form, a measure, and with it a certain finitude, to destroy which would be lacking in objectivity and, in consequence, unscientific, even though it were done in the name of 'the spirit of pure science': '*Ecrire contre ceux qui approfondissent trop les sciences,*' (as Descartes wrote).[55] Any tendency in searching out the origins of things to lose sight of or to dissolve the form arouses Pascal's deep suspicion: '[Man is] a middle point between all and nothing, infinitely remote from an understanding of the extremes . . . equally incapable of seeing the nothingness from which he emerges and the infinity in

[54] P 5–6 B 543, 243 L 190, 463; P 366 B 242 L 781; P 728 B 549 L 191; P 730 B 547 L 189; P 602 B 556 L 449.

[55] P 193 B 76 L 553. [Write against those who probe science too deeply.] *Cf.* P 262 B 340 L 741, where the limitations of the adding machine are pointed out: it certainly appears to have more intelligence than the beasts, but it, like the beasts, can do nothing of its own will—from which one can add that Pascal does not agree with Descartes' mechanistic theory of animals. This is more important than might be thought, for it is in the realm of animal life that it is decided whether a philosophy can conquer not only matter and intelligence but also the forms of life that are transitional between the two.

which he is engulfed. What else can he do, then, but perceive some semblance of the middle of things . . . ?'[56] And so the method of proof cannot run in a straight line, but is essentially circular: 'For what we are trying to prove always seems obscure, and what we use for the proof seems clear; for when we put forward something to be proved, we first imagine that it must therefore be obscure, whereas the thing that is to prove it is clear. . . .'[57] What more contradictory of Descartes could be said!

According to Pascal 'exact science', which he calls geometry,[58] cannot prove its own principles. It has to presuppose that we know naturally what space, number, movement, correspondence and time is;[59] the idea of a *mathesis universalis*, that defines all its concepts and presupposes nothing can certainly be imagined as an idea, but to put it into effect is 'absolutely impossible'.[60] Any definition of man is more obscure than what everyone knows spontaneously about him; and a definition of being is impossible, because it would presuppose its being known.[61] Exact science remains bound to the experience of the senses—*expérience*—and therefore to the testing of this experience by fresh experience—*expériment*. All rational conclusions are deduced from experience only and mediate fresh experience,[62] but thereby the inner presuppositions of experience are illuminated. In his 'Treatise on Conic Sections' by developing the projective geometry of Desargues, Pascal had derived all modifications of conic sections from the possible variations of perspective, and had equally discovered a simple and ingenious geometrical formula that corresponded to this simple, sensible, point of view. From this the sixteen-year-old Pascal had been able to derive all the properties of conic sections.[63]

[56] P 84 B 72 L 199.

[57] P 67 B 40 L 527.

[58] In a broad sense geometry covers for Pascal that science that is distinguished within itself into arithmetic, mechanics and geometry in the narrower sense: *De l'esprit géométrique*, 583.

[59] *Ibid.*

[60] *Ibid.*, 577–578.

[61] *Ibid.*, 579. *Entretien avec M. de Saci*, 566.

[62] *Préface pour le Traité du Vide*, 530, 535.

[63] Of this treatise there is only an extract and a table of contents preserved by

But the forms of the sections—circle, ellipse, parabola, hyperbola—are developed in a basically infinite and therefore formless space. This space is characterised by an unlimited divisibility (into the infinitely small) and a corresponding extensibility (to the infinitely big). This proposition appears to Pascal to be quite evident and perspicacious, although the *process* of such a division into infinity is wholly unimaginable. Any physicist who wishes ultimately to stop the process of division at some determined point, because he has reached the indivisible, the atom, shows, according to Pascal, his complete lack of the most elementary geometrical intelligence: 'For what could be more absurd than to pretend that in dividing space one will at last arrive at a division such that the two bits thus divided are indivisible and without any extension, so that the two nothings (as regards extension) together form something extended?'[64] The imaginable and intelligible figure therefore presupposes for its imaginability and intelligibility a double infinite—the infinitely small and the infinitely large—which as such cannot be experienced and are beyond understanding and yet which must be posited, because if they are not posited, what is comprehensible remains incomprehensible. In no sense are these two infinities simply subjective modes of conception, as for Kant. For Pascal they can be read off the phenomena themselves (as their objective presupposition); the cosmological antinomies are therefore not to be resolved by 'transcendental idealism'.[65]

The discovery that the finite figure has need of an infinite medium for it to exist and be understood became for Pascal the key to much else. If one takes the form as the centre, then the infinite appears to extend on two opposite sides: into the infinitely great and the infinitely small. But if one sets the form in the, so to speak, already-posited medium, then this form is a single thing in itself: there is nothing about it that is large or small, and one can put the figure in any place one likes in the medium without anything being changed. The finite is in the

Leibniz, 60–70. On this see Jacques Chevalier, *Pascal* (1923, cited according to the edition of 1957), 49f.

[64] *De l'esprit géométrique*, 586.

[65] Kant, *Kritik der reinen Vernunft* (Insel 1922), 389 (In Norman Kemp Smith's trans.: *Critique of Pure Reason* (London 1933), 439).

infinite without being in any way fixed; it slides, it is fragile, indeed, unstable, it falls into the abyss. *Il n'a pas de bornes dans les choses.*[66] Here perspectives open up into a possibly infinite repeatability of the *universum* in the dimensions of space (the atom as a new solar system, et cetera);[67] why not with time too? That is the initial sense of the title, *disproportion de l'homme*, Pascal's heading for the long fragment 84, a sense that may not be simply left behind, but which must be included in all developments that seek to go further. The condition of everything finite (including therefore man) can in an exemplary manner, be read off the geometrically infinite. Between the geometrical figure and the infinite space in which the figure stands, there reigns disproportion, just as there does between the finite figure of man with its differentiation into orders and the infinities in which he stands. There is in man no necessity that he should stand in one place rather than another: 'Why have limits been set upon my knowledge, my height, my life, making it a hundred rather than a thousand years? For what reason did nature make it so, and choose this rather than that mean from the whole of infinity, when there is no more reason to choose one rather than another, as none is more attractive than another?'[68] '[I do not know] why I have been put in this place rather than that, or why the brief span of life allotted to me should be assigned to one moment rather than another of all the eternity that went before me and all that will come after me.'[69] From this follows what is fundamental: 'I feel that it is possible that I might never have existed. . . . I am therefore not a necessary being. I am not eternal or infinite either, but I can see that there is in nature a being who is necessary, eternal and infinite.'[70] The accidental penetrates every aspect of infinite form; even the most important is dependent for its life on accidental conditions.[71] Is not then the finite form itself threatened by the infinite, is it not patient of infinite division, on

[66] P 229 B 380 L 540. [There are no boundaries in things.]
[67] P 84 B 72 L 199 (p. 1106 in Chevalier).
[68] P 89 B 208 L 194.
[69] P 335 B 194 L 427.
[70] P 443 B 469 L 135.
[71] P 127 B 97 L 634.

the brink of a destruction that would allow it no unchangeable core of its own?[72] 'Nothing can fix the finite between the two infinites that enclose and that yet evade it.'[73] If no necessary place can be assigned to the finite within the infinite, then it follows that no relationship subsists between the two, and that therefore, viewed from the absolute, 'all finites are equal'.[74]

The status in being and truth of all creaturely being, and especially of man, is an indefensible middle position between the nothing and the Absolute (God): 'Such is our true state. That is what makes us incapable of certain knowledge or absolute ignorance. We are floating in a medium of vast extent, always drifting uncertainly, blown to and fro.'[75] 'Everything here is partly true, partly false. Nothing here is essentially true. . . .'[76] The status of being in the sliding middle position makes any radicalism impossible: 'It is not man's nature always to go on in one direction; it has its ups and downs ... *itus et reditus*.'[77] Extremes turn into their opposites, lead back to the point from which they started. The wish to be extreme betrays madness; moderation (*médiocrité*) alone is good: 'It is deserting humanity to desert the middle way.'[78] No category of worth can be given absolute value and set above the others. Power, beauty, intelligence, piety—each has its own realm.[79]

The dread that Pascal lets his 'unbelievers' feel before the infinite spaces of the cosmos[80] is for him unconditioned by the geometrically infinite as such—spatial extension would never have terrified a soul such as his: 'What is there in the vacuum that could make them afraid? What could be baser and more ridiculous than such fear?'[81] The spatially infinite is for him only a pointer (which even the dim-witted can grasp) to a metaphysical status in being that makes it impossible for the finite

[72] P 305–306 B 322–333 L 104, 688.
[73] P 84 B 72 L 199 (p. 1109 in Chevalier).
[74] *Ibid.*, (p. 1110 in Chevalier).
[75] *Ibid.*, (p. 1109 in Chevalier).
[76] P 228 B 385 L 905.
[77] P 318–319 B 354–355 L 27, 771.
[78] P 323–327 B 353, 357, 359, 378–379 L 57, 518, 674, 681, 783.
[79] P 244 B 332 L 58.
[80] P 91 B 206 L 201; P 88 B 205 L 68.
[81] P 191 B 75 L 958.

being to come to terms with its ultimate cause, so that all its being and knowing rests on a foundation of something that it neither essentially is nor grasps.

Only so, in the context of the whole of Pascal's testimony, is his penchant for the sceptics' argument about dreaming to be understood. Finite reality itself, compared with the infinite, possesses the coefficient 'unreal': 'Life is a dream, but somewhat less changeable.'[82] And so the category of 'image' is again suggested: 'we perceive an image of the truth',[83] indeed the infinities of the most diverse orders that our finite being presupposes are for us as such an image and likeness of God, who in this way has imprinted upon all things the stamp of his incomprehensibility.[84] The beginning and the end of everything, even of finite beings, remains hidden.[85] So the hiddenness of God is nothing surprising to the understanding, but rather a confirmation that he is genuinely perceived.[86] Therefore, genuine knowledge of God and the world is united with a genuine ignorance. Pascal embraces alternately one and the other, dogmatism and pyrrhonism; he can say with complete seriousness: 'All their principles are true, sceptics, stoics, atheists, et cetera ... but their conclusions are false, because the contrary principles are also true.'[87] Only from this point of view does this assertion become comprehensible: 'Incomprehensible that God should exist and incomprehensible that he should not; that the soul should be joined to the body, that we should have no soul; that the world should be created, that it should not. . . .'[88] Everything comprehensible manifests itself against a background of incomprehensibility.

It would not be surprising if Pascal's experiments as a physicist, in repeating and developing Torricelli's experiment and drawing from it a wide range of conclusions, laid the foundations of hydrostatics and led to the invention of the

[82] P 380 B 386 L 803.
[83] P 438 B 434 L 131 (p. 1207 in Chevalier).
[84] P 84 B 72 L 199 (p. 1107 in Chevalier); *cf.* P 416 B 580 L 934.
[85] P 335 B 194 L 427 (p. 1175 in Chevalier).
[86] *Ibid.*, (pp. 1172–1173 in Chevalier).
[87] P 389 B 394 L 619.
[88] P 447 B 230 L 809.

hydraulic press; if his bitter fight against a concept of the *horror vacui* in nature—which rested on pure speculation—had its metaphysical starting point here. Not for Pascal the fear of the vacuum and of nothingness! Being has been utterly nullified, so why should not the vacuum and nothingness occur experimentally and be rendered comprehensible in the realm of beings?

However, the whole foregoing consideration stems from the notion that the finite is set—in a place that is never necessary—in the medium of the infinite. But what if we start with the opposite notion? What if God wished to posit finite things, and if both infinite greatness and infinite smallness should receive their meanings and realities as the mediums of these finite things only when viewed from the central positions that they occupy? And indeed greatness and smallness are meaningful only in relation to this regulating central position. Without it, infinite division would not reach nothing (the negative infinity), nor would infinite addition reach the positive infinity. And the regulating central position, as the great fragment on the disproportion of man (84 B 72 L 199) eventually concludes, is man in his incomprehensible composite unity of body and soul, man who for this reason can neither grasp the material in itself apart from the soul, nor the soul in itself apart from the material, but who combines matter and soul in an essentially intermediary being, which certainly renders their difference and their interrelatedness, but neither of them in their purity.[89] The

[89] Ernst Wasmuth, the profound writer on Pascal in Germany, who, more than any other, has laid bare in his careful analysis the philosophical system immanent in the fragments, draws attention to an important thought, later crossed out by Pascal, at the end of the fragment, that has otherwise never been noticed. 'Instead of receiving ideas of these things [matter and spirit] in their purity, we colour them with our qualities and stamp our own composite being on all the simple things we contemplate'—so runs the sentence now. But originally Pascal had written: '. . . empreignons de notre être composé toutes les choses simples qu'il (man!) contemple. . . . C'est ainsi qu'il borne l'univers parce qu'étant borné il borne l'univers et . . .' (*Pensées*, Edition paléographique by Z. Tourneur, Vrin 1942, 244). [. . . let us stamp our composite being on all the simple things that he (man) contemplates. . . . It is thus that he limits the universe in that being limited, he limits the universe and. . . .] *Cf.* E. Wasmuth, *Die Philosophie Pascals* (1949), 87. See further his 'Abhandlung über die Lehre von den Ordnungen und von der Vernunft des Herzens', the appendix to the

figure that man forms is composite, made up of two elements or orders, and possesses no other instrument for measurement, either of matter or of soul, than this figure. Thus the fundamental concepts, which geometry has to accept as given without proof, are the ways in which the material world presents itself within the finite, composite figure. Only from this perspective can we posit the point, beyond any infinite division of space, as the indivisible that all divisions approach asymptotically; that is, essentially without ever being able to reach it. The indivisible point is necessarily presupposed and yet is of another order than the line, just as the line is presupposed for space and is yet of another order than space; and just as, on another level, zero is presupposed for the numbers that 'copy space, though so different by nature'.[90] This thoroughly analogous relationship, which led Pascal to the threshold of the differential and integral calculus, appears within the mathematical realm on a purely quantitative level, and in this sense he set out the nature of these mathematical hierarchies in his research into the sum of the series of powers of a number:

> In continuous quantity, whatever quantities of a certain order are added to a quantity of a higher order, they add nothing to it. Thus points add nothing to lines, nor lines to surfaces, nor surfaces to solid figures; nor, in the case of numbers . . . are roots commensurate with squares, squares with cubes, nor cubes with the fourth power, et cetera. Thus the inferior grades do not come into consideration as being of no significance. These things are familiar to those who study indivisibles: I have mentioned them here so that in this example that close union might become apparent in which the nature desirous of unity draws into one things that seem most remote—a close union that can never be sufficiently wondered at.[91]

It is clear now what an immensely compelling image this absolute order of different grades, even in matters quantitative,

translation of the shorter writings of Pascal (*Die Kunst zu überzeugen*, 2nd ed., 1950) and the afterword to the translation of the *Pensées* (Über die Religion, 5th ed., 1954).

[90] P 31 B 119 L 698. The analogy of equal relationships is raised in *De l'esprit géométrique*, 590.

[91] *Potestatum numericarum summa*, 171.

presents for philosophical consideration—since every being in each possible summation remains for ever 'as nothing' over against being itself—and hardly less for theological consideration—since everything natural, even the greatest achievement of the created mind, remains 'as nothing' over against the being of grace, for neither 'carnal nor intellectual greatness . . . has any relevance' to the kingdom of the saints, 'for it neither adds nor takes away anything.'[92]

But for the moment the point he wishes to make is that the subdivisions within the quantitative order occur only because of the qualitative otherness of the finite, regulating figure that engenders the 'two infinities' in their opposition through its own being and which at the same time, by virtue of its own division into spirit and matter, soul and body, makes something like a figure possible at all, a figure that itself presupposes the '(bad) infinities' of its own medium. In the quantitative 'in between' (between zero and infinity) man should, in Pascal's opinion, 'come to know himself . . . and learn to assess himself according to his proper value and entertain considerations that are more valuable than all the rest of geometry.'[93] This 'is the finest craft in the world, but in the end it is only a craft. And I have often said that it is a good way of testing our power but not of putting it to effect.'[94]

In the foregoing line of thought the finite figure appears set in an already existing, infinite (material) medium, and there the 'dread' before 'the eternal silence of these infinite spaces' finds its place. But it was the dread of the atheist—today we would say of the evolutionary materialist, for whom the form of the universe has emerged from formless matter—whom Pascal undertook to convert. Although Pascal, like a great dramatist, draws this opponent and partner in the conversation from out of his own soul ('It is not in Montaigne but in myself that I find everything I see there'),[95] and one can therefore call Pascal the first 'dramatic theologian',[96] yet this dread is only a feeble echo

[92] P 829 B 793 L 308.
[93] *De l'esprit géométrique*, 591.
[94] Letter to Fermat, 522.
[95] P 79 B 64 L 689.
[96] Mesnard, *Pascal, L'homme et l'oeuvre* (1951), 156.

of a quite other dread, which comes not from looking up but down and is derived from the fact of the *distance* of spirit from all orders of lower nature. The world is not as such a 'strange' place for man, but only for those men who bring to it a sense of strangeness from themselves, who have lost their sense of being at home and having a home. The decisive fragment '*Infini-rien*' (wrongly called 'The Wager') situates man between the infinite (where he is truly at home) and nothingness, which as such yawns before him only because he has lost the true infinite. The qualitative distance (between spirit and body) is the point of departure for the recognition of all quantitative distance, and the lack of relationship between the lower and the higher quantitative orders (between point and line, or between zero and number, et cetera) is only the strange echo of a quite different lack of relationship that there is at the qualitative level. But is the distance between the orders so great that no ascent from the lower to the higher is possible, but only a jump? The question about the measure of the distance tormented Pascal.[97] And yet it was a problem he had to make his own, a problem especially for him. He, the Augustinian theologian, who knew in his heart that any intensification of a lower order could not produce the least effect on a higher order, he who had originally discovered this *theologumenon* in the realm of geometry—it fell to him to establish the relationship between such separated orders and to discover ways of calculating them.

The solution can only be found from a point of view that looks from above downward. For in fact the line presupposes the point; the number, zero; space, the surface: the approximation unobtainable from below has already been taken for granted from above. So the intellectual order includes

[97] 'I cannot judge a work while doing it. I must do as painters do and stand back, but not too far. How far then? Guess . . .' P 28 B 114 L 558. That this point is not to be found in the existential is stated by another fragment: 'If we are too young our judgment is impaired, just as it is if we are too old. . . . If we look at our work immediately after completing it, we are still too involved; if too long afterwards, we cannot pick up the thread again. It is like looking at pictures that are too near or too far away. There is just one indivisible point that is the right place. Others are too near, too far, too high or too low. In painting the rules of perspective decide it, but how will it be decided when it comes to truth and morality?' P 85 B 381 L 21.

in itself the carnal order, and the order of charity includes both. By being thus sustained and presupposed, the order that is embraced becomes a figure of the higher. The figuring is therefore not simply a matter of a lower order closed in itself in a horizontal extension; it contains in itself at the same time a vertical relation, which admittedly cannot be discerned from below, but only from above.

An early letter of Pascal's to his two sisters develops in a completely Augustinian way the idea that God had given to the children within the family both the figure and the reality of the spiritual family, of God's covenant in Christ, 'for, as we have often said amongst ourselves, corporeal things are only an image of spiritual things, and God has represented the invisible things in the visible. This idea is so general and so useful that no significant period of time ought to be allowed to pass without our thinking of it attentively. We discussed in great detail the relationship between these two sorts of things . . . , a relationship too *beautiful* for it not to remain in your memory, and what is more, it is absolutely necessary that it should, in my opinion.' And now Pascal spells out that the fall has transposed man from the order of truth into that of images, and that 'it is necessary that we should make use of the place into which we have fallen, in order to raise ourselves from our fall.' God in his goodness 'has always left for us to contemplate an image of the goods that we have lost'; we are 'like criminals in a prison full of pictures of their redeemer and the instructions that have to be followed if they are to escape their servitude, but it has to be confessed that these holy signs cannot be perceived without a supernatural light'.[98]

This theological aesthetic rests therefore completely on a relationship that is established from above. *Rapport* and *proportion*, *mesure* and *correspondance* are the key concepts. Relationship (*rapport*) between our nature and the thing that pleases it establishes 'a certain model of delight and beauty. . . . Everything that conforms to this model delights us, be it a house, a song, a speech, verse, prose, a woman, a bird, rivers, trees, rooms, clothes, et cetera'; the model is unique; failures to

[98] Letter to Gilberte and Jacqueline (1. iv. 1648), 484.

measure up to it can, however, be infinite.[99] On the knowledge of this relationship rests the art of rhetoric, so highly prized by Pascal (as it was in Antiquity, the Middle Ages, and the Baroque period), the nature of which was aptly caught by Gilberte in her biography of her brother: 'He conceived this art to consist in certain proportions between the mind and the heart of those to whom one is speaking, and the thoughts and expressions that one uses, whereby, however, the proportions could only be properly attuned one to another by the creative turn that one gave them [*par le tour qu'on y donne*].'[100] Similarly, again as Gilberte tells us, the rational proofs of the existence of God, in contrast to those of the Holy Scriptures, did not seem to her brother to be 'sufficiently proportioned to the man's heart'.[101] This aesthetic proportion plays a role that penetrates right into the analysis of faith;[102] it clarifies also the possibility that there can be for Pascal, completely on the margin, on the basis of genius in being able to discern relationships, something like a *fides naturalis* without any supernatural illumination.[103] It is moreover the motto of the '*honnête homme*' who strives to find the right relation, attainable in this world, between the harmonious 'whole man' and the whole spiritual world.[104] Proportion even becomes the soul of the 'argument of the wager' and thus removes the accidental character of the fictitious presupposition that God's existence is unprovable and that one must therefore opt either from him or against him: 'The proportion between the uncertainty of winning and the certainty of what is being risked is in proportion to the chances of winning or losing.'[105] This sentence, torn from its context and thus here not completely comprehensible, is intended to show simply how for Pascal, who had also discovered how to measure probability, the concept of proportion sets, as it were, from above the realm of the 'accidental' into the framework of that

[99] P 37 B 32 L 585.
[100] Mme Périer, *Vie de M. Pascal*, 14–15.
[101] *Ibid.*, 16.
[102] J. Russier, *op. cit.*, 164.
[103] *Ibid.*, 200–202.
[104] P 40–44 B 35–37, 14 L 195, 605, 647, 652.
[105] P 451 B 233 L 418 (p. 1215 in Chevalier).

which is regulated by law, as indeed he proudly points out against the Paris Academy: *Sic matheseos demonstrationes cum aleae incertitudine jungendo . . . stupendum hunc titulum jure sibi arrogat: aleae geometria.*[106]

It remains however a proportion that is established from above and that thus provides no insight into vertical symmetry but only into horizontal symmetry.[107] From a vertical perspective man can only survey what lies beneath him, what he has either naturally or spiritually fashioned. In his relation with God he can fashion nothing—rather is he fashioned—and therefore he understands his relationship to God only in the measure that he understands the grace of his own fashioning, in faith and love.

This explains the searching conversation at the beginning of the fragment 'Infinity-nothing' between the Christian and the atheist.[108] It is given here, reduced to its essentials.

Atheist: Our soul is cast into the body where it finds number, time, extension; it reasons about these things and calls them natural, or necessary, and can believe nothing else.

Christian: Unity added to infinity does not increase it at all, . . . the finite is annihilated in the presence of the infinite and becomes pure nothingness. So it is with our mind before God, with our justice before divine justice. There is not so great a disproportion between our justice and God's as between unity and infinity. [The quantitative gap is a likeness of the qualitative gap between God and the world, and yet, according to the Christian, this gap allows a certain relationship, *aliqua proportionalitas*.]

Atheist: God's justice must be as unproportioned as his

[106] *Celeberrimae Matheseos Academiae Parisiensi*, 74. [Thus by joining mathematical demonstrations to the uncertainty of the die . . . he justly arrogates to himself this stupendous title: the geometry of the die.]

[107] P 50 B 28 L 580.

[108] It is only comprehensible if the parts of the dialogue are correctly distributed. Decisive for an understanding here is Jean Levillain, 'Exégèse du Fragment sur le Pari', in *Ecrits sur Pascal* (1959), 125–154.

mercy. Now his justice toward the damned is less vast and ought to be less startling to us than his mercy toward the elect. [The atheist wants to destroy even the appearance of a proportion between God and man; if there is such a slight relationship between merciful love and sin, then it will be equally slight at the level of justice.]

Christian: We know that the infinite exists without knowing its nature. [Thus we know that there is an infinite number, but because it can be neither odd nor even, something that every (finite) number must be, we do not know its nature.] Similarly, we may well know that God exists without knowing what he is. [This is the old patristic distinction between the 'that' and the 'what', supported with an arithmetic simile.] Is there no substantial truth, seeing that there are so many true things that are not truth itself? [The Christian extends the conclusion from the being of the world to the unknown being of God by means of the Augustinian-Thomistic *argumentum ex gradibus*, moving from truth by participation to essential truth.]

Atheist: We know the existence and nature of the finite because we too are finite and extended in space. We know the existence of the (quantitatively) infinite without knowing its nature, because it too has extension but unlike us no limits. But we do not know either the existence or the nature of God, because he has neither extension nor limits. [The atheist calls into question the analogy between proportion (over the gap) in the mathematical and the proportion (over the gap) in the metaphysical. There is missing any common medium between the magnitudes, which the *analogia entis* only presupposes but does not prove. Thus we remain within the confines of the world.]

Christian: But by faith we know his existence, through

	glory we shall know his nature. . . . [This retreat to theology dispenses with any rational proof of the existence of God.]
Atheist:	Let us for the time being continue to talk in terms of natural reason. If there is a God, he is infinitely beyond our comprehension, since, being indivisible and without limits, he bears no relation [*rapport*] to us. We are therefore incapable of knowing either what he is or whether he is. That being so, who would dare to attempt an answer to the question? Certainly not we, who bear no relation [*aucun rapport*] to him.
Christian:	Who will then condemn Christians for being unable to give rational grounds for their belief . . . ? They declare that it is folly in expounding it to the world, and then you complain that they do not prove it. . . . It is by being without proof that they show that they are not without sense. [The Christian has now abandoned the metaphysical proofs and has retreated to the good sense of faith, which would be senseless if it allowed itself to be enforced by reason.]
Atheist:	Yes, but although that excuses those who offer their religion as such, . . . it does not excuse those who accept it.[109]

Now the Christian offers a justification of faith by means of the proof that choice and decision are demanded by existence itself and that (this is explained by a parallel drawn from the calculation of probabilities, which, however, as a geometrical method is not itself probable but certain) only the decision for God can be regarded as rational.

In the prelude to the new existential argument that the Christian brings forward, he is pressed hard by the atheist. The atheist refuses to accept his metaphysical proof of God's existence, because between God and man there is no common medium of 'extension'; that is, no common concept including

[109] P 451 B 233 L 418.

both. Nor will the argument from degrees of being work. In his retreat to faith, the Christian's 'folly' is readily conceded, but that everyone has to succumb to such folly is disputed. The negative aspect of the mathematical analogy is admitted: that one, added to infinity, does not add anything to infinity. But the positive aspect is rejected and with it the whole traditional patristic and Scholastic idea of an 'ascent to God' and of a negative theology understood as ecstasy is rejected as well. If we include also the subsequent attempted proof from the analogy of the game of chance we can say that Pascal, who here appears to espouse a reformed, fideist theology, remains nevertheless faithful to his geometrical analogy, inasmuch as such a theology presupposes that the higher orders can in no way be derived from the lower (not the line from the point, nor infinity from the unit), but that on the contrary the lower orders are included in the higher and determined thence. Man cannot understand God, but through God he can understand himself—but not, precisely, by means of the 'God of the philosophers' and the *analogia entis*, but through the free, living God of inconceivable grace, as he has been manifest in the Cross of Jesus Christ. It is really by contrast with Descartes's *cogito* that Baader's *cogitor (diligor) ergo sum* is made distinct. If this is posited as an a priori, then Pascal will permit any thought process within this presupposition: he has amply undertaken such himself in the apology. Philosophy as a function of a personal relationship to God, at most as an existential training in such a relationship through demonstration of the gaping disproportion that cannot right itself—that is the post-Reformation situation that Pascal embodies.

3. PROPORTION OF THE DISPROPORTIONS

'*Disproportion de l'homme*' is the heading of the already much-quoted fragment. Pascal had at first written '*incapacité*', but he wanted to emphasise the objective lack of harmony more than any subjective inability. The philosophical anthropology that the piece develops and which is developed in many other fragments to the same purpose is unfolded in two stages: first as an inventory of facts, without any metaphysical or theological elaboration, and second as the grounding of the state of being that had been shown to exist: *raison des effets*. The presupposition of both steps is that it is possible to read man as a form. The result of the first part is that this form cannot be grasped simply by the analysis of being, for what emerges is formlessness, contradiction (*contrariété*), monstrosity. So the second part must raise the question: from what perspective must man be seen so that the deformed is integrated into a true form, the disproportion into a true proportion? This second part will in turn also be accomplished in two stages: first, the cause of the disproportion has to be indicated, but that is not enough; the cause of the transcending of the disproportion must be shown, which is something quite other. The first part ends in the blindness of dialectic. But Pascal does not deduce from this the blindness of faith, for it is a fundamental demand of reason that it should be able to see. The understanding of faith (*intellectus fidei*), that he works toward, is true vision in true blindness.

A wonderful fragment expresses this aesthetically: 'We think playing upon man is like playing upon an ordinary organ. He is indeed an organ, but strange, shifting and changeable, with keys that do not follow the scales. Those who only know how to play an ordinary organ would never be in tune on this one. You have to know where the keys are.'[110] There is then a certain knowledge, and consequently a harmony that can be produced by playing that appears unmethodical but is in reality superlatively methodical. Similarly, on the higher historical levels the same image as before repeats itself: as the geometrical figure presupposes unimaginable infinity as a medium, so the true image of God in man, which will be called Jesus Christ, becomes delineated against the background of the imagelessness, the lack of harmony and the absurdity of existence.

We need not trace the development of the disproportions here, for they are lodged in the memory of even the casual reader of the *Pensées*. They form—whatever Pascal's conception of the complete structure of the work—the first part, to the

[110] P 172 B 111 L 55.

working out of which Pascal gave most detailed attention.[111]

Man cannot place himself—not only because, like all finite beings, he is suspended at the level of being within the infinite,

[111] So much so that L. P. Couchou (1948) has attempted to isolate this anthropological part and stamp it Pascal's main concern: originally he had intended to make it alone the content of his apology and put it forward as a 'Discours sur la condition de l'homme'; only the objections of one of his theological friends had moved him to add the second, biblical and historical, part. This unprovable thesis would certainly destroy the decisive articulation of the structure of the whole which we have sought to prove, and would stamp Pascal not only as the father of the 'method of immanence'—as something he thoroughly approved—but of a 'system of immanence' of a Schleiermacherian colouring.

The exact plan of the apology cannot be reconstructed. It does not seem that Pascal, who had a clear *idea* of the work before his mind, worked out this plan in detail. Recent philologically orientated research into Pascal has certainly established that Pascal had himself classified almost half of his fragments into twenty-seven sections with headings (something that has been long known) and that we have the original transcript, which follows this order unchanged (see the preface to the *Edition de Port Royal* by Etienne Périer [1670], p. 1468), in MS Bibl. Nat. 9203 (something only known for certain since Louis Lafuma's research). But this first disposition of the material took place in all probability with a view to the lecture that Pascal gave at Port Royal in 1658 to communicate a first outline and idea of the work; it had necessarily therefore a quite limited aim and leaves the greater number of fragments unordered. One can try, as Lafuma did in his first edition (Delmas 1947), to distribute the unclassified fragments over the twenty-seven classified groups or, because this is not satisfactory, simply reproduce the 'first copy', with the classified and then the unclassified fragments (as in the *Collection Astrée*, no. 19, 1958). One can also try, as did, most ingeniously, Jean Mesnard (*Pascal, l'homme et l'oeuvre*, 1951), to demonstrate 'a cunning interweaving of themes, a subtle, almost musical mode of composition' (p. 139 ET p. 148) in Pascal's classification, something which cannot however be done without much supporting elaboration.

There remains, therefore, the older method, represented today most credibly in Chevalier's edition, still the best despite everything: by various converging ways to approach a never completely simple basic plan (1) through the inner criteria contained in the fragments themselves, which allow one to recognize in their cross-references the main lines of the thought; (2) through Pascal's provisional classification; (3) through the detailed plan of the whole work, as it is explained by Filleau de la Chaise, one of those who heard Pascal's lecture in Port Royal, though not without examining the remaining fragments of 1672 (*Discours sur les Pensées de Pascal*, ed. Chevalier, 1474–1501). The inner logic, as well as the external witnesses, clearly show that the proof moves from the disproportion of man to the express posing of the religious

but also because, at the epistemological level, he hovers as a spirit in a void that he cannot understand, and therefore is unable to root his (real) knowledge in the Absolute. 'I see too much to deny and not enough to affirm.'[112] So self-knowledge is required,[113] and yet concretely self-knowledge is rejected as something vain and impossible.[114] If man were to know himself, he would need to know the world, but that is impossible, for 'how could a part possibly know the whole?'[115] Besides, such knowledge would distract one from what one sought to know. Through knowledge of the world one cannot attain self-knowledge.[116] Man is as body one with the world, and as spirit he is the other; yet he is both at the same time and this, at the level of being, puts him out of relation with regard to things: *Concevons donc que ce mélange d'esprit et de boue nous disproportionne.*[117] 'Limited in every respect, we find this intermediate state between two extremes reflected in all our faculties.'[118] In *all* our faculties, not only in our less-than-spiritual faculties and attitudes, as Augustine and the more Platonist fathers pointed out—in the outer senses that deceive us, in the imagination that makes a fool of us, in 'opinion', the *opinio* of 'convention', or 'illusion', that rules the private and public lives of men and their social intercourse—but also in the spirit that remains for the most part enclosed in a 'circle' of 'opinions'.[119] Pascal frequently makes reference here to the dialectic between 'healthy popular opinion', enlightened criticism and the insight that, transcending the criticism, perceives the deeper truth of popular opinion, which is certainly

problem, and, after eliminating the other attempts at religion, to the historical proof of the truth of the biblical religion. The beginning (man's situation) and the end (the religion of Jesus Christ) are laid down with absolute clarity, while the middle cannot be reconstructed with complete plausibility; even for Chevalier it exhibits certain obscurities and discrepancies.

[112] P 414 B 229 L 429.

[113] P 81 B 66 L 72; P 210 B 146 L 620.

[114] P 76 B 62 L 780.

[115] P 84 B 72 L 199 (p. 1110 in Chevalier).

[116] P 80 B 144 L 687.

[117] Deleted sentence in P 84 B 72 L 199 (n. on p. 1111 in Chevalier).

[118] *Ibid.*, (p. 1108 in Chevalier).

[119] P 26 B 6 L 814.

open to objection: 'There is certainly some truth in these opinions, but not as people imagine [*se figurent*].'[120] In practice it applies above all to the social order of representation and of law, which can nowhere be realised in its pure form, which expresses itself in power and is figured by it, in such a way that one cannot simply say that naked power can replace an illusory, unavailable law.[121] Pascal expects—say, in his 'Three Discourses to a Prince'—that one who possesses power should array himself in the mere imaginary (even illusory) display of the social order and then affirm this as the true human condition.[122]

Here it is again characteristic of Pascal that all this does not lead to scepticism but to a truth, everywhere pointed to but never grasped. This is expressed for religion as follows: 'Men could not possibly have imagined so many false religions unless there were a true one.'[123] 'We have an incapacity for proving anything that no amount of dogmatism can overcome. We have an idea of truth that no amount of scepticism can overcome.'[124] So the Platonic idea of images and copies appears again; from Montaigne Pascal takes over a quotation from Cicero: *veri juris germanaeque justitiae solidam et expressam effigiem nullam tenemus; umbra et imaginibus utimur* (*De Offic.* 3.17).[125] And yet it is not Platonism, for the images are not illuminated by any natural light whether from above or below. Pascal envisages no *anamnesis* of the heavenly truth. Rather, everything is concentrated on demonstrating the coexistence of the opposites of *grandeur* and *misère*, toward which already the dialectic in the conversation with M. de Saci had been directed—to the never-ceasing change of one into the other, the exhibition of the one by means of the other, the mutual reflection of the one in the other: 'Man's greatest humiliation is the quest for glory, but it is just this that most clearly shows his excellence.'[126] 'If he exalts

[120] P 310 B 335 L 92; *cf.* P 287, 295–297, 307–312 B 313, 320, 324–325, 327–328, 330, 335–337 L 26, 83, 90–94, 101, 525, 977.

[121] P 104 B 82 L 44; P 238 B 299 L 81.

[122] *Trois discours sur la condition des grands* (c. 1660), 615–621.

[123] P 825 B 817 L 734.

[124] P 273 B 395 L 406.

[125] P 235 B 297 L 86. [We possess no solid and express image of true law and authentic justice; we are shadows and images.]

[126] P 276 B 404 L 470.

himself, I humble him. If he humbles himself, I exalt him. And I go on contradicting him, until he understands that he is a monster that passes all understanding.'[127] If Pascal calls man *monstre*,[128] *chimère*, *chaos*, *prodige*, *contradiction*,[129] he does so not to emphasise man's dreadfulness or depravity but the indecipherability as a whole of his figure. Every feature is brought into prominence by its opposite, but also held in check, both fostered and threatened.

If one asks about the 'reasons for these effects', then the sole solution offered, which is constantly and exclusively invoked, is the doctrine of original sin, or, more exactly, the patristic doctrine of *katastasis*, radically understood. Man is not in his rightful situation; he is, at the level of being, in a situation of self-estrangement. Here, in this vertical relationship between the higher being that he is by right and the lower being that he has now unnaturally assumed, can be found a first line of approach to the deciphering of his form. 'Man's greatness is so *obvious* that it can even be deduced from his wretchedness, for what is nature in animals we call wretchedness in man. . . . He must have fallen from some better state that was once his own. Who indeed would think himself unhappy not to be a king except one who had been dispossessed?'[130] 'Man's dualism is so *obvious* that some people have thought we had two souls.'[131] That we should find the word 'obvious' throughout this discussion is notable. Here lies 'the knot of our condition':[132] in this '*double capacité*', these '*deux états*', these '*deux natures*'.[133] The often-quoted '*l'homme passe infiniment l'homme*'[134] is nothing else than the expression of the normal teaching of the early fathers that man transcends the human in his participation by grace in God in his primordial state, in redemption and in glorification, and that only in this

[127] P 330 B 420 L 130.
[128] *Ibid.*; P 144 B 406 L 477; P 438 B 434 L 131.
[129] P 438 B 434 L 131 (p. 1206 in Chevalier).
[130] P 268 B 409 L 117.
[131] P 315 B 417 L 629.
[132] P 438 B 434 L 131.
[133] P 482 B 430 L 149.
[134] P 438 B 434 L 131 (and the different, deleted versions: pp. 1206–1207 in Chevalier).

transcendence can he be understood. In this way a proverb like '*se moquer de la philosophie, c'est vraiment philosopher*'[135] is taken to refer to the transcendence of the true (theological) philosophy over the passing endeavours of immanent philosophy; and this also renders intelligible the statement that the whole of human ethics and politics is but a '*fausse imitation*' of true love,[136] a construction from the *débris* of the original wholeness, '*mais quelle différence, que de vides, que de disproportions! Ce n'est qu'une misérable copie de ce divin original*'.[137] But it is still a sign of human greatness that, outside love, man has achieved '*un tableau de la charité*'.[138]

It is only in this context that we can understand the saying about the '*moi haïssable*',[139] which Pascal frequently and carefully explains. Man must unconditionally hate his estrangement from God and from himself,[140] for what he is then hating is his lack of love, his abysmal egoism, which is ultimately hatred. On the other hand, man, who has a double nature, should both love and hate himself: 'Let him love himself, for there is within him a nature capable of good. . . . Let him despise himself because this capacity remains unfulfilled; but that is no reason for him to despise this natural capacity. Let him both hate and love himself.'[141] What is important is that he should 'hate the self-love within him and the instinct that leads him to make himself into a God',[142] 'that makes himself his own centre',[143] 'the bias toward self'.[144] The member severed from the mystical body of love, which wills to be its own life-principle,[145] deserves our

[135] P 24 B 4 L 513.

[136] According to Filleau de la Chaise's expression, 1493.

[137] *Ibid.*, 1500. [But what a difference, whether in vacuums or disproportions! It is only a miserable copy of the divine original.]

[138] P 284 B 402 L 118.

[139] P 136 B 455 L 597; P 707 B 476 L 373; P 564 B 676 L 475; P 689 B 545 L 271; P 700 B 468 L 220.

[140] P 130 B 100 L 978: '*La nature de l'amour propre et de ce moi humain est de n'aimer que soi.*' [The nature of self-love and of the human ego is to love only the self.]

[141] P 331 B 423 L 119. Similarly, P 435 B 494 L 450.

[142] P 434 B 492 L 617.

[143] P 483 B 430 L 149.

[144] P 703 B 477 L 421.

[145] P 710 B 483 L 372.

hatred, 'but as we cannot love what is outside us, we must love a being who is within us but is not our own self. . . . The kingdom of God is within us, universal good is within us and is both ourselves and not ourselves.'[146] Therefore, here too we have to do with a relationship between two orders of image and reality separated by a gap, so that the private and public order of self-love is '*une fausse image de la charité, car au fond ce n'est que haine*'.[147]

This is true even if it has to be conceded that it is a sign of man's greatness '*d'avoir tiré de la concupiscence un si bel ordre*',[148] '*d'en avoir fait un tableau de la charité*'.[149] 'We have established and developed out of concupiscence admirable rules of polity, ethics and justice, but at root, the evil root of man, this evil stuff of which we are made, is only concealed; it is not pulled up.'[150] Therefore, an inner dialectic prevails between image and reality, which does not at all destroy the character of image, but which means that it is just in the contrariness, which emphasizes the gap between the orders, that the similarity must emerge. *Corruptio optimi pessima.* The man who does not seek his true greatness in God must seek it in himself, something that is at the same time both a perversion of his true greatness and a caricature of his true humility and lowliness.[151] In this context we find those words that designate man as *nouveauté*, *monstre*, *chaos*, *contradiction*: 'We perceive an image of truth and possess nothing but falsehood.'[152] The image is in reality reversed, as in a mirror, whence follows the perpetual dialectical change, '*renversement continuel du pour au contre*'.[153]

Here is rooted the concept of madness, *folie*, which in a similar dialectic to that developed by Erasmus expresses the self-estrangement of reason from its (Christian) self—whether it be

[146] P 712 B 485 L 564.

[147] P 134 B 451 L 210. [A false image of charity, for essentially it is just hate.]

[148] P 283 B 403 L 106. [To produce such excellent order from his own concupiscence.]

[149] P 284 B 402 L 118. [To make it the image of true charity.]

[150] P 135 B 453 L 211.

[151] P 276 B 404 L 470; P 284 B 402 L 118.

[152] P 438 B 434 L 131.

[153] P 309 B 328 L 93; P 312 B 337 L 90. [Constant swing from pro to con.]

our existence as in a sunken mirror (as fancy and imagination)[154] that is thus described, or whether this worldly reason sees its own restoration as reason in the Cross of Jesus Christ as a heightened *folie*.[155] The relationship appears again in a dialectical way when the Christian appears as subject to the *folie* of the world out of obedience to God,[156] and so in the end the *folie* of the Christian emerges incomprehensibly exalted above the *sagesse* of all apologetic proofs of its truth.[157]

Finally too the profound ontological concept of *divertissement* belongs to the doctrine of *katastasis*; it has the same significance as the concept of *kinésis* in Origen and Evagrius: becoming distracted, slipping from the centre, through diversion, through turning away. The mysterious range of associations of *se divertir* is always present to his mind: the apparent harmlessness of amusement, deeper still the apparent natural necessity of games and exercise which for the organism itself are in fact functional. But always there is to be found, whether conceded or not, the flight from being present to oneself; that is, from communion with God, from the '*redire ad cor*'. From sport, to any form of communal entertainment, to scientific work, Pascal sees all human striving as coming under the law of this secret, nonsensical flight—to life in the past or to hope for the future, to escape at all cost the present.[158] For, present to himself, a man begins to feel 'his emptiness, nullity, boredom, his despair, and gloom, depression, chagrin, discontent'.[159] From himself—that is, without grace—he can never rediscover the lost source, there remains no other way open to him than self-deception through activity. 'Man is so unhappy that he would be bored, even if he had no cause for boredom, by the very nature of his temperament.'[160] Take away from men their diversion, 'and they will be bored to extinction, for they feel their nullity

[154] P 185 B 414 L 412; P 294 B 331 L 533; P 297 B 330 L 26; P 334 B 195 L 428; P 364 B 257 L 160.

[155] P 448 B 445 L 695.

[156] P 313 B 338 L 14.

[157] P 827–828 B 587–588 L 291, 842.

[158] P 168 B 172 L 47.

[159] P 201 B 131 L 622.

[160] P 205 B 139 L 136 (p. 1142 in Chevalier); P 217 B 171 L 414.

without recognizing it'.[161] Without grace there is in this emptiness no sort of longing for God; here Pascal turns away from the Middle Ages and its natural *desiderium* to the Modern Age, to existentialism. Man's emptiness of love is *as such* the opposite of loving longing. Everyone indeed seeks happiness, but this is only 'the empty print and trace' of the lost love, which man 'vainly tries to fill with everything around him'. But this void can be filled only by God.[162] In everything nature points to a God who has been lost.[163] It is not that man is as such incapable of comprehending God, but that he no longer has that dignity that would render him proportionable to the divine love.[164]

To have fallen from love is the mystery of original sin, something rationally insoluble and yet nevertheless the illuminating presupposition for an understanding of the human condition. But for Pascal such a reference to original sin is already the content of the Christian revelation. Anthropological analysis brings us only to the point where we recognise the incomprehensibility of the situation, where we renounce any attempt to build a thought pattern out of the contradictions. Original sin as the *nœud de notre condition*[165] cannot be discovered by our unaided reason.[166] But even as revealed, it is not the last word in wisdom, for while it reveals our remoteness from our true nature negatively, it cannot justify it positively. It cannot break through the '*cercle sans fin*' between the greatness and the misery of man.[167] Within the human realm, the greater the insight one achieves, the wider gapes the opposition between *grandeur* and *bassesse*[168]—so much so indeed that for Pascal the conclusion of the way of philosophy consists in this: in conceding to both Epictetus and Montaigne their conflicting views, both that which demands greatness of man and that

[161] P 211 B 164 L 36.

[162] P 370 B 425 L 148.

[163] P 421 B 441 L 471.

[164] P 603 B 557 L 444.

[165] P 438 B 434 L 131 (p. 1208 in Chevalier).

[166] '*Tout son état dépend de ce point imperceptible. . . . Le péché original est folie devant les hommes.*' P 448 B 445 L 695.

[167] P 314 B 416 L 122.

[168] P 427 B 443 L 613.

which shows that he has no such greatness: accepting them as contraries that cannot be made to complement one another in a picture of a harmonic or tragic-heroic majesty of man, as a contradiction, the opposing extremes of which expressly destroy one another instead of complementing one another.[169] Pascal's 'method of immanence' therefore tends in no way to derive Christian truth from existence, for, in his opinion, not even original sin can be proved immanently—it is the most obscure, unbelievable dogma that no one could hit upon except through revelation. And if that is true of the doctrine of original sin, it is even more true of the Incarnation.

And yet the 'method of immanence' is correct in so far as the content of revelation, the fact of the love of God and its formulation, strikes the heart immediately as truth. 'Those who believe without having read the Testaments do so because their inward disposition is truly holy and what they hear about our religion matches it. They feel that a God made them, they want to love only God, they want to hate only themselves. They feel that they are not strong enough to do this by themselves, that they are incapable of going to God, and that if God does not come to them they are incapable of communicating with him at all. They hear it said in our religion . . . that God made himself man in order to unite himself with us. It takes no more than this to convince men whose hearts are thus disposed.'[170] Love therefore—beyond the knowledge of original sin and the dualism of the conditions of nature—is that element in which nature becomes whole and consequently understands itself—but love in its truth, as grace from God, and so with the insight that apart from God it cannot be attained, but the love that comes from God is Jesus Christ, and therefore he is man's possibility of wholeness and the restoration of the proportion that resolves in itself all lack of proportion, embracing it and drawing it into itself.

Christ is for Pascal the human image that can evidently only be established by God and which is unattainable, even impossible, in the world. For if Christ is to be understood, he

[169] '*Il ne résulterait de leur assemblage qu'une guerre et qu'une destruction générale.*' *Entretien avec M. de Saci*, 574.

[170] P 837 B 286 L 381.

must be read as God's free act of grace that nothing in the world could demand or suggest or construct. What in man is by nature irreconcilably contradictory, in him is bound together into a unity, the meaning of which was not the revelation of man as such, but the revelation of God's love for man. The synthesis, which draws everything together immanently, has its possibility manifested in the transcendent. 'In Jesus Christ all contradictions are reconciled.'[171] The *bassesse* is not done away with for the sake of a one-sided *grandeur*, but the *bassesse* becomes the expression of *grandeur*. 'As man and as God he has been everything that is great and everything that is abject in order to sanctify everything in himself.' Death 'without Jesus Christ is horrible. . . . In Jesus Christ it is wholly different: it is lovable, holy, and the joy of the faithful.'[172] Everything finds its true proportion, the right temperature: 'The grace of the redeemer . . . so nicely [*avec tant de justesse*] tempers fear with hope . . . that it causes infinitely more humiliation than mere reason, but without despair, and infinitely more exaltation than natural pride, but without puffing us up.'[173] And although the teaching of Christ is 'so contrary to nature', it does everything so 'gently'[174] because it restores everything inwardly to its proper place.[175] 'There must be impulses of abasement prompted not by nature but by penitence, not as a lasting state but as a stage toward greatness. There must be impulses of greatness, prompted not by merit but by grace, and after the stage of abasement has been passed.'[176] The undiscoverable in Christ remains the revaluation of lowliness in love: the Cross. And that is the act of God. Here and only here is established 'the harmony of the two opposing truths', here all names fit: 'righteous sinners, living dead, dead living, reprobate elect—*élu réprouvé*'.[177] Therefore the Cross is beyond all the wisdom of apology—'*après avoir étalé tous ses miracles et toute sa sagesse*'—

[171] P 558 B 684 L 257.
[172] Letter on the death of his father (17.10.1651), 493.
[173] P 439 B 435 L 208.
[174] P 487 B 289 L 482.
[175] P 75 B 527 L 192.
[176] P 392 B 525 L 398.
[177] P 788 B 862 L 733.

and towers above all this as the eternal foolishness of God, and for its sake the Christian believes.[178] And because it transcends all wisdom, it remains forever contested—it is not at all the simple, judicious fulfilment of mankind—and Christianity clings to it lest it be debased to the status of a human ideal.[179]

Christ is thus simply the one who embraces; he is the mystery. His suffering is not proportionate to the sufferings that all sinners cause him, but beyond that it is the suffering of a God in human form, caused by God himself: God abandoned by God in the wrath of God. Therefore this agony lasts 'until the end of the world'[180] and is even an 'eternal suffering that Christ as our substitute brings on himself'.[181] So too 'Jesus Christ has existed from the beginning of the world',[182] 'Jesus Christ is the purpose of all things, the centre toward which all things tend. Whoever knows him knows the reason for everything. . . . The world exists only through Christ, for Christ. . . . But for Christ the world would not go on existing, for it would either have to be destroyed or be a kind of Hell.'[183] Christ is therefore not dependent on any picture or figure to point us to him historically: 'The figure was drawn from the truth. And the truth was recognized from the figure.'[184] The Old Testament is figure, as is the believing Christian, and especially the suffering Christian, who only finds meaning through the archetype that attains expression in him. This is sublimely expressed in the 'Prayer for a right use of sickness': 'I find nothing in myself that is agreeable to you. I see nothing there, O Lord, other than my sorrows alone, which have a certain resemblance to yours . . . O God, who were made man only to suffer more than any man. . . . Enter my heart and my soul to bear there my sufferings and to continue to endure in me all that remains for you to suffer of your Passion that you complete in your members until the perfect consummation of your Body; so that being filled with

[178] P 827–828 B 587–588 L 291, 842.
[179] P 776–777 B 613–614 L 280–281.
[180] P 736 B 553 L 919.
[181] Ninth letter to Mlle de Roannez, 518.
[182] P 768 B 846 L 878 (crossed out line).
[183] P 602 B 556 L 449.
[184] P 572 B 673 L 826.

you it may no more be I who live and who suffer, but you who live and suffer in me, O my Saviour.'[185]

This is for Pascal the rational justification of existence: the embracing of all contradictions and nights of being in the mystery of Christ. The 'Memorial's' sole aim is this: to keep alive this thought, once grasped. 'Certainty, heartfelt joy, peace' is not explained by itself, oscillating, as it does, freely between feeling and experience, but by the following line: 'God of Jesus Christ. "My God and your God".'[186]

The 'empty trace' of lost love in the sinner does not allow him to calculate the distance that separates him from his authentic, 'original' condition. The relationship between the two conditions yields therefore no shape. This occurs only at the moment when the hypostatic union, the essential unity of God and man, of redeemer and sinner, of reprobate elect and elect reprobate, embraces both conditions, drawing them into one another, and by revaluing them transcends them. The act of the love of God not only confers meaning, but a form: it creates and at the same time fulfills the figure.

4. HIDDENNESS AND LOVE

In the revelation of Jesus Christ the crucified, two things are revealed at the same time, each in its own way essentially something hidden: the ever-greater love of the incomprehensible God, and the sin of man that appears ever greater in its light. Thus the revelation that takes place in Christ is in the highest degree paradoxical: the double hiddenness is that which, manifest *as such*, becomes really *manifest*. All a priori objection to such a possibility can arise only from the unhistorical realm of constructive reason, but this is contradicted by the 'history of truth'.[187]

Our task is thus to treat successively: (1) the revelation of the hiddenness of God, (2) the revelation of this hiddenness in the hiddenness of sin, (3) the true, historical way of reading and

[185] *Prayer for a right use of sickness*, 610f, 614.
[186] *Memorial*, 554.
[187] P 778 B 858 L 776.

depicting this hiddenness, and (4) the relation of love and figure.

1. God is in his nature *deus absconditus*; 'this is the very name that he gives himself in Scripture', and if men complain about God's obscurity, then they forget that 'the obscurity in which they find themselves and which they use as an objection against the Church simply establishes' its teaching.[188] The usual proofs of God's existence are, from this point of view, naive: 'to tell [men] that they have only to look at the least thing around them and they will see in it God plainly revealed; to give them no other proof . . . than the course of the moon and the planets,' is much too feeble. 'This is not how Scripture with its better knowledge of the things of God, speaks of God. On the contrary, it says that God is a hidden God,' and 'only through Jesus Christ is any communication with him possible: *Nemo novit patrem*. . . .'[189] God cannot completely hide himself; otherwise, faith would be impossible. Still less can he become completely manifest, for then there would be no merit. 'But he ordinarily hides himself and rarely reveals himself. . . . He remained hidden beneath the veil of nature, which concealed him from us, until the Incarnation; and when he had to appear he still more hid himself by concealing himself in humanity. He was much more recognisable when he was invisible than when he made himself visible'. And finally, he hid himself in 'the strangest and most obscure secret of all, in the eucharistic forms of bread and wine . . . the last secret place where he can be'.[190] So increasing hiddenness corresponds to an increasing manifestation of what is essential; that is, of love. This gives the decisive key to Pascal's discarding of the rational proofs of God's existence: God is here too little hidden, for them truly to make him manifest; on the other hand, the final hiddenness of the truth in the proofs is for him a decisive indication of their truth, just as he interprets the obscurity of the prophets as an important way of drawing attention to the truth that they contain.[191] God, as the highest value, wills to be sought, for such seeking is alone

[188] P 335 B 194 L 427 (pp. 1172f in Chevalier).

[189] P 366 B 242 L 781.

[190] Fourth letter to Mlle de Roannez, 509f.

[191] J. Russier, *La foi selon Pascal* (1949), 389.

worthy of him.[192] And God, as love, wills to be found only by love, 'perfect clarity would [only] help the mind. . . . Their pride must be humbled.'[193] But it is the 'between' that is truly humbling, for just as perfect clarity satisfies reason, so would perfect obscurity satisfy the radicalism of faith. 'I may well love total darkness, but if God plunges me into a state of semidarkness I am displeased by such darkness as is there, and because I fail to see in it the same merits as in total darkness, such a state does not please me. This is a fault and a sign that I am making an idol of darkness, separated from God's order. Now we should worship only his order.'[194] There must therefore be enough light available for the darkness of the true religion to be *seen*, and contrariwise, darkness enough for the image of God that is appearing not to be rendered improbable. This hiddenness of God certainly allows his revelation always to remain subject to objection,[195] but it also allows the encounter between God and man to take place in the freedom of the heart and without the reason being compelled by logic.[196] There is thus 'evidence and at the same time obscurity . . . , enough evidence to condemn [the refractory] and not enough to convince by force.'[197] 'I am angry with those who absolutely insist that one believe the truth when they have demonstrated it, something Jesus Christ did not do in his created humanity.'[198]

And because God revealed himself in Christ in this unity of evidence and hiddenness,[199] there truly lies in this the divine mystery of predestination; in the same figure, which he sets up before the world, he chooses the one and rejects the other. Pascal, who was greatly agitated by this *theologumenon*, believed that he could discern it in the phenomenon of revelation itself. It was for him, moreover, the exact expression of the incomprehensibility of his own election, of which he never

[192] P 579 B 574 L 472.
[193] P 596 B 581 L 234.
[194] P 597 B 582 L 926.
[195] P 776–777 B 613–614 L 280–281.
[196] P 637 B 795 L 237.
[197] P 831 B 564 L 835.
[198] Fragment d'une lettre, 526.
[199] *Cf.* P 599 B 586 L 446; P438 B 430 L 149 (pp. 1227f in Chevalier).

doubted. The acts of judgment in the Old and New Testaments assured him that he was himself not in the realm of the God of the philosophers (according to which all is a vain harmony), but in that of the living God of love.[200] It is a strange mystery of the Western heart that it flees back, past all the lights offered it by philosophy, even by Christian philosophy, ever again to the moment of decision in this darkest region of the biblical message of judgment, as if it were only then, when it returned from the furthest horrors of dereliction to the heart of God, that it could be finally assured of love.

2. The hiddenness of God in Christ bears the colours of judgment because of sin; God hides himself not only in being raised above sin, he hides himself in lowliness and humility among forms that can be confused with the accustomed forms of sin. 'For thirty of his thirty-three years he lives without showing himself. For three years he is treated as an impostor. The priests and rulers reject him. Those who are nearest and dearest to him despise him. Finally he dies betrayed by one of his disciples, denied by another and forsaken by all.'[201] 'Just as Jesus remained unknown among men, so the truth remains among popular opinions with no outward difference.'[202] In contrast to Mohammed, he did not place himself in the light; he was 'wretched and alone'.[203] He did not kill but let himself be killed, he did not wish to be 'humanly successful' but to 'perish humanly', and this had to be if he was to be recognised as the hidden one.[204] For the proportion between ordinary human '*médiocrité*' and the dazzling darkness of God, manifest as veiled in it, appears now to be strangely exact. But *médiocrité* means for actual, historical man the inextricable dialectic in himself between *grandeur* and *misère*, exaltation and lowliness. And this dialectic is not destroyed by Christ but fulfilled and thereby revalued, and in such a way that he too, in order to be true man, must be 'doubled', must be both the one brought low from his

[200] P 563 B 675 L 503; P 582 B 578 L 236; P 589 B 758 L 255; P 613 B 735 L 347.
[201] P 636 B 792 L 499.
[202] P 638 B 789 L 225.
[203] P 404 B 596 L 1.
[204] P 402 B 599 L 209.

majesty, and the one exalted because of his humiliation: *deux avènements*.[205] The unity of this doubling is uniquely love—nothing else. And everything capable of form and figure can refer to nothing else than love, for love alone embraces its opposite, the condition of the sinner, and enfolds it into itself. '*Elu réprouvé*, et cetera.'[206] And from out of this unity of love in Christ there can be only two types of men: 'the righteous who think they are sinners, and the sinners who think they are righteous'.[207]

3. The unity of dialectical and figurative thought makes Pascal seem to be predestined to bring the traditional *theologumenon* of the Old and New Testaments to its consummation as *the* proof of the truth of Christianity. The whole apology of the *Pensées* leads up to this point. The anthropological perspectives, which served to unsettle sated reason, are completely overshadowed by the great sign that God has himself unmistakably buried in the public history of the world. Here all the motives in Pascal's thought converge: exact perception of the actual proportions combined with sharp separation of the mutually related orders, in both of which the evidence and the incomprehensibility of God is equally manifest. The relationship of the Old and the New Testaments, of Jew and Christian, is the 'double witness' of God's historical truth.[208] They form together, as a diptych, a comprehensible figure, but only because one of the wings prefigures the other, which is itself beyond the figurative. Figure is here therefore used in an internally analogous sense: on the one hand as prefiguration (*typos*) by the Old Testament of the New, which is beyond figure, and on the other as a manifest relationship between the figurative and what is beyond the figurative. Both aspects belong intrinsically together, because figurativeness in the first sense is a function of the whole figure.

This leads to two assertions: (1) 'Charity is not a figurative precept. It is a horrible thing to say that Christ, who came to replace figures by the truth, came only to set up the figure of

[205] P 566–567 B 678–679 L 253, 260.
[206] P 788 B 862 L 733.
[207] P 681 B 534 L 562.
[208] 'Les deux Témoins': P 772 B 852 L 859.

charity. . . .'[209] (2) 'Everything that does not lead to charity is figurative. The sole object of Scripture is charity. Everything that does not lead to this sole goal is figurative.'[210] From these two propositions together it follows that charity is of an order qualitatively different from that of figures, but that the figures, which belong to a lower order and can attain to love by no approximation, are born and made possible by a striving after love that penetrates their being. Therefore again it is the higher order that bears the lower and interprets it, although by comparison it is 'as nothing'. This strange dialectical relationship, which is necessarily so, is illustrated now by the whole historical actuality of the history of salvation and is set up before our eyes as an historically located occurrence in the past and yet—because the Jews continue to exist and perpetuate this relationship in history—as a '*miracle subsistant*'[211] for all times and places. For Pascal this historical form is the integration of all the other proofs; the individual miracles take second place to it.[212] Occasionally the whole evidentiality of the Christian religion is summed up in this single picture, '*le reste doit en être cru*';[213] In any case, this picture distinguishes the Christian religion from all others, which can produce nothing similar.[214] Pascal has hardly brought forward any new biblical material—this must be said against Filleau[215]—but he has handled the already available material in such a way that even Lagrange, who draws attention to the outmoded character of his exegetical approach, can identify himself completely with Pascal's fundamental thought[216] as it was expressed in the two theses just outlined.

The problem to which these theses give rise is, at the level of reason, only representable dialectically—that is, not concretely—but the biblical relationship of the Testaments makes

[209] P 608 B 665 L 849.

[210] P 583 B 670 L 270.

[211] P 526 B 706 L 335; P 620 B 830 L 718.

[212] P 407 B 619 L 454.

[213] P 581 B 576 L 594. [The rest of them ought to be believed.]

[214] P 393 B 693 L 198; P 400 B 598 L 218.

[215] '. . . *la découverte de quantité de choses* [*dans l'Ecriture*] *qui avaient jusques ici échappé à tout le monde*': *Discours sur les Pensées*, 1477.

[216] M. J. Lagrange, 'Pascal et les prophéties messianiques', *Revue Biblique* 3 (1906), 533–560.

this dialectic obvious beyond contradiction in the public realm of history. The dialectic lies in this; that the promise to Israel, in order to be proportioned to fulfilment, must belong to the order of charity—it must spring from it and move towards it and therefore must be understood in a sense that is alone not 'unworthy of God'[217]—but still the order of promise must leave that door shut, the opening of which can only be the work of the redeemer, and must therefore remain by contrast with him picture, figure, *typos*. Pascal is concerned that the intrinsically dialectical character of prophecy (to which also the law belongs) be manifest as exactly as possible; it promised completely unmysterious earthly goods, and yet the prophets remain obscure, they say that the meaning of their utterances cannot be grasped; indeed, their sayings 'are contradictory and cancel one another out . . . sometimes in the same chapter'.[218] The contradiction lies in the fact that in everything the order of love is intended, but that as a form of pedagogical concession by the Word of God parables and indirect reflections of love are at first set up, which, as something for the time being only comprehensible by the 'carnal people', must be misunderstood carnally, in the sense of *concupiscentia*. The blame for this lies with the carnal heart, for which the carnal promise is a temptation, leading to conviction and judgment, while the spiritual heart, which was hoped for in Israel and presupposed by the economy, would indeed have been able to interpret the picture as a picture pointing to a religious reality. Pascal distinctly says: 'Each man finds in these promises what lies in the depths of his own heart; either temporal or spiritual blessings, God himself or creatures; but with this difference, that those who are looking for creatures there find them indeed, but with many contradictions: they are forbidden to love them, bidden to worship and to love God alone (which comes to the same thing), and finally they find that the Messiah did not come for them; whereas those who are looking for God find him, without any contradictions, and find that they are bidden to love God alone and that a Messiah did come at the time foretold

[217] P 556 B 659 L 501.
[218] *Ibid.*, with Lagrange's remarks; *loc. cit.*, 543f.

to bring them the blessings for which they ask.'[219] The picture becomes a means of judgment separating *caritas* from *cupiditas*, and in this sense it is very easy to hold the view that God, who as a form of concession by the Word sets up this picture before the heart, wishes 'both to blind and to enlighten'.[220]

The picture that the Old Testament formed had therefore, in God's eyes, to be a picture of love—hence, a picture derived from love and drawing men to it, indeed containing it—without, however, excluding its opposite. 'Two supernatural foundations of our wholly supernatural religion, one visible, the other invisible. Miracles with grace, miracles without grace. The synagogue, treated with love as figurative of the Church and with hate as being merely figurative, was restored when about to collapse, when it stood well with God, and was thus figurative.'[221] The synagogue was a figure, and to that extent it did not perish; it was only a figure, and to that extent it perished. It was a figure that contained the truth, and it continued to exist until it no longer contained the truth.[222] But that means that the synagogue united in its visible form things that in the invisible order are opposed, things that could only be united at the level of the figure and that, when the truth came, had to be separated: 'Nothing is so like charity as greed, and nothing is so unlike. Thus the Jews, rich with possessions to flatter their greed, were very like Christians and very much unlike them. And thus they had the two qualities they had to have: being very like the Messiah in order to prefigure him, and being very unlike so that they should not be suspect witnesses.'[223] The figure, that the Messiah will form himself and that only would reveal man's sublimeness and his humiliation in their unity, could not be anticipated by any picture; thus the Jews were deceived both as to the true greatness of the Messiah (they did not think of him as God) and as to his true lowliness (they did not regard him as mortal: Jn 12.34).[224] Only in Christ 'are all contradictions

[219] P 563 B 675 L 503.
[220] P 581 B 576 L 594.
[221] P 771 B 851 L 903.
[222] P 772 B 852 L 859.
[223] P 575 B 663 L 615.
[224] P 577 B 662 L 256.

reconciled',[225] and this includes the essential contradiction between the image and Christ himself and, hence, also the contradiction of the image in itself. And so the Old Testament must be both 'pleasing [to God] and displeasing': displeasing, in so far as it absolutizes itself though only a picture—that is, as it understands itself as the reality that it prefigures—but pleasing, in so far as it is a picture of reality and, hidden within the reality, is justified by it.[226]

Therefore Pascal loves, next to the word 'figure', the word 'cipher', because this is an encoded figure that can be interpreted only when the code is broken. 'Figure includes absence and presence, pleasant and unpleasant. Cipher has a double meaning, of which one is clear and says that the meaning is hidden.'[227] Pascal's accompanying theory, that the prophets knew that they were talking only in pictures and that they had glimpsed beforehand the mystery of the Messiah, need not be taken over and would rightly be rejected by modern exegesis. But it is not necessary that they should have themselves used the code to produce the cipher; it is enough if the Christian has found the key in the New Testament and 'in the picture seen the thing represented'.[228] 'The Old Testament is a cipher',[229] certainly in the first place in so far as it relates to the New as nature does to grace, and therefore it is full of visible miracles so that the invisible miracles of the Messiah might be believed,[230] but more deeply it is not simply pure nature, but the incomprehensibly encoded medium (*le milieu*) between nature and grace, between paganism and Christianity,[231] which can produce no picture of itself except when it passes over into the truth to which it refers.

In so far, however, as the Messiah appears in a hidden way in the Jewish world of images and in his death participates in the collapse of the faithless Jerusalem, so far the Christian reality too is still half veiled in images so that there emerge (at least) three

[225] P 558 B 684 L 257.
[226] P 559 B 685 L 259.
[227] P 565 B 677 L 265.
[228] P 566 B 678 L 260.
[229] P 558 n. B 691 L 276.
[230] P 560, 563 B 643, 675 L 275, 503.
[231] P 496 B 608 L 289.

orders: 'As nature is only an image of grace, . . . even grace is only figurative of glory. . . . It was prefigured by the law and itself prefigures glory.'[232] And this glory too has its degrees, because the Church as the kingdom of the Holy Spirit is already the revelation of the mystery of the Messiah. For the Church the relationship of Old and New Testament has been decoded and can be understood, and yet it too partakes of the hiddenness and becomes an image of the eschatological glory. The retrospective view of the history of salvation from the point of view of the Church in itself constitutes an imposing apocalypse: 'How beautiful it is to see with the eyes of faith Darius and Cyrus, Alexander, the Romans, Pompey and Herod, working unwittingly for the glory of the Gospel!'[233] 'How beautiful to see with the eyes of faith the story of Herod or Caesar.'[234] Charles Péguy later, in his 'Eve', develops this world historical contemplation on the grand scale. What in truth is to be seen is something Augustine contemplated in his *de Civitate Dei*: the presence of piety, of love from the beginning, but also of the struggle between 'Jerusalem' and 'Babylon' from the beginning,[235] and therefore too of the struggle between the figurative and the transfigurative order, which yet includes all images within itself as the source and justification of all images—just in so far as these are *only* images and therefore inimical to it. Rightly taking as his guide the hermeneutical principle that 'to understand an author's meaning all contradictory passages must be reconciled',[236] must be made clear from a point of unity as an inner unity, Pascal construes the tensions and incompatibilities of the Old Testament from the perspective of the New. Such a procedure is for him, on the level of the interpretation of revelation, a thoroughly exact science that renders the historically extant material in the highest degree 'intelligible'. He has no need of any artificial allegorization; he mistrusts one-sided allegory.[237] It is for Pascal

[232] P 560 B 643 L 275.
[233] P 544 B 701 L 317.
[234] P 545 B 700 L 500.
[235] P 696–697 B 458–459 L 545, 918.
[236] P 558 B 684 L 257.
[237] '*Parler contre les trop grands figuratifs*': P 551, *cf.* 552 B 649f L 217, 254.

no contradiction of this notion of an exact science that the decisive light that makes things visible and comprehensible comes from revelation itself (and therefore from faith itself), and that the love of God can be perceived only by a heart with at least an inchoate love, which is at least set on love. If it is already true in the Old Testament that the one who loves God can distinguish the relativity of law and ceremony and can also see beyond the promises of earthly happiness to the reality of love, how much more in the New Testament will love be the decisive presupposition of true knowledge! 'We make ourselves an idol of truth itself, for truth apart from charity is not God but his image and an idol that we must neither love nor worship.'[238] That is also the final reason why the God of love wills to be hidden: only the pure heart penetrates beyond the truth to love, because precisely in God love is also the heart of truth. So the reciprocity of Old and New Testament remains in its inextricable criss-crossing the eternally valid, eternally actual, inexhaustible picture in which may be read by all men the dialectic of image and truth, of sin and redemption, of nature and grace, of earth and Heaven.

4. Truth is love, which is beyond the figurative. But love is God's love for us in his surrendering his Son for the life of the world. So what is beyond the figurative is God's action that makes him manifest—for this reason the Son is the making visible of the Father—and so all love that flows from the Son's action and which, in following him, returns to it, also shares in this making visible of God, taking shape from his fulness. Christ is the fulfilment of all images,[239] and so one can ask: 'Why did Christ not come in an obvious way instead of proving himself by previous prophecies? Why did he have himself foretold figuratively?'[240] He did this presumably in order not to put himself in the light, but rather to illuminate everything else from his own hiddenness, to judge by separation, to do things in God's way. Thus he is the manifestation of the hiddenness of God, who, without manifesting himself, makes every manifestation his image and likeness. 'Beautiful deeds are most

[238] P 597 B 582 L 926.
[239] P 619 B 766 L 607.
[240] P 632 B 794 L 389.

admirable when kept secret. When I see some of them in history . . . , they please me greatly . . . , [and] the most beautiful thing about them was the attempt to keep them secret.'[241]

Here the poor man becomes the epitome of Christian figurativeness. He is the hiddenness of Christ, but the Christian's love enables him to read in the poor man the image of the presence of Christ, the sacrament of Christ, and, most particularly, to read it in the act of love. The poor are the permanent presence of the picture world of the Old Testament; and to encounter Christ in the poor is the realisation of this '*miracle subsistant*', the always already-accomplished transition from the Old to the New Testament, the fulfilment of the promise. Pascal had, especially at the end of his life, grasped this with the utmost exactness. He visited the poor and gave them alms. He took them into his own house. He refused to support charitable, social institutions with financial contributions, although he recognized that this was a right and worthy activity for others; but such a way was not for him; rather, he sought to meet Christ in personal encounters with the poor. When he was denied communion in his mortal sickness in spite of his pleas because his condition was not regarded as hopeless, he said: 'Since I am not to be granted this grace, I would like to make good its lack by some good work, and not being able to communicate in the Head, I would like to communicate in the members, and for that purpose I have thought to have some poor, sick person brought here to whom can be rendered the same services as to me. . . . Go, please, and ask such a one from the priest.'[242] And in the *Pensées* he wrote: 'I love poverty because he loved it. I love goods because they afford me the means of helping the needy'—and this with an un-Jansenist universalism: 'I love all men as my brothers, because they are all redeemed.'[243]

In fact, the mystery of predestination is divine and does not concern the loving man. It affects Pascal existentially only at the point where he feels himself personally elect and therefore knows that of him the highest is demanded. But this highest is

[241] P 148 B 159 L 643.
[242] Mme Périer, *Vie de Pascal*, 33.
[243] P 732 B 550 L 931.

the universalism of love (while all desire is particular), through which the heart opens itself to what is beyond images, to the Holy Spirit.[244] Here there develops for Pascal the idea of the Church. It is the integration—through self-opening love—of persons who exist for themselves: *un corps plein de membres pensants*.[245] '*Adhaerens Deo unus spiritus est*: he that is joined to the Lord is one spirit. We love ourselves because we are members of Christ. We love Christ because he is the body of which we are members. All are one. One is in the other like the three Persons.'[246] In so far as someone is covetous (and that means hating), he must hate himself and seek that other whom he can love. 'But as we cannot love what is outside us, we must love a being who is within us but is not our own self. And this is true for every single person. Now only the universal being is of this kind; the kingdom of God is within us, universal good is within us, and is both ourselves and not ourselves.'[247] This heart of the Church, which builds itself up in the love of Christ—a Church that is always built up already in the head, Christ—does not seduce Pascal into a mysticism of the invisible. But he sees the Church as bound up in a living way in the redemption of the world: 'For it is the Church that merits, with Jesus Christ, who is inseparable from it, the conversion of all those who are not in the truth; and these converts are then those who help the Mother who has delivered them.'[248] That is said specifically of the visible, institutional Church, for in the next sentence unity with the Pope is emphasized; there is never any question for Pascal of a Church other than the Roman, in spite of all the persecution of Jansenism by Rome and despite all the qualms of conscience he endured as a result. 'I will never separate from her communion, . . . else I would be lost forever.'[249] Thus for Pascal the visible and invisible aspects of the Church are wholly inseparable, and by the same token he can in no way hypostatise the visible aspect alone in an image. But he does see in the model

[244] P 703 B 477 L 421.
[245] P 704 B 473 L 371.
[246] P 710 B 483 L 372.
[247] P 712 B 485 L 564.
[248] Letter 6 to Mlle de Roannez, 513.
[249] *Ibid.*, 514.

of the kingdom of God that the Church represents, that the ratio between the outer and inner, between the institution and the event, can vary in accordance with the capacity of the individual. 'For the people must understand the spirit of the letter, while the educated must submit their spirit to the letter.'[250] The model of the Church must be preserved intact through all variations and even all practical defections; this ideal spurs Pascal on to struggle against laxity in essentials. 'For it is an evil much less dangerous and much less general to permit irregularities while at the same time upholding the laws that forbid them, than to pervert the laws and justify the irregularities.'[251] In accordance with his view and intention Pascal placed himself, in this resistance to any fundamental weakening or false reassurance, in the phalanx of the saints who, for him, in the closest unity of the Spirit with Christ, form the frontline of the *résistance*, of the militant kingdom of God. The saints must not be thought of as 'renowned demigods'; they were simply men like us. 'St. Athanasius was a man called Athanasius, accused of several crimes, condemned by such and such a council for such and such a crime. All the bishops agreed, and in the end the Pope. What are those who resist told? That they are disturbing the peace, causing schism, et cetera. . . . They are excommunicated by the Church but yet save the Church.'[252] 'And is it not obvious [*visible*] that, just as it is a crime to disturb the peace when truth reigns, it is also a crime to remain at peace when the truth is being destroyed?'[253] The saints are the core of the *ecclesia militans* just because they love the true peace. Pascal at the end of his life consciously enlisted in their ranks at the same time that he withdrew himself from the *résistance* as he had understood and practised it in the *Provinciales*, and from the still sharper conflict (comparable to Kierkegaard's last struggle) over the subscription to the anti-Jansenist formulary, in a retreat that one should see neither as a retraction of his faith in its sympathy

[250] P 834 B 251 L 219.

[251] *Factum pour les Curés de Paris*, 907; *cf.* P 796 B 894 L 679: 'Some who love the Church complain when they see morals corrupted, but at least the laws survive. But these people corrupt the laws. The model is spoilt.'

[252] P 803 B 868 L 598.

[253] P 822 B 949 L 974.

for Jansenius (though he never held the 'five propositions') nor as a hardening of it, but as in reality the naked, heroic transcending of his own particular standpoint as he achieved a new standpoint within the unseen totality of the Church. This is indicated in his final letter, probably sent to Domat:

> When we want by our own power to bring something about, we are irritated by obstacles, because we feel in these hindrances something that is not inspired by the motive that moves us to act, and we find things that our own spirit, which moves us to action, has not formed. But when God truly moves us to act, we sense nothing outside ourselves that is not inspired by the same principle that inspires us . . . the same mover who prompts us to act encourages others to resist us, or at least he permits them, so that . . . this agreement does not disturb the peace of a soul and is one of the best signs that one is moved by the Spirit of God. . . . And as there is no doubt that God permits hindrances, one has the right to hope humbly that it is God who inspires our passions. And yet! One acts as if one had a mission to cause the truth to triumph, instead of simply having a mission to fight on behalf of the truth. The desire to conquer is so natural. . . . One thinks one is seeking the glory of God, when one is in reality seeking one's own.[254]

Thus has Pascal again, within the Church, indeed within its very highest rank, struggled out of a purely figurative sanctity, which could conceal its opposite beneath the image, to its imageless and invisible truth, most deeply perfecting his own doctrine by a true leap from one order to another. He remains the theologian of both image and leap, taken together, because in the wake of Augustine and the Reformation he undertakes to unite the concept of incomprehensible grace (interpreted as election and reprobation) with the concept of the universalism of love. At each stage then there is the figure that transcendentally justifies the invisible and infinite of the lower order as well as being deeply marked and threatened by this order that embraces it. Man is the figure in and above the two infinities, which question him so deeply, and Christ is the figure in and above man, who without Christ would be incomprehensible chaos, but who in the Passion draws him down into

[254] *Fragment d'une lettre* (1661), 524–526.

his night. But even Christ remains an unintelligible mystery without his Holy Spirit, who gives us 'the eyes of faith' that we may truly see in love what *is*, not however in ourselves but in the Church, to which we must ascend by renouncing our own standpoint. And so the leap to the higher order that makes sight possible is in every case a leap into the invisible, and so and only so is the ever-new daring of the heart ultimately the self-glorification and self-understanding of absolute love.

It is only in this context that the celebrated 'argument du pari',[255] in which Pascal uses the form of the reckoning of probability to lead man to God, can be justified. This attempt, the details of which we cannot discuss here, rests on the triumphant insight of the mathematician that what on a lower level is not subject to law can be grasped, held and transformed from above by a geometry subject to law, 'and thus by joining mathematical demonstration to the uncertainty of the die' (*et sic matheseos demonstrationes cum aleae incertitudine jungendo*), in the midst of uncertainties certainty can be attained.[256] But the analogy goes no further. Man is confronted with the inescapable necessity of choosing on the basis of his being thrown into existence, his *Geworfenheit*, to decide either for or against the existence of God. In this choice the possibility of a rational proof of the existence of God is systematically bracketed off, for such a comfortable resolution is to be denied to man; his eternal happiness, which is God, is to be attained by the movement of his heart, by the daring of a man's staking himself, for it is through this that the certainty of truth is perceived: '*à chaque pas . . . vous verrez tant de certitude du gain et tant de néant de ce que vous hasardez, que vous connaîtrez à la fin que vous avez parié pour une chose certaine, infinie, pour laquelle vous n'avez rien donné.*'[257]

5. PASCAL'S AESTHETIC

Pascal wrote no aesthetics, and if one sets his *Discours sur les passions de l'amour* on one side as inauthentic, there remain only a

[255] P 451 B 233 L 418.

[256] *Cel. Matheseos Academiae Parisiensi*, 74.

[257] P 451 B 233 L 481: 'At every step . . . you will see that your gain is so

few fragments in his work to indicate what its outline might have been. On the other hand, a concern with beauty and harmony is found in his whole work, and indeed in such a mysterious and unique way that there will always be the temptation to seek more from the reflection of what he achieved with such simplicity. Because his aesthetic is at its deepest theological, drawing hardly at all on other, extratheological traditions, such an attempt is all the more profitable in our context. It may help us finally to overcome the romantic picture, which ever bewitches the Germans, of a Pascal 'torn apart' in himself.[258] But such rents and gaping distances are not the greatness of this soul—it would be a cheap idea of greatness! His greatness is that of Romanesque architecture, throwing bridges across abysses and indeed incorporating the void within its structures. Recent French research has shown that in his *Pensées* Pascal thinks and writes more dialectically than had been thought, and that many of the expressions of terror, which had been taken as the deepest confessions of his heart, are only meaningful on the lips of his atheist partner. He himself never doubts the truth of Christianity.

The embryo of the *Pensées* is embedded in an amniotic fluid of the most general considerations, to which Pascal would most likely have given the name of rhetoric in its all-embracing sense—considerations of right form, of the right measure of presentation, of utterance, and also of deporting oneself generally; teaching about the *justesse* of the expression, not only of the literary but of existential expression too, and that again not simply in the sense of an ethic of conventions but of an unwritten wisdom in which converge ethics and the logic or metaphysics of existence. Such a wisdom certainly finds Epictetus and Montaigne on its flanks, and yet the central position is still left free. This teaching about *justesse* remains a bare idea that floats before Pascal, both for himself, so that he

certain and your risk so negligible that in the end you will realize that you have wagered on something certain and infinite for which you have paid nothing.'

[258] As Reinhold Schneider depicted it, projecting himself into his hero, in the introduction to his selections from Pascal (Fischer-Bücherei, 1954), or as Hans Ehrenberg (*In der Schule Pascals*, 1954) expressionistically and ecstatically sketched it.

may have the 'right taste' (*goût bon*) in thinking and speaking (*da nobis in Spiritu recta sapere*), and also for his partner, to whom he wishes to communicate wisdom with good taste. The credibility of the Christian truth should finally be grasped by a judgment of taste. That is to say, one must come not only to a conviction that it could not have been discovered by men,[259] but also to a conviction in its inner measuredness and its outward fitness.

If there is an objective measuredness of the thing in itself, a fitness for the subject whom the thing pleases, then there emerges in the relationship between the object and the observer the decisively right measure. 'There is a certain model of attractiveness and beauty based on a certain relation between our nature, weak or strong as it may be, and the thing that pleases us.'[260] According to Pascal this model is given expression in different contexts—it can be a house, or a poem, or a woman—and it will always please and will always be, as a model, one and the same. The ideal/model imposes itself therefore on the faculties; it is in accordance with it that 'geometrical beauty' or 'medical beauty', just as much as 'poetical beauty', are formed, the more so even, in that we can

[259] Filleau de la Chaise has in his somewhat garrulous manner revealed Pascal's intention in placing before his reader the complete picture of the Bible. 'What a beautiful system that is! . . . Could there be a man of sense and good faith who would not recognize that nothing could ever be said approaching this, and that those who have thus spoken, however little proof there be, assuredly merit being believed? There are indeed many men for whom it would already be a powerful proof that this had been said at all, for indeed it would not seem easy to one who examined it closely that it had been invented; it would only be necessary to look at what the most skilful of those who had wished to discourse on this subject had said. . . . In truth these are not their ways, and it is strange that they have not noticed it and that they have not availed themselves in this of a certain delicacy of discernment that they show in other matters. For there is no one who would deny that in regard to those things that fall beneath our senses we have in ourselves a certain sense that enables us to judge, simply by their manner, whether what is presented to our eyes is a work of nature or of men. . . . Why not extend this principle that thus guides us and not discern, by what we feel in ourselves and by what we experience, that these great ideas have a character quite different from what the human spirit is capable of producing [1485–1486]?

[260] P 37 B 32 L 585.

much better discern the relationship between ideal and realisation in the case of mathematical or medical correctness than in the case of the poetic, where the ideal remains obscure to us.[261] This leads Pascal inevitably to the '*homme universel*' or the '*honnête homme*' who, instead of being a specialist in a particular field, corresponds in the completeness of his relation to reality to the model or correct relationship. 'This universal quality is the only one I like.' 'It is much better to know something about everything than everything about something.'[262] But Pascal properly never considers the *honnête homme* from an aesthetic point of view—that is to say, as a complete work of art—but from the point of view of his effectiveness—that is to say, 'rhetorically' or, if one wishes, apostolically. '*Il faut donc un honnête homme, qui puisse s'accomoder à tous mes besoins généralement*',[263] who can awaken in me the truth, who 'has shown us not his own wealth but that which we have in common, and this kindness makes him agreeable to us, quite apart from the fact that our shared insight necessarily moves us to like him'.[264] The fashionable definition of the *honnête homme* by the Chevalier de Méré required of him the 'art of pleasing', of 'making oneself loved',[265] but for Pascal this amiability soon takes on earnest, Christian tones. It is a matter from the very beginning of a model that is both subjective and objective: '*Il faut de l'agréable et du réel; mais il faut que cet agréable soit lui-même pris du vrai.*'[266] Only then does such 'pleasing' (*plaire*) make contact with the *esprit de finesse*, which in a glance takes in the overall proportions of things and from that standpoint forms a judgment,[267] as also with the *sens droit* and the *esprit de justesse*.[268] But then it suddenly becomes clear, that the secret model, in accordance with which the heart takes pleasure in and judges

[261] P 38 B 33 L 586.

[262] The last sentence is crossed out. P 40, 42 B 35, 37 L 647, 195.

[263] P 41 B 36 L 605. [What I need is an all-round good man who can adapt himself to all my needs generally.]

[264] P 44 B 14 L 652.

[265] J. Mesnard, *Pascal* (*op. cit.*), 52f (ET p. 48).

[266] P 47 B 25 L 667. [There must be elements both pleasing and real, but what is pleasing must itself be drawn from what is true.]

[267] P 21 B 1 L 512.

[268] P 22 B 3 L 751.

things, is determined by the innermost inclination of the heart, and that the great either-or between *cupiditas* and *caritas* cuts right through the norm of beauty. The 'whole' of fitness is either open to the love of God as it is, or it is closed to it so as to be purely worldly.[269] Pascal is relentless in his exposing of the way the heart succumbs to the powers of worldly delusion and of the entanglements of personal and social conventions; he attempts to loose the heart of the Christian individual from them in order to bind it to the true wholeness as measure and model. On the other hand he is enough of a realist to know the power of automatism over a soul sunk in the realms of matter and also to demand in the service of the highest synthesis that 'we must combine the outward and inward ... we must go down on our knees, pray with our lips. ... If we expect help from this outward part we are being superstitious, if we refuse to combine it with the inward we are being arrogant.'[270] 'Custom and habit provide the strongest proofs and those that are most believed. They influence the automaton, which leads the mind unconsciously along with it. ... *Inclina cor meum, Deus.*'[271] And so finally there is required, as a formula for aesthetics, a model in which the higher order of love informs the lower order of sensible pleasure without prejudice to the far-reaching judgment of *caritas* over *cupiditas*. Pascal, to whom one vainly imputes the Cartesian absolute dualism between matter and spirit, who did not regard animals as automata and who knew about the role of vital powers,[272] here does not overlook the unifying role of woman and Eros.[273] The 'heart' is the organ of the aesthetic and the ethical alike, because it is at every level the organ of love.[274] Correspondingly, Pascal does not demand in the social sphere the abolition of all ceremony (on which rests any beauty in political and public life), but its being rendered transparent, through the most profound ascesis in the heart of

[269] *Cf.* E Wasmuth, 'Von der Vernunft des Herzens', appendix to *Pascal: Die Kunst zu Überzeugen* (1950), 356f.

[270] P 469 B 250 L 944.

[271] P 470 B 252 L 821.

[272] P 260, 262 B 342, 340 105, 741.

[273] P 37–38 B 32–33 L 585–586.

[274] J. Russier, *op. cit.*, 163–165.

the prince, to the archetype of the kingdom of *caritas*. He therefore demands much: beyond naive popular piety (which is relatively in the right) and the critique of the enlightened (which is relatively in the wrong), the *ignorance savante qui se connaît*, which without succumbing to it, can justify the beauty of appearance.[275] What he demands as a Christian, is what, after Philip II, the French Baroque of the *grand siècle* had demanded for its own order: an aesthetic that has room in its heart for the most demanding asceticism. And this not purely as a matter of individual preference but as the presupposition for allowing and recognising earthly beauty. It is just this hierarchical ordering of illusion, disillusion and again an embracing illusion in the power of love that forms the fundamental Catholic response to the Lutheran dialectic. It is the attempt—which in its way the great German romantics continued—of human sensibility,[276] employing all its resources of judgment and taste, to depict reality at every level of being without abridgement or concealment. This ideal of a heart attuned to every level of the universe—*le cœur a son ordre*—manifests itself to Pascal as the human imitation of that archetypal and inimitable consuming of the heart of God in the death of love and in Christ's eternal transfiguration of love, for '*la grandeur de la foi éclate bien davantage lorsque l'on tend à l'immortalité par les ombres de la mort*'.[277]

[275] P 308 B 327 L 83; *Trois discours sur la condition des grands*, 615–621.

[276] On Pascal's *sensibilité* and *tendresse raisonnable* and the relationship of *charité* and *amitié*, *cf.* Gilberte Périer, *Vie de Pascal*, 25f.

[277] Letter of 17 October 1651, 498. [The greatness of faith is much more brilliant when one approaches immortality through the shadows of death.]

HAMANN

1. ON THE EVE OF IDEALISM

Hamann, with his theological *Aesthetica in nuce*, stands in the background of the whole idealist movement, which he mysteriously overshadows yet equally mysteriously supersedes and frames, for no one, not even his closest friend Herder, not even Jacobi and the Münster circle, still less Kant, really understood his purpose; he points to a dimension that has never been filled, reaching out his hand over the decades, to Søren Kierkegaard and to the Léon Bloy of *Salut par les Juifs*. Hamann, more than anyone, has always been a solitary, indeed unique, figure in German letters: 'I work alone—with nobody to come to my aid with his understanding, judgment, even taste.'[1] And again: 'I have a feeling . . . that those who write for a few have more sense than those who write for many; unless you first have the few on your side, you will never win over the many.'[2] Christianity is the front on which he takes up his outpost, and he defends it from sinking in any way into humanism: from breaking down into poetry (Herder), philosophy (Kant), agnosticism for the sake of faith (Jacobi), pseudobiblical humanism (M. Mendelssohn) or pseudomystical freemasonry (Starck)—(to say nothing of the vapid Enlightenment of Nicolai and the 'Nicolaites;, or that 'crowned philosopher',

[1] Written to Lindner, 30.12.1760 (Z 2, 55). Throughout, when quoting Hamann's works, I shall refer to Nadler's critical edition (Vienna, 1949–57) = N. Quotation of letters follows the critical edition of Ziesemer and Henkel (Inselverlag, 1955; so far 4 vols.) = Z. Quotation of letters to Jacobi follows Gildenmeister: *Hamanns Leben und Schriften V* (1868) = G. I also use the valuable but as yet incomplete edition with commentary published by Fritz Blanke and Lothar Schreiner (*Hamanns Hauptschriften erklärt*, Hrsg. von Fritz Blanke und Lothar Schreiner, Bertelsmann, 1956; so far 3 vols.) = H. Josef Nadler: *J. G. Hamann. Der Zeuge des Corpus mysticum* (Mueller, Salzburg, 1949) = Na.

[2] To Lindner, 5.5.1761 (Z 2, 85). Cf. the letter to Herder of 3.4.74: 'I live as though in the wilderness. I cannot endure any society. . . . Not one friend do I possess—except in Lindner an analogon and pillar of salt of friendship' (Z 3, 76).

Salomon de Prusse in Berlin, whom he courted so ardently and finally damned as the Antichrist). Yet these men are his friends, the circles in which his spirit moves, so that he fights with 'flesh and blood' and at the same time with the 'mighty despots of this darkness'. The friend must be the bitter foe; Hamann must, for example, spare Mendelssohn when, as the conscience incarnate of German idealism in its advance, he may not do so. 'Have pity upon me, have pity upon me, o ye my friends; for the hand of God hath rested upon me also.' And here he bids farewell, already in the twilight of death: 'Think not to add one single ell to me or to my stature. Let not the measure of my "greatness" be that of a giant or an angel, no not a handsbreath more than the common human ell. Lest the world be plundered to disguise and transfigure a putrid sinner with the aureole of a saint, make me, I beg you, no moustaches in my life, so long as I can still laugh with the rest of you. I myself will strip off my clothes, spread forth my hands as he that swimmeth spreadeth forth his hands, and swim over the quiet-flowing waters of the past, or sink beneath them.'[3] In this, his last testament, Hamann speaks of undressing because, throughout his life, he went under masks and pseudonyms, as Kierkegaard was to do; but Hamann's disguise was even better. Both fight the religious fight in the heart of the hostile camp of the aesthetes, and thus Hamann can say that his testamentary 'undressing' will likely enough only make him more obscure to his critics than his masks.[4] Kierkegaard used *aesthetic* as a sharply defined concept, with an exact place in his triadic system. Hamann's concept has much the same range of meaning, but almost always with a touch of irony to it; for him, *aesthetic* means the jejune, bodiless attitude, typical of the Enlightenment, that finds the crude, physical, earthly quality of Christianity, its fleshliness, its crucifixion and resurrection and *corpus meum* too unrefined, preferring to withdraw to the airy castles of rationalism, or, indeed, into the 'ethereal edifice' of the 'purisms of Pure Reason'.[5] Few thinkers have demanded conceptual clarity with Hamann's insistence, and the climax of his critique of Mendelssohn's *Jerusalem* comes

[3] *Fliegender Brief, 1. Fassung* (N 3, 404).

[4] *Ibid.*, 366.

[5] *Anzeige der Kritik der reinen Vernunft* (N 3, 279).

when he accuses Mendelssohn of being vague in order to deceive.[6] But this ironical use of the concept *aesthetic* is only part of the story; while Kierkegaard, who to begin with had sharply distinguished between the *aesthetic* and the *ethical*, subsequently strives toward a balance of the two,[7] Hamann allows the aesthetic to regain, without further transposition, the religious and Christian fulness of dimension inherent in it, and he even feels free to speak of the 'aesthetic obedience of the Cross'.[8] The title *Aesthetica in nuce* also makes use of this fully developed concept. A sentence like the following well illustrates the affinity and subtle difference between him and Kierkegaard: 'Talking to half-blinded art critics . . . I have to use what they give me, an aesthetic language of their own, with only one difference: theirs are the marks of arid fibres, mine, the better marks of a fresh green wood, theirs are trees whose fruit withereth, without fruit, twice dead, plucked up by the roots (Jud 12), mine, such as are planted by streams whose waters flow out of the Sanctuary.'[9] Hamann thus confronts a withered aesthetic with one that is full-blooded, finds his way straight back from the one to the other; but without having to espouse a Kierkegaardian dialectic to do so, for it was Hamann's belief that the act of *aisthēsis*, if it is not curtailed, is the original religious act itself, for all things are God's word and language, and therefore one who apprehends these things hears God himself speaking. For both Hamann and Kierkegaard, Socrates is a mythical and paradigmatic figure, but what seems to be a meeting point between the two men turns out to demonstrate the gap better, perhaps, than anything. For Kierkegaard, Socrates, the Socratic art of midwifery and Socratic ignorance are all the marks of the human, in sharp contrast to the divinely human, that which is of Christ. For Hamann, however, Christ

[6] *Fliegender Brief, 1. Fassung*. 'The πρωτον φευδος, or principal mask, of the whole of that play of Mendelssohn's "in which our reason is deceived" consists in the way clear, definite concepts are missing.' (N 3, 394)

[7] 'Either-Or', II. Two of the titles are: 'The aesthetic validity of marriage', and 'The balance between the aesthetic and the ethical in the development of the personality', (in Hirsch's edition 3 and 165).

[8] *Zwey Scherflein I* (N 3, 234).

[9] *Fliegender Brief*, 1. Fassung (N 3, 378).

himself appears directly through Socrates and his maieutic art, and Socratic ignorance is transfigured, becoming the 'oracular utterance of the great teacher of the heathen. If any man think that he knoweth any thing, he knoweth nothing yet as he ought to know. But if any man love God, the same is known of him.'[10] And this brings Hamann directly to the inference 'that the grain of all our natural wisdom must decay, pass into ignorance, and . . . out of this death, this nothing, there must spring forth, in new creation, the life and being of a higher knowledge.' That is a sentiment that German mysticism and Kierkegaard's sworn enemy, Hegel, would have echoed.[11] Kierkegaard had no liking for Hamann's idea that the Christian and theological may appear directly through the secular and philosophical: 'Sometimes there seems to me to be an element of blasphemy involved.'[12] For Hamann, the Socratic *daimōn* and *Scheblimini*, the good Christian 'homely spirit', are secretly one and the same, and Socrates is, all unwitting, a Christian humorist. Hamann is speaking at the beginning of German idealism, and the hope that one could show how the mythical *in toto* led into, was transparent to revelation—the great theme of the old Schelling, upon whom, according to Horst Fuhrman, Hamann exerted a decisive influence[13]—belonged as yet to the future; Kierkegaard, writing at the end of the era, will have to set in order the borders of Christianity because of the infringements that have occurred.

Hamann never wrote a philosophical aesthetic; even in his *Aesthetica in nuce*, which constitutes the main part of *The Crusading Philologist* (*Kreuzzüge eines Philologen*), he is speaking as a 'philo-logist', that is, as a lover of the Word, understood by him in its unity as divine and as human word. Since his conversion experience (in London, Easter 1758), which all his life he treated as undeniably an act of supernatural grace, since his great 'memorial', *The Diary of a Christian* (*Tagebuch eines Christen*), he could see the world only as the glory of God's love, emptying and abasing itself. All creation is *schechina*, a gleam

[10] *Sokratische Denkwürdigkeiten II* (N 2, 74).

[11] Quoted by Hegel in *Über Hamanns Schriften* (Werke [1835] XVII, 64).

[12] *Nachlass-Papiere 1833–43*, p. 142 (quotation from H 1, 49).

[13] H 1, 40f.

from the glory of the presence of the Lord, and at the same time a pillar of clouds and fire; just as the visible word and the Scriptures are the invisible thought of the Spirit made gloriously manifest: '*Schechina*, tabernacle and *merkaba* of our feelings, thoughts and ideas through audible and visible signs of language.'[14] 'Speaking is a translation—from the language of angels into the language of men—so that thoughts become words, objects become names, images become signs; these may be poetic or kyriological, historic or symbolic or hieroglyphical, and philosophical or characterical.'[15] *Kyriological* means 'taken in its proper sense', but underneath we have Hamann's idea that this proper meaning is the Logos of the *Kurios*, the Word of the Lord Christ, and that also pertains for the 'poetic' words, the 'historic' words, and so on. For it is God who speaks, speaking as Creator and creating through the Word. And thus he is 'the powerful Speaker' and 'free Potter',[16] 'the poet at the beginning of days',[17] and the word is, as Herder and Novalis will also say, a poem, (Claudel's *art poétique*) in a wider sense than the word had hitherto possessed. But God 'crowned the physical revelation of his glory (*schechina*) with his masterpiece, man. He created man in the form of God—in the image of God created he him. By this decree of the Creator's, the most intricate knots of human nature and destiny are loosed. Blind heathens have recognised that invisibility is something man has in common with God. The concealed shape of our bodies, the countenance of our heads and the extremities of our arms, these are the visible form in which we go our way'—here he alludes not just to the hidden spirit that appears by means of the body, but to the trinitarian nature of the body's form: the Father begetting in secret, the Son appearing, and the Spirit as active extremity. 'But the creation of the scene relates to the creation of men as does epic to dramatic poetry. The former came about through the Word; the latter through action.'[18] The outside world has

[14] *Zwey Scherflein II* (N 3, 237). For some reason the meaning of this fundamental concept of Hamann's escaped Nadler, who identifies the *schechina* with the tabernacle (N 6, 337).

[15] *Aesthetica in nuce* (N 2, 199).

[16] *Ibid.*, 200.

[17] *Ibid.*, 206.

[18] *Ibid.*, 198, 200.

had its place given to it, but through his freedom man is intrinsically destiny and event, a truth that already comes to light in the creation myth. Not until man does the profundity of existence unfold itself and yield a present with the scope of history, of past and future, each being an expression of Spirit. Man comes from God and goes to God, and as present he can be interpreted only protologically and eschatologically; and so, when Hamann speaks of man as the highest word of the Poet-God, at once he must also speak of the Fall and of how man came to clothe himself with the skins of animals, which he explains derives originally 'from the general durability of animal characters,[19] which became known through Adam's association with the Old Poet, (whose name in the Hebrew tongue is Abaddon, but in the Greek tongue Apollyon)'. When the Devil too is a poet, 'the aesthetic' is again being understood in its fashionable meaning, as fiction and unreality; in the Fall, aesthetics of this sort made chaos of the ordered poem, so that we were 'left with only a jumble of verses and *disiecti membra poëtae* for our use. The scholar's role is to collect them up; the philosopher's, to interpret them; and the modest role of the poet is to imitate them—or, yet more daring! . . . to give them a destiny'.[20] But it is not quite clear what Hamann means by *poet* here. Is it the poet in the narrower sense who thus becomes a renewer of the divine creative act? Such an idea would be quite typical of Hamann. Nevertheless, the task of reassembling a fragmentary world and giving it a destiny is not simply the privilege of the poetic individual, but of man as such—for Hamann, ethics and religion have an essential part to play, for only thus can man and creation be healed. 'But how are we to raise up the extinct language of Nature from the dead?' Hamann answers by showing us 'a shortcut via hyperbole', (a reference to 1 Cor 12.31); here we have an exuberant aesthetic, embracing the whole man and his whole existence. 'Let us now hear the conclusion of the whole' of the 'newest aesthetic, which is the oldest: Fear God, and give glory to him for the hour of his judgment is come, and worship him that made Heaven and

[19] *Ibid.*, 198.
[20] *Ibid.*, 198f.

earth and the sea and the fountains of waters!'[21] In this aesthetic, then, beauty is treated unequivocally as a trascendental concept constituted by analogy, and analogy is given the status of its central method, so that no objective or historical sphere of existence is excluded nor given open or secret identification, for although he bounds from one step to another, or rather, precisely because we can see him doing so, we are nonetheless shown an all-embracing beauty that can ultimately be none other than the glory, the *schechina*, of God.

Now we have an outline, however hasty, of the area and can measure it out more carefully and trace the hidden proportions of theological aesthetic. Let us begin this time at the centre.

'The revelation in the flesh is the midpoint of everything. This is the meaning of the divine Word in its entirety, and the reason why it is given to us.'[22] 'The best part of heaven ... containing the heart and bowels of God's mercy ... is in the sending of his only begotten Son.'[23] 'Thus even the furnishings and animal housekeeping of our bodies are a prophecy; everything is made through him who has redeemed us. Had he not wanted to redeem us, nothing would be there; this life, this existence in him and in his love, is the light of men.' Thus is 'Christ the head' of the *whole* body, thus the 'measure of each part'.[24] This he is both as creator and as redeemer, and therefore as representative, of each man, who has his measure and his rightness in him and through him. 'The witness of the Holy Spirit in our souls is not dependent on memory, and even if we forget everything, Jesus the 'Crucified represents all wisdom and all strength, all reason and all senses. It would be more possible to live without one's heart and head than without him. He is the head of our nature and all our powers and the source of the movement that in a Christian can no more stand still than the pulse in a living man. But only a Christian is a living man, an eternally immortally living man, for he lives, moves and exists in God, with God, indeed, for God.'[25] Christ is in the fullest

[21] *Ibid.*, 211, 217.
[22] *Biblische Betrachtungen* (N 1, 242).
[23] *Ibid.*, 263.
[24] *Ibid.*, 237.
[25] *Gedanken über meinen Lebenslauf* (N 2, 48).

sense 'the only man upon whom the Spirit of the Lord rested, just as Gideon's fleece alone lay soaked in dew amid the barren land all about',[26] 'and all the Scriptures are the life story of the only righteous man, who came into the world to atone for the crooked ways of men and restore the royal way through his suffering and life'.[27] We, however, 'cannot answer God, appear before his judgment, reply to his questions, without first consulting with the Spirit of his Son and in faith, in trust in his intercession, seeking hearing and forgiveness, grace and freedom'.[28] From *Biblical Reflections* (*Biblische Betrachtungen*) to *The Final Page* (*Das letzte Blatt*), Hamann never deviated one iota from this consistent and unbroken Christocentricity; the commentary on Mt 22.42 'What think ye of Christ?' is a good example of this:

> Man is a thinking creature. The Fall cost him his brain, his spiritual brain. For us, all thoughts of Christ or God are hidden, indeed repugnant. A supernatural change of heart, a beatific illumination, is indispensable if we are able to think rightly of Christ. We men must expect God to examine and test us through thoughts as well as actions—above all, we must test and examine our thoughts of Christ, for God will base his judgment on them. ... What think ye of Christ? ... Of his glory? ... Whose son is he? What think ye of his person? What think ye of his anointing—of him who anointed him, the Father; of the office to which he was anointed; of the Spirit with which he was anointed; of the measure of his anointing; of the spices and sweet odours thereof; of the beauty and charm; of the worth and delightfulness; of the virtue and power your redeemer has to soften your hearts and heal your wounds? ... Without right thoughts of Christ, it is impossible to think rightly about God. ... This question is the best guide to self-examination. ... This question puts a gag on all impertinence and useless curiosity. ... This question overturns all prejudices and errors in respect of Christ himself and of all other things. And at the same time this question clarifies Christ's thoughts towards us. As we think of him, he thinks of us, and as he thinks of us, we become, for his thoughts are creations, secrets and miraculous. ...[29]

[26] *Bibl. Betrachtungen* (N 1, 48).
[27] *Ibid.*, 120.
[28] *Ibid.*, 134.
[29] Written around 1760 (N 4, 249f.).

2. BEAUTY AND KENŌSIS

The God-Man is the key to God as to the World. 'None but the only-begotten Son, which is in the bosom of the Father, has given an exegesis of his fulness and grace of truth', in that in his unity he represents both the unity and the trinitarian nature of God and, likewise sums up within himself the unity and multiplicity[30] of the world: 'Omnes-Unus παντας-Εἷς.'[31] In that he is the visibility of God, the truth of the world and man, the Incarnation of the Word of God becomes the absolute canon of all aesthetics in accordance with its principal qualities: (1) to have become man in an act of gracious freedom, (2) to have done so in a most pristine act of self-emptying, (3) to have embraced the flesh through becoming flesh and through the flesh to have healed the spirit, and (4) to have superseded all the unreality in human thought and imagination through his reality in the flesh, bringing them back into the realm of reality. These are the four principal aspects of Hamann's theology, and they open the way for a formulation and critique of his idea of beauty as a whole.

1. God's appearance in Christ is free. It is grace, not nature, and therefore cannot be reduced to the schema with which we are familiar within the world, 'ground and appearance', 'content and form'. Although his emphasis on the senses borders on pure empiricism, he never, not even in the secular sphere, acknowledges a mere schema of matter and form. The language of men, unlike that of animals, always unites two things, an organic relationship and a free determining act, so that it is possible for men 'to join together quite opposing ideas using the external signs and sounds of words' and 'to express a single image of our souls using quite different signs. Here we find simultaneously a reminder of the likeness of God and of the Fall. To the first belonged Adam's freedom to name the animals as he wished; through the second, the misuse of this freedom arose and with it all the inconvenience that it caused.'[32] And if it is true that all subhuman nature contains an abundance of images of

[30] *Golgotha und Scheblimini* (N 3, 315).

[31] *Das letzte Blatt* (N 3, 410).

[32] *Bibl. Betrachtungen* (N 1, 220).

human life, Providence and the properties of God—indeed 'that the whole of man's physical nature, from his conception to his decay'—is 'a typical history' of mankind, 'still the only key to their understanding is redemption itself', God's free, forming intervention from above. 'All our limbs are claves [i.e., violin pegs] for our souls, which exist in a wonderful relationship to the merely audible sounds. Their harmony is not the wood, not the strings, nor the fingers; yet it is brought forth by all three in union.'[33] There is harmony, then, between the expressing body and the expressed soul, and yet a lasting freedom in the relationship of expression; if this is true even of the spirit within the world, how much more so of the divine spirit.

Here is the basis of Hamann's entire linguistic philosophy, which, incidentally, develops further after his reading of Aristotle; it is a philosophy in which there is clearly a peripatetic element. Repudiating Herder's enthusiastic naturalism in a devastating caricature,[34] he moves directly from the organic character of man to the 'judicial and magisterial dignity' that corresponds to his freedom, and it is here that Hamann perceives the essential quality of the spirit. 'So do neither instinct nor *sensus communis* define man, neither natural nor national rights the prince.' 'Consciousness, attentiveness, abstraction and even moral conscience seem largely to be energies of our freedom', but again, this is the freedom of a body and soul; 'thus there is nothing in our understanding that was not first in our senses, just as there is nothing to our entire bodies that has not at one time been through our or our parents' stomachs. The *stamina* and *menstrua* of our reason are therefore, in the truest sense, revelations and traditions that we receive and make our own. The analogy provided by animal metabolism is the only ladder to the anagogic knowledge of the spiritual economy.'[35] 'The secret of the marriage between such contrasting natures as the outer and inner man, or body and soul', true receptivity and free spontaneity, this genuinely Aristotelian mystery of a free spontaneity within the very process of reception, of a spiritual apprehending, then, of sensible material, of a transformation

[33] *Ibid.*, 228f.

[24] *Philologische Einfälle und Zweifel* (N 3, 42f.).

[35] *Ibid.*, 37–9.

into spiritual revelation of what arrives as sensible revelation is the reason that 'man is not just a living soil, but also the son of the soil, and not jut soil and seed (according to the systems of the materialists and the idealists), but the king of the field'. Applied to language, this means that 'man *learns* to use and direct all his limbs and senses, including, of course, his ear and tongue, because he *can* learn, he *must* learn, and he is glad to, *wants* to, learn. It follows that the origin of language is just as natural and human as the origin of all our actions, skills and arts. Yet despite the fact that every apprentice contributes to his instruction . . . *learning*, in the true sense of the word, is no more invention that it is mere recollection.'[36] Man has freedom, then, to self-determination, yet predetermination to be free; the necessity of interpreting sensible revelation through the spirit, by analogy logically brings with it the possibility of failing to apprehend that revelation. If man's language is a function of this peculiarly human factor, the possibility and necessity of freedom, his word will always be a right or wrong answer to the word he receives from the self-revealing Creator, and he himself is, to the depths of his being, intended for and disposed to dialogue. For all its Aristotelian and sensualist foundations, Hamann's theory of language is a Christian anthropology quite without parallel in its time; neither Herder nor the idealistic theory of language (of Humboldt) showed any interest in it, and it was not taken up again until our own century by the masters of the dialogical principle. Here it must be said (in refutation of Unger's interpretation) that this theory is ultimately unified; Hamann's logic leads him to understand the Creation and nature as God speaking and proclaiming himself, but man as fallen, unable to achieve his self-determination, no longer able to respond with interpretation, and thus coming to need the revelation of Christ in the form of inward grace and outward history of salvation (as it appears in the Scriptures) in order to apprehend what God intended the world to mean.

When Hamann says that God has revealed himself to men 'in nature and in his word', 'each revelation declaring and supporting the other',[37] or when he declares that 'nature and

[36] *Ibid.*, 40f.

[37] *Bibl. Betrachtungen* (N I, 8f.).

history are . . . the two great *commentarii* on the divine Word',[38] this doctrine of the 'Two Books' should not be taken in a neutral sense, for Hamann explicitly decrees that the Book of Scripture is to be ranked higher than the Book of Nature; he 'shows the primacy of the former'.[39] 'Is there any book, indeed, is even the Book of Nature itself like unto that which alone can uncover for us the veil of nature and her own heart, yes, the heart of her Creator?'[40] 'Nature vanishes before thy word. Here is the Holy of Holies; the whole of creation is but a forecourt.'[41] 'This is the Tree of Life, whose leaves are to heal the peoples, whose fruits are to nourish the souls.'[42] In God's Word lies 'the only key that can open to us the knowledge in both books'.[43] 'I found the unity of the divine will in the redemption of Jesus Christ, so that all history, all miracles, all commandments and works of God converged upon this midpoint.'[44] Therefore 'all history is . . . like nature, a sealed book, a concealed witness, a riddle that cannot be solved unless we plough with some heifer other than our reason'.[45] If the two revelations relate to each other as what is general and open relates to what is particular and secret, still 'the unity of the Originator' is reflected 'in the very dialect of his works—in all a single Note of immeasurable height and depth'[46]—and that note is the eternal Son, who as the Word, is the end toward which all things begin truly to speak, including even man.

2. If the Word of God in Creation finds interpretation in the Word of Christ in his Incarnation, and if this note rings on in the Word of the Holy Spirit in the Scriptures, then the immeasurable height and depth of the One Note are the simultaneity of exaltation and abasement, 'a proof of the most glorious majesty and most empty depletion—a single miracle of such endless repose, likening God to nothing, that you must in

[38] *Brocken* (N 1, 303).
[39] *Bibl. Betrachtungen* (N 1, 202).
[40] *Ibid.*, 119.
[41] *Ibid.*, 49.
[42] *Ibid.*, 92.
[43] *Brocken* (N 1, 303).
[44] *Gedanken ueber meinen Lebenslauf* (N 2, 40).
[45] *Sokr. Denkw.* (N 2, 65).
[46] *Aesth.* (N 2, 204).

all conscience deny your existence or be a dumb beast; but at the same time of such infinite power, which fills all in all, that you are caught up helplessly in fervent devotion'.[47] And this is so because freedom is 'the maximum and minimum of all our natural powers',[48] and because God speaks to his creature as befits its limits and laws: in the 'condescension' to very nothingness, even thus to reveal his all. Even in Creation, not just in redemption through the flesh and the Cross, this was a fundamental law, yet it involves no paradox, because in the guise of the utmost humility God really does show his utmost love and glory, and because 'Golgotha', God's final *kenōsis*, already contains within itself '*scheblimini*': 'Sit thou at my right hand.'[49] Here Hamann, in Luther's footsteps, makes his strongest statement, which at the same time governs the whole form of his aesthetic, saying that God 'condescends to the blindness of Adam', that 'a dissimulation by God toward men'[50] takes place, that he hides himself in the form of wretchedness just as King Saul did 'amid the refuse and the sweepings',[51] that he 'sought out' for himself 'the most contemptible of nations',[52] that he left 'Heaven and everything to cleave to his wife' and share 'with her her fate, her poverty, her sin and shame'.[53] But the same wonder that fills Hamaan at the depletion of God in the servant figure of Christ fills him when he contemplates it in the Holy Scriptures, for there 'old rags' are twisted into ropes to pull man out when he lies trappped like Jeremiah, in the miry pit,[54] and one must, with Paul, venture to speak of the foolishness and infirmity of God,[55] because 'God has adapted as much as he could, condescending to man's tendencies and thoughts, indeed, even to his prejudices and weaknesses'.[56] 'The

[47] *Ibid.*

[48] *Philol. Einfälle und Zweifel* (N 3, 38).

[49] *Cf.* L. Schreiner's commentary on *Golgotha und Scheblimini* (N 3, 291f.; H 7, esp. 47, 136).

[50] *Bibl. Betrachtungen* (N 1, 19).

[51] *Ibid.*, 97.

[52] *Brocken* 3 (N 1, 303).

[53] *Bibl. Betrachtungen* (N 1, 211).

[54] *Ibid.*, 5.

[55] *Ibid.*, 6.

[56] *Ibid.*, 10.

Holy Ghost became an historian of actions such as men perform, foolish, nay sinful', and like David, whose pose as a madman was sheer cunning, 'he daubs the doors of the gates so that no Achish could make any sense out of them, signs people took for the handwriting of an idiot, and, worse still, he lets his spittle run down onto his beard. The inspiration that he gave as God's word makes him seem to contradict and pollute himself. He has the lies of an Abraham, the bloodguilt of Lot, he distorts the man pleasing to God into the figure of one who, as is thought, lies under God's greatest punishment.'[57] 'Thus the Scriptures are the *kenōsis* of the holy *pneuma* in an empty 'wind' that has become an invisible 'nothingness',[58] 'the still small voice that we . . . hear in our hearts',[59] so small that it has shrunk to the voice of 'the small understanding of men'. He lays this principle down forcibly: 'It is an aspect of the unity in the divine revelation that the Spirit of God abases itself through the human pencil of the holy men that it itself impells, divesting itself of its majesty just as much as does the Son of God through the servant figure, and in the same way as the entire Creation [of the Father] is a work of the highest humility. Merely to admire God, who alone is wise, in the Creation is an insult perhaps not unlike the abuse accorded to an intelligent man when the rabble estimates his worth by the coat he is wearing. If, then, the divine style, to put to shame the strength and ingenuousness of all profane scribes, even chooses the foolish, the trivial, the ignoble, it must be admitted that the eyes of a friend, a confidant, a lover, illuminated, enthusiastic, armed with jealousy, are needed if the rays of heavenly glory are to be perceived in such a disguise. . . . The sublime in Caesar's style is its carelessness.'[60] Clouds in Hamann always have a deliberate ambiguity; they refer to the

[57] *Ibid.*, 99.

[58] *Golgotha und Scheblimini* (N 3, 310). Also the symbolic 'Apology for the Letter H' (N 3, 91f.); this has to do with a neologist who was anxious to do away with this letter because it cannot be heard (in speech), and in defending it Hamann was defending both himself and the breath of the Spirit, thus dismissed by the Enlightenment as superfluous.

[59] *Bibl. Betrachtungen* (N 1, 121).

[60] *Kleeblatt hellenistischer Blätter 2* (N 2, 171). On the whole subject, see Helmuth Schreiner's *Die Menschwerdung Gottes in der Theologie J. G. Hamanns* (Tübingen 2, 1950).

Jewish pillar of cloud, Aristophanes' satirical play, and the clouds of glory upon which the Son of Man comes to judgment.[61] If faith is to be possible, offence must always be possible. God has emptied himself so he could write a children's book for us, and Hamann is fascinated by the thought that his friend Professor Kant should be commissioned to write a physics book for children; he gives encouragement and instruction in two magnificent letters: 'To win oneself praise out of the mouths of babes and sucklings!—to share in this ambition is no mean task, and one must not begin by stealing brightly coloured feathers, but by divesting oneself of all superiority in age and wisdom of one's own free will and renouncing all vanity. A philosophical book for children would therefore have to appear as simple, foolish and tasteless as a book written by God for men.' 'The greatest law involved in the method for teaching children therefore consists in condescending to their weakness. However, nobody can understand this practical principle or put it into practice unless, to use a vulgar expression, he is crazy about children and loves them without really knowing why.'[62] Thus in the simpleness of childish stammerings, the simplicity (*monotēs*) of the infinite God becomes visible and comprehensible, although, of course, only for an understanding that through *kenōsis* of itself in the simple act of faith, has itself become a suitable organ for the divine simplicity. This is where Hamann's entire Socratism belongs; the point is not just to clear a space for the unpretentiousness of the senses and imagination in the face of the lofty claims of the reason, but to have reason itself pass away in Socratic ignorance, which is only Pauline ignorance (1 Cor 8.2), gnosis finding expression in faith, in concealed form. For 'the grain of all our natural wisdom' must 'decay, pass into unknowingness', so that 'out of this *death*, out of this *nothingness* the *life* and *being* of a higher knowledge can spring forth in new creation'.[63] The fact that 'the father of modern philosophy was forced to forget, deny and reject all that he knew and saw this as the only means

[61] Cf. *Wolken* (N 2, 108); *cf.* N 1, 204, 221.
[62] *Zugabe zweener Liebesbriefe* (N 2, 372f.).
[63] *Sokr. Denkw. 2* (N 2, 74).

of finding the truth'[64]—although it shows that this is the law that governs our natural thinking—cannot by itself guarantee that any alternative will be found other than 'newly polished errors'; the question is what *spirit* lies behind this self-denial. 'What is meant by the distinction between natural and revealed religion? To my mind nothing is involved other than the difference between the eye of someone who sees a picture without understanding at all painting or drawing or the story being depicted and the eye of a painter, between the natural ear and the musical ear. When Socrates referred to his familiar spirit, could one not say the same of him as we read of Peter: he knew not what he said?'[65] For he was inspired by a prophetic spirit. 'Socrates entices his fellow citizens out of the labyrinths of their learned sophists to a truth that lies in a hidden realm, . . . to the service of an unknown God.'[66] Socrates's ignorance was a feeling',[67] says Hamann, meaning the organ for the reality of the living, hidden God, called by him elsewhere *faith*.[68]

It is this organ that enables man to transcend reason, which has fallen into the distinction between good and evil, and find his way back to a complete affirmation of the world and of God in the world. Here Hamann is close to Augustine's aesthetic theodicy, while having a clearer insight into the inner analogy of the concept *aesthetic*. It is 'the Father of lights' who 'declares the darkness to be his creature'.[69] 'God is everywhere—in Heaven, on earth, in the miracles of Moses, in the obstinacy of Pharaoh; he caused the serpent to speak and Adam to eat; by him Israel was sent into Egypt and led with glory out of slavery there; he made the children of his anger into children of his grace. If God has his prophets, his Church, his altars, then he has granted some to Satan as well.'[70] In pictorial language: 'The carpenters of Solomon and of Hiram had a common share in the

[64] *Bibl. Betrachtungen* (N 1, 222).

[65] *Brocken* 3 (N 1, 303f.).

[66] *Sokr. Denkw. 2* (N 2, 77).

[67] *Ibid.*, 73.

[68] *Cf.* H 2, 139; 'Thus there is no distinction between faith and feeling' (Blanke).

[69] *Einfälle über die Begierde, ein Original zu sein* (N 2, 378).

[70] *Bibl. Betrachtungen* (N 1, 96).

building of the temple and the city of Zion. Light and darkness, earth and water, were equally necessary for the Creation of the earth. . . . Esau was after all blessed for the sake of Isaac and Abraham. . . . There was, then, the spirit of Wisdom in Israel and in Tyre; it taught Moses the secret story of creation and redemption. . . . It prospered the Tyrian craftsmen in their brass work, filling them with wisdom, understanding and invention.'[71] In the first place, certainly, these words are spoken against the aesthetics of the Enlightenment, which called for a mere imitation of 'the beautiful' in Nature; Hamann's answer to that was to restore the *whole* of nature, the universe, complete with its 'left-hand side', especially its physicality and irrationality, its *Sturm und Drang.* But with him this contradiction is only in the foreground, and he means much more: the unity of the supernatural world, in which the 'left-hand side' is the state of fallenness, and the 'right-hand side', God's redemptive movement descending even to the darkness, his wisdom become foolishness. Here, then, Dionysus does not stand over against him who was crucified but becomes rather his mask, the mask of him who is the true 'critic' and who 'will shiver the aesthetic bow of the fine arts into pieces in the valley of beautiful nature. Idols of porcelain and glazed earth, these are the ideas of our fair spirits; their brightest notions, springing from the tenderest feeling and hurrying back to the sensations, are filthier than the soiled garb of a treader in the wine press, whose eyes laugh like the doves that pull Venus's chariot, who hath washed his coat in the blood of the grapes and hath teeth like a dragon; pitch-blacker than the black juice of Circe . . . through which the reflections of the fair spirits, whose object is always the fairest beauty, achieve their noblest expression'.[73] With Hamann, the aesthetic rules of Enlightenment poetry are set on a level with the Old Testament law, and when one transcends it to enter into the truth, that is called 'becoming naked of all dramatic rightness' and being delivered up 'to the God of love', 'who never ceases to be a child, though his little arm performs great wonders. . . . The prize of his bow is the

[71] *Ibid.*, 117f.

[72] *Leser und Kunstrichter* (N 2, 346).

fulfilment of the entire law, the sting of his arrows is the heart and death of every commandment.'[73] This is evangelical *Sturm und Drang* of the Holy Ghost: 'When Diderot rejects the burlesque and the marvellous as dross, things human and divine lose their truest character. Breasts and loins of the art of poetry dry up. The *mōron* of the Homeric gods gives his muse the quality of marvel, is the salt of her immortality. The foolishness of the *xenōn daimoniōn* that Paul seemed to be proclaiming to the Athenians was the secret of his joyous message of peace'.[74] To understand Hamann and his aesthetics one must not stray far from the miracle of 'divine foolishness'; the whole world is a free descent by the divine spirit into the hells of createdness and materiality, and it is this very descent, this humility and poverty of God, that radiates forth in glory from all things: that is what is actually manifest and therefore the heart, too, of all beauty. If Christ reveals the Trinity in the flesh,[75] the entire creation of the Father and the entire writings of the Holy Ghost reveal the glory of the Son's humiliated love—and the art of men receives no other canon from Hamann.

3. With this in mind, we can understand why in the descent of the Logos the principal stress is laid on the flesh, and therefore on senses and physicality. Hume's empiricism becomes the ally in the struggle against the citadel of rationalistic Enlightenment in a Babylonian Berlin. 'Not just the whole warehouse of the reason, but even the treasury of faith, rest upon this staff', upon the 'five loaves of barley', the 'five senses'.[76] By means of our senses we make contact with reality, and although it is true that the reason has the power to abstract concepts from it, these cannot replace or vie with that experience. 'Thus the foundation of religion lies in our existence as a whole',[77] and this 'sensing' of reality is expressed chiefly in images. 'Senses and passion speak and understand nothing but images'.[78] Hamann agrees with Herder's 'oldest document' to the extent that the first creation,

[73] *Fünf Hirtenbriefe 4* (N 2, 362f.).
[74] *Ibid.*, 5 (N 2, 367).
[75] Texts in Na, index under 'Trinität' (p. 507).
[76] *Brocken* (N 1, 298).
[77] *Zweifel und Einfälle* (N 3, 191f.).
[78] *Aesth.* (N 2, 197).

the first statement of reality, necessarily found expression in images in the Genesis story; in the way he receives images from the world and in the way he creates images man is an analogous fellow creator with God[79]—'hence that mythical and poetic vein in all religions, their foolishness and offensive form in the eyes of an heterogeneous, incompetent philosophy, cold as ice and lean as a hound.'[80] Hamann is profoundly anti-Gnostic; the flesh, if it was chosen by God, can least of all be called impure.[81] By the same token, he is no sensualist à la Heinse, for he means 'the senses of a Christian',[82] those senses that can see, hear and feel God through the flesh. 'The witness of the ears, of the eyes, of the feelings, this is the foundation of the Gospel. How can any revelation be surer that these?'[83] If God expresses himself physically in the Creation, Christ's becoming man and the incorporation of the world within him are the fulfilment of God's poetry. Therefore all theology was originally poetic, and Hamann quotes the words of Martin Opitz: 'In the beginning, poetry was none other than a concealed theology and an instruction in divine matters', and he deduces from this: 'for this reason drama was a part of the heathen liturgy.'[84] 'Poetry is the mother language of the human race'[85]—but only when our senses rest with simplicity in the Word of God, and the peace of God on earth is not 'made too salty' by the 'whoring taste of Reason'.[86]

But that is the state of affairs the Fall has brought about. That absolute poetry in which everything belonging to the senses was God's Word to man and man's reply to God is a paradisial and lost state. 'All tasted and saw, at first hand, the deed still fresh, the goodwill of the Craftsman as he played in his own earth and delighted in the sons of men. Not yet was any creature made subject against its will to the vanity and slavery of the transient

[79] *Ibid.*, 206f.
[80] *Zweifel und Einfälle* (N 3, 191f.).
[81] *Aesth.* (N 2, 200).
[82] *Bibl. Betrachtungen* (N 1, 118).
[83] *Ibid.*, 244.
[84] *Fünf Hirtenbriefe* 5 (N 2, 365).
[85] *Aesth.* (N 2, 197).
[86] *Konxompax* (N 3, 224).

system. . . . All that nature displayed was a word—the sign, symbol and pledge of a new, secret, inexpressible, but for that all the more intense union, communication and association of divine energies and ideas. Everything man in the beginning heard, saw with his eyes, looked upon and with his hands touched was a living word; for the Word was God.'[87] If one wishes to understand the fundamental meaning of man, broken apart in sin and dualistic as he is, one must always bear in mind this lost protological state in which everything was unity of body and soul, God and man, and was therefore word and dialogue.

Language, taken in its original meaning, is the reason that *ab origine* always either hears words by means of the senses or else expresses itself in the realm of the senses by means of words; by contrast the realm of the senses is for Hamann centred in the act of begetting and giving birth. Thus the original biblical idea of *knowing*, that is, begetting, is taken seriously again. But it is this same original unity that has disintegrated in the Fall, becoming a dualism—empty reason and sensuality bereft of reason—that originally expresses itself in knowledge as 'knowledge of good and evil' (that is, man's departure from a naive acceptance of faith in goodness) and in the realm of the senses as the emerging 'nakedness' of sexual distinction. Not that Hamann would wish paradisial man conceived of, in Gnostic fashion, as sexless—after all, as we saw, the power to beget and bring forth is the most original image of God;[88] but even upon this image disorder and devastation have fallen, as is proved by the phenomenon of shame. 'The knowledge of good and evil and the sufficient reason of a system depending upon this contradiction—in these is the oldest and highest problem of reason . . . Furthermore, the basic concept of good and evil is as undifferentiated and transcendent as the natural difference between the sexes is a *verum signaculum Creatoris*';[89] this contradiction permeates reason and sex alike. And again: 'The secret parts of our nature, upon which all taste for, all enjoyment of beauty, all truth and goodness are founded, bear relation, like that tree of God's in the

[87] *Ritter von Rosenkreuz* (N 3, 32).
[88] 'To be a father is the highest authorship . . . ' (Z 3, 98).
[89] *Schürze von Feigenblättern* (N 3, 212).

midst of the Garden, to *knowledge* and *life*. Both are causes as well as effect of love. The coals thereof are coals of fire and a flame of the Lord; for God is love, and the life is the light of men. These three bear witness for us in Heaven and in earth. Innocence knows of no difference between good and evil and therefore knows of no disgrace or shame. Guilt, dreading neither witness nor avenger, is not sullen or ashamed; but mounts up to marriage with a Hel when God dwells within. In the same way as one can speak of *burning cold* and *cold fire*, two opposing effects can be deduced from any cause and two opposed causes from any effect.'[90] Thus Hamann settles the ancient dispute of the Church fathers—whether the Tree of Knowledge and the Tree of Life in Paradise were one or two trees—in favour of the one tree; usurped knowledge is usurped sex, when, according to the will of the Creator, both should have fallen out of grace and in faith. Life and light could have been one, as love, but with sin there enters into both, Logos and sex alike, the contradiction of burning cold and cold fire. Hamann had profound things to say about the insatiable curiosity of sinful reason,[91] in the face of which the spirits of Scripture and nature remain, 'like the Saviour before Herod', dumb, and there can be no doubt that he is also referring to his own, insatiable lust for knowledge and reading, just as, in sexual lust, he depicts the other side of his inner infirmities.[92] Together the two are the issue of 'the oldest pet sin of self-idolatry'.[93]

In the case of reason it is easy to show its contradictory

[90] *Das stellenlose Blatt* (N 3, 213).

[91] *Bibl. Betrachtungen* (N 1, 10f.). From birth the sinner is without a sense of hearing; *ibid.*, 14, 91 and *cf.* 116. We must renounce the superstition of human darkness if our eyes are to be opened; *ibid.*, 218f.

[92] To M. Mendelssohn, 13.9.70: 'Meanwhile there still dwells in my breast the original sin of scholarly curiosity, addiction to reading and a kind of ill-defined lust for things that are not worthwhile, or at any rate beyond my horizon at present.' (Z 3, 4). *Cf.* to J. F. Reichardt, 28.7.82: 'I am always afraid that my heart evaporates away or has its taste spoiled because it can only communicate via the retort of a brain that, alas, is burnt out; yet love atones for all these sins, many though they are.' (Z 4, 408). To F. H. Jacobi, 12.8.82: 'But really my whole life is more stupefying than cultivating—builds up rather than breaks down the seat of the evil' (Z 4, 416).

[93] *Konxompax* (N 3, 224).

dialectic: the 'dilemma' between 'nothing and something', which become 'opposed like good and evil'; 'the perception of the One in the many', which nourishes[94] 'the extra and suprasensual, or transcendental, light of reason' in its empty abstraction—these false mysteries (naked reason is by definition absolutely without secrets, as *Konxompax* shows) are revealed by Socrates, but in fact they reveal themselves in the end as clearly as they did to the couple in Paradise who had to perceive their nakedness. But while Enlightened and Kantian reason meets this crisis by putting on a fig leaf, it is in fact Socrates who, having brought about the stripping of reason in her sin and shame, is truly chaste. The thirst for knowledge (in terms of the distinction between good and evil) is a usurping of divine judgment, for 'the true element of right and wrong are unknown to us',[95] and the will to achieve what is right by one's own efforts 'turns into the greatest wrong';[96] only when the reason becomes dependent upon Socratic and Pauline ignorance can it be brought into the realm of salvation.

But how is the dialectic of sex (and with it the whole realm of the senses) to be approached? Here Hamann's groping speculation reached its summit, but inevitably this was at the same time its crisis. Two tendencies struggle for supremacy, and neither can show the way independent of the other. In the one tendency (prominent in the early period) there is an eagerness to return to the innocence of the original state; shame would be reduced to mere convention, and sex would have the poison taken from it and the naturalness of Paradise restored. Hence the constant reference to sexual matters, to the pudenda, seen as man's good and fruitful natural source—a kind of Lutheran Freudianism. But at the same time Hamann knows that reintegration is not a matter for fallen man, for he as sinner is the real pudendum of Creation, the disgrace of God himself:

> The human race and the Fall are the nakedness of God, the shame of Creation—the drunken Noah is simultaneously a symbol for the human race, whose natural corruption is expressed through

[94] *Ibid.*, N 3, 218.
[95] To Herder, 18.11.82 (Z 4, 462).
[96] *Golgotha und Scheblimini* (N 3, 299).

> an intoxication and the consequent inability to be aware of its own disgrace. Let us no longer join Ham and jeer at the nakedness of our father and our own nature in the barbarians, savages, et cetera. What did the Jews and the wiser heathens—Shem and Japheth—achieve? Did the law and philosophy they had suffice to repair the Fall of Adam? They went both of them backward (Is 44.25). They knew neither of them the corruption of their nature—they did no more than spread a coverlet over it, a cloak so much their shoulders were able to bear. Further than that their justice, their strength, their wisdom did not go. What Ham was mocking when he jeered at the nakedness of his father and attributed it to wine was, like all sin, a mystery of God's, who used it to reveal his wisdom, power and goodness and justice. It was the same spirit of Ham that fell into mockery when it heard the disciples talking in tongues.[97]

'A dying man is like Noah when he awoke from his drunkenness, for things of the senses and the growth of our vineyard take possession of our heads, and we are no longer aware of ourselves. Happy he who upon this awakening finds about him a cover to rescue him from eternal shame and disgrace—and who sees how greatly he needed it.'[98] There can be no covering up, then, of this shame through human effort—in that sphere the truth would inevitably be revealed—but as the end shows, only covering through the cloak of the grace of Christ, for he has already uncovered and borne the real disgrace in his flesh.

And thus the later Hamann turns his gaze away from an unattainable protology to the eschatology toward which man and the world are making their way. Thus, as Nadler in particular had depicted, the thought that *sexus* (and with it the split between *logos* and life) might be overcome becomes increasingly prominent, especially in *The Flying Letter—Undressing and Transfiguration*.[99] And yet Nadler forces the Magus into a systematic development that ends up with almost Gnostic or Origenian traits, abandoning what matters, the centre: the incarnation of the *Logos*, which is 'the one mystery of

[97] *Betrachtungen über Newtons Abhandlung* (N 1, 316f.).
[98] *Ibid.*, 318.
[99] *Fliegender Brief, Entkleidung und Verklärung* (N 3, 347–407).

Judaism and the *prolēpsis* of his hidden name, the thousand-tongued mystery of the Gentiles. But the unification of both these tinctures, the New Man, after the likeness of the Creator', is simultaneously the unification of man and woman, head and body. This was why the Song of Solomon was so sacred to Hamann and why he translated it.[100] The Bridegroom, who has taken away all our badness and given us all his goodness, who is therefore 'so near to us that nothing can part us from him; bone of our bone, flesh of our flesh', in whom, as our true neighbour, we truly love ourselves:[101] he is the original image of man. 'Every sinner bears on himself the likeness of the crucified Saviour. Behold the man! said Pilate. As God said: Behold, Adam has become as one of us. We all have upon us not only the image of God, but of him who takes away sin.'[102] Thus and only thus are we 'the betrothed of God. The adultery of sin, when we go a-whoring after the spirits of darkness, divorces us from God. . . . Not till the first-born has won shape in us, till Jesus is brought forth in us and we are born again in the Holy Ghost, does God once more acknowledge our souls as his true and lawful wife.'[103] So fulfilment is 'the marriage of the human race, or rather, of the Church of God, with Jesus'. This is 'indisputably more than a mere figurative idea. . . . As Mary became a mother and yet remained a virgin, not having known a man, thus too must we imagine the spiritual marriage of the Church with her bridegroom, Jesus Christ. Our being already capable, here in the world, of feeling the raptures of a heavenly love for our saviour is an anticipation by faith of the bliss to come.'[104] Hamann cannot in this context leave out a reference to the sexuality of the Redeemer (which is certainly virginal), for this, in view of Paradise, the Song of Solomon, the eschatological marriage and fulfilment of the reality of Creation, is indispensable.[105] The way Eros thus finds shelter in Agape

[100] N 4, 251–6.

[101] *Bibl. Betrachtungen* (N 1, 212).

[102] *Ibid.*, 213.

[103] *Ibid.*, 199.

[104] *Betrachtungen zu Kirchenliedern* (N 1, 255f.).

[105] Thus—rightly—Nadler's interpretation of the beginning of *Schürze von Feigenblättern* (N 3, 207).

is crucially important for Hamann's aesthetics. Even when we have repudiated anything that might suggest an excessive interest in the sexual sphere or an underrating of the Catholic idea of virginity, it still remains valid. He never finally settled the question—who could? But the dotted lines pointing out beyond this fragmentary scheme indicate the right direction.

Language, however, is a begetting by the spirit within nature, (for even free language is no arbitrary contrivance but a body born of the stamina of feelings and sensible traditions). As much and more, language is a begetting by nature into the spirit in that in the spirit sensual experience of the world and of God become understood statement. This two-in-one, primary phenomenon is the basis for Hamann's criticism of all philosophy, especially Kant's: 'Now to what purpose such a violent, unwarranted, wilful divorce of what nature has joined together (namely, sensibility and understanding)?' Why is the 'common root' split up in this way, when it can only lead to both stems drying up? The branches come forth from a single root, which is the organic and spiritual (what the epigones will call the imagination); 'music was the oldest language, and along with the sensible rhythm of the pulse beat and the breath in the nose, the original embodied image of all measure of time and its numerical relationships'.[106] This Pythagorean and Augustinian element, no longer infected with Platonic spiritualism nor with the naturalism of a Herder or the parallelism of a Leibniz, has in consequence a colouring all Hamann's own; for the rhythm that unites body and soul is language itself in its origins, and consequently the place where the paradisial, christological-pneumatic revelation of God occurs. In so far as language in its unity with begetting and birth is understood as an expression that creates only in fellowship and by imitation, this very revelation is also the central mystery of what it means to become man: the state of marriage.

4. For Hamann, the jurisdiction of reason (as conceived in the Enlightenment) does not extend into the decisive areas of truth; as we define this thesis more closely it becomes apparent how near to and how far from Kant he is. Reason is absolutely

[106] *Metakritik* (N 3, 286).

dependent on the senses, and its knowledge does not go beyond their sphere. As early as 1758 he had written in *Biblical Reflections*: 'The nature of objects provides the *material*; and the laws according to which our souls experience, think, conclude, decide and compare provide the *form*. It follows that all natural knowledge is as old as nature herself, and, since she remains unchanging, in the real sense nothing new can occur in our experience of her.'[107] Here he means that something truly new, and not just a permutation of whatever happens to be present in man already, can originate only with God's revelation. Man's longing for novelty is therefore ambivalent: it is either sinful curiosity, 'an itch that all external satisfactions and earthly medicine can make only more dangerous, burning and rife', or a true longing for God, 'the thirst of one who is weary, parched', one who longs for 'a pure spring'.[108] But if reason were limited to the process of 'forming' sensible reality, there would be another sense in which its jurisdiction was restricted: in its formalising *reality*; that is the real God and the real, historical man slips through its hands, for these can be grasped in their reality and relationship only by faith, 'faith in a single, independent and living truth that, like our existence, can only be older than our reason', for the latter cannot possibly penetrate 'the entire historical riddle of our existence, the impenetrable night of its *terminus a quo* and *terminus ad quem*'.[109] Reason cannot be esoteric, for its forms are common knowledge—that is the blow aimed at Starck's false masonic neoreligion in *Konxompax*[110]—but when it does have pretensions to mystery it becomes 'the very sign of contradiction', the inept fig leaf that reveals its own need and shame even as it tries to conceal them.

Here what is original and anti-Kantian is the idea that in *faith* the two are brought together, immediate experience of reality proclaiming itself immediately and sensibly; this description of faith as 'sensation' goes back to Hume, for whom experience of existence is based upon an instinct. 'Our own being and the

[107] *Bibl. Betrachtungen* (N 1, 222f.).
[108] *Ibid.*, 224.
[109] *Zweifel und Einfälle* (N 3, 191f.).
[110] *Konxompax* (N 3, 217ff., esp. 220).

existence of all things outside us must be believed, and cannot be worked out in any other way'.[111] Socrates is in possession of the organ whereby reality may be perceived and expresses it as 'ignorance'; therefore Socrates's ignorance is hidden faith.[112] Because it is rooted in the senses, this faith is reminiscent of Hume, but its transcendence into the religious sphere associates it with Kant; Hamann can accomplish this seemingly impossible synthesis by virtue of his philosophy of language: the immediate experience of reality is word and dialogue. For the same reason, language is human freedom expressing itself, the personality put into action; therefore Hamann identifies faith with 'fidelity and trust', *fides* with *fidelitas*, seeing in this the actual foundation that makes reason—individual and sociopolitical alike—possible.[113] The wide arc thus performed by the concept faith is for Hamann neither strained nor artificial, if the statement that 'Original being is truth, imparted being is grace'[114] is correct, if, that is, contact with reality (through hearing, sight, touch) and revelation are inevitably one and the same. 'Experience and revelation are one . . . meaning and history are the foundation and ground.'[115] And therefore the 'analogy of man to the Creator confers upon all creation its content and form, and on this are dependent fidelity and faith in the whole of nature',[116] which again is only the converse of the statement that in this 'fidelity and trust' the basis of reality, analogy, truth and grace is truly to be found. Thus following the Church fathers and adopting the Ancient Greek idea of faith, the Aristotelian Δει γαρ πιστευειν μανθανοντα[117] as well presents no problems. All this shows the contrast with Jacobi too, for there is no question of a desperate attempt to burst out of the prison of reason, to attain to faith in a *salto mortale*; rather does one with each simple experience abide ever, childlike, in the truth that is God, and

[111] *Sokr. Denkw.* (N 2, 73).

[112] *Cf.* F. Blanke's commentary (H 2, 136ff.).

[113] *Golgotha und Scheblimini* (N 3, 300f.). *Cf.* the commentary by L. Schreiner (H 7, 84f.).

[114] To Jacobi, 1.12.84 (G 21).

[115] *Ibid.*, 14.11.84 (G 16).

[116] *Aesth.* (N 2, 206f.).

[117] *Fliegender Brief, 1. Fassung* (N 3, 370).

from this vantage point alone look down upon our reason and its desperate inability to capture reality in concepts. Hamann's simple answer to Jacobi's torments is enjoyment: 'There can be no existence in words and concepts, that being a property of things and objects alone. Enjoyment never broods—and all things, among which, logically, even the *ens entium* must be included—are there for enjoyment, not speculation. The Tree of Knowledge costs us the Tree of Life, which ought yet, ought it not, to be the dearer; do we then wish to become children, to take to us flesh and blood, take upon us the Cross, like the new Adam? The upshot of all metaphysical terminology is this historical *factum*'.[118] And why should not then the way of reason for once be right as well, if only there is faith? 'To the pure all things are pure; any method, mystical, logical or mechanical. Everything human and earthly is liable to misuse; and what God has made pure ceases to be common. . . . Not our love, but his inexpressible love in the Son of love, this is the node, the sun of our system. What I write to you is always the same; I am sorry. I would so like to be able to extricate you from the labyrinths of worldly wisdom, and set you down in the childlike simplicity of the Gospel . . . to make you sick of that arid ὄν.'[119] 'Not *cogito ergo sum*, but the other way round, or, yet more Hebraically, *est, ergo cogito*.'[120] Here it should be remembered that Hamann, like Herder and many other contemporaries, does not acknowledge that the Hebraic and Greek worlds are in conflict; he sees Hellas rather as being completely rooted in the Orient,[121] so that the conflict is for him one of attitude (which is all-pervasive), and not of culture.

But how can Hamann's concept of faith reconcile the immediacy of sensible experience with the historical factor emphasised previously, which after all lies in the past and beyond our grasp? The question sets the stage for the decisive encounter between Hamann's philosophy and aesthetics and those of the Enlightenment. On the first page of the *Aesthetica* we read how overpowering is the 'experience of the presence of

[118] To Jacobi, 14.11.84 (G 15).
[119] *Ibid.*, 23.1.85 (G 55).
[120] *Ibid.*, 2.6.85 (G 81).
[121] Unger, *Hamann und die Aufklärung*, p. 259.

things'.[122] But this is a presence of the Infinite, necessarily transcending the fragile creation that is the vehicle of his glory; a present that needs past and future, and therefore, as Hamman says, not only the spirit of observation, but also the spirit of prophecy, if it is to be approached. 'Spirit of observation and spirit of prophecy are the pinions of human genius. Everything present belongs to the sphere of the former; everything absent and of the past and future, to the sphere of the latter.' And now we come to the important definitions: 'The philosophical genius expresses its power by means of abstraction, by striving to render absent what is present; by *undressing* real objects, so that they become mild concepts, mere tokens of the mind, more appearances and phenomena. The poetic genius expresses its power by means of fiction, by *transfiguring* the visions of absent past and future so that they become present depictions.' The true attitudes, which, unlike philosophy and poetry, do not each perform vanishing tricks with a side of reality (and to which Hamann here gives designations at first sight scarcely comprehensible, 'criticism and politics'), 'resist the encroachments of both powers and ensure that they are in balance through the same positive forces and means, those of observation and prophecy'.[123] This in practice means a demand that present reality be experienced in its historical, ontological dimensions, pointing to creation (protology) and transfiguration (eschatology); these dimensions alone can give a true account of experience in all its profundity. But these are dimensions of reality and as such *historical*, for that which is present is absolutely an historical instant.

In this resides the whole force of Hamann's argument, developed in *Golgotha and Scheblimini* and *The Flying Letter*, against Moses Mendelssohn's construction of an enlightened Jerusalem, timeless and ideal. The *analogia* between God and man of which we have just spoken finds concrete interpretation in an *analogia temporum*, which, when known and understood, yields the key of truth. 'With what precision God has determined the periods of time in their symmetry and equal

[122] *Aesth.* (N 2, 197).
[123] *Fliegender Brief, 1. Fassung* (N 3, 382–4).

relation!'[124] '*In periodis temporum, divinitus definitis, perpetua est Analogia.*'[125] Because time and states of being are established by decree, the use of magical, philosophical and aesthetic tricks with mirrors to create the illusion that Jerusalem's present state is anything other than nonbeing cannot succeed; 'the spirits of observation and prophecy', 'by turns assuming each other, relating to one another and cooperating', and 'expressions of a single positive force. ... What would the most precise and painstaking knowledge of present things amount to without a divine renewal of what is past, a presentiment of what is to come?'[126] The Old Covenant without the New therefore shares the same basis of unreality as mere philosophy (without theology), and *law* and *idea* are both of them alive only through love; but the measure of that love is the Golgotha between Paradise and *Scheblimini*. The interpretation of 'the literal fragments of the archetypal Jerusalem' can be only a Christian one, just as Hamann himself could make sense of the collapse of his own existence only in Holy Scripture. 'Should anyone care to compare the map of Israel's journey with the course of my life, he will see how exactly they correspond. . . . It was the story of my life that I read there.'[127] Of the real Jerusalem we read: 'The prophetic riddle of a theocracy is mirrored in the shards of this shattered vessel, like the sun "in the droplets on the grass, that tarrieth not for man, nor waiteth for the sons of men", for *yesterday* the dew of the Lord was upon Gideon's fleece alone, and it was dry upon the whole earth; *today*, dew upon the whole earth, and dryness upon the fleece alone.'[128] By this majestic image Hamann means that God himself, using the example of sacred history (whose image is the fleece), reveals what is meant by fulfilment; 'manifestness of real fulfilments',[129] 'glorious progress of [that] life that enacts its own development in depictions "from glory to glory", until in the apocalypse comes the complete uncovering of the mystery, at first hidden and

[124] *Bibl. Betrachtungen* (N 1, 193).
[125] Taken from Bengel; to his brother, 21.3.60 (Z 2, 13).
[126] *Fliegender Brief, 1. Fassung* (N 3, 396–8).
[127] *Gedanken über meinen Lebenslauf* (N 2, 42, 40).
[128] *Golgotha und Scheblimini* (N 3, 311).
[129] *Ibid.*, 305.

believed, in the fulness of the beholder, face to face';[130] the reference to the central text of Pauline aesthetics (2 Cor 3) is well justified here. Here, then, is biblicohistorical *and* existential interpretation of reality, through 'observation' (also called experience, sensibility) and 'prophecy' (*daimonion* and '*Scheblimini*, spirit of the home') in one, and each in and through the other, since both 'the whole mythology of the Hebraic economy'[131] and that of the fallen and redeemed individual were nothing other 'than the type of a more transcendent history, the horoscope of a heavenly hero, through whose appearance everything is already completed, yet still to come'.[132] And thus he can say, with a Lutheran emphasis: 'Unbelief, in the most literal and historical understanding of the word, is therefore the only sin against the *spirit* of the true religion, whose heart is in Heaven, whose Heaven is in the heart. The mystery of Christian bliss does not consist . . . in services, offerings and vows; but rather in promises, fulfilments and sacrifices that God has made and performed for the benefit of mankind.'[133] Thus for Hamann the 'eternal truths of reason' concerning man and God lie in these selfsame 'chance truths of history', although (bearing in mind the *analogia temporum*, the relationship of promise and fulfilment) not in what by its nature is destined to pass away, such as Heaven and earth, but in what even then does not pass away, being earlier and the origin of all things: the Word[133]—word not yet as letters, but as that abundance of address through all created things. 'Everything that in the beginning man heard, saw with his eyes, beheld, and his hands touched, was a living word.'[135] If letters then become the vehicle of this word, it must be true that 'the literal or grammatical, the fleshly or dialectical, the Capernaitic or historical sense are all mystical to the highest degree . . . so that without going up to Heaven one cannot bring down the key to their understanding'.[136] The letter itself

[130] *Ibid.*

[131] He means the *oiko-nomia*, the divine order of salvation.

[132] *Ibid.*, 308.

[133] *Ibid.*, 312.

[134] *Ibid.*, 304–7.

[135] *Ritter von Rosenkreuz* (N 3, 32).

[136] *Aesth.* (N 2, 203, n. 23).

contains the holy spirit of prophecy; in *Aesthetica in nuce* we find the quotation; 'The testimony of Christ is the spirit of prophecy' (Rev 19.10). In that real reality shows itself to be fulfilment of divine promise, it becomes the pledge of divine glory; just as Eve is the glory of the man, and the new Jerusalem is the glory of the new Adam, that glory that throughout the whole history of the world, the earth and salvation is in the process of coming, of propagating itself. This is how the *Aesthetica* puts it: 'The hieroglyphic Adam is the history of the whole race in a symbolic cycle—the character of Eve, meanwhile, the original for beautiful Nature and the systematic dispensation, not written with methodical holiness upon a plate borne on the brow, but wrought in the lowest parts of the earth and lying in secret in the bowels—in the reins of things themselves.' Eve, the glory of man, is the new aeon, born out of the Golgotha of the Old: 'The next aeon will awaken like a giant from his cups and embrace your muse [that is, the muse of the "virtuosi of the present aeon"], joyfully crying out to her and bearing witness: But that is bone of my bone, and flesh of my flesh!'[137] Thus when men follow Christ into the begetting hour of Golgotha they enter the actual birthplace of the highest art, brought about by the believing and holy man as instrument of grace, although its glory is only to be revealed eschatologically, as Hamann piously reflects in *The Magi from the East*:

> There are actions of a higher order for which an equation cannot be produced using the elements (rudiments) of this world. That very divinity that makes signs out of the wonders of nature and original works of art sets apart the ways and deeds of those called to be saints. Not the end alone, but the whole winding course of a Christian is the masterpiece (Eph 2.10) of the unknown genius whom Heaven and earth does and will acknowledge for the one and only Creator, Mediator and Ruler in transfigured human shape. We read that our lives are hidden with Christ in God. But if Christ—our life—is to reveal himself, then we too shall be revealed with him in glory.'[138]

Thus Hamann can—half in jest, half in earnest—speak of an

[137] *Ibid.*, 200.
[138] *Die Magi aus Morgenlande* (N 2, 140).

'*ars poetica* of brotherly love'.[139]

To round off this section, it remains to describe the social and political side of this process, since it possessed great importance for Hamann and explains to us his earlier description of the right attitude as being 'critical-political'. His lifelong struggle for the kingdom of Heaven to be incorporated into the structures of the state; his impassioned pleas in French to Frederick the Great to set up his banner under the star of Jerusalem, not Babylon; the torment of his drudgery under the French customs officials, who made life more and more intolerable for him, increasingly begrudging him the bare necessities of life; the union with free thinking that Berlin (and that meant Germany, too) was entering upon as he watched in suffocating anxiety, and the glorification of this union perpetrated by that bogy, Mendelssohn's New Jerusalem; the slow but sure degeneration of the German intelligentsia (in which Kant, but also Herder and, in his own way, Jacobi participated) in a second, more subtle enlightenment: because of all this the political hour came to seem apocalyptic to him, and he himself sank into the isolation of the 'witness who is slain' in the midst of the great city, which spiritually is called Sodom and Egypt (Rev 11.8). But out of the rubble of Babylon, Jerusalem shall be awakened: 'The faithful waiting of a city that has a foundation and whose builder and creator is God will always be opposed to the political experiments of a Cain and the basic principles of a Nimrod and their successors. The first revelation of the most holy name occurred in a famous bush of thorns that does not burn, and the preservation of the weeds until the harvest is the best theodicy of the best housefather. In the horrors of the last days there is nonetheless consolation, the promise of his future and our redemption, approaching to raise up our heads.'[140]

As he continually affirms, Hamann's entire theological aesthetic has its sole nodal point in Jesus Christ, who, present from the beginning as Word, as Man is in the process of coming and as the Man who has come, nevertheless remains he who comes eschatologically. For him as for Pascal, Christ is the

[139] To J. Fr. Reichardt, 27.10.1782 (Z 4, 432).

[140] To C. Fr. v. Moser, 10.11.63 (Z 3, xxix). Na 138–145, 175ff., 211ff.

geometric point where the contradictions of the world are resolved. And in truth *coincidentia oppositorum* is the final formula to which Hamann clings (not knowing that Cusanus invented it and its christological use, he assumes that it derived from Giordano Bruno).[141]

As early as *Biblical Reflections* we read: 'Yet in this consisted the mystery of divine wisdom, in uniting things that could not exist together, that contradicted one another, that seemed to destroy each other. This is more than creation out of nothing. This—to create evil and make it into an enemy, to create darkness and form it into light—no one but God can do (Is 45.7).'[142] But since these contradictions are permitted only because at the place where the Word becomes man they are, through his divinely human power of suffering, resolved—and 'Even contradiction itself, against himself, he tolerates'[143]—the way rebellious enlightened reason contradicts Christ is always something already resolved and unreal, and 'the truth of God' becomes 'yet more glorious for his praise through the inner lies or contradictions of reason; but her damnation is still quite right'.[144] But the inadequacy of human judgment as such—'since *summum ius* and *summa iniuria* are, like light and shade, inseparably related in time within the underworld of the senses'[145]—is also superseded and justified in Christ's judgment, which brings the truth concealed in it creatively to light. There is a splendid passage in a letter to Kant: 'Altogether truth is of such an abstract and spiritual nature that it cannot be grasped other than *in abstracto*, in its element. *In concreto*, however, either it appears in the form of a contradiction, or it is that famed stone of our sages, whose original application is to transform every crude mineral, even stone and wood, into *true* gold.'[146] This stone of our (that is, the Christian) sages is Christ, and Hamann

[141] To Jacobi, 16.1.85 (G V 49). *Cf.* to Herder, 19.11.82: 'Giordano Bruno's *principium coincidentiae oppositorum* is worth more in my eyes than all Kantian critique (Z 4, 462). For other passages, see Na 407–409.

[142] *Bibl. Betrachtungen* (N 1, 264).

[143] *Konxompax* (N 3, 222).

[144] *Ibid.*, 227.

[145] *Zwey Scherflein I* (N 3, 233).

[146] To Imm. Kant, April 1774 (Z 3, 88f.).

incessantly demands a 'grammar' suited to Christ as the Word; according to Hamann it does not yet exist,[147] it being anyway dubious what kind of a science it could be. 'The unity of the head and, equally, the splitting up of the body . . . are the mysteries of the kingdom of Heaven from genesis to apocalypse—the focal point of all the parables and types in the entire universe, of the *histoire générale* and *chronique scandaleuse* of all times';[148] and that is anything but the general 'unity in multiplicity', being rather 'uniqueness', which (being unique and incomparable) in inscrutable fashion unites what cannot be united and thereby forms the universal principle of aesthetics. 'O a muse like a refiner's fire, and like fuller's soap'—Malachi's words point to the Day of the Lord.[149]

This, then, is the hyperbolic aesthetic[150] which, to reach its goal, must transcend the entire old aeon just as God, in that the Son became man, has already, in the middle of history, transcended the aesthetics and poetics of the Old Covenant. 'After God, through nature and Scripture, creatures and seers, causes and figures, poets and prophets, had exhausted himself and spoken until he was out of breath; there, in the evening of days, he spoke to us through his Son—yesterday and today—until the promise of his coming—no longer in the form of a servant—shall also be fulfilled':[151] from the Old to the New Covenant and from both to the Second Coming—together, a two-fold transformation from water into the headiest of wines.

3. THE EVANGELICAL DOCTRINE OF ANALOGY

Finally, we take a glance at the inner premise and the limitations of Hamann's philosophy. The principle Hamann follows and to which everything he writes is related he himself called that of analogy. He took it originally from Bengel, and quoting from Young ('analogy, man's surest guide below'), he attributed it to

[147] To Jacobi, 1.12.84. (G V 22).
[148] *Konxompax* (N 3, 226).
[149] *Aesth.* (N 2, 207).
[150] *Ibid.*, 211.
[151] *Ibid.*, 213.

his first hero as the real heart of the Socratic method. 'Analogy was the soul of his arguments, and he gave them irony to be their body.'[152] Kierkegaard was content with irony; now while this is undoubtedly a crucial aspect of Hamann, no understanding of him can afford to ignore the ubiquitous principle of analogy.

Analogous in Hamann means in the first place simply 'corresponding', 'in accordance with'. In so far as God is *causa prima*, everything that happens in the world is divine; 'however, everything divine is also human, since man can be neither active nor passive save after the analogy of his nature. . . . This *communicatio* of divine and human *idiomata* is a fundamental law, and the principal key to all our knowledge.'[153] In this original *communicatio* lies the second and higher conception of analogy, expressing the relationship between *causa prima* and *secunda* in terms of the relationship between the senses and spirit in this world. Language presupposes an original 'relationship and connection between our soul, with its ability to know, and our body, with its ability to make signs'.[154] Life—organism—mechanism: this trinity is 'similar in its stages'[155] in man and beast. But between God and man there is the similarity of the word, with its naming power, and here Hamann specifically uses the term *analogy*. 'The analogy of man to the Creator bestows on all creatures their content and their form.'[156] In so far as God's revelatory word has primacy of effect, and man is obedient to the dispensation of the Spirit of Christ, his obedience becomes what Paul calls *analogia fidei*, and what Hamann takes up when he gives Herder, who had been speaking of his planned interpretation of Genesis, the following advice: 'Believe me, dearest friend, your theme is happily chosen . . . always assuming that the imagination too is given a

[152] *Sokr. Denkw.* (N 2, 61).

[153] *Ritter von Rosenkreuz* (N 3, 27).

[154] *Versuch über eine akademische Frage* (N 2, 121).

[155] *Philol. Einfälle und Zweifel* (N 3, 37). *Cf.* 39: 'The analogy provided by animal housekeeping is the only ladder to the anagogic perception of the spiritual economy.' Here the analogical process presupposes an analogy between the lower and the higher realms.

[156] *Aesth.* (N 2, 206f.).

free rein—but not so that obedience, the analogy of faith, is thereby denied.'[157]

It is typical of Hamann that 'the infinite wrongness of man's relationship to God'[158] (this idea, which places him between Luther and Kierkegaard, he takes absolutely seriously) in his view finds such great redemption through the *communicatio idiomatum* in the Holy Spirit and in faith, now that it has been renewed and restored in Christ; and that in consequence, by virtue of Christ's becoming man, everything that has been created, in nature as in history, can and must become a redemptive image and word for one who has mastered that spirit and faith. To be sure, there is the contradiction of sinful reason in its blind vanity; but she too, her contradiction borne and overcome by Christ, must in the end, albeit against her own will, serve and acknowledge that One is Lord. Here as elsewhere Hamann follows Paul's confession: 'We destroy arguments and every proud obstacle to the knowledge of God and take every thought captive to obey Christ' (2 Cor 10.5). Hamann's way of taking apparently 'natural' data 'captive' is to turn them into organs, potential or real, of Christ's unique revelation. For example, the poetic disorder found in the Bible is a copy of the 'regular disorder in nature' and becomes the style of the Holy Ghost in its higher disorder. 'The imagination of poets has a thread, invisible to the ordinary eye, that seems to connoisseurs a masterpiece.'[159] It is here that the question—the decisive one—arises. Is the (genuine) poetic 'disorder' in itself an analogon to the 'disorder' of the Holy Spirit, or is it solely through the Spirit that it is enabled to become such? To raise this question, or to attempt to solve it with an either-or, would be to ask too much of Hamann. Consider the following quotation: 'Paul does a poet the honour of calling him a prophet of his nation (Tit 1.12). True poetry is a natural form of prophecy. . . . Mythology, say the experts, is the soul and inspiration of poets.'[160] Here the relationship is both descending and ascending. Again and again Hamann testfied to his certainty that there were prophets

[157] To Herder, 13.1.73 (Z 3, 35).
[158] *Golgotha und Scheblimini* (N 3, 312).
[159] *Bibl. Betrachtungen* (N 1, 229f.).
[160] *Ibid.*, 241.

among the heathen, too, and 'that we ought not to despise this cloud of witnesses, that Heaven anointed them to be messengers and translators and initiated them into the very vocation in their race that the prophets enjoyed among the Jews'.[161] This, as I have mentioned, is the basis of the profound difference between the Socrates of Hamann and of Kierkegaard; the ignorance of Hamann's Socrates is in a hidden way what Paul's was openly,[162] and his genius or *daimon* may very well have had something of the holy *pneuma* about it, for he bore a reverential love for this genius,[163] and his foolishness may have been a form of the holy, evangelical foolishness.[164] In that case, why should not the babble of Apollo in the oracle be understood as a likeness of the servant, form of the divine word, since rays of grace and illumination are to be found in ancient wisdom?[165] And further: 'Plato makes of Socrates's voluntary poverty a sign of his divine mission. What is more significant is his sharing the final destiny of the prophets and the just'?[166] The analogous breadth of Hamann's understanding of 'belief' I have already described; also, that it is capable of interpreting Socrates not only as a likeness but as a medium of Christ. That Hamann, the true Christian, undertakes to do this shows that a relationship such as this to him who is absolutely unique can be meant only as a work of the Holy Spirit of Christ himself, who chooses his vessels as he will.

And thus a final point becomes apparent: that Hamann's aesthetics can be called Christian and theological because at the critical point he brings nature and supernature into a relationship of hiddenness and openness; in other words, that the categories he imposes of nature have so radical and sweeping an effect because, ultimately, they derive from the sphere of supernatural revelation. Poetic inspiration is (hidden) prophecy. Language is (hidden divine) revelation. The realm of the human senses conceals the mystery of Christ's incarnation. Created

[161] *Sokr. Denkw.* (N 2, 64).
[162] *Ibid.*, 74.
[163] *Ibid.*, 75.
[164] *Wolken, 3. Aufzug* (N 2, 107).
[165] *Sokr. Denkw.* (N 2, 70f.).
[166] *Ibid.*, 81.

sexuality is the hidden mystery of the heavenly Eros of Christ and Church. Genius is hidden *pneuma*. Beauty is hidden eschatological transfiguration.

'Holy Scripture ought to be our dictionary, our art of rhetoric, so that all a Christian's ideas and speech would be based on it, would consist and be composed of it.'[167] This is so central a truth for Hamann that occasionally he fears he has gone too far. 'What Homer was for the ancient Sophists, the Holy Books have been for me, and perhaps I have even misused that source, and my drinking has been—εὐκαίρως ἀκαίρως—too deep.'[168] Not that there is such a thing as an excess of Scripture, but when the peculiar structure of created being, which, it is true, is conceived and prepared with a view to grace, finds itself all too hastily overpowered and replaced by it, that can be an encroachment into the sphere of philosophy. Here we find Hamann's limitations and perhaps a way of justifying the obtuse rejection, the refusal to understand, that became his lot in the age of Goethe. Perhaps it was that the leaps and bounds of his logic demanded structures for the Christian sphere that did not exclusively belong to it and for which philosophy and poetry had the prerogative of investigation; it may even be that his view of these structures was inadequate, so that he put himself somewhat in the wrong. His unquestioning rejection of all Catholicism (which he hardly knew) shows the same limitations, suggestive of a self-sufficient philosophical orthodoxy (which perhaps comes out most clearly in the writings against Mendelssohn).[169]

And yet, how close he was to achieving a role far beyond his actual historical influence, to becoming (instead of Schleiermacher) the theological mentor and 'familiar spirit' of German idealism and so to determining the theological attitude of more than a century. Such an interpretation would be a falsification. But for one prepared to understand and apply

[167] *Bibl. Betrachtungen* (N I, 243).

[168] To Jacobi, 7.1.85 (G V 38).

[169] This is the grain of truth in *Natuur en Genade bij J. G. Hamann* by Jansen Schoonhoven (Nijkerk, 1945), which otherwise presents a far too systematised theology.

Hamann's work with sufficiently generous breadth, his lightning mind, despite its elliptical speech, can bear fruit in the future for theological aesthetics as few others in German-speaking lands.

SOLOVIEV

1. VISION AND FORM OF WORK

Soloviev,[1] writing a century after Hamann, was heir to all that had occurred during the intervening period; the French Revolution, German idealism, the Hegelianism of the Left

[1] Unfortunately, I am obliged to quote Soloviev's works in translation, so far as they are available (there is a complete Russian edition in 9 volumes, 1901–1907, and another in ten volumes, 1911–1914, plus four volumes of letters, Petersburg, 1908–1911, 1923). There is one work in French, *La Russie et l'Eglise universelle* (Paris, 1889).

A German 'collected edition', which brings together the major works, has been appearing under the imprint of Verlag Erick Wewel since 1957 (four volumes have appeared so far, *II*, *III*, *VI*, *VII*; these are quoted as W). The deficiencies in this edition can be supplied from other translations, above all from that of Harry Kohler, which appeared as *Wladimir Solovjeff: Ausgewählte Werke* (two volumes, Diederichs, 1914, 1916). The projected third volume never appeared. This edition (=D) becomes the fourth volume in the *Philosophical and Anthroposophical Library* published by Verlag Der Kommende Tag (Stuttgart, 1918–1922; = A). What is not available in D, we shall quote from A.

Other translations referred to include: the French version of Soloviev's doctoral thesis, *Crise de la philosopie occidentale* (translated by Maxime Herman, Aubier, 1947); *Drei Reden über Dostojewsky* [*Three Addresses on Dostoyevsky*], translated by Th. Gräfin von Pestalozza, Grünewald, 1921: *Die historischen Taten der Philosophie* [*The Historical Achievements of Philosophy*], an inaugural lecture, translated by E. Keuchel, Sarja, Berlin, 1925. There are some shorter pieces, particularly letters, translated for the first time in *Wladimir Solovjew: Übermensch und Antichrist* (selected and translated by L. Müller, Herder, 1958). Parts of the work on *Judaism and the Christian Question* are translated in Bubnoff-Ehrenberg, *Östliches Christentum, Vol II*, 299–332 (Beck, Munich, 1925). A short passage from the *Critique of Abstract Principles* is reproduced in Kobilinski-Ellis, *Monarchia Sancti Petri* (Grünewald, 1929), an extensive anthology of texts on the ecumenical question from Soloviev's writings.

What is not translated of the major works had to be taken on the basis of the painstaking and brilliant analyses of Soloviev's work by D. Stremoukhov in *Vladimir Soloviev et son oeuvre messianique* (Strasbourg, 1935; quoted as Str.) and other studies (such as that of Szylkarski, in *Solovjews Philosophie der All-Einheit*, Kannas, 1932).

To provide some general perspective, we here list Soloviev's major works:

The Crisis of Western Philosophy (1873); quoted as *Crisis*, following the French translation.

together with Feuerbach and Marx, Comte's positivism, Darwin's evolutionism, Nietzsche's doctrine of the superman;

The Philosophical Principles of Integral Knowledge (1877); quoted as *Princ.*, following Stremoukhov.

The Critique of Abstract Principles (1877–1880); quoted as *Crit.*, following Str., one chapter in Kobilinski-Ellis.

Twelve Lectures on Godmanhood (1877–1881); quoted as GM, from A III (ET, *Lectures on Godmanhood*, trans. by P. Zouboff, Poughkeepsie, 1944).

Three Addresses on Dostoyevsky (1881–1883); following the translation already mentioned.

The Spiritual Foundations of Life (1882–1884); quoted as GG [*Die geistliche Grundlagen*], from W II (ET, *God, Man and the Church*, trans. by D. Attwater, London, 1938).

The Great Schism and Christian Politics (1883); quoted as GS, from W II.

The History and Future of Theocracy (1885–1887); quoted as Th., from W II.

La Russie et l'Eglise universelle (1889); like the smaller French works, this will for the sake of simplicity be referred to in the German version in W III, and quoted as R.

The National Question in Russia (collected essays from the period between 1883 and 1891); quoted as Nat., following A IV.

The Justification of the Good (1897); quoted as RG [*Die Rechtfertigung des Guten*], following D II (ET, by N. A. Duddington, London, 1918).

Theoretical Philosophy (1897–1899); quoted as *Th. Phil.*, following W VII.

Essays on aesthetics, sexual love, *The Drama of Plato's Life* (1889–1899); from W VII.

Numerous articles on philosophical matters in Brockhaus-Ephron's dictionary; quoted from W VI.

Sunday and Easter Letters; quoted as SO [*Sonntags-und Osterbriefe*], from D II.

Three Conversations (1899–1900); quoted as *Gespr.* [*Drei Gespräche*], from D II (ET in *A Solovyov Anthology*, ed. by S. L. Frank, London, 1950).

Soloviev's poems (about 190) are in part available in German translation. The following editions are noted:

Gedichte von Wladimir Solovjew, trans. by L. Kobilinski-Ellis and R. Knies (Grünewald, 1925).

Gedichte von Wladimir Solovjew, trans. by Marie Steiner (Dornach, 1949).

Wladimir Solovjews religiöse und philosophische Lyrik, trans. by Hunnuis and Engert at the end of the above-mentioned work by Szylkarski (Kaunas, 1932); relatively speaking, the most complete collection, but poetically unsatisfactory.

Russische Lyrik, selected and trans. by W. von Mattey (Schwabe, 1943).

Neue russische Lyrik, ed. and trans. by J. von Guenther (Fischerbücherei, 1960).

Bibliography in Stremoukhov; on Soloviev's aesthetics in particular, Leonida Gancikoff, *L'estetica di Wladimir Solowiow*, in *Sophia* (Naples, 1935), 420ff.

and the fashionable pessimism of Schopenhauer in the form finally given it by E. von Hartmann. The controversy between the religious confessions had acquired a broader, worldwide perspective, turning into a dialogue between East and West, the Byzantine-Muscovite world and Rome. The Great Schism had once again become an issue of present relevance and its theological meaning was being reexamined. Soloviev's thinking has an urgency attained by no one since Hegel, and it operates on the same level as Hegel's, dealing once more in purely and consistently universal, 'catholic' terms. It has an almost hallucinatory spiritual clarity, like the northern Alpine valleys when the dry warm wind of that region is blowing: all objects seem to be brought very near to the eye; they can be grasped in sharp outline and arranged in ordered relations one with another. The reason why this, the 'most universal intellectual construction of modern times',[2] has its place in the context of this present work is not only that it is 'a work of art on a massive scale', a drama and epic, a hymn of the universe; nor is it just because it is 'beyond question the most profound vindication and the most comprehensive philosophical statement of the Christian totality in modern times'. It is, rather, that this system aims at bringing a whole ethical and theoretical scheme to perfection in a universal theological aesthetic—a vision of God's coming to be in the world. By this means, Soloviev both delivers his final verdict on Kantian and Hegelian formalism, and at the same time secures a place for the theological aesthetic already in existence but not hitherto recognized as a proper discipline of thought, by giving it at least the outline of a formal structure. He is also 'the only Russian writer to have left us an aesthetic system'.[3] This is no accident: he alone among the Russians had had some feeling for the specifically Roman form of the Church, not, as one might suppose from an exclusively aesthetic standpoint, in the manner of the Romantics or of the *Action Française* (with whose precursors he did indeed come into contact),[4] but from an ethical and social perspective.

[2] Keuchel, in the introduction to the inaugural lecture, ed. cit.

[3] Herman in the introduction to *Crisis* (ed. cit.), 137.

[4] GM, lectures 11–12 A III 219, n.

Soloviev arrived at the Catholic conclusion[5] because, for him, it provided a link between two formal concepts. The first originates with Hegel and corresponds to his distaste for any kind of subjectivism, any clinging to particularity and differentiation. The subject is a person only because it becomes objective spirit: this spirit mediates between the subject and that which lies outside it, and as such it has structure and form. But so long as this form remains limited by the particular—especially the national—the spirit has not yet acquired the universality that properly belongs to it. Confronted by this Hegelian law, the scales fell from the eyes of the young slavophile Soloviev: even the greatest spokesmen of this school—Khomiakov, Kireevsky, Aksakov—stay within their national frontiers and inevitably, for good or ill, are bound to impose this limitation on Orthodox Christendom as such. Hegel's all-embracing intellectual structure in its systematic as well as its historical aspects has been of invaluable service to Eastern Christianity, a means for it to transcend its national limitations, leading it back to its true identity.[6] Even the cyclical view of culture defended by Danilevsky (the Russian Spengler) is entirely superseded by it.[7] And the catholic spirit can be attained only through the mediation of an objective form that is itself international and catholic; so adherence to the form of Roman Christianity is a means, not an end in itself.

But there is a complementary Hegelian principle, the law of process, understood as the progressive determination of the undetermined, so that by this means determinacy and universality or plenitude develop simultaneously. This principle provides the transition to the second ultimate formal concept. *Process*, or *evolution*, is the great word of the century, a concept in which temporal and historical consciousness encounters the metaphysical question of meaning and is brought within the

[5] The proof that Soloviev actually converted in earnest to Catholicism—a fact ever more strongly contested time and again from the Orthodox side—is to be found in Heinrich Falk, *Wladimir Solowjews Stellung zur katholischen Kirche*, in *Stimmen der Zeit*, 1949, 421–435.

[6] Th., foreword W II 374–375.

[7] Reply to N. J. Danilevsky, W II, 347–360; art. on Danilevsky in Brockhaus-Ephron, W VI.

latter's sphere. And for Soloviev this concept stands at the centre of his system. It is securely grounded upon the abiding intuition that was the basis of German idealism, and it is confirmed by the cosmology that was established empirically only subsequently (cosmology seen in terms of a process of hominization) and by the study of cultural history (seen as a preparation for the incarnation of God); confirmed, finally, by the evolution of christological truth in the dogmatic development of the Church—sketched by Soloviev almost more painstakingly than by Newman and deployed against the rigidly retrogressive Eastern Church.[8] By this means, the total meaning of the world's evolution is clearly established for the future: the development of humanity and the totality of the world into the cosmic body of Christ, the realisation of the eschatological relation of mutuality between the incarnate Word and Sophia, who receives through the Word her final embodiment as his Body and his Bride. The theme and content of Soloviev's aesthetic is nothing less than this: the progressive eschatological embodiment of the Divine Idea in worldly reality; or (since the Divine Spirit is indeed in and for itself the highest reality, while the material being of the world is in itself no more than indeterminacy, an eternal pressure toward and yearning after form) the impress of the limitless fulness and determinacy of God upon the abyss of cosmic potentiality. This also means the bringing into submission, the conquest, of the nondivine on the basis (in Baader's terms) of the image of God already printed upon it. This is the complete triumph of God's omnipotence, which can manifest his plenitude and totality and cause it to prevail even in what is opposed to it—in what is finite, separated, egotistically divided, evil.

Here, then, is the same universal trend of thought as in Hegel; but in place of the Protestant 'dialectic', which relentlessly transcends all things to find its term in the absolute Spirit, the basic conceptual model in Soloviev's thought is the catholic '*integration*' of all partial points of view and forms of actualization into an organic totality that annuls and uplifts (*aufhebt*) all things in a manner that preserves that which is

[8] Th. XXIII W II 476ff.

transcended far more successfully than in Hegel. It establishes God's becoming man as the abiding pivot and organizing focus of worldly reality and its relation to God. What is preserved is the eternal, ideal kernel of every person in so far as it has been integrated into the entirety of the cosmic body of God; which means that its real bodily form is preserved in the same way. There is no ultimate absorption of all things into an absolute spiritual subject; instead there is the resurrection of the dead. So for Soloviev aesthetics and eschatology coincide, in practical terms; and in connection with this we must note simply that if God has become man in Christ, the Kingdom of God does not break in 'unilaterally' from above and from outside; it must necessarily grow to maturity just as much from within. Soloviev's skill in the technique of integrating all partial truths in one vision makes him perhaps second only to Thomas Aquinas as the greatest artist of order and organization in the history of thought. There is no system that fails to furnish him with substantial building material, once he has stripped and emptied it of the poison of its negative aspects. This process succeeds smoothly and painlessly even with wholly anti-Christian ways of thinking like ancient Gnosticism and contemporary materialism; and the integration is so powerful that no trace is left in the completed structure of eclecticism or of a process of compilation; just as, through the skill of composer and conductor, all the instruments of an orchestra articulate precisely that symphonic consonance (for the production of which their parts were differentiated in the first place) as a consequence of the ideal pattern worked out beforehand. It is not so much that integration is made possible by the capacity to distinguish necessary and unnecessary aspects in a system—though such a capacity is eminently present and available and is indeed brought into play. Far more importantly, such integration is achieved by a technique of allocating to each element in turn a place in the system in accordance with its value and specific gravity. And by this means, the limitation of the particular original world view appears of its own accord in the perspective of an inclusive totality of vision. This style of thinking is made possible primarily by means of a concept of God that is alike beyond personalism (God as the free *hen*) and beyond vulgar pantheism (God as *pan*). The Greeks emphasized the *pan*, the Jews the *hen*; but the Christian God is in the truest sense both *hen* and *pan*. 'God is not exhaustively defined in terms of personality. He is not only an independent entity, He is everything, not only a distinct individual but the all-embracing substantial being of things, not only an existent but Being itself'[9]—and precisely in that respect freely exalted and all-powerful over every individual existent, so that his being as totality is in no way simply the sum of all finite substances.[10] Thus the Christian reality of participation by grace in this *hen-kai-pan* in Jesus Christ must mean the opening up, in full consciousness, of the limited, finite spirit to this total plenitude; it must mean the breaking apart of every variety of egotistic will-for-self, allowing it to emerge as a love free from jealousy, which lets all things be (and so is a self-negation).[11] The divine and eternal integral wholeness is answered from the side of created reality by a progressive integration into that integral wholeness.[12]

If Soloviev is set against the background of the Christian *past*, one can say that it is idealism (especially in the form given it by Schelling) that has provided for him the impulse to free himself from the limited forms of mediaeval and Eastern Christianity—as it provided the same impulse for Karl Barth (in the form of Schleiermacher and Hegel), who used it in overcoming the limited vision of Luther and of Calvin (in their doctrine of predestination). Schelling confronts Soloviev with ancient gnosticism as an attempt to reduce Christianity to its own terms in a systematic way. Valentinus is hailed by Soloviev as 'one of the greatest intellectual geniuses of all time';[13] all the main motifs of his cosmic poem are taken over, but their direction is reversed. As Valentinus builds the Christian doctrines of incarnation and salvation into a surrounding system alien to them, so Soloviev integrates gnosis into Christianity. This implies also that the two streams that here flow together—the

[9] GM, lecture 5 A III 91.
[10] *Ibid.*, lecture 6 A III 105.
[11] *Ibid.*, lecture 1 A III 15.
[12] *Ibid.*, lecture 7 A III 138.
[13] Art. on Valentinus, W VI.

Oriental (including the Indian doctrines of freedom and of *nirvana* and their resurrected modern forms in Schopenhauer and Hartmann) and the Greek (most centrally in the shape of Plato and all his imitators, Eastern and Western)—are employed in the most positive and deliberate fashion and with distinct tasks to perform. India provides the first form of the doctrine of pan-unity, and so also of the doctrine of freedom; but this alone remains negative and exclusive. It presents a theory of the world as infinite potentiality ('thirst', or 'urge', or Schopenhauer's 'blind will'), but redemption from this world remains again something negative.[14] Greece, in the person of Plato, discovers the divine in the shape of the Idea that fully answers the 'urge' or 'longing' (*Drang*). The latter can be understood as Eros directed toward the good and the beautiful; but the divine world of ideas does not embody itself, and the Idea is manifested only in a contemplative sense, its embodiment in ethics and politics comes radically to grief. There is no thinker whom Soloviev, the ostensible Platonist, takes to task so severely as Plato. Soloviev saw the greatest tragedy of human history in the fact that Plato, who owed the whole of his philosophical impulse to the liberating influence of Socrates, had finally and shamefully (in the *Laws*) betrayed his master and his master's ideas—in that, in this late work, he judges anyone who subjects the authority of the state's laws to any kind of critique to be worthy of death.[15] But even without this catastrophe, the Platonic Eros remains only a beginning, incapable of following itself out to a proper conclusion, or indeed of understanding itself to the limit. Plato had not unravelled the mystery of what the process of 'generation in the Beautiful' means.[16] He could not, for he had no knowledge of it from within; for that, some sort of radical conversion was necessary, like that provided by biblical religion in its transferring of the initiative from God-seeking Eros to the gratuitous descent of Agape, and in its making humanity the object of God's quest. To understand what is central in

[14] GM, lecture 3; A III 51f.

[15] *The Drama of Plato's Life* (*Lebensdrama Platons*) XXX W VII 333. Similarly, in the very detailed article on Plato for Brockhaus-Ephron, W VI, and further, in GG W II 53ff. 66–67.

[16] *The Drama* . . . XXII W VII 318–319.

Soloviev's turning away from Plato and the whole of Platonism, one has to let the following statement sink in.

> Before Christianity, the natural principle in human nature was the given object (the fact); divinity was something that was sought for (the ideal), and it worked on man in an 'ideal' way, simply as the object of seeking. But in Christ what was sought was given to us, the ideal became fact: 'Here the inaccessible (that is, the unattainable) happens, the indescribable is here enacted.' The Word became flesh, and it is this new spiritualized and divinized flesh that remains the divine substance of the Church. Before Christianity, the firm foundation of life was human nature (the old Adam); the divine was the principle of change, motion, progress. After the appearance of Christianity, the Divine itself, incarnate now for evermore, stands over against man as a firm foundation, as the element in which our life exists; what is sought is a humanity to answer to this Divinity; that is, a humanity capable of uniting itself with it by independent action, appropriating it for itself. As the object of seeking, this ideal humanity here becomes the active principle of history, the principle of motion and of progress. . . . The outcome must be man divinized, that is the humanity which has taken the Divine into itself.[17]

Or, briefly put: 'In Christianity, Plato's ideal world is transformed into the living, active Kingdom of God, which does not operate "over against" the material being of the factual reality of this world with indifference, but rather endeavours to make this world the vessel and the vehicle of absolute being. . . . The harmony of the ideal world, the inner unity of all things, reveals itself in Christianity through the power of the divine-human personhood of Christ as its living reality'.[18]

Logically, then, Soloviev's true starting point in the Christian past is Greek patristic thought before the Schism, especially in its definitive form in the work of Maximus the Confessor, who systematically makes the Chalcedonian dogma (that is, the synthesis between God and man in Christ) the foundation upon which the entire structure of natural and supernatural reality in the world is erected. To the static element provided by this

[17] GG II W II 134–135.

[18] Inaug. lecture 10–11.

world picture, Soloviev added nothing of substance except the dynamic element of German idealism—the evolution of nature towards man, of history toward Christ, and of the Church toward the Kingdom of God in its completeness. The christological development of patristic thought in the great councils constitutes for him an adequate basis for discussion between Eastern and Western churches. Maximus in particular—'the most significant philosophical spirit in the Christian East after Origen, the only significant philosopher of that era in the whole Christian world, the link between Hellenic Christian theosophy and the mediaeval philosophy of the West'[19]—is repeatedly cited as chief witness for the fundamental idea of Soloviev's evolutionism: that, since Christ God has been given to men: that now it is man who is sought; everything from now on depends on the free acceptance of the grace of this gift—the 'art' of the Kingdom at work, and the redemption of the cosmos. Maximus's defence of the free human will of Christ against all the encroachments of platonizing monophysitism provided a decisive vindication of the Christian cause.[20] If Maximus, with his christological philosophy of Godmanhood,[21] represents the truth at the heart of Hegel's thought, so it is Hegel who gives Maximus his topical relevance at the end of the nineteenth century; in the pattern thus arrived at, all the theoretical and practical strivings of the age find their magnetic centre.

[19] Art. on Maximus in Brockhaus-Ephron; W VI.

[20] GS 3 W II 231, 242. Clarificatory comments in W II 328–329, 332; Th. 17, W II 449. *On St Vladimir*, W III 123; R introd., W III 163, 170–171; ch. 9 W III 239, etc. On the meaning of Chalcedon: GS 3, W II 24ff.; Th. 16, W II 444ff.; ch. 23, W II 475 (Chalcedon as a criterion); R ch. 14, W III 319–324 (Chalcedon and Rome).

[21] The extent to which we have to speak of a christological philosophy in Soloviev is illuminated by this principle: 'A free and interior union between the absolute divine principle and human personality is possible only on the basis of allowing human personality itself an absolute significance. Human personality therefore can unite itself with the divine principle only in freedom, out of its own interiority, since it is itself, in a certain sense, divine, or, more accurately, participates in the divine' (GM, lecture 2; A III 22). This 'divinity' of man, however, has its preeminent and supreme instance in Christ and thus has its foundation in Christ.

This is so much so that Soloviev also anticipates in prophetic fashion the great developments of the twentieth century. As compared with the methods of eidetic classification used by Dilthey (forms of Spirit), Spranger (forms of life), Leisegang and Rothacker (forms of thought) and Spengler (forms of culture), Soloviev is indeed well in advance with his method of integration. He analyses independent forms only within the context of the whole and in order that they may fructify the whole. In the approach of his theoretical philosophy (1897f.), he comes very close to Husserl's earliest approach to philosophy. He surmounts the monadic idealism of this system simply by implanting the whole of theoretical philosophy in the context of an ethical reference, the sphere of act and freedom (like Blondel and his disciples). In his presentation of themes, his kinship with Scheler is astonishing: there is the same religious approach as in *The Eternal in Man*, the same struggle against Kantian formalism in ethics (for both of them the decisive impulse and point of departure for their own particular concerns), the same phenomenology of the ethical—the sense of shame, the sharing of suffering (*Sympathie*) and the sense of honour and reverence (*Pietät*). There is the same broadening out into sociology (society and the forms of knowledge),[22] the same basic tension in man between the materially real and the divinely ideal. But where the later Scheler is broken by this tension, Soloviev holds out as a Christian and avoids that fatal philosophical notion of the twentieth century that sees driving instinct as power and spirit as impotence. Nonetheless, he comes close to Freud in freely accepting the theory of sublimation as something pervasive within this tension: the forces of egotism are given to man not to be destroyed but to be transformed, just as God himself creates good out of evil. The dark 'ground' is constantly in need of being brought to illumination.[23] Most astonishing of

[22] All this appears most clearly in *The Justification of the Good* but is also to be found in the earlier *Spiritual Foundations* and *Lectures on Godmanhood*.

[23] GG II 4: 'The essence of the Good is made present through the activity of God; but nothing other than the transformation of the self-assertive power of personal will, when overpowered and converted into a condition of potentiality, can provide the energy to produce the manifestation of the Good in man. So in the holy man, potential evil is the precondition of actual

all, though, is the relationship of the whole vision to that of Teilhard de Chardin. One might well say out that none of the latter's intuitions is alien to Soloviev. He accepts the process of the hominisation of nature as established fact, as much on the idealistic and speculative level as on the empirical scientific level of palaeontology; it is so self-evident as not to need recapitulation. Likewise, he accepts the progress of cultural and religious history toward the God-Man, Christ. And on the basis of both these assumptions, the collective evolution of humanity and the cosmos toward the complete coming into being of God in the world, in the mystical Body of Christ, appears no less self-evident to him. If Christians eighty years ago had taken Soloviev's world picture seriously, there would be no cause today for all the anxious efforts to refute Teilhard. But, quite apart from Soloviev's incomparably greater speculative power, his picture has this in its favour: at the end of his career, Soloviev was confronted by the apocalypse, by Antichrist; and this serves as a salutary counterpoise to his evolutionism, a counterpoise lacking in Teilhard right up to the end.

Soloviev's achievement for his own age was to have affirmed so far as possible all the distinct paths and streams in the construction of world views. If he went along with German idealism in its basic concerns, the idealism to which all the varieties of rationalism since Descartes had been leading, so also he agreed with the check to idealism offered by Feuerbach's humanism. After all, if it is true that the human spirit has developed out of nature, why then refuse any justification to the material aspect of man?

> The material principle in man that links him with the rest of nature, which Buddhism attempted to deny, from which Platonism sought escape and liberation—this principle, according to Christian belief, has an established role in the life of man and of the universe. Christianity sees material life as the necessary foundation for the realisation of divine truth, the embodiment of divine spirit. . . . It asserts the resurrection and

---

salvation: the saint is great in his holiness because he might also be great in evil.' W II 85–86. Likewise GM, lecture 10, A III 201; RG I 2, 4, D II 55ff.; *ibid.*, 62, RG II 8, 7, D II 192f.

> eternal life of the body. . . . The reinstatement of the rights of matter was a necessary operation in the process of liberation wrought by philosophy, for it is only the acknowledgment of matter in its true significance that sets us free from actual slavish dependence upon it, from an involuntary materialism. So long as man does not feel material nature in himself and outside himself as somehing that is his own, something akin to him, he does not love it, and he is not yet free from it.[24]

But in the same connection Soloviev exposes crude materialism as philosophical naiveté and the concept of pure matter as a contradiction in itself, a contradiction that Leibniz and, more particularly, Schopenhauer and Hartmann, show him how to resolve. With materialistic socialism, the same contradiction breaks through in the ethical sphere,[25] and its concerns must find a haven at a higher spiritual level, in a christological socialism, in what Soloviev dreamt of and sketched out as 'universal theocracy'. This integration will be bound to take its aspect of formal absoluteness from rational idealism, but the real fulness of substantive historical content from empirical 'materialism'. In Christ, the real and the ideal have become archetypally one, and so Soloviev now seeks ideological schemata that can chart the process of the world's divinization that begins at this point.

These schemata must in each case be developed with an encounter in mind: the encounter between a divine reality, understood in its maximal, most concrete fulness, and a human and worldly reality, taken equally in its maximal concrete fulness. In this way they must indicate the basic form of the *hieros gamos*, the sacred marriage, of Heaven and earth. Thus Soloviev harks back to the gnostic idea of *syzygia* (the primordial couple, *Ur-Paar*), a syzygy between the fully incarnate deity (as Logos and Christ) and the fully divinized reality of the world (as the *Sophia* that is led upward to God, back to its source in God). Intently and enthusiastically, he follows through the history of Western Sophiology in its various changing guises, from Valentinus by way of the

[24] Inaug. lecture, 13–14.

[25] GM, lecture 1: the opposition between a renunciation of egoism and individual separateness in the interests of a collective egotism of material welfare.

Kabbala to its baroque representatives—Böhme, Gichtel, Pordage, Rosenroth, Arnold—to Swedenborg and to Franz von Baader. But because in reading all these and many others he fully appropriates them for himself, the muddy stream runs through him as if through a purifying agent and is distilled in crystal-clear, disinfected waters, answering the needs of his own philosophical spirit, which (in contrast to that of so many of his speculative compatriots) can live and breathe only in an atmosphere of unqualified transparency and intelligibility.

Sophia is the eternal feminine in the world, the eternal object of God's love; it is the essence of the world, gradually moulded, elevated, purified, emerging in its proper selfhood in the primordial image of the Church, the *Panagia*, the spotless virgin and mother of Christ, but then broadening out to become the real principle of the whole of redeemed humanity and creation. This Sophia is Soloviev's 'immortal beloved'. To her he dedicates most of his poems, though there too, as normally elsewhere, she is still not named directly. She appeared to him in visionary form three times during his life,[26] and it is worth at least airing the question of whether these are not in fact apparitions of Our Lady. Soloviev always saw and acknowledged that Mariology and Sophiology pervaded one another from within and so welcomed the application of Sophiological texts in Scripture to Mary and the promulgation of the dogma of the Immaculate Conception by Pius IX. Despite occasional and impassioned relationships with earthly women, which remained, however, unrequited or unconsummated, signifying for him no more than transitory embodiments of his 'secret mistress', Soloviev lived in an habitual state of 'baptized Eros' directed toward Sophia. His only desire was to see all things in her light; not only relations with the individual human 'Thou', but also relations with human

[26] These visions are described in the great poem frequently translated, 'Three Meetings: Moscow, London and Egypt'. Soloviev said of this that it contained the most important thing that had ever happened to him so far. Kobilinski-Ellis (see n. 1) provides, together with his translation, a commentary on the whole of Soloviev's Sophiology, in which more extensive confirmation of and testimony to its mariological significance is adduced.

society and the cosmos in general must be 'a living relationship of syzygy.'[27]

It is out of Sophiology that there issues the outline of that system that might be called 'theosophy' (in Baader's sense), that is, a science conceived as the integration of philosophy and theology. It is not, however, an integration in the way in which it was conceived in German idealism, which simply assimilated both into the ideal of absolute knowledge; it is based rather on the foundation of the Christian assumption that the free acts of a free God are a revelation of the highest kind of rationality surpassed by nothing else and so are *necessitates* in the Anselmian sense. Once we know that God has redeemed and divinized the world in Christ, the immediate issue of that knowledge for human understanding is the recognition that everything in history and nature, as far back as the act of creation itself, must be intelligible in this perspective, which excludes all others, and that it could not be otherwise. Within the total overall scheme, then, the logical connection of the several elements can manifest itself in the form of a 'postulate',[28] as 'logical inference',[29] as something 'entirely natural, necessary and rational' (this expression is used in connection with the resurrection of the body).[30] 'By virtue of their deepest meaning, and because they are absolutely congruent with reason, [Christian dogmatic statements] can be developed into the most perfect of philosophical systems.'[31] This holds true even for the doctrine of the Trinity, so far as its 'formal aspect' is concerned.[32] What this means is clarified by the statement that

> the eternal and divine world . . . as the ideal plenitude of all things and the actualization of the good, the true and the beautiful, presents itself to the understanding as something that must stand as a norm, in itself and for itself. As the absolute norm, it is logically necessary to the understanding; and if understanding as such cannot assure us of the presence and accessibility of that

[27] *The Meaning of Sexual Love* 4 W VII 269.
[28] GG I 4 W II 87.
[29] GG I 5 W II 91.
[30] SO 12 D II 176.
[31] GG II 2 W II 129–130.
[32] GM, lecture 6 A III 127–128.

> world, that is because the understanding alone is in no way the organ by means of which we can know any *actual* reality. Such reality can be known only through genuine experience. The ideal necessity of a divine world and of Christ as the centre and pivot of this world, absolutely universal, and at the same time, for that very reason, absolutely, uniquely individual, a central point in whose complete fulness the world participates—all this is plain to speculative thought.[33]

Accordingly, Soloviev (contradicting the traditional affirmations) says that God's *essence* is accessible to reason while his *existence* must be the object of faith.[34] Soloviev's ecumenical purpose is 'to vindicate the faith of our fathers and to raise it to a new level of rational consciousness: to show how this ancient faith, when freed from the fetters of local isolation and national egotism, coincides with eternal and ecumenical truth'.[35] The role of philosophy in all this is that of 'defactualising' the Christian and churchly reality that had by its superficiality obstructed the understanding of faith, both in the mediaeval Western world and in the East.[36] What is achieved is an enrichment of the patristic and of the mediaeval Christian world view with all the contributions made by modern speculation and the results of modern science. In this way, all partial aspects are integrated into the central theosophic and 'logosophic' system as *logoi spermatikoi*. And among these also there actually appears the Roman Catholic ethic of ecclesiastical obedience and practical discipline; for Soloviev this seems to be demanded unconditionally by the idea of a social world-organism, just as it saves to complement the strongly individualist-ascetical component in his spirituality.[37]

In Russia and in the West as well, Soloviev was a completely solitary figure. However, various bonds linked him with his most important contemporaries: between him and Dostoyevsky there was the closest friendship and the most

[33] GM, lecture 8 A III 150.

[34] *Ibid.*, lectures 2 and 3 A III 28f., 40f., 43: 'That God is, we believe; who he is we experience and know.'

[35] Th., foreword W II 363.

[36] Inaug. lecture, 11–12, 15.

[37] Particularly clear in GG.

intimate commerce of soul and mind, so that (for instance) we do not know which of them first conceived the figure of the Grand Inquisitor or the notion of applying the three temptations of Jesus to the Church and to Catholicism in particular. It is in fact more likely to have been Soloviev.[38] The two of them went on pilgrimage together to Optina Pustyn (in June 1878) to visit its renowned Starets Amvrosy. Both were equally impressed: the Starets was to become the prototype of Zosima, and Soloviev, the 'secular monk', the model for Alyosha Karamazov. Soloviev lived out his ideal of practical Christianity to the point of folly: 'He was almost always without money, he let all and sundry take advantage of him, he would give the contents of his wallet to anyone who asked anything from him, and, if his wallet were empty, he would take off his coat and give that, so that in winter he regularly had to borrow clothes from his friends. He would even give his shoes to beggars in the street.'[39] Animals loved him, and flocks of birds besieged his hotel room. He died far too young, worn out by a quixotic life of constant wandering and by overwork. A lasting affection drew him to Tolstoy, so different a character from himself. Soloviev always believed that he could win Tolstoy back to a genuine Christian belief, although Tolstoy dismissed the *Lectures on Godmanhood* as 'rubbish' and 'childish nonsense'. Common social concerns brought them together again; it was only reluctantly that Soloviev, obedient to his convictions, attacked Tolstoy's pacifism and moralism in the *Three Conversations*. His encounter with Leontiev, however, was crucial. At first, Leontiev beset him with an impassioned adoration, an almost unhealthy love; but he became less and less willing to forgive him his religious belief in progress. Leontiev, torn between an aesthetic and an ascetic and religious existence, a Russian Kierkegaard, could not cope with Soloviev, the supreme Hegelian. If Soloviev's ideological constructs seemed to him far too deceptively lucid, his very style of life seemed

[38] W. Szylkarski, *Solowjew und Dostojewskii* (Schwippert, Bonn, 1948). By the same author: *Messianismus und Apokalyptik bei Dostojewskii und Solowjew*, which appears as an epilogue to Antanas Maceina's *Der Grossinquisitor, Geschichtsphilosophische Deutung der Legende Dostojewskijs* (Kerle, 1952).

[39] Herman, introd. to *Crisis*, 149f.

opaque and ambiguous; so the ardent love turned to a hatred that embittered his last years. He demanded Soloviev's exile from Russia and elaborated a complete campaign of persecution. In an article written after Leontiev's death,[40] Soloviev had no difficulty in showing him to be a contradictory thinker, never able to unite his Byzantine hostility to progress, his asceticism and his cult of beauty.[41] But the encounter with Leontiev was unexpectedly portentous for Soloviev; it was on this rock of opposition that his firm and rounded faith in progress splintered (though indeed it had already been undermined by his disappointments in ecumenical negotations). There now rose up on the horizons of his spirit the dimensions of the scriptural apocalyse: it might be that the line of development from the head of the Church on his cross to the Kingdom in its fulness and the deified cosmos would run only through the eschatological battles between the opposing forces in the world, finally revealed in all their contradictoriness. So Leontiev's objections to Soloviev (as Ludolf Müller impressively demonstrates) in fact led him to a conclusion in the theology of history that—as the theologian of the three temptations of Christ—he could have drawn for himself and would have been obliged eventually to draw for himself: the conclusion 'that the ways of history do not lead directly upwards to the Kingdom of God'; they pass by way of the final unveiling of the Antichrist, who conceals himself under the last mask to be stripped away, the mask of what is good and what is Christian.[42] We shall see how this tension between progress and apocalypse (which is missing in Teilhard) moulds the shape of Soloviev's aesthetic. Here the total opposition between Hegel and Soloviev comes out into the open, between Hegel's dialectic of absolute knowledge (which again first takes flight—as the 'owl of Minerva'—in the twilight of the end of history) and Soloviev's Christian programme of integration. For the former,

[40] For Brockhaus-Ephron; W VI.

[41] On the relations between the two men, see N. Berdyaev, *Constantin Leontjeff* (Paris, n.d.) 201–229.

[42] Ludolf Müller, *Wladimir Solowjew: Übermensch und Antichrist. Über das Ende der Weltgeschichte*. Selections from the complete works. Herder-Bücherei 26 (1958), 148–149.

evil can be no more than Socratic ignorance; for the latter, it is a clearly acknowledged act of saying No to love. And this contradiction shatters any systematic clarity in the cosmic 'process'; it explodes into a battle to the death, a battle of mounting intensity, that, in Soloviev's eschatological consciousness, could not be other than directly imminent. And so it is into this fiery inferno that his entire system flows.

Soloviev's work divides into three clearly delimited parts. The first period is dominated by the construction of the theosophical system (1873–1883); the second is taken up with the ecumenical project for reconciliation between the churches of East and West and with paving the way for the advent of 'universal theocracy' or 'free catholicity' (1883–1890); the third period, after the failure of his union schemes, returns again to philosophy, outlining the system in its final form, with the accent this time on 'theurgy' and apocalypse (1890–1900).

After a preliminary enquiry into *The Mythological Process in Paganism* (1873), which takes its bearings from Schelling, the first period opens with a critical survey of modern Western thought from the Middle Ages to the present. *The Crisis of Western Philosophy* (1874) was already internally adumbrating the method of integration and indeed was already making use of it to a limited extent in pointing beyond rationalism (idealism) and empiricism (positivism) to the true point of departure for philosophy. The first positive outline of a system, in fact, was to be entitled *The Principles of Universal Religion*; never in fact carried through to completion, it nonetheless led in to the later structure. The earliest extant outline seems to be the foreword to the next work, which remained no more than a fragment, *The Principles of Integral Knowledge* (1877).[43] According to this, philosophy should be made up of three parts: first, the logical part, which has for its object the Absolute in its necessary a priori determinations; then the metaphysical, which investigates the Absolute in its relations with the created world; then the ethical part, which deals with the integration of the world into God and God into the world. While the book aforementioned treated of

[43] Stremoukhov, 52f., 69–78.

logic, it is the work that follows it, the *Critique of Abstract Principles* (1877–1880) that undertook to set out an ethical system (or a religious doctrine of self-realisation). In this work, which deals in an epilogue with Kant's formal moral principle, the parallels with Scheler are particularly striking; not only do we find a substantial ethic of value, but a new ethic of being (developed from idealism) in process of construction. In this latter, human self-realisation is seen within the framework of the total self-realisation of God in the cosmos, so that the close connection, close to the point of full identity, between ethics and aesthetics is evident.[44] The appropriate metaphysics, though partly overlapping with ethics, is represented by the *Twelve Lectures on Godmanhood* (1877–1881), while the aesthetics remained unwritten. Instead there appeared an outline treatment of spirituality, *The Spiritual Foundations of Life* (1882–1884).

After the assassination of Alexander II, Soloviev, who had pleaded for Christian compassion to be shown to the murderers, resigned his chair at Moscow. Dostoyevsky urged him to be more active; so, even more strongly, did Fyodorov (for whom, in his *Philosophy of the Common Task*, the only legitimate account of the world was to be found in the resurrection of the dead, the fathers being raised to life by their children). But Soloviev's concern about the state of the Russian Church led to his rather abrupt turning toward the Roman communion (1882);[45] and the works of his second period stem mostly from his residence abroad. First there came *The Great Schism [sc. between East and West] and Christian Politics* (1883); and after that a *magnum opus* in three volumes was planned, *History and the Future of Theocracy: An Examination of the Path Towards True Life in World History*. Of this, only a foreword and a first book, *An Introduction to the Whole Work*, appeared (1885–1887). The second part was to have included a 'philosophy of biblical history', and the third a 'philosophy of church history'.[46] The essence of this work was preserved in his French essay, *La Russie et l'église universelle* (1889). Side by side with this went studies on

[44] *Ibid.*, 60–62.

[45] Details in Wladimir Szylkarski, *Solowjews Weg zur Una Sancta*, in W II 153–205.

[46] W II 363.

Israel and its relation to Christianity and theocracy, as well as prolonged polemical debates with representatives of Eastern Orthodox nationalism and slavophilism.

The failure of his schemes for reunion led him, now a much-fatigued man, back to theosophy and the final stage of construction of his system. From the second period there still remained a belief in the primacy of ethics, so much so that the theoretical element, much restricted as to its sphere of competence, was only just squeezed in between ethics and aesthetics. The new ethics was first to have been a revision of the earlier version (in the *Critique of Abstract Principles*), but it grew into a major independent work. *The Justification of the Good* (1897) emerges as the most luminously serene work of this wise man. The *Theoretical Philosophy* (1897–1899) remains fragmentary; the radicalism of its approach makes it extremely difficult to see how it might have been developed. Cartesian methodological doubt is pursued to its conclusion; as regards the object as well as the subject, the essay suggests no way out of a phenomenalist position; that is, it denies to pure thought any capacity for breaking through into being. Whatever was to have followed, we may be sure that the further step upward would have derived from consideration of the ethical claim. Everything flows into Soloviev's aesthetics, and for this only sketches and drafts survive: *Beauty in Nature* (1889), *The Universal Meaning of Art* (1890) and the essay on Eros, *The Meaning of Sexual Love* (1892–1894). The early material shows how much his controlling interest drew him toward this conclusion to his work. 'The task of humanisation now emerges as the solution of an aesthetic question, a solution for which the Beautiful in nature prepares the way and which art continues. Contemporary art, then, is obviously inadequate to the embodiment of Wisdom: what is needed to fulfil such a task is a genuinely theurgic art.'[47] The essay on Eros witnesses to something of this: it achieves meaningfulness only in connection with Christ's 'humanisation', his becoming Man. 'Aesthetics thus becomes the science of the progressive embodiment of the idea. . . . The new position of the philosopher is that he now

[47] Str. 225.

treats the world process from the aesthetic viewpoint, instead of confining himself to the theocratic dimension.'[48]

2. LOGIC AND METAPHYSICS

Soloviev paves the way toward his system of pan-unity by a preliminary delimitation of the field of philosophical thought. Only the independent subject is capable of self-reflexive philosophising, and this activity contains as much reality as the independent being as such. The subject, however, finds itself belonging to a common, suprapersonal, generic nature, finds itself caught up in a social and political life; and the realities of language and religious expression itself belong of necessity to this social and political life—an individual can as little 'invent' them as the individual bee can invent the honeycomb. But the subject also acts beyond and outside himself in aesthetic work, which expresses a more than individual inspiration.[49] In the *Crisis of Western Philosophy*, Soloviev shows the consequences of philosophy's identification of these suprapersonal relations with the subject itself. Such a move inevitably condemns philosophy to formalism; that is, to confusing the demonstration of the conditions of the possibility of suprasubjective knowledge within the subject with the reduction of what is known to the subject itself. In the late and fragmentary *Theoretical Philosophy*, the same point of departure appears in radicalised form. Here what is given in the finite subject is strictly reduced to a *noesis* and a *noema* conceived, respectively, simply as 'appearance' and that which appears; while the positing of the *noema* as real transcends the whole sphere of what is merely *theoretically* given and derives in fact from that sphere of act or will, which is also the only thing capable of giving the subject itself its ontic dignity. The separation of the subject from the total cosmic subject and the divine subject is, as it stands, as much a fiction as the act of isolating the phenomenal object from the total interconnectedness of existing reality.

[48] *Ibid.*, 267; *cf.* Herman, 132f.
[49] *Crisis*, 162–163.

The major currents of Western philosophy—rationalism, from Descartes, by way of Spinoza, Leibniz and Wolff, to Kant, Fichte, Schelling and Hegel; and empiricism, from Bacon by way of Locke, Berkeley and Hume to Mill and Spencer—have absolutised either one aspect or the other of the structure of cognition, either the concept or the experience, and turned a merely formal element into the whole of the reality. This ultimately issues in the identifying of an abstract function with the concrete reality that perform that function; in Hegel everything is reduced to '*the* Reason', in Schopenhauer everything is reduced to '*the* Will', in Hartmann to '*the* Unconscious'. But who is it who *is* rational, who wills, who is unconscious or superconscious? The twofold historical development can be expressed in two syllogisms. For rationalism, the major premise is this: 'what is truly knowable is known by a priori thinking' (Descartes to Wolff). The minor premise runs thus: 'but a priori thinking can know only the forms of our own thought' (Kant). And so the conclusion is: 'therefore what truly exists is the forms of our thought; being and concept are the same' (Hegel). Likewise for the empiricist tradition. The first premise is: 'what truly exists is known experientially' (Bacon); the second: 'but only discrete empirical states of consciousness can be experientially perceived' (Locke, Hume and Berkely); and the conclusion: 'therefore what truly exists is discrete states of consciousness' (Mill).[50] These statements are mutually exclusive, but they are at one in the one respect of elevating a single element in actual knowing into the whole act. Soloviev dubs this 'abstract formalism', 'because where there exists neither knowing subject nor known object, only the form of knowledge remains'.[51]

In the *Crisis*, Soloviev generally finds his stimulus in those philosophies that carry on the train of reflection beyond the primitive Cartesian allocation of 'spirit' exclusively to the subject (*noesis*) and 'matter' to the object (*noema*). Matter (the concept of the atom in particular) conceived as pure extension and pure passivity is a contradiction in itself. Leibniz rightly sees

[50] *Ibid.*, 318–320.
[51] *Ibid.*, 320–321.

the need for some active principle in matter, a power working against infinite divisibility, analogous to the spiritual principle, and so also a kind of unity in plurality—whether it is that a temporary state of affairs unites plural elements in a unity (*perceptio*, cognition), or that the power working within effects an unbroken transition from one cognition to another (*appetitio*, will).[52] In Schelling, this analogy of subjectivity (the idea of a principle existing in the object as 'nature' and in the subject as 'spirit') is acknowledged as a starting point; but it loses its primacy in the process of advance toward final identity. This identity (of subject and object), however, remains a questionable conclusion, since the 'absolute subject' is conceived on the pattern of the finite subject, which achieves its selfhood from what is *not* identical with it; and thus formalism is still present in the system.[53] Schopenhauer emerges as the first to break through that formalism that culminates in Hegel; he clarifies the whole sphere of cognition from the perspective of the will that surrounds it on all sides. But if will, understood as a blind urge—that is, as something preceding all cognitive activity—is postulated as absolute, then once again it remains vacuous and meaningless; the world is as little illuminated as God, and its real existence as little vindicated. An absolute 'will for life', an infinite, unsatisfied striving, a hunger for being and so also for suffering, is a contradiction in terms; and the ethic of 'sympathy with the finite creature' erected on this basis, the ethic in which every sufferer transcends the egoism of his own particular existence to identify with the Other, is no less contradictory.[54] But if the obscure drive within all finite reality is not itself the Absolute, then equally it is not to be identified with the finite knowing ego; it is rather that reality that alone can illuminate the objective world in its existence as matter and as phenomenal life and that comes into its own in the knowing subject as knowledge and will. On the other hand, these elements that come into their own in the reflective activity of the human subject—will and perception, reality and ideality—must always have been part of each other if the formal and

[52] *Ibid.*, 180–181.
[53] *Ibid.*, 198–201.
[54] *Ibid.*, 256–260.

elemental realities are to be rendered intelligible. In other words, the world process *exists* as truly as does the Absolute that must be posited before and beyond any world process—as truly, that is, as God, understood as that which is not in process of becoming but which exists eternally in the perfect identity of spirit and nature, ideality and reality.

The 'crisis' in the attempt to explode the formalism of Western philosophy comes, therefore, in allowing the self-reflexive finite subject to make a twofold claim as the condition of its own possibility. On the side of the 'object', the demand is for a total reality that is always volitional but not identical with the particular subject (this will be christened the 'world-soul' in subsequent books), although it is at the same time the 'real' condition presupposed for the subject's own existence. On the side of the 'subject', what is required is a subjective reality in which the two moments of finite cognition, each of which presupposes but never becomes identical with the others—that is, general concepts (form) and particular perceptions (content) —have a prior identity. In other words, what is required is God.[55] Soloviev grounds this second demand for the time being by means of inner experience (Jacobi), which he describes as 'faith' (as opposed to finite objective knowledge) or direct intuitive penetration (*Mystik*); but it would be unfair to accuse him at this point of a flight into the irrational. His path toward God is (as with Baader) philosophically precise, well thought out and logical. Later, at the beginning of his *Theoretical Philosophy*, he shows that he is also able to dispense with appeal to supposedly 'direct' mystical experience. It is only a terminological question whether or not one wants to call the (finite) personal subject's reflection on his act of knowing 'philosophy'; if one does so, no problem remains about calling the actual step beyond the boundaries brought to light by this reflection (boundaries that themselves demand this step beyond), 'ethics' on the one side—the step toward the world—and 'theosophy' on the other—the step toward God—leaving the name of 'metaphysics' for the relation between God and the cosmos (the world-soul).

[55] *Ibid.*, 329–331.

So at the end of the *Crisis*, we are confronted with three postulates (though they are not as yet clearly articulated) for a comprehensive ontology, coming clearly to light in the subsequent works of the first period correspondingly as they are worked out in detail.

1. We must be committed without qualification to the achievements of modern philosophy as regards the world process in its twofold cosmological and historical shape (hominisation and divinisation), but without identifying the subject of this process with God. It can only be a comprehensive subjective reality over against God, in process of self-integration; it may be designated as world-soul, cosmic will, humanity or, finally, 'Sophia'. If this assumption is not made, even the most limited of material objects will remain inexplicable.

2. God's existence over against the cosmic process makes it impossible directly to identify the finite with the infinite subject; and above all it makes possible the relation of love that had always been impossible in idealism. The merely formal (ideal) sign of the divine in man cannot be given content except through God's free opening of himself (grace, revelation). God, as the identity of real and ideal, being and spirit, identity and nonidentity, is also the totality of what is outside himself, since he is wholeness *in* himself. He exists 'for himself' only in so far as he exists as 'not for himself' (as love), as totality both within and without himself.

3. Thus there falls a shadow over any being that exists 'for itself', in a state of separation that is not wholly and purely a condition of and an opening to wholeness in the world. The individual ego (as philosophising subject) is bound on its own level to degenerate into formalism, since pure separation is ontically abstract and unreal, a state of fallenness from the concrete fulness of God; it is exiled from fulness, so that it has to recapture this fulness in the process of integration, starting from the opposite pole, from sheer nullity, so as to be 'God outside God,' the representation of God in the twofold freedom of creator and creature and therefore the absolute form of artistic activity.

We shall now proceed to deal with these three metaphysical

perspectives in turn, though in different order.

1. Since the doctrine of the world-soul and the world process presupposes the doctrine of God, we shall first present this latter in the form in which it appears in subsequent works, above all in the *Principles of Integral Knowledge* and the *Lectures on Godmanhood*. God is the Absolute in the twofold sense of being both a reality detached from (unconditioned by) all that he is not, and a reality subsisting entirely independently in isolation (and perfectly); which is possible only if, while being limited by no other reality, he also possesses the power and freedom to be himself *in* any other reality.[56] He is in fact not a part of all things; if he were only that, he would be the actual being of what is other to him. But if in fact he has free sovereignty over what is other to him, if he is its principle, then he is himself both in himself and in what is other to him, which therefore cannot be the negation of God in its otherness from him. And it is as the one who in his freedom and power possesses what is other to him as both subordinate to himself and behind himself, that he is Trinity: this important and suggestive conclusion Soloviev shares with Schelling, though he does not understand it in quite the same way, since he fills up the idealistic form with what he considers to be (and wants to be grasped as) Christian content. As the ground of all that is (*quod est*, the subject), God is Father; as paradigm of existing reality (*essentia*, the object), he is Son; and as that which unites both (*esse*, identity),[57] he is Spirit or being. This explains why it is that the finite subject cannot in itself attain by philosophical reflection to the ground of being (and of spiritual being); it can do this only by self-transcendence—by its subjectivity (*noesis*) transcending itself in movement toward the absolute subject, the Father, and its object-reference (*noema*) transcending itself in movement toward the absolute object, the Son. Soloviev can dispense with the Cartesian self-affirmation of the finite subject in its intuition of itself as 'thinking substance' only because he has in the background this conception of the *imago Trinitatis*.

Because God the Father has by his side a Son identical in

[56] Str. 70.

[57] *Ibid.*, 72, 74; *cf.* R III 1 W III 327.

substance with himself,[58] he has within himself the perfect reproduction and self-presentation of his own totality, independently of whether this is manifest in himself or in the other that is also himself. In his Logos, he contemplates his own absolute divine power and freedom—freedom to do all things, and so power over all things.[59] The infinity of this free power becomes truly present for God in the Son; he possesses this in himself both as his potentiality and as his own actuality. But he does not wish to possess it only in and for himself, as he is unenvying Goodness; he wishes to give this freedom and power to his potentialities by giving them self-subsistent actuality. By this means, in the first place, he demonstrates fully that 'he is an absolutely unified reality in his innermost essence, which cannot be superseded or negated by any plurality within his unity'.[60] He rules from all eternity over all the plurality that stands against him as power and as ideal reality; but he also wills to rule over it as Good, and to do this he must let it attain real plurality.

> God cannot be content with being stronger than chaos only *de facto*; he must also be so *de jure*. . . . Thus he must separate off his perfect wholeness from the chaos of plurality and respond in his Word to every possible expression of plurality by an ideal expression of true unity, a rational ground that demonstrates the intellectual, or logical, impotence of chaos when it seeks to maintain itself *as* chaos. . . . God's absolute superiority must emerge not only as *against* chaos but also as *for* it, in that it gives to chaos more than it merits, allows it to share in the fulness of absolute life, allows it to perceive the truth that divine plenitude is superior to the empty multiplicity of an unredeemed and corrupt infinity by living inner experience, not only on the grounds of objective rationality.[61]

This rather later formulation softens the abruptness of certain expressions in the earlier writings, in which the distinction between the necessary begetting of the Son and the free creation of the world seems to have been obliterated; in these texts God appears to be obliged by his own eternal character to create the

[58] Th. 13 W II 435.
[59] GM, lecture 6 A III 110.
[60] *Ibid.*, 110–111.
[61] R III 3 W III 341–342.

world, to let his free power triumph over chaos and to let the glory of his love illuminate the self-orientated life of his creatures.[62] The immanent Trinity would then have to be seen as in its very expression already orientated toward the world itself. 'The Logos is God revealing himself; but that presupposes an Other for whom or with reference to whom God reveals himself; that is, it presupposes man.'[63] Accordingly, in *The Principles of Integral Knowledge* the relation between the Logos and the material principle, *Hyle*, seen as the external presupposition of the intradivine being-other of the Second Person, becomes very close.[64] Finally, Soloviev makes the link between God and the three transcendentals: in that he comes forth from himself, God is Goodness; in that he knows himself, he is Truth, in that he experiences himself, he is Beauty. But these determinations are in each case made in relation to God's revealed existence in the 'otherness' of the world; so that Truth is at the same time God's self-manifestation as the Kingdom of God, brought to perfection in Christ, and Beauty is God's full actualisation of his selfhood in the other, his highest degree of materialisation. 'Good is the prescribed goal, Truth the necessary means for determining it, and Beauty the actual realisation of it. In other words; because Being itself affirms the ideal as Good, it bestows upon it, through the mediation of Truth, a realisation in the Beautiful.[65]

But what precisely is this ideal reality or totality of ideas? What (to introduce the term that now becomes necessary) is God's *Sophia*? Is it the plenitude of the modes in which his essence can be imitated (which exist already as absolute reality in his essence), coming to light through his power and freedom? or is it the plenitude of possibilities realised through his free power and grace, possibilities that are (eschatologically) linked with the form of preexisting ideas? The question is of some importance for aesthetics; from the viewpoint of the aspirations of reality, does the Beautiful lie in the sphere of ideal being only? or does

[62] *Cf.* for example, GM, lecture 5 A III 75, and *ibid.*, 88; also lecture 6, *ibid.*, 105; lecture 7, *ibid.*, 142, and lecture 8, *ibid.*, 152.

[63] *Ibid.*, lecture 8, 153.

[64] Str. 73.

[65] *Ibid.*, 75.

ideality eternally include reality in itself? For Soloviev, however, the question can be left as insoluble, since for him the opposition of real and ideal no longer had ultimate significance as in the idealist system of God's coming to be; in God, the idea is always his own reality, and it is this reality that draws the still imperfect creation, existing for itself alone, home to himself.

This also becomes clear from the fact that the process of the subjectivising of the idea, its fulfilment in being properly and independently itself, is curiously underemphasised in all this. In the Logos there exists, first of all, 'the sphere of pure intelligences, objective ideas, hypostatic thoughts of God . . . and these constitute the world of ideas; they are entirely contemplative, passionless and immutable essences, fixed stars in the firmament of the invisible world, and so they stand above any desire, any will and thus also any kind of freedom'. Over against this world stands the sphere of the 'responsive activities of the Holy Spirit, which are more concrete, subjective and lively and which constitute the spiritual world, the sphere of pure spirits or angels. . . . They experience not only intellectual contemplation but states of emotion and will, they possess motion and freedom' (the significance of the fall of Lucifer is illuminated by this).[66] In the former sphere, the intelligences are so much 'in' God that they exist only beyond themselves; in the latter, the spirits also exist *in* themselves. The former have 'only an ideal individualisation', while for the latter 'the divine will seals their independent unique subsistence'.[67] We may properly observe here that for Soloviev, individuation is in no way accomplished *ratione materiae*; for him it is precisely the personal that is truly and properly 'ideal', while, conversely, that which is purely generic and anonymous is assigned to matter. The tendency to 'neutralize' (so to speak) the act of creation, and in certain respects to negativise it is of importance here. This is the old neo-Platonic-Gnostic-Kabbalistic tradition, about which more will be said later on.

Sophia, then, is the divine substance *qua* 'pan-unity', 'the plenitude or absolute wholeness of being', in which

[66] R III 5 W III 354–355.
[67] GM, lecture 9 A III 171.

'indeterminate plurality has never existed as such but has from all eternity submitted itself and reduced itself to the absolute unity of being in its three inseparable hypostases'.[68] In a figurative sense, it can be described as 'the body of the divine, the material being of the Godhead, penetrated by the divine principle of unity'. Or else it may be described as his 'nature'; since it is precisely in this way that God distinguishes himself absolutely from the nature of the world, it is necessary that 'an eternal nature of his own, a special eternal world of his own, be accorded him'.[69] As such, though, it also includes in itself 'the power that unites the fragmented and disrupted being of the world'. It includes this not in its form as active divine Logos, but rather as 'the feminine origin or the feminine consummation of every entity'. 'If it *exists* substantially in God from all eternity, then it comes into actuality in the world, embodying itself progressively in the world. In the beginning, it is *reshith*—the fertile idea of absolute unity, the only power whose calling is the unification of all things. At the end, it is *malkuth*, the kingly rule of God, the perfect, wholly realised union of creator and creature. It is not the world-soul—this is only the vehicle, the means and the basis for its realisation.'[70] On this basis, then, Sophia is defined in terms of the tension between, on the one hand, God himself in his perfect presence and perfect representation in the totality of being (thus over against the Logos, understood as the locus of divine generation and the active moulder of that totality), and on the other, the Kingdom of God as the perfected issue of the world process, together with the humanity that is brought to completion through that process. But if humanity is necessarily threefold—Man, Woman and Society—'then its union with God is also necessarily threefold, though forming only one unique divine-human essence—Sophia incarnate, whose central and perfect personal expression is Jesus Christ; whose feminine complement is the Holy Virgin; and whose universal extension is the Church', this last-named being officially held together by the person of Peter. Nevertheless, Christ remains in himself the

[68] R III 3 W III 339–341.
[69] GM, lecture 7 A III 145–146.
[70] R III 5 W III 352–353.

incarnation of the Logos as the divinely personal power that actively shapes the world. Over against him, as both fertile feminine womb and his created, formed issue, stands Mary, who is also the Church, *Maria-Ecclesia*, eschatologically the 'Bride and Consort of the Lamb', the personal and social form taken in the world by Sophia in the stricter sense of the term.[71] The bodily element in this process of incarnation is essentially that of the one eucharistic body of Jesus, made ready beforehand in the animation of all bodily existence in the world, but finally given concrete structure by God. This living form of the body of the world, which finally finds its own plastic expression, is the form of God's Sophia, of his divine mode of articulation itself.[72] This is not contradicted by the *Lectures on Godmanhood*, where he sees Sophia as 'the ideal, complete humanity, determined for eternity in Christ',[73] not only collectively but thoroughly individually, since it is a reality in which 'each single individual is eternal as a part of total humanity' and has 'an eternal and unique substantiality'.[74] The world-soul was previously distinguished from Sophia as being only an 'outer husk' for the perfection of humanity; but in so far as it is structured in all respects by Sophia and so enters into it as its goal, it also can now be called Sophia in its own right; it is 'the complete organism, simultaneously universal and individual, total humanity as the eternal body of the Godhead and the eternal soul of the world'.[75]

2. Both the remaining aspects of Soloviev's metaphysics—the complex of ideas centring on creation, separation from God, and the Fall, on the one hand, and the question of the world-soul and the world process on the other—are in fact inseparable, and this inseparability is precisely what characterises the contribution of Eastern Christian theology to the *Una Sancta*, the theme that it brings to be incorporated in it. The actual coincidence of Creation (the creature's emergence from God and from ideal form) and Fall (the creature's falling away from

[71] *Ibid.*, III 7 W III 366–367.
[72] *Ibid.*, 368.
[73] GM, lecture 8 A III 152.
[74] *Ibid.*, 158.
[75] *Ibid.*, 157.

God) is expressly taught by Maximus the Confessor,[76] epitomising a long tradition that is by no means exclusively Gnostic. The 'subject' of the world process as a whole, normally called the 'world-soul', begins its development in a position of extreme inferiority, a state of absolute fragmentation and separation. In accordance with gnosticising Christian tradition, Soloviev believes that this state cannot be comprehended without supposing a dimension of turning away from God, a dimension of guilt, embracing the whole process.

Before we introduce the question of 'process',—that is, of the essence of Creation, Fall and development, a word about the essence of the world-soul is in order. According to the article in Brockhaus-Ephron, 'The world-soul is the uniform inner nature of the world', in so far as this unity is conceived not only as 'the highest ideal unity, which reposes in the absolute principle', but also as a real 'subordinate principle', as in Plato's *Timaeus* and in Plotinus. 'The idea of a world-soul, which disappeared in the Scholastic period, becomes a matter of pressing concern once again in the Renaissance Platonists and at the beginnings of the modern era,' in Goethe and Schelling, for instance; while Schopenhauer and Hartmann go further back still, beyond the Greeks, to the monism of Indian thought. Soloviev himself dismisses this monistic conception of the world process: 'If we presuppose a world-soul as the unique fundamental principle, such a world process would have to be a constant generation of something absolutely new, an uninterrupted creation *ex nihilo*; that is, pure miracle.' However, natural philosophy makes it perfectly plain that there is a uniform centre of nature (as, indeed, the Soloviev of the *Crisis* had demonstrated): 'If the component elements of the cosmic whole, the atoms, are to be traced back to a dynamic source of determination (centres of active powers), a determination that in turn finds its exhaustive definition in the psychic characteristics of aspiring and imagining, then we are necessarily bound to grant that the natural ground of unity in these powers also possesses the same psychic nature.'[77]

[76] *Cf.*, my *Kosmische Liturgie. Maximus der Bekenner*, 1961, 184–185.
[77] Art. 'Weltseele' in Brockhaus-Ephron W VI.

If 'atoms' are active centres of energy in reaction against a principle of passive dissolution proceeding *ad infinitum*, then 'pure matter' is a limit concept, a 'postulate', that is entirely imaginary; it cannot even be followed through to a logical conclusion.[78] 'In order to act upon another reality outside itself, any power or energy must strive to go out of itself. In order to receive the influence of another energy, it must, so to speak, make room for the other, draw it to itself or set it before itself. It follows from this that any fundamental or primordial energy necessarily finds expression in this way, in aspiration and representation.'[79] In action, it becomes real for others; in experiencing outside influence, other things become real for it. So the purely quantitative dimension is already superseded: the centres of atomic entities are acting and aspiring monads, living elemental substances (if they were not so, they would have no rationale for their aspirations). 'In nature there is no such thing as pure mechanism or absolute soullessness.'[80] If we start our investigations at the lowest levels of the process, it is still the forward-striving energy of nature that appears as 'elemental basis of the cosmic whole, as blind natural will'. In this, two tendencies are simultaneously recognisable: there is the capacity for a deeper submission to the ideal principle of the cosmos, and thus the readiness to receive forms; and at the same time, because of the blindness of the act of aspiration, there is the opposite capacity for resistance to the ideal principle, the tendency toward chaos.[81] Pure 'striving', 'blind yearning' (*désir aveugle*) is what characterises this stage, precisely because the energy has not yet achieved any kind of interiority, and cannot transcend the separation of the particular individuated centres of energy that 'exist side by side with one another in the formal unity of infinite space—a completely external and empty image of the objective substantial wholeness of God'.[82] This 'pure striving' is 'pure indeterminate potentiality',[83] and as such, it is 'the first of

[78] GM, lecture 2 A III 30.
[79] *Ibid.*, lecture 4 66.
[80] RG, introd. 4 D II, 20, n.
[81] 'Beauty in Nature' ['Die Schönheit in der Natur'] 8 W VII 152–153.
[82] R III 4 W III 349.
[83] *Ibid.*, 348.

all creatures, the *materia prima*, the true substratum of our created world'.[84] Soloviev does not want to abandon to their own inner and autonomous fertility and creative fantasy the products of the world-soul as they follow one upon the other, the gradations of astral, geological and biological processes leading up to humanity; rather, in reaction against a monistic idealism, he puts them all under the irradiating activity of the divine creative Logos, but in such a way that in the inmost depths the mother and matrix of all forms shares in the successive acts of their information, since this matrix itself attains a deeper interiority in every one of its products and so acquires greater generative power. On its own, it is a 'barren womb';[85] but when it is fertilized by the Logos, it is no longer possible to say whether the forms generated are more the product of the Logos or more the product of the world-soul. What at first is imposed upon the world-soul as an external 'law', (what, therefore, it experiences as pure limitation) it now takes into itself and, as it ascends towards consciousness, experiences as inner life and light and so as liberation. Whereas the world-soul 'originally, as simply aspiration, does not know what it should aspire to and does not possess the idea of pan-unity', the Logos for its part cannot realise 'its ideal purpose directly in the divided elements of material existence'. So the world-soul is the necessary principle of mediation, just as much for the Divine Logos (whose desired goal is the coming to be of God in the world) as for the world itself, which can only attain to freedom through a process of prolonged assimilation of the ideal 'law' into its own distinct life. So if the question is asked as to why the goal is not reached 'by one single act of creation', 'why such pain and fatigue is necessary in the life of the cosmic whole', 'the answer [lies] in a single word that expresses something without which neither God nor nature is conceivable: freedom'.[86]

Now the world-soul becomes 'free' and 'self-aware' for the first time in man: 'In man nature transcends herself and, in attaining her conscious being, passes over into the sphere of

[84] GM, lecture 10 A III 180.
[85] R III 6 W III 357.
[86] GM, lecture 10 A III 181–183.

absolute being.'[87] In man the world-soul 'comes to itself': all that has gone before is only a process of 'hominisation'; and so the world-soul can be identified in its meaning and its goal with humanity.[88] 'As the living core of all creatures and at the same time as the real form of the divine, the unified wholeness of humanity, or "world-soul", is both the true subject of creaturely existence and the true object of divine acton.'[89] Man is the one truly free being who stands between God and the world; his freedom may, of course, be no more than a natural exercise and thus be limited and conditioned, but it has only itself to blame for this. So if we say that 'by a free act of the world-soul, the world that it held together as a unity has fallen away from God and fragmented into a multitude of warring elements',[90] then this cosmogonic 'falling away' (at least in so far as it includes an element of guilt) has to be seen as one and the same event as the fall of man. 'Eternal humanity' (the 'Adam Kadmon' of the Kabbala) is, in the ideal purpose of God, the world-soul that has 'come to itself': only in man does it attain to that state of suspense between God and the world that can result in a falling away from God. Man 'possesses first the elements of physical existence that link him with the natural world; second, an ideal consciousness of total unity linking him with God; and, third, because he unites himself exclusively neither with one nor the other, he emerges as a free ego. . . . He is free to will the total unity that God possesses; and by willing it as God wills it, he can will to exist beyond himself, as does God.'[91]

It would be nonsense to think in terms of two 'falls', especially as Soloviev consistently impresses on us the identity of world-soul and humanity (*qua* content of the cosmos of which it is the consciousness). But Adam Kadmon is man in a general no less than an individual sense; Soloviev recognizes no

[87] *Ibid.*, 186.

[88] *Ibid.*, 187. *Cf.* 174: 'The world-soul, or ideal humanity', 'the prototype of humanity or the world-soul'; 188: 'The world-soul in man, or man himself'; 190: 'Human consciousness, i.e., the world-soul.'

[89] *Ibid.*, lecture 9, 174. *Cf. The Meaning of Sexual Love* I, W VII 215: '[Man] is aware of himself as the centre of the general consciousness of nature, as the soul of the world, as the self-realising potentiality of absolute total unity.'

[90] GM, lecture 10 A III 183.

[91] *Ibid.*, 187.

such thing as an hypostatized universal, only 'ideas' concretely filled out with their individual content.[92] He speaks of 'the sinfulness of universal man', as a consequence of which humanity, 'which ought to constitute the unifying rationality of the universe, found itself fragmented and scattered over the globe'.[93] Like Maximus the Confessor, he speaks of the 'splitting of a single human nature into many individual natures'.[94] He sees the totally unified essence of man and the world as having emerged from God's eternity into a sphere that is not historical ('fallen') time, in which preexistence (the preexistence in unity of all things) and immortality (after time) are absolutely one and the same and support each other. 'That which comes into being only in time must also disappear with time; the notion of an entity eternally perduring after death cannot be logically harmonized with belief in its antenatal nonexistence.'[95] The paradox is inescapable that for Soloviev the temporal world process (the world-soul's coming to consciousness in man) depends upon a supratemporal decision of the same reality in its freedom—depends, that is, upon its 'eternal humanity'. This indeed is the only possible resolution of the apparently contradictory assertion that death came into the world through one man's sin (Rom 5.12) and yet must have existed, in terms of evolutionary history, long before the first man. It is possible that Soloviev also has in mind here Schopenhauer's doctrine of the unconditioned will and its subjugation at the level of phenomena to the principle of sufficient reason. He offers a painstaking exposition of this: 'Every willing individual is, from one point of view, entirely conditioned in its manifestations; but, from the other side, it is entirely free in its inmost essence. Although all its acts are determined by its innate character, this

[92] GG II 1, 5 W VII 89: 'By the figure of the natural Adam we should understand not merely an individual person over against other persons, but a wholly united personal being, including in itself the entirety of natural humanity.'

[93] R, Introd. W III 151.

[94] RG II 7, 10 D II 164.

[95] GM, lecture 8 A III 159–160. *Cf.* 167–168: 'The efficient cause of evil cannot be in the individual as an earthly phenomenon, conditioned in advance; *rather it must be sought in an absolute, eternal essence, in which the direct, pristine will of this individual is contained.*'

innate character of the person is at the same time conditioned in its metaphysical essence by its own free will.'[96] Quite apart from the fact that, in Soloviev's work, the whole process is set out in dualistic rather than monistic terms (in terms of the distinction of cosmic will from God), the resolution of the world-soul problem must be sought in this direction. The world-soul itself is aspiration and will, but in an indeterminate condition (it is *aoristos dyas*),[97] 'an unconditioned and unconfined principle' (*apeiron kai aoriston*);[98] in order to define itself as will, it requires the consciousness that it attains only in man.

Once again, it is clear from all this that the world-soul is in no sense to be equated with Sophia,[99] although as the wisdom and the total unity of God progressively embody themselves in it, the more the activities of the creative Logos are taken up by it, at an ever more interior level, and marked as its own. In this sense, at any rate, Sophia and the world-soul can be equated,[100] or rather the world process can be described as Sophia coming to be.[101] Thus it could be envisaged as in one way comparable to the Augustinian City of God (*peregrinans*), or else as the universal Church.

3. The world-soul is that which carries forward the cosmic process that begins with Creation. At the point of Creation, the only thing established as the ground of created being is pure potency (the world-soul as *materia prima*, as mother or matrix of all things); and there then follows the bestowing of form on this by the irradiation of the creative Logos (which represents the ideal world, *divine* Sophia, over against this primal matter). So Soloviev, following Augustine on the one side and Schelling on the other, can describe the act of creation almost in negative terms as the 'removal' of God's triumphant power, that power for which the chaos of pure potentiality is always a possibility that is already in the past, already transcended. God 'wills chaos to exist since he is able to lead back into unity the rebellious life

[96] *Crisis*, 249.
[97] R III 4 W III 348.
[98] *Ibid.*, III 5 W III 356.
[99] As Stremoukhov rightly stresses (82, n. 65).
[100] GM, lecture 9 A III 174.
[101] *Ibid.*, lecture 10 A III 182.

of creatures and fill the infinite void with his overflowing life. Thus God gives freedom to chaos, he denies himself . . . the power of reacting against it in his omnipotence.'[102] This negative guarantee of security for the order of potentiality by means of the already victorious power of God holding itself back is at the same time a positive act of will, 'since this other reality only attains its existence by a free act of the divine will'.[103] God

> desires that finite essences should possess a real life of their own. It is to this end that he brings his divine will out from its absolute substantial unity and directs it toward the multiplicity of the ideal objects and thereby confirms their independent and individual existence. . . . God confirms and establishes the 'other'—that is, being (*to apeiron*)—by not retaining this will in himself as the One, but objectivising and actualising it for himself as total unity. However, because of the natural unique particularity that belongs to the life of this 'other'—that is, to every divine idea, every objectivised form, and in virtue of which it is simply '*this*' reality—these forms with which the divine will has linked itself do not behave at all indifferently with regard to the divine will; they remould the activity of this will to conform to their own particularity, pouring it, so to speak, into their own particular form. . . . In this way, the will ceases to be exclusively divine. . . . It now both belongs to the objectified form in its particularity as well as being an expression of the activity of the divine essence. The infinite energy of existence (*to apeiron*) which in the Godhead always remains hidden behind and within its realisation . . . , ceases to conceal itself in an individual essence behind its realisations, since these actions are not the whole but only a distinct part of the whole. So every individual essence loses its direct unity with the Godhead, . . . it separates the divine *act* of will from the absolute and immediate unity of the divine will as such, taking it *for itself*, and through it acquiring the living power of reality.[104]

Here one need only replace the word 'will' with the word 'being' (*actus essendi*)—as indeed Soloviev himself does—to see appear the classical Thomist doctrine of the *limitatio actus essendi*

[102] R III 4 W III 345; *cf.* 354.
[103] R III 4 W III 346.
[104] GM, lecture 9 A III 171–173.

per essentiam ut potentiam, with the whole profoundly problematic element that this contains (since the inner potentiality, or 'openness', of this divine act of being, as it externalises itself in the cosmic act, the *apeiron*, is already articulated in and with the process of *limitatio*). The consequence also follows that the world-soul (*qua* humanity), which has already been designated as *apeiron*, is nothing other than this divine act of being itself, transcending itself in the Other and pouring itself out into the Other.

The world then becomes 'the God who is coming to be' vis-à-vis the God who exists as eternally contemporary to all things. It becomes, as Soloviev constantly reiterates, a mirror image of God's reality,[105] which constructs itself a second time beyond itself, constructs itself out of a pure potentiality for being. Why so? So as to point to the ultimate proof of its Divine Being, to the fact that he is both *hen* and *pan*; that, in its total being, it is contained by no 'other' reality and limited by no 'other'. It is wholeness both in himself and outside himself.

This is where the difficulties start, at the point where the limitation of the act of being is described as a separation and a 'taking for self' of the divine will. To avoid identifying the coming into reality of nature with the Fall, identifying separateness with egotism, we must stick to those texts that are quite clear in tracing the Fall back to a (transcendental) free decision, which establishes the form of fragmentation in cosmic life. It is through this decision that evil enters in at the root of the sensible world as the contradiction between the infinity of the basic blind urge or 'thirst' and the finitude of the forms in which it is realised and which it wills to make absolute. The central phenomenon in which this destructive contradiction becomes manifest is the life of the various species; though when thus manifest, the contradiction is ipso facto denied and resolved at a higher level. Such a life is based on sexual desire and necessarily ends in death. It nourishes itself from an alien life (killing so that it itself may live) and yet can live only in order to die.[106] Again this is a decidedly Eastern way of thinking. The positive concept

[105] R III 4 W III 346. 'A negative counterpart to the divine'; RG III.8, 3 D II 184.

[106] GG I, Introd. W II 13–15.

of form means the removal and elevation of this endless and unsatisfied craving in finite being to another level: 'The boundary of matter is to be found in God.'[107] Thus the world's condition is evil, since all beings burn with the hellfire of insatiable craving, they burn with 'false and evil life'. Only from God can it receive definition and limit—initially, by means of an external and harsh law that, as it is gradually interiorised, brings this dark blaze of desire into the light; and by doing so it shows itself to be truly grace, something the creature can never bestow upon itself, something, therefore, that requires faith in a higher gift, given from outside,[108] something that thus requires prayer.[109] The finite in itself is parasitic and insatiable; the infinite, on the other hand, is always a matter of a definite task, a definite responsibility, and so constitutes the form that determines the 'matter' provided by the basic urge or drive.[110]

Adam exists in three conditions. He is, first, wholly real in God and potential in himself. He then becomes real in his own right, and *as such* has only potential (ideal) reality in God. Finally, in Christ, he becomes real both in himself and in God—*en duo physesin*.[111] 'The animal shape in which humanity appears to us at the dawn of history is only a distortion of the image of God in man.'[112] So far as it includes the process of hominisation, the establishment of the world's reality is indeed the result of alienation. The latter is 'a displacement of certain essential elements'[113] and thus 'a false relation' of individual entities to one another,[114] whereby 'the root of the perversity of our existence is constituted by impenetrability; that is, by mutually exclusive essences standing in opposition to each other'.[115] The centring of the self *in* the ego and the stubborn clinging *to* the ego, clinging to the differentiated existence of separation and division, this above all puts individual existence 'outside the

[107] GG I 1 W II 33.
[108] GG I, Introd. W II 19–25.
[109] *Ibid.*, 25f.
[110] GS I W II 211–212. Also R III 6 W III 357.
[111] GG II 1, 5 W II 92–93.
[112] GG I 2 W II 51, n.
[113] GM, lecture 9 A III 165.
[114] GG II 1, 2 W II 74.
[115] *The Meaning of Sexual Love* 4 W VII 268.

truth' and condemns it to death and decay.[116] 'The oppressive, tormenting dream of our egotistic separateness',[117] the contradiction of wanting to be at one and the same time the whole of reality *and* one's own self, this 'root of all suffering',[118] existing in opposition to the corporate fulfilment of nature, is transcended first and foremost in Christ and in the Mystical Body. In ordinary sexual relationship, the contradiction is at best only masked—that is why sexual Eros is so close to cruelty and to rending hostility;[119] and thus too, marriage is not a real means of salvation—sexual continence is far better. Again, childbearing can only be the transmission of the same finite, egotistical and therefore mortal life, despite the hope that the temporal world will get 'better' with the children; the sacrament of marriage does not alter any of this.[120] For that one would have to be able to elevate the meaning of Eros, purified and clarified by sexual continence, into true love. And then to pass beyond both marriage (which will always remain the only possibility for the common run of men) and negative asceticism (beyond which the Christian monastic tradition has rarely penetrated), into that rare and supreme possibility of authentic love, in which the eternal, androgynous syzygy which is the heart of Eros, now redeemed from its fallenness to sexuality, is taken up into God, into the relation of Logos and Sophia.[121]

But it is worth remembering at this point that matter—that is, a state of absolutized separation and fragmentation—is no more than a limit concept (a 'postulate') that is in reality impossible, and that the 'will', energy or impulse, that constitutes the kernel of all life is already in reaction against this tendency toward a flight into chaos. However, the power to penetrate and overcome this chaotic tendency toward absolute separation varies: the cosmic process is the gradual illumination and redemption of the will (of the world-soul), its deliverance from this perverse potentiality that it possesses. Here we should

[116] *Ibid.*, 2 VII 215.
[117] GM, lecture 9; A III 162.
[118] *Ibid.*, 164.
[119] GG II 1, 3 W II 77.
[120] RG II 7, 4 D II 15 154f.
[121] This is the theme of the essays on sexual love; VII 201–272.

note merely that it is only when it becomes conscious in the free human subject that the blind 'impulse to separation' opens up to the diabolism of freely willed evil; and so the world process can be perfected only in a process of historical and apocalyptic decision for or against the true Good.

We shall not attempt here to trace out the stages of the cosmic process in detail, though the description given of them (modelled on the accounts of Schelling and Hegel) is of the highest visionary power. God does not create directly, but only through the medium of the world-soul: this is an indispensable notion of which we must never lose sight.[122] Through 'blind groping', 'through unfulfilled projects for never-realized creatures', the world-soul ascends with difficulty, from chaos to cosmos. So the stages of the world's coming to be are to be interpreted as the steps leading up to the coming to be of man and of Christ. The 'universal force of gravity' binds disparate things to one another in a mechanical and external fashion; it is 'a primordial expression of cosmic altruism'. Subsequently, a new, refined and dynamic form of matter, the 'ether', embraces the elements and binds them together as light, electricity and so forth; 'this active energy is characterised by pure altruism, an unlimited extension and a continuous act of self-giving'. 'The world-soul, the earth, beholds in the radiance of the ether the ideal image of its heavenly beloved, but it does not in reality unite with it'; it strives toward it by absorbing the light into itself, by 'transforming [it] in the fire of life', and now begins to develop organic forms. These represent the Logos in so far as it has come into being as immanent in the world, the Logos that finally, after endless efforts, struggles through to come to consciousness in man, and so too to come to the form of total being, that form in which the God, who is all in One, can be present as ideal structure. At this point, the historical process begins, the process that so deepens and alters the ideal forms of thinking about God that the dwelling of God in a real man, as the constitutive reality of a real man, becomes possible in consequence. By these stages the world ascends toward its peak in the God-Man. Soloviev constantly goes over them again:

[122] R III 6 W III 157–159.

from the abstract Indian idea of God (corresponding to the abstractness of the principle of gravity) we move to the luminous, contemplative ideal world of the Greeks (corresponding to the stage of the irradiation of matter, but still lacking active interiority of life) and thence to Israel's real and active relation to God (corresponding to the organic process of nature)—a relation, though, in which God still remains 'Other'.

'That which is fresh and original in Christianity does not lie in general conceptions but in positive facts, not in the speculative content of its ideal structure, but in this idea's embodiment in a personality. This fresh and original character can never be taken from Christianity; it is not at all necessary in establishing this to demonstrate, in the face of all historical fact and all sound human understanding, that the ideas of Christian dogma come on to the scene as something entirely novel, fallen from Heaven, so to speak, in their perfected shape. Nor would this be a view shared by the great fathers of the Church.'[123] Soloviev does not mean to say that Christ is only a particular case of the genus 'Godmanhood': he is much more its unique and all-transcending peak, God's becoming real in man—previously no more than an unrealisable ideal for humanity. He is 'the absolute synthesis of the infinite with the finite',[124] 'manifestation of the new man . . . [as] the focal point of world history'.[125] However, this is not 'a miracle in the crude sense of the word, not something alien to the general order of existence; this new and unprecedented phenomenon was being made ready in all that had gone before; it represented what all the earlier phases of life had yearned for and striven for and hastened toward: the whole of nature had aspired and gravitated toward man, and the whole history of humanity had been directed toward the God-Man'.[126]

Soloviev's Christology reaches its climax in the affirmation that the realisation of the God-Man Christ is to be seen as

[123] GM, lecture 6 A III 102–103. *Cf.* lecture 7, 141: 'Christianity has its own proper content . . . , and this is uniquely and solely Christ'; and 142: 'The only novelty, the only specifically distinguishing feature, [is] Christ's teaching about himself, this pointing to his own person.'

[124] R III 11 W III 408.

[125] GG II 3 W II 136.

[126] GG II 1, 5 W II 91–92.

grounded upon a reciprocal sacrifice—God's sacrifice in entering into humanity no less than man's in entering into God. In this lies the perfection of human love, and thus too the perfection of human freedom. In the state of total 'innocence', Adam Kadmon existed really in God while existing only potentially in himself; then, when he came to be real in (and for) himself, his being in God was only potential. The pristine unity cannot be simply reproduced, it must be 'achieved; it can be only the issue of free action, of a free deed, in fact, of a twofold deed: a self-abandonment on the part of the divine just as on the part of the human'. Now the whole cosmic and historical process rests upon 'a kind of self-sacrifice' by the Logos, 'since on the one side, the Logos here renounces, by a free action of his divine will or love, the manifestation of his divine glory. He forsakes the repose of eternity and engages in the struggle against the principle of evil, subjecting himself to the whole consequence of the rebellion of the cosmic process by appearing within the imprisoning constraints of an existence external to himself, within the limits of space and time . . . hidden rather than manifest. On the other side, however, is cosmic and human nature, in the form of its actualisation at any particular point, unceasingly divesting itself of itself as it experiences an unremitting yearning and strives after ever new modes of appropriating the divine prototypes.' Nevertheless, for the time being this twofold *kenosis* remains incomplete; 'it first comes to perfection when the divine Logos truly empties himself and takes the form of a servant (Phil 2.7)', since at this point he

> determines [the human principle] no longer by means of external action, by setting limits to it without himself changing at all but rather by an interior self-limitation making space in himself for the Other and taking up into himself what is human. So on the one hand, the divine Logos takes human limitation upon himself; not indeed in such a way as wholly to enter into the limits of human consciousness, which would be impossible, but by experiencing these limits in any actual given moment as his own. And this self-limitation of the Godhead *in Christo* sets free his humanity, since it allows his natural will freely to renounce itself in favour of the divine principle—regarded not as an external force (which would mean that the self-renunciation was

unfree) but as an interior good through which man can then come to share this good in full reality.[127]

This is a crucial text for the whole of Soloviev's theology and theological aesthetic: in God's *kenosis* (which perfects the whole process of creation by transcending it from within), human *kenosis* is freely given space in God so that the human consciousness may give itself over absolutely to the divine. In this act, man is freed from all sinful isolation for him who is total unity; and this indwells in him, no longer simply as a pure abstract form of thought (Western rationalism from Descartes to Hegel remained fixed at this level), but rather as real plenitude. And this is possible, not through some Promethean will to understanding on the part of 'absolute Spirit', but through loving dedication in response to the eternal Father. This twofold *kenosis* is the essence of the person of the God-Man no less than of his work, his death on the cross, and it is at the same time absolute glory in twofold form—the self-glorification of God in his creation as much as the glorification in God of the whole man, the man who, in the voluntary death of love, is victorious over all the disastrous contingencies of the material world and so has achieved for himself and for all humanity and the cosmos the resurrection of the body.[128] In this connection, Soloviev insistently stresses the necessity of the christological doctrine of Christ's twofold will, which alone guarantees the *kenosis* and the glorification of the God-Man himself as well as of the whole creation through him. This doctrine alone makes possible the threefold temptation of Christ, which becomes intelligible precisely in virtue of this developed Christology (the idea that Christ's human nature exists in and because of a surrender to the person of the Logos who makes space for it in himself). It is a temptation to bring more and more of the divine power into play for the work of salvation—which would, however, mean the loss of life lived in self-surrender and so the loss of the only possible salvation. The renunciation of a glory that can be deployed at will is the attainment of an authentic 'glory in the act of all-conquering

[127] GG II 1, 5 W II 94–96 (collated with Kohler's translation in D I 78–80).
[128] GG II 1, 5 W II 99–101.

love: "We beheld his glory, glory as of the only Son from the Father, full of grace and truth".'[129]

With Christ, the spiritual man comes on to the scene; the law of his being lies in the saying that only he who loses his soul (in so far as it is separate, limited and worldly) will save it.[130] And he wins in exchange for it not only his own self in Christ and so in God, but also, as a necessary consequence, the divine and worldly total unity itself. He has consecrated himself to the work of atonement, to the coming to be of God's Kingdom; and that Kingdom in its coming to be is the Church.

3. ETHICS AND ECCLESIOLOGY

Soloviev's basic idea is the notion of 'realisation', realisation as the becoming real of the ideal, as the descent of Heaven to earth, as the setting free of man for God and for himself by the process of God's becoming man. To this end it is of first importance that the level of *theoria* (as pure knowledge and perception of the idea) be transcended; and it is transcended by God as he makes himself known in the Judaeo-Christian tradition as the *realissimum* (beyond the Greek ideal of contemplation and the formalism of Kant), which in its work of grace sets limits on human freedom for the actual task of collaborating in the building of God's Kingdom in the cosmos. Thus the 'will' of God, that which he has invested in the world as his own reality in the Other, returns again to him in a threefold manner.

So clearly does Soloviev see in the process of the absolute ideal—God becoming real—the abiding and obvious achievement of Christianity for the human race, that he does not consider it as a philosopher might, going back behind the process, abandoning what has actually been attained in the interests of some kind of pure philosophical method. Still less is he minded to offer a rationalistic unravelling of the Christian phenomenon in order to surpass it. For if God's coming to be real has not been consummated on the soil of historical and

[129] GG II 1, 5 W II 96–99.
[130] GM, lecture 5 A III 59.

empirical fact in the uniqueness of the God-Man, then everything remains still in the partial and prejudiced state of *theoria*, 'absolute knowledge'. However, the projected system of the late 'theoretical philosophy' shows a concern to build into itself this realm of absolute knowledge as pure phenomenalism and formalism. The later ethics, the *Justification of the Good*, accomplishes both steps at once: worldly reality (of the so-called 'external world' as well as of the ego) is unfolded and secured primarily in ethical fashion—and the reality of God unfolds itself in the same act as the inner reality that makes possible every ethical action and is presupposed by it. For in order to exist, man must act; and in order to act he must presuppose that existence has some meaning; but this presupposition implies the existence of a *giver* of meaning.

> Any creature striving toward the goal of its existence necessarily becomes convinced of the fact that the attainment of its goal or the final satisfaction of human desire does not lie in human power; that is, any creature endowed with reason comes to recognise its dependence on an invisible and unknown reality. Such dependence is impossible to deny. The only question is whether that on which man depends has a meaning or not. If it has no meaning, then a life conditioned by this meaninglessness is itself meaningless. . . . We are able consciously and rationally to do good only if we believe in the Good itself, in its objective, independent significance in the world—only if (in other words) we believe in a moral order, in a purpose, in God. . . . We must believe that the good that reason demands of us is no subjective illusion but has a real ground, and that it brings truth to expression.[131]

Soloviev has no trouble in showing that all the great ethical systems (all those, that is, with religious content) of the various races are constructed on this assumption, and that the ethical systems of eudaemonism on the one hand[132] and Kantian rigorism on the other[133] extract only one aspect from the total

[131] RG I 4, 4–5 D II 98–100.

[132] RG I 6 D II 128–148.

[133] RG II, 713–714 D II 170–177. 'Morality is in reality autonomous; Kant was not deceived in this respect. And this massive issue from the sphere of human consciousness, which is implied in its very name, will not forsake man.

phenomenon. He himself constructs his system (as always) with an eye to the final integration of the 'total unity'; the norm is the wholeness of man,[134] and a broad inductive survey of ethical phenomena, conducted with magisterial sureness of touch, demonstrates 'from below', from the concrete facts of history, what Kant proves a priori (and thus no more than formally).[135] The three basic phenomena of shame (the elevation of spirit over the world of instinct), sympathy (communication with one's fellow man, with everyone who is a neighbour) and *pietás* (in the sense of reverence for the higher reality upon which one depends—parents, clan, country, ancestors, gods, the living God) support the cosmos of virtues and duties, the universal human integration as personality, society and Church, or Kingdom of God.[136] Here again the concept of process, this time at the historical level, is for Soloviev 'an historical fact that cannot be contested with any well-founded degree of certainty'.[137] Each man on his own level can of course, in some way do what is right, strengthened by providential grace. 'But just as neither a formless organic piece of matter nor an inadequately evolved living body such as a sponge, polyp or cuttlefish can produce a human being, even if it possesses it potentially within itself, so also the Kingdom of God (in the sense of the perfection of human and cosmic social life) cannot take shape directly out of a horde of savages or an inadequately evolved and barbarous political organism.'[138] Just as the first Adam's arrival on the scene was a seed sown in the world requiring infinite time to evolve, so too the seed of the second Adam will require a long passage of time before the whole

Morality is autonomous precisely for this reason, because its essential core is no abstract formula, hanging in the air; rather it is autonomous because it carries in itself all the conditions of its own reality. And those realities presupposed by a moral life, the existence of God and an immortal soul, do not represent the demand for something other, added on to the sphere of morality; they are its own inner basis. God and the human soul are not postulates of the moral law, but the very formative powers of moral reality.' *Ibid.*, p. 175.

[134] RG II 7, 10 D II 162f.

[135] RG, foreword *ad fin.*; D II xxii–xxiii.

[136] *Ibid.*, I, ch. ii–iv.

[137] *Ibid.*, II 7, 14 D II 176.

[138] *Ibid.*, II 8, 5 D II 188.

'dough' of world history and the cosmos is leavened. However, the eschatological Kingdom of God does not fall from Heaven any more than Christ's own advent occurs without mediation; it comes in the fulness of time, when the womb of the virgin—and the womb of earth itself as well—is perfectly ripe for the reception of the divine seed. While the Church fathers had to answer the question of why Christ came so late, at the end of the ages,[139] Soloviev has to deal with the opposite question, why he came so early and delays his return so long. If 'the Kingdom of God could be revealed as little among cannibals as among wild animals, if it is necessary for humanity to make its way from an animal, formless and chaotic condition to intelligible organization and unity, then it is as clear as day that this process is not yet concluded, that the idea of Christ has not yet leavened all the dough'.[140] Soloviev is no Pelagian,[141] so little does he recognise any independent achievement by men and by humanity without the prevenient assistance of the 'nourishing' work of grace,[142] that we must fear almost the exact contrary—a dissolution of the natural order (where, at the end of the day, nature would still exist really only as pure potentiality, while an ideality stems from the Logos) in the order of grace. But the expressions he uses here should not be pressed too far: Soloviev thinks as a Christian who can never posit a pantheistic dissolution of creation and creaturely freedom in God; his teaching on the Kingdom of God seeks indeed to integrate all particular individual freedoms in the one mystical Body, in the communion of saints, but seeks precisely in this integration to preserve and eternalise the authentic freedom of authentic personalities.

Since the event of Christ, this process of the integration of humanity into the Kingdom of God is necessarily bound to the reality of the *Church*. The Church is, on the one hand, the God-Man really living on in a community of love, realised ethically as well as sacramentally; but, on the other hand, it is also, necessarily, the pattern of the ideal universal form of the

[139] Henri de Lubac, *Katholizismus als Gemeinschaft* (1943), 145f., 216f.
[140] RG II 8, 5 D II 189.
[141] *Cf.* the detailed article on Pelagius in Brockhaus-Ephron; W VI.
[142] RG II 7, 14 D II 176.

Kingdom of God. It is ideal in so far as it has not yet really been integrated and realised in the historical process; but in Christ it is already real, and, in inchoate form, it is realised in the Church and in humanity. The Church as founded by Christ is the place where the ultimate is made present; in it the false and contradictory species life that exists in the flux of temporality is done away with: in the Church is abiding fatherhood and abiding filial *pietas*; it is 'natural humanity transsubstantiated'.[143] And it is so from a starting point in the real and particular that the ideal sought for is no longer simply God but the perfected body of humanity.

> The God-man is individual, the true Man-God is universal: as the radius is the same for the whole circle and determines equally the distance from the centre to any given point on the circumference, it is thus in itself the formative principle of the circle, while the points on the circumference can make up the circle only in the sum of their totality. Outside this totality—that is, outside the circle—they have taken individually no definition; and the circle also is unreal without them. In the human world, the Church represents this circle. When human personality is united with the Church, man comes to be *integrated*. He receives true and healthful life, and the Church itself is fertilised and can now act effectively.[144]

Everything then depends on the integration of humanity into the Church, so that it can receive there a share in the form of divine-human universality, and on the other hand, on the Church's integration into humanity, so that it can shed the abstractness that is foreign to it because of its essential centre, but which it still retains because of the refusal of men to accept it. It is of course equipped by its founder, for the sake of its task of integration, with a *form* of universality, that removes it from the limits of any finite worldly form (nationalism in particular); but this form, which culminates in the finality of papal authority and in the doctrine of infallibility, is not *in itself* abstract. For in the first place there is absolutely no such thing as abstract truth in the Church; further, the *form* of being in truth corresponds to a

[143] R III 10 W III 396–397.
[144] GG II 2 W II 135.

real existence; in truth, an existence which has its ground in the immaculate virgin Mary,[145] and finally, the form of infallibility is always embodied in a concrete Church order, 'grounded in the real and living unity of the prince of the apostles,' the one who, in the place of all and in the name of all, was the first to make a free confession of the divinity of Christ, to 'the messianic idea in its absolute and universal form,' and thus the one to whom the keys of the Kingdom have been entrusted.[146] So the concept of form that is practically applied in the polity of the Catholic Church is, as was noted at the onset, the concept of a means, a way of mediation; but it is only possible and meaningful if it arises out of a form that has its end in itself (the Godmanhood of Christ as the expression of God in the world) and advances toward a form that equally has its end in itself (the complete embodiment of Christ in humanity, the Kingdom of God). Only when considered in the light of this purposive dynamism is the form of the Church not vacuous or abstract, but a plenitude in the process of coming to be, supernatural ethic in practice and so itself an expression of Christian love. For it is love alone, and can only be love alone, that transcends all forms of egotism, whether of individuals, or of groups, so that it may liberate them in 'a real act of submission or love toward the Church'[147] for Christ who is total truth and total unity. It is in virtue of this love, which is at work beyond all limited personal or racial loves, that 'the Church as a whole is more real and more alive than all persons and races, just as the whole body surpasses the individual organs and cells in its vital power'.[148]

In the *Spiritual Foundations of Life*, Soloviev had already, in a superb survey, outlined the forms of ecclesial catholicity; it is a survey oriented to the practical 'catholic' task of the permeation of all humanity but does not yet enter into the debate between the Western and Eastern Churches. Although, as Soloviev says in this work, the Church stands above all natural organisms, it possesses in common with them those qualities that belong to any kind of life in the world. 'Any real determinate life also

[145] R II 1 W III 249.
[146] *Ibid.*, 250–253.
[147] *Ibid.*, II 4 W III 267.
[148] Th. 23 W II 476.

requires a corresponding determinate form', a body. This is more than a mere aggregate of parts; it involves (1) the entirety of its component elements, (2) the organic form that produces the real body out of these elements, (3) the actual vital energy itself, which expresses itself in all the operations and movements of the separate parts in subordination to the whole. In the Body of Christ, the elements are human beings, the form is the Church and the vital energy is the Divine Spirit. By virtue of the ecclesial form, the Divine Spirit elevates particular individuals above their limited existence, so that they come together formally in the total unity of Christ; and it further happens, again because of the ecclesial form, that the enduring limitations of sinners do not damage the dignity of the Church as a whole. A natural body too can be diseased in particular members, but it will die only if the central organs are affected. But in the Church these organs are invulnerable: the head is the God-Man, the heart is the immaculate Virgin and, with her, the whole invisible Church of the saints. So the ethical task proper to all who belong to the Church becomes the conforming of its life to the divine life, whose seed and whose structure are preserved in the sacred form of the visible Church. Any form originating with man is innerworldly; by contrast, everything 'provided by the Church universal, has the form of unconditionality (absoluteness).' This comprises (1) the true faith as the Church understands and proclaims it in her role as representing the powers of human knowledge penetrated by Christ's spirit, to which the individual has to surrender his isolated, 'fleshly' understanding; (2) the right relationship to all men, which the Church in her hierarchical form is able to uphold, the hierarchial form 'in which every member occupies his place and fulfils his destiny not in his own name, but in the name of him who has commissioned that member for his work, in which this whole ordered existence leads directly up to the source of all truth, to Christ, the one true High Priest and King'; (3) the human destiny to rule over the cosmos and mould it into the body of God. But for this last the Church carries in itself only the seed, the germ of the new and higher nature (in the Eucharist), 'the absolute form of transfigured matter,' with which we communicate in the organic existence of the Church, so that, starting from there, freed in principle from the servitude of the material order, we can actively help the world to be transfigured.[149] The universal form of faith, universal hierarchical obedience, and the receiving in the sacraments of a universal eschatological quality of life, these three things together elevate man in his fragmented and limited existence to a state of participation in the fulness of divine catholicity. And the ecclesiastical form directed toward that goal cannot be invalidated by the 'matter' that is unified by it: 'The Church is not only the assembly of believers; it is, before all else, that which assembles them—that is, a substantive form of unity given to men from above, by means of which they can come to share in the Godhead.'[150]

Soloviev emphasises very strongly the mediatorial nature of ecclesiastical form. We are not to 'confuse the bed with the stream'; the Church is the Kingdom, not in the state of fulfilment but only in becoming, and there can be no doubt that the grace of God has always been at work in the world. But since Christ's incarnation, this grace has taken on a visible and tangible form: 'In the Christian Church, the divine is not only an interior and intangible working of the Spirit, it appears also in determinate shape, already realised, in bodily manifestation. The Old Testament Church too had its forms, but there they were only allegorical foretypes and signs. On the other hand, the sacred forms of the New Testament Church are true and authentic images of the presence and work of God in humanity.' Because of the imperfection of the human beings who enter the Church, 'these forms appear only as the inception, the pledge, of divine life in humanity . . . but even at the present time the New Jerusalem, the city of the living God, does not consist purely in the thoughts, wishes and inner feelings of Christians: the divine forms represent the real foundations, here and now, of that city of God, on which the divine building will be erected—which, indeed, is already in process of construction in a mystical sense. So, of course, not everything in the visible Church is divine, but the divine is already something visible within it. And these

[149] GG II 2 W II 108–111.
[150] *Ibid.*, 112.

visible foundation stones are unshakeable and unchangeable; without them there is no Church.'[151] The Church is, it could be said, the process of gestation, the perfected Kingdom is the event of birth.

Soloviev's doctrine of the necessary interpenetration of an immutable structure with the living evolution of the same structure arises out of this conception: if an entelechy is vital and active, then precisely for that reason it must change as to the forms of its manifestation if it is to remain itself. 'Thus the visible forms of the divine, though always present in the Church, were at first very rudimentary and imperfect, just as the visible form of a seed is rudimentary and imperfect and shows very little correspondence as yet to the full form of the plant, although it contains this form potentially in itself.' So it would be foolish for someone to reject the full-grown tree so as to preserve the seed, to 'reject the more fully revealed forms of God's grace in the Church, preferring absolutely a return to the structure of the primitive Christian community'.[152] And yet the whole plant is present in the seed; and thus the choice of a new apostle to complete the original number is made at Peter's suggestion. It is not done 'aristocratically', with the Apostles exercising their own plenitude of power, nor 'democratically', by ballot, but 'theocratically', through prayer and the drawing of lots. In this way, the divine influence on the community is the outcome of the free concord of the disciples under Peter's leadership; so that 'already the polity of the Church emerges with complete clarity as a free theocracy'.[153] The Church that is sent out into the arena of world history will always have to express its life in the fact that, through the indwelling Spirit of God, it is equal to ever-new historical situations and tasks. It will, in consequence, have to elucidate its faith in the rich Graeco-Roman systems of learning and conceptuality and to develop the expression of it accordingly, precisely if it wishes to remain true to its own primitive tradition;[154] and the definitions promulgated in its ecumenical councils as the expression of the self-understanding

[151] *Ibid.*, 114–115.
[152] *Ibid.*, 118–119.
[153] *Ibid.*, 120.
[154] *Ibid.*, 121.

of its faith will be binding on all believers.[155]

At this point, the Great Schism intervened, the schism between East and West, between the Byzantine-Muscovite world and Rome, and between the slavophiles and Soloviev, with Soloviev pleading the cause of Rome—but also the cause of the ecumenical councils—with such superiority in his grasp of the issues involved. We need not and cannot summarize here this brilliant apologia, although in its clarity, verve and subtlety it belongs among the masterpieces of ecclesiology. One or two observations must suffice. Both the great schisms, Eastern and Protestant, are pure scandal; they cannot be justified from a Christian point of view in any way at all. The East, which adhered to the legitimacy of the great ecumenical councils, had in fact acknowledged the authority of Rome in these very councils (especially at Chalcedon); no council ever condemned Rome, and, since the time of Photius, the East has recognized its inability to convene an ecumenical council on its own behalf. It has ossified in the position it held at that time, whereas Rome has never ceased to renew itself in vital fashion, facing up to the contemporary historical situation. Before the separation of the churches, the Byzantine Church, out of loveless political envy and the lust for honour, had surrendered itself to the service of the emperor and so deprived itself of its catholic, supranational liberty. This bondage to the state was its legacy to Russia, which totally dispensed with the Church's liberty by finally establishing the tsar as head of the Church in 1885. By rejecting the living, contemporary polity of the Roman Church, Byzantium had no alternative but to elevate the stagnated tradition and, in consequence, formalism into a principle; thus it became the Church of the past.[156] It was a profound historicophilosophical logic that the heir of Byzantium was Islam.[157] Whoever, as a Christian, only preserves without creating has indeed suffered the interior loss of his treasure: 'When cut off from its living form of *coming to be*, existing only in the forms of expression that *have* already *come* to be, the Church's holiness necessarily loses its infinite quality. It becomes

[155] Th. 7 W II 414f.

[156] GS 3 W II 240. *Ibid.*, 4, 258f., 5, 268f., 272f.; and SO 12 D I 183f.

[157] GS 3 W II 243–248; R, Introd. W III 174–177.

hidden and bound by limited, dead, ... already-exhausted forms that weigh upon the living consciousness as purely external things.'

'In such a situation, what is essential and eternal in ecclesiastical structure is confused with the contingent and the past; the stream of Church tradition itself, forced into narrow channels by the dead hand of fundamentalist literalism, no longer has its proper unbounded ecumenical breadth.'[158] Thus the flight into contemplative monachism was likewise logical, a flight by which the profane world and the Christian nation were abandoned to a purely secular political order and left without Christian nurture.[159] Byzantium is now no more than 'a deserting Church'.[160] Indigenous Russian Orthodoxy, with its healthy and vigorous beginnings under St Vladimir, was too heavily weighed down by its fateful heritage to be able to escape the disease of sterile conservatism. The indigenous Russian schism, the controversy between Avvakkum, the leader of the *raskol*, and the patriarch Nikon, revealed the hopelessness of the inner situation and the cruel lack of any decisive ecclesiastical court of appeal. Peter the Great did the only possible right thing when he abolished the patriarchate and established the Synod: 'Russia, thank God, was rescued both from the Oriental stasis of the Old Believers as well as from a superfluous and belated parody of the mediaeval papacy!'[161] On both sides we see the lack of interior catholicity; but the saviour figure, Peter, who 'legitimately and lawfully abolished'[162] the ecclesiastical power that had been so abused, was also the one who opened a door to the West—and thus to the universalist thinking of German idealism. Compared with this, Peter's own rationalism and that of the slavophiles who followed was something already surpassed from within. If Khomyakov understood the notion of an ecumenical Church 'as a living organism of truth and love, and still at the same time wished to cling to Russian national messianism, then logically he ought to have accused the whole

[158] GS 5 W II 272.
[159] R I 1 W III 192–193.
[160] *St Vladimir* W III 105.
[161] Th., foreword W II 367, 370.
[162] *Ibid.*, 371.

of the West of a falling away from love. For Soloviev, this is a 'monstrous assertion' from the Christian point of view as much as the historical (when considered in the light of the actual events leading to the Great Schism).[163]

Soloviev himself is unsparing in criticism of the Roman Church, but only so as to separate wheat from chaff, to set out the Petrine principle in its purity and indispensability. Rome is the form of the sacred, the living counterpart of the frozen Byzantine Icon,[164] grounded upon the resurrection of Christ, which demonstrates 'that bodily existence is not excluded from the covenant between God and man, and that external, palpable objectivity can and must become a real instrument and a visible likeness of divine power'.[165] But this sacral form is holy only as a means to the realisation of God's Kingdom;[166] the more it appears as a humble servant and the less attention it draws to itself, the more Christlike it is.[167] 'The authority of the Roman See was never more generally acknowledged or more powerful than under the least assuming popes.'[168] The besetting temptation for Christian Rome, as the heir of the pagan caesars, was, again and again, the exploiting of power to achieve spiritual goals. An 'authority possessed of a mystical religious foundation had no need of reinforcement from without or of formal juridical documents'; but an 'all-too-active concern with their own power' led the popes to strive for such secular guarantees, and in this way they inevitably became entangled in politics and even in waging war. 'The Church militant became the Church in arms', and the spiritual theocracy to some extent assumed 'the character of a coercive regime'.[169] So little does Soloviev extenuate these abuses and what he calls the 'abstract clericalism' of Rome,[170] that he can portray Protestantism's

[163] *Ibid.*, 375–377.

[164] 'The apostolic chair in Rome: this wonderworking icon [sic!] of universal Christianity': R, Introd. W III 161.

[165] *Ibid.*, 160. On the theology of the icon, *cf.* Th. 17 W II 450–455.

[166] R II 2 W III 259.

[167] R II 8 W III 284. 'So it is clear that the central authority of the papacy has a purely conditional and functional meaning': GS 6 W II 288.

[168] GS 6 W II 289.

[169] *Ibid.*, 288–291.

[170] W II 161.

reaction in the direction of Christian liberty as in fact inevitable,[171] although he denies that Protestantism has the character of a Christian Church because of its refusal of an objective and universal ecclesial form.[172]

The great lesson to be learned from the twofold schism is that the Roman form is still necessary for the Church's survival, but that the Church cannot be united by force, any more than it can rule the world by force or man be saved by force.[173] There is nothing more needful for the stability of Christianity on earth and its effectiveness among men than the reunification of its three branches. Each of them preserves one distinctive element of Christian life: the Graeco-Russian East preserves tradition (the past); Rome preserves the means of spiritual power (the present, as the constant renewal of the presence of Christ); Protestantism preserves freedom and prophecy (the future), though this can in no way present itself as authentically Christian without both the other principles.[174] Soloviev is not arguing for the 'branch theory' of the Oxford Tractarians; but he does see the values that have been stolen from the Church's centre in Rome and are still withheld from it because Orthodox and Protestants stand aloof. Only a pure act of love can help the Church over these difficulties, a love, though, that renounces any kind of egotistical clinging to the national or to a freedom of conscience conceived in purely individualistic terms, a love that acknowledges the form of universality. What is required is an 'ethical act of self-denial on the part of persons and nations'; this alone can open the way for the total unity of the Church of Christ;[175] for it is only when animated by the Spirit of the Church that the individual can be free: 'Such men as surrender religiously to the Church in its holiness and obey it humbly in its authority share in the Church's freedom in full measure; for in their life the Divine Spirit lives and works, and where the Spirit of the Lord is, there is freedom. Any other kind of freedom,

[171] GS 4 W II 257. *Ibid.*, 6 W II 304f.; GM, lecture 2 A III 22.

[172] GS 6 W II 306. *Ibid.*, 7, 323.

[173] *Ibid.*, 6 W II 307–308.

[174] *Ibid.*, 4 W II 263f. *Cf.* the rather different division in Th., foreword W II 382–385, and R, Introd. W III 152–153.

[175] GS 4 W II 253.

which is not purchased at the high price of self-denial in faith and obedience, is counterfeit coin in the ethical world.'[176]

For Soloviev, with his lucid spirit and its search for order, one thing self-evidently, necessarily and immediately needed resolution: the ecumenical problem of the mutual estrangement and hostility of the churches. He made a representative confession of faith to the Roman Church in the name of all Russians:

> As a member of the true and venerable and rightly believing Eastern or Graeco-Russian Church ... I acknowledge ... as supreme judge in matters of religion him whom St Irenaeus, St Dionysius the Great, St Antony the Great, St John Chrysostom, St Cyril, St Maximus the Confessor, St Theodore the Studite, St Ignatius, et cetera also acknowledged: namely, the apostle Peter, who lives on in his successors and did not receive that Word of the Lord in vain: 'Thou are Peter ...' et cetera. You know, O immortal spirit of the blessed Peter, invisible servant of the Lord in the government of His holy Church, that there is need of an earthly body for its revelation. Twice, indeed, you have granted it to be embodied in a society, first in the Graeco-Roman, then in the Romano-German world ... and after those two preliminary incarnations it awaits the third and final one. A complete world, full of forces and longings but lacking a clear consciousness of its destiny, is knocking on the door of world history; what word is to be spoken to it, O peoples of the Word? ... Your Word speaks of a free universal theocracy, the true solidarity of all nations and classes, the realisation of Christianity in social life, a christianised politics, freedom for all the oppressed, protection for all the weak, social justice and true Christian peace. ... I have come to utter this Amen in the name of one hundred million Russian Christians in the firm and full conviction that they will not dissociate themselves from me. ...[177]

4. AESTHETICS AND APOCALYPTIC

The protests against Rome failed;[178] Rome possessed that form of catholicity that alone can unite the world and lead it toward

[176] *Ibid.*, 255.
[177] R. Introd. W III 188.

the Kingdom of God. Soloviev wished to see this formal principle applied entirely realistically in the free subordination of the state—that is, of particular states—to the spiritual authority of the representative of Peter. Only so can national egotism be overcome, and 'the universal brotherhood of races' be realised.[179] 'The free ethical sacrifice of the national spirit' could make real the 'supremely free unity of the Church', whose ecumenical reality would appear to us 'no longer as a lifeless idol, nor as a body possessed of soul but bereft of consciousness, but as self-conscious, ethically free, a nature itself working for its own actualisation, as Sophia, the true Beloved of God . . .'[180] Soloviev's dream was to open up the sphere of realised secular achievements, of state and culture, to the influence of a Church that is unified and thus fully aware of its task, in the kind of free reciprocity that the Middle Ages had indeed sought, but never wholly realised. Only through the Church can the concerns of the state achieve a supratemporal significance for the Kingdom of God, only through the Church can the indubitable fruits of cultural and technical progress be given meaning in the light of eternity. 'If social progress aims to be authentic progress, it must have an absolutely worthy, an ideal and perfect purpose.'[181] Like Dante, Soloviev dreamt of the unification of the world, not in a totalitarian monarchy, but in a total free theocracy, into which all things, secular and spiritual, must be integrated. Did he seriously hope to see this distant goal of his ecumenical efforts attained? In any event, after his failure to achieve the proximate goal of ecclesiastical unity, his hopes vanished into thin air, leaving him a disappointed man.

And so the last years of his life—the years that take up again the speculative work of the first period and attempt to bring it to a conclusion—move into a curious twilight. The direct activism in ecclesiastical politics which marks his ecumenical period recedes, to give place to his own theoretical work, which (as was demonstrated at the beginning) seeks to open the whole of philosophy to aesthetics, starting with ethics and working

[178] GS 6 W II 308–310.
[179] Th., Introd. W II 384.
[180] *Ibid.*, 385.
[181] GG II 3 W II 149.

through to theory. The aesthetics which has to perfect the whole scheme was never written; we have only fragments of this. It was to have been an aesthetic that was the issue both of the 'realisation of the good' (the idea taking form) and of perfected truth (the idea, that which is worthy of being, becoming real), and so a 'science of the apocalypse', of the revelation of God's Kingdom, God's ultimate coming-to-be in man and the world. In the light of Rom 8.19f., both basic words, *apocalypse* and *glory* move closer together: 'This revelation, and the glory of God's children that all creation awaits in hope consists in the fact that the free union of God and man is to be fully realised in the whole of humanity, in every sphere of its life and activity . . . , all these spheres must be led into the condition of divine-human, harmonious unity, must enter the state of free theocracy in which the Church Universal will attain to the full measure of Christ's maturity.'[182]

But if the meaning of *apocalypse* is here reduced entirely to 'aesthetics as ultimate harmony', the other meaning of apocalypse in the Bible makes its impact felt ever more strongly as the years pass. Indeed, it swells to thunderous volume until at last it produces a quite opposite result and completely swallows up the first meaning, 'aesthetics as harmony'. Free obedience, free sacrifice, free theocracy, all will flow into the divine freedom in an apotheosis of creaturely freedom. But what if the creature uses its freedom to say no? Had not Soloviev's earlier philosophy already established that all true freedom rests upon the overcoming of the power to say no, and that the depth of denial that is possible increases in proportion to the increase of consciousness and spirituality? The unconscious world-soul is chaotic, but only the free spirit is demonic. Thus there errupts into Soloviev's world picture a force that had always been latent there but had never been given its true weight. At the beginning Soloviev had attacked Western abstract thought; but was not the construction of the historical process, as a continuation and a reflection of natural process, still itself abstract? Did it take seriously enough the freedom of the creature? Even if we want to assume that the historical process is entirely in the hands of the

[182] GG II 2 W II 107.

Logos, who is becoming and finally has become man—this 'real suprahuman field of activity, giving nourishment to the whole life of humanity and conditioning its ethical progress by the fulness of this nourishment'[183]—even so, we still have to ask whether what we know of the incarnate Logos gives adequate grounds for expecting this kind of progress within history. As the powers of good advance through history, so too do the powers of evil, since progress can in no case outplay the free decisions of humanity, least of all if we conceive the world-soul as 'coming to itself' in man, and if man is not cast down from his throne to be a mere function of a monistic *Weltgeist*.

But what then is the content of the total aesthetic scheme? It is a revelation (an apocalypse) of the truth of God and of man—of God as God-Man and man as man-God—each opened to the other in their apocalyptic depth; and above all it is the unimaginable and incomprehensible justification of the good in and through this death-dealing reciprocity. But this means that the law of death and resurrection remains the ultimate law for world history, no less than for the individual. Certainly we would be less than just to Soloviev if we did not acknowledge that even in the period of his undisturbed faith in progress, he always had the resurrection of the dead before his eyes as the horizon of his eschatological aesthetics, and that the whole of the aesthetic element in nature and art appeared to him purely as an adumbration of the resurrected cosmos. But this view so dominated his thinking that he was in consequence inclined to overlook the realism of death or to cloak it in the enveloping terms of the 'process'. For him, 'the Kingdom of Death' was subspiritual nature, which included the sexual sphere; all truly spiritual entities in which the eternal, ideal world is already to be seen appeared to him to constitute the unique path to immortality and resurrection. The heavenly crucifixion of the Logos was for him (as it was in Valentinus' myth) a painless, dialectical matter, and the earthly crucifixion was something viewed exclusively from that standpoint. In the very few places in his work where the cross appears, it is only as 'the sign of spiritual power that can overcome all suffering'.[184] In this area

[183] RG II 7, 14 D II 176.

[184] GG II 1, 6 W II 105.

there was a great deal still to be done. Soloviev wrote his *Three Conversations*, including the *Tale of Antichrist*, with his last failing energy, and he did indeed say a decisive word with these. But death itself left him no time to deal more thoroughly with the mystery of death.

It remains for us to deal in order with the first fragmentary outlines of an aesthetic, then with the subsequent, apocalyptic aesthetics that extend so far beyond the first.

From the very beginning, Soloviev wanted to complete his theosophy with a universal aesthetics.[185] He prefaced his essay on natural aesthetics with Dostoyevsky's dictum that 'beauty will save the world.'[186] The *Critique of Abstract Principles* had proclaimed that 'the realization of pan-unity in its external actuality is absolute beauty', so it is as little something 'given' as is 'pan-unity' itself; it is a task assigned to humanity, and human art is a vehicle of its realisation. Soloviev promises to develop, at the end of his work, 'the common axioms and rules of this great and mysterious art that brings all beings into the form of beauty'.[187] According to another declaration, the sphere of aesthetic realisation should be divided into three areas: the material (technology), the formal (the 'fine arts') and the absolute (mysticism).[188] For Soloviev, however, mysticism is not only passive devotion to the divine or direct contact with it; it also is the active art of bringing the divine from Heaven to earth, and, in this sense, 'theurgy'[189]—it is concerned, that is, with the realisation of the ideal: this is why Soloviev becomes a bitter opponent of classical idealist aesthetics, according to which beauty is allowed to be 'only' appearance, not reality, only an illusory reflection, not even a true promise or foretaste. 'An infinity that existed solely for an instant would be an unbearable contradiction for the spirit; a bliss existing only in the past would be a torture for the will.'[190] Thus too Goethe's

[185] As in the outline of the *Philosophical Principles of Integral Knowledge*, Str., 75. He refers back to this in his later philosophy of art: W VII 174, n.

[186] *Beauty in Nature*, W VII 119.

[187] *Cf.* the introd. to *Shorter Writings on Aesthetics* W VII 337.

[188] *Principles of Integral Knowledge*; Str. 114, 273.

[189] Article on 'Mystik' in Brockhaus-Ephron; W VI.

[190] *Sexual Love* 5 W VII 257.

Faust cannot embody any authentic idea: 'The heavenly powers and the "eternal feminine" appear from above, and so from outside; they do not reveal themselves from within, in the very content of reality itself.'[191] Even Dante's Paradise is 'not sufficiently living and concrete—an essential deficiency that not even the most euphonious verse can make good'.[192] 'According to Hegelian aesthetics, beauty is the embodiment of a universal and eternal idea in individual and transitory phenomena; in this embodiment, moreover, these phenomena remain transitory, disappearing like individual waves in the stream of the material process. Only for a moment do they reflect the light of an eternal idea. This is possible only if the relation between spiritual principle and material phenomenon is accidental. True and perfect beauty, on the other hand, since it expresses the full solidarity and mutual penetration of these two levels, must necessarily allow one of them (the material) to come really to share in the immortality of the other.'[193] If true embodiment is lacking, 'the powerlessness of the Idea to give its inner content a direct external expression' becomes manifest. Thus Soloviev welcomed the shift toward literary realism, even in the materialistic form that it assumed in Chernyshevsky:[194] he was a declared enemy of all 'art for art's sake'.[195] In ancient culture, 'poets were at once prophets and priests', and it is only in the subsequent division of labour that poets elevated an isolated art to the status of an idol: 'For such priests of pure art, perfection of external form comes to be the main consideration.' Realism quite rightly reacted against this; but 'in the ineffectual hunt for pseudo–real detail, the actual reality of the whole is once more lost'. Dostoyevsky had an eye for true inner reality, and he is the pledge of the poetics of the future. In this way he unmasks in prophetic fashion the anti-Christian side of modern utopian social progress—movements orientated to the future; his vision grows in the true 'houses of the dead', of the 'insulted and injured', as he recognises the solidarity of saints and sinners. His

[191] *The Meaning of Art* 3 W VII 188.
[192] *Ibid.*, n.
[193] *Ibid.*, 2 W VII 179–190.
[194] *First Steps Towards a Positive Aesthetic* W VII 351.
[195] *Ibid.*, 346f., and the essay on Lermontov W VII 405f.

ideal is the Church, the Kingdom of God, and not a particular nation. 'The Church as positive ideal was intended to become the central idea ... of *The Brothers Karamazov*.'[196] The more truth, the more beauty, always: 'The full truth of the world consists in its living unity as one spiritualised and God-bearing body; in that lies the world's truth and the world's beauty.'[197] Following on from that, the task in hand is 'to embody the content of salvation and truth in the sphere of things perceptible to the senses by giving it the form of beauty'—and that immediately means ascesis for the soul that lives through its senses, a submission of blind, inordinate impulse that has no interior goal to the chains of the spiritual idea that captures it and gives it form.[198] But what exactly is the idea that seeks thus to incarnate itself?

Soloviev defined it quite strictly in relation to his aesthetic. Ideal being is being such as merits to be and therefore *shall* be. It is existence in complete unity such that in it (1) 'the elements do not exclude one another but stand in complementary relationship and exist in solidarity'; (2) these elements 'do not exclude the whole, but maintain their individual existence on the one common ground'; (3) 'the ground in its totally unified character does not suppress or absorb the individual elements, but gives them full play within itself by developing itself in them'. Being of this kind is at once true, good and beautiful. If one of the three elements is lacking, falsehood, evil and ugliness arise. 'Anything is ugly where a part grows disproportionately and unchecked, dominating other parts, where unity and wholeness are absent, where, most particularly, there is no free diversity.'[199] In short: 'The plenitude of the Idea requires that the greatest unity in the whole be realised in the greatest independence and freedom in the partial and particular elements *in* them themselves and *through* and *for* them.'[200] This idea of beauty is indeed eternally real in God himself, in so far as he exists as the eternal actuality of all his potential in the fullest

[196] First address on Dostoyevsky, in *Drei Reden* (1921), 9–26.
[197] GG, foreword W II 10.
[198] GG I 3 W II 64.
[199] *The Meaning of Art* 2 W VII 176–178.
[200] *Sexual Love* 3 W VII 266.

degree of freedom. It is, at the same time, the reality of the Kingdom of God in its coming to be in the world as it realises itself eschatologically through the ascent of natural and historical forms. Christ and Mary, the Logos incarnate and Sophia incarnate, represent in this process the ever-perfect primordial form of beauty, the norm by which reality as it takes on form can measure and align itself.[201] The threefold characterisation of the Idea (as the mutuality of parts, their free submission to the whole and the whole's allowing the parts to be themselves) can be summed up in one word: love. 'Love in the extended sense in which this concept coincides with that of unanimity, harmony and peace, the concept of the totality of the world, the concept of *kosmos*. In this sense, the Good, the True and Beautiful are only the various images of love. . . . The will of the Good, however, is in its essence genuine love, or love's source, the Idea of the Idea.'[202] And as the good that is longed for, this love is Eros, and, as that which is realised out of God's plenitude, it is Agape. It is plain that, for Soloviev, to distinguish between Eros and Agape in their essences is completely unthinkable: Christian love is the level where natural Eros is fulfilled, where what it vainly longed for and sought to embody is granted to it—the true presence of God in man, immortality, resurrection.

The essays *Beauty in Nature* and *The Universal Meaning of Art* belong among the best of Soloviev's work, but this is not the place to rehearse their argument in their particular details. For our purposes it is important that in the essay on nature the idea of progress, which allows the beautiful to be perfected as a free and living organism, only gradually and with dramatic setbacks (monstrosities in nature, the disproportionate growth of individual functions, excesses, et cetera), provides the basis of the eschatological hope of glory for the entire cosmos in its interior development. The Kingdom of God is coming into being from the beginning of the world process onward. Beauty in nature is neither pure illusion nor can it be simply explained in terms of psychological stimuli; it is just as objective in its forms

[201] W VII 199.

[202] GM, lecture 7 A III 138–139.

as it is subjective for the one who beholds or experiences it. It may be encountered anywhere where the more spiritual reality overcomes the material and makes it transparent: in the diamond, for instance, where the light so shines through and plays with the material reality that both seem to have become one, 'what results is translucent matter and embodied light.'[203] In living beings, the penetration becomes more and more an interior thing; the lower level of being can be changed, illuminated, sublimated in different degrees by the Idea. 'Thus the material instinct of sexuality can, in the nightingale's song, clothe itself in the form of harmonious notes', 'the instinct comes to embody the idea of love'.[204] Of course the beautiful is not to be found simply in the adequate embodiment of any kind of content (otherwise an animal such as a pig, embodying pure voracity, would be beautiful, as would a worm, embodying formless and blind instinct), but only in the embodiment of a content worthy of existence, which alone merits the name 'Idea'. In order to embody the latter, the art of the creative Logos struggles with the chaotic element in the world-soul;[205] and so long as the supreme equilibrium is not reached, any harmony is menaced from within, because it is only provisional: 'Every fresh victory opens the possibility of a fresh defeat', since the primaeval chaos, which is pure hunger for existence, the 'necessary background of any earthly beauty', is not yet finally informed and transfigured.[206] 'Even the most beautiful of butterflies is no more than a winged worm';[207] in the higher animals, the 'worm-like' element is forced inward and made unnoticeable by a beautiful outer covering. But such a covering is not yet a complete transfiguration: only in the resurrection of the body is the inwardly necessary goal of the world process achieved, the resurrection as the complete illumination of chaotic matter by the loving spirit; but only God can bring this to perfection.

Human art is not a copying of nature, but rather an imitation

[203] *Beauty in Nature* 2 W VII 127.
[204] *Ibid.*, 128–129.
[205] *Ibid.*, 6, 144–147.
[206] *Ibid.*, 140, 146, 153.
[207] *Ibid.*, 9, 159.

of the *natura naturans* that forms images, 'the world process as it is drawn forward in its aesthetic aspect'.[208] Truth and goodness are not enough—or, better, they are both pressing toward embodiment. But only someone who believes in immortality and resurrection can ascribe an ultimate meaning to artistic activity. The one who 'reconciles himself (even if only theoretically) to the triumph of an all-destroying material process must treat beauty and, in particular, all that is "ideal" in the world, as a subjective illusion of the human imagination—as indeed the most consistent minds of this school do'.[209] Today there can no longer be a third standpoint between Christian hope and faith and pure materialism. There may have been such in the pre-Christian period, when the ideal had yet to be incarnated, when myth served as the aesthetic anticipation of Godmanhood. The Egyptians were right to organize their culture and art around the idea of resurrection, even if it could in no way be actualised;[210] Plato likewise was right in wishing to let his Eros be creative in the sphere of the Beautiful, even if the content sensed in this could nowhere actually be grasped.[211] A true work of art is simply 'the perceptible representation of an object from the perspective of its ultimate condition or (which is the same thing) in the light of the world beyond'.[212]

It is in this context that one must set the *Essay on Eros*, in which the authentic personal love of man and wife appears as the central 'theurgic' work of art. Such love aspires to a superhuman wholeness above and beyond the separation and struggle of the sexes in a purposiveness that transcends

[208] *The Meaning of Art* 1 W VII 172.

[209] *Ibid.*, 2 W VII 181.

[210] GS 2 W II 223–224: 'The Egyptians were above all else artists. The final goal of this art was the vision that it gave of a victory over death, the eternalisation of life, the bringing to life of the dead. . . . This great religious idea of a general resurrection or restoration of all things is a specifically Egyptian one.'

[211] *The Drama of Plato's Life* 22 W VII 318: '[Plato's] theory of love, unheard of in the pagan world, profound and bold, remains unelaborated'; and 320: 'The proper activity of Eros can be nothing other than the rebirth or resurrecting of life into immortality.'

[212] W VII 194.

enslavement to the concerns of the species and of sexuality[213] (with which marital love in its personal core has nothing to do—so little, in fact, that there exists no direct proportionality between sex and Eros).[214] The Western theme of an androgynous unity in humanity, found from Plato to Dante to Böhme, Novalis and Baader, is thus resumed and brought in classical fashion to its conclusion. And yet this does not imply a process in which the person is transcended; the human being as 'the reasoning power of truth' can indeed 'infinitely perfect its life and nature without transcending the limits of its human form. . . . Therein lies the essential distinction between the cosmological and the historical process.'[215] The power of Eros is that it can creatively perceive the (objective!) ideality of the personality in the beloved and can work to make this real: Eros as looking up to the ideal ascends; as embodying the ideal in a real beloved human being it descends.[216] Its essential theurgic power lies in the faith by which it 'accords unconditional significance' to the beloved, a significance that an empirical and temporal nature cannot as such have. Only he can love who believes in the eternal meaning of his love for this particular finite substance; and this does not occur without a parallel belief in God, immortality and the resurrection, not only of the I and the Thou, which is impossible, but of the whole cosmos. Only in such a context does this love have space and scope.[217] The emotion of love (being 'in love') can of course be a prefiguration of Eros, but it first becomes real when realised actively and creatively.[218] The true lover 'actually sees something, perceives with his eyes, something other than that which other men see': he sees the ideality that is the true reality; in an inchoate way he sees the beloved person as God sees him, which is indeed the

[213] RG II 7, 8 D II 159f.

[214] *Sexual Love* 1; W VII 201–211.

[215] *Sexual Love* 2, art. 1 W VII 213. 'To bring into being the true man, the union in freedom of the masculine and feminine principles, to preserve, in both, their formal separateness, while having overcome their essential distinctness and dividedness—this is the proper and most immediate task of love'; art. 3, 1: 272.

[216] *Ibid.*, art. 4, 7 W VII 255.

[217] *Ibid.*, art. 4, 6 251–253.

[218] *Ibid.*, art. 3, 2 229.

only way God wills to see him. And to let this ideality be true, to make it true, is 'the beginning of the visible restoration of God's image in the material world.'[219] Here Soloviev, in accordance with the most characteristic concerns of his programme, has allowed the power of (platonic) Eros to merge into the power of the agape of the Sermon on the Mount. The Christian, therefore, is obliged because of this to see his neighbour as God the Father sees him in his redeeming Son, and to take this ideal vision as a guide in his actual dealings with others.[220] Soloviev therefore expressly subsumes the model of androgynous Eros under the twofold norm and prototype of God's relation to the world as the divine Sophia, and Christ's to the Church as the incarnate Sophia. This at the same time implies that the individual relationship of syzygy must, because of these prototypes, open itself out into an erotic relationship with the whole of the rest of the world. The person who believes and loves must embrace in his love the whole of humanity and the cosmos, as well as Christ and God, since they are Sophia in the process of coming to be, God's own beloved.[221] It is in this context that Soloviev's most significant poems have their place. His cosmic lyricism is both Christian and erotic in the highest sense just defined; for here he senses and glorifies in all worldly forms only the veilings and hidden revelations of his eternal secret beloved, the divine Sophia. Her eschatological glory he takes on faith alone; but with the eye of Eros he sees into the future, sensing her presence, as he lives out of the cosmic love of God.

But Sophia's apocalyptic unveiling is not the same as the apocalypse of world history. In Soloviev's last years, the lyrical intuition of an eternal presence of love takes on an ever-darker hue, turning to an apocalyptic foreboding of the imminent incarnation of evil in history.[222] And since for Soloviev there is no individual fulfilment without the collective fulfilment of all men and all creatures—'no one has the right to separate his own

[219] *Ibid.*, art. 3, 3 230–231.
[220] *Ibid.*, art. 4, 5 248f.
[221] *Ibid.*, art. 5, 4 268–272.
[222] Text in Ludolf Müller, *Übermensch und Antichrist.*

welfare from the true welfare of all living things'[223]—then the revelation of Sophia too is bound to recede into the collective mystery. Evil, according to the *Three Conversations*, is 'not only a natural lack, an imperfection,' it is the power of the lie, of seduction, especially in the name of the Good.[224]

The first question to be posed from a standpoint high above the human stage concerns war: is its abolition possible? Is the Tolstoyan gospel of nonresistance a correct interpretation of the Sermon on the Mount? Soloviev was as sceptical as Péguy would be not long afterward. Two orders are here being confused with each other. 'Why did Christ not employ the power of the Gospel spirit in such a way as to arouse the good hidden in the soul of Judas, Herod, the Jewish high priest—and finally of that impenitent sinner whom we normally overlook when we discuss his penitent fellows. If he forgave his enemies, why—to use your own [Tolstoy's] words—did he not release their souls from the fearful darkness in which they lay? Why did he not conquer their wickedness by the power of his meekness?'[225] But Christianity, after all, is not moral rearmament; it demands a Yes or a No. 'In earlier times, Christianity was comprehensible to one, incomprehensible to another; but only our age has succeeded in making it repellent and mortally boring.'[226] This moralisation reflects a seriously anti-Christian spirit, for Christ did not come to bring peace, but a sword. Otherwise Christ's disciples would have to 'perform greater moral miracles (on the higher level of moral development we have now reached) by their meekness and nonresistance to evil than was possible eighteen centuries ago'.[227] Man remains as he is. And, above all, death remains what it always was: 'in this respect, there is no cultural advance to be recorded of any kind'.[228] What has Christ succeeded in changing on earth? His work was 'an astonishing failure'. Historically, 'in any case, far more evil than good has resulted from it', since

[223] *Sexual Love* art. 5, 1 W VII 260.
[224] *Three Conversations*, foreword D I 227.
[225] *First Conversation* D I 266.
[226] *Third Conversation* D I 315.
[227] *Ibid.*, 319.
[228] *Ibid.*, 327.

Christ's resurrection is, of course, not itself a part of the historical process.[229] 'We have only one refuge: the real resurrection . . . all else is only the condition, the path, the step toward it . . . and in reality it is still a Kingdom of Death.'[230]

The Antichrist will blur the edges of the apocalyptic rift between morality and the cross, between cultural progress and the resurrection of the dead. He will permit Christianity to merge into this synthesis as one positive element. 'Christ divided men in terms of good and evil; I shall unite them through the benefits of salvation, which are necessary to good and evil alike. Christ brought the sword, but I bring peace. He threatened the earth with a terrible Last Judgment; but I shall be the last judge, and my judgment is one of grace.' Satan fills his son with his spirit; his soul is filled with a glacial abundance of enormous power, courage and effortless skill. He composes a manifesto, *The Open Path to World Peace and Welfare*, an all-embracing programme that unites all contradictions in itself—the highest degree of freedom of thought and a comprehension of every mystical system, unrestricted individualism and a glowing devotion to the general good. He establishes a European union of states, then a world monarchy, satisfies the needs of all the poor without perceptibly affecting the rich and founds an interconfessional institute for free biblical research. He seeks to be elected by the general assembly of the churches as head of the Church (from now on ecumenically united), and receives the approval of the majority. But resistance comes from Pope Peter II, John the Elder, leader of the Orthodox and Professor Ernst Pauli, representing Protestantism: under the pressure of persecution the three churches in this eschatological situation at last unite. Peter's primacy is recognised, and the Pauline and Johannine churches come into the Roman fold. The spokesmen of Christianity are persecuted and killed, but they rise again; the last Christians journey to the wilderness, the Jews raise a revolt and the Christians join with them. They are slaughtered; but then Christ appears, robed in the imperial purple, his hands outspread with the marks of the nails upon them, to rule for a

[229] *Ibid.*, 335f.
[230] *Ibid.*, 338–339.

thousand years with those who are his own.[231]

What is important in this story is not its novelistic features, but the fact that Soloviev quite unconcernedly surrenders great parts of his philosophy of cosmic process into the hands of the Antichrist. As regards the *facts* of the process, he has not abandoned a single detail; the one thing he has given up is the idea that the process comes to perfection within history. The harvest of the world is brought home, but not by man; it is brought home by Christ, who alone lays the whole Kingdom at his Father's feet. He is himself the integration of all things. And if we believe ourselves capable of establishing within history some kind of signs of the end—perhaps in the unification of the world or in this ideal seen as the way in which 'the whole of humanity gathers itself around an invisible but powerful focus in Christian culture'[232]—even such indications will never suffice to gain an overview of the real course of the historical process as it appears from God's own standpoint. In this respect, Soloviev humbled himself before the all-conquering Cross.

[231] *Ibid.*, 348–380.

[232] *First Steps Towards a Positive Aesthetic* W VII 350.

HOPKINS

1. OXFORD, IGNATIUS AND SCOTUS

A sharper contrast with Soloviev than Hopkins[1] is scarcely conceivable; yet Hopkins too administers a great inheritance in a way at once unique, sovereign and pregnant with future implications. It is the English inheritance, which this other convert with a finely discriminating mastery brought home to Mother Church when he trod the path from Oxford, beyond Newman's oratory, into the novitiate of the Jesuits. Formed through and through by the English spiritual tradition, he retained not only in his choice of the religious life but also in all his aesthetic decisions an astonishing independence: 'The effect of studying masterpieces is to make me admire and do otherwise.'[2] Nowhere is there attachment; he passes back beyond all his lineage to the origins.

The artistically very gifted boy, who came from an artistic family, early began to draw, to make music, to write poetry.

[1] Gerard Manley Hopkins' works are cited with reference to the editions published by the Oxford University Press:

Poems of GMH, 4th ed., ed. by W. H. Gardner and N. H. MacKenzie (1967; reprinted with corrections, 1970) = P (with the number of the poem and, for the longer poems, number of the stanza).

The Sermons and Devotional writings of GMH, ed. by Christopher Devlin SJ (1959) = S.

The Journals and Papers of GMH, ed. by Humphrey House, completed by Graham Storey (1959) = J.

The Letters of GMH to Robert Bridges, ed. by Claude Collier Abbott (1935; revised 1955) = B.

The Correspondence of GMH and R. W. Dixon, ed. by Claude Collier Abbott (1935; revised 1955) = D.

Further Letters of GMH, Including His Correspondence with Coventry Patmore, ed. by Claude Collier Abbott (1938; 2nd ed. revised and enlarged 1956) = F.

Bibliography in *GHM's Gedichte, Schriften, Briefe*, ed. by Hermann Rinn, trans. by U. Clemen and Fr. Kemp, introduction by Wolfgang Clemen (Kösel, 1954); in *The Shaping Vision of GMH*, Alan Heuser (OUP 1958), a concentrated and critical account of the spiritual world of the poet; and *GMH*, Geoffrey Grigson (*Writers and Their Work*, no. 59, 1955).

[2] B (25.9.88) 291.

Fragments of his early poems, which he destroyed on his entry into the novitiate, betray the predictable influence of English Romanticism, above all of Keats. In 1863, when he was nineteen, he went up to Balliol College, Oxford, to study classical philosophy; he had Matthew Arnold and Walter Pater as teachers, the latter also as a tutor, and he was therefore completely immersed in the whole aesthetic world view that characterised the mid-Victorian period. Nowhere in Europe had the word *beauty* such a magical sound as in the England of that time; nowhere else had the Platonic and Epicurean antiquity so immediate a presence, nowhere else had the Dante of the *Canzoniere* and the *Vita Nuova*, the world of the Troubadours and the Florence of the *quattrocento* awakened to such a life as with the English pre-Raphaelites. All that in continental symbolism—from Flaubert and Baudelaire to Maeterlinck and d'Annunzio—was set aside in a very programmatic and polemical manner, was in England completely bathed in the ancient and mediæval tradition. And where on the continent ecclesiastical modernism sought to take over the ideas of the imaginary character of concepts and also of dogmatic *symbola*, thereby earning the sharpest of censures—so that the two worlds were violently split in two—just there English theology, reared in an hereditary empiricism, sensed no danger and preserved the native rights of imagery in religious thought, and therefore in Christian theology, right up to the present day. Newman's *Grammar of Assent* cannot be understood apart from this tradition of the place of the imagination in thought (as Coleridge, in a way somewhat parallel to Schelling, gave it classical expression in England), and still today theologians like Austin Farrer (*The Glass of Vision*[3]) and E. L. Mascall (*Words and Images*[4]) keep this tradition alive.

A mistrust of the value of universal concepts, a consciousness

[3] Dacre Press, Westminster, 1948, with chapters on 'Images and Inspiration', 'Archetypes and Incarnation', 'Prophecy and Poetry', and the 'Poetry of the New Testament'.

[4] Longmans, Green 1957, with discussions of the relationship between sense experience, the intellect and mysticism and on the role of analogy and of images in theology.

is as old as English intellectual life. The formulations of Locke and Hume are secondary to this consciousness—they express something of it, but not the whole—and again the poetical intimations of Wordsworth and Coleridge's speculations about God as nature are secondary and temporally conditioned; they are a possible interpretation, but not the sole necessary and all-embracing one. Yet again the symbolist theories of the pre-Raphaelites and the mythologists and Platonists of the Oxford of Hopkins' time are a variation of an ancient theme and not at all the theme itself.

Hopkins had himself passed by the nineteenth and eighteenth centuries; behind them there rose up for him Milton, Purcell and Shakespeare, and behind them Duns Scotus. He set no store by a warming up of the ancient world of mythology.[5] He had at an early stage taken a dislike to Swinburne—he mentions him in the same breath as Wagner and E. von Hartmann[6]—and it was the same with Browning. He finally turned from the once beloved Keats, whom he still quite late defended in correspondence with Coventry Patmore until he was convinced by Patmore of Keats's entanglement in a sensuous immanence;[7] of the idealist imagination as understood by Wordsworth he retains only 'his spiritual insight into nature', which appears to him to be more of a philosophical than a poetic accomplish-
of the irreducibility of the individual, be it material or personal,

[5] To Bridges: 'Believe me, the Greek gods are totally unworkable material; the merest frigidity, which must chill and kill every living work of art they are brought into'. B (17.5.85) 217. To Dixon: 'Mythology is something else besides fairytale: it is religion, the historical part of religion. . . . First it is as history untrue. What is untrue history? Nothing and worse than nothing. . . . For myself literally words would fail me to express the loathing and horror with which I think of it and of man setting up the work of his own hands, of that hand within the mind the imagination, for God Almighty who made heaven and earth'. D (23.10.86) 146.

Both letters deal with the mythological dramas of his fellow student and life-long friend, the poet laureate Robert Bridges, who, thirty years after the poet's death first published Hopkins' poems (1918).

[6] To Baillie: F (15.9.67) 228–229; to the same, F (22.5.80) 246; about Browning, D (12.10.81) 74; B (26.11.82) 164.

[7] To C. Patmore (20.10.87 and 6.5.88) F 381, 386: 'He lived in mythology and fairyland the life of a dreamer'.

ment.[8] Blake's invention of myths remains for him 'crazy',[9] although he recognised here 'an exquisite freshness and lyrical inspiration',[10]and there are too places in his own speculation, where he approaches, quite unconsciously, Blake's religious inspiration.[11] But only in face of the Christian poetry of Milton is there posed for him the problem of the mythical image that, throughout English Romanticism up to Hopkins' times, had retained an astonishing, almost archaic, liveliness. In his early poem 'Pilate' (1864) he had once trodden such ways, but never again. What remained valid for him in Milton was only the unattained power of form; it was in Milton that he would soonest see anticipations of his own rhythmical innovations in an English context (leaving aside Pindar and the choruses in Greek tragedy). And beyond, towering over all, was Shakespeare, the greatest creator of unique, incomparable characters, marked out from all others—God alone can assign him his rank[12]—and close to him the mighty Purcell, to whom Hopkins dedicated one of his finest sonnets, 'and that not so much for gifts he shares, even though it should be in higher measure, with other musicians as for his own individuality'. He compares this 'arch-especial spirit', his 'forgèd feature', his 'own abrupt self', with a 'great stormfowl', who, after he has rustled his thunder-purple plumage on a stormy seabeach, unfolds his 'snow pinions' and scattering 'a colossal smile', himself intent only on flight, 'fans fresh our wits with wonder'. 'So that while he is aiming only at impressing me his hearer with the meaning in hand, I am looking out meanwhile for his specific, his individual markings and mottlings.'[13] Always for Hopkins it is a matter of such uniqueness, of a vision that penetrates beyond all laws, all Platonic ideas and Aristotelian forms, to the incomparability of just this individuality, whether it be, as with Milton, Purcell, Shakespeare, the uniqueness of genius[14] or the

[8] D (7.8.86) 141.

[9] D (25.10.86) 148. *Cf.* (22.10.87) 153: 'mingled with the good work a great deal of rubbish, want of sense, and some touches of ribaldry and wickedness'.

[10] D (22.12.87) 153.

[11] *Cf.* for example the end of the sermon of 25.1.80: S 66–67.

[12] P 126: 'God . . . see what his place is. . . .'

[13] P 45; B (4.1.83) 170.

[14] 'Every true poet, I thought, must be original and originality a condition

uniqueness, unnoticed by men, of each image met with every day in nature or the world of men. Hence Scotus becomes his thinker, 'who of all men most sways my spirits to peace; / Of realty the rarest-veinèd unraveller; a not / Rivalled insight, be rival Italy or Greece'.[15] The Scotist *haecceitas* as 'individual form' is the basis for any consideration of universal constructions of things; only here do they touch the ground of reality. In the unique, the irreducible, there shines forth for Hopkins the glory of God, the majesty of his oneness,[16] to whose ultimate, creative artistry the incomprehensibility of worldly images bears witness.

At this level the English genius gathers together the results of the experience of Antiquity into itself. Any consideration of 'form in general' at any stage of universality becomes preparation for what Hopkins intended by the always unique oneness of the individual form that only emerges in the Christian encounter between the absolutely personal and free God and the fully personal creature—here alone truly *monos pros monon*—and just this fundamental experience had to lead Hopkins back to Ignatius and his *Spiritual Exercises*, where for the first time in the history of Christian spirituality everything is placed on the knife edge of the mutual election that takes place between God and man, behind which retreats any consideration of 'perfection in general'. Here are dissolved all the confusing clouds of the mythical in order to uncover the absolute, hard reality in which alone the true glory of being shines forth. The impatience of this breaking through to the uniquely true glory determines Hopkins' whole ethos; here lies the unity of his personality as poet and religious, that unity of which he was most sharply conscious even when it finally broke him, for neither his poet friends nor his brothers in religion had any eyes for it. In the end, as Wolfgang Clemen rightly says, the 'supposition of any conflict between priest and poet, between

of poetic genius; so that each poet is like a species in nature (*not* an *individium genericum* or *specificum*) and can never recur'. To C. Patmore (6.10.86) F 370.

[15] P 44.

[16] J 215: 'Of a tree he writes, 'the inscape markedly holding its most simple and beautiful oneness up from the ground'.... S 146: Generally of the self: 'Self is the intrinsic oneness of a thing'.

his religious and artistic vocation, cannot be maintained'; this is also the reason why in the case of his poems, which 'stand forth as an almost incomprehensible miracle, the conventional methods of literary criticism are inadequate',[17] and Hermann Rinn is in agreement with him, when he maintains 'that the priest, the theologian and the poet in Hopkins are not to be separated. Despite all the obvious tension, any attempt to find inner contradictions in him seems hopeless, a radical misunderstanding even.' He is also 'a singular case in modern times' in that with him 'the theoretical concept and the poetic "conceptus" are completely congruent.'[18] Through the consuming impatience of his ascent Hopkins achieves a position in which he can become, next to Keats, the greatest English poet of the century[19] and at the same time not only the sharpest critic of his own and others' poetry and works of art, a subtle philosopher and theologian, but also a spiritual man, to whom the hardest sacrifices, among them the sacrifice of art and the whole aesthetic sphere, are wholly justified. This consuming passion devoured him—whether deservedly may be questioned—but in such a way that in the fearful isolation into which it drove him, he alone—unlike his whole generation on whom time was running out—knew himself to be a beginning. To Bridges he wrote thus about his compositions: 'If you do not like it [my music] it is because there is something you have not seen and I see. That at least is my mind, and if the whole world agreed to condemn it or see nothing in it I should only tell them to take a generation and come to me again.'[20] And a sonnet ends in a melancholy vein:

> This to hoard unheard,
> Heard unheeded, leaves me a lonely began:

that 'wisest word', which his heart breeds and which Heaven or Hell hindering frustrate: to store up this thing unheard while

[17] Introduction to the German selection, op. cit., 16, 15.
[18] Afterword to the German selection, op. cit., 732f.
[19] Alan Heuser, op. cit., 103.
[20] B (1.4.85) 214.

even what is heard remains unheeded causes him to remain a lonely beginning.[21]

If we now try to trace this first curve more carefully, it will be helpful to go back behind all his experiences of upbringing to an almost primeval experience that characterizes Hopkins both as poet and man and touches his reader very directly. From the poems, the diaries and letters there breathes everywhere, uniquely and unmistakably, the English countryside: woods, hills, green upon green, always a strong wind, driving clouds, the closeness to the sea, the moors and highlands with quick-flowing brooks and heather, the surge of the waves, islands wild and yet with a Southern mildness. But it is no cultural landscape, not at all a romantic or mythological landscape, but, as it were, a primeval landscape. The word *wild* is everywhere and is literally meant, but it enters even into the loftiest Christian utterances: as when Mary is described as 'worldmothering air, air wild',[22] and Christ's Advent, in the great shipwreck poem, as 'sealed in wild waters'.[23] In the first place it is simply landscape as wilderness, as celebrated in the poem 'Inversnaid': the gloomy, brown mountain stream, rushing down between heather and dripping fern:

> What would the world be, once bereft
> Of wet and of wildness? Let them be left,
> O let them be left, wildness and wet;
> Long live the weeds and the wilderness yet.[24]

He had another poem, 'On the decline of wild nature', which began something like this:

> O where is it, the wilderness. . . .[25]

It is of 'brute beauty',[26] that he intends to sing, which will find again 'the true Arcadia of wild beauty',[27] and equally his works

[21] P 68.
[22] P 60, at the end.
[23] P 28, st. 23.
[24] P 56.
[25] B (22.2.79) 73.
[26] P 36.
[27] To C. Patmore, F (6.10.86) 370.

should reflect this formally. Once when he read again some verses from one of his own poems, 'it struck me aghast with a kind of raw nakedness and unmitigated violence I was unprepared for'.[28] To achieve this impression of the harsh, the abrupt, the unruly, this ear, most sensitive to beauty and melody, discovered his new 'sprung rhythm', which he established on the most rational foundations and distinguished from rhythmic schemes hitherto attempted (including Milton's and Coleridge's).[29] A tense, utterly objective contemplation of the primal power of nature, the language of nature expressing itself free from any hindrance—such seemed to him the authentic school for the senses of the poet: '*Laus Deo*—the river today and yesterday. Yesterday it was a sallow glassy gold at Hodder Roughs and by watching hard the banks began to sail upstream, the scaping unfolded, the river was all in tumult. . . . Today the river was wild, very full, glossy brown with mud. . . .'[30] Or 'Bitter north wind, hail and sleet'[31] or the breakers of the sea, whose structural laws the poet searches out through a penetrating, ever-new contemplation,[32] or the formation of ice,[33] or the forms of freely growing trees,[34] the curves of water flowing over stones,[35] the subtle shading of colours in the sunset,[36] meteors, comets, but ever again, endlessly, the changing forms of the clouds[37]—all this was a complete attentiveness that has nothing to do with romantic outpourings of the feelings but rather reminds one of the attentive eye of a Goethe; with a desire for objectivity[38] that lays claim to the

[28] B (22.4.79) 79.

[29] Most important explanations: to Dixon (6.10.78) 14f.; (4.3.79) 21f.; (14.1.81) 39f.; to Bridges (21.8.77) 44f.; (18.10.82) 155f.; (11.10.87) 263. Comparison with Pindar and the Greek tragedians, B (18.10.82) 157.

[30] J (20.10.70) 200.

[31] J (11.11.74) 261.

[32] J (10.8.72) 223; J (16.8.72) 224; J (16.8.73) 235; J (13.8.74) 251.

[33] J (29.4.70) 201.

[34] J (17.3.71) 205f.

[35] J (1863) 8f.; also the sketches, fig. 8, 28 and 31 in J after p. 455.

[36] J (24.9.74) 260 and frequently.

[37] J (24.7.68) 181; J (29.7.68) 184; J 195f.; J (25.10.70) 201; J 204; J (21.4.71) 207, etc.

[38] J 58: 'Addis says my arguments are coloured and lose their value by personal feeling. This ought to be repressed'.

whole man through and through. A companion, with whom one must converse, is a hindrance to such total concentration.[39] Hopkins is sensitive to any mutilation of pure, wild natural form: fallen trees 'unselve' a whole landscape ('unselve the sweet especial scene') and 'after-comers cannot guess the beauty been'.[40] Above all devastation there flies—in his favourite, untiringly varied picture—the bird in the free, untamable air. If Hopkins thought he had achieved his poetic best in the 'Windhover',[41] then it was not least because of the unity of vision and thing seen: the 'daylight's dauphin' who, in 'brute beauty and valour and act', spiralled upward with 'air, pride, plume' on his wing tips against the powerful wind, so that, called by the poet as he hovers on high ('here buckle!'), he may pour forth all his most dangerous power, motionlessly, like falling embers.[42] At a quite early stage the ascending bird became Hopkins' signature,[43] later the 'dare-gale skylark', emprisoned in his cage, becomes a parable of the soul in its earthly 'bone-house',[44] while in the sonnet 'The Sea and the Skylark', there is placed between these two primeval sounds—the roar and lull of the tide and the 'rash-fresh re-winded', descending note of the lark—'this shallow and frail town' with its 'sordid turbid time' and all culture, which, in its longing for the original purity of being, is fated to 'drain fast towards man's first slime'.[45] The theme is raised again and brought to a conclusion in the prodigious poem, 'That Nature Is a Heraclitean Fire and of the Comfort of the Resurrection', with its picture of nature, noisy, stormy, joyfully romping about, pillows of clouds tossed by the winds of the storm:

> Delightfully the bright wind boisterous ropes, wrestles, beats earth bare

[39] J (12.12.72) 228.

[40] 'Binsey Poplars', P 43. *Cf.* J (15.9.71) 215; J (8.4.73) 230; J (18.12.73) 240: 'The ashtree growing in the corner of the garden was felled . . . there came at that moment a great pang and I wished to die and not to see the inscapes of the world destroyed any more'.

[41] B (22.6.79) 84.

[42] P 36.

[43] P 16: 'Let me be to Thee as the circling bird. . . .'

[44] P 39.

[45] P 35.

Of yestertempest's creases; in pool and rutpeel parches
Squandering ooze to squeezed dough, crust, dust; stanches, starches
Squadroned masks and manmarks treadmire toil there
Footfretted in it. Million-fuelèd, nature's bonfire burns on.

All that was human culture is 'drowned . . . in an enormous dark' after its dank outlines have been parched by the 'world's wildfire' and dissolved in dust. Certainly the end of the poem speaks suddenly of the Resurrection, but this shines out only in the dying down of the fire, and only in so far as man is 'this Jack, joke, poor potsherd, patch, matchwood' is he also 'immortal diamond'.[46]

It is in terms of this rhythm, which sweeps the whole cultivated world of beauty of the Victorian age into the dustbin, that the turning points of Hopkins' life are to be understood: (1) from Walter Pater, (2) through his conversion, (3) to Ignatius, and (4) to the interpretation of the *Exercises* in the light of Duns Scotus.

1. The Oxford classical student had made himself at home in the world of beauty of the Greeks, which as *kalokagathia* (the beautiful and the good) pervaded and dominated every sphere of existence, including personal and political ethics. And the English poets had always, in the most diverse ways, had this totality in view. Even unworldly poets like Blake or Shelley had in view in their poetry the *polis*, the community of humanity; and again the contemporary representatives of a 'total aesthetics', in particular Ruskin, saw their goal as the informing of every realm of existence with beauty. Ethics and sociology are subordinated by Hopkins to the canon of the soul's harmony; the crying ugliness of the English industrial towns betrayed the lack, the total loss, of any spiritual equilibrium, of any hierarchy of values in the individual and in the social consciousness. The isolation of the economic world from the entire human harmony rendered first man, then his world, ugly, turned man egoistically back upon himself and his dull selfhood, and robbed him of the capacity to understand nature as it reveals itself: as the glory of God. Already in *Modern Painters* (1843f.)

[46] P 72.

Ruskin's concern was clear (as will later be true of Hopkins): to discern the forms of the world, trees, rocks, clouds as objectively as possible—and such objectivity includes for him the whole dimension, from scientific observation to Christian and religious contemplation.

If Hopkins in his first efforts was occupied with the nature of beauty—for instance, in 'On the Origin of Beauty: A Platonic Dialogue' (1865),[47] composed, we may assume, for Walter Pater—and in so doing initially saw only harmonic laws (proportion, balance and their subtler form, contrast, illustrated by the structure of a chestnut leaf), if he further attempted to interpret these fundamental, numerical laws as a polarity between a 'transitional or chromatic opposition' of imperceptible change and increase and an abrupt, diatonic contrast ('Poetic Diction', 1865),[48] then already he ranged the creative power of imagination with the abrupt moulding that imparted unique form. The only slightly later essay on 'The Probable Future of Metaphysics' (1867)[49] took issue with the positivism, psychologism and materialism of the time, which destroy the substance of metaphysics; for without metaphysics all these supposedly exact sciences would in future become aimless and remain atomistically separate, and if there is talk of there being within metaphysics a temporal rhythm of development, leading from formal Greek and Scholastic thought, through the scientific and positivistic, to the Hegelian and evolutionary, the last-named seeming to be the one to govern the future, then, Hopkins argued, there lies in the concept of a pure, absolutely orderly development a self-contradiction, which automatically calls forth the reaction of a new Platonism or formal system. Hopkins saw the return of three basic concepts in the near future. First, he saw the return of the type or the species, which, instead of a pure, chromatic transitionalism of all forms one with another, presupposes a diatonic determination of fixed differences, both quantitative and qualitative, that provide form and meaning for the continuum—it is the return of the Pythagorean world view—

[47] J 86–114.
[48] J 84f.
[49] J 118–121.

and only when these basic forms of natural being have been laid down and the 'determined differences' between them established is it possible to speak meaningfully of development. Second, it is therefore necessary to take the basic forms or ideas as one's starting point, if the multiplicity of the forms that are empirically encountered is to be accounted for, which means, third, taking issue with the 'atomistic personalism' of contemporary thought. And here it is important for the later Scotist that at the same time he professes himself to be 'in an even prostrate admiration of Aristotle' and gradually comes to think 'that he is the end-all and be-all of philosophy',[50] that even later he holds fast to and uses the doctrine of the soul as form and shaping power as if it were obvious.[51] The Platonic idea for him was thoroughly incarnated in nature; this aspect remained an integral part of his thought even when the Aristotelian *morphê* took separate form as the personal, Christian self, as the person. So again it is important to note that Hopkins developed his henceforth indispensable coinings of word and concept, with which he expressed his heart's intent and from which from this time on he never again is separated, on the occasion of an essay on Parmenides (1868):

> His great text, which he repeats with religious conviction, is that Being is and Not-being is not—which perhaps one can say, a little over-defining his meaning, means that all things are upheld by instress and are meaningless without it. An undetermined Pantheist idealism runs through the fragments, which makes it hard to translate them satisfactorily. . . . His feeling for instress, for the flush and foredrawn, and for inscape is most striking. . . . But indeed I have often felt when I have been in this mood and felt the depth of an instress or how fast the inscape holds a thing that nothing is so pregnant and straightforward to the truth as simple *yes* and *is*. 'Thou couldst never either know or say / what was not, there would be no coming at it.' There would be no bridge, no stem of stress between us and things to bear us out and carry the mind over. . . . Being and thought are the same. The truth in thought is Being, stress, and each word is one way of

[50] To Baillie, F (2.2.68), 231.
[51] To C. Patmore, F (24.9.83), 306f.

> acknowledging Being and each sentence by its copula *is* (or its equivalent) the utterance and assertion of it.[52]

Hopkins interprets Parmenides; he does, it is true, defend himself against his 'pantheism' and yet he reads into him his own best. With 'inscape' and 'instress' his world view is expressed in cipher. Both concepts lie no less deeply in being than in the thought of the Greek; it is only that being is differently experienced: it is en-selfed as person. Hopkins was by the time of this essay already a convert, and he was teaching in Newman's Oratory in Birmingham. At the same time, he was making notes on the nature of words and language. 'A word then has three terms belonging to it . . .—its prepossession of feeling; its definition, abstraction, vocal expression or other utterance; and its application, "extension", the concrete things coming under it.'[53] The first moment of prepossession has clearly to do with instress. *Instress*, as in-stress, im-pression, intention in existing beings, is used by Hopkins for both the object and the subject: things express their instress, their deep, unique act, which establishes them, holds them together and holds them in tension,[54] and there is required in the subject an answering stress, so that it can hold communion with the stress of things and experience them from within and can also through a feeling prepossession of their nature find the word that exactly expresses it. This communication is everywhere presupposed; Spinoza is mentioned even before Parmenides, invoked against the 'atomism of personality'.[55] The objective instress is taken up by the subject that is open to it, that is moved in its depths by the depth of its power of being. On seeing a comet Hopkins says: 'I felt a certain awe and instress. . . .'[56]

[52] J 127–130.

[53] J 125.

[54] J (18.5.70) 199: 'All things hitting the sense with double but direct instress'. J (23.2.72) 218: 'I could not but strongly feel in my fancy the odd instress of this'. J (11.5.73) 231: The blue of the bluebells 'beating up from so many glassy heads, which like water is good to float their deeper instress in upon the mind'. J (8.8.74) 250: 'A lovely coomb that gave me the [same] instress'. J (17.8.74) 253: 'There was an instress about this spot'. J (6.9.74) 258: 'Looking all round . . . I felt an instress and charm of Wales'.

[55] J 121.

[56] J (13.7.74) 249.

If *instress* refers to the power of a thing, then *inscape* refers to its form. What is intended is not a separate form, resting in itself, but a form released from its creative source and at the same time shaped and held by it, radiating from a focus from which the whole form (whether it be a curve or a play of colours or a landscape) can then be brought to completion. Increasingly, it is the uniqueness of the personal 'inscape' that Hopkins aspires to and for which he looks in nature and in art. Of the young Keats he said: 'a poet . . . full of feeling, high thoughts, flow of verse, point, often fine imagery and other virtues, but the essential and only lasting thing left out—what I call *inscape*, that is species or individually distinctive beauty of style.'[57] In the poem on Purcell (and in his explanations) the sense of inscape is perfectly expressed: for genius unfolds its wings, and 'also unaware gives you a whiff of knowledge about his plumage, the marking of which stamps his species'.[58] The word is everywhere,[59] as also 'all the world is full of inscape.'[60] All one has to do is find the point where it discloses itself, from which, for example, an animal is built up.[61] The form thus grasped is the key to the word, is itself already an objective word. *Formed* can also mean *worded*.[62]

In the period before his entry into the Society of Jesus and thereafter during his studies, Hopkins kept a diary through which he preserved the sharpness of his eye in reading the signs of inscape. In the creative sources of natural things, whether they be enduring or completely transitory, like water and clouds and the light and shade of landscape, the novice, the

[57] To C. Patmore, F (7.11.86) 373. On instress and inscape see especially A. Heuser, op. cit., 23–39, and the literature discussed by him on 105f.

[58] B (26.3.79) 83.

[59] J (14.5.70) 199: The chestnuts in blossom, tossed by the wind, 'crossed one another without losing their inscape'. J (18.5.70) 199: The inscape of the bluebells is mixed of strength and grace. J (17.3.71) 205: 'This is the time to study inscape in the spraying of trees, for the swelling buds carry them to a pitch which the eye could not else gather'. J (9.5.71) 209: The bluebells 'baffle you with their inscape, made to every sense'.

[60] J (24.2.73) 230.

[61] J (6.4.74) 242: 'caught the inscape in the horse . . ., following that one may inscape the whole beast very simply'.

[62] J (20.4.74) 243.

scholastic, trained himself in this encounter with the Creator of all nature. 'Unless you refresh the mind from time to time you cannot always remember or believe how deep the inscape in things is.'[63] The openness of the soul for particular forms changes; 'for a certain time I am astonished at the beauty of a tree, shape, effect etc, then when the passion, so to speak, has subsided, it is consigned to my treasury of explored beauty, and acknowledged with admiration and interest ever after, while something new takes its place in my enthusiasm'[64]—so wrote the nineteen-year-old. Later he experienced the diminishing power of the memory of inscape,[65] of an immediate relish for things,[66] he weighed this loss very carefully against the gain in clarity and perceptive power.

Inscape in nature is for Hopkins beautiful in itself.[67] 'I thought how sadly beauty of inscape was unknown and buried away from simple people and yet how near at hand it was if they had eyes to see it and it could be called out everywhere again.'[68]

2. Most of these references come from Hopkins' diary, from the time of his early days in the religious life. But it was not inscape that drove Hopkins to conversion and entry into the religious life, at least not inscape in the sense he gave to it in his maturity: an experience exact, aesthetic and religious at the same time. The divine image of his Anglican period is rather—in several poems that welled up from the depths of his heart—that of negative theology. 'Nondum' takes its motto from Scripture: 'Verily, Thou art a God that hidest thyself', and makes a division between the revelation of the glories of the world and the complete unapproachability of the Creator:

We see the glories of the earth
But not the hand that wrought them all:
Night to a myriad worlds gives birth,
Yet like a lighted empty hall. . . .

[63] J (Beginning of March, 1871) 205.
[64] To Baillie, F (10.7.63) 202.
[65] J (20.4.74) 243; *cf.* to C. Patmore, F (28.9.83) 313.
[66] D (22.12.80) 38.
[67] J (20.4.74) 243: 'beautiful inscape'.
[68] J (19.7.72) 221.

> We guess; we clothe Thee, unseen King,
> With attributes we deem are meet;
> Each in his own imagining
> Sets up a shadow in Thy seat. . . .

The soul reels, stunned,

> That dares to cast its searching sight
> On being's dread and vacant maze.

The prayer goes forth to God to bestow the 'sense beyond' and to lead her by the hand through the total darkness of the night.[69] 'The Habit of Perfection' praises the 'elected silence' of the infinite and puts to sleep all bodily senses; it is the year of his conversion, which echoes with Newman's word, 'surrender':

> Shape nothing, lips; be lovely-dumb:
> It is the shut, the curfew sent
> From there where all surrenders come
> Which only makes you eloquent.

The marriage with poverty begins.[70] But 'Lines for a Picture of St Dorothea' already open a new door; starting from the legend, Hopkins lets the dead martyr bring her executioner a basket full of fruit from Paradise, but the fruit melts away into the world of nature, which is like the visible husk in which the 'bright remainder of a miracle' is left:

> My eyes hold yet the rinds and bright
> Remainder of a miracle.[71]

What draws Hopkins, together with some of his friends, to the Catholic Church is—in so far as this mysterious, hidden event can be made plain—certainly a dissatisfaction with the theological position of the Tractarians; neither Liddon nor even Pusey could justify the incoherence of their position in regard to Rome, as Hopkins depicts it in his dignified letters to his dismayed parents.[72] It is simply not the aesthetic that draws him

[69] P 23.
[70] P 22.
[71] P 25.
[72] To his father, F (16.10.66) 92: 'The Tractarian ground I have seen broken to pieces under my feet'. On Pusey, *ibid.*, 98.

to Rome: 'I am surprised you shd. say fancy and aesthetic tastes have led me to my present state of mind: these wd. be better satisfied in the Church of England, for bad taste is always meeting one in the accessories of Catholicism.'[73] Everything looks much more like a breaking out from the closed aesthetic world of Oxford, within which not even a Ruskin could successfully encompass reality. The bitter, horrifying reality of today and tomorrow is continually before Hopkins' eyes: 'I must tell you I am always thinking of the Communist future. . . . I am afraid some great revolution is not far off. Horrible to say, in a manner I am a Communist.' The condition of the workers in 'very rich' England is terrible, and if they have to 'live a hard life without dignity, knowledge, comforts, delight, or hopes in the midst of plenty', who can blame them if 'they profess that they do not care what they wreck and burn, the old civilisation and order must be destroyed!?[74] Hopkins will be sent to the poor as a simple pastoral priest, and among the poor he will gladly spend his time. 'Tom's Garland' is the name of a sibylline sonnet in which he depicts the nature of the state in the image of a man: the monarch as the head, crowned among the stars, the day labourer as the foot, shod with dirty hobnailed boots, but the soles crowned with a crown of hobnails, which signifies a second crowning, stamping the form beneath.[75] To the end Hopkins gives expression to his abhorrence for the great cities of misery, which slowly but surely suck up the population of the country and bring them to ruin both of soul and body.[76]

At his conversion Hopkins offered himself to the real God, the God who addressed him personally, the God of the Cross and the God of this fearful world, and with himself offered his love of beauty and his art. Without doubt the poems of his youth breathed the atmosphere of an immanent aesthetic: 'I burnt [them] before I became a Jesuit and resolved to write no more, as not belonging to my profession, unless by the wish of my superiors; so for seven years I wrote nothing.' The first great poem to be written after that, which marked the beginning of

[73] *Ibid.*, 93.
[74] B (2.8.71) 27f.
[75] P 70; the interpretation to Bridges: B (10.2.88) 272–274.
[76] To Baillie, F (1.5.88) 293.

the masterpieces of his maturity, owed its origin to a chance remark made by his rector.[77] Between the poems of Hopkins' youth and those of the Jesuit there yawns then an abyss: that of a determined and fundamental ascent beyond all the beloved forms of the world—no matter how religious the view that one takes of them—to the naked God; and what on the far side of this gulf is perceived and praised as the manifestation of the glory of God in nature and the Church is pure gift, without any necessity and without any accent.

3. Two years after his conversion Hopkins entered the religious life. This raises the difficult question of Hopkins' encounter with the father of his order, Ignatius. Could he, was he to find in his new son one who could make known his ideal in poetry? No convincing poet had emerged in the order since Spee, Balde and Bidermann.

To his friend, Canon Dixon, who continually urged Hopkins to publish something, or at least not to oppose the publication of a few of his poems by him, Dixon, Hopkins offered resistance with an ever-categorical No. 'You say truly that our Society fosters literary excellence. Why then it may be left to look to its own interests.'[78] To the uncomprehending Dixon he explained that his vocation 'puts before me a standard so high that a higher can be found nowhere else'; also that if he made a sacrifice to God with 'reserves . . . in my heart', he must expect a severe judgment from God: 'a purpose may look smooth and perfect from without but be frayed and faltering from within'. He had burnt his earlier poems, but a man, learned in spiritual matters, had said to him, 'with things like composition the best sacrifice was not to destroy one's work but to leave it entirely to be disposed of by obedience. But I can scarcely fancy myself asking a superior to publish a volume of my verses. . . . And to be sure if I chose to look at things on one side and not the other I could of course regret this bitterly. But there is more peace and it is the holier lot to be unknown. . . . I know I shall not regret my forbearance. . . . PS. I should tell you that my letters now are opened.'[79] In his next letter he explains to Dixon that the Society

[77] D (5.10.78) 14; to Baillie, F (24.4.85) 256f.
[78] D (31.10.79) 30–31: 'I forbid its publication'.
[79] D (2.11.81) 88f.

of Jesus does not place any emphasis on the aesthetic. Pure poetry is only rarely a serviceable means in the search for God's greater glory; literature and culture are certainly prized, but only as means to higher ends. Jesuit poets have, anyway, always been an irregular phenomenon. Genius attracts fame, and it was just this that seemed to St Ignatius to be dangerous. Campion could have been a great poet, but it did not interest him. 'But his eloquence died on the air, his genius was quenched in his blood. ... Brilliancy does not suit us. Bourdaloue is reckoned our greatest orator: he is severe in style. Suarez is our most famous theologian: he is a man of vast volume of mind, but without originality or brilliancy; he treats everything satisfactorily, but you never remember a phrase of his, the manner is nothing.' So too the saints: Ignatius, one of the most extraordinary men, lived such an unremarkable life in Rome that in the process of his canonisation one of the cardinals said that he had never noticed any higher qualities in him than in any other good priest. Much the same may be said of Aloysius, Stanislaus and John Berchmans. 'I quote these cases to prove that show and brilliancy do not suit us, that we cultivate the commonplace outwardly and wish the beauty of the king's daughter, the soul, to be from within.'[80]

While Hopkins continually urged his friends, Bridges, Dixon and Patmore, to publish, not to shun fame but to consider that the poet represented a spiritual power in the nation and the world and must seek such power for moral reasons,[81] that admiration belonged to the work of art as much as reward to moral deeds,[82] he seemed to claim for himself completely the opposite. But even his career in the order was one of an ever more fundamental failure: he was a joke, an oddity; because of his Scotist leanings, even with his great speculative gifts he could not continue his studies beyond his priestly ordination. After that as an occasional preacher in the industrial cities he was never able to achieve a sufficiently common touch, something that became increasingly a problem. After the tertiate he first had to

[80] D (1.12.81) 92–96.

[81] To C. Patmore, F (4.6.86) 366; to Bridges, B (13.10.86) 231; to Dixon, D (4.6.78 and 13.6.78) 1–6.

[82] D (13.6.78) 6f.

be a schoolteacher of Latin and Greek, and then, in hated Dublin, he taught classics in a dilapidated University College. All inspiration deserted him; a continuing, total exhaustion hindered any fruitful intellectual work; his life, like his work, crumbled away under his fingers. During the scholasticate, in the blessed Welsh countryside, those few poems that make him immortal were completed; then later there trickled a few more, then everything dried up except for a few fearful sonnets 'written in blood'.[83] There were many pieces he began but never finished, 'ever so many . . . ruins and wrecks'.[84] 'The melancholy I have all my life been subject to has become . . . rather more distributed, constant, and crippling.'[85] 'Every impulse and spring of art seems to have died in me. . . . I have . . . been so completely ruined for life by my alleged singularities.'[86] Completely misunderstood and pushed about in the order, 'I have long been Fortune's football and am blowing up the bladder of resolution big and buxom for another kick of her foot.'[87] 'My muse has long put down her carriage and now for years "takes in washing". The laundry is driving a great trade now.'[88] 'It kills me to be time's eunuch and never to beget.' His spirit was so broken 'that madness seemed to be making approaches'.[89] But if his friends to whom he thus wrote became indignant, he explained to them that there is nothing to be done, it must ever be so.[90] He referred to the destiny of Christ, who certainly as man had hoped also to have success and saw all his earthly work fall to ruins.[91] He referred also to his vows that rendered him dead to the world.[92]

Who will disentangle this inner tragedy? If Hopkins acknowledged the view of Ignatian indifference that he was

[83] B (17.5.85) 219.
[84] To Baillie, F (24.4.85) 255.
[85] *Ibid.*, 256.
[86] B (3.4.81 and 27.4.81) 124, 126.
[87] B (26.7.83) 183.
[88] D (29.7.88) 157.
[89] B (1.9.85) 221f.
[90] B (21.8.84) 197; B (17.5.85) 216: 'which must be and will be'; B (1.9.85) 221: 'alas, so it must be'.
[91] D (3.7.86) 137f.
[92] D (17.10.81) 75.

taught as just—namely, that he himself could undertake no step in the matter of his poetry but must wait for the clearly never to be expected initiative of his superiors—then things could have turned out no differently. But behind this conflict there lay another still deeper, indicated in a letter to Bridges: 'The only person that I am in love with seldom, especially now, stirs my heart sensibly and when he does I cannot always "make capital" of it, it would be sacrilege to do so.'[93] It is the problem of the conflict between divine consolation in prayer and poetic inspiration. The first *could* overflow into the second, but the poet did not will it, particularly when such consolation became rare. It is the ligature, to which Baruzi draws attention in the case of John of the Cross, and which Brémond's superficial book, *Prière et Poésie*, does not sufficiently perceive.

On the one hand there is justice in the remarks of Fr Devlin, S.J., who has said some of the most acute things about his fellow-Jesuit, Hopkins:[94] 'Hopkins the Jesuit behaved to Hopkins the poet as a Victorian husband might to a wife of whom he had cause to be ashamed. His muse was a highborn lady, a chaste matron, dedicated to God; but he treated her in public as a slut, and her children as an unwanted and vaguely sinful burden. . . . It is certain that Hopkins was keenly and even agonizingly aware of his duty to these children, his poems, and that in secret he loved them passionately.' But Hopkins belongs, in Devlin's opinion, to that type of nineteenth-century convert who had brought with him into the Church a certain Kantian-Victorian and crypto-Jansenist 'hero'-ideal and thereby excoriated himself in self-laceration.[95] Thus there were many times when his whole destiny must have manifested itself to him as completely coherent and logical: he wanted to transcend the aesthetic sphere and confront God in his nakedness—indeed the living God appeared to him in decisive moments as Heraclitean cosmic fire (almost with the aspect of Shiva), as the roaring winter sea in which the *Deutschland* with her five exiled nuns, and later the *Euridice* with her fine young sailors, foundered and

[93] B (15.2.79) 66.

[94] In the three introductions to the sermons, the spiritual writings and the private notes: S 3ff., 107ff., 213ff.

[95] S 119–120.

were destroyed. He knew very well that this God of majesty, to whom the created dust owes praise, reverence and service, is at the same time the mystery of the noblest tenderness, the wounded Heart of the World breaking with sweetest love, of which so many of his poems speak. But how far he is in all of this Ignatian, it is hard to say. The *Exercises* were for him the breath of life, an ever fresh occasion for self-examination and conversion, an occasion too for the most daring speculations, which, however, betrayed more interest in Scotus than in the father of his order. Hopkins and Ignatius do not look one another full in the face.

4. Duns Scotus, whom Hopkins first encountered in the summer of 1872 and in the reading of whom he 'was flush with a new stroke of enthusiasm',[96] was for Hopkins from the beginning the confirmation of his own vision of the nature of things: 'Just then when I took in any inscape of the sky or sea I thought of Scotus.' Scotus had been the first to maintain philosophically the uniqueness of things, withstanding the temptation to dissolve them into general ideas, forms or laws. This too was Hopkins' object: to express the irreducibly unique, or at least to evoke it, which clearly brought with it the danger of 'oddness'—'No doubt my poetry errs on the side of oddness. . . . Now it is the virtue of design, pattern, or inscape to be distinctive and it is the vice of distinctiveness to become queer. This vice I cannot have escaped.'[97] Where the distinctiveness of things is emphasized and the unifying laws are not allowed to drown such distinctiveness, there the world becomes essentially surprising,

> All things counter, original, spare, strange . . .[98]

they are 'dappled', 'brinded', 'fickle', 'freckled', each has a different and peculiar taste, which is its worth, its irreplaceability. Scotus had an eye for the uniquely individual; that meant that his vision outstripped his power of expression, as Hopkins pertinently remarks: 'And so I used to feel of Duns Scotus when I used to read him with delight: he saw too far, he knew

[96] J (3.8.72) 221.
[97] B (15.2.79) 66.
[98] P 37.

too much; his subtlety overshot his interests; a kind of feud arose between genius and talent, and the ruck of talent in the Schools finding itself, as his age passed by, less and less able to understand him, voted that there was nothing important to understand.'[99]

In the great essay on the *foundation* of the *Exercises* ('*Homo creatus est*')[100] the mystery of the 'I', of the being of the self, moves into the centre and becomes in its determined, irreducible uniqueness the touchstone of every world view and the proof of God's free, sovereign, creative act. The diatonic points in the Pythagorean picture of the world are given a new, much sharper characterisation: 'I find myself both as man and as myself something most determined and distinctive, *at pitch*'— that is, exactly aimed, like an arrow that hits the bull's-eye, set on its course, marked out, harmonised, picked out—'more distinctive and higher pitched than anything else I see.' But whence is this concentration of being into this unique knot, whence this selving? Clearly not from anything less dense, anything more blurred, more shallow, more general; 'but only by one of finer and higher pitch', which alone could 'force forward the starting and stubborn elements to the one pitch required'. This is already true generally in the case of man, still more so in the case of mind, of self-being, consciousness and feeling of self: 'that taste of myself, of *I* and *me* above and in all things, which is more distinctive than the taste of ale or alum, more distinctive than the smell of walnutleaf or camphor, and is incommunicable by any means to another man. . . . But to me there is no resemblance: searching nature I taste *self* but at one tankard, that of my own being.' In other cases two things have always something in common; but here all things rebuff him and 'in no way help me to understand [my being, myself]'. To clarify the phenomenon, the hypothesis of chance is first rejected, but then a second hypothesis, thought through by Hopkins with some subtlety, that some universal spirit of nature or the world is 'enselfed in my self' ('here we touch the *intellectus agens* of the Averrhoists and the doctrine of the Hegelians and

[99] To C. Patmore, F (3.1.84) 349.
[100] Dated 20.8.80; S 122–129.

others'), for neither could this universal spirit enself itself in different selves as the same 'I', just as little as I, considered as an individual, can be a part or a member of some universal spirit, for 'either way self tastes differently to him and to me'; still less can the universal spirit be thought of as a mere centre or point of reference for consciousness or action attributed to it, for whose self would this point be? It is true that a self has its centre and its periphery (as, for instance, a man and his body), but this is just the periphery of its self, and not a self in itself. In the animal realm, a central life may display itself in individuals, but neither are really selves. In mankind there may be community of selves, but this does not abolish them. God as the highest self may indwell all created persons in virtue of his uniqueness and transcendence, but only because he has in freedom singled out these selves (from the infinite possibility of other determinations and self-ings) and set them in being.

In this way the whole world of myth is finally transcended, but not through some demythologisation, but rather through a transmythologisation: because of the immanence of the absolute the free self in all determined selves is the truth of the impossible, imagined, romantic self as a whole. And from this springs the basic conception of Bonaventure, from which the way leads on to Scotus: 'God's utterance of himself in himself is God the Word, outside himself is this world. This world then is word, expression, news of God. Therefore its end, its purpose, its purport, its meaning, is God and its life or work to name and praise him.'[101] The free word of a free self can only express this, can only radiate his solitary glory, and therefore the whole world must speak of God. All nature's language is in Bonaventure's sense *reductio*: 'As we drove home the stars came out thick: I leant back to look at them and my heart opening more than usual praised our Lord to and in whom all that beauty comes home.'[102]

But in all this the real mysteries of the self have not yet emerged. These only disclose themselves when we pass beyond the general philosophical *analogia haecceitatis et personalitatis* to

[101] S (7.8.82) 129.
[102] J (17.8.74) 254.

the theological problem: what is the human self, the person in the face of God's gracious election in Christ? It is only here that Hopkins, taking his lead from Scotus, develops his speculative originality.

2. GOD'S THOUGHT OF THE WORLD AND VISION OF THE WORLD

This speculation is developed principally in two very dense pieces: 'On Personality, Grace and Free Will'[103] and 'Creation and Redemption: The Great Sacrifice'.[104] Again, the starting point of Hopkins' reflections is the notion of the self, or rather the person as a rational self: 'Self is the intrinsic oneness of a thing, which is prior to its being and does not result from it *ipso facto*, does not result, I mean, from its having independent being.' Of course a self cannot exist without a nature, but as an intention (of the Creator) it is yet something 'positive' and distinct from each other possible self. This Scotist distinction between person and nature exactly meets the point that Anton Günther has made the centre of his thought. The same nature can be imparted to different selves, and the same nature can even more readily undergo in the different subjects different destinies. But that act, through which God wills to elect a self in its uniqueness—to possibility or reality—is indivisible and imparticipable. The personal self, which can only exist clothed in a nature and can only be and be effective in it as itself, has its freedom precisely in this distinction: it can and must determine itself as the self that it is—'in freedom of pitch'—and this self-determination has to be worked out within the area of manœuvre that its nature grants to it—'freedom of play'—to which belongs logically a certain range of objects from which to choose—'freedom of field'. But it is self-determination as self-choice that is decisive, which is then perfected when it integrates

[103] S 146–159.

[104] S 196–202; to which add the individual passages from the fragmentary commentary on the *Exercises*, especially the meditation on Hell (135–142), the remark on the composition of place (S 185), on the Resurrection appearances to Mary (S 190f.), on the meditation *De Amore* (S 192–195).

itself to the innate sound and taste of this individual, preconceived and chosen by God from eternity, to a 'pitch' in which at all times the self-determination (and therefore 'self-creating') of the creature is included.[105] Here the choice (*elección*) of the Ignatian *Exercises* complements this Scotist primordial choice, as praxis complements theory, for Ignatius trains the human will to choose what God has chosen for it from all eternity (*Exercises*, no. 135). Here Hopkins engages in polemic against the Thomists and a bare freedom of indifference in the creature in which the constraints of pre- and self-determination are undervalued. It is in this sense that Hopkins wants to take the *videre personas* and *videre locum* of the Ignatian contemplation, for 'every real person living or dead or to come has his quarter in the round of being, is lodged onewhere and not anywhere, and the mind has a real direction towards him'.[106] But because the refusal of self-determination, which is present in every sin, is potentially a refusal to choose the archetype of the self, conceived and chosen by God, (which rests in God and ultimately is God himself), there is hidden in every sin a manifest tendency to develop into the murder of God: whence sin receives its meaning and structure, and to which it is in fact related by the Cross of Christ.

Now if we are indeed from all eternity predetermined and called by God to be brothers and members of Christ, the core of our personal 'pitch' lies in the supernatural, and thus our self-choice can only be perfected concretely within the grace of God. It is not that Hopkins wants to define the person (as, it might be, by contrast with the individual) only in a supernatural way, for he posits quite clearly creaturely, rational freedom as the presupposition of any cooperation with grace; but he tends to oppose quite bluntly naked personal freedom (*arbitrium*) on the one hand and the freedom of the rational nature (*voluntas ut natura*, affective will) on the other, and to entrust to the former alone the work of the deciding choice.[107] But how can God's

[105] J 197: 'Taking part in their own creation'.

[106] S 186; in which context Scotus is introduced: God reveals his triunity so that believers might give their thoughts of God a completely determined direction to a completely determined someone, who is God.

[107] S (5.9.83) 138f.: 'The memory, understanding and affective will are

grace bring the human person to choose and determine itself beyond nature in the supernatural? It can achieve this through a threefold work that is effected by *gratia praeveniens*, *concomitans* and *perficiens* (*elevans*, *uniens*). The prevenient or 'forestalling' grace operates on the *voluntas ut natura*, which moves naturally toward the (absolute) good, and can do no other: 'It is prevenient grace which *rehearses* in us our consent beforehand, when for the moment we find ourselves to have consented, without finally consenting; and I suppose this to be a true and proper consent.'[108] It is the Augustinian being drawn (*delectatio*) to God, expressed here in more personal terms, that cunning of grace by which God takes to himself in advance the natural motion of our agreement[109] and holds it out as a trophy in front of our still hesitating *arbitrium*. As his grace penetrates us, there opens up for us a new horizon, a new 'strain' for the exercise of freedom, a new plane of cleavage, a new 'cleave' through the round ball of the self,[110] though not on the same level as before but displaced in a 'shift': 'It is into that possible world that God for the moment moves his creature out of this one . . . *shewing it to itself* gracious and consenting; nay more, clothing its old self for the moment with a gracious and consenting self. This shift is grace.'[111] It is only now that the personal *arbitrium* has to decide for itself for this highest self, to aim to hit it ('pitch'), drawn by the accompanying grace, in a decision that man can achieve only inchoately, only in a 'sighing of consent', only in the acknowledgment of the prevenience of grace. This decision of the creature 'is found to be no more than the mere wish, discernible by God's eyes, that it might do as he wishes, might correspond, might say Yes to him . . . and this least sigh of desire, this one aspiration, is the life and spirit of man. . . . And remark that prayer understood in this sense, this sigh or

incapable themselves of an infinite object and do not tend towards it. . . . The arbitrium in itself is man's personality or individuality and places him on a level of individuality in some sense with God.' S 153: 'For a self is absolute which stands to the absolute God as an infinitesimal to the infinite'.

[108] S 150.

[109] S 157: 'God's forestalling of man's action by prevenient grace, which carries with it a consenting of man's will. . . .'

[110] S 151.

[111] S 154 (my italics).

aspiration or stirring of the spirit toward God, is a *forestall* of the thing to be done, as on the other side grace prevenient is God's forestall of the same, and it is here that one creature, one man, differs so much from another: in one, God finds only the constrained correspondence with his forestall . . . ; in another, he finds after this an act of choice properly so called. And by this infinitesimal act the creature does what in it lies to bridge the gulf.'[112] If this work of *gratia praeveniens* is like 'a prophecy, a forecast, not of the certain future, for it leaves us free still to discard and unmake that future', then is the future thus opened up such that in it 'God has already acted, nay we have done so too. . . . The sigh of correspondence links the present . . . to the future . . . : it *begins* to link it, is the first infinitesimal link in the chain or step on that road which is to created power impassable.' And 'even the sigh or aspiration itself is in answer to an inspiration of God's spirit and is followed by the continuance and expiration of that same breath which lifts it, through the gulf',[113] and in which grace is finally immanent to freedom as *gratia sanctificans* and *uniens*. While the first grace must be appropriated to the Father, who raises us to the image of the Son, the second is the genuinely crucifying grace of the Son; the third, however, is the unifying and sanctifying grace of the Holy Spirit. The first (as the experience of being drawn affectively) is the grace of the novice, the second (as independent choice) is the grace of the mature Christian, the third 'is truly God's finger touching the very vein of personality which nothing else can reach and man can respond to by no play whatever, by bare acknowledgment only, the counter stress which God alone can feel . . . , the aspiration in answer to his inspiration': perfecting grace.[114]

But all this revolves round the basic Scotist idea that the sacrifice of the Son is God's first thought of the world; we have met this in Bonaventure. Hopkins, like Bonaventure, is interested only in the actual world order (and not in the question of what would have happened if Adam had not sinned), but this is founded on the 'great sacrifice' of the Son, to which Idea of

[112] S 155.
[113] S 155f.
[114] S 158.

sacrifice all the rest of the creatures are related at the level of idea. The 'great sacrifice' on which everything is founded is, however, the primary way in which the self-emptying, the pure being for another of God's personal, trinitarian being can be manifest externally:

> The first intention then of God outside himself . . . the first outstress of God's power, was Christ; and we must believe that the next was the Blessed Virgin. Why did the Son of God go thus forth from the Father not only in the eternal and intrinsic procession of the Trinity but also by an extrinsic and less than eternal, let us say aeonian one?—To give God glory and that by sacrifice, sacrifice offered in the barren wilderness outside of God, as the children of Israel were led into the wilderness to offer sacrifice. This sacrifice and this outward procession is a consequence and shadow of the procession of the Trinity, from which mystery sacrifice takes its rise; but of this I do not mean to write here. It is as if the blissful agony or stress of selving in God had forced out drops of sweat or blood, which drops were the world, or as if the lights lit at the festival of the 'peaceful Trinity' through some little cranny striking out lit up into being one 'cleave' out of the world of possible creatures.[115]

From here Hopkins proceeds to his breathtaking speculations. Scotus had, in view of the eucharistic presence of Christ, revised the Aristotelian categories and found that quantity, though secondarily signifying the being of parts outside themselves, primarily signified only the relatedness of parts one to another within a being; that is, its harmony or corporeal form. God therefore has the power to cause the eucharistic body of Christ to be present universally in any position in space and time throughout the cosmos, and Scotus adds: 'I say then, but without insisting on it, that before the Incarnation and "before Abraham was", in the beginning of the world, Christ could have had a true temporal existence in a sacramental manner. And if this is true, it follows that before the conception and formation of the Body of Christ from the most pure blood of the Glorious Virgin there could have been the Eucharist.'[116] On the basis of this *auctoritas* Hopkins continued

[115] S 197.

[116] *Op. Oxoniense* IV, dist. 10, qu. 4 (cited after Devlin, S 113f.)

the already quoted passage on sacrifice thus: 'The sacrifice would be the Eucharist, and that the victim might be truly victim like, like motionless, helpless, or lifeless, it must be in matter. Then the Blessed Virgin was intended or predestined to minister that matter. And here then was that mystery of the woman clothed with the sun which appeared in heaven.'[117]

This eternally universal temporality and spatiality of God sacrificing himself in matter is primary; in Paul's account of the *kenosis* of the Son, who 'could not but see what he was, God, but he would see it as if he did not see it, and be it as if he were not . . . [there] seems to me the root of all his holiness and the imitation of this the root of all moral good in other men.'[118] And indeed this is true already for the angels, who were created not in time but in eternity to accompany the lamb of self-sacrifice, and who in the midst of their eternal world encountered the real presence of the eucharistic Son and the woman clothed with the sun following him and then had to decide[119] whether 'to contribute . . . towards the Incarnation'[120] or not; that is, whether they would realise in the eternal foundations of the world the spirit of the sacrifice of Christ, would allow Christ an 'embodiment' in the angelic world, or not. Here Hopkins likes to take up motifs that have flitted through the history of theology from Origen to Soloviev; they fit in with his line of thought, and he uses them in poetic vision of the world. He uses too the notion that Scotus made seem possible of the simultaneity of happenings in the

[117] S 197. Apropos of the appearance of the risen Christ to his mother, as Ignatius depicts it in the fourth week of the Exercises, Hopkins draws out the implications, showing as beyond a doubt that 'at the Last Supper Christ invisibly but sacramentally communicated his Blessed Mother (as many ecstatics and others have been communicated)'. 'In her then as well as on the cross Christ died and was at once buried, her body, his temple, becoming the sepulchre. At his rising the soul entered the body in her as in the sepulchre and, issuing from her breast, the two presences passed into one': S 190f. So too is Michael's battle against the serpent who is threatening the woman a sort of 'crusade' to liberate the 'Holy Sepulchre' in which 'the sacrifical victim had lain and from [which] he had risen': S201.

[118] B (3.2.83) 175.

[119] S 197f. On the basis of the Scotist theory of *adductio* (S 200) Hopkins can speak of a 'real fetching, presentment, adduction' of Christ and of Mary into the world of the angels. *Cf.* Devlin's notes, S 308f.

[120] S 200.

aevum and in time, for 'a single event in angelic duration could be coincident with the whole of our time.'[121] If creation in its entirety is traced from the pinnacle of Christ and therefore from this height is unfolded, then the key to the Pythagorean distances of the spheres and the cosmic harmonies of them all is found in Christ, then Christ 'passed', as the last blossom of the world, through the whole 'pedigree' of the angelic world as well as through the material and organic world.[122] Then is Lucifer's sin a refusal to follow the 'great sacrifice', a 'dwelling on his own beauty, an instressing of his own inscape, and like a performance on the organ ... of his own being; it was a sounding ... of his own trumpet and a hymn in his own praise'.[123] It is (following Scotus again) the sin of 'luxury', which is one with that of pride, in Heaven as on earth[124]—which explains how there can be 'beautiful evil'—while the explanation of 'ugly good' lies in the resistance of matter to the (Aristotelian) power of form.[125]

Thus, if the creation of the world is seen in this way, as an implication of the decree of the Incarnation, then it follows that the cosmos as a whole possesses, either manifestly or secretly, a christological form. And it further follows that through all the raging of the elements, all the wildernesses of matter, all shipwrecks and ruins, Christ can be coming and truly is. For the sake of this vision, Hopkins began again, as a religious, to write poetry.

> I admire thee, master of the tides,
> Of the Yore-flood, of the year's fall;
> The recurb and the recovery of the gulf's sides,
> The girth of it and the wharf of it and the wall;
> Stanching, quenching ocean of a motionable mind;
> Ground of being, and granite of it: past all
> Grasp God, throned behind
> Death with a sovereignty that heeds but hides, bodes but abides;

[121] Devlin's explanation in S 112f. *Cf.* the beginning of the sonnet, 'The shepherd's brow ...': P 75. So can Satan lay hold of man, before he, Satan, has himself finally fallen from heaven; he draws man into his own pride, and it is a single, universal fall ('move' = the Origenist, Evagrian *kinesis*).

[122] S 200.

[123] S 201.

[124] S 132, and Devlin's notes, 286f.

[125] To C. Patmore, F (24.9.83) 306f.

With a mercy that outrides
The all of water, an ark
For the listener; for the lingerer with a love glides
Lower than death and the dark;
A vein for the visiting of the past-prayer, pent in prison,
The-last-breath penitent spirits—the uttermost mark. . . .[126]

Christ girds chaos in his descent into Hell—and his coming is always a descent—but he determines too the decisive selving of all created persons who achieve their 'pitch' only in their victory over self for him. This their victory over self is, for the elect, included beforehand in the act of their creation, so that in their act of decision they have only to remain true to themselves, while the wicked and the lost 'are like halfcreations and have but a halfbeing',[127] because they are shut up and immured in their natural selves (which they doubtless possess) without hope of being able to ascend. This self is experienced by the sinner, and still more sharply by the man who feels himself bereft of transforming grace while he is left behind in his own night, as 'myself unholy':[128]

Selfyeast of spirit a dull dough sours. I see
The lost are like this, and their scourge to be
As I am mine, their sweating selves; but worse.[129]

The murderer in the St Winifred drama is wrapped up in the 'despair' of such 'keen self-feeling',[130] while on the other side there answers the grace of that innermost 'selfless self of self', which no man can trace in advance or sound out, or imagine, and which will say Yes or No to the great sacrifice:

Man lives that list, that leaning in the will
No wisdom can forecast by gauge or guess,
The selfless self of self, most strange, most still,
Fast furled and all foredrawn to No or Yes.[131]

Finally it is Christ himself, who is enselved in all his members if

[126] P 28, st. 32–33.
[127] S 197.
[128] P 16.
[129] P 67.
[130] P 152 (Gardner and MacKenzie 191).
[131] P 157.

the believer will let grace work in himself and together with it breathe forth a sweet perfume to God:

> Acts in God's eye what in God's eye he is—
> Christ. For Christ plays in ten thousand places,
> Lovely in limbs, and lovely in eyes not his
> To the Father through the features of men's faces.[132]

'For grace is any action, activity, on God's part by which, in creating or after creating, he carries the creature to or towards the end of its being, which is its selfsacrifice to God and its salvation. . . . So far as this action is God's it is divine stress, holy spirit, and, as all is done through Christ, Christ's spirit; so far as it is action, correspondence, on the creature's part it is *actio salutaris*; so far as it is looked at *in esse quieto* it is Christ in his member on the one side, his member in Christ on the other. It is as a man said: That is Christ playing at me and me playing at Christ, only that it is no play but truth; That is Christ *being me* and me being Christ.'[133]

This then is the theological centre from which we can develop the laws of Hopkins' aesthetics. For a complete picture it would be necessary to separate out the tangled and yet always extremely lucid threads of his formal and critical reflections—on verse form; on rhythm; on the nature of poetry and prose; on the role of number, proportion, chromatics, counterpoint, fugue, canon in verse and music—it would be necessary to trace his word creations, his powerful conciseness, his poetry's assonance and inner rhymes, his subtle, critical remarks on his own poems and those of others; it would be necessary to build out of these countless fragmentary aspects a complete edifice, whose coherence with Hopkins' philosophy and theology would then have to be shown.[134] We must content ourselves with a theological approach.

The principle lies in the fact that all truth is grounded in

[132] P 57.

[133] S 154.

[134] Alan Heuser has made such an attempt, though he carries his attempts at systematisation too far. W. H. Gardner's two-volume study is fundamental: *GMH, a Study of Poetic Idiosyncracy in Relation to Poetic Tradition:* I, 2nd ed. London, 1948; II, 1st ed., 1949.

[135] P 157.

Christ ('Christ is truth')[135] and that all beauty belongs to him, is related to him, is yielded to him in the 'great sacrifice' and must rest with him ('give beauty back, beauty, beauty, beauty, back to God, beauty's self and beauty's giver').[136] In the sonnet, 'To What Serves Mortal Beauty?', which sets out from the danger of its bewitching power—'the O-seal-that-so feature'—this power serves to keep alive a man's sense for things as again and again he is left speechless at the sight of them: as at that of the beautiful English boys whom Pope Gregory noticed in the slave market in Rome, and who moved him to send missionaries to convert such a people. Man would worship blocks and stones did not human beauty speak to him, human beauty in which 'self flashes off frame and face', and say that love is intended for a 'thou': in a real encounter, but in what is only an encounter, that allows the beloved other to be—'then leave, let that alone'—and wishes it eternal beauty and grace.[137] Christ alone is the repository and the judge; as he is the ethical judge of mankind, so he is the highest aesthetic judge of all human art. 'As I am criticising you, so does Christ, only more correctly and more affectionately, both as a poet and as a man.'[138] 'The only just judge, the only just literary critic, is Christ, who prizes, is proud of, and admires, more than any man, more than the receiver himself can, the gifts of his own making. And the only real good which fame and another's praise does is to convey to us, by a channel not at all above suspicion but from circumstances in this case much less to be suspected than the channel of our own minds, some token of the judgment which a perfectly just, heedful, and wise mind, namely Christ's, passes upon our doings.'[139]

But now the glance that God casts on man and his work is the glance of his grace and election. He hears man's inchoate sigh of assent, which is included in the picture of his election:

> Thou heardst me truer than tongue confess
> Thy terror, O Christ, O God.[140]

[136] P 59.
[137] P 62.
[138] B (22.2.79) 73.
[139] D (15.6.78) 8; *cf.* D (1.12.91) 93.
[140] P 28, st. 2.

If He would prove
And search me through
Would he not find
(What yet there must
Be hid behind. . . .[141]

And so God sees, complementing what is failing in the creature itself:

God, lover of souls, swaying considerate scales,
Complete thy creature dear O where it fails,
Being mighty a master, being a father and fond.[142]

So too it must be left to God to see the most fearsome destruction in worldly terms as a gentle spring:

Surf, snow, river and earth
Gnashed: but thou art above, thou Orion of light;
Thy unchancelling poising palms were weighing the worth,
Thou martyr-master: in thy sight
Storm flakes were scroll-leaved flowers, lily showers—sweet heaven was astrew in them.[143]

This doctrine of grace changed the natural doctrine of instress and inscape, for the true inscape of all things is Christ; God's grace is the stress within them, by which indeed (as has already been said) the arguments of our self-taste against mythical pantheism are not rendered powerless but are, rather, transcended. For now it is really God who has the true taste of the human self in his mouth. In the great shipwreck poem, man is the succulent fruit that God bites in order to know its innermost taste, and in being this fruit for God, mankind treads, willy-nilly, the way to Calvary:

. . . How a lush-kept plush-capped sloe
Will, mouthed to flesh-burst,
Gush!—flush the man, the being with it, sour or sweet,
Brim, in a flash, full!—Hither then, last or first,
To hero of Calvary, Christ's, feet—
Never ask if meaning it, wanting it, warned of it—men go.[144]

[141] P 127.
[142] P 34.
[143] P 28, st. 21.
[144] P 28, st. 8.

The Holy Ghost is the Paraclete within us, since he is 'stress' in us: 'Who comforts, who cheers, who encourages, who persuades, who exhorts, who stirs up, who urges forward, who calls on; what the spur and word of command is to a horse, what clapping of hands is to a speaker, what a trumpet is to the soldier, that a Paraclete is to the soul: one who calls us on.'[145] But Hopkins insists that this 'stress' does not come unmediated to us from above, from Heaven, but also from the temporal history of the Cross:

> Not out of his bliss
> Springs the stress felt
> Nor first from heaven (and few know this)
> Swings the stroke dealt. . . .
>
> But it rides time like riding a river. . . .
>
> It dates from day
> Of his going in Galilee [. . . and]
> The dense and the driven Passion, and frightful sweat:
> Thence the discharge of it, there its swelling to be.[146]

And because the Cross was invented and laid on him by men but grasped by God as a sign and then in turn imprinted by him on men, the stroke and stress he inflicts touches men both humanly and divinely, just as the imprint of the seraphic signs sealed Francis in a divine and human way.[147]

For this reason, and also because God, in virtue of his predestination of man to his eternal self, already possesses a measure of man's acceptance in advance, there is in the 'great sacrifice' for men not only darkness, but always too a kind of light. It is the light of faith, whose strength is precisely proportional to the measure in which man has surrendered himself to God and God has bestowed on man the totality of his vision, for 'it is God—in man—knowing his own truth. It is like the child of a great nobleman taught by its father and mother a compliment of welcome to pay to the nobleman's father on his visit to them: the child does not understand the words it says by rote, does not know their meaning, yet what they mean it

[145] Sermon at Liverpool, S (25.4.80) 70.
[146] P 28, st. 6–7.
[147] P 28, st. 22–23.

means. The parents understand what they do not say, the child says what it does not understand, but both child and parents mean the welcome.'[148] And that it is so is understood by the child too, and the child is glad, not in himself but in the one addressed, that he can bring joy. So too can it be with the joy of Christian faith: 'We must put a stress on ourselves and make ourselves find comfort where we know the comfort is to be found. It *is* a comfort that in spite of all, God loves us. . . . We have only to force ourselves to see it, to dwell on it. . . .'[149] In the same sermon the emphasis is laid ever more firmly on God: 'It has been said that God prays to men more than men to God: Christ called to us from his cross more than we call to him there. . . . His servants rejoice in him, at least St. Paul says they should, but much more does Christ rejoice in them. . . . He admires them more than they can, more than they *justly* can, themselves, for he made all these things, beauty, health, strength, and the rest. But we admire ourselves and pride ourselves: we should leave that to him, he is proud enough of us. If we do well he smiles, he claps his hands over us; he is interested in our undertakings . . . more . . . than we are.'[150] A sonnet on soldiers draws out this thought in poetry. Why, he asks, are we inclined at the sight of our redcoats, our tars, to bless them, although they are only frail clay, even foul clay? Because the heart hopes and fancies that the man in the uniform will answer to his calling, because it judges the artist by the standards of his art.

> Mark Christ our King. He knows war, served this soldiering through;
> He of all can reeve a rope best. There he bides in bliss
> Now, and seeing somewhere some man do all that man can do,
> For love he leans forth, needs his neck must fall on, kiss,
> And cry 'O Christ-done deed! So God-made-flesh does too:
> Were I come o'er again' cries Christ 'it should be this'.[151]

God therefore sees in us the true beauty, because by his

[148] S 157.
[149] Sermon at Bedford Leigh, S 47f.
[150] *Ibid.* 49.
[151] P 63.

looking he sets within us his beauty; yet with Hopkins this is grasped completely undialectically, in a quite unprotestant way. Everything depends, at the stage he is considering, on the assumption of the human deed, of the human act of assent, by redeeming grace—so much so that this assumption becomes something absolutely original and already occurs where God in his freedom calls man to rise from nature to grace: 'for redeem may be said not only of the recovering from sin to grace or perdition to salvation but also of the raising from worthlessness before God (and all creation is unworthy of God) to worthiness of him, the meriting of God himself, or, so to say, godworthiness.'[152] And here the whole world order—and within it the whole of aesthetics—depends on the inextricable linkage of Christ and Mary: on the interweaving, by grace, of the human act of assent into the redeemer's own act of assent, which is one with the assent of the love of the Trinity. Thus is Mary everywhere present in the work of Hopkins and indeed compared to the air we breathe:[153] in her the whole of creation is worthy of God, is objectively, and without any dialectic 'as if', beautiful. Thus we see again that at the deepest level theological aesthetics as a whole stands or falls with Mariology.

3. SACRAMENTAL POETRY

The fact that all natures and selves are fashioned and determined for Christ, who is both their ultimate inscape and instress, means that there is no other possibility of reading them objectively and understanding them than in relation to this centre in which they are integrated. Hopkins does not thereby confuse nature and grace, but the concrete *telos* of natures and persons is none the less that for the sake of which they exist; and out of the glory of the Incarnate God there breaks forth the truest and most inward glory of forms both of natures and persons. Christ therefore stands once more in the place of the eternal idea, which shines through the phenomena: but he is idea as living God and living man, as personal majesty, self-sacrifice, love in mercy

[152] S 197.
[153] P 60.

condescending and emptying itself, so that Hopkins can even frequently call him hero, the beloved, deified ideal hero.[154] The Christian, who is able to read this picture of the manifestation of the glory of God knows that here all truth and therefore all beauty lies, that he owes it to himself to surrender in love to this archetype, because he owes him his being and existence and can therefore only glorify him in an ascent to him in his life and work.

So Christianity is really 'an inspiration'[155] such as is expressed both in the ethical sphere (above all as love of one's neighbour) and in the aesthetic (as an exact experiencing of the forms of the world) with the most careful, most sober endeavour. It is precisely the duty of the one who ascends to Christ in faith, hope and love to interpret all the forms of God's revelation in Christ throughout the universe, and this task is achieved by Hopkins the poet. For what has to be interpreted is not concepts (of 'universal', abstract truths), but images (of the unique, personal, divine-human truth), and here poetry is the absolutely appropriate theological language, and Hopkins brings the great English tradition back into the Church by his own creative achievement.

His constant efforts and schooling in reading the forms of nature is therefore not 'aesthetic' in the usual sense nor 'mystical' nor one-sidedly 'exact and scientific', but rather, it subsumes them all under the higher Christian law.[156] It is, in a real sense a 'learning to read'. Of certain clouds he can say: 'its make easily read';[157] of a moonlit landscape with clouds and trees: 'I read a broad careless inscape flowing throughout'.[158] Inscapes are 'discovered',[159] they unfold ('the scaping unfolded'),[160] they are

[154] S 21, 34f., 48; P 28, st. 8; P 41, st. 28. He is also called 'giant': P 28, st. 33; and designated as 'greatest genius': S 36f. And there is here certainly no dependence on Carlyle, whom Hopkins regarded as an impostor, a false prophet, and in whose style he discerned pretence: D (2.10.81) 75.

[155] B (10.9.88) 287.

[156] Clemen's introduction to *GMH's Gedichte, Schriften, Briefe* (ed. by Rinn, cited in n. 1), 19.

[157] J (24.5.71) 210.

[158] J (23.2.72) 218.

[159] J (14.5.70) 199.

[160] J (20.10.70) 200.

caught flowing ('I caught an inscape as flowing');[161] indeed it is just in their movement that they unfold and become legible: 'Indeed a floating flag is like wind visible and what weeds are in a current.'[162]

The idealists and romantics were right when they understood that the inscapes would only open themselves to the poet in some creative consummation between him and the spirit of nature; but for the Christian the final creative unity lies higher, and he must raise himself to this in his faith, in the great sacrifice; his enthusiasm may have no other source than does his faith. It is of this exaltation as the whole man's engagement and effort that the poetic form must speak; the unprecedented character of Hopkins' language is a theological phenomenon and can be understood only in this way. It was unintelligible to a non-Christian like Bridges, who found Hopkins' language (although in some way magically attractive) mannered and outrageous,[163] and even a convert such as Coventry Patmore, with his dutifully traditional diction, had no antennae for it.[164] Hopkins himself heeded a warning from his friends: 'It is plain I must go no farther on this road: if you and he [Dixon] cannot understand me who will?'[165] 'Dividing a compound word by a clause sandwiched into it was a desperate deed, I feel.'[166] But he will not give up; language must be revalued, at whatever price, it must be equipped anew so as to be able to express in a plausible and fine way the unique and extraordinary, even if not everyone will go along with it at first: 'Plainly if it is possible to express a subtle and recondite thought on a subtle and recondite subject in a subtle and recondite way and with great felicity and perfection, in the end, something must be sacrificed, with so trying a task, in the process, and this may be the being at once,

[161] J (17.9.72) 227.

[162] J (22.7.73) 233. *Cf.* the 'beautiful instance of . . . successive sidings of one inscape': the successive stages of the iris: J (13.6.71) 211; the Horned Violet 'even in withering . . . ran through beautiful inscapes', 'it is not that inscape does not govern the behaviour of things in slack and decay': J (19.7.71) 211. Inscapes can also run together in the observer: J (14.9.71) 215.

[163] B (30.5.78) 54; B (6.11.87) 265.

[164] His letter to Hopkins, F (20.3.84) 352f.

[165] B (10.2.88) 272.

[166] B (6.11.87) 265.

nay perhaps even the being without explanation at all, intelligible.'[167] At the deepest level Hopkins was not to be diverted. If he renounced any publicity, any fame on his own part, then it was because he sensed that his hour had not struck, and he could wait.[168] 'The verses stand or fall by their simple selves.'[169] But a Hopkins renaissance in a purely aesthetic or stylistic sense would be as fundamental a misunderstanding as his former neglect; with him, form and content stand and fall together.

Together with the man, the language must reach out beyond its immanence because the mystery of God does not hold sway as something incomprehensible *behind* the forms of the world; rather, the divine Word was made flesh. Bridges regarded the dogmatic formulation of the mystery, above all of the Incarnation, as profanation; to the extent that the mystery diminishes, he said, so also is diminished its power to captivate the mind. Hopkins replied that mystery was not 'an interesting uncertainty' that held the mind only so long as one had not got to the bottom of it; he cited examples from the realm of the arts that prove that the delight—say of certain musical cadences—'is keenest when they are known and over'. How must it then be when the very answer is the most tantalising statement of the problem and the truth one is to rest in the most pointed putting of the difficulty! And so it is in the dogmatic explanation of the Trinity, which for Christians is 'news of their dearest friend or friends, leaving them all their lives balancing whether they have three heavenly friends or one—not that they have any doubt on the subject, but that their knowledge leaves their minds swinging; poised, but on the quiver. And this might be the ecstasy of interest.'[170] For an understanding of the way the mystery of God takes form in the world, the concept of the sacramental is at hand, which certainly contains within itself the power of the 'symbol', while it goes far beyond it; the form of the image is a likeness to the primordial form in that it has the

[167] *Ibid.*

[168] B (1.4.85) 214: 'take a generation and come to me again'; D (1.12.81) 95: 'it may be that the time will come for my verses'.

[169] D (27.1.87) 150.

[170] B (24.10.83) 187f.

'stress' of the latter in itself: *sacramenta continent quae significant.*

But the mystery incorporated in the inscapes is not to be grasped as a straightforward picture, as, it might be, a simple allegory. The mystery of Christ is, on the one hand, of infinite depth, penetrating all the levels of being from flesh to spirit and beyond into the abyss of the Trinity; on the other, it is an infinitely dramatic event that in the kenotic descent into man and matter exalts and changes them, redeems and deifies them. The poet of the cosmic rapture will be, if he is a Christian, at the same time the poet too of the intimate dialogue between the lost sinner and the crucified Redeemer; as one who beholds he will be also the obedient believer, in the analogies he must always consider and express the reversals and the erasures. The image that should interpret the mystery of Christ is, in itself as an image of nature, utterly overtaxed, but in so far as it is grounded in Christ as the presupposition of nature, it is allowed to say by grace of the archetype what it cannot say of itself.

So it is the mystery of the sonnet, 'The Windhover'—dedicated 'To Christ our Lord'—to draw out the image in an immense, ascending intensity, which starts by spiritualising the bold soaring of the wild bird in order then to interpret the utmost, now motionless, suspension at the highest point, with outstretched wings, as the final unfolding of power from which the embers drop down: a sacramental image of the Cross. At the natural level the image is overstretched, but as a whole it is not; it accomplishes no *metabasis*, no allegory; Christ's Cross is indeed not one historical fact among others to which a natural process can more or less arbitrarily be related: it is the fundamental, ontological presupposition of all natural processes that all, knowingly or not, intrinsically signify or intend by pointing beyond themselves. The 'Windhover' allows this connection to appear expressly only in the dedication; in the poem itself the image must say all. But there are other ways in which this connection can manifest itself in a poem.

First of all there is the Christian's simple 'cosmic experience of God'. Here Hopkins' world view is very close to that of Claudel; many of the images he uses could be Claudel's.[171] God

[171] For example in the sonnet, 'Hurrahing in Harvest' (P 38), whose beginning immediately reminds one of the '*Cantate à trois voix*'; 'The Starlight

is immediately visible in the beauty of the world.[172] In 'God's Grandeur',

> The world is charged with the grandeur of God.
> It will flame out, like shining from shook foil.[173]

In the summer glory of a harvest day, the poet wanders beneath wild wind-walks and silk-sack clouds and lifts up heart and eyes:

> Down all that glory in the heavens to glean our Saviour;
> And, eyes, heart, what looks, what lips yet gave you a
> Rapturous love's greeting of realer, of rounder replies?

The next verse discovers in the rise of the azurous hung hills Christ's world-wielding shoulder. And all these things were here and waited for the one who could truly behold them,

> ... which two when they once meet,
> The heart rears wings bold and bolder
> And hurls for him, O half hurls for him off under his feet.[174]

In the encounter then of nature and the beholder the mystery of the 'great sacrifice' is thrown up in both of them. It is not 'projected into' the landscape; it has long tarried there in order finally to be discovered. Harvest means the world harvest, and the gleaning gaze gleans the Redeemer. In 'Pied Beauty' it is the contrariety and perverseness of natural things that proclaim immediately in their incomprehensible beauty the glory of God:

> Glory be to God for dappled things,

for 'whatever is fickle, freckled (who knows how?) ... He fathers-forth whose beauty is past change: Praise him'.[175]

Night' (P 32), where the sight of the stars becomes immediately, as with Claudel, a vision of all the saints, or the way in which the poet 'kisses his hand' to the stars and the wind (P 28, st. 5), et cetera.

[172] Sermon, S (18.1.80) 59: 'he let himself be seen'.

[173] P 31, and the explanation to Bridges, B (4.1.83) 169: 'I mean foil in its sense of leaf or tinsel, and no other word whatever will give the effect I want. Shaken goldfoil gives off broad glares like sheet lightning and also, and this is true of nothing else, owing to its zigzag dints and creasings and network of small many cornered facets, a sort of fork lightning too.' An example of the exactness of Hopkins' poetic diction.

[174] P 38.

[175] P 37.

. . . nature is never spent;
There lives the dearest freshness deep down things

—in contrast to the world, trodden down under men's feet, 'seared with trade; bleared, smeared with toil': a virginal creation embraces the fallen cosmos,

Because the Holy Ghost over the bent
World broods with warm breast and with ah! bright wings.[176]

This pure, wild nature—in contrast to the fallen culture, returning to dust, swept away and burnt up in the Heraclitean fire—we have already encountered; between 'the sea and the skylark', whose sound and rejoicing are pure, there stretches the sordid city of men:

We, life's pride and cared-for crown,

Have lost that cheer and charm of earth's past prime:
Our make and making break, are breaking, down
To man's last dust, drain fast towards man's first slime.[177]

Here the periods of world time overlap one another: 'earth's past prime'. Is then Paradise the past and mankind the present? 'It is the blight man was born for', and the child's grief over the fallen blossoms finds its truth in the tears of the grown-up over himself.[178] The sonnet, 'The Lantern Out of Doors', sees a little light, a human destiny, a human beauty, lose itself in the night: no eye, following its course, can perceive it to the end. But there is one who knows every line, every fate, who lovingly pursues and rescues as 'first, fast, last friend';[179] in him is the world of men, however vainly it disports itself, hidden, embraced, brought home, set to rights.

It is impossible to say where the natural perception of God in the world ceases and the supernatural, Christian perception begins, which presupposes a dogmatic knowledge. Faith is so deeply involved in flesh and blood (the Word indeed has become flesh), that the transfer of interpretation from

[176] P 31; the theme of the brooding dove is found again in the sonnet 'Peace', P 51.

[177] P 35.

[178] P 55.

[179] P 40.

sacramental signs to the indwelling grace of faith proceeds imperceptibly, ultimately indeed because the christological-mariological has been *understood* as the inner condition of the possibility of the whole natural order. So in the sonnet 'The Starlight Night', looking at the 'fire-folk sitting in the air', at the 'bright boroughs, the circle-citadels', at all the treasures poured forth—'all a purchase, all is a prize'—passes over immediately into the Christian: 'Buy then! bid then!—What?—Prayer, patience, alms, vows', and what is above is really

> . . . the barn; withindoors house
> The shocks. This piece-bright paling shuts the spouse
> Christ home, Christ and his mother and all his hallows.[180]

The transparency of nature to the mystery of salvation makes it equally as easy to look from the mystery into nature: Mary is the kernel of unfallen nature, she is effective mediation to her Son, she *is* the atmosphere in which we live, not metaphorically but really; she is in no way a personification of mother nature; on the contrary, she establishes and supports the natural spring at a much deeper level, as 'The May Magnificat' sings:

> All things rising, all things sizing
> Mary sees, sympathising
> With that world of good,
> Nature's motherhood. . . .
>
> This ecstasy all through mothering earth
> Tells Mary her mirth till Christ's birth
> To remember and exultation
> In God who was her salvation.[181]

The ode 'The Blessed Virgin Compared to the Air We Breathe' praises the nature of Mary's gentle mediation: what would the sun be without the blue sky? 'Whose glory bare would blind'—it would be a fearsome, fiery ball in the darkness. But now Mary is mediatrix—'let all God's glory through'—she is the web, the robe, the 'sweet alms' self' in whom everyone must participate simply in order to live:

[180] P 32.
[181] P 42.

She, wild web, wondrous robe,
Mantles the guilty globe . . .
Nay, more than almoner,
The sweet alms' self is her
And men are meant to share
Her life as life does air.

So through her there is extended to men the possibility of new Nazareths and new Bethlehems, for in faith they breathe in Mary's fruitfulness, her Son, who insinuates himself into their selves as a nobler self and I and as eternal life:

Men here may draw like breath
More Christ and baffle death;
Who, born so, comes to be
New self and nobler me. . . .[182]

Hopkins had then during his years of pastoral activity among the poor come to see men and women ever more strongly as a sacramental form of God: on the one hand, in their fearful threatenedness[183]—Hopkins has a mimosa-like feel for purity and could hardly bear the pollution of young, innocent souls—and on the other, men and women in their homecoming, as sinners, to God, in the bursting forth from him of love in all its cunning: here the tenderness of the priest and the poet are fused into one.[184] His eye gives him a scarcely bearable insight into the heart; in human love he can catch an almost naked glimpse of the love of God holding sway there; it is as if the heart stood still for him ('The Handsome Heart', 'Felix Randal', 'Brothers').[185] The Christian neighbour becomes for him a most transparent sacrament of the Incarnate God, a symbolism of Christian fashioning without reverie or giddy enchantment, in which obligation and inclination, ethical self-transcendence and aesthetic rapture have become one.

But the ultimate for Hopkins remains still his shipwreck poems, because here the foundering and shattering of all

[182] P 60.
[183] P 47, 48, 62, 157.
[184] P 53.
[185] P 47, 53, 54.
[186] P 28, st. 24.
[187] P 28, st. 31.

worldly images and symbols yield a final picture of the sacrament of the world: perishing and ascending to God—death as Resurrection: Resurrection not beyond death, but in death. The nun on the foaming deck, who from the midst of the tumult of the elements cries 'Christ, come quickly'—she cries to her Redeemer in and through the elements: 'christens her wild-worst Best'.[186] The wreck is as a harvest ('is the shipwrack then a harvest'),[187] the beach as a goal ('the goal was a shoal');[188] everything alive was washed away ('lives at last were washing away').[189] Foundering in God—that is the high point of the poem—man finds nothing more to cling on to, not his longing nor reward nor Heaven nor any of God's attributes, for beyond all that there is nothing but him alone: '*Ipse*, the only one'[190]—the self beyond any nature. Here the poet rejoices because the 'heart right' (*cor rectum*), the 'single eye' of the parable, is capable of the highest: to interpret the formless and unformable chaos of the night as form and in the senselessness of pure question to know the who and the why:

> Ah! there was a heart right!
> There was single eye!
> Read the unshapeable shock night
> And knew the who and the why. . . .[191]

[188] P 28, st. 12.
[189] P 28, st. 15.
[190] P 28, st. 28.
[191] P 28, st. 29.

PÉGUY

1. THE BASIC PATTERN

For the opening years of the twentieth century, there is no better representative of the concerns of a theological aesthetic than Charles Péguy,[1] because, from within the Catholic sphere, he

[1] Péguy's works will be quoted as follows. Since the volumes of the standard collected edition (*Oeuvres Complètes*, vols. 1–15, Paris, Editions de la Nouvelle Revue Francaise, 1917–1933, and vols. 16–20, Paris, idem, 1952–1955; not strictly speaking a critical edition), as well as Péguy's own periodical, the 229 issues of the *Cahiers de la Quinzaine*, are not easily obtainable outside France, references will be to the modern India paper edition in the Bibliothèque de la Pléiade: two volumes of this contain the full texts of the works included; the third unfortunately does not, though the full texts are promised for future editions.

A = *Oeuvres en prose 1898–1908* (edited—like the two following volumes—by Péguy's son Marcel, Paris 1959). This contains all the major works of the first period, beginning with a selection prepared by Péguy himself: *De la cité socialiste*, *Marcel*, *Premier dialogue de la cité harmonieuse*; then a group of texts from the *Cahiers*, the most significant being *De la grippe* (three parts of a serial); *Réponse brève a Jaurès*; *Personnalités*; *De Jean Coste*; *Zangwill*; *Notre Patrie*; *Les suppliants parallèles*; the three studies directed toward his projected theses (*De la situation faite à l'histoire et à la sociologie dans les temps modernes*, *De la situation faite au parti intellectuel dans le monde moderne* and *De la situation faite au parti intellectuel dans le monde moderne devant les accidents de la gloire temporelle*). The same volume contains a number of pieces not included in Péguy's selection: *Pierre* (an autobiograpical fragment), *Pour ma maison*, *Pour moi* and a few others.

This volume, A, should be supplemented by the numerous published articles that appear in the *Cahiers* and the *Oeuvres Complètes* (some of which are also available in 'Péguy et les Cahiers: textes choisis par Mme Ch. Péguy', *Nouvelle Revue Francaise* 1947), and the extensive and important writings remaining from this first period collected in:

Par ce demi-clair matin (1952) (= D). This contains the two continuations of *Notre Patrie* (1905–1906), the fragment of a monograph on Bernard-Lazare (1903) and *Hervé* (1906).

L'esprit de système (1953) (= S), containing the fragment of this name, various fragments for the *Situations* essays, the beginning of a work entitled *Brunetière* and other fragmentary pieces.

Deuxième Elégie XXX (1955) (= E), a fragment in the same area as the *Situations* pieces.

B = *Oeuvres en prose 1909–1914* (1957) [2nd ed. with some additions from

conducts precisely the same polemic against the 'spirit of systematisation' that Kierkegaard conducted against Hegelianism. In this respect, he speaks for the same existential preoccupations as Kierkegaard; but he does so in consequence of a more radical anchorage in the Bible than the Danish writer possessed and so avoids his major failing—the separation between aesthetics and ethics (and, equally, religion). As for Hamann—indeed, even more fundamentally than for him—the aesthetic,

unpublished sources, 1961; Tr.]. This volume contains the completed prose works (though the order of items and the commentary are open to question): *A nos amis, à nos abonnés* (with the suppressed sequel, *Nous sommes des vaincus*), 1909; *Clio, dialogue de l'histoire et de l'âme païenne* (1909–1912), together with the important essay arising out of this, composed in 1909 but originally suppressed, *Dialogue de l'histoire et de l'âme charnelle*, which was published (along with the *Deuxième Elégie XXX*) and given the title *Véronique* on the basis of a chance remark by Péguy; *Notre jeunesse* (1910); *Victor-Marie, Comte Hugo* (1910); *Un nouveau théologien, M. Fernand Laudet* (1911); *L'argent and L'argent suite* (1913); *Note sur M. Bergson et la philosophie bergsonienne* (1914); and from the posthumously published works, *Note sur Victor Hugo* and *Note conjointe sur M. Descartes et la philosophie cartésienne* (1914).

C = *Oeuvres poétiques complètes* (1941). This contains the early play *Jeanne d'Arc* (1897), the published text of the three *Mystères* (*De la charité de Jeanne d'Arc* [1909], *Du Porche de la deuxième vertu* [1911], *Des Saints Innocents* [1912], the poems, especially 'Tapisseries' and the great 'heartbeat' *ballade* (*Quatrains*, written in 1912) and finally the epic *Eve*, with its more than 12,000 stanzas (1913). The volume also includes the unpublished continuation of the first *Mystère*, but the first complete edition of the unpublished text, found among Péguy's papers after his death, is that of Albert Béguin, *Le mystère de la Charité de Jeanne d'Arc*, Club du mielleur livre, 1956 (=J). Quotations of this *Mystère* will be from Béguin's edition.

L = Péguy, *Lettres et Entretiens* (1927), containing letters to Mme Geneviève Favre (more fully in Maurice Reclus, *Le Péguy que j'ai connu*, 1951), to Louis Baillet, OSB, and above all, the important letters to and conversations with Joseph Lotte. Further letters in *Cahiers de l'Amitié* (v. infra).

Bibliography: A brief general survey in Louis Perche, *Charles Péguy*, 1957. For Péguy's life in the context of the history of his times, various books of recollections by friends and acquaintances: Fr. Porché (1914), André Suarès (1915), Daniel Halévy (1918, 1940), Jérôme and Jean Thauraud (1925, 1948), Romain Rolland (1944—an intensive exposition, which is, however, crucially deficient because of their entirely diverse and unreconciled perspectives), Jules Isaac (1959, important for the early period, a corrective to false and legendary pictures), Geneviève Favre (*Souvenirs* 1938, in the review *Europe*). On Péguy's achievement as a whole, Jean Delaporte, *Connaissance de Péguy* (1944); Emmanuel Mounier, *La Pensée de Ch. Péguy* (1931); Elsbeth

for Péguy, is in its depths identical with the ethical, and this on the basis of God's becoming man in Christ: the spiritual must put on flesh, the invisible must give proof of itself in form, and only that which is just and justifiable in the sight of God can be right in worldly terms. The Augustinian and Anselanian key word, *rectitudo*, gave expression to this in earlier ages, and Péguy's twofold language of *justice* and *justesse* takes up the same idea. While Kierkgaard retreated before Hegel and the aftermath of his thought and threw up his defences against it, Péguy goes immediately into the heart of the anti-Christian position, the extreme of left-wing Hegelianism, in order to bring all of it home or, better, to unfold from within what is Christian in it. But this does not happen by means of any kind of synthesis or compromise; the form that is achieved and lived out must be a pure and seamless fabric. The words *pur* and *pureté* appear again and again as fundamental concepts, employed in an almost sacral fashion.

What drove the young Péguy out of the Church was precisely the same thing that brought him by a direct route back to it. 'My past needs no apology. I require no defence. I do not stand arraigned on any count.'[2] 'We have been walking continuously in the same direction, and this straight path has led us to where we now stand. It was not a "development", as people rather foolishly say, unthinkingly using one of those words in current speech that has become so loose in meaning: it was an *approfondissement*. It is through a steady *approfondissement* of our heart along the same path, and not through any kind of develoment, that we have rediscovered what it is to be a

Gremminger, *Péguy. Vom Sozialismus zur christlichen Weltschau*, with an introduction by A. Béguin (Olten 1949—the best introduction in German); Karl Pfleger, 'Péguy, der gute Sünder' (Hochland, 1933–1934; included in 'Menschen, die um Christus ringen', 1946[5]); Alexander Dru, *Péguy* (London, 1956). On Péguy's theology and spirituality, Albert Béguin, *La prière de Péguy* (1942); *L'Ève de Péguy* (1948); André Rousseaux, *Le prophète Péguy* (3 vols. 1942, 1944, 1945). On his aesthetics, A. Chavanon, *La poétique de Péguy* (1947); Bernard Guyon, *L'Art de Péguy* (1948).

The society 'L'Amitié Charles Péguy' publishes both more extended studies in its *Cahiers* (1947–) and smaller essays, bulletins and reviews in its *Feuillets* (1948–).

[2] B 561.

Christian. Not through a return home, but as the last end of all. We may have been in advance of the letter; but we have never resisted the spirit.'[3] In this course of unswerving consistency lies the mystery of Péguy's character, which, despite all the oscillations and depressions of his personal life, was in itself so unshakeably secure. Never yet have I felt so strongly that I myself am nothing, and only what I do is everything.'[4] 'Unimaginable trials in private matters, enormous graces for my works'[5]—by this he means that mission whose true scope impresses itself upon him ever more plainly, strengthening him and yet also threatening to shatter him. 'Mine is no ordinary life. My life is a wager. At the deepest level, there is a Catholic renaissance coming to fulfilment through me. One must see this for what it is and stand one's ground. I am a sinner, I am not a saint. You can recognise a saint at first glance. I am a good sinner. A witness. A Christian in the parish, a sinner, but one possessed of the treasures of grace. . . .'[6] Nonetheless, the most clear-sighted of his contemporaries, notwithstanding all their misunderstanding and hostility, their conspiracy of silence, had some sense of the incomparable quality of the event before them—like Gide, writing on the appearance of Péguy's first *Mystère*: 'Nothing since Claudel's *Arbre* has impressed me so much. I am still disturbed as I write, still quite intoxicated.' Or Alain-Fournier: 'It is absolutely wonderful. . . . I know what I am saying when I make the claim that no one since Dostoyevsky has been so patently a man of God.' Or Jacques Copeau: 'It is wonderful, uniquely beautiful.'[7] After reading the second and third *Mystères*, Romain Rolland wrote in his journal: 'After Péguy I can read nothing else. How hollow the greatest men of today sound in comparison with him. Spiritually, my place is at the opposite pole to his, but I admire him unreservedly.' And on the conclusion of the poem about the holy innocents: 'A unique creative achievement amongst the literature of all ages.'[8]

[3] B 998–999.
[4] L 30.
[5] L 168.
[6] L 158.
[7] These and further remarks are assembled by Béguin, J 397–398.
[8] Rolland, *Péguy* I 283–284.

Péguy's work reaches out to pagan, Jew and Christian alike; and even when Péguy is misunderstood by non-Christians, they are not able to resolve his wholeness into its parts and deal with his aesthetics independently of this ethical and religious dimension. He remains indivisible; and so he stands both inside and outside the Church. He is the Church *in partibus infidelium*, the Church in those places where the Church will be one day, and he is so thanks to the fact that he is rooted in the depths where world and Church, world and grace, meet together and interpenetrate to the point of indistinguishability. Perhaps, after the long record of Platonic variations in the history of the Christian spirit, the Church has never been placed so firmly in the world as in Péguy's thought; and, as a result of this, the idea of the world is allowed to remain free from any taint of uncriticised enthusiasm, whatever its source—whether in mythology or eroticism or in optimism about the future. The biblical sobriety and chastity of his thought provides an incorruptible clarity of vision for the world as it really is, *grandeur et misère*. In this respect Péguy, quite deliberately and consciously, sails in Pascal's wake; it is Pascal above all who is in Péguy's mind, it is by Pascal's stature that Péguy measures himself, through him that he acquires both nearness to and distance from things; even at those points where he is bound to go further than Pascal, he brings his ideas to completion.

In that he plunges back into a ground below all secondary oppositions, Péguy is still in the eyes of all those who cannot follow him there a contradictory spirit, or a unifier of all the things that cannot be unified: Communist and traditionalist, internationalist and nationalist, a man of the extreme Left and the extreme Right, ecclesiastically minded and anticlerical, mystic and polemical journalist, and so forth. But on the other hand, for anyone who can see the basic pattern, all these strands that appear to cross one another converge like radial lines toward the central point. From this point he can deal with opposite notions as complementary pairs. From this point too he can indulge an all-pervading humour, less intellectual than Chesterton's, less pedestrian than Claudel's, a kind of superior peasant shrewdness and good nature by which he sets himself apart from the ecclesiastical and antiecclesiastical intelligentsia around him as the only one left with his feet on the ground, incarnated afresh again and again. If he is, in common with Kierkegaard or Nietzsche and like scarcely anyone else, an 'individual', he is nonetheless an individual whose roots run deep, who is bound to family, people and race. 'A task like mine is not the work of an individual; it is nourished, often without their being aware of the fact, by what is best in the life of all those who are present in it. This life reverbeates in the work, in almost incalculable ways.'[9] Only in this lived relation is the mission at all possible, for it is itself existence as representation. Whom would the man speak for who is deprived of his roots, even if he is a genius as an individual? 'What a bitter irony there is in words themselves!' What in any case will the genius that is cut off from its grounding in the national life represent? Only itself; it will depict itself, a poor, pitiful representation. It repents itself, itself as man, and then always only as a poor and pitiful man, just as we all are.'[10]

But what a nation is in the natural order—an interrelation of human beings that is more than the sum of its individuals—the communion of saints is in the Christian sphere, except that here true saints stand out with the stamp of authoritative vocation. The shape that gives focus to everything is here, for Péguy, the figure of Joan of Arc, that unique point of intersection of spiritual and secular action, and this precisely because she *is* 'the people', and—Péguy ascribes this to her from the very beginning—acts out of a sense of total solidarity. Behind Joan, 'as her master and model', stands King Louis, saint and ruler, spiritual and earthly crusader, who was again a prototye for the Sire de Joinville in his own life's path as in the chronicle that he wrote to depict the saint. Péguy has now found the geometrical location of his mission: 'In just the same sense Joan of Arc is my model, since I undertook to devote all that belongs distinctively to me to the representation of this great saint. In that respect, Joinville is my master . . . My attitude toward Joan of Arc is in spirit exactly that of Joinville towards St Louis. Everything hinges upon the dependence and loyalty that we have to these great exemplars. Joinville too was a sinner. But that is not in

[9] J 389. [10] D 158.

question, that is not the issue. What we look to him for is what he has made of St Louis, what portrait of him he has bequeathed to us, what faithfulness he has preserved in the representation, what degree of certainty, what depths of representation his reproduction has achieved.'[11]

The key word 'representation' here combines all its possible meanings: presenting oneself, making onself present—but doing so by making someone else present, the saint who for his part makes present and personifies the people, profane and holy as the people are, and brings them to full reality. At this focal point where the word's meanings intersect we have, as in a flash of lightning, a complete view of Péguy's universe: representation means standing forth on behalf of someone or something, on behalf of others, of all men, so it means solidarity, love as service. And of course, since this is the fundamental definition, it is in principle unlimited. In secular terms, this is where ethics, self-forgetful involvement, belongs, but it is also where aesthetics, the life of genius, belongs. Woe to the genius who is not 'the voice, the expression, the revelation of the whole people!'[12] In spiritual terms, however, it is the holy that again, in its real nature is the life of the Church. Thus, missions and mandates in both areas always have connexions in a vertical direction: the hero's relation to the people, the saint's to the mass of sinners. But if the sinner is at the same time hero or poet, then—like Joinville or Péguy—he can ascend toward the saint in this vertical relation and represent him by depicting him (in his work) and imitating him (in his life). The two are, for Péguy, self-evidently inseparable. But it is not that he, the poet who has been given a mission, portrays in the secular realm what Joan achieved in the spiritual; the decisive thing is that Joan herself does what is spiritual in a worldly fashion. In that respect she is Christ-like, the disciple of Jesus the Jew. Jesus is the fulfiller of the Old Covenant and of the people of the Old Covenant, not their destroyer. At the basis of the Christian demand to take root in the world lies the eternal concern of Israel, obscured by Platonism and rediscovered by Péguy. He completes the circle back to our own point of departure, to Irenaeus.

[11] B 1023.

[12] D 160.

Ecclesia verus Israel: but Israel is a people, and its solidarity is simply that of a people. The Church is the 'people' of all mankind, and its absolute solidarity is with humanity as a whole. Jesus wants to redeem the world as a whole; he is the Son of Man, and his absolute solidarity is with each person, with the least of the brethren. Only the ideal of total solidarity permits the ideal of the genius and the hero in the secular sphere and of the martyr and the saint in the spiritual. The ideal of solidarity creates an analogy between the two orders (and not that separation that the Protestant Kierkegaard carries through in his book *The Eagle*, the separation between the genius and the apostle). Péguy's central problem is thus laid out before us, the question that illuminates the shape of all his life and work: the problem of the eternal loss of a part of humanity—damnation, Hell. Joan '*est mon seul atout (temporel) dans ce terrible jeu*',[13] and so he can say: '*la damnation est mon seul problème*'. Thus he ties together inseparably both themes, Joan and Hell, from the first of his works onwards. Joan, with her holy obstinacy, must and will force the door that Church tradition since Augustine has closed in what for her and for Péguy seems an incomprehensible resignation. Joan and Péguy do not understand how *charité* can understand itself in any other way than as *solidarité*. This was why the young Péguy rapidly determined to abandon the Church to devote himself to the Socialist (Communist) Party. 'All my colleagues from the *lycée*, whether they became workers with hand or brain, peasants or factory hands, whether or not they became socialists and republicans, all of them alike shook off their Catholicism just as I did.'[14] A religion that has resigned itself to giving up brothers eternally for lost without eternally regretting this has a fundamentally egotistic view of salvation and thus is at bottom utterly bourgeois and capitalistic. It is only logical that the bourgeoisie in modern times should chose this kind of Christianity of *charité—a dole for the socially destitute, the proletarians—and that the people, the working class, should opt out of any involvement in this to choose that is, to preserve—solidarité*, and accordingly to oppose *humilité* with simple *modestie*.[15] If *solidarité* after all demands a higher

[13] B 675. [14] A 182. [15] A 451, 489.

involvement than bourgeois *charité*, then it is not possible for it to lead into what is only an augmented earthbound egotism of *fécondité* (this point is sharply established in opposition to Zola).[16] Earlier Christianity, whatever its theology might be, 'laid hold on the essential thing; one and the same blood animated the vast body, one and the same thought dominated, one and the same heart beat, in full community, indeed, in a full communism. One breath, one conscience pervaded the whole flesh, and they possessed one and the same eternal character. Today, we pay the same taxes and have the same political representatives. There was more security in the comradeship of any age than in the friendship of today. They did not talk incessantly about solidarity, but they knew what it was.'[17] What prevailed was not today's horizontal 'dust-storm of individuals' but a vertical structure of representation and of rootedness in the life of the people. So it is clear how Péguy could at the same time attack the (Augustinian and Bourgeois) ideal of *charité* and demand the reinstatement of a Christian and organic form of society, and how there could be no possible understanding from the supporters of the Left, any more than with those of the Right, the *Action Français* group. For these, it is a question of forms, but, for Péguy, form grows only out of the depth of the living spirit. They were aesthetes, but Péguy's concern was with a Christian aesthetic that could most easily be attained through a Christian world revolution. The finger directs us inexorably toward one single point: a cosmic harmony dependent upon the definitive abandonment of those beyond salvation means tolerating (as did Augustine and Dante) the *città dolente* within a theological aesthetic and limiting hope in an individualistic fashion *lasciate ogni speranza*; and so also it means finally giving an aesthetic justification of Hell as an accepted fact, just as Augustine does. But that in turn means accepting a general exodus from the Church into the bargain. For Péguy this can never yield a viable aesthetic. Such an aesthetic would, for him, have to stand or fall by the 'principle of hope', which in his earlier period he understands as the 'principle of solidarity'.

Thus the shape of his life and his work is marked by an

[16] A 548. [17] D 109–110.

enduring warfare on two fronts: against the clericalist and ecclesiasticist bourgeoisie is set the liberating and broadening prospective of socialism as an effective programme for changing the world (the Old Testament ideal) no less than as total personal solidarity (the Cross of Jesus). And therefore, on the other hand, the deep mysteries of salvation in Christ are set against the narrow-minded philistinism of anticlerical socialism: *solidarité* is most easily achieved if it goes together with the original biblical depths of *charité*. The *Cahiers de la Quinzaine* from 1900 to 1914 carry on this war on two fronts, not indeed in the lonely fashion of the journals of Kierkegaard or Karl Kraus, but, from the very beginning, in solidarity—Péguy with a group of friends and fellow workers of the most diverse tendencies seeking to act as a leaven and a magnet. Christians are reminded that they cannot shrug off their responsibilities with a few charitable works. 'The alarm has been well and truly sounded on the subject of a certain kind of intellectual modernism that hardly attains the measure of a major heresy but is only a sort of witness to the poverty of the modern intelligence. Infinitely more serious is the modernism of the heart; Christianity is no longer socially an underground religion, a religion of the people, a temporal and eternal people, a religion rooted in the deepest foundations of temporality, but a pathetic kind of "better" religion for people who are supposed to have "bettered themselves" . . . . But it will not win back the centres of labour if it is not prepared to bear the cost of an economic, social and industrial revolution—in short, an earthly revolution for the sake of eternal salvation'.[18] What is said to the socialists is just the opposite: the earthly revolution is made for the sake of the freedom of the person. This freedom, which Péguy demands as a primary condition,[19] immediately collides with the interests of the party politician. More and more, he exposes such men as concerned only with power, betrayers of the spirit and the person; their anti-Christianity is nothing but a new and more insubstantial counter-Church,[20] their atheism a new mythology with massively unexamined metaphysical

[18] B 592–595.

[19] A 1112; B 10; B 61.

[20] B 810.

assumptions,[21] their free thinking a new variety of clericalism.[22] Péguy's first creative period (1900–1905) is taken up in this struggle against the dragon of socialist pseudoreligion that had sunk to a position well beneath authentic Christianity rather than itself surmounting it. 'There is nothing to be compared with a total life such as Christian and above all Catholic life was other than a new totality of life, a total revolution—that is, a deeper grounding; *res nova*, the Latins said, *vita nova* we shall say, for a revolution consists essentially in a deeper entrenchment in the unexhausted resources, the wellsprings of the inner life. And therefore the great figures in revolutionary action are men whose greatness lies in their inner life: meditative and contemplative men; it is not the men of external concerns who make revolutions, but the men who live an interior life.'[23]

These deeper sources are in fact nothing other than early Christian ideas; the breach with the Church for the sake of solidarity must be followed by a second breach with shallow political socialism. But woe to the man who makes a break twice in his life. It is only this 'second wind of courage'[25] that makes him absolutely alone, isolated; it gives him authority as a witness to truth and makes him an exile from any party. Neither his first nor his second group of friends will forgive him this 'second leap'.[25] He experiences the 'modern social and secularized version of Hell'; the 'scientific methods of contemporary ostracism, total boycott'.[26] For the sake of his campaign for the truth, Péguy travels this path of suffering to the ultimate degree of privation for himself and his family. Betrayed by his comrades,[27] he defends his work to the last breath, the work that appeared to him 'the most important of undertakings',[28] the one solitary sanctuary of absolute truth and freedom,[29] '*la misérable petite boutique essentielle des Cahiers*',[30] which at least had stood for '*un certain noyau de résistance*.'[31] In his darkest hours, he cannot avoid the realisation of his 'wretched

[21] A 1072–1073.
[22] A 1297.
[23] A 1388.
[24] A 1017.
[25] A 1022.
[26] A 1024–1026.
[27] A 458; B 56.
[28] B 6.
[29] A 468.
[30] S 318.
[31] B 61.

situation' between the times, in a sterile present that is only a period, not an epoch,[32] and can only admit the shame of his total defeat. 'We have been conquered. There is a secret gnawing certainty that tells us that in success there is always a residue of impurity, in victory always a residue of coarseness, . . . that there is and can be complete purity only in misfortune, and that therefore historically the great and secret honour and glory are always the lot of the fallen.'[33] But it could also be that this secret glory remains completely invisible in worldly terms, that a deed of the highest courage may be entirely wasted. Clio does not concern herself with the vanquished, and if they appeal to history for vindication—as to the juster judgment of later generations—these naive folk do not realize how powerless Clio is.[34] She is concerned with results;[35] and so she can 'never do more than bring to light the suns that have set'.[36]

The second period (1905–1909) is marked by a retreat from direct involvement in the times, a distancing, in order to get a general view of the period itself, the event of the present. Péguy's youth drew its finest inspirations from a threefold, through still unified, taproot: Antiquity (the natural piety of the pre-Christian era), Christianity and national history that for Péguy flowed in an organic stream from the Middle Ages up to and including the French Revolution. In 1880 occurs the first catastrophic interruption: the three sister worlds sunk down together to yield to the *monde moderne*, the rising tide of the post-Christian era. Its characteristics are these: a view of man as a mere calculating intellect, Kantian formalism, Hegelian systematising, the ant-like labours of German philology, psychology and sociology in place of philosophy, the loss of relationship with God, the loss of all real nourishing roots, the quantifying of all value, the triumph of mathematics and technology all along the line, the shallow optimistic ideology of progress, and money as the only real force in the world. Péguy's great analyses of contemporary nonculture, analyses related in many ways to those of Nietzsche, Bloy and Chesterton, are the

[32] B 508–509, 511.
[33] B 36–37.
[34] B 19; B 207–214.
[35] B 19–28.
[36] B 35.

warning cries of a Cassandra faced by the threat of total loss. How restricted on earth are the zones of true culture and authentic humanity![37] And these small islands are capable of being swamped, really and irrevocably;[38] as of old, the barbarian stands at the door once again, more terrible than ever.[39] From the time of the Tangier episode of 1905, Péguy knew with absolute certainty that war was unavoidably drawing near;[40] resisting all pacifist and internationalist illusionism, he steered himself and held himself constantly ready, in the utmost of alertness and tension, for battle and death.[41] He fell in the first days of the World War in an attack, shot through the heart.

One great name besides those of the detested lesser idols of the contemporary Sorbonne—Lavisse, Lanson, Durkheim—dominates Péguy's critique of the age: that of Renan. The embodiment of apostasy,[42] elevated by the contemporary anti-Church to be its official symbol (with the dedication of his monument in Tréguier),[43] surrounded by an atmosphere of elusive and unreal melancholy,[44] but the father of modern insubstantiality,[45] spiritually speaking he can generate afresh apostates who are loyal to him only because they are disloyal to him.[46] The basic textbook of the modern world for Péguy is Renan's *L'avenir de la science* (written in 1848), which dreams of the absolute progress of man and builds up the atheistic hope of a human collectivity higher and higher in an asymptotic approach to the divine consciousness by way of general cosmic evolution and the totally comprehensive sciences of the world and of human history. Much in Péguy's astonishing and lengthy quotations from Renan sounds like an anticipation of Teilhard de Chardin; no doubt Péguy would have felt the same metphysical horror at the latter's work.[47]

Although this critique of culture was continued until the last years of his life, Péguy had resolved in 1909, after along pause

[37] D 24–25.
[38] D 36–38; A 927–928, 932–934, 939.
[39] A 736–737.
[40] A 811, 849–853; D 52–55.
[41] A 1251–1253.
[42] A 1016–1017.
[43] A 1031f., 1044–1047.
[44] A 1004.
[45] S 157–174.
[46] A 1051.
[47] A 700–740.

due to exhaustion, to devote his remaining powers to constructive work. He knew perfectly well that the modern world had not begun over night, that the spiritual apostasy of Christians had brought it slowly and unavoidably into being,[48] but also that a *ressourcement*, a plunging back into the wellsprings of primitive Christianity, was more important than any accusations. He reworked his socialist drama of Joan of Arc into a contemplative mystery play (the first part of which appeared in 1909)—the problematic issue of solidarity and damnation are not in the least muted as a result; rather they receive a far more truly Christian response and *approfondissement*. In all, some fifteen such 'mysteries' were projected, all of them circling more or less closely about the ideal figure of Joan, but only two were completed: the one on hope (1911), and the on on the holy innocents (1912). But from Joan the view leads on to the broadest Christian horizon. In *Eve* the whole of salvation history is unfolded: Jesus, grace, the new covenant are here in dialogue with the first mother of mankind, the origin of the Old Covenant: the relation of *enracinement* in the world on the part of God is here understood as belonging to the original source of the Incarnation. In the great poems on Chartres (*La tapisserie de Notre Dame*) the interpenetration of spirit and flesh is celebrated in its final simplified manifestation in the realised symbol of Mary.

During his period outside the Church, Péguy had married the sister of Marcel Baudouin, a friend of his youth who met an early death; she bore him four children. But the marriage was ill-starred; it was solemnised in a civil ceremony, and Péguy's wife resisted the idea of a Church wedding up to the time of his death. Péguy did not want to put pressure on her in this respect, and so he too abstained from the sacraments after his return to the Church, and his children remained unbaptized (after his death, his wife converted to the Church, and the children were

[48] On this, see especially the analysis of the epochs of Philip the Fair, and of Mazarin and Richelieu, D 112–116, B 1376–1378, the treatment of the philosophy of the Enlightenment, D 116f., the evaluation of the French Revolution as an attempt to restore a primitive and natural ethic, A 1377–1378 and elsewhere, the judgments on Michelet, D 133, 190f., A 278–279, and on the history of the 19th century, D 127–132, B 520–522.

baptized). No resentment on this score embittered the lonely Péguy. He always mentions prayer and sacrament in the same breath,[49] and against a one-sided clericalist overvaluation of the sacraments, he simply makes the point that prayer 'is at least the half of it'.[50] His sacramental theology is distinguished by a deep sense for what is proper for the life of the Church; he stresses the distinct character of each one. The Eucharist and confession he puts in the foreground as the sacraments of life, seeing in the other five nonrepeatable acts of consecration (to life and death) and of the sanctifying of particular states of life.[51] His desire is to have a 'sacramental heart'. He aims to demonstrate the 'indelible' nature of Christianity by appeal to the indelible character of some of the sacraments.[53]

In 1910 Péguy lost his heart to a Jewish girl. It was a great and painful love, an experience that shook him to the core. But the demand for purity in his life preserved him from any ambiguity, any aesthetic transfiguration of earthly Eros. He gave up any claim on the girl and led her to marry someone else. 'I worked uninterruptedly so as to bring myself to my senses. Rather be a little unwell from overwork than endanger my mission because of an aberration of the heart. True Christian resignation is no apathetic affair; it is the extremity of being torn apart.'[53] He calmed himself in Chartres before the Mother of the Lord:

> Et pour bien nous placer dans l'axe de détresse,
> Et par ce besoin d'être plus malheureux,
> Et d'aller au plus dur et de souffrif plus creux
> Et de prendre le mal dans sa plein justesse
> Par ce vieus tour de main, par cette même adresse,
> Qui ne servira plus à courir le bonheur
> Puissons-nous, ô régente, au moins tenir l'honneur,
> Et lui garder lui seul notre pauvre tendresse.[55]

[49] B 259; B 1187, 1235.
[50] L 138.
[51] B 431–436.
[52] Missing Copy?
[53] B 431.
[54] Letter to Mme Favre, 4 Sept. 1910.
[55] *Prière de Confidence*, C 698.

All this is no less important for the understanding of Péguy's theological aesthetic than Kierkgaard's broken relationship with Regine Olsen, or Dante's relationship with Beatrice or Claudel's with his Polish sweetheart, the original for Dõna Prouhèze. But here there is neither a theological transfiguration of Eros nor a flight from it, but a lacerating faithfulness to an indissoluble marriage without any kind of transfiguration. *Axe de détresse* rhyms with *pleine justesse*, but also with *pauvre tendresse*. It is precisely these freely sought hardships and an entirely un-Kantian disregard for his own predilections, his own tender feelings, that brought to Péguy the grace to penetrate more deeply than any other Christian poet into the secrets of the tenderness of God's heart, which is more deeply within the heart of man than the heart of man itself and is, most purely and simply, Agape. A man humbled in every way has been granted the privilege of uttering words, beyond all the fluency of theology to date, spoken as from the centre of God's fatherly heart, that reveal the glory of the *kenosis*.

2. PROPHECY AND THE TRUE ISRAEL

Péguy's destiny and his thought are indissolubly bound to Israel. Two major encounters made a decisive impression upon him at the outset of his career: the Dreyfus Affair and the philosophy of Bergson. Together they furnished him with his determinative pair of categories (comparable to Kierkegaard's pair of 'aesthetic' and 'ethical' but entirely opposed to it): *mystique* and *politique*. '*Tout commence en mystique et finit en politique*':[56] everything begins in an original intuition and a truth lived out and ends in its subordination to other ends and so in untruth. So one might paraphrase and elucidate the basis meaning of these two basic concepts (awkwardly chosen, perhaps, and not fully corresponding to Péguy's ultimate inclinations). 'The founders come first. Then come those who exploit their work'.[57] For Péguy, involvement in the Dreyfus business was a holy, almost sacramental symbol of ethical purity and integrity; but it is

[56] B 516. [57] B 619.

precisely a symbol that develops itself in the public arena of the *polis*, the state. The adoption of Bergson's governing idea presses him into direct intuitive contact with reality, beyond all the conceptualisations of scholasticism, dialects or the 'exact sciences' of the modern world, toward a contact that is directly revelatory and of binding force.

It is clear from the convergence of these two influences that Péguy was working his way toward the Jewish prophetic tradition, which emerges clearly in the third decisive figure, that of Bernard-Lazare. In this atheist, 'overflowing with the Word of God',[58] Péguy saw 'the secret friend, the hidden inspirer, I might gladly and quite rightly say the patron of the *Cahiers*',[59] precisely because he was 'the prophet and interior master' for God's renewed testing of Israel,[60] which had experienced its usual fate in the political mishandling of the Affair. 'The complete misunderstanding, the disappearance from view, the isolation, neglect and contempt into which it was allowed to fall, or made to fall, or by which it was allowed to go to its ruin. Or abandoned to its death. The misunderstanding of the prophets by Israel, and yet the leading of Israel by the prophets: that is the whole history of Israel.' Péguy adds (drawing on Pascal): 'The misunderstanding of the prophets by Israel is a figure of the misunderstanding of the saints by the sinful.'[61] Bernard-Lazare first taught Péguy the old Jewish virtue of 'gentleness, goodness, mystical tenderness, even-temperedness, experience of bitterness and ingratitude, perfect assimilation of bitterness and ingratitude',[62] and then also the 'eternal trembling and resonance' with inner events, the concord that gives to the critical judgment a keenness that cannot be deflected, an essential 'exiledness' that is half essential terror, half essential courage. It is this that characterises the situation of all Israel and again and again thrusts it against its will into a dreaded and unwanted heroism. This mortally sick man whose last remaining friend Péguy was, showed him the present age in its true colours; 'he was, like all authentic prophets, a prophet of dis-

[58] B 572.

[59] Rolland, *Péguy* I 77.

[60] B 549. 'One of the greatest prophets of Israel', B 14.

[61] B 551.

[62] B 552.

aster, at least of temporal disaster',[63] well versed in temporal affairs precisely because he knew the real distinction between the eternal and the temporal and the character of their interrelation.[64] This gave him an 'elemental freedom, primordial freedom'[65] and thus a distanced perspective to see even the greatest historical systems—Judaism, Christianity, Islam, et cetera—from outside in an 'international perspective', a distance 'that none of us has attained'.[66] In his fragment of a portrait of his friend, Péguy relates the whole matter in Bersonian categories: the springs of historical events lie far deeper than the level allotted them by the judgments and evaluations of scientific history. This method will and must always control its material by making evaluations of a juridical and political nature. But only the prophetic vision (which Péguy allows to Michelet as well)[67] can 'accompany in everlasting movement the everlasting movements of everlasting spiritual reality'.[68]

Alred Dreyfus, a general staff officer of Jewish extraction, was convicted in 1894 of espionage; Colonel Picard, convinced of Dreyfus's innocence, was exiled; after Bernard-Lazare, Clémenceau and Zola took up the battle on behalf of the innocent man. The real culprit, Major Esterhazy, a proficient confidence trickster, was expelled from the army in 1898, but only on the grounds of other crimes. In 1899, the sentence of 1894 was commuted: Dreyfus was sentenced to ten years' imprisonment in consideration of mitigating circumstances, and a week later he was pardoned. The Parliament determined to resist any further reconsideration of the trial. Dreyfus's innocence was never fully recognised. 'What matters is that a statement of plain justice has never been accepted in this matter. It means that no court of law in the France of the Third Republic possessed sufficient authority actually to administer justice'.[69] Even when Clémenceau came to power, he could not risk a legal confirmation of Dreyfus's proven innocence. Péguy

[63] B 15.
[64] B 570.
[65] B 587.
[66] B 598–590.
[67] A 278f.
[68] D 235.
[69] Hannah Arendt, *Elemente und Ursprünge totaler Herrschaft* [*The Origins of Totalitarianism*] 1955, 155.

gave his loyalty to this reluctant hero to the last the Affair, which was soon hushed up and petered out, not least because the hero himself 'betrayed his own renown',[70] remained for Péguy what it truly was; the concrete symbol of injustice in the world, the *politique* that betrays *mystique*, the textbook case of how a people, a state, can 'sell its good faith and lose its soul',[71] 'fall into a state of mortal sin' and 'gamble away its eternal salvation'.[72] Theologians of a juridical cast of mind may treat sin as a 'finite, limited act'; but in doing so they fail to see how guilt can become, for an individual as for a nation, an atmosphere, an all enveloping reality.[73] Péguy investigated this condition more extensively in his analysis of the 'modern world', a condition that, in the hollow life of the intelligentsia, 'becomes a lasting state of sin, and even—quite evidently—because of the gravity of its matter a material state of mortal sin, in which the evil intention is only formally absent'.[74] The illusionism of scientific activity is shown up in the Judaeo-Christian light of the Sermon on the Mount: 'Whoever is unfaithful in spirit has already committed adultery in his heart. Any unfaithfulness in respect of reality itself is, almost before it has been entertained (and such entertaining is always the beginning of its realisation), for us something of infinite and eternal import'.[75]

The Jew is condemned, willy-nilly, to reality. Although no hero by nature, he must play the hero and martyr on the stage of world history. 'Whoever is marked down must march. Whoever is called must answer. He is appointed to be a public person.'[76] It is true of Dreyfus, as it is of Israel; Israel's history is in its depths the same as that of the Christian world. Jews, like Christians, naturally have 'a fear of violent assault, a fear of *affaires*, a fear of their own greatness', and thus always use *politique* against their own *mystique*. The Jewish Dreyfus party demonstrated this with sufficient clarity: 'They could think of nothing but sacrificing Dreyfus to still the storm.'[77] Jews are indeed possessed of 'a good memory, fifty centuries of wounds and scars, of neurasthenia. They were so frequently whipping

[70] B 637.
[71] B 524–525.
[72] B 643, 646.
[73] B 820–822.
[74] S 211.
[75] S 219.
[76] B 637–638.
[77] B 545–546.

boys for the whole world, for ourselves. Israel's *politique* consists essentially in never making a fuss. But Israel's *mystique* consists essentially in Israel's pursuing in the world its painful mission, which resounds to the furthest corners of the earth. It is the prophetic race. It is as a whole, in one single body, a single prophet.'[78] It lives as a people *à l'intersection* and is left there doubly defenceless. '*Ils subissent ensemble l'inquiétude verticale et 'inquiétude horizontale ... verticale de la race, ... horizontale de l'âge, du temps.*'[79] Here one can recognise the hidden kinship with Joan's mission, who likewise lived at this point of intersection: '*Elle est à un point d' intersection unique dans l'histoire de l'humanité*', she lives 'in the deep eternal contradiction between the temporal and the eternal'.[80] But Joan's point of intersection is, on the level of her unique mission, the same place as that in which the everyday Christian in the world has to live; 'he has the experience of touching the very point of articulation, the point of intuitive penetration' reciprocally between time and eternity.[81]

So it may be that when Christians evade the pain of this 'intersection' and take refuge in the spiritual, the Jews are brought in to remind them of their mission. 'If God in his Church were to receive a full measure of service (he is served there with punctiliousness, but with such a meagre punctiliousness), then perhaps he would not need to recall, when he wished to bestow some great grace in the life of intellect and reflection, that he still has the people of his original servants at his disposal.'[82] For Péguy the Old Covenant is not simply persuaded, all the less so because he sees its relation to the new as very close to the relation between nature and supernature. Christianity eternally rests upon the foundation of the ancient world as on the foundation of Israel, and thus

> the perspectives of the first law can in no case be surrendered. Jesus came to bring us a second law. He came to crown the order of nature by the order of grace, but not by means of the devaluation of the natural order. He would be wrongly understood and wrongly served if people sought to establish his

[78] B 546–547.
[79] B 1017.
[80] B 627.
[81] B 1246.
[82] B 1355.

kingdom on the destruction of the primary foundations. Creation was the preparation for salvation; the Fall required the atonement. The mystery of the first and of the second convenants, the mystery of God the Father and the mystery of God the Son, are in direct interplay as the two essential elements in the mechanism of our salvation. Any disposition of the spirit that tended to lose sight either of nature or of grace, of the first law or the second, God the Father or God the Son, would by a symptom of some profound loss of balance. One may search the gospel in vain for any trace of contempt: all there is love (and nothing is more opposed to contempt). The terrifying wrath that flows beneath the surface of the Gospels is not wrath against nature or against man confronted by grace, but wrath directed only against wealth. But wealth, the axis on which the modern world turns, is no less opposed to nature than it is to grace.[83]

The fact that Jesus was a Jew, in solidarity with his people and their destiny, remained for Péguy the starting point for the attainment of a right balance between *spirituel* and *charnel* (or temporel).[84] God does not come into flesh, into historicity, simple to turn away from the world. Péguy reproached the clergy and the monks for having upset the balance in favour of the spiritual, leaving behind the concerns of Israel instead of bringing them to fulfilment. As a disciple of Pascal, he was well aware that Israel is a figure—'*la figuration est un des mécanismes essentiels du sacré*'[85]—but a figure that in Jesus is filled out and perfected.

Jesus came as a creative personality in order to save the whole world. He was neither a 'secular' nor a 'regular'. That is to say, he was neither exclusively. He was not exclusively and strictly secular, nor exclusively and strictly regular. You could well say that the question did not arise. He was simultaneously and truly worldly and spiritual, both together without separation or any possibility of separation. He was what we have ever since (after their separation from one another) called the secular and monastic Christian, both together in unity. Nevertheless, the original Christian enterprise was one that entered into the world, not one that retreated from it. Worldly existence is evidently the

[83] L 186–187.
[84] J 68–70.
[85] B 792; *cf.* B 551.

> object; the norm (or that which has since become a norm) was that from which nourishment was drawn.

'Spirit' in ancient culture was certainly no more than it was in Israel; it was a source of nourishment, a force for the transformation, a distanced cast of mind, simply 'registering' its view of the world.[86] Thus Joan of Arc serves as a representation of Jesus and thus too as a representative of Israel.

Right up to the end, Péguy continued in persistent dialogue with Israel. Even in his last work, the *Note conjointe*, he extended his discussion with the Jew Benda (an anti-Bergsonian) about Bergson and gave it an eternal dimension. Here it is the ancient people (who in their experience of suffering, their endurance and rejection, and with their Scriptures and their culture are so much ahead of the younger people, who still persist in their rebellion against the order of this world) whose voices are heard urging their own concerns and carrying the day.[87] Many Jews, in more or less close association, were companions in Péguy's destiny. These included Albert Lévy, librarian at the Sorbonne, who had made the pilgrimage to Domrémy and Caucouleurs with Péguy; Jules Isaac, who followed and defended the path Péguy had taken, and Pierre-Marcel Lévy; the poet André Spire; Gaston Raphael; Julien Benda; Eddy Marix, to whom the book on hope is dedicated; Daniel Halévy, with whom Péguy had a vigourous dialogue in *Notre jeunesse* about the *mystique* of Dreyfus—a contest, with no holds barred, about friendship and mission—and who dedicated a report to him; and Edmond Fleg. The *Cahiers* constantly carried information on the situation of the Jewish community in the world at large; and articles by Aaron (Delahache), and the long short story *Chad Gadya* by Zangwill (with a long introduction by Péguy) were also given space. The great love of Péguy's life was a Jew; and Pauline Benda (Mme Simone) was a confidante of his.[88]

Over and above all these, Bergson remains the spiritually decisive figure, the Bergson who in those initial years of his

[86] B 367–368.

[87] B 1311–1321.

[88] Jules Isaac, 'Les amitiés juives de Péguy', in *Expériences de ma Vie* I (1959), 304–311; Mme Simone, *Sous de nouveaux soleils* (1957); Rabinovich, 'Péguy, témoignage d'un juif', (*Esprit*, June 1939).

career was not yet unequivocally clear in his teaching; he is the great source of stimulation, from whom a variety of pathways branch off in diverse directions. One line of development led directly from the *Evolution Créatrice*, with its evolutionary optimism (in which life finally attains to spirit), to Teilhard de Chardin; another was seized on by the neo-Thomists and employed in bringing Aquinas to life (Maritain, Sertillanges and the school of Maréchal, which on this point was also fertilised by the influence of Blondel, and which has had so powerful an effect in Germany as well). Péguy, however was not interested in a Bergson interpreted in these ways: his reality is the historical existence of humanity withits deeply-rooted decisions, and for him the revered master is a religious thinker standing between Judaism and Christianity. And Bergson, who once said of Péguy to Tharaud, 'He has come to know my most secret thoughts as I have never expressed them myself but as I would have wanted to express them'—Bergson in his own development, perhaps not without some covert influence from Péguy, was to vindicate this statement, setting the concept of incarnation at the heart of everything, from the ethical as well as the aesthetic point of view.[89] What Péguy demanded—and took over—from Bergson was his vision of reality, which is unjustly 'thought of as agnostic, domineering and superhuman, as opposed to the discursive method, which is thought of as scientific, human, modest, clear and distinct'. The exact opposite is true.[90] The desire to capture reality and to offer an exhaustive representation of it by means of an infinite discursive process is the real 'titanism', the graspong of modern science after equality with God;[91] but reality is inexhaustible, the more so the better one comes to know it.[92] The courage to engage with reality directly and without defence is in fact humility; this alone gives promise of success. Bergson's abiding merit is to have shown this simple and direct relation to reality (which

[89] E. Mounier, 'Bergson et Péguy'. A. Béguin, 'Note conjointe sur Bergson et Péguy', both in A. Béguin and P. Thévenaz, *Bergson. Essais et Témoignages* (1941), 319–335; André Henry, *Bergson, Maître de Péguy* (1948).

[90] A 699.

[91] A 1083; B 95, 324–329, 811; S 203.

[92] B 34; A 736.

Husserl again was to call for and to work through in his own fashion) as the pristine impulse in all the sciences. So 'in scientific work itself, in scientific discovery and development, the methods of art, the insights, intuitions and flexible responses of art, the inventive dimension of art' are at work.[93] Modern systematic thought, 'in its foolish arrogance' wants to omit nothing from its purview, and it believes that in this way it will avoid the need for decision and the choice of one thing rather than another. But 'it has nonetheless made a choice, against its will, in this attitude—a choice in favour of extinction'.[94] The correct choice, the free choice is the basis of intuition—indeed, it is one and the same thing as intuition: 'Choosing is an artistic medium. Choosing means to take the shorter way. And how shall one choose among the inexhaustible immensities of reality without a definite intuition, a definite and direct grasp, a definite interior grip on reality?' Anyone who creates, in however modest a way, who selects, leaves things out, has preferences, is behaving as an artist.[95]

This is the point at which the 'ethical' and the 'aesthetic' coincide for Péguy. The prophetic books of Israel bear witness to their identity, bear witness all the more clearly because the ethical dimension in the prophets always makes its appearance as the temporal and social and demands not only the interior, spiritual decision of faith, but also an exterior, national and often enough, genuinely political decision. It is to promote such a decision that the Word of the Lord is given, removing all illusions and yet laying claim to nothing less than the height of poetic utterance. By analogy with this, all the great poetry of the ancient world has a sacral character; but in Israel there is a complete absence of any kind of mythological fog, and the precision of God's pronouncement in the situation of decision becomes one with the potential precision of the human being as he makes a determinative decision for himself and thus becomes one with the immanent condition of the world itself. André Rousseaux recognised that this was the theme closest to Péguy's heart, rightly entitling his three-volume study, *Le prophète*

[93] B 809. [94] A 774.
[95] A 739.

Péguy. Prophecy here, of course, does not mean foretelling the future but knowing what God's righteousness demands in any particular instant; knowing how, from the standpoint of God, to assign to things and to human beings, to events and their configurations, their place in the overall pattern. The tangled threads of time are unravelled, and 'the system, as our geographers call it, is laid bare.[96] But one cannot wish to play the role of the conscience of the age' without being oneself involved centrally in it. Péguy founded a 'truthful review', *un journal vrai*,[97] in which he repeatedly heard the confessions, as it were, of France and of the modern world. And this he could do only in so far as he himself constantly 'confessed' before the general public, in so far as he was himself crystal clear and transparent. He understood that this was also the principle of Christian sanctity (and consequently of canonisation): however deeply the interior and hidden contemplative life may reach into God, 'the Christian of the early centuries was nonetheless always prepared for, always submissive to the discipline of public confession, a communal and, as it were, mutual confession. The ancient principle of public confession undergirds all Christian living.'[98] This openness, this complete externalising, opens one's eyes to the signs of the times and one's ears to the promptings of the Spirit: '*Des sourds avertissements profonds intérieurs, des pentes intérieures, de ces admonitions sévères et justes.*'[99]

It is perfectly clear that religious and poetic inspiration have their common roots here and stand in an interior relationship and analogy to each other so long as the poet is someone who tells a story for the whole nation, not a private aesthete, whose inspiration can have no deep roots because it cannot bear any ethical weight, and whose work will therefore never be truly influential in history. Péguy directs his polemical shafts against Laudet, who had claimed with regard to Joan that 'all visions are projections': 'By no means; they are communications, occasions of communion, occurrences of direct possession. Because of this and in respect of this they are visions. The other ways in which

[96] A 1027.

[97] A 96, 97, 99, 131, 444–446, 482, 742. *Cf.*Rolland, *Péguy* I 85.

[98] B 875.

[99] B 674.

God speaks with his creation and which amount to something less than visions, these are in greater or lesser measure projections.'[100] Beauty is found only in the exact self-presentation of what emerges from the accuracy of the innermost vision. 'After all, we are forty years old. We know what life is. It no longer satisfies us if we find a marble that is without blemish. We want to know whether the organic construction beneath the harmonious and incomparable folding of the rock is correct, whether indeed there is such a construction at all, whether being itself is correct, organised, organic.'[101]

The word that recurs again and again is *exact*. In his earlier, non-Christian days, Péguy wrote to a religious with whom he had become friendly and with whom he wanted to maintain his friendship: 'That an exact-minded humanist can keep up an exact-minded friendship with an exact-minded Catholic may turn out to be something indispensable for an honest clarification of our most important common origins.'[102] In a splendid fragment, he compares ancient culture to a great trireme: 'A miracle of exactitude, born of an exact people, with the perfect accuracy of its curves, a work of unadorned sincerity, which is still subtle, inventive πολύμητι'[103]—'perfect exactitude in the curvature of the flanks. And one should not even say "perfect". The word is a pleonasm.'[104] 'But the ἀκρίβεια of the Greeks has been wrecked, the delicate exactitude of the Greeks has sunk beneath the waves.'[105] After haunting Western humanism like a ghost ship, it has at last given way to the rigidity of mathematics, which arrogates to itself a monopoly of exactitude, 'confusing, as it does so, the abstract and the scientific'.[106] 'And now they talk indefatigably, inexorably, imperturbably, about exactitude!'[107] In his *Polyeucte* (which Péguy considered the supreme artistic achievement of French literature), Corneille had established a certain equilibrium in the relations between the ancient and the Christian worlds, between the pagan wisdom of the judge Sévère and the Christian wisdom of the martyr Polyeucte, a

[100] B 920.
[101] B 783–784.
[102] L 45.
[103] S 274–275.
[104] S 284.
[105] S 288.
[106] B 814.
[107] B 816.

balance that brings the ethical and the aesthetic into thoroughgoing correspondence and thus realises the concept of the classical. 'What constitutes the sublimity of the prayer [of Polyeucte for his wife, who is still pagan], what gives him his detachment and, at the same time, his exactitude, his strong, hard exactitude', is that it is first and foremost the completely human, incarnate prayer of an individual; but then, more deeply, it is that, in the situation of martyrdom, it is 'a secret, humble, Christian anticipation of the heavenly authority soon to be his. It is this that gives his prayer fulness, preeminent authority and complete exactitude.' It is an earthly prayer, and it is primarily 'a prayer of the whole Church triumphant that prays for the whole Church militant'.[108] 'The depths of the eternal aesthetic' are, so to speak, incarnated in the most transparent of earthly situations.[109] It is tempting to think back to Augustine's doctrine of number, in which numbers are transformed analogically into the realms of spirit and grace; or, again, to hark back to Pascal, in whom the same analogy of exactitude is repeated, this time in the leap forward from one level of order to the next. All true art is either classical or is not art at all—any other concept of the classical would be no more than Alexandrine.[110] The exact, the classical, is that which is correctly placed in relation to an 'axis'—that is indeed itself an axis and thus is the deeper point of illumination on the far side of phenomenal objects. The word *axis* appears everywhere. Genius, for instance, lays its span of life 'precisely along the axis of an age'.[111] That Christ came to save the world as a whole is 'the axis of Christianity'.[112] And within Christianity there is 'an axial, central level on which saints and sinners meet; around this axis they oscillate, forming in common an indissoluble system'.[113] And again, it is something 'at the axis and heart of Christianity' that looks for eternal salvation in the pursuit of temporal salvation.[114] Formally, the axis is the place of *justesse*; materially, it is the place where Heaven and earth, time and eternity, flesh and spirit, contemplation and action, grace and

[108] B 795–796.
[109] B 833.
[110] B 832–833.
[111] B 303.
[112] B 398.
[113] B 400.
[114] B 645–646.

achievement penetrate each other—not as two factors external to each other, but as realities that internally require and condition each other. This axial point is never attainable in terms of a synthesis, by way of a process of thinking, but only as the decisive involvement of a whole life. German idealism, and then, in Péguy's lifetime, the Sorbonne, imagined that Christianity could be decisively dealt with by some such systematic process. But just as the prophets resisted any synthesis between Yahweh and Moloch or Astarte, so Péguy resisted this modern amalgam. If one is a Christian by the decision of faith, then, to be sure, the ethical dimension brings the aesthetic with it; the latter does not remain as an indeterminate or supradeterminate neutral area over and above the basic decision about one's life. It is impossible to enjoy Christian truth, the Christian form of life, Christian liturgy or poetry in an aesthetic way and to defend them as culturally valuable (like the supporters of *Action Française*), without deciding for faith and discipleship. 'There are Christians for whom the Joan of Arc of M. Anatole France means next to nothing (and is certainly incomparably more dangerous than a mere nothing), and there are non-Christians for whom the Joan of Arc of M. Anatole France means everything.'[115] It is the eyes of faith that see the beauty of faith and the vacuity of its seductively dazzling opposite. These beauties are shut off from those who do not have the eyes of faith; in their existential depths they own a different aesthetic.

And yet, Péguy had set out by assuming the union of all who truly act in good will, be they Jews, pagans or Christians, and his concern was for the transformation of reality. Because Christian action failed, he appealed to socialist action. He was convinced, and he remained convinced throughout his life, that anyone who commits himself totally will find his way through the entanglements of all systems to the ground of reality. 'Let us study the book of reality, one of the rare books in France that are not written in German!'[116] What he valued in Descartes was 'that he deliberately pursued his thinking as if it were action itself. But the goal of his resolve was no less theoretical than

[115] B 960.

[116] D 41.

ethical'.[117] In contrast, he refused to allow the validity of the basic axiom in Kant, the idea that the maxim of every action should be capable of universal legislative force. 'We have other and infinitely deeper concerns. How many of our acts would be incapable of ever being elevated into general rules—and these are precisely such acts as are most valuable in our minds; acts done with trembling, with feverish shudderings of emotion, completely un-Kantian, acts done in mortal anxiety, perhaps our only good acts, by no means full of self-confidence, in no way without remorse, in no way securely guaranteed; but always challenged, always accompanied by the interior gnawings of conscience, our only good deeds, or just our least evil ones, perhaps the only ones that will count toward our salvation.'[118] They are the enterprises of our own selfhood, by which we alter both ourselves and something of a genuine reality as well.

To do this rightly is what the prophet seeks and requires from us, and what art, in its way, seeks from us, like the headless, eyeless archaic torso of Apollo in Rilke's words: '*Denn da ist keine Stelle, die dich nicht sieht. Du mußt dein Leben ändern.*' [For there is no place where you are unobserved. You must change your life.']'[119] Thus the problem of analogy, central for Péguy, arises again in connection with inspiration. Artistic inspiration too is directed toward incarnation: spirit becomes flesh. The idea that the great art of classical Antiquity has significance in relation to Christ as part of the Advent hope; that, despite its opposition to Christian faith, or rather precisely *because* of the opposition, it is engaged in the most lively dialogue with it—this is not for a moment in question so far as Péguy is concerned: it can simply be read off from the facts. But there can also be the post-Christian phenomenon of what might be called naive paganism, without any interior relation, either positive or negative, to the Christian reality; and yet even there the incarnational tendency can, astonishingly, be clearly discerned. In this connection, Péguy was throughout his life preoccupied by the figure of Victor Hugo (Balzac he never touches upon)—

[117] B 1281.
[118] B 825–826.
[119] *Sämtliche Werke* I (1955) 557.

Hugo, whose personal as well as poetic ambiguity he knows accurately enough and illuminates in a very humorous style;[120] and yet 'any weakness seemed to him preferable to the curse of barrenness. And who knows whether the waters that look so brackish and dirty to us from the bank were not just as precious to him, the parent stream?'[121] Occasionally he had what Péguy prized above all else: 'Eyes that saw the world as it was on the first day of creation. One thing that that man possessed was a fair share of Θαυμάζειν—triumphant mornings, the breaking of unbelievably glorious dawns. He could boast of having got himself a real pair of spectacles!'[122] Boaz lies sleeping in the harvest field, a slender crescent moon above him, and Ruth catches sight of it and wonders, 'What god, what reaper of the eternal summer has left this golden sickle so carelessly by the wayside in the cornfield of the stars:' Boaz dreams of an oak tree growing up out of his body as far as the blue heavens: '*Une race y montait comme une longue chaine. Un roi chantait en bas, en haut mourait un Dieu.*'[123] There is an atmosphere of primordial, chthonic time, 'where man the nomad wanders restlessly over the earth, an earth still damp and soft from the waters of the flood, soft enough to show the tracks of the giants' and a primordial pagan vision of all things bearing fruit on this earth, of the commingling of man and woman, and the heavenly fields of harvest above: 'never perhaps has any creature so directly penetrated into the fleshly core of creation, [*dans le ventre de création*]'; and it is from these bowels of creation (*sorti de son ventre*) that there rises the shoot, the stock, upon whose topmost point a God will die.

> Christians are accustomed to viewing the Incarnation as something communicated from the eternal realm, to viewing it from the side of eternity. But what gives this poem its value is that here we have a pagan (and a Jewish) vision of the Incarnation as emerging out of the Jewish and the pagan worlds, as a bodily

[120] '*Hugo était un faiseur*', B 705. '*D'avoir hasardé de bafouiller, tant, si carrément*; S 313. '*Rusé comme un lapin, double, duplice, avisé, retors. . . . Un vieux malin, en somme*', B 316.

[121] A 841.

[122] B 316.

[123] Victor Hugo, 'Booz endormi', in *La Légende des Siècles* II 6.

culmination, a bodily maturation, a fulfilment and a completion, the bodily bringing to fulness of a bodily sequence. The Incarnation is simply the supreme instance, the superabundant instance, a peak, a limiting case, the ultimate drawing together into a single point of this everlasting infusion of the eternal into the temporal, the spiritual into the carnal, which is the hinge, the cardinal point, the joint, the elbow and knee, the entire creation of the world and man and which indeed brings it into being. . . . Any kind of sanctification that is abstract, withdrawn in a crude manner from the world of the flesh, is a process without meaning or consequence. But there are still two ways of regarding the *et homo factus est*. Normally, Christians see it as issuing forth from the eternal; they contemplate this supreme insertion, this point of concentration, this drawing together in one point where the wholly eternal enters the wholly temporal. To find the counterpart to this, the view from the other side, the countervision, as it were, for a story that had happened to the earth—namely, that it had given birth to God—for this the earthly, the fleshly and the temporal realms, the pagan world (and also the mystics of the elder Law, the Jewish people) would need to see the Incarnation from their side. But this is just what they do not do; and, God knows, they can hardly be blamed for it. The Incarnation would have to present itself as the full flower and the temporal fruit of the earth, as an extraordinary triumph of fertility, as a superabundant but yet not unnatural growth; in order that we might consider God as he is on the side of his creation, emerging out of his creation, from a succession of creatures, from the lineage of David, which issues in God as it might in an ordinary bodily issue.'[124]

'Matthew the peasant' traces the succession of Jesus' ancestors according to the flesh: 'few men perhaps have so many criminal forebears.' Luke on the other hand moves backwards and upwards, 'he goes in search of Jesus and his temporal pedigree right back as far as the first Adam: *qui fuit Adam qui fuit Dei*. Homogeneously, unobtrusively and modestly, he goes back to our father Adam, and to Adam's Father, God'.[125] Creation too was a begetting; we pray to God as 'Our Father'. Luke 'puts great stress on the record of Jesus' paternity' and arrives back at the eternal Father who begets his Son through the medium of

[124] B 729–732.

[125] B 734–737.

humanity. And it really needed a pagan like Hugo for someone to 'hit on the idea, for someone to receive the vocation of contemplating one of the central mysteries of the Christian *mysterium* as a *témoin de l'extérieur*, a pagan'.[126]

So Péguy can write (in bold type) 'a pagan prophecy',[127] and the conditions of its possibility are weighed: there is 'some sort of mysterious osmosis between the realm of genius and the realm of grace, a mysterious outflowing and overflowing, a derivation, a discharge, an outpouring (in a carnal and spiritual manner) from the realm of grace into the realm of genius.' Despite all distinctions of 'orders', for the proof of such interpenetration 'we need only to look at the pagan pride of which this poem is so exuberantly full, the sense of well-being, the fleshly fulness, the sense of playfulness and entertainment, the constant provocations in its very vocabulary.[128] And Péguy, unperturbed by all warnings, all apocalyptic oppositions between Man-God and God-Man, makes directly for the point where both sides must meet on theological ground.

Genius is defined by its incomprehensible power to look into the deepest origins of things, and out of that to bring forth its fruits—against all the forces of alienation and existential obsolescence.

> The question about genius's residence among us poor men is one of the hardest ever posed to psychology, ethics and metaphysics. In the sphere of human psychology, human ethics and human metaphysics, it has precisely [*exactement*] the same problematic status as does the question about Christ's divinity in religious divine things. If one wants to regard theology (qua investigation of, or knowledge of God) as the limit toward which psychology and ethics (qua investigation of, or knowledge of man) is striving, as a part of metaphysics (qua investigation of, or knowledge of being), one might suggest that the question of the divinity of the Son of Man is, as it were, the limit toward which the problem of human genius is striving, and that both together are two distinct expressions of the overall problem of personality within being itself.

The modern science of man prides itself on its discovery of the

[126] B 738, 740. [127] B 746.
[128] B 752.

splitting of the personality. 'I am not claiming that the problem of genius can be completely reduced to these terms, but I do avow and profess boldly that it is a related question.' And if the problem of Incarnation in theology is one like that of dual personality, then the problem of genius appears as an immanent stage on the road toward a destiny that outreaches our longings, toward which 'the being that we already comprehend within our own selves and that we know in man' is orientated.

So our clever modern psychologists are making a great mistake in ridiculing the difficulties that beset our theologians. Whether for psychologists or for theologians, the difficulty is still the same, the concerns of both are equally alien to the inquiries of the logicians. The *mysterium* is the same. On the one side: God becomes man, God becomes the Son of Man, God descends into a man, living and abiding in him. On the other: genius becomes man, is born, lives, dies in a man; simply put (using Scholastic language for once), the divine problem or *mysterium* is a transcendent problem or *mysterium*, a transcendent form, and the human problem, *mysterium*, is an immanent problem and *mysterium*, an immanent form. I am amazed that it has not yet occurred to our young clerics, with their self-congratulation and their sporadic attempts to modernise the most ancient faith for the benefit of the Western nations, to rescue the dogma of the Incarnation by placing it under the sign—or under the cloak, let us say—of the psychological dogma of the splitting of the personality. I do not want to say that they will thereby serve their God as he asks to be served; they possess the eternal and yet see the temporal as a prop to lean on, they have the sacraments and yet occupy themselves with sophistries, they have the Mother of God and yet hurry to resort to any and every kind of psychophysiological laboratory; I am only saying that if our young clerics, who these days are so eager to imprison their ancient faith within the system of the modern world just at the moment when this modern world is creaking in every joint and stammering out the confession of its inability to interpret the course of human life—if these clerics were to bring to light the *mysterium* of the two persons, or to put it in the exact terms of Catholic theology, the *mysterium* of the two natures in one single person, which is the correlate of the mystery of the one person in two natures, and then, starting from there, and in analogy with this, to bring to light the *mysterium* of the one single God in three persons as the limiting case in the system of splitting of personality, then, I believe, they could seriously embarrass the *grands seigneurs* who influence the modern world.'[129]

That would depend, admittedly on the willingness to waive the claim that genius can be dealt with according to the rules of a psychology, ethic and metaphysic designed only to deal with the average, perhaps (and Péguy develops this in a lengthy satire) in such a way that the genius's immediate perception of the sources of things might be compared with the immediate perception of the child; so that, from the fact that we were all children once, we could broaden the argument into a generalisation that genius is only a more or less dormant potentiality in every human being.[130] This would in turn depend on the willingness to recognise the inalienable obligation and necessity attaching to genius, the obligation to live in a 'representative' way. 'The man of genius has behind him a whole mute nation, abandoned to the fate of historical (if not, indeed, eternal) death. He is the only person in today's world who can convey to us some idea of what the ancient chiefs or kings were when the whole nation represented itself, crystallised itself, concentrated and personified itself in one outstanding personality.' He is supported by all of this silent throng, produced by them, nourished by them; he is indebted to them and remains always in their debt. They have no other earthly immortality except through blood (their next of kin) and through him.[131] 'The true hero thus draws on the resources of his origins as from an inexhaustible well.' But it is this too which is the natural ground on which the saint's life grows. The saint does not merely represent; he transfers the virtues of hero and genius on to a higher plane. 'The melody, the *cantus firmus*, is identical—each in its own order, of course.' In the hero and the genius it is a game; in the saint, it is in deadly earnest.[132] And 'however various may be the living sources, adaptations and fresh resources of grace, there is still undeniably a certain technique, a certain hierarchy of expertise, a rule of the trade and a kind of skeleton structure for heroic virtue and sanctity

[129] D 204–208.
[130] B 319–329.
[131] D 156–157.
[132] A 1200.

alike', a definite 'measure of venturesomeness,' which was indeed *required* but never fully encompassed by the feudal laws of the Middle Ages.[133] The analogy between the two realms, then, is not only an external one, lying in the category of pictorial representation, but an internal one, despite all the contrasts between the two orders (as seen by Pascal).[134]

> It is precisely when the temporal sets itself up in diametrical opposition to the eternal on the matter of the object and the mechanics of the relation between end and means that it nevertheless continues to provide the eternal with a temporal shape, a temporal representation of the universal form. The temporal hero represents in his own mode the eternal saint. As the former is continually drawing his strength from his historical and racial origins, so the saint is continually drawing his strength from the strength of God's grace; and in a certain sense, *mutatis mutandis*, the communion of saints is for the saint, by analogical relationship, a kind of race, a point of origin; it means for the saint what race and roots mean to the hero. As the inheritance of blood wells up and overflows into the heart of the hero, so the blood of grace wells up and overflows into the heart of the saint—the temporal power of blood; the eternal power of grace; the eternal power of the eternal blood.[135]

But this eternal blood of Jesus Christ was itself temporal blood: in Christ the analogy is transformed from an external into an internal one; it becomes the inner mystery of his dual personality. Grace is in blood, and grace does not exist without blood.

Péguy develops the enormous consequences of all this again with reference to *Polyeucte*; because the Christian martyr must depict, represent, to the heathen sage who condemns him what is truly Christian in a way the latter can understand—on the level of the human, in the human mode. Polyeucte must hold up to Sévère his own ideal image, he must make what is Christian credible to him on the level of the human; it cannot be realised in any kind of 'as if' presentation (as Pascal's separation of the two spheres would dictate). Polyeucte must 'see his own likeness' in Sévère. And this appears clearly where nature exists in its

[133] B 1012. [134] A 1202.
[135] *Ibid.*

maximal form (as genius and heroism), and grace likewise in maximal form, in the witness given by the shedding of blood.[136] Here is a fair standard for self-measurement: the struggle is a matter of 'integral loyalty' and *noblesse*, although it is the saint who is the 'measure' of the hero, not the other way round.[137] And though Péguy acknowledges Pascal's competence in all this discussion, especially as regards the choice of Epictetus as the only figure in Antiquity ultimately worthy to be a partner for the martyrs, still, for him, Corneille here 'makes a significant step beyond even the *Pensées*' in that he, as a 'unique poet of the heroism of blood', becomes also 'a unique poet of the eternal blood . . . of grace'.[138] He brings the classical drama of the *analogia entis* to its supreme theological stage of creative development.

However, this interior quality in the analogy between culture ('Antiquity') and Christianity, as should now at last be clear, is not possible without the mediation of Israel and its prophetic tradition—both aesthetic and ethical, natural and supernatural. Where this mediation is absent, Jesus is no longer seen as emerging from a race and a particular history, but drops straight out of Heaven in Gnostic fashion. And when this happens, the relation between culture and Christianity becomes Platonic and 'aesthetic', in the dubious sense of the word: culture (classical Antiquity) becomes a symbolic system that is in no way indispensable (and which can simply be discarded by Luther), a system that (as in Pascal) is no longer recognised as belonging together at the innermost level—in virtue of the Incarnation—with what it symbolises. And so Christian reality becomes 'deed without image'.

3. THE METAMORPHOSES OF HELL

Péguy had abandoned the Church because the dogma of an eternal Hell seemed to him intolerable, yet he returned to the Church in such a way as not to have to foreswear the least

[136] B 1393–1394.
[137] B 1396, 1394.
[138] A 1203.

portion of his past. How did he manage this? If 'prophecy' has been singled out in the preceding pages as the formal focus of his world, 'Hell' must likewise be singled out as its material focus. His world stands or falls with the question of Christian exclusivity; and so too, therefore, does his theological aesthetic.

The starting point is to be found in a twofold work. Since 1892, when he was nineteen, Péguy had studied the life of Joan of Arc, which he turned into a powerful dramatic work, completed and published in 1897. At the same time at school he was an enthusiastic advocate of socialism, involving himself actively in relief work for the hungry poor, and in 1896 planning with his friend Marcel Baudouin a manifesto, *De la Cité Harmonieuse*. After Baudouin's death in 1898, Péguy completed this, and again published it—a kind of 'Holy Writ' of thoroughgoing socialism, a sacral *Utopia*, which set out the aesthetic-ethical ideal toward which humanity must strive, after the failure of Christianity, simply by its own innate powers of good will.

Both these earliest works of Péguy, contradictory as they seem, must be seen as a unity; the concern of both is the overcoming of Hell. The *Cité* is a *civitas Dei* constructed from below out of the stuff of the world and in which, essentially, there is no more possibility of exile. *Jeanne* is the interior overcoming of exile through a total engagement on behalf of one's condemned and banished brethren (even to the point of an interior experience of Hell).

The *Cité* in its very title presents the aesthetic category of harmony as the supreme value. It is an eschatological harmony, which everyone except Péguy would have regarded as merely utopian since it could seriously be realised only in the overcoming of any and every economic cultural and ethical disharmony, in a comprehensive work of art fashioned from the whole of humanity and effected by the whole of humanity, a work of art to which all egotistic and private sectional interests must be surrendered. Solidarity does duty for Christian *caritas*, and the whole is penetrated by the ideal of spiritual and bodily health, *santé*. The sacral term *pur* is everywhere, signifying a sense of life and a style of life that rest upon a personal and social relation to life and to being that has been completely healed and renewed—not upon a diseased relation, as with the Christian notion of purity.[139] In the *Cité* only healthy relations are worthy of attention, and thus only such relations are the object of scientific study. Men have 'discarded and renounced all knowledge of social disease'[140] from their historical tradition and themselves 'experience nothing that is in any way unwholesome'.[141] Since the human world, like all organic living being, is inseparably and equally both personal and collective, both sides are taken into account at once in a perfect harmony: collective entities, when they are established in progressively integrated stages will not overwhelm personalities but rather develop them; and persons will discover their freedom precisely in their integration by service into the community's life. 'In the harmonious *Cité* a soul is born for the *Cité*, and this soul lives and attains its full-grown form without ever displacing individual souls, the souls of families and friendships or nations, being born from all of these.'[142] The salvaging and defence of the personal world and of freedom from the threat of being overwhelmed by political force, the basic concern of Péguy in later years in his opposition to Jaurès and Socialist Party politics,[143] is already an aspiration here. But the horizon of the human spirit remains, for the time being, immanent being, the self-manifestation of the *logos physeōs*, as in Stoic thought; freedom and law here coincide. However, the transcendent horizon (of a personal relation to God) is not simply shut out. If human reason is essentially free,[144] then the state has no right to prescribe a normative metaphysic,[145] as for instance in the elevation of atheism into a state religion.[146] The consequences of this will be drawn out in the years immediately following, in the realistic light of a *cité désharmonieuse*; and this is why the inspiration of the original vision is never allowed to disappear. The primary requirement of the *Cité Harmonieuse*, that it should be a *cité sans exil*,[147] is never abandoned; and the second requirement, that within it the social apparatus should have a

[139] A 34f., 37f.
[140] A 77, 44.
[141] A 78.
[142] A 41.
[143] A 260f., 443, 447–448, 972–973.
[144] A 407–427.
[145] A 1075– 1076.
[146] A 313f.
[147] A 259.

subsidiary place in relation to the free creative working of the spirit in art and science and philosophy, is still more strongly emphasised.

In the *Reponse a Jaurès* (1900) we find the clearest formulation on this subject: 'We demand that science, art and philosophy should not be socialised, precisely because the socialising of the large-scale means of production and commerce, or, better still, of the means of manual labour (which is indispensable for the securing of the fleshly life of the *cité*), guarantees for the *cité* the leisure and freedom not to have to socialise any and every thing that does not lie within its sphere of competence but rather belongs to mankind as such.'[148] 'We have to learn how to distinguish humanity and society. We mean to prepare the way for this *cité* of mine, where *société* will organically cater for the concerns of the citizen so that he can occupy himself in complete freedom with the concerns of *humanité*.'[149] Even the idea of beauty as the supreme value is never rejected in later years by this ethical polemicist: it was at this point that he drew the dividing line between himself and Zola, with whom he was at one in his political programme. 'His works are for the most part intent on showing us the numerous mean and ugly features of humanity. I think the message of these books was damaging; it is not through horror at what is ugly but by the attraction of what is beautiful that we should teach people about beauty. The beautiful should ignore the ugly, just as Aristotle's God ignores the imperfect world.'[150] Péguy was later to feel obliged to go beyond the proposition formulated in these terms: the goal of inclusion came to take the place of simply ignoring what is ugly. But in spite of this, beauty as the standard of value is never surrendered.

Only one rift, a curiously revealing one, appears in the artistic construct of the *Cité Harmonieuse*. Although bodily defects are to be reduced to an insignificant minimum, it is nevertheless part of the greatness, the harmony and health of the human spirit to suffer. This is an idea, like so many of the younger Péguy's, that reminds one of Nietzsche, although it derives

[148] A 264.
[149] A 258–259.
[150] A 556.

from completely different sources 'The sane and healthy sorrows of the harmonious soul are endlessly nuanced; occasionally they can increase to the point of extreme agony and extreme suffering. They increase in power and beauty to the utmost point of the endurance of God's absence, especially in doubt, separation and death.'[151] Here the poet who celebrated Joan of Arc leaves room for his socialist heroine, who had made her way to the *Cité* only through the experience of Hell.

In progressing from the socialist drama, *Jeanne d'Arc* (1897), to his Christian work *Mystère de la Charité de Jeanne d'Arc* (1909), Péguy did not need to delete a single sentence: he simply added clarificatory material to the text. The *Mystère*, in Péguy's overall plan, proceeds by way of interpolation until the end of the first part of the first third of the trilogy is reached. But because this is where the inner drama of Joan's election is enacted, everything essential is in fact said in the account of the motivation of this election. The remaining two thirds of the trilogy simply develop the consequences of this, retelling the external history—the battles, the imprisonment, the interrogations and attempts at intimidation, the recantation and its subsequent withdrawal, the execution at the stake. Thus the *Mystère* could properly be restricted to the making explicit of the latently Christian themes of the initial conception, displaying them in all their breadth, height and depth.

The drama is dedicated to all those who gave their lives and deaths 'to remedy the general ills of mankind', and those who 'knew the way of salvation, which is to stake life and death on the task of bringing near the universal socialist republic.'[152] Joan suffers because of these 'ills', and her friend Hauviette recommends daily work on the land for her and the giving of alms to the hungry; but this is a drop in the ocean. Madame Gervaise has left her aged mother and taken the veil to pray for the world; but she cannot free herself from the suspicion of having deserted her post. Secular and spiritual tasks must be done together, and since destructiveness rages in the world in the shape of war, war to the death must be waged against war.[153] But destructive power is from the beginning seen by Joan, in a

[151] A 35.
[152] C 949.
[153] C 954.

wholly radical fashion, as the violation of the soul, the loss of salvation, damnation itself, all this rising like a flood ('*la damnation va comme un flot montant*').[154] And since Joan has not committed her whole life and death in the struggle against this Hell, she feels herself to be 'hopelessly cowardly, in collusion with the general evil'. Gervaise, reading her inmost thoughts, poses the decisive question: basically, it is no longer possible to love those of one's fellow men, one's brothers and sisters, who work their own damnation—'*tu ne peux pas les aimer*'. According to the Church's teaching, there is no expiatory suffering for the damned, just as their own suffering is fruitless. But Joan feels the loss of those she has loved as an eternal void in her soul: '*tous ceux–là que j'aimais sont absents de moi-même*'. And so she offers to God her own soul to suffer loss of God in order to save the souls mad with the pain of their loss of God. When Gervaise remonstrates with her, saying that the Saviour did not let himself be damned in our place but could offer only his human suffering, Joan does precisely that. But Gervaise transcends the limits of her own thinking as she now proceeds to describe the Godforsakenness of Jesus on the Cross: Jesus' suffering for the Hell-bound despair of Judas, for the impossibility of redressing his eternal damnation by his own temporal suffering, so passes our understanding that it becomes itself infinite.

Étant le Fils de Dieu, Jésus connaissait tout,
Et le Sauveur savait que ce Judas, qu'il aime,
Il ne le sauvait pas, se donnant tout entier.
Et c'est alors qu'il sut la souffrance infinie,
C'est alors qu'il sentit l'infinie agonie,
Et clama comme un fou l'épouvantable angoisse . . . ,
Et par pitié du Père il eut sa mort humaine.[155]

Before this paradox, Gervaise halts and stays: all that a Christian may do is to want to do no more than Jesus did, to adore God's will and seek to live in it. But Joan presses on into the heart of the darkness. She knows that Gervaise is right, that God is always right in what he ordains, but she is no longer able to pray so long as the thought is in her mind that there are souls damning

[154] C 957.

[155] C 960.

themselves. And so as not to be 'mad, in company with the rebellious spirits', she asks for a sign. She asks that the venerable shrine of Mont St Michel on the seashore, besieged for months, may be relieved. The sign is granted, the news of the liberation arrives, and the victorious battle at Mont St Michel at once becomes for her transparent to the apocalyptic battle of the archangel against Satan. Image and prototype merge with one another; the eternal battle againt Hell must be fought on earth. Praying alone, in place of acting, is cowardice; but soldiers in such a battle must be ardent for their good cause without anger, without any of the lower passions. How shall a leader be constituted who might tame all that is impure and brutish by the power of complete purity and so lead the way to righteousness?[156]

In what follows, there is a twofold thread of development in the drama. The one who is called by God is in the highest service and is answerable to God alone; Joan follows her voices consistently through all that happens, and that constitutes her freedom which is unintelligible to those around her, that freedom which others interpret as her arrogance.[157] Her commands are not open to discussion;[158] she will carry through the attack on Paris against the king's command;[159] she knows nothing of diplomacy,[160] and so she loses her best comrades in arms and inevitably becomes a stone of stumbling for churchmen, theologians and bishops. She submits humbly to the Church as far as its sphere of competence extends: '*Dieu premier servi*'.[161] So she is condemned as a heretic: the ecclesiastical judges (Péguy excels at this point in the drama) torment her. If she does not submit to the injunctions of ecclesiastical diplomacy, she is to be condemned not only to temporal but to eternal fire.[162] And Joan, shorn of all power, ratifies this condemnation in a long monologue: yes, she is damned and she will pass from the earthly to the everlasting fire.[163] The theologians' blasphemous playing with the idea of damnation is only the incidental music that leads from their

[156] C 971–972.
[157] C 1084, 1120.
[158] C 1038f., 1048, 1065, 1097.
[159] C 1080, 1108, 1113.
[160] C 1055f., 1072f., 1108f.
[161] C 1161.
[162] C 1181–1183.
[163] C 1187–1193.

playing with predestination,[164] by way of the trivialising of Hell itself ('*qu'importe qu'elle se damne*'),[165] to the justifying of torture and the stake as a means of saving Joan's soul[166] (Jesus' trial too only brought the world good), and to the idea that 'she must be burned in any case': 'for if she is a witch, she has deserved no less, and if she is a saint, it will win her a better place in Paradise where she will be better able to pray for us'.[167]

The second sequence of motifs is less happy than the first; it is meant to show that even the purest soul, when it comes into close contact with earthly reality, cannot remain spotless. Already, to free herself from her parents, a kind of lie is necessary, which continues to weigh heavily on Joan's conscience; and she is pursued ever anew by involuntary lies and defilements.[168] But this motif is necessary in that it gives Joan an inner consciousness of guilt and so of solidarity with the damned. She suffers the pains of Hell not as something imposed from without, but as her own proper fate. The great concluding emphasis is wholly on the willing acceptance of damnation in the night of the spirit. What comes afterward has little power—the prayer to God to forgive and 'if possible' to save all. The strongest positive stress is at the beginning, where Joan, after receiving her sign from God, is able to pray again and, in the spirit of the *Cité Harmonieuse*, can utter an eschatological and socialistic Paternoster for the salvation of the whole creation.[169]

Péguy's point of departure in these two works, the *Cité* and *Jeanne*, is a dialectical knot; the task of its unravelling is pursued through all his works. Why then does Péguy, for the time being a non-Christian, build so irremovably into his world picture the Christian problematic of Hell? Because (he said), the question, once it has been raised by Christianity, can never again be silenced, even though the answer remains unacceptable. In the Cross an 'infinite terror' burst forth on the world, and 'twenty centuries of Christianity have instituted a kind of ritual presentation of this infinite terror. Christianity has introduced the infinite everywhere, pushed up the prices in the market of

[164] C 1083–1084, 1128.
[165] C 1082; *cf.* 1095.
[166] C 1129.
[167] C 1201.
[168] C 1062f., 1102, 1110, 1150f.
[169] C 966.

values'.[170] 'You Christians', says Clio, 'are the most unhappy of people. And you are also the happiest. You have made everything infinite. You have made the measure of value infinite.'[171]

Even as a small child, Péguy (in the fragment *Pierre*) had encountered the devil in the stories told by his grandmother, the devil who longs to draw souls into Hell and from whom they are snatched at the last possible instant by the angels or by the pastor.[172] Later the question was posed in earnest: can any member of humankind be lost to the realm of God, which is also the realm of humanity? Can any member be lacking from the sum of all the others? Or, more clearly: is it possible that the others when saved will not feel his lack? The manifesto denies this: '*Aucun vivant animé n'est dans le cité harmonieuse comme un banni de la cité*'.[173] It is *la cité sans exil.*[174] Anything else leads to bourgeois egotism about salvation. 'You do not save your soul as you might save a treasured possession. You save it as you lose a treasured possession: in surrendering it. We must save ourselves collectively, we must arrive together before the good Lord. What would he say if we arrived before him, came home to him, without the others?'[175] It would be bad if someone were to 'love God against the interests of his neighbour, were to pursue his own salvation at his neighbour's expense'.[176]

What the young socialist writer of *De la Grippe* admired in Pascal (bearing it out in long quotations from the biography) was the latter's love for the poor: the fact that when mortally ill he wanted to be no better off than the destitute in the hospital 'who are infinitely more poor and sick than I'; that he wanted to be taken there himself and, when this was not permitted him, wanted at least to have one sick pauper sharing his house with him.[177] It is then that the problem of exile appears in relation to Pascal. A man of the ancient world would have experienced exile from the *polis* as something dreadful and longed with all his might for a return home, for νόστος. 'But when the *polis* had become universal, had become the eternal *Civitas Dei*, then the

[170] B 420.
[171] B 485.
[172] A 1218.
[173] A 23.
[174] A 259.
[175] J 44.
[176] B 1390.
[177] A 169–171.

earth itself became the place of exile, horror and death that we fear, and the longing for a homecoming came to be of ultimate importance.' The Christian God, 'slayer of other gods, was also their heir; in succession to Zeus, he became the god of the hospitable: his own hospitality is infinite, merciful toward all.' And in this system it is understandable that many Christians are over-eager to hasten away from their earthly banishment to the eternal *polis*. Pascal did nothing of the sort; his prayer was to persevere on earth as long as his mission from God consigned him to be here.[178] But why stay? Here Pascal's *cœur* points the way: we stay out of compassion for the suffering, out of solidarity, *charité*—as one does if one takes the word 'as Pascal understood it, in an absolutely fully operative sense',[179] and distinguishes it from any other sort of effectiveness in human activity and effort by means of a qualitative 'leap' (*saut*).[180] This 'leap' (out of the realm of the mathematical and quantifiable) into the realm of love displays Pascal as 'a perfect geometer and equally a perfect Christian',[181] because the leap itself had its own exactitude, and also because Pascal as a Christian did not renounce terrestrial, mathematical exactitude. Yet because Péguy was a good Christian, the temporal realm must have been for him banishment. 'Christians cannot have this deep-rooted taste for life and health, this kind of bondage to animal nature—I might almost say, to vegetative life'. Hence, in their lives the ruling influence is 'something uncertain, inexact, standing over against their own life—though it would not be difficult for me, even within Christianity to find a means of salvation despite all this. But it does seem to me to have been demonstrated that Christianity is especially complicated.' Under the pretext of uniting all extremes it is nevertheless a 'violation of life itself'. And when Christians had once reached the point of loving and affirming, for God's sake, the heavenly sentence of damnation on earth, it naturally followed that they were able to become familiar with the thought of an eternal exile, a Hell, 'this shocking hybrid of life and death.' 'But no one who has experienced the human lot or who has devoted himself

[178] A 182.
[179] A 184–185.
[180] A 188.
[181] A 179.

to it could accept this. No fellow citizen who has done no more than grasp the idea of solidarity could consent to it.' 'Our solidarity is with those who are eternally damned. We cannot bear that human beings should be treated inhumanly. We cannot bear that human beings should be turned away from the gate of any *polis*. That is the grand passion that animates us. We will tolerate no exception in Heaven or on earth. An eternity of living death is a perverse and unnatural piece of fantasy.'[182]

But even in Antiquity do we not already find just such a conception? Did not Creon let Antigone be immured alive in a subterranean cavern full of terrors? Lengthy quotations from the *Antigone* show that there is here, beyond any doubt, 'a pagan adumbration of Hell'. The reply to this objection is weak: 'The harmonious laments of Antigone and the harmonious but cowardly consolations uttered by the chorus seem to me dubious, but in no respect horrifying like the fantasies of the Christian Hell. The pagans, with their love of life and beauty, neither could nor would construct such a horror. At the root of Christian consciousness there must exist a repugnant accommodation with sickness and death, and that's an idea I cannot get out of my head. . . . Here there is indeed a *non possumus*. Whether or not Hell was invented as a deterrent for sinners, it has certainly succeeded more in horrifying the best sort of Christians.'[183] Such was the tone and timbre of the argument in 1900, the tone of the socialist manifesto.

In 1902, *Jean Coste*, a story about the condition of the poor by the writer Lavergne, appeared in the *Cahiers*; Péguy wrote a long introduction to it, and tackled the problem of Hell afresh from a new perspective. It has now become a question of the immanent Hell of the wretched of this earth, a question of the sharp demarcation between poverty (with the minimum necessary for life) and *misère* (with less than the minimum necessary for life). Destitution may be known from within or without: Zola knew it and described it from without, Lavergne from within. In the face of such destitution a Christian *charité*, which 'lowers itself' to help is an inappropriate, bourgeois stance. That such misery, such an exile from human society,

[182] A 192–193. [183] A 198–199.

should cease from the earth, is a matter of elementary social obligation. In terrestrial terms it corresponds exactly to Hell in Christian theology. Péguy remarks in passing that Heaven and Hell are related to each other in diametrical opposition as regards the question of time: Hell is 'being deprived of all time'; the horizon of the damned is built of infinite constraint, Hell is fenced around and not the slightest glimmer of hope filters through. In contrast, Paradise is an infinite openness to every kind of companionship and fulfilment. Even Purgatory belongs on this side of the divide; it is within the sphere of communion, while Hell is outside.[184] However, the reality of destitution on earth is more than merely an image of Hell. Whoever lives in real destitution has no hope of escape. 'The perpetual gaze he directs toward his own destitution is itself a look of destitution. What this produces for him is a uniform impression of total despair: destitution is his whole life, an unrelieved servitude; a taste of death is intermingled with the whole of life. Death, for the sages of Antiquity, was a final release, but for the destitute it is only a filling to the brim of the cup of bitterness and defeat, the very peak of despair. The destitute person is at the heart of destitution itself; he understands only in a destitute fashion, precisely because he has no belief in eternal life. The destitute person as we know him, as he has become through his exclusion from religious belief, has only a single room left to live in, and this is filled for him to the limit with destitution.' This cannot be imagined from without. From without it looks like a finite kind of suffering, but from within it is as infinite as the Christian Hell: '*Une absence particulière peut causer une privation totale*.' 'Human suffering extends its range to seize the place previously occupied by religious anguish, religious suffering', which was indeed qua human suffering, no less objectively limited.[185] 'Serious Catholics have always been preoccupied with the question of Hell—whether it has been out of concern with the question of whether or not their own souls would be damned (the problem of salvation was of capital importance; hence the many efforts to do away with Hell); or when they became heresiarchs and impugned the threatened pains of Hell; or as they sought to save

[184] A 496–498. [185] A 503–507, 501.

souls by faithful perseverance and immersion in the depths of their faith; or when, as nowadays, they decide in favour of unbelief and abandon the Catholic faith so as not to have to accept the doctrine of Hell. And it is quite certain nowadays that requirement of belief in a Hell of eternal torment is, for the great majority of serious Catholics, the most serious reason for apostasy.'[186]

But Péguy feels no relief after disposing of this dogma, because destitution, exile and hopelessness are still there. 'The cost of life has not gone down since the elimination of the Catholic faith. The value of suffering is undiminished. The value of the struggle to cope with it is always the same.'[187] 'To succour the destitute is one of the oldest concerns of true humanity throughout every culture; from age to age, fraternity—whether it appears as *caritas* or as solidarity, whether it proves its mettle in hospitality to a guest in the name of the hospitable Zeus, whether it receives the destitute as a figure of Jesus Christ or forces through a minimal wage for workers—fraternity in an eternal human sentiment.'[188]

Péguy always adhered to this equation.[189] Indeed, at the nadir of his own life, he himself experienced *misère* as bodily and spiritual indigence and deprivation and depicted it in moving words.[190] At the furthest limit, the idea of death or suicide prevails over life as a whole, 'sours life itself, the whole sum of existence, in a total interpenetration of life and death; it is a "living death", as I then (in *Jean Coste*) expressed it'.[191] This throws some light on the concept that (with only slight modifications) haunts the whole of Péguy's work: the concept of *tourisme*. Zola's depictions of destitution are indeed far blacker and more dramatic than those in *Jean Coste*, and yet, 'The conditions of the destitute in Zola are those we might find in a description given by a rigorously observant and often conscientious tourist, by someone on an excursion to view the poor.[192] Even where the French Revolution and the campaigns of Napoleon are concerned, it is still said that this is '*du tourisme*

[186] A 508.
[187] A 509.
[188] A 510–511.
[189] A 1131.
[190] B 63–64.
[191] B 64–65.
[192] A 519–520.

aussi. Naturellement du très grand tourisme'.[193] Clio had a similar comment to make on those historians who bustle around on the field of reality like demigods: '*Les historiens perlustrent le monde comme des amateurs.*'[194] The category gains importance above all in the controversy with Halévy. Halévy is a Jew of the wealthy bourgeoisie; he likes to travel and to talk amicably with ordinary people. Péguy *is* himself the people. For the peasants and vintage labourers Halévy is always '*un monsieur qui passe, qui leur fait l'honneur de venir les voir, un visiteur (je ne dis certes pas un étranger)*'.[195] The idea that even Christians in the Holy Land can only 'visit' the holy places like foreigners and tourists drives Joan of Arc (in the *Mystère*) beside herself.

> A pair of pilgrims, poor shabby pilgrims, go and ask the infidels for permission to 'visit' the Holy Sepulchre.
> Visit, visit! anyone would think it was an object of curiosity.
> Well, we shall see whether permission must be asked of them to conquer the Holy Land![196]

And now, at last, comes the relating of all this to Dante, whom Péguy wanted to rival in things concerning Hell and Heaven. 'Of course I know no Italian. But despite that, I have read this *Paradiso* of his. He invents, I discover. He is far stronger in his *Inferno*. But they all do this: they need evil and sin to make things interesting. I do not work in sin. I am a sinner, but there is no sin in my work.'[197] In *Eve*,

> everything is in the first-person plural. That means that nowhere in the course of this great long pilgrimage does the author appear as an historian or a geographer of Heaven and earth, as a visitor, an inspector, or, so to speak, a tourist—as a grandiose kind of tourist, perhaps, but still a tourist. At no point here is the poet someone on a trip—a grandiose trip, maybe, but still a trip. At no point does he take up a position on the sidelines so as to observe what is going on in front of him, because what is going on in front of him is himself—that is to say, it concerns his damnation or salvation. At no point does he take up his position on the pavement to watch the sinners go by, because the sinners are

[193] A 1192.
[194] B 276.
[195] B 688; *cf.* 680.
[196] J 316.
[197] L 170.

> himself. This immense multitude is what he is himself within, not something alongside it. The whole task consists in the right orientation of mankind, turned full-face toward the Last Judgment.[198]

Les Suppliants parallèles (1905), one of Péguy's finest works, offers a response to *Jean Coste*. Here he introduces a poem of Porché's, celebrating the bloody events of 1905 in Petersburg when the Russian workers marching to the Tsar's palace to present their famous petition to the monarch were greeted by the imperial guard opening fire on them and were decimated before the palace gates. 'Sire! We, the workers of the city of St Petersburg, our wives and children and our aged and infirm parents, have come to you seeking justice and protection. . . . We have fallen on hard times, we are destitute . . . we are treated not as men but as slaves who must endure their bitter and wretched lot with patience and accept it in silence. We do not ask for much, only for that without which life is not life at all but prison and endless torture. . . . Whoever among us dares to raise his voice . . . is thrown into prison, condemned to exile. . . . Sire! Is this the divine law in virtue of whose grace you reign? . . . We speak to you as to our father, honestly and openly.' Then follows the list of requests. 'But if you will not answer our pleas, then we shall die right here, before your palace.' Péguy's heart was touched at the innermost level. He contrasts the workers' document point by point with the ancient text that forms the prelude to the *Oedipus Rex*; both utterances illuminate one another, both evoke the eternal threnody of man's pleading for succour. But the one to whom the plea is addressed in the classical text is himself a suppliant, 'besought by men, he beseeches the gods; he does not separate himself from the suppliants who are his subjects.' And 'the formula of Christian supplication and, more generally, of Christian lamentation, drawn originally from the Messianic lament, is to be found, both in its full perfection and in its completest purity, in the words *Misereor super turbam*. I weep, I grieve, with compassion for the multitude.'[199] Only lately has the modern ruler abandoned his solidarity with those outcast from society.

[198] L 180–181.

[199] A 897.

The formulation of the theme is new and prepares the way for a motif soon to increase in importance: that of the *monde moderne* that has become inhuman juxtaposed as a contrast with the classical and Christian worlds (the latter understood in terms of its messianic origins) as the *humanum*. What is astonishing for Péguy is that the petition of the Petersburg workers is made in the most authentic tone of the supplications of Antiquity, which gives the suppliants their unique human and superhuman stature. For the Greeks, the suppliant, and the one who pleaded for succour, was the truly great man, for he represented humanity to the gods. But the fortunate man was the one to be pitied, because he is menaced by fate, because he falls victim to fate. The suppliant at his feet is in fact superior to him, for

> he is a representative. He is no longer himself alone—no longer even himself. Thus every other person must be on his guard. Dispossessed as he is by the same events that brought such precarious good fortune to the one being besought, a citizen without a city, a head without an eye, a child without a father, a father without children, a belly without food, a back without a bed, a head without a roof over it, a man without possessions—he no longer exists as himself. He is moulded by the human and suprahuman fingers of God, moulded and turned to the lathe. The gods and the Fate that stands behind the gods have deprived him of the *polis*. But the gods have given him his own city in return. It is in no sense a compensation, not even a sign of justice; and naturally it is not a romantic antithesis. It is something much deeper, much truer. Here men have put on record that they were the plastic material beneath the sculpting fingers of Fate.[200]

Thereby they achieve the 'higher tone'; they have received promotion (*élection* would no doubt be the Christian term) to the highest aristocracy that the essence of classical tragedy can delineate,[201] in which the 'opposition between the just and the unjust' is mysteriously transcended and balanced out.[202] Péguy here spoke only of supplication in the ancient world; Christ's supplication is no longer mentioned. But the line connecting Oedipus with Christ is drawn in cryptic fashion; each of them, as the one besought who is himself a suppliant, cast a bridge

[200] A 905–906.

[201] A 908–909.

[202] A 912.

between the hellish world of exile and the shelter of the *polis*.

The works that follow complete this turning toward the existential in various distinct forms of expression. *Notre Patrie* (1905) had already broached the problem of the relation between genius and the people: the mortal people, cut off from posthumous celebrity, have their immanent temporal salvation in the genius (and this is where Péguy sees his own burdensome mission as lying). 'His only true equal, his only brother, his only father, his only begetter is this poor, destitute and ignorant mass; to them he is bound for ever by a vertical bond'.[203] 'Dreadful responsibility! He is the voice, the expression, the revelation of this whole people!'[204] If he ceases to be a witness to what they cannot themselves be witness to, 'he annihilates himself, he destroys his genius'.[205] He becomes fair game for the sociologist: 'Neither the genius nor the people allow themselves to be sociologised—only talent allows that.'[206] In the *Cahier Mangasarian* (1904), the relation between conservation and revolution is dealt with: the conservation of a status quo requires only talent, but revolution on the contrary requires genius, whether it is that of individuals or the deeper genius of race and people 'or finally that specially profound variety that rises up out of a long-lasting experience of destitution (*misère*)'. The removal of organisation and the diminution of conservation will not create freedom; this emerges only where the revolution of the depths of national life and the focal point of genius bring with them and develop out of themselves and their own freedoms the power of organisation.[207] To eliminate this power, through the levelling alike of the springs of national life and of genius, is the programme of the *monde moderne*, and Péguy feels that he is its sacrificial victim. His destiny is inexorable ostracism; he will perish through total neglect, through deadly silence and the deprivation of air to breathe (*Situations* I, 1906). He experiences 'the modern, secularised, social Hell'[208] that is far more dreadful than any banishment in ancient times. But then the poet (in *Notre Jeunesse*, 1910), as he reflects on his origins, recognises that this fundamental exile was from the beginning

[203] D 161.
[204] D 160.
[205] D 166.
[206] S 253.
[207] A 1382–1385.
[208] A 1024.

rooted in his intentions and earliest decisions. The one who in the *Cité Harmonieuse* and in the Dreyfus trial had opted for absolute truth and justice could expect no other fate at the hands either of a bourgeois Catholicism or of a politicised socialism: 'There was infinitely more Christianity in our socialism than in the whole of the Madeleine together with St Pierre de Chaillot, St Phillippe du Roule, and St Honoré d'Eylan [the affluent parishes of Paris]. It was essentially a religion of worldly poverty. We had received so strong a vocation to poverty, even to destitution [*misère*], so deep, so interior and at the same time so historical, so event orientated a calling, that we could never extricate ourselves from it; and I begin to believe that even in the future we shall never be able to.'[209] Péguy again saw his fate as an exile side by side with the Jewish destiny, especially that of the poor Jews who in the *monde moderne* are cut off by the same horizontal dividing line from the wealthy world above them and are thus doubly destitute and exiled by their religious destiny. Péguy the poor man felt and knew himself to be 'in a common state of *misère, dans cet enfer commun*', with them.[210]

The negative idea of existence as exile united Péguy more and more inseparably in this period with a conception of the modern world as seen in Bergsonian categories, a conception of the modern world as one in which, yet again, only the features of an existence alienated from God, distorted into grotesquerie, appear. For Bergson, indeed, everything rigid, complete and conceptual is a degenerate form of what is living, flexible, fluid and intuitive; it is the sinking down of life and existence toward the limits of complete petrifaction. But all existence is as such a growing old, *vieillissement*, a transition from originality to habit and so to lack of authenticity and individuality; thus too subsequent generations allow the historical achievements of genius to decline into something accustomed and dull. For that now seems to be 'the greatest mystery of events'—that what is completed once and for all still 'remains always incomplete' and cries out for a crowning completion in the vision of the observer, the reader, the one who shares in the task. The sublimest works of art, stowed away in museums and 'flung

[209] B 579.

[210] B 629–630.

down before the dogs', before our unworthy and unseeing gaze, perish from lack of receptive response. 'A futile gaze, an empty gaze, something that is no gaze at all is—so to speak—the most malignant gaze, for it is the gaze of ultimate distancing and lovelessness, ultimate annihilation; the gaze, ultimately, of disintegrating oblivion.' 'We are free to contribute as much collaboration as we wish,' and if we refuse it, the waves of barbarism will once again swamp civilisation for centuries, 'like a temporal image of the Last Judgment'. Such is the 'terrifying responsibility' we have for the survival of civilisation.[211] The origins of this disintegration are thus completely internal; in this respect, the ethic of the Sermon on the Mount is quite right. 'Whoever has merely conceived the idea of disloyalty has already committed sin, he is already an adulterer in his heart. All disloyalty to reality is already, even when it has hardly been conceived, the beginning of its realisation, an infinite and eternal disloyalty.'[212] And Clio, the muse of history, is incapable of halting this process of disintegration; therein lies her *misère*. Péguy sees only two alternatives for history: either great events perish entirely for it, or else they become powerless in the memory of the succeeding generation. Any other option, 'apart from salvation', which comes from God, is not open for man in history.[213] This is the language of extreme pessimism, at least as regards the effects of history; there is no possible appeal to future generations. But—and this is the other side of the coin—grace always remains available in the present and is always offered for the future; a life lived in increasing hope can always salvage something from the process of decline and fall toward death and Hell. All that is in decline exists only in virtue of what is growing and rising ('What does it matter if they mock us? They themselves live only through us, they *are* only through us. Even the insubstantial beings that they are, they would not be without us. Even their hatred stems from us, it is our handiwork, parasitic upon us').[214]

Péguy here draws attention to the coincidence of Bergsonian and ecclesial language:[215] 'It is in the highest degree remarkable

[211] B 109–111.
[212] S 218–219.
[213] B 119.
[214] B 540–541.
[215] B 1344.

that spiritual death, the death of the soul, in the traditional language of the Church, is understood as the result (we might also say, as the limiting case) of a process of hardening. As the encrustations penetrate more and more deeply, they at last reach the heart; it is all simply a matter of this process of encrustation.'[216] Now this means that for Péguy, in the light of what his philosophical mentor said, Hell, which was for him the one utterly unacceptable thing, suddenly became a conceivable, almost a tangible reality. Bergson explained 'the mechanism of the gradual death of the soul', the process of mummification, of ageing, stiffening and hardening in the soul in which what is completed (*le tout fait*) defeats what is still in the process of shaping itself (*le faisant*). The insolubly tangled contest between freedom and grace can here no longer take place; everything is crammed to the limits with 'finished results', with memories, records and bureaucracy. As organic life presses toward the death of the body, so all spiritual life presses toward the second, historical and moral death, and only a suprahistorical principle in the heart of history itself can save it from this descending path. 'If we speak of the eternal promises that the Church has received, this means strictly that it possesses the promise that it will never succumb to its own ageing process, its hardening and rigidifying, its habits and its memory. Never will it become dead wood, dead soul, never will it collapse under the weight of its archives and its history. Never will it be entirely crushed by its recollections. Never will it succumb to the accumulated paperwork and the inflexibility of its bureaucracy. And it is the promise that the saints will rise up ever anew'[217] (*Note Conjointe*, 1914).

So it is a twofold experience by which Péguy comes into contact with the reality of Hell: the experience of his own expulsion from the modern world, and the experience of the modern world's state of expulsion from authentic life. And thus the two contrary experiences encounter one another at their roots: the illusionism of the modern world is a catastrophic expression of the general frailty of finite being that Péguy experiences in his own self (*Eve* will testify to this theme) and

[216] B 1343–1344. [217] B 1346–1349.

that makes clear to him that he still remains in solidarity with that modern world he hates. 'I too am a modern, I too am fired by the modern demagogy I am struggling against.'[218] 'Against our will we are infiltrated by barbarism, by the modern and modernism.'[219] 'Every modern man is a tattered newspaper. Not just today's, but a battered old daily on which every morning the day's news has been printed on the same paper.'[220] 'In the modern world, everything is modern, even those who struggle against the modern'; they live 'in the same terrible privation, the same dreadful lack of a holy reality [*du sacré*]'.[221] *L'Argent* (1913) describes the personal dialectical experience of Hell as the universal experience of the age: under the rule of money (the quantifying of all value) there is no longer any room for a 'spiritual marriage with poverty'; only an 'adulterous coupling'. The mysterious exchange that made such a marriage possible in the old world has now vanished—so how shall a Christian live the Christian life in such a dispensation? 'Ancient culture and Christianity went hand in hand—both kinds of ancient culture, the Hebrew and the Greek. Hitherto, the Christian was a man belonging to this culture; today he is bound to be a modern man.'[222] How can he be so 'in this contemporary Hell where anyone who does not play along is lost?'[223] It is the immense problem of dechristianisation, as set out in *Véronique* (= *Clio* II, 1909), in which Péguy distinguishes three levels of the problem: (1) the possible loss of the individual soul within the Christian community—where this is concerned, as Joan of Arc first showed, there can be no resignation to it; (2) excommunication from the Christian community—but this act of expulsion, so Péguy forcefully shows, is still a juridical-mystical bond, and it is precisely this that connects the person excluded in a continuing relation to the community of salvation—(3) the dechristianising of the world *in toto*, the loss of any connection to a sacral universe, whether antique or Christian—the condition of managing entirely without God. It is here that the question posed in the drama of Joan expands to the most comprehensive and contemporary dimensions; it is

[218] S 152.
[219] S 285; *cf.* B 627.
[220] B 1325.
[221] L 196.
[222] B 1075.
[223] B 1073.

here that the most decisive statements about the essence of being a Christian are made.

Corneille's Polyeucte had made men familiar with the idea of a figure who could strike an equilibrium between Christian and pagan by means of his representative activity as a Christian. But this equilibrium of secular and spiritual to the point where it is a true complementarity rests upon the principle of incarnation: the *enracinement* of the divine and spiritual in the secular and carnal by means of representation—that is, by acceptance of the world's descent into Hell—by means of mortal anguish. Accordingly, deadly sin in Christian thought is the refusal of this *enracinement*, the fruitlessly agonized effort to spiritualise and desecularise, the anguished struggle to avoid anguish, the bridge of anticipation reaching out to Easter, as a result of which Good Friday is never fully realised—Easter as a mythical, pagan or Jewish festival: the joy of the seasonal return of spring, bracketing out the historically and eternally unique anguish of God.[224] Besides, we are all so glad that Jesus has borne it on our behalf. All are agreed in this respect, agreed 'in a dark instinct of self-preservation'. 'Our metaphysical anguish feels itself diminished by all this. We are liable to look upon this tragic agony with a complaisant eye. We tolerate it with a truly disarming naivete and cruelty.' You men, says Clio, are used to living in illusion, but when, in the interstices of existence, the unhealable chasm of your nothingness yawns open once again, 'then I counsel you not to look into it or to turn your heart toward that agony, be it ever so tragic, toward that helplessness—to open your heart to that unfathomable heart. Be content with hearsay, do not seek to go back to the original text. Do not bend your heart, your feeble heart, down toward this infinite heart.'[225] Yet everything rests upon his agony. Everything else, even Peter's denial, Judas's betrayal, is less than the true reality. But the agony is. 'God himself was in anguish even unto death. *Tristis usque ad mortem*. Though this densely packed text does not make it plain whether it is a question of a single datum only—"unto the hour of death"—or also, at the same time, of a mortal sorrow that in itself extends to the point

[224] B 441–443. [225] B 444–447.

of death, constitutes a kind of death.' The whole drama of the Passion is made ready: everything in the world waits upon that one totally decisive event; God himself waits, from all eternity he has made himself ready for it in complete freedom and love, he has engaged himself in it. '*De toute éternité il s'était embarqué dans cet affaire.*' 'But between will and deed there is after all a chasm, between the knowledge of death and death itself.' Thus a pause falls in between, 'the moment of terror and amazement, the moment, we might say, of stumbling or of retreat, so that this appalling prayer can sound loud and clear, out of a fleshly agony, an agony like the eternal agony of a boundless torment, *Transeat a me . . . si possibile est.*'[226]—'Dreadful words, which we venerate so as to avoid having to hear them. Your own concerns intrude on you, egoism pulls at you, the calendar lends its assistance, and the historical record and the catechism (three little works of approximately equal value)—all three have conspired together: the historical record so as to set the event firmly in the past (whereas it is in fact universally present); and the calender could do no other than set it firmly in the springtime, where nature lives through the illusion of an eternal rebirth![227]

Upon this event the world rests absolutely; but only Christians know it and run up against it from every angle. 'You bring everything to God, you relate everything to God. From every side you touch him. From all sides you reach out to God, you wound him. Therefore you can no longer move yourselves. The least of your sins shares the guilt of the Roman spear, it reaches personally to the flesh of Jesus. How can you survive this? Only if the nature, the carnal nature concerned has retained a great capacity for resisting death in the power of its instinct for self-preservation and its will. But also, and above all, if such an exchange is to occur, God's grace must be infinite, and the merits of Jesus must cancel out the peculiar horror of their manner of realisation.'[228] Only to the believer's eye is the appalling phenomenon upon which all things depend translucent to the glory of grace. 'We may wonder how you can

[226] B 448–460.
[227] B 462, 461.
[228] B 491–492.

endure it. It is so *disproportionné* as to be virtually cowardly. It is so excessively heavy for you that you become defenceless and dumb, without any appropriate response; it becomes a pressure constantly exerted upon you—to put it plainly, an eternal blackmail. And this brings you, even on the most trivial occasion, face to face with the flesh of Jesus, in the Host, on the Cross, face to face with the Passion. By this mechanism the crucifixion begins ever anew in the world for all eternity. So, you ask yourself, from where can you draw the courage to keep on going to Mass?' The Jews, the Romans, Caiaphas, Pilate, Barabbas 'have simply been working on your behalf. You are the ones who stage the play.'

> You are bound to the body of Jesus by a mystical mechanism, bound to that sacrificial body, that body that writhes in death, that body of destitution, by an incredible, improbable, certainly nonhuman mechanism, by an unbalanced mechanism, staggering on its way, out of joint, out of true, a mechanism that yet is the only authentic one; by this bond, so profound, so essential, so centrally Christian, which is thus the only authentic bond between man and God, between infinite and finite, eternal and temporal, even between spirit and matter, spirit and flesh, soul and body, by this inconceivable union of a fleshly soul; with God and in God, with man and in man—this unbelievable, uniquely effective union of the Creator with his creation.[229]

'Innumerable connections bind all beings to Jesus, bind every soul and every body to Jesus—through this community, this communion. What an inextricable mesh, my children! Everything is linked with everything. You are all linked together and linked to all. Everything is linked with everything and everyone, and at the same time all this is linked with the body of Jesus.' And so—as the *Suppliants* had begun to show—all the fortune of the world is based upon misfortune, 'upon the contemplation, the consideration, the representation of misfortune'. This is so for the ancient world as much as for Christianity. 'For the pagans it is more a matter of misfortune [*infortune*], for you as Christians, more a matter of *misère*'. The *polis*, no less than the *civitas Dei*, rests upon exile and the

[229] B 493–495.

experience of Hell.[230] Only in this descent into the anguish of dereliction is the bliss and salvation of love in all its purity realised.[231] Here is '*l'axe de détresse*' and '*le centre de misère*'.[232]

Now too it becomes clear how much in the Christian system the saints and the sinners together constitute the pattern of the Church and are complementary qualities in it—a theme Péguy constantly emphasised afresh.[233] Because Dante could not give a genuinely christological foundation to his *Inferno* (in so far as it is to be taken in an ontic sense, not merely as a phase of his wanderings), the idea of reciprocal representation broke down for him. For Péguy there is in addition the possibility of a representation of the saints by the sinners—St Louis by Joinville, Joan of Arc by Péguy himself.[234] This ultimate solidarity and thus complementarity between the few saints and the multitude of sinners is to be found only in the Church. 'Whoever does not enter into her system, whoever does not lend his hand is no Christian, he has no kind of competence in the affairs of Christianity. He is a stranger. But the sinner does extend his hand to the saint, offers him his hand, because the saint has already given his hand to the sinner. And all of them together, the one by means of the other, the one drawing the other, advance upward and reach Jesus.'[235]

So Péguy, instructed and chastened by his roundabout journey, could now, for the first time, sort out the form of his second *Jeanne d'Arc* (1909). Everything was now immersed in, impregnated with prayer. The work opens with a prayerful meditation on the Lord's Prayer. The 'kingdom on earth'—this is also, even after Jesus' coming, the risk of perdition. 'It seems as if "thy kingdom" has gone away.' No bread, no forgiveness of sins, no deliverance from evil. Must not something wholly new and unheard of be established? 'But whoever will venture to say—for God's sake!—that there might still be something new to come after fourteen centuries of Christianity?'[236] Then comes once again the encounter with Hauviette, Joan's friend, and with the nun, Madame Gervaise; and it is in conversation with

[230] B 497–498.
[231] B 36–37.
[232] C 698.
[233] B 1021.
[234] B 1023.
[235] B 1022.
[236] J 17.

the latter that the real breakthrough is accomplished. Gervaise sacrifices herself for the individual soul, and to this end she risks the ultimate in prayer and suffering. Who would ask more from God? In the end she stands awestruck and silent before the divine mystery of predestination. Even Hauviette knows about the communion of saints: sinners and saints belong together. This is a barb directed against the cloister: Jesus, after all, was not the founder of an order, he did not withdraw from the lost world.[237] To remedy the world's destitution, one must act in a worldly, not only in a spiritual way. Joan becomes immersed in contemplation of the Cross, its reality in space and time. She envies those who can encounter the flesh of Jesus in a fleshly way; she envies the Jews who were his kin according to the flesh.[238] Then, as if in a single leap (and in the same moment Gervaise appears—they are both in ecstasy, both forming together the communion of saints), the historical suddenly becomes perfectly present.[239] It is as they confront each other that their long altercation takes place. Joan points to the world's dereliction and the complicity of Christians in it.[240] Gervaise understands her: even her first communion brought her no consolation; so long as the ideal of Hell haunted her, it remained powerless and 'worm eaten'. And now there arises the question of the cry from the Cross: it can only belong, says Gervaise, on the side of fruitful, profitable suffering, not the meaningless pain of the damned, even if Jesus cries out more teribly than a damned soul,[241] and his cry echoes through Church and world for all time and eternity.

O clameur culminante, éternelle et valable
Comme si même Dieu se fut désespéré.[242]

God the Father measures the depth of this suffering: 'Even the wretch who had just condemned himself was yet in his presence only as a condemned human being'; but here his Son cries out to him from the heart of time, and yet in his cry binds together both ends of eternity.[243] Everything in the atoning work of Jesus

[237] J 41f.
[238] J 55–70.
[239] J 70.
[240] J 81.
[241] J 97–98.
[242] J 107.
[243] J 116.

moves toward this cry—the birth, the shepherds and the kings, the years of manual labour, the episode in the temple when he was twelve years old. And now the long lament of Mary too enters in, as the weeping mother follows on the way of the Cross[244] and ponders on the destiny of this child who caused her such anxiety, her own son. Rarely indeed have Mary's thoughts been displayed with such realism, clearly from the perspective of the poor, uneducated woman from Nazareth; it is a masterpiece of Christian poetry. But her whole destiny too runs on to the cry that is coming, flows toward this precipice. Then again, there is the meditation of the crucified Christ on the men who are to be saved—on Judas, the betrayer, who hanged himself—and at this (as the earlier Joan had already pictured it), 'infinite agony' seizes him, and it is then that he 'lets out that insane cry'.

But Joan rebels: why did the apostles forsake him? She would not have done so. Charlemagne and Roland, Geoffrey and King Louis, they would not have done so, nor yet would Martin nor Bernard nor Francis. Gervaise replies: you are dividing Christendom, playing off the later saints against the earliest ones. Your saints would never have done that. They all began by submitting themselves to judgment, they all humbly recognised themselves as sinners and only then sought to be imitators of Christ. Beware: arrogance is close to sanctity. Joan now aims directly at the other's heart: 'I say that you, even you, Madame Gervaise, you would not have tolerated it.'[245] Gervaise wavers, wounded to the depths. Joan has dragged her unwillingly over a threshold. Gervaise will adduce against her the deep mysteries of the Church's teaching: that Peter was subsequently crucified as well, that the grace of Christ crucified must always be grasped and realised by men, that prayer and suffering carry such infinite weight before God that, if one offers onself for the salvation of the world, one excludes no one from his hope,[246] that one can offer to God only what is given one freely, that one can never know whether any soul has condemned itself. Joan counters this by saying that one sees and

[244] J 122.
[245] J 205.
[246] J 217.

knows that Christianity 'gradually and of its own free will is drawing toward its own ruin, toward perdition'. Gervaise attributes this to the evil times; other and better days will follow, God is in command. At this point the two women take leave of each other. The *Mystère* ends abruptly with an anticipatory sight of Orleans. Péguy initially had the rest of the play typeset, but he then suppressed it.

In Péguy's posthumous work, the dialogue is continued—a dialogue, like that of Bernanos's Carmelites, on the highest level of sanctity as the Church conceives it. Gervaise has nothing personally narrow about her, let alone anything in the least hypocritical; she represents the noblest and most daring efforts of an Augustinian and mediaeval theology. She begins by confessing her own humiliation—an involuntary humiliation, as true humiliation only is. Then she refers to Joan's vocation, her particular and superior mission. 'Listen for a little while more. Do not dismiss me scornfully yet, and consider this: we must work in the little way. Our place is behind our shepherd, my daughter, behind Jesus Christ, not ahead of him. We must not run ahead like stray sheep.'[247] You have recognised what solidarity means: that we remain linked with every tragic occurrence, even when we do not bear guilt for it, and we feel remorse just because of this link. But anything more than prayer and sacrifice is not vouchsafed to the Christian. Thus Gervaise concludes: '*Elle sort. On ne la reverra jamais.*' And thus Péguy, with decisive solemnity, closes the door on an epoch of Christian thinking.

Joan is alone, her own path is a solitary one, a struggle with God. She offers herself and acknowledges in that moment the perfect justice of God. 'You are the only judge, you are the whole machinery of justice; you always give just judgment.'[248] But when her prayer becomes powerless, she begs for the sign, the relief of Mont St Michael. She reflects on Gervaise's attitude: 'Fundamentally, she has resigned herself. She suffers a great deal, but fundamentally, in the very last analysis, she has resigned herself. Hauviette too, they both put up with it, they are used to it. But you, my God, are not used to it; the saints are not used to

[247] J 235. [248] J 250.

it; and Jesus, your Holy One, is not used to it. Are we to say, my God, that we are in your debt, through our sin, our sin-laden dereliction, in your debt for repentance, for a kind of repentance in you? In prayer, Joan is drawn unexpectedly right into the heart of God. 'My God, I have secret prayers. You know it. I have come to an understanding with you, and you with me. I implore you—we shall begin with that, begin with something very small. Afterwards, of course, we shall see. You know what you are doing, and it is always well done. The damned. The damnation of the damned. Grant us again to make communions that are complete and pure. There is a secret between the two of us, a secret we share. I have risked sharing a secret with you.'[249] Hauviette brings her the news of the liberation of the Mount. Joan rejoices at this confirmation and breaks out in a great prayer of thanksgiving.[250] In this she shows that there is no longer any kind of rebellion in her (as in the earlier Joan). The simultaneity of her total *fiat* and her plea to God, her secret shared with God, is itself the inmost mystery of Christian theology, which permits nothing but a Trinitarian solution. The world is given afresh to Joan, 'it is as if it came forth afresh from your own fresh hands'. 'Tomorrow I shall celebrate my true first communion.' Here is Christian existence at the very sources of its inspiration—an account composed in Bergsonian tones. But the sign of Mont St Michael is at the same time an example with implications for earthly engagement and action. Both must be one: prayer and struggle.[251] Once again we see how for Péguy these two things are connected internally and inseparably: the problem of earthly and eternal exile, the question of the *real* actualisation of the kingdom of God both here and beyond. The Paternoster that Joan now prays is both contemporary and eschatological.[252] It includes martyrdom, but only as the culmination of the earthly battle. The thought is cast in the contemporary categories of the crusade, but Péguy means by this the taking in hand of the earthly task. Christianity and humanity are ultimately one. The goal is not to ask permission 'to visit the Holy Land', but to conquer the land that belongs to

[249] J 257–259.
[250] J 269f.
[251] J 293–294.
[252] J 300–306.

Jesus. Otherwise, Christians would merit only the scorn of the infidels, and so would be unfaithful to their own mission.

Que la chrétienté croisse au cœur d'humanité.
Que cette chrétienté se fasse humanité.[253]

God's earth, says Joan in her prayer, is like the steps leading up into the church. 'It is our right that the earth should become the gateway to your Heaven. The church steps are, if you will, outside the church, they are in the marketplace. But they are also in the church, for they are the beginning of the church.'

The final section (first published in 1956) makes the transition to the point where Joan rides out from her home. The village has been burned and the church with it. God has taken back his gifts. The people have fled: Christians are always cowardly; they have 'flight in their bones'. So finally we are left with the question of the saint who may be at the same time a hero, of the soldier who might fight without taking revenge. This question is of course for Joan the beginning of her exposure, her God-forsakenness: '*Pourquoi m'avoir laissée en exil de vos cieux.*'[254] '*Faible et seule et pleurante en la terre exileuse*?'[255] Péguy had no need to take the revision of his play any further; all that was to be said had been said, and anything liable to misunderstanding had been set right. And the 'door into the mystery of hope' is pushed open, the door that leads directly into the heart of God. There, in God's grace and love, the secret between God and man becomes one of mutuality. Joan even expresses it in these words: 'Never yet has God been so much in need of man.'[256] The *Note Conjointe* enlarges on this theme: 'I think I said this (in my *Mystères*): that the lover enters on a state of dependence upon the beloved, and that therefore God himself arrives at a state of dependence upon the one he wants to save. When the good shepherd sets out to seek for the lost sheep, he enters a state of dependence upon the lost sheep, and you could say that, to find the sheep again, he takes his bearings from it and from its wanderings.'[257] 'If two people fail one another, they both fail together. Human guilt causes something to be lacking in God

[253] J 317.
[254] J 356.
[255] J 358.
[256] J 255.
[257] B 1400.
[258] B 1275.

himself. When man fails God, God fails man. When one fortress falls, Versailles too suffers the loss, the kingdom loses an outpost.'[258]

So there still remains a twofold job for us to do: to describe the *enracinement* of the Christian identity in the world and humanity, and—thus anchored—to outline also its entry into the triune communication and conversation within the Godhead.

4. THE ENRACINEMENT OF CHRISTIAN IDENTITY

The characteristic movement of the Christian life is that of God's own approach to man. Life in the public eye and suffering are the highest degrees of this approach to man: the supreme involvement of Jesus, the supreme outpouring into all the world of the blood of the God-Man.[259] 'The whole point is embodiment, becoming concrete, becoming flesh. The whole is this process of engrafting, and this succeeds only very rarely.'[260] 'Being Catholic is, sadly, not enough; one must in addition act in the temporal order if one wants to save the future from temporal tyrannies.'[261] In all earthly affairs, this law holds: 'A body, a temporal form of flesh is needed as a material carrier, as the matter for an idea. We know of no historical movement of the spirit, be it political, social or even religious, that could become manifest without a certain *corpus*, a fleshly form of actualisation. The sage had need of the Greek *polis*; the prophet of the race and nation of Israel; the saint of the Christian people—and of certain Western nations, at least as a starting point. This extends to the formation of the Roman empire, which germinated around the time of the advent of Christianity and in view of it—such a heavy, fleshly, corporeal and material phenomenom, to which an almost exaggerated and certainly disquieting significance seems to attach.'[262] The Christian apex is neither possible nor conceivable without the earthly, historical substructure,[263] and this is always twofold, since the Church

[259] B 370, 381.
[260] B 1286–1287.
[261] B 1214.
[262] B 42.
[263] L 186–188.

consists of Jews and Gentiles alike: it is both biblical and classical. Christian identity always presupposes the two foundations so as to bring both to completion in transcending them; but when the foundations are shaking, where the deepest feeling for the *humanum* is clouding over, what will be the possibilities for Christian existence and Christian orientation? Péguy's anxious thoughts constantly wander up and down the one highway, articulated in a fourfold curve: natural origins, the Christian fulfilment in transcending the menance of the modern world, and the exposed, apocalyptic situation of the Christian today. To make this anxiety intelligible, the fourfold path can be measured three times over; once in the area of nature, then in the area of time and history, and finally in the area of creative originality, where temporal man makes contact with the saving wellsprings of his being, the ever-springing wells of salvation.

1. The natural roots of Christian identity lie as much in classical Antiquity as in Scripture; here Péguy appeals to the Church fathers.[264] 'The doctor of the Christian Church would on no account be what he is without Plato, Aristotle and Plotinus'; Christ is the heir of all philosophy, just as he is the heir of the ancient *polis* and the universal claims of Rome. He is above all else a founder, and Christian worship resembles the classical ritual and sacral worship offered to the founders of cities. He inaugurates, initiates, takes possession of the soil and makes tradition out of it. He is founder and father, the procreative fertility of the City of God in the midst of temporality and history. This divinely valid, supratemporally valid aspect throws into still sharper relief the process of the assumption of power in the temporal order: 'For the more life boasts of having overcome death, and eternity boasts of having overcome temporality, the more does the power and value and sublimity and, so to speak, the range and scope of death, the power, value, sublimity and scope of history and temporality, come eternally to expression and make its mark.'[265] As against a socialistic, political world internationalism[266] that no longer has any roots anywhere, Péguy emphasises the native soil, 'our

[264] L 191–192.

[265] B 347, 341–346, 885.

[266] A 924.

native land'; for him his own youth among peasants and workers is the source of all his power.[267] His strength comes not from the intelligentsia, but from the people;[268] it is the family, with its self-containment, its fertility, its direct contact with happiness and powerlessness at once, its care and responsibility for temporal existence, that is the model for earthly life, not the cloister.[269] Jesus lived in the bosom of a family for thirty years, but even the last years represent a grounding in the world, 'an unending movement toward the world'.[270] The great founders of the Christian religious orders, the fathers of what is in each case a powerful spiritual kindred, '*d'une cité mystique dans le siècle même, dont le siècle était la matière*', repeated in a twofold correspondence, both to classical Antiquity and to Christ himself, the same act of initiation or foundation.[271] Life in the family, the people and the *polis* has its roots deep in obscure sustaining powers: waking his its roots in sleep, the public in the secret and private, action in contemplation and prayer. Péguy's anger raged almost without limit against Fernand Laudet, who as *nouveau théologien* opposed this basic principle with the intellectualist thesis that the meaning of Christ and the saints for us is in exact proportion to what we can know of their public activities through historical documents.[272] All roots stretch without end into the night. And so too all acts that have effective power in the world are rooted in the ethic of a hidden pattern of daily work, in jobs decently done. Even revolutions must be decently done; sabotage is the death of any and every culture; and the machine, which dispenses with labour and 'service', poses, at the least, the severest threat to any culture.[273] A certain quality of celebration, celebration of events, of the passage of time, belongs to an existence that has proper roots; even what seems insignificant wins some attention in such a context.[274]

[267] A 1217–1247; S 263–270; B 666–668.
[268] A 815; D 18; A 1286; B 1047–1049, 1319–1322.
[269] B 372–376.
[270] B 380–381.
[271] B 381–382, 349.
[272] B 857–885.
[273] A 247–248, 255; B 1051, 1053; S 151–153.
[274] B 685f.

Likewise frugality, even property, which is the fertile soil of all ethical greatness[275] belongs to such a mode of existence, as does *areté*, ethical skill, self-awareness, proper pride (which is the only thing that can be the foundation of Christian humility);[276] and as does also the conflict of man with man, the personal trial of strength, and thus war, in the classical sense, war that is an inalienable form of the human proficiency that must be historically brought to light and is always to be gained afresh.[277] All the great men and movements of history have had to fight for their authority; the category of struggle is coextensive with historical existence itself. Péguy's life was the perpetual bitter struggle of an individual who all but succumbed to the superior power of forces hostile to the personal; but for him—and here he goes beyond Kierkegaard's supernaturalistic picture of the 'individual'—the roots of this life of witness are actually in the depths of historical existence. It is precisely in warfare, in the total and crucial time of trial, that what is uniquely and properly human—solidarity—emerges in decisive fashion. The individual risks and offers himself for the whole. Péguy refused to identify war with hatred: true human conflict presupposes an underlying fellow feeling. Enemies 'cannot engage in the struggle without beginning to engage with each other, mutually interpenetrating each other, and so gradually coming to stand on common ground, having adopted the same rules of play'.[278]

In order correctly to grasp Péguy's understanding of the Christian *enracinement* in the natural order, we must beware of seeing in him a romantic yearning for a 'new Middle Ages'. Above all, he had no wish to preserve 'traditions'; he had nothing in common with the *Action Française*. He was a revolutionary socialist who traced the path back to the ultimate ground of the human so as to create a genuine breakthrough into the future.[279] There is nothing in the foundations of human existence that we can afford to overlook, and it is precisely in these inmost structures that the Christian God has revealed himself. Christian heroism in its faith, hope and love draws out

[275] B 129, 1071–1073, 1083.
[276] B 536f., 572.
[277] B 1162–1163.
[278] D 69.
[279] D 1377.

of the natural man what he cannot of himself attain. 'Heroism is essentially a skill, a condition and an act of sound health, good spirits, joy, even merriment, almost of frivolous playfulness—in any case, an act of pleasure, well-being, an act of the unconstrained, relaxed, productive person, of security, self-mastery, self-possession, almost (so to speak) of custom and routine, of good manners. It is without any posturing or ulterior motive, and, above all, without any self-pity; without sighs and lamentations, without the wish to win a reward. The person who only wants to win is a bad player. What makes a great player is the will to play. He would far rather play without winning than win without playing.'[280] This is how Péguy saw the Christian hero Polyeucte, the martyr for Christ, who matches his wits against the highest representative of classical wisdom in a contest that engages his whole life, in an 'immense unprotectedness. He has no cloak of virtue, of our own poor and false virtues; only faith, hope and love. It happens so seldom that the advocates of a good cause are free from anxiety. There is no accumulation of proofs, no piling up of furniture. Clothes and weapons are cast aside in grace. He does not devalue the world to exalt himself, and therein he is very sharply distinct from a certain tendency in Pascal. He gives the temporal order its due.'[281] This allows him the possibility of being superior even within the terms of the pagan system, since the pagan can only make judgments within his own system.[282] What Péguy admires in the Christian classical culture of the martyrs and the great doctors of the Church, in mediaeval chivalry and in the Christian classicism of Corneille is the health and joy of true involvement—life as a 'noble game' in the presence of God,[283] a game that concerns the most serious matters of life, though not in a spirit of Kantian and Kierkegaardian anguish, not in a bitter conflict between 'duty and inclination';[284] there is at most the conflict in Corneille between honour and love.[285] It is undertaken as a matter of course in free human involvement, undertaken out of a sense of decency,[286] without making any

[280] A 1198–1199.
[281] B 1387.
[282] B 1397–1401.
[283] B 1380.
[284] B 1382–1385.
[285] B 1382.
[286] B 1187–1189.

problem over 'recompense' (which is a concern that always tends toward a spirit of resentment). 'The man who allows full play to prayer and sacrament only to exempt himself in the time of war from work and, action is breaking the divine ordering of things. It may be generally accepted, a fine and profound thing, to beg in prayer, through prayer, for the crown of good fortune on an enterprise, to pray for the outcome of a battle (an outcome dependent only on the event); but equally it is stupid and subversive of obedience to want the good Lord to work on our side and to have the audacity to ask this of him. To ask for victory without the desire to fight—this would be indecent'.[287] So, from *Le Cid* to *Polyeucte*, we see 'the development of this wholly youthful and chivalrous generosity toward another kind of youthful generosity: the generosity of sanctity'[288]—all this in the hiddenness of the everyday life, of the petty tasks of Nazareth, yet done in such a way that the new task of love for God and man is performed also;[289] in the hiddenness of caring for the sheep and the life of prayer at Domrémy, out of which emerge the battles and the great martyrdoms.[290] It is precisley the Christian task of representation that presupposes this rootedness in the hidden. 'And it must be said that the *Mystères* of M. Péguy would lose their entire crowning glory if this mystical representation ceased even for a single moment to be the great inner regulative principle of his work.'[291] Thus, once again, everything rests upon what has already been noted once—the vertical network of solidarity (between the tip that appears and the hidden base, people and prince, people and genius, action and prayer)—and it is this network alone that is 'perfect communism'.[292]

Péguy's struggle against the *monde moderne* is also a struggle against the total deracination of the natural order and thus, consequently, of the Christian man; this does not need to be spelled out in detail. It is in its origins the denial of vertical solidarity,[293] the loss of the dark and invisible roots, the shift to the horizontal, the displacement of *mystique* by *politique*,[294] of

[287] B 1188.
[288] B 802.
[289] B 848–863.
[290] B 844f.
[291] B 878.
[292] D 109; B 802, 1060.
[293] A 1138f.
[294] B 506–507.

personal and natural values by money.[295] It is the dissolution of all exactitude of living into mathematics and thus into the mechanistic[296] and a false notion of *égalité*;[297] the replacing of resilient material (wood and stone), which educates man in respect for things by the weak and shapeless paste of concrete, which adapts itself in characterless fashion to everything;[298] the replacing of the classical geometrical idea of equivalence by the idea of interchangeable elements.[299] It also means the advent of the concept of 'progress', which is properly at home only in the quantitative sphere but now draws into itself the whole meaning of existence, so that this meaning now can be only in 'results' and 'achievements',[300] resulting in an overall loss of contact with that reality with which alone the philosopher, no less than the Christian, wants to deal: those essentially poor souls who can never achieve a condition of measurable progress.[301] It means internationalism, but internationalism as loss, because we no longer know the value of the homeland;[302] pacifism, but pacifism as loss, because we have lost the skill of the warrior and have become anxious about war, which thus only approaches all the more inevitably.[303]

Finally, what can the Christian do in such a time? He can, of course, do nothing but be the 'individual'. 'The great civilisations are protected by no one so much as the poor and wretched like ourselves; they still are maintained only by beggars like us, by unauthorised individual existences.'[304] Today, everyone is organised in terms of parties, and whoever does not cooperate is left out in the cold. 'I have been banned by the Catholics for having become a Freethinker, by the bourgeois for being a socialist and later on by the antisemites for being a Dreyfus supporter; one day I shall be banned by the socialist party for being an anarchist, and I have no doubt at all that later still some anarchist will condemn me for being a bourgeois (1902).'[305] And yet it is always 'personalities', not

[295] B 179, 1074, 1474–1476.
[296] B 813–814.
[297] D 252–254.
[298] E 20–36.
[299] E 50–85.
[300] E 85–98.
[301] E 88.
[302] A 924.
[303] A 819f., 828f., 835f., 848; D 58f., 65–71; A 920f.; B 41, 1161, 1198.
[304] B 808.
[305] A 441.

concentrations of power, that, again and again, achieve fruitful results, outside and inside the Church. Such people must make good out of their own plenitude what the age has taken away and is no more able to supply them with. 'Those who were all too richly endowed with goods remained sterile. And we, who had received nothing, had to find in our own selves a fertility that came only from our own selves.'[306] Solitary to the end, we must be the fathers of the future; our utmost degree of involvement occurs in the hope for our children.[307] 'And this is not one of the most secret of mysteries, for everyone knows it and simply no one talks about it: I mean that sense of being ashamed, perhaps less of shame than of despair, this terrible sense of responsibility that is part of fatherhood, for having brought children into the world. There is almost a kind of remorse, which one will never again be rid of. We want to protect ourselves and, out of a deep need for compensation and forgiveness, we become bold and courageous, so that we would now do anything for our children.'[308]

Here Péguy reveals something that is at the very heart of all living traditions, which never get off the ground without some such almost despairing act of self-giving—something fresh, and yet, surpassing all familiar and routine tradition, primordially Christian. By means of this self-giving he wants to recreate what is of elementary importance. In his earliest years he refers to it as '*refaire un public*'.[309] Later, he makes the more important statement: '*Ce qu'il faut refaire avant tout, c'est la paroisse.*'[310] He was never willing to rely for this on the clergy, on the official life of the Church. '*Les catholiques n'on jamais soutenu leurs hommes.*'[311] '*Il faut se méfier des curés. Ils n'ont pas la foi, ou si peu.*'[312] This assertion is broadly confirmed by the posthumous *Véronique*. Péguy laid the blame for the de-Christianising of the modern world almost exclusively at the door of the clergy and the religious. They have spiritualised everything in Christianity. They have betrayed the earth. 'In their ignorance of the temporal order there is a great deal of unbelief, a great deal of

[306] B 934.
[307] B 1244.
[308] B 1245.
[309] A 467.
[310] L 164.
[311] B 1091.
[312] L 138.

pride as well, no doubt, and a great deal of laziness.' They have underrated 'the essentially complementary, indispensable, completing element', the created world,[313] and thus they are bad workmen; they 'sabotage the eternal gardens, trampling down the garden of the Lord—what little still remains of it—with elephantine feet'. 'The dreadful thing is that they are never willing to voice their *mea culpa* and that, by a curious reversal of roles, those who should have been praying for the world are precisely those who will one day stand in need of the world's intercession for them.'[314] 'In all their piety (in prayer and sacrament) they forget the havoc they have wrought, forget it dishonestly, obscurely and yet clearly, cunningly, forget it and deny it . . . and so they have made null the effect of so many cloistered lives, so many prayers and sacraments. So eternity miscarries in time, because those entrusted with the authority of the eternal have forgotten the temporal, underrated and despised it.'[315]

We can now understand what Péguy means by 'civil war in the Church', a struggle more terrible and unhappy than any other. It is not simply that today, in contrast to the mediaeval situation, every Christian is in the forefront of conflict, that the decisive battles have to be fought out in each individual life and no safe interior sphere remains,[316] since everything now falls under the 'fortunes of war'; it is that, against the Bergsonian process of petrifaction, against the overgrowth, of organization and (as the unfinished conclusion of Péguy's last work, the *Note Conjointe*, puts it with incomparably delicate humour) against the dominance of the milestone over the road itself and the love of travel—against all these an interior struggle must be kindled, a struggle that 'even if it turns out victoriously, still comes into the category of the infinitely regrettable, the category of unholy warfare.' But since 'Jesus has to wage both wars at once, the inner war against the Jews and the external war against the Romans', the Christian even in his struggles is still part of the same axis.[317] Joan, who does indeed begin her warfare as an 'individual', who fights it through in the powerlessness and

[313] B 355–356.
[314] B 363–365.
[315] B 366–367.
[316] B 906–915.
[317] B 1409.

defencelessness of Jesus himself, stands yet again as the patroness of the modern Christian.[318] Péguy's whole life was lived under the sign of war. He was well aware (from 1905 onward) that a world war was approaching, and he held himself in readiness for it. What was required of him was the hardest thing of all: to exercise the virtues of peacetime and of wartime simultaneously, the virtues both of the child at play and of the man at war.[319]

2. *Enracinement* in the soil of time and history is no more than the complementary aspect of what has gone before. But an unexpected profundity appears as it becomes clear that all the highest aspects of humanity can be realised in this medium, which does not simply threaten them, but ineluctably destroys them. Historicity, the moment, the event—these fundamental and constantly recurring concepts are not taken in a Kierkegaardian, and certainly not in an idealistic, sense as the vertical breaking of eternal meaning and activity into the stream of time, but in their classical and Catholic sense, as categories of transient time that bring wealth precisely in and through their poverty, true being in their insubstantiality, Godward plenitude in their deathbound emptiness. And if these ideas of time and history clothe themselves once more in a Bergsonian conceptuality, the veil is here more transparent than elsewhere. *Durée réelle* (as opposed to alienated chronological time) does not, properly speaking, exist on earth; it is for Péguy a theological, not a philosophical category. All actual time is a state of alienation from divine, paradisial time; it is time declining and hastening toward death, the fateful process of ageing, *vieillissement*.

Nevertheless, there is a confluence of two distinct basic conceptions, each of which predominates at a certain period of Péguy's life. The first period of ethically heroic socialism is dominated by the notion that, amidst all the official, organised history, these are points of an absolute clarity and compression in events, sources and wellsprings where man must abide and from which he must live and learn to interpret history in prophetic fashion. The decision of the Dreyfusards was an

[318] B 1018.

[319] B 819, 1251–1255.

exemplary case of this,[320] a holding fast to the 'infinite value of the real presence'[321] (and that against the current of a historical process declining into official, mediocre and generally mendacious judgments) in the effort to return upstream toward the sources. *Remonter* is the basic word here,[322] and it approaches more the Augustinian than the Bergsonian concept of memory. 'History is essentially horizontal, remembrance essentially vertical.'[323] To think 'against the stream' means to persevere in the examination of conscience (as against one's peculiar propensity for forgetting).[324] This pair of concepts is extended in *L'Esprit de Système*, where any process of actualisation directed toward a possible systematisation is seen as already a declension toward the unreal; while true (realistic) philosophy is the effort to stick faithfully to reality and thus to make itself, as concept and expression, redundant.[325] Thus from the start Péguy denies the possibility of belonging to anyone's philosophical school: '*les philosophes n'ont pas d'élèves*',[326] while the systematisers, who have sacrificed the reality of truth, inevitably ramify into innumerable schools and subschools—Scholastics, Kantians, Hegelians—whose insubstantiality provides inexhaustible fodder for Péguy's wit. The formalism of the schools and of modern scientific and learned enterprises, however, is the 'final distortion' of the true and eternal philosophical problem, 'the ancient Platonic and pre-Platonic idea, the ancient and venerable idea of age-old humanity, the Indian, Brahmanic and Buddhist idea, the idea of the people of Israel, that there is in fact a difference, a distance, a margin between being and the phenomenal world, and that therefore it is necessary to undertake the journey back to the source [*remontée*], a journey of transcendence and dialectic. The metaphysical task is to grasp the more truly real under the forms of the phenomenally real, a metaphysical *approfondissement* that must be carried through with infinite reverence', and that is the opposite of 'modern scientific enquiry in which the phenomenally real is replaced by a less phenomenal ideal of truth'.[327]

[320] D 220–238.
[321] D 199.
[322] D 211f.; S 150; B 951.
[323] B 270.
[324] B 642.
[325] S 10; E 14.
[326] A 86.
[327] S 238–240.

A second variation on the theme follows on the first one, especially in the *Clio* books. The ancient Clio, muse of history, can never, as a writer of historical records, lay bare the origins of events. 'Reality' in its 'inexhaustibility' is her 'enemy';[328] Clio herself can never offer more than an echo of this, since she is subject to the laws of the ageing process, the laws of attrition; she has to let things pass away and so is inevitably cruel and unjust.[329] She can at best offer 'truth', never 'reality'.[330] And precisely in so far as she is the process of recollection, she is the one who obscures the origins of things, the primordial, unimpeded vision, such as the child, and perhaps, exceptionally, the genius possess.[331] Of any historical achievement we can ask, 'How old is it?'—that is, 'How far is it from the source?'[332] or even, 'At what *kairos* did this work enter history?' A play that has no real premiere cannot survive in a living way.[333] In what epoch did a genius embed himself? Was this embedding a successful and profitable thing for him, or was it located between the wheels of two overlapping epochs?[334] Was it able to bring its own ascending progress into line with the ascent of a whole period?[335] One way or another, however, we are debarred from a Faustian lingering over the unique moment;[336] we are waves in the ocean of transience, and the greatest prospect for us is still the threefold peak of human existence: *la mort, la misère, le risque*.[337] This is why the men of Antiquity, though subject to destiny, are greater than their gods; they have the consecrated status that mortality bestows. And thus Christians are ill-advised if they shield themselves against the risk of death behind a screen of nontemporal Platonic ideas or nontemporal modern rationality. God has put his own self at risk in the medium of death, and so all rationality and all consciousness of God as well hangs upon this event. 'Man must take the risk of freedom; and so, in the last analysis, it must remain a risk, and we must return ever anew to the theme of Pascal's wager. Thus Christianity has never produced proofs in

[328] B 95.
[329] B 113–119.
[330] B 28.
[331] B 311–312.
[332] B 331–340.
[333] B 159–163.
[334] B 260–262, 296–298.
[335] B 298–301.
[336] B 665.
[337] B 257.

the sense given to the word by gross men; its best and only proof is just that it offers none.' In this way, the world after the death of Jesus may be no different, no better, no further advanced, since proofs of this kind would have destroyed the completely free character of the wager, which expresses at once the *misère* and the *grandeur* of man.[338] Clio can never penetrate to this level of inner reality, she cannot grasp it. She remains a stranger to destiny,[339] she is only the 'ageing process' of time;[340] so, on the one hand, history is the replacing of life by self-propagating recollections,[341] and thus again, not a genuine remembering but the replacing of memory by documents.[342] Men, the more insubstantial they themselves become, seek to understand this aggregation as progress; they dream, with Hegel and Renan, of a divine consciousness in process of coming to be, a consciousness that would equal the totality of historical occurrence. 'They secularise the Last Judgment and turn it into the paltry verdict of history. And for this they have sought me out, Clio, the most wretched of creatures, the princess of the past.'[343] Yet whence comes this senseless, deluded hope in the historical future—whence if not from a reflection of grace and eternity: 'and perhaps God loves misdirected virtue more than no virtue at all'? But God is constantly demolishing intrahistorical hopes so as to disclose the ultimate ground of them all—the roots of time and the past in a reality that has no ground. And if Christians still shrink back so much before such a prospect, they must enter upon it—history itself compels them.

Looking back on *Clio*, Péguy hoped to have shown 'that there is no kind of opposition between culture and faith, but far more a deep relationship, a deep nourishment that faith receives from culture, even a vocation for faith drawn from culture'.[344] Both rest upon the mystery of death, that monstrous presence to which no man can accustom himself; for every man, death is always a new thing—the death of friend and loved one, of father and mother, a death that really impinges upon a life. In death there is an insoluble mystery before which spirit no less than

[338] B 479–480.
[339] B 261.
[340] B 266–267.
[341] B 268.
[342] B 269–270.
[343] B 221.
[344] B 966–967.

flesh recoils, before which even God himself recoiled on the Mount of Olives.[345] And if time, like space, gives life a measure and a limit, it is still only in the mode of a groundless reality from which Platonism is powerless to save us. The whole modern world is one great campaign against risk and uncertainty; as a money-dominated world, it is a world of life insurance. 'The modern world as a whole is a world that thinks only about its own old age. It is a monstrous old people's home, an institution for pensioners. In economics, politics and constitutional law, as in ethics, psychology and metaphysics, we should, if only we had better eyes, be able to see one thing and one thing only: how much this terrible need for peace and quiet is invariably a principle of enslavement. It is always freedom that has to pay the bill. It is always money that is master. The glorious insecurity of the present is always sacrificed to the security of the moment immediately following.' That is the real psychology of the contemporary idea of progress: man would like to live his life in the future, to live in advance of the event, so making his present into his past.[346] Taking thought for the morrow, saving for the morrow, actually means throwing away its freedom, castrating its fertility and potency, which are the supreme blessings for human beings. 'Every financial transaction is an expense of spirit; the only genuine miser, storing up his treasures, is the lover. That is the most profound teaching of the gospel. And we are so much under the domination of money, the Antichrist, that even when we do not openly name it, we constantly take its name for granted.' In this commercial world, everything is commercial, even metaphysics, and theology; they too fall into line and cease to have any true presence in their own right. Christianity, like everything else, is detemporalized and thereby deprived of its 'salt'. Avarice in the form of anxiety about tomorrow is the lord of all the world. The drying up of the heart makes itself felt both spiritually and temporally. The person who rejects the fluidity of the living heart, preferring the rigidity of money and conceptual thought, has already chosen the other kind of fluidity, the liquefaction of the corpse.[347] 'The question is simply

[345] B 439–441. [346] B 1438–1441. [347] B 1422–1450.

what in any given world is a commercial commodity and what is not. It is by this standard that every world will be judged.'[348] And yet Clio looks with an indulgent and absolving eye upon mankind taking flight into the future. Who knows, she says, whether, in this desacralising of hope, the true divine hope may not yet prevail in spite of all? Grace travels by tortuous routes; 'if you turn it from the door, it will climb in through the window. The men God wants, he has; the humanity Jesus sought to redeem, God's grace has given to him.'[349]

Here is the starting point for the third modification of Péguy's idea of temporality. It dominates his last years and is crystallized in his massive poem *Eve*. This modification is the essentially Christian variation on the theme. Clio, the wonderful, elegiac and witty spokeswoman of the middle period, was a personage of classical mythology, an abstraction. But Eve, the mother of fallen mankind, is a real person, and she as an individual has experienced the difference between primordial, paradisial time and the time of a fallen and sinful world. She both possesses and constitutes the measure of such difference. Yet is is not Eve who speaks, but Jesus who speaks to her, to 'the much-beloved mother of his mother',[350] about the time that is lost and that is restored in him; here Péguy's work is also the theological redemption of the unredeemed epic of Proust. It is, to put it with precision, the only major attempt (after Augustine's *Civitas Dei*) to deal poetically with the three theologically distinguished existential conditions (*katastaseis*) of actual humanity: the primitive state at the time of innocence; the sinful state of the time after the Fall, a time flowing toward death and waste; and the redeemed state in Christ and Mary, who take up the whole world's heritage and bring home the harvest of death to the Father. Péguy's uniquely felicitous touch (whose internal necessity we shall later trace) lay in the fact that he treated these conditions not, as did Augustine, in a theoretical way, but in the situation of dialectical solidarity between Eve

[348] B 1451.
[349] B 211–222.
[350] C 718 (st. 93. In what follows, *Eve*'s quatrains are referred to by page number, so that even the incomplete quatrains (1226 and 1300f.) are included in the sequence along with those projected but never actually written.

and Jesus; and also that, unlike Dante, he did not conceive the love that governs all things on the scale of a human Eros enlarged to cosmic dimensions, but in terms of the all-surpassing Agape of the Cross—though this itself, in the dialectical solidarity that exists between the second Adam and the first Eve and because of the perfect *enracinement* of grace in nature, issues in a unique natural-supernatural tenderness, which prevails throughout the whole epic. Nothing has yet been said in explicitly Christian terms, but behind this fresh aesthetic possibility stands a theology that opens up new possibilities, a theology that can be established with precision. It begins with the evocation of the 'atmosphere' ('*ce climat de la grace*') of the paradisial creation—fully earthly, yet completely pure, a completeness beyond any possibility of addition, yet above all a temporal reality, the passage and the rhythm of the seasons, a dying into new life.[351] The eye of God rests upon all, the eye of a God who is ever young and yet eternal, who watches with love over the youthfulness of the world and time. Eve has known all this, this 'cloak of tenderness cast about the shoulders of the world'.[352] Everything was a source, a spring, and there was no need to save, to channel resources; everything was loving faith, requiring no dogma, no scripture, no formula or rule;[353] everything was abundant plenitude, and there was no need of 'mine' and 'thine'.[354] Then came sin (its form is of no interest to the poet—only its consequences), and with it plenitude disappeared, existence became meagre and Eve became a housekeeper, a steward, a provider. *Ranger* becomes the catchword for hundreds of verses: the process of orderly provision for house, laundry, children, husband, everything, even God himself, is carried on upon a foundation of anxiety for their sakes, and, on the other hand, in order to control poverty and forget care. 'Women, I tell you, you would look after God himself if he should drop into your house one day; you would look after the wrath of God and grace and forgiveness of sins and the host and the chrism and the viaticum. . . .[355] The endless work of tidying up is an effort to cope with an essential disorder,

[351] C 707–711 (st. 9, 15, 17f.).
[352] C 716 (st. 70).
[353] C 723 (st. 126–129).
[354] C 728 (st. 173f.).
[355] C 726 (st. 151–156).

and it proves in this very process to be itself a thing of futility and impotence and thus an expression of that same disorder. Eve as the one who 'tidies up', as the calculating housewife, here takes over the characteristics of Clio; she sets in order the *temple de mémoire*,[356] taking care always and above all of what has happened, even of the death of Christ, as events of past history:

Et vous rangez le mort: après qu'il est bien mort.
Et vous rangez les temps: quand ils sont revolus.
Et vous rangez les jours: quand ils sont absolus.
Vous rangez le vaisseau: quand il est dans le port.[357]

Eve classifies and quantifies, and at the end of the day it is from her activity that the *monde moderne* too will spring. But meanwhile her work of 'looking after' and providing is only an expression of the poverty of contingent existence. She knows the human condition and its flight from God, she knows what man has taken on board '*vers le déportement d'un éternel exil*',[358] she knows the fruitlessness of man's endeavour—and she has to incorporate all this into her domestic accounts, everything, even eternal salvation, which, however, cannot be part of any reckoning.

Éternelle économe, éternelle ouvrière,
Vous rangez le salut, quand il est écoulé.
O femme médicale et femme infirmière
Vous épongez le sang, après qu'il a coulé.[359]

Here Mary herself takes on the features of Eve, the primordial mother '*qui a pu ranger la muette agonie*'. Eve indefatigably sets in order the unending fatigue and futility of the world, the futility of buying and selling, of commercial value or lack of value;[360] she picks up what is left of the trampled flowers after the procession has made its way over them. 'You gather up grace when it has been spent, you gather up the spring when it has run dry.'[361] But how will the housewife of the temporal order survive the judgment of God with all this refuse heap around

[356] C 735 (st. 224); but *cf.* C 784 (st. 617), where Clio is the 'Temple of Memory', since she alone remembers the origin of things.
[357] C 759 (st. 420).
[358] C 734 (st. 214).
[359] C 741 (st. 273).
[360] C 744 (st. 295–297).
[361] C 746 (st. 313, 316).

her? Suddenly, we have a great vision of the way toward this judgment,[362] a curiously sunless, entirely earthy vision, an awakening of the earth, in which the dead have first to get used once again to their flesh—verses that could have been written by Rilke. Again, and more urgently, comes Jesus' call to Eve—'*O mon âme, ô ma mère*'[363]—and now, when the judgment has been revealed as that which lays bare ultimate discrepancies, the question is one of the intrahistorical discrepancy in the human condition: between the task of setting things in order and the reality of disorder that it deals with, between calculations and the fact that all calculation is resolved in God alone and in God's uncalculating grace. Here there is a clear passing shot at Anselm's teaching, and Eve stands for the earthbound, theologising Church:

Vous pouvez calculer, voici l'encre et la table,
A quel taux j'ai prêté le sang que j'ai donné . . .
Vous avez pu compter, implacable régente
Ce que j'avais tenté d'avec ce que j'ai pu . . .
Vous avez pu compter à combien revient l'homme,
Et qu'il fallut payer du sang même d'un Dieu.[364]

Everything in this unfathomable vanity of time is 'wormeaten' and hollow: law, virtue, morality, religion. Everywhere, man in his failure wants to manage God, to outwit God, to come to an exactly defined relationship with God; but God's ever-flowing love is the sole truly exact reality, and Eve's calculations will always be hopeless in face of that. And she knows,

. . . que l'être de Dieu remonte incessament
A son niveau de force à la même altitude,
Et qu'il fait de lui-même et son redoublement
Et sa force éternelle et son exactitude.[365]

Everything that man is able to take in hand is in the grip of

[362] C 748–758 (st. 327–411).
[363] C 761 (st. 433).
[364] C 760–761 (st. 426, 428, 430).
[365] C 764 (st. 455; the next stanza replaces *redoublement* with *retriplement*, alluding to the threefold generative power of God). On law, C 768; on virtue, 768, on morality within the sphere of original sin, 790–794.

futility, decline, the loss of the inheritance of past events. In this respect, *Eve* is a recapitulation of Augustine, Anselm, Luther and Pascal.[366] But what Jesus says to Eve, the '*reine de disgrâce*',[367] has such tenderness of filial love about it that it presupposes something very different from what the theologians of original sin have as their stock in trade. This fresh element is thrown into sharp relief by the second part of the poem: it is the path toward the Incarnation seen from below (what had earlier been described in the name of Victor Hugo) and, following from this and building upon this terrestrial solidarity, the pathos of the Greek fathers in their sermons on the descent into Hell. The tone in which Péguy's Jesus addresses his first mother is immediately reminiscent of the tone in which the dead saviour in Hades addresses the submerged figure of his first father, Adam: 'Thou first image of my father, what dost thou here?'[368] Suddenly in stanza 943 the tone shifts abruptly: '*Heureux ceux qui sont morts pour la terre charnelle!*'[369]

All those among the sons of Eve who have fallen in a just war for the sake of their homeland, the heroes who have perished sacrificially, they are 'an image and a first beginning of the house of God', they are 'the body of the *Civitas Dei*'. 'This pledge to the earth is the beginning of, and the first attempt at an eternal troth.' And when, as the 'mighty vanquished', they return again to the 'plastic clay' out of which 'God's thumb has shaped them', then their reunion with the ground of all is a sign of hope and promise for the whole being of the world within the life of God.[370] It is the classical and biblical lament for needlessly shed blood, the celebration of the lives of heroes, taken up into the sphere of redemption. 'May they not be weighed with a primitive severity, by fleshless standards or with eternal weights; may it still be remembered that they had blood flowing in their veins, *un sang artériel*.'[371] And in the same tones Jesus adds his own blood, shed just as humanly, just as

[366] C 770–771 (st. 506–513).
[367] C 773 (st. 532).
[368] *Cf.* for instance the homily of pseudo-Epiphanius, PG 43, 440–446.
[369] C 800.
[370] C 800–802 (st. 743–761).
[371] C 805 (st. 784).

pointlessly, just as heroically in company with the hero fallen in war[372]—shed blood, shed word, shed life of time and eternity together, inexhaustibly real and sacramental.[373] And now the endlessly flowing intercession of Jesus to his Father begins, the Father who has 'moulded from earth and clay and mire' these his brothers and so cannot be surprised to find them so earthy, so soiled with clay and mire.[374] Here for the first time theology returns to its home port with Irenaeus of Lyons. And the inextricable interpenetration of nature and grace is celebrated in solemn verses:

Car le surnaturel est lui-même charnel,
Et l'arbre de la grâce est raciné profond
Et plonge dans le sol et cherche jusqu'au fond,
Et l'arbre de la race est lui-même éternel.

'And eternity is itself within time, and time itself is timeless time. And the tree of grace and the tree of nature have their roots so fraternally intertwined that they are one single essence, one figure. The same blood flows through the veins of both, the same glory flows through the sufferings of both. Each soul that finds salvation saves its flesh also. Grace and nature have bound themselves together in so fraternal a knot that both have souls and both have bodies, both sail on the same ocean, both cradles float upon the same abyss of nothingness. And neither can perish without the other dying also, and neither can survive without the other surviving also.'[375]

An unexpected image of Christmas appears—'even Jesus is

[372] C 805 (st. 789–799).

[373] C 807–808 (st. 805–813).

[374] C 811–813 (st. 837–846); and on this subject see also the stanzas (298–418) from the posthumous material (*Suite d'Ève*), C 1242–1255, and again, C 1290–1292 (st, 729–750).

[375] C 813–814 (st. 847–861). Alongside this runs the theme to which widespread allusion is made in the posthumous material, the notion of body and soul as a married couple. Body is the knight-errant, boldy embarking on earthly enterprise, soul is distracted by the things of Heaven, recalling its origin in God: both together constitute the anthropological image of the central nuptial union, that of nature and grace. So the Platonic inheritance is conscripted into the service of a quite un-Platonic theology (C 1285f., 1292f., 1295f., 1298f.).

the fruit of a mother's womb':[376] the child, dreaming of Paradise, is only milk and blood, dew and wine (*rosée*), and he sleeps, sheltered in his mother's arms, the sleep of the source of all things, for all begins in the fruitfulness of sleep.[377] He is sheltered too by the warm breath of the two animals, those hirsute representatives and delegates of Mother Nature, of the cosmos in which God has made his bed; Péguy lets his humour play tenderly upon them in a long litany.[378] And as God slumbers within nature, so he does in history; and as Péguy lets Joan of Arc's whole destiny be determined in advance in the contemplation of Domrémy, so he makes the history of the world focus itself proleptically around the sleeping heir. He lies in the crib like Moses in the bullrushes; he is the heir of the Old Covenant[379] and of much more besides: the whole ancient world, Egypt, Greece and Rome; priesthood; wisdom; world power. All their sacrifices, all their speculation, all their battles, all were done for him. Here Péguy develops a true renaissance *Trionfo*, but one with the theological point that in Jesus the world's movement toward nothingness and death is arrested, brought to a standstill and turned in its right and proper direction; from this point on, the movement is upward, toward the source, which has itself been manifest within history in Jesus.[380] Rome, the midpoint of the historical world, is established afresh in him, and if the roads of the world radiate outward from Rome like the cracks in a glass mirror into which someone has thrust the shaft of a spear, so too the roads of the world of grace radiate from the heart that was pierced by a Roman spear. On this theme, the lines flow freely.[381] It is the great theme of the Church fathers and of Dante that here finds its haven and comes to rest, a theme that Péguy had long sought since for him the *praeparatio evangelica* of classical Antiquity seemed to lie not simply on the side of the spiritual and

[376] C 815 (st. 862).
[377] C 833 (st. 1006f.).
[378] C 822–832 (st. 925–1005).
[379] C 837–840 (st. 1042–1062).
[380] C 834–869 (st. 1014–1299).
[381] In the posthumous material, C 1210–1211, 1213–1218, 1231, 1255–1268, 1283–1285, 1294–1295, 1301–1307, 1314–1315.

philosophical, the Hellenic world, but also in the political and juridical and strategic world, in the mastering even of these apparently supremely worldly spheres in the world's redemption.[382] Nonetheless, he did not ignore the distinct role of Byzantium, and he illuminated the relation of the Eastern and Western worlds in this respect with a few lapidary remarks.[383] But above all, in this motif of the Roman roads, he did not omit to note how much Rome, with its lance striking at the heart of Jesus, its own new centre, pierced its own secular power. The roads went out from Rome,

Comme si d'une lance on eût frappé le monde,
Ainsi qu'on a frappé le flanc de Jésus-Christ,
Il s'était étoilé d'une étoile profonde
Et des rayons d'un cercle inscrit et circonscrit.

Et comme si l'injure et la lance romaine
Etait redescendue au cœur même de Rome,
Ainsi que le parjure et la faiblesse humaine
Etait redescendue au cœur même de l'homme. . . .[384]

Thus the Dantesque theme has its sting drawn: the old Rome was and still is a precondition, but one that enters the new city only when transfixed by its own spear. Jesus is the heir of the ancient world; he is not the heir of the 'modern world', the world that imprisons itself in its own denial of the Christian vision, which has become sterile, rushing forward into the futility of an empty future—the Johannine *kosmos*. After Péguy's maledictions against this world have been wearily recited,[385] he concludes with the 'parallel deaths' of two saints, Geneviève and Joan, who point in exemplary fashion to the route by which humanity returns to Paradise. Both are shepherdesses of peasant stock, signifying what Péguy so often turned his mind to (and which Thérèse of Lisieux was equally concerned to pursue): the duality of the road to salvation—being sheltered from the world, and being proved and tried by the world; the child's innocence, and the attrition of suffering.[386]

[382] A 1383; B 250, 348f., 803–805, 1163–1165; L 188, 192.
[383] B 337–339.
[382] C 1231 (st. 201–202).
[385] C 869–929 (st. 1300–1778).
[386] B 1410, C 255–257.

But they both are equally of the people and the soil, and in each the significance of the earth itself is once again glorified, that significance that can bring fleshly man, even the saint, in his form, dimension, limit and contour into the absolute sphere, into the reality that eternally abides:

Or la terre est chargée, et c'est la terre seule,
De faire long âge et l'âge révolu,
Et de faire une enfant et de faire une aïeule,
Et de marquer les bords de notre âge absolu . . .

'and to mark out the frontiers of our actual age, so that none can alter, none can undo, the curve that it describes. So it is the earth that triumphs at last and that pleads for us in the trial of our ageing, the earth that disposes of us and provides our record and registration.'

Rien ne peut suppléer cet enregistrement
Et cette inscription et cette expérience.[387]

The poem to Eve does not fail to recognise the role of Mary. The long sequence on the 'only two bodies' that, without being dissolved into cosmic nature, travel back along the road to Paradise, the bodies of Jesus and Mary—all this clearly emphasises the dogmatic position of Mary over against Eve.[388] If Jesus is the God-Man and thus the source of all things made present in the temporal order, then Mary is the unfallen creature and thus Paradise made present in a fallen temporal order. In *Eve*, Jesus speaks with Eve, eternal time with fallen time. But in the six great *Chartres* poems, which must be considered as Péguy's supreme artistic achievement, he appeals from the fallen temporal order to the presence of unfallen time in the holiness of Mary.[389] Chartres, standing amidst the limitless golden cornfields of the Beauce, is a symbol of the harvest of the world come to fruition around a Paradise made present. Péguy, the weary but indefatigable pilgrim on his solitary way, established

[387] C 934–937 (st. 1821, 1825–27, 1836, 1843).

[388] C 1290 (st. 728), 1296–1298 (st. 788–805), 1312–1313.

[389] *Présentation de la Beauce à Notre Dame de Chartres* (C 676–687), *Prière de Résidence, Prière de Demande, Prière de Confidence, Prière de Report, Prière de Déférence* (C 688–704).

and initiated the pilgrimage that today many thousands of Parisian students and intellectuals still follow. His prayers are nothing other than the surrender of the earthly, which can find no ultimate measure in itself, to that which is right without qualification, the measure of Paradise and the fallen world that gives to all things their true direction and their peace. It is sacrifice as submission, as the abandonment of all now meaningless rebellion and bitterness, all the disorder of the covetous and presumptious heart, all anxiety in the face of death and judgment. The request is not for an alleviation of suffering, but rather for the maintenance of fidelity and honour in service. Everything becomes crystal clear and plain down to its foundations, every line is dominated by a penitent desire for transparency, like the Marian canto at the end of the *Commedia*, and like many lines of Eichendorff's.

Eve and Mary in their reciprocity determine the manner in which Péguy understands the Christian *enracinement* in time and history. The loss of this in the 'modern world' is self-evident; the long invectives of Péguy against contemporary idols need only be mentioned by their titles. Against the humility of this *enracinement*, the modern man, in flight from his roots, sets the concept of evolution—a German import, according to Péguy, resting on the shallow modern interpretation of a quantification of reality,[390] whose internal contradictions are set forth with particular penetration in the fragment *Brunetière*.[391] 'Neither life nor death, neither love nor hate, neither law nor morals, neither homeland nor family, neither marriage nor children, neither salvation nor suffering, and above all neither destitution nor poverty have declined in market value.' Nor will they ever do so as long as humanity exists.[392] Who would seriously want to improve on a child?[393] After Péguy has exposed the reader—without comment—to pages and pages of Renan's fantasies of the future it is enough for him, leaving aside questions of 'interplanetary morality', to select as a counterpoise to such fantasies two of the major atrocities of modern civilisation: 'Europe's decay has spread to the whole world.'[394] 'Naturally,

[390] B 125–127, 400f.; D 35f.
[391] S 177f.
[392] B 1237.
[393] B 324.
[394] A 158; similarly, the discussion that breaks off at A 736.

after the invention of telephotography mankind will invent new "-ographies" and "-phones", each more "tele" than the last, and we shall be able to whistle round the earth in next to no time—though still only around the temporal earth. But still, if Plato had never existed, would you be able to invent him, do you think?'[395] Who is there today who still thinks about philosophy? Sociology is the slogan of the new Sorbonne, the slogan of 'exact human science', which means fundamentally a comprehensive cataloguing of facts, statistics. Péguy never tires of pouring out his most bitter and caustic wit on such fabrications[396]—bitter, because those people who are secretly glad to see the great philosophical and religious systems of mankind in decline are those who are the true gravediggers of humanism.[397] But there is irony here too, as he exposes the ludicrous nature of an enterprise that seeks to translate the values of sanctity (Joan's, for example) into psychological terms.[398] Let the world progress as it wills; there is in Christianity 'no progress of any kind [Péguy puts these words in bold type]. Only modern men make progress. But we are, once and for all, no more clever than St John Chrysostom.'[399] To improve Christianity would be like wanting to 'improve' the North Pole.

If we ask about the theological situation of the Christian in this modern world, then, as Péguy sees it, what is left for him to do is roughly what Péguy himself has done: to discern the signs of the times in the power of Christian prophecy and to demonstrate in exemplary fashion in his own person (and that is again a form of prophecy) what Christian *enracinement* means, over against the loss of substantiality in the world around. No more can be required, and the task will need, and will demand and consume, all the resources the witnessing Christian possesses.

3. The third aspect of *enracinement* will be recapitulated only briefly, since its features have already appeared in many respects.

[395] A 1106.
[396] A 253, 992f., 999f.; S 76–81, 215–217.
[397] A 1108–1110.
[398] B 900–905, 1219.
[399] B 918.

In the midst of the nothingness of time as it dissolves, even in the natural sphere, are resources, wellsprings, which are like a present token of eternal life, or at least a promise and foretaste of redeemed existence. There is the child and his unspoiled world, his freshness, still moist from the divine dawn. It is as if the astrological moment of birth were really decisive: 'We all have only one kind of innate knowledge, the mother-wit that we receive from the world; at the particular place and time at which we come into the world, there our whole existence is forged, there is life, truth, the starting point of our path through life; there is the innermost axis, the mystery and the power.'[400] It is out of these remote areas that there breaks out, around the family table, those unpredictable children's remarks that so entertain the grown-ups, and yet also, at the end of the day, may make them tremble, because they can themselves no longer come up with such words, they cannot even hold them in their memory to retail to others.[401] We have already noticed how close the child for Péguy is to the genius in his capacity to see without illusion and to formulate his vision accordingly. The attempt to abide in and hold to the power of the source usually takes the form of philosophy and so can never be imitated externally in its products but only internally in its striving. Any 'division of labour' here would be absurd, so there can be no 'progress' in philosophy, but only the manifestation of abiding types.[402] And indeed the third point to be taken up in Péguy is the experience of fatherhood, where human thought masters that ungraspable fruitfulness and responsibility that drives the father to any and every degree of involvement on behalf of his children.[403] This 'source experience' is perhaps—even in Péguy—the deepest of all: not the experience of Eros between husband and wife, which in Bloy's work wanders so far off the beaten track and is still confused in Claudel, yet is almost overlooked in Bernanos and Péguy (none of the four had a happy marriage); but the experience that occurs between father

[400] D 90–91.

[401] C 430–433; *cf.* S 232; B 320.

[402] A 1005–1006; S 99f., 184; A 1092–1097; D 244–245.

[403] B 344, 372f., 1245–1246; C 179–188.

and son, which becomes for Péguy the terrestrial point of entry into the inner mystery of the Trinity.

It is with good reason that the Christian consummation of this natural *enracinement* in the springs of life takes the path that leads to the Cross, the humiliation, the thrust that opens up the heart. But once again, it is Péguy's unique contribution always to see the broken heart upon the Cross, the source of all temporal-eternal life, all hope and all innocence, exclusively in relation to its rootedness in natural greatness—to see heroism and holiness as *one* single phenomenon,[404] natural kinship and grace reflected in one another and ultimately one in Christ;[405] the classical hero marked by divine fate and the Christian saint marked by the Father's mission.[406] Christian heroism (as that of Polyeucte, for example) must 'display a natural supernaturality, not a free-floating kind of holiness (which would be a terrible danger), but a heroism that is close to eternal reality yet cleaves to all its temporal origins, to its roots in time, to its rootedness, *enracinement*, in time; a heroism that can indeed tear itself away from all this without uprooting itself and so does not become a merely intellectual thing, but remains fleshly, not only in virtue of its source and starting point, of its whole flavour, its sap of life, but at the very least because it has to fulfil the duty of praying in a representative fashion. Thus this heroism of sanctity always remains fleshly with respect to its process of generation. And that is what constitutes its infinite value, for it is precisely the mystery of incarnation. And that also gives it its accuracy.'[407]

This is exactly the balance sought in the eleven hundred quatrains of the 'Ballad of the Beating Heart'[408] (dating from 1911 but published in 1941), which Péguy had made no further effort to 'organize' (that is, to set in order). In the brief hammer strokes of their heartbeat rhythms, a well-nigh innumerable succession of free-flowing *aperçus* on two constant and basic themes follow one another in turn: the naked, proud, humiliated heart, and the comparison between the four cardinal

[404] A 1200–1203; B 641.

[405] A 1202–1203.

[406] *Cf.* B 532.

[407] B 720.

[408] C 479–618.

and the three theological virtues; that is, between classical and natural perfection and its Christian counterpart. The unending garland is plaited in a wonderful fashion with perfect Christian tact and humour; in this garland, the praise of the cardinal virtues is followed each time by a still higher praise of the theological, achievement is followed by grace, exact figure of classical perfection by the unexpected outpouring of grace, seriousness by childlike playfulness.

Les quatre Cardinales
Sont des gendarmes.
Mais aux Théologales
Le don des larmes.

Aux quatre Cardinales
Les revenus.
Mais les Théologales
Marchent pieds nus.

The heart beats in accordance with this system; it must always both fulfil and transcend, and there can be no transcendence without fulfilment. As in the prayers, so it is in the reflections on French history and in Péguy's secret struggles at the time of his great love. But what always triumphs in his work, as in Corneille's, is honour, the demand for purity.

O cœur tissé de joie
Sur fond de peine,
La joie est une proie,
La peine est reine.

Nous perdrons le bonheur
Virgilien,
Mais perdrons-nous l'honneur
Cornélien.

It is a poem celebrating the heart as centre of life and being, as the pulsating point of unity between flesh and spirit, between pride and humility, between pleasure and pain. The point of equilibrium here is heart, not spirit, and it is in the heart that Péguy finds his jumping off point for venturing an attempt at capturing the very heart of God—the heart that beats between father and child and thus both heart and spirit; the heart that bears the cost of all life out of its own strength and creative resourcefulness, its own original genius; the heart that depends on nothing else for its beating, that never judges or compares, but in its own naked poverty gives protection and security to all things. Quite simply, it is a symbol of any and every creative source, and one that does not remain inaccessibly transcendent, but is alive and active in the midst of our own reality.

There is nothing to be gained in detailing the forms of contemporary degeneration, the withering away of the heart's power by the philosophical and scientific 'systematics' that dries up everything, and attempts to 'write up' reality and so loses sight of every possible experience even before any experience has occurred, the breaking forth of original freshness as well as faith's vision of it. It loses sight of it because it has to leave being itself out of account so as to have left only essences capable of classification and, ultimately, formal definitions and no more. With this blinkered claim, all genuine culture is abandoned, and we see before our very eyes the ruin of the entire heritage of Antiquity.[409] The advances of the modern age are purchased by surrenders and losses that can never be made good. And all that is left for the Christian is an act of 'ultimate courage'[410] and 'weary hopefulness',[411] to hold up his heart to the unfeeling teeth of the machines in the theological hope that, against all hope, the sacrifice of the heart may yet contribute to humanity's self-discovery.[412]

5. THE HEART OF GOD

Péguy carefully gathered together all the component parts of his theology and built these stones into a wall, so as finally to be able to set his last reflections in place like the keystone of an arch—a keystone that, however much it had been trimmed and dressed, had never yet really fitted any structure. It had not found a place in the theology of the Greek fathers (of which Péguy had some

[409] B 810; S 288; A 1075.
[410] B 1244.
[411] B 56f.
[412] B 1247; L 160.

idea);[413] they had developed the idea of comprehensive human solidarity through the comprehensive character of the Incarnation, but their concept of God was still overshadowed by a particular philosophical perspective (the idea of immutable, self-diffusing goodness). Still less could it find a place in the theology of Augustine and the West, in which the concept of predestination consistently ruled out any ultimate solidarity—according to Augustine, man can hope only for himself, not for his neighbour.[414] Péguy, who was certainly not a theologian given to compartmentalising, had brought his insights, once achieved, to completion in a breakthrough into a comprehensive theology of hope—by means of patient contemplation of the one reality that is at once natural and supernatural, by an unceasing process of *approfondissement* and assimilation. And this theology of hope makes its presence felt today, gently but irresistibly, by a structural shift in the whole theological edifice.

This is evident in the two works, *The Mysteries of Hope* and *The Holy Innocents*, which fundamentally constitute one single piece, the crown and consummation of Péguy's theology and so too of his aesthetic. Everything flows together in the 'principle of *hope*'. While all things in the world sink down toward the entropy of death, hope is the only thing that swims against the stream and moves upward: '*quand tout descend seule elle remonte*'.[415] And so the principle of hope inherits all the legacy of Bergson and indeed of all true philosophy. But Péguy's Bergson was, as we saw, the spokesman of Israel, the philosopher as prophet; and so, once more, Péguy's theology of hope is the heir of the Old Covenant. He took up, in broad terms, the ancient patristic and Pascalian *figura* relationship between the two Testaments, and, as will later become clear, developed it to a level more profound than did Pascal.[416] Yet for Péguy nothing

[413] B 337–339.

[414] *Enchiridion* 8: *spes non nisi bonarum rerum est . . . et ad eum pertinentium, qui earum spem gerere perhibetur* (PL 40, 235). The development of a theology of hope was blocked for a millennium and a half by this statement. *Cf.* Pierre Charles, S.J., '*Spes Christi*', *Nouvelle Revue Thèologique* 1934, and my own book, *Sponsa Verbi* (1961), 67.

[415] C 250.

[416] C 368–422.

was biblical that was not also human (classical). Such a phenomenon is the hope of humanity for the future, the hope that Clio smiles indulgently upon; this feeling that is refuted day by day and yet is never annihilated, the feeling that despite everything things will get better; this need and longing connected not so much with the life of the individual as with the race as a whole, deeply embedded in the mystery of fatherhood; the need to do everything possible so that things may be better for one's children. That is why Péguy began his *Mystery of Hope* as he did: after some introductory theological thoughts, he moves at once to the reflections of a woodcutter in the forest in winter, slaving away for the sake of his children. 'Wherever do men get this from?' asks God. 'These poor children surely see every day how the world goes, and yet daily they think that things are bound to go better tomorrow. Only tomorrow . . . *Ça ça me confond. Ça ça me passe. Et je n'en reviens pas moi-même.*'[417] But Péguy's woodcutter is a Christian, and the Christian hope from the start intermingles with his human hope. So Clio's critique loses its validity here; and when, at the end of the book, the secret pact between the people of France and the idea of hope is celebrated, the union between human and Christian hope is indissolubly sealed. 'Immediately, at once, almost in advance, they forget all the evil days, the evil days that descend like a grey, unremitting rain. They soak this rain up like the good Lorraine earth, transforming it at once into flowing water, living, clear and sweet. That is what amazes me, says God; and yet I am not easily surprised.'[418] The woodcutter is, through his children, in solidarity with all Christendom, and that is why he pins his own hope, in one and the same moment, upon the whole communion of saints. With a determination so bold that it shocks him, he has bypassed all the usual patron saints to go straight to the Mother of God, laid his sick child in her arms and left it there. This means that Péguy's socialist hope, resting as it does upon the universal solidarity of all men, upon the intolerable pain of a single shared exile, has now, without breach or interruption, become part of the equally universal solidarity of the communion of saints, whose apex is Mary, the

[417] C 267–268.

[418] C 268–269.

one created being who is entirely pure and yet entirely fleshly, 'infinitely pure because infinitely poor, infinitely exalted because infinitely humbled, infinitely young because infinitely maternal, infinitely upright because infinitely inclined in mercy, infinitely joyful because infinitely sorrowful'.[419] This is the statement finally achieved in the first *Mystère*, and it remains the necessary foundation for everything that follows; Péguy feels no desire now to return again to deal with the dimension of totality in this consciousness of solidarity. The communion of saints is not only a horizontal extension in historical time but equally a vertical line extended between the heavenly and the earthly Church (with Mary as its summit in Paradise)—the unconditional medium into which hope dares to enter. The existence of such a mediating reality assumes that unfathomable link, forged by God alone, between body and soul, nature and freedom;[420] assumes an incarnation of spirit that the angels will never know. But here Péguy is no longer philosophising in the abstract about the physical unity of human nature: he is reflecting within the bounds of the mystery of God's becoming man. To have bodily form already means to be in contact with the body of Christ[421] in the sense worked out by Péguy in *Véronique*.

So now all the elements are assembled for the curtain to rise on Péguy's drama: the risky venture of the soul's *enracinement* in the material world is, in so far as the soul is free, spiritual reality, a response to the deeper hazard of the eternal Divine Spirit as it puts down its roots in the nothingness of the created world, the nothingness of creaturely freedom. Taking for granted Clio's notion that the great historical event must constantly be borne, preserved and brought back to life responsibly by each subsequent generation, the chronicle of hope moves on: even God's Word and God's being can only entrust themselves to the world in such a way that they must be accepted by men and responded to in love; otherwise, everything could have been in vain. And this is a risk that God must run if he is to trust himself to creaturely freedom. Here there is no 'eternal knowledge' that

[419] C 206.
[420] C 217–219.
[421] C 220.

will transcend and arrest the risk involved in this entrusting of self, no eternal 'power' that will neutralize the risk by exploiting the world's powerlessness. That would debase the whole process to the level of a children's game. Here, in the heart of God, there can be nothing but hope alone.

Péguy introduces this concept unobtrusively in speaking of the Good Shepherd who follows the trail of the lost lamb with an anxious heart; and this theme once raised is then taken up time and again till its depths are laid open. 'This sinner who wandered away and was all but lost has unlocked the doors of anguish and so too the springs of hope in the heart of God himself, in the heart of Jesus—the fear and trembling of anguish, the tremor of hope.'[422] 'God has known the dread that he will have to condemn . . . the dread that he will never find the lost lamb again, the dread of not being sure. But finally he is rescued; he himself, the rescuer, is rescued—rescued from having to condemn it.'[423] And this rescue depends on us, who must catch and hold God's Word and God's blood, who 'in our hearts must nourish the fleshly Word of God with the flesh and blood of our own hearts'.[424] God sets his hope on us, and it is his hope that 'guarantees in advance and promises a temporal form for eternity, flesh for the spirit, a Church for Jesus, a creation for God himself, his own creation'.[425] 'And so it depends on us whether or not hope in the world is a deceit. It depends on us (ridiculous though it is!) whether or not the creator loses his creation.'[426] This preserving in oneself of the God who risks himself is faith, which can also be called hope ('the faith I most prefer, says God, is hope').[427] 'We must have sufficient trust in God to hope in him. To hope in God and to believe in God are one and the same. We must trust God; he has already trusted us sufficiently.'[428]

In this free, mutual movement of risk, Péguy sets out the origin and content of all that is. Everything ultimately depends on this reciprocal hope, which, however, has its source in God. 'This is what God began with. All feelings, all emotions that we

[422] C 209.
[423] C 215–216.
[424] C 227.
[425] C 233.
[426] C 235.
[427] C 169.
[428] C 240–241.

owe to God, he has already experienced with regard to us.'[429]—and this not at all in any predestiniarian election, but in creation as a whole. 'So it is not the will of your Father in Heaven that one of these little ones should perish. "See that you do not despise one of these little ones." And does not the shepherd leave "the ninety-nine in the desert to seek the one, *quae perierat*, that has been lost until he finds it? I tell you, there is as much joy in Heaven over *one* sinner who repents as over ninety-nine righteous men, who need no repentance."' Over that *one* unfaithful sheep there is as much—'perhaps even more'—joy as over all the faithful. 'For it was dead and has come back to life. It has made God's heart tremble with anguish. It has brought the theological virtue of hope into God's heart. It has caused an unfamiliar feeling to well up in the heart of God himself, made his heart new, as it were. The heart of God made new—I have weighed these words, I know what I am saying: the heart of God eternally new.'[430]

All this is infinitely far from Hegel, yet it is the truth in what Hegel says transferred into the sphere of the reciprocal freedom of love. 'When someone loves, he commits himself thereby to dependence upon, servitude to, the one he loves. That, my child, is the state to which God has come by his love for us.'[431] 'As Jesus has left his body in the wretchedly poor Church throughout all ages, exposed to the malice and mockery of the humblest soldier, so God has left his hope throughout all ages exposed to the malice and mocking of the humblest sinner. He has, so to speak, condemned himself to this.'[432] But in this way, as he relates the parable of the prodigal son, which no one can hear without tears, 'he has awakened in man's heart I know not what unique little point of response'; and this parable 'is perhaps the one thing to stick fast in the heart of the betrayer, like a nail of tenderness'.[433] So God plays with man the children's game of 'loser takes all'.

'I have often played with man, says God. But what a game! I still shudder at the mere thought of it. But my grace has its secret methods, it is more cunning than a woman. It plays with man,

[429] C 241.
[430] C 243–248.
[431] C 250.
[432] C 252–253.
[433] C 262.

spins him around and spins the outcome around. Often I play against man, says God, but he will insist on losing, the idiot, when I want him to win. Now and then I succeed in getting him to win. You might indeed say that we are playing "loser takes all". At least he is, since it is only when he loses that he wins. An extraordinary game: I am his partner and his opponent. He wants to beat me and so to lose; and I, his opponent, want to let him win.'[434]

There are two points here. One is that, no matter what the sinner may do, he is always in contact with the throbbing heart of God as a reality enveloping and bearing him, a reality into which he inevitably falls back as the waking man falls into sleep, as day falls into night. And there is also the point that God must train man in making his own venture: in freedom. He is like the father (says Péguy, in a thought-provoking image) who stands in the river 'wanting to teach his little son to swim and torn between two impulses: if he goes on holding him with his hand all the time, the child will come to depend on it and never learn to swim; but if he does not snatch him up at the right moment, the child will choke. On the one hand, men must work out their own salvation. That is the law, there is no breaking it. Otherwise it would not be interesting, they would not be men at all. They must be manly and win their spurs on their own. On the other hand, they must not be left to choke as they are immersed in the malice of sin.'[435] So grace must coach them in freedom and at the same time teach them how one truly serves the cause of one's own freedom. They must learn to understand the generous, gracious, gratuitous character of love, so as to respond 'with liberality of heart' to the heart of God. This is the essence of Christianity, that in the heart of man 'a reflection dawns of the gratuity of my grace'.[436] This is the aristocratic courtesy of the heart that grace shows to men, in whose context indeed grace sets them. That is why sanctity is aristocratic courtesy, *largesse*, at the same time that it is humility, because God's *largesse* itself takes the risk of humiliation—*largesse* and the bloom of well-being and comfort (*aisance*), of the

[434] C 345.
[435] C 352.
[436] C 359.

profoundest kind of health: '*nos saints sont sains. Sanctos esse sano*'.[437] Péguy quotes extensively from the memoirs of the Sire de Joinville and the reprimand given him by St Louis because the unfortunate man had said that he would sooner have committed thirty mortal sins than become a leper. Louis knew the nobility of heart that was in this sinner; God himself knows him and delights in his open candour. Louis does not reproach him as the Pharisees might. 'The Pharisees would like others to be perfect. I am easier to please, says God.'[438] The royal saint knows human nature all too well; only at the deepest level is he saddened. He speaks firmly but with gentleness and humility: 'firm in his meekness, meek in his firmness'. 'He, the king, speaks in the name of God and of himself. On behalf of God and the King of France he speaks humbly, like a trembling petitioner. He trembles out of anxiety that his faithful knight may not act for his own salvation.'[439] He shudders like God himself, but, like God, he cannot for one moment cease to be in solidarity with the sinner; the saint along with the sinner together form the 'Christian system'. Undoubtedly, though, the saint is the 'representative of Jesus'[440] and only in this sense the representative of the sinner. This means simply that the Christian vision has its truth and its manifestation in Jesus and, consequently, in the saints. It can be understood only from the perspective of Jesus and, consequently, of the saints. Hence, it is uniquely from this point that its glory and beauty break forth. The radiance of glory in sanctity is identical with its rightness, its exactitude, and this radiance is again nothing but the reflection of God's own holines, which is itself that hope that risks the utmost. So there comes about that wonderful moment when the son has grown up and can encounter the father on equal terms as a free man.

> Ask any father whether the best of all moments is not that one
> When his sons begin to love him as full-grown men,
> To love him as himself a man, freely and for nought.
> When subservience is done with, and the sons, grown into men,

[437] B 904.
[438] C 372–373.
[439] C 367–370.
[440] C 453.

> Now deal with him and love him man to man, like those who have a right to judge.[441]

That is what God has always willed—that his grace should educate man in freedom, in the same spirit of risk that constitutes God's own heart.

But God's heart still remains a wounded heart, rendered helpless by love, an exposed and undefended flank where the enemy, man, can force a way through. The most famous image in the *Mystères*, that of the prayer 'fleet', illustrates this phenomenon. Its presuppositions include first a Christology in which the Incarnation is always capable of an ambivalent reading: as God's revelation to man and as man's to God. And it is precisely this second aspect that is properly Trinitarian, since the tension between Father and Son is never greater than there, at the point where the Son as man returns from the world to the Father bearing all the concerns of mankind. The other presupposition, as is obvious from the theology of freedom, is that the 'merit' of man, his empowerment by creation and grace, will be taken fully into account. This creaturely fulness of power is, as is evidenced in the *Mystère* of Joan of Arc, itself something possessed of an internally Trinitarian form: it is the interpenetration in prayer of the total submission of the will and its total 'revolt' in the sense of the articulation of its own wishes; and this avoids being a contradiction (it becomes, rather, a Trinitarian mystery) only when the saint, as he says his Yes to God, rightly divines with his own wishes the most deeply hidden wishes of the Father's heart.

In this case it is the prayer of the Son, the Our Father, that rises from the world to the Father, laden with all the pleadings, all the requests, of the whole creation like some antique warship with its pointed prow; and behind it, shielded by it, the immense fleet of all the world's prayers follows after in its spreading wake—the massive Paternosters and the light galleys of the Ave Marias and all other prayers uttered or only thought or even unconscious. It is an irresistibly successful assault on the Father's heart. And here appear those words of the Father of which Romain Rolland said: 'I know of no writer in the world who

[441] C 376–377.

has ever made God speak in such a manner.'[442]

'Father, who art in Heaven—naturally, when a man begins to speak thus, he can go on to say whatever he likes. You can see quite clearly that I am disarmed. My Son knew that well enough. . . . This, then, is the way I am attacked. I ask you, is this fair? No, it is not fair, for all this belongs to the power of my own mercy. The kingdom of Heaven suffers violence, and the violent men will take it by force—violate it, you could even say. How can anyone defend himself in such a state? My Son has told them everything. And not only that, he, in his turn, has put himself at their head. And now they are like some great fleet of ancient times, countless in number, mounting an attack on the High King. Behind that foremost spur they cluster, tightly locked together like a bundle I cannot break apart; the massive triremes come recklessly closer and closer, shamelessly smashing through the surging waves of my wrath. They present themselves to me at this angle, and only at this angle can I receive them. They approach, crouching down like warriors taking up their positions for the attack; together they make a spearhead, they make a covering with their shields and often even with their own bodies. And the tip of the spearhead is formed by the clasped hands of my Son. How do you expect me still to be able to pass judgment after all this has happened? Our Father, who art in Heaven—my Son knows full well how the plot should be laid, to bind the arm of my justice and loose the arm of my mercy. And now I shall pass judgment on them as a father. For once, a father will be judge. "There was a father who had two sons." You know how a father judges; there is a well-known case. You know well enough how the father judged the son who had left home and then returned. All the father could do was to cry over it. That's the kind of story my Son has told them. My Son has given away the secret of my justice to them.'[443]

Not for a moment did Péguy oppose the Father's standpoint to the Son's. For the same God who weeps softly over the Son's 'treachery', his *traditio*, because he has given away the Father's secret to men, himself gave away, handed over, 'betrayed' his

[442] Rolland, *Péguy* I, 270. [443] C 334–344.

own Son to the world out of love. The powerlessness of the Father, whose justice is fettered by mercy, is the expression of his own omnipotence, and the powerlessness of his omnipotence is equally the omnipotence of his powerlessness; this is the *kabód*, the true glory of God that Péguy seeks to extol, and the aisthesis of which he cultivates in all possible ways.

The corollary is that man too has power with God and for God only on the foundation of the divine powerlessness, which remains the supporting and nurturing ground from which all earthly illumination and form grows and to which it will return again. This is the place where we encounter in Péguy the symbol of night, corresponding to John of the Cross's *noche oscura* (the intermediate stage of Novalis's *Hymnen an die Nacht* is an essential point of transmission in this); but Péguy's night is, in its profoundest core, still within the bounds of biblical theology.

'"O night", says God, "my daughter in your great cloak, it is through you that I sometimes win the self-surrender of man so that he gives in, relaxes and above all, finally for once falls silent, he who never stops talking."'[444] This 'night' is in one of its aspects simply the mother soil of nature, sleep as a falling back into the sources of life, the grown man becoming a child, a release from all the business and cares of the day, God's loveliest creation, since it both allows and prayerfully requests the lifting of the day's heavy load. 'As if I were not capable of the least anxiety or wakefulness over it; and perhaps you will find all the oppressive matters of today set right tomorrow when you get up, because I have overlooked them in the meanwhile.'[445] Night—the time in which children make up the sum of what they have released during the day as if drawing from the inexhaustible fountain of youth from which their strength flows, yet without any counting up or reckoning, since sleep is without reckoning; the Bergsonian night of the infinite reserves of being, of which the fanatical apostles of duty, the Kantians, have no inkling.[446] And what of the examination of conscience in the evening? Well and good: a brief glance backward, a passing regret; but then to immerse oneself in the abyss of grace

[444] C 347.
[445] C 296–298.
[446] S 113–118.

that is the night, in the inconceivable miracle of a new beginning;[447] the Bergsonian night, but one already wholly saturated with the mysteries of the divine presence and love. Hence follows the unbroken transition to the second aspect: night as the supportive basis, the continuum, in which the days form only intervals, openings, discontinuous segments. 'The nighttime is what is permanent in the life of a child, constituting the basis of his existence. It is into this that he returns, falls back. It is his very own place, his being, in which he swims, where he gets his nourishment, creates himself, forms himself. The days are interruptions. The nights join hands with one another in a beautiful dance around the days. The days only break in, they are like islands in the ocean, scattered islands broken up by the sea. But the ocean goes on while the islands are astray.' The days constitute time, but night is a 'foretaste' of something beyond time, that great 'bed in which I, the Father, shall lay my creation down to sleep. These days are never more than an appearance, an ambiguity; and you, night, you are my great and dark light.'[448] Thus above all, in these first and second aspects, the creaturely dimension and the dimension of grace are indissolubly linked. Night is not (as for John of the Cross) simply an expression of divine transcendence and of faith; it is already established as the basic form of creaturely existence itself. Man must each night again become a child, and each night the child draws from the night his strength for the day. Only from this perspective can Péguy go forward to his concluding treatment of the mystery of night, to give it its final theological location: night as the calming, silencing, reconciling curtain that falls upon the dreadful drama of Good Friday; and thus the night into which God himself sinks back from the draining day in which the Father has had before his eyes the spectacle of his Son on the Cross. 'All was finished. We shall speak of it no more, this incredible descent of my Son among men, and what they have so far made of it. And about the ninth hour my Son let out that cry that will never again die away. The soldiers had gone back to their barracks, laughing and joking because their turn of duty had been done. Only a centurion was still left and a

[447] C 322–330. [448] C 298–302.

few men to keep guard over that meaningless gallows. A few women too: his mother; perhaps one or two disciples as well, though that is less certain. Now any man has the right to bury his own son. Only I, God, whose arms have been bound all though this adventure—I could not bury my Son. And then it was you, night, that came. . . .'[449]

As if this creaturely night now had power even over the heart of God, as if it could silence and bury the bleeding mystery in God's heart, as if God's heart should yield to the law of his 'loveliest creation', as if the 'uninterrupted' night of the world might now at last flow into the uninterrupted night of God—Péguy has recognised the problem of the continuum that endures throughout all the quantified intervals that both measure and interrupt as the deepest of all problems, and he returned to speak of it again and again.[450] All images and concepts are an interruption of the night of the race as they are of the night of that understanding that is beyond concepts.[451] Ultimately all creation is an interruption of God's eternity: 'I have cut time out of the fabric of eternity, says God.'[452] The return of time into eternity, however, is not a philosophical problem, but rather a problem that is theological through and through; for its resolution nothing less is required than the entire history of salvation: the history of human death, but also of God's love, which empties itself even to death on a cross, of the infinite weariness of the evening of Good Friday, in which God himself sinks back into his own eternal life—death as the noiseless opening of the eternal gates. So *Eve* ends with the image of snow falling silently and endlessly on the grave of Geneviève.[453]

Yet in the *Mystery of the Holy Innocents* the poet seeks to transcend this image of night yet again. His last word cannot be of weariness, of soothing descent into sleep, for he is the poet of hope, and so he probes insistently through the night, looking for a further extremity again.[454] The ultimate point must be the child, the youthfulness, the blossoming spring of eternity

[449] C 307–308.
[450] B 1413–1415.
[451] B 1326.
[452] C 419.
[453] C 945 (st. 1904f.).
[454] C 349, 382–383.

itself.[455] Dante gave the holy innocents the lowest place in his celestial Rose; Péguy accorded them the highest. God himself enumerates ten reasons for this decision of his. One of them is that the children who safeguarded the flight of the infant Jesus with their blood 'were in a way his representatives'; they managed to witness by shedding their blood without departing from the source of their primordial innocence, and no one else apart from the Mother of God has succeeded in doing that. 'And so these urchins, these less-than-urchins, acquired a claim on us', 'these Infant Jesuses who will never grow old', who never needed to tread the whole path of futility and destruction, who 'play with palms and crowns' in Paradise, as the festal sequence that Péguy sets out in conclusion puts it, playing no doubt that game where you have to catch a hoop thrown to you on a short stick. 'That is how it is in my Paradise. What other game can you play with palms and crowns? I imagine they play quoits—at least I think so—for you must not suppose that people always have to ask my permission.'[456]

So the whole of Péguy's art and theology flow more and more towards prayer without one ever being able to say precisely whether this prayer is a dialogue or a monologue on God's part. It is a dialogue with God (predominantly so in *Jeanne*), but one which is constantly developing into a monologue of God the Father, addressed without distinction to his Son, to the men he has created and to himself. It is a form of 'theology as Trinitarian conversation', never realised prior to Péguy, which could only be risked by a poet using a simple and popular style of utterance that avoids any show of sublimity and yet does not for a moment degenerate into 'mateyness' and false familiarity. Only faith in the Holy Spirit can allow God to speak in such a way: in a meditation not only on the basic relationship of creation (*analogia entis*, of the ever-greater unlikeness of God in contrast to the world), but also on the basic relationship of the gospel and its *analogia fidei*—of the ever-greater unlikeness of the divine-human person of Jesus in contrast to sinners. And yet, presupposing and surpassing all this, the Church can speak and pray adequately in the Holy Spirit; it can (as Péguy makes God

[455] C 384.

[456] C 461.

the Father say) put words liturgically into the mouth of God himself: '*Or je ne démentirai jamais une liturgie, . . . je m'engage autant dans les enseignements de l'Eglise que dans mes propres enseignements.*'[457] 'My daughter the Church', in which Mary constitutes the innermost foundation, can treat the Word of God with precision, and in the Spirit of the Church, the poet too can treat the divine-human Word with precision if he has received the necessary humility, simplicity and *parrhesia*, boldness, from the Holy Ghost. Péguy is personally aware of himself as a sinner, and his life is not that of a saint.[458] 'But my work is not performed in sin. There is no sin in my work. . . . I am a sinner with rich resources of grace and an astonishing guardian angel. . . . I see issues absolutely simply. That amazes the priests. The liturgy is full of this simplicity, but they have never spotted it.'[459]

Dialogue is the basic form of Péguy's art, in contrast to Kierkegaard, who always delivers monologues, always speaks as an individual. The *Cahiers* are simply composed of conversations with real human beings, often cast in dialogue form (as with *De la Grippe*). Very frequently, a personal address breaks unexpectedly into the middle of a prose discourse—*mon cher Halévy*, *mon cher Isaac*, et cetera. When Péguy speaks about a fundamental issue, it is always in dialogue with those others who have dealt with it: Corneille or Racine, Michelet or Hugo, Renan or Taine, Jaurès or Herr; only human beings make history. The basis of history itself is the dialogue between the *polis* and the exiles, dialogue as supplication, the dialogue between the people and their spokesman. Only once does Péguy permit an unhistorical figure to speak or take part in a dialogue, and that is History herself, the colourful, humorous and elegiac muse, who however, immediately gives way before the still more profound conversation between Jesus and Eve. Jews speak with Christians; what is more, in the *Note Conjointe* Péguy and Benda go off together for a walk and a never-ending conversation. Christians speaks with pagans, as Polyeucte does does with Sévère. Saints speak with saints, Gervaise with Joan.

[457] C 434, 439.
[458] L 158.
[459] L 170, 158, 168.

Ultimately, though, it is God alone who speaks with all. We never find in Péguy truth abstracted from the world of persons—only truth that rests in the bosom of Trinitarian communication and so evolves out of a source in personal life, in a conversation that is as awesome as it is tender. Of his *Eve*, the poet had this to say: 'How can one fail to see that this total awe, this sort of profound and serious universal tenderness is here not only given representation in eminent form, but is summed up in eminent form in the respect, the great tenderness, of Jesus toward his first fleshly ancestress? It is precisely in this respect that the work shows itself to be profoundly Catholic, if indeed *tendresse* is the mark of the Catholic.'[460] *Tendresse* is not simply a matter of emotional tenderness but is an essential gentleness as it belongs to the heart of all existence: to the child, to the swelling bud, to hope and all the mysteries in the bosom of being.

If Péguy is constantly appealing to the mysteries of the communion of saints, to the intercession of the saints for sinners, this task of representation belongs (in accord with his conviction of the naturalness of this intercession) to the innermost structure of his life as of his work. In this respect he is in a particular sense a French poet, who draws on the riches of the grace of the great French saints alike in his life and in his own creative writing. Thus a foreign reader of his work must allow him some indulgence when, again and again, he sings the praises of the French soil, making God himself praise it, and of that 'garden-loving people who are best at ploughing both soil and souls, who always have fresh waters flowing in their wonderful and tragic gardens, those deeply sorrowful gardens of the soul.'[461] Likewise when he praises the 'order' and 'clarity' in which prayer and suffering occur, and when he spells out what 'secret sacrifice' is signified by these orderly ranks in the 'garden of the King'.[462] He thinks above all of Louis and Joinville, Geneviève and Joan, but he could equally well think of Ars and Lisieux, of the tears of La Salette that occupy a central place in the work of Léon Bloy just as Jean-Baptiste Vianney does in the work of Bernanos; and Joan is significant for all of them and for Claudel

[460] L 193–194.
[461] C 272–273.
[462] C 274–275.

as well. The subterranean links between the message of little Thérèse and that of Péguy have already been touched upon elsewhere; they are indissoluble bonds, and the messages of both are in many respects identical, both in what concerns the ideas of childhood and the heart of God and in what touches the ideas of loss and destruction and of hope.[463] Their missions are inextricably interwoven, for Joan herself stands in succession to Louis, and Thérèse in succession to Joan. But Péguy, whose central point is Joan, projected onto her the figure of Louis no less than that of Thérèse. In the communion of saints all these vocations exist in mutual connexion with one another and emerge in reciprocal relation. But the vocations of poets—as sinners who dedicate themselves in their work to an ideal of sanctity and serve this ideal by giving it artistic representation—are like separate emanations from the order and beauty of the saints. In the lineage of theological beauty, it is they who witness to it and make it present.

6. AESTHETICS AND SANCTITY

Our aim in this section is not to elevate Péguy to the rank of one of the greatest Christian poets or even theologians. It is simply to gather from his work those elements of a theological aesthetic that could only with difficulty be found elsewhere in comparable fulness and clarity of organization. He has many features that also point us forward to the best figures of the period following—to Charles de Foucauld or Konrad Weiss—and has every right to represent them in advance. His work as an essayist, like his work as a poet (to outward appearances, sometimes standing in opposition to his inner poetic sense), is a mass of fragments, a jumble of unfinished, disproportionately conceived things: the planned number of the *Mystères* varied from twelve to fifteen, *Eve* is spun out endlessly, the wide-ranging prose style can for pages appear almost empty and pretentious in its repetitions, the absence of plan is self-conscious and (as with the prophets) is treated as imperative: '*Car nous*

[463] *Cf.* my book, *Bernanos* (1954), 291f.

n'avons pas de plan, nous ne devons pas en avoir.'[464] Yet in the litany-like character of his style there is, as Gide recognised, a profound stylistic principle: something of the Kierkegaardian trick of repetition, something too of Bergsonian continuity, the never-ceasing stream of reality as it passes on its way and is experienced in its unfolding. The characteristic feature of the Alexandrine line employed in his strict verse is that its mechanical measuring of syllables is constantly at odds with the rhythmical stress; the latter is superimposed upon the former without destroying it and is repeatedly held back and restrained by it. But the interferences are innumerable, and the whole structure is always suspended in midair without ever losing the ground beneath its feet. This is also the reason why Péguy, after such a long apprenticeship in prose, showed an immediate mastery of strict rhythmical form, a great improvement upon his early essays in drama.

The starting point of his aesthetic was the *Cité Harmonieuse*, that utopian aesthetic ideal that was intended as the earthly substitute for the *Civitas Dei*: harmony as the ultimate value, but a harmony won by means of a struggle involving the highest ethical achievement—the abolition of any kind of exile, the abandonment of any kind of disease of the spirit, an ethical classicism that roots out all romantic muddle in life or thought. The absolute striving of life toward this vision of beauty was then itself the embodiment of beauty in contrast to all Socialist Party programmes relating to art[465] and to any designs for a distinct, demarcated artistic sphere. Beauty is what is 'given in addition' (*par surcroît*), a gift gratuitously bestowed on men and events.[466] But since in Péguy the success of the outcome always remains interlinked with the effort involved in arriving at it, it is also possible to speak of the beauty of an authentic revolution. 'Nothing is so agonizingly beautiful as the spectacle of a people raising itself up and doing so by means of a fresh and profound renewal of its origins, by immersing itself in its most ancient pride and dignity.'[467] Right up to the end, the beautiful for Péguy does not have its primary location in beauty of form, but

[464] S 214.
[465] A 244f.
[466] A 249.
[467] B 1247.

rather in the fresh-springing blossoming forth of life itself as it reveals its victorious achievement in achieved forms. This is why for Péguy the aesthetic is ultimately rooted entirely in the religious; he takes no account of any kind of art other than a religious one, an art of worship. Cathedrals are for him 'the prayer of fleshly people, a glory, almost an impossibility, a miracle of prayer';[468] they are 'embodiments of adoration'.[469] The argument with the clergy that ends the *Note Conjointe*, full of subtle peasant malice, yet without bitterness, turns upon the role, the utility, the indispensability, of milestones on the road. The cleric defends these external forms (in practical terms, this has to do with the Index—more specifically, with Bergson's being placed on the Index), while Péguy speaks for the fine, straight road itself and the longing to travel along it. And it may even be just as well, out of a surpassing desire for certainty, as it were, to cast a glance once in a while at the stones that mark the distance; their 'indispensability' is admitted in the long run, but they are 'not indispensable in the sense of having utility'.[470]

Already in the socialist period, the concept of ethical and aesthetic *justesse* is paired with that of prophecy. Bernard-Lazare, as an atheistic prophet, has an unfailing instinct for what is right and just in history as it is happening. This is the Old Testament ethic; this is why the prophet is a 'poet', since he finds the right words to utter from God in the strength of the correct divine reading of the times, and so with the creative power of the word that imprints itself on the prophet. For the prophecy of the ancient prophets is a path toward the Incarnation, as the divinely just reality embodies itself in what is ethically and aesthetically just and right and manifests itself in these terms. And the more firmly the total Incarnation of the Word in Jesus Christ is established as the supreme norm, overflowing in its abundance, the more it becomes clear that what is humanly right and just is not simply and unilaterally inserted into the world from above, but is simultaneously drawn up from below, out of the roots of the order of creation itself; and that therefore, in Péguy's understanding, there is no disputing the reality of the

[468] B 333–334.
[469] B 897.
[470] B 1490.

encounter and interpenetration between classical and Christian reality. The 'classical' for Péguy means the phenomenon of perfect human proportion, as developed from within, out of the interior, existential, primordial proportions in human nature itself. Here he opts for the classicism of Corneille as against the 'romanticism', the 'passion', the 'morbidity' and 'secret cruelty' of Racine's characters.[471] For it is not in the difference between Paradise and the Fall that we find the element of the compelling and the beautiful; it is uniquely in the overcoming of that difference by 'power from on high', by grace, which bestows righteousness on men. There is neither a beauty in sin (*Fleurs du Mal*), nor a beauty that can be taken seriously in pure form alone—anything like that is patently the consequence of sin. Wherever beauty (*justesse*) may be, *justice* is required along with it; and this is ultimately grounded only in justification by grace.

Jesus is God and thus is infinite; but he is also man and as such is finite. Péguy guards against a Christology that makes out of Jesus an abstract, nonconcrete and thus inhuman compendium of the supreme values, a summary of the *summum bonum*. Since he is some particular thing, a some*one*, 'a living, clearly delineated personality', he cannot simply be 'everything'. He is 'circumscribed in space and time. He enters into a finite scheme of things.' It is precisely 'because he accepts Incarnation in its exact sense, without qualification, without limit or condition' that human finitude on this basis can 'tune in' to his perfect being. If he were simply a compendium of all virtues, 'we should not have required any Gospels. We should not have needed any narrative record. But he ranges himself in the ranks of humanity. He ranges himself among the saints—as the first among them, but still among their ranks. *Il se range*. He is certainly not just anyone and everyone. He does not swallow up the whole world in himself. He leaves something for the others. So it is that the freedom of God as well as historical freedom can be seen in him; as a man and a saint, he is metaphysically beyond the sphere of calculation or fabrication. And the freedom of his existence thus and not otherwise as a human being is the most necessary reality there is, 'for it alone expresses itself exactly on

[471] B 778f.

the basis of the gratuity of grace.' This freedom in the event of Jesus is shown, for instance, in the sovereignty with which he fulfils the prophecies; there is nothing mathematical or mechanical in this correspondence.[472] It is for this that he needed historical witnesses and willed to have them, that he commissioned scriptures and therefore also scribes; that he set in motion as an historical human being an unending historical process, 'becomes a sacrificial offering to historical criticism', 'delivered over to the exegete, the historian and the critic, just as he was delivered over to the soldiery, delivered to these other judges, these other fellow countrymen. It is one and the same *traditio*, one and the same delivering up, handing over.'[473]

This is of decisive importance for a theological aesthetic. A Jesus (like the Jesus of so many theological systems) who is no more than the abstract (and necessarily false) sum of 'perfections' or, more precisely, of the things that look like perfections to human eyes and that they thus attribute to the God-Man—such a Jesus can never be the canon of a 'classical' beauty; his image is bound to degenerate from the already vacuous *beaux Christs* of Gothic art to the style of modern 'sacred heart' kitsch. For such a Christ does not take his place in a series, *il ne se range pas*, so as to form an authentic figure along with prototypes and imitations alike. Only when this visible figure emerges is the transcendence of his Godhead credible in the same moment. And so it is possible to apply to him what Péguy wrote about *Polyeucte*: '*Un texte ferme et précis, parfaitement [dé]limité, parfaitement classique et qui pourtant on ne sait comment sans aucune dégradation baigne dans un bain de dépassement de sa propre grandeur*'.[474] So it is also an aspect of the 'classical' quality of Jesus that the divine love is in him fully incarnate in righteousness, which can only be *justice* when it is *justesse*; and so once again it can only be itself when it is immersed in what transcends it.

Again, the relationship between Old and New Covenant is decisive for aesthetics. Péguy discusses this exhaustively in the *Holy Innocents*, where he tells the whole story of the Egyptian

[472] B 1418–1420.
[473] B 1420–1422.
[474] B 792.

Joseph. 'There was a man who had two sons'—but first, 'There was a man who had twelve sons.' And in both cases it is the youngest child, who seems to be dead, who is found again. 'That is a symbol, my child, a single story that is told twice. And for the one who has eyes to see, each version appears in the other *en transparence*.' But the parallels only hold when both wings of the diptych correspond to each other as mirror images, reversed images. The one son is found seated on a throne, the other arrives coming from a pigsty. 'The Old Covenant always has a perspective that includes the idea of lordship. And in the New Covenant the idea that is always in the background is that of service, of being a servant, of obedience, of the ordinary condition of man.' In the former the idea in the background is of 'the kingdoms of Egypt and Babylon'; in the latter, it is the idea of affliction, destitution and poverty. 'She is the much-beloved and most holy Lady Poverty.' But the diptych is equally a moving process, a movement forward: 'The temporal kingdom advances toward the eternal.' Thus the Old Covenant is indeed a kind of progressive 'image', 'but as an image, it is at the same time wholly faithful and yet completely the other way round, going in the opposite direction, faithfully and exactly reversed, precisely the contrary: *fidèlement inverse, exactement inverse*'.[475] Jesus is the coping stone of the arch, toward which both sides mount upward. 'The last stone before the keystone is John the Baptist, but the first one after it is Peter the Founder. Thou art Peter, upon this rock. . . . And he was crucified upside down; that is, on the descending plane.'[476] Despite all this, the parallels are not exact, for 'the Old Covenant is a line, while the New occupies a surface, an area'. And the ridge that mounts up 'swells upward from the earth, and it is a fleshly ridge, but the surface that flows downward stems from the spirit and is a spiritual surface'. Or again it can be put in these terms: 'The Old Covenant is a deep ocean in which a lofty forest is reflected. And the forest is entirely in the ocean and yet is not in it. And the dark sea, the deep sea rests upon the foundation of the earth, and in the depths of the sea lie the heavens. But the lofty forest strives toward the heights. The lofty forest, the real and substantial

[475] C 386, 415–418. [476] C 420.

forest, lifts itself upward away from its reflection in the water, allowing the real and substantial sap to rise up towards the only deep and real and substantial Heaven.'[477] Previously, the Old Covenant had been fleshly reality in its rising upward. Now the substance of the Old Covenant, reversed in the mirror, has become the water that moistens the roots of the New. In both images there is a real relationship involved, going beyond the purely aesthetic, symbolic relationship with which Pascal had stopped. Péguy, faithful to the classical side of Corneille, rejected the Jansenist aspect all along the line. He retained what is evangelical while rejecting what is Protestant.

Apart from this, there was no aspect of Pascal that would not be taken up positively by Péguy: his *royale détresse*;[478] his vision of the *grandeur et misère* of humanity,[479] of the present actuality of sin;[480] his sense of exactitude and geometrical precision;[481] his assessment of genius;[482] his praise of Epictetus and the Stoics in general;[483] his leaving out of consideration of rational proofs of God so as to leave plenty of room for his 'wager', for the freedom to stake a bet;[484] his treatment of biblical imagery;[485] and above all his own particular quality, the sanctity, which finally has to do with love alone.[486] But Pascal reasons too much and looks too little; he proves too much, a dangerous trait,[487] and Corneille has more than he does of that Christian and human peace and plenitude that is its own evidence.[488] This is not to be found without a full affirmation, stemming from the heart of faith and all the secrets of its life, of that freedom, given and bequeathed to man by the Creator, to cultivate the earth, to create *cultura*. Christianity and culture—but culture does not have the onesided meaning of 'civilisation', certainly not of 'technology'. Culture is the triumphant achieving of form out of landscape, history and human nature itself. Péguy cannot be a Christian without landscape and locality; but it is not the wilderness of Hopkins, but rather the Beauce, awaking to an

[477] C 422–423.
[478] B 1312, 1315.
[479] B 405.
[480] B 822.
[481] E 81, S 284–287.
[482] D 200–201.
[483] B 1392–1393.
[484] B 1386.
[485] B 792.
[486] D 169–183, 187; A 539, 735, 939.
[487] D 189–190.
[488] A 1203, B 1387.

infinite fruitfulness,[489] the royal Loire with its chateaux, its vineyards, its customs and speech,[490] and, ever and anew, the inexhaustible scenery of Paris, 'monument of all monuments, city of supreme culture'.[491] It is an ethical landscape that from the very first exists in achieved perfection, effortlessly classical,[492] 'sacramental', noble, 'without any striving for special effect'[493]—a landscape that has been organised, in which a foreordained order reposes, in which man can trustfully establish himself so as to learn what order is; and yet a landscape already set in order by man as well, in which human and divine order interpenetrate. 'Neither too much or too little of anything; proportion. Neither barbarism nor Byzantinism (casuistry, Scholasticism, pedagogics, philology, sociology). Nothing in polychrome. Nobly sloping hills, situated in just the right places, clothed in natural nobility, clothed by nature in classical and Christian dignity. Not simply in the sense of Christian art, for it is far more than art, even Christian art. For this reason, this landscape corresponds with unique exactitude to an exact point of maturation and fulfilment, the point at which the Christian vision achieves its goal.'[494] It is classical harmony: not, however, an angelic, heavenly, eschatological harmony, but rather a harmony between Heaven and earth, between grace and sin, the solidarity of all the world's sounds in the all-embracing motif of poor and powerless Christian love, powerful in its powerlessness. Christians, indeed, often make music that transports them to the supraterrestrial level, music in which they imagine they have a foretaste of the sounds of Heaven.

> Mystical, heavenly revelations, fragments, anticipations of Heaven. But even when these sounds seem to us most poignant, most upward soaring, mounting most surely, precisely at these peaks, or perhaps when these have already been surpassed, they still remain human prayers, human harmonies, human mystical visitations, the music of human organs, in human registers; even when, just when these registers dub themselves *vox coelesta*. The Christian is entirely human. He is indeed the most human reality

[489] A 1181–1190.
[490] A 1204f.
[491] A 1165–1178.
[492] S 308–310, 323; E 114–117, 128f.
[493] A 1183.
[494] E 130–135.

there is. He is the only one who has put on humanity a price equal to the market price of God, who has valued man, even the last and least of sinners, the most wretched of sinners, at the price of God himself. So his music is something entirely different from that of the angels: a paltry human music, a wretched music, that sinners and saints perform together, the hymn that is in sum, all told, a hymn of sinfulness—the music of Christian hearts.[495]

[495] B 396–397.

INDEX OF PROPER NAMES